PRAISE F[...]
THE FOOD [...]

"Health authorities advise us to eat less fat, salt, and sugar, but that doesn't tell us what to put in the shopping cart. With *The Food Book,* you can learn which of hundreds of foods meet those recommendations and which do not. Anyone concerned about high blood pressure, heart disease, allergies, or just plain good health will find *The Food Book* indispensable. In clear and simple English, it helps answer that vital question: Is this food good for you?"

—BONNIE LIEBMAN, Director of Nutrition, Center for Science in the Public Interest

***

"How can you be serious about losing weight or having a healthy heart without knowing what you are eating? *The Food Book* gives you clear, concise information about nutritional value that will help you make healthful food choices. Buy this book."

—HAROLD S. SOLOMON, M.D., Director, Healthstyle Program and Assistant Professor, Harvard Medical School

***

"In their search for more complete information about prepared foods, consumers will find *The Food Book* to be an excellent and useful resource. Nutritional labeling is enhanced by including sodium, fiber, and cholesterol data—all in commonly understood terms and in practical portion sizes. Comments are included after each food that help consumers make better food selections. Helpful food hints that encourage better eating habits are also included—ideas that can easily be put into action."

—KATHLEEN RAU, Nassau Branch, Cornell University Cooperative Extension

**WHICH BREAKFAST CEREAL
IS NUTRITIONALLY SUPERIOR,
WHEATIES OR WHEAT CHEX?**

IS CAMPBELL'S SOUP GOOD FOOD?

**SHOULD YOU MAKE IT PROGRESSO . . .
OR MAKE IT YOURSELF?**

The answers in this book may not be what you'd expect! You'll discover the often dramatic differences in nutritional value from brand to brand of the same item—*information you can't find summarized anywhere else!*

Along with full nutrition data, including sodium, fiber, and cholesterol counts and an ingredients list for each food, you'll find recommendations and evaluations based on the latest guidelines from nutrition experts.

THE FOOD BOOK synthesizes the most important facts about your favorite brand name foods in clear, readable, easy-to-use entries. It provides you with nutritional tips and helpful hints—and arms you with the facts you need to eat wisely and well.

QUANTITY SALES

Most Dell books are available at special quantity discounts when purchased in bulk by corporations, organizations, and special-interest groups. Custom imprinting or excerpting can also be done to fit special needs. For details write: Dell Publishing, 666 Fifth Avenue, New York, NY 10103. Attn.: Special Sales Department.

INDIVIDUAL SALES

Are there any Dell books you want but cannot find in your local stores? If so, you can order them directly from us. You can get any Dell book in print. Simply include the book's title, author, and ISBN number if you have it, along with a check or money order (no cash can be accepted) for the full retail price plus $1.50 to cover shipping and handling. Mail to: Dell Readers Service, P.O. Box 5057, Des Plaines, IL 60017.

THE

FOOD

BOOK

The Complete
Guide to the Most Popular
Brand Name Foods
in the United States

BERT STERN
Producer

LAWRENCE D. CHILNICK
Editor in Chief

LYNN SONBERG
Project Director/Writer

Nutrition Consultant: Sharron Dalton, Ph.D., R.D.
Research Director: Matthew Ostrowski
Production Coordinator: Julie Surrey
Computer Services: Ari Computer Systems, Inc.

A DELL TRADE PAPERBACK

Dell Publishing
a division of
The Bantam Doubleday Dell Publishing Group, Inc.
666 Fifth Avenue
New York, New York 10103

Chart for United States Recommended Daily Allowances on page 10 has been adapted from the FDA consumer memo, "Nutrition Labels and U.S. RDA." 81-2146, 1981.

ISBN: 0-440-52570-5

Printed in the United States of America

June 1987

10 9 8 7 6 5 4 3

MV

CONTENTS

PREFACE   x

INTRODUCTION   1

    Why You Need This Book   1
    Guidelines for Healthy Eating   2
    What the Profiles Tell You   6
    Where We Got Our Data   12
    Label Information Isn't Always Enough   13
    Using the Profiles to Shop More Healthfully   15
    How to Use This Book   18

THE BRAND NAME FOOD PROFILES   23

BABY FOOD   25
    cereals   25
    fruits and fruit juices   27
    meat and vegetables   31
BISCUITS AND BISCUIT MIXES   36
BREAD AND ROLLS   40
BREAD CRUMBS AND STUFFING MIXES   61
BUTTER AND MARGARINE   65
CAKES AND CAKE MIXES   77
    mixes   78
    ready to eat   86
CAKE ICINGS   91
CANDY (NONCHOCOLATE)   95
CEREALS   100
    cold   102
    hot   134
CHEESE   137
CHOCOLATE   145
COFFEE CREAMERS   154

COOKIES AND GRANOLA BARS 156
CRACKERS 168
DESSERT TOPPINGS 173
FISH 177
    canned 178
    frozen 183
FLOUR AND BAKING NEEDS 189
FRUIT 196
FRUIT DRINKS 205
FRUIT JUICE 212
GELATIN DESSERTS 219
GRAVY AND GRAVY MIXES 222
ICE CREAM AND FROZEN DESSERTS 225
INSTANT BREAKFASTS AND DIET BARS 233
JAMS, JELLIES, AND PRESERVES 235
KETCHUP 240
MAIN DISHES AND DINNERS 242
    canned 243
    dry 247
    frozen dinners 253
    frozen entrées 271
MAYONNAISE 293
MEAT AND POULTRY PRODUCTS 297
    bacon 297
    bologna 301
    canned meat and poultry 305
    ham 308
    hot dogs 312
    salami 318
    sandwich meats 322
    sausages 332
MEXICAN FOOD 335
MILK PRODUCTS AND FLAVORINGS 341
MUFFINS AND MUFFIN MIXES 349
MUSTARD 356
NUTS AND COCONUT 358
OILS AND VINEGAR 363
OLIVES 369
ORIENTAL FOOD 371
PANCAKES AND WAFFLES 379
PASTA 385
PEANUT BUTTER 389
PICKLES AND RELISH 393

PIES AND PASTRIES   398
PIZZA   405
POTATOES   413
POTATO CHIPS, POPCORN, AND SNACKS   417
PUDDING   421
RICE   425
SALAD DRESSING   429
SAUCES AND SEASONINGS   440
SNACK CAKES AND PIES   448
SOFT DRINKS   458
   canned   459
   mixes   468
SOUP   475
SPAGHETTI SAUCE   500
SUGAR AND SUGAR SUBSTITUTES   507
SYRUPS AND HONEY   511
TOMATO PRODUCTS   514
VEGETABLES AND LEGUMES   520
   beans/pork and beans   521
   canned vegetables   526
   frozen vegetables   534
YOGURT   545

BASIC FOODS: A NUTRITION COUNTER   551

GLOSSARY OF BASIC TERMS   569

SOURCES   573

INDEX   575

PREFACE

Choosing foods that add up to a nutritious diet seems a difficult, often discouraging task. *The Food Book* offers usable, sensible information for quick decisions regarding a wide array of convenience foods such as packaged breads, soups, cereals, and frozen dinners. Everyone uses these products in varying amounts with varying degrees of concern regarding their health value. Cold cereal is a good example of a processed food with a wide range of excellent to poor nutritional choices. *The Food Book* evaluates a variety of nutritious, less processed cereals for everyday use as well as those that should be eaten only once in a while. The supporting information helps you make an intelligent choice. Additives are another area of concern for some consumers. *The Food Book* offers guidance for persons who must avoid certain additives, such as sulfites, as well as for those who simply want to know more about the chemical ingredients in their foods. Nearly all of us, on the other hand, can benefit from reducing excessive fat in our daily diet. An excellent feature is mention of the percentage of calories from fat compared to the recommended 30 percent in products such as prepared frozen meals. This does not mean that a food high in fat calories needs to be avoided, but that it requires careful use. Less of it or less often! No single food is a "junk" food, because a high fat, high sugar, or high sodium food can be balanced with other foods low in these ingredients. But there are "junk" diets. A junk diet contains *many* foods with high amounts of these problem ingredients. *The Food Book* provides useful, easily understood information for balancing your diet.

SHARRON DALTON, PH.D., R.D.
PROFESSOR OF NUTRITION
NEW YORK UNIVERSITY

INTRODUCTION

Why You Need This Book

The foods we eat affect our health. If you're like most health-conscious Americans, you already know that you and your family should eat less fat, salt, and cholesterol. You also know you should eat more dietary fiber and complex carbohydrates. You've heard that your chance of developing serious illness such as heart disease and certain types of cancer are directly affected by the foods you eat. But when faced with the daily task of shopping for your family, it's hard to translate these generalities into wise food choices.

The Food Book does the work for you. It is the only book that provides a complete evaluation of the most popular brand name foods, including hard-to-find information on cholesterol, fiber, sodium, and controversial additives. This all-in-one reference will help you identify the most nutritious brand name foods before you step into the supermarket, while planning your family's meals or before going on a special diet.

We decided to focus the book on brand name foods for several reasons. In 1985, American spent more than 190 billion dollars, or sixty percent of every food dollar, on brand name foods: Soups, cereals, frozen pizzas, and "gourmet" frozen entrées are just a few of the convenience foods that are eaten daily by millions of Americans. As the book clearly shows, there are dramatic differences in nutritional value from brand to brand or within the same brand, from one style of preparation to another. In order to make *The Food Book* a complete reference we also included a nutrition counter for basic foods such as fresh fruit and vegetables, and unprocessed meat and poultry.

The recommendations in this book are based on guidelines about healthy eating from the following organizations and authorities:

1

Dietary Goals of the McGovern Committee (1977)
Surgeon General's Report on Preventive Medicine (1980)
National Academy of Sciences–National Research Council (1980)
National Cancer Institute (1984)
American Heart Association (1986)

Guidelines for Healthy Eating

—Reduce overall consumption of total fats, and especially saturated fat and cholesterol abundant in red meats, butter,
cheeses, and whole milk products. Also avoid processed foods
high in saturated fat. Americans currently consume more than
40 percent of their calories as fats. This should be reduced to 30
percent or less.

—Reduce consumption of protein from fatty meats, cheese,
and eggs, and increase consumption of plant sources of protein. Animal protein is the main source of unwanted cholesterol and saturated fats.

—Increase consumption of complex carbohydrates (whole
grains, legumes, starchy vegetables, pasta, potatoes) and dietary
fiber. Americans currently get 28 percent of their calories
from complex carbohydrates and natural sugars instead of the
recommended 50 percent. Average dietary fiber intake is estimated to be about 15 grams per day instead of the recommended 30 grams.

—Increase consumption of fruits and vegetables, especially
those rich in vitamins A and C and cruciferous vegetables (such
as broccoli, cabbage, Brussels sprouts, cauliflower).

—Increase consumption of fish and shellfish containing
Omega 3 fatty acid (such as salmon, tuna, sardines, scallops, and
mussels). Fatty fin fish are the richest source.

—Decrease consumption of salt and refined sugar. Americans
now get about 18 percent of their calories from refined sugars
and processed sugars instead of the recommended 10 percent.
Salt intake should be limited to 5 grams daily (about 1 teaspoon) instead of the current 10 to 20 grams.

—Limit consumption of processed, salt-cured, smoked, and
pickled meats.

These guidelines can have a direct impact on you and your family's health. For instance, the McGovern Committee predicted that if its goals became a reality, there would be an 80 percent drop in obesity among Americans, a 25 percent drop in deaths from heart disease, and a 50 percent drop in deaths from diabetes!

You probably remember being told that good nutrition meant eating a variety of foods from the four basic food groups. Unfortunately, nothing was said about *which* foods to choose from each group. No mention was made of fat, cholesterol, saturated fat, salt, sugar, or dietary fiber. The Center for Science in the Public Interest publishes a chart, which corrects

NEW AMERICAN EATING GUIDE*

	ANYTIME	IN MODERATION	NOW AND THEN
Group 1 **Beans,** **Grains,** **and Nuts** *four or more* *servings a* *day*	bread and rolls (whole grain) bulgur dried beans and peas (legumes) lentils oatmeal pasta, whole wheat rice, brown rye bread sprouts whole grain hot and cold cereal whole wheat matzoh	cornbread **8** flour tortilla **8** hominy grits **8** macaroni and cheese **1,(6),8** matzoh **8** nuts **3** pasta, except whole wheat **8** peanut butter **3** pizza **6,8** refined, un-sweetened cereals **8** refried beans, commercial **1**, homemade in oil **2** seeds **3** soybeans **2** tofu **2** waffles or pan-cakes, syrup **5,(6),8** white bread and rolls **8** white rice **8**	croissant **4,8** doughnut (yeast leav-ened) **3 or 4,5,8** presweetened break-fast cereals **5,8** sticky buns **1 or 2,5,8** stuffing, made with butter **4,(6),8**

KEY: **1**-moderate fat, saturated **2**-moderate fat, unsaturated **3**-high fat, unsaturated **4**-high fat, saturated **5**-high in added sugar **6**-high in salt or sodium **(6)**-may be high in salt or sodium **7**-high in cholesterol **8**-refined grains

*Adapted from *New American Eating Guide* which is available from the Center for Science in the Public Interest, 1501 16th Street, N.W., Washington, D.C., 20036, for $3.95/$7.95 laminated, copyright 1983.

continued

	ANYTIME	IN MODERATION	NOW AND THEN
Group 2 **Fruits and Vegetables** *four or more servings a day*	all fruits and vegetables except those listed at right applesauce (unsweetened) unsweetened fruit juices unsalted vegetable juices potatoes, white or sweet	avocado **3** cole slaw **3** cranberry sauce (canned) **5** dried fruit french fries, homemade in vegetable oil **2**, commercial **1** fried eggplant (veg. oil) **2** fruits canned in syrup **5** gazpacho **2**,**(6)** glazed carrots **5**,**(6)** guacamole **3** potatoes au gratin **1**,**(6)** salted vegetable juices **6** sweetened fruit juices **5** vegetables canned with salt **6**	coconut **4** pickles **6**
Group 3 **Milk Products** *two servings a day*	buttermilk made from skim milk lassi (low-fat yogurt and fruit juice drink) low-fat cottage cheese low-fat milk, 1% milkfat low-fat yogurt nonfat dry milk skim milk cheeses **(6)** skim milk skim milk and banana shake	cocoa made with skim milk **5** cottage cheese, regular, 4% milkfat **1** frozen low-fat yogurt **5** ice milk **5** low-fat milk, 2% milkfat **1** low-fat yogurt, sweetened **5** mozzarella cheese, part-skim type only **1**,**(6)**	cheesecake **4,5** cheese fondue **4**,**(6)** cheese soufflé **4**,**(6)**,**7** eggnog **1,5,7** hard cheeses: blue, brick, Camembert, cheddar, Muenster, Swiss **4**,**(6)** ice cream **4,5** processed cheeses **4,6** whole milk **4** whole milk yogurt **4**

	ANYTIME	IN MODERATION	NOW AND THEN
Group 4 **Poultry, Fish, Meat, and Eggs** *two servings a day* Vegetarians: nutrients in these foods can be obtained by eating more foods in groups 1, 2, and 3	FISH cod flounder gefilte fish (6) haddock halibut perch pollock rockfish shellfish, except shrimp sole tuna, water packed (6) EGG PRODUCTS egg whites *only* POULTRY chicken or turkey, boiled, baked, or roasted (no skin)	FISH (drained well if canned) fried fish **1 or 2** herring **3,6** mackerel, canned **2,(6)** salmon, pink, canned **2,(6)** sardines **2,(6)** shrimp **7** tuna, oil-packed **2,(6)** POULTRY chicken liver, baked or broiled, **7** (just one!) fried chicken, homemade in vegetable oil **3** chicken or turkey, boiled, baked or roasted (with skin) **2** RED MEATS (trimmed of all outside fat!) flank steak **1** leg or loin of lamb **1** pork shoulder or loin, lean **1** round steak or ground round **1** rump roast **1** sirloin steak, lean **1** veal **1**	POULTRY fried chicken, commercially prepared **4** EGG cheese omelet, **4,7** egg yolk or whole egg (about 3 per week) **3,7** RED MEATS bacon **4,(6)** beef liver, fried, **1,7** bologna, **4,6** corned beef **4,6** ground beef **4** ham, trimmed well **1,6** hot dogs **4,6** liverwurst **4,6** pig's feet **4** salami **4,6** sausage **4,6** spare ribs **4** untrimmed red meats **4**

these omissions; it tells you how to choose from the basic four food groups, while still following the latest dietary recommendations. "The New American Eating Guide" is an excellent practical guide to healthy eating.

Scientists know a great deal about human nutritional needs, but the science of nutrition is not a single fixed body of information. Every month new studies are published which change the way scientists view the relationship between food and health. It is beyond the scope of this book to discuss nutritional issues and controversies in any detail, but if you are interested in gaining a better understanding of this complex field, consult the listing of excellent books and newsletters at the end of this chapter. Additional publications of general interest are listed in "Sources" at the back of this book.

What the Profiles Tell You

Each profile in *The Food Book* contains a huge amount of information—everything from USRDAs for vitamins and minerals to brand comparisons, to hard-to-find data on cholesterol, fiber, and additives. To make all this information instantly accessible and easy to understand, it had to be carefully organized. We started with the structure provided by standard nutrition labeling, then expanded it to include information *not* found on labels. We also added a written evaluation.

For example, let's start with a popular brand name food: Weight Watchers Chopped Beef Steak in Green Pepper and Mushroom Sauce with Shoestring Carrots.

The package label gives you the following information.

CHOPPED BEEF STEAK
in green pepper and mushroom sauce
with shoestring carrots

NUTRITION INFORMATION
Serving Size: 1 Package (8¹⁵/₁₆ oz.)   Servings Per Container: 1
CALORIES 320   CARBOHYDRATE 12g
PROTEIN .... 24g   FAT 20g
**PERCENTAGE OF U.S. RECOMMENDED
DAILY ALLOWANCES (U.S. RDA)**
PROTEIN 30   VITAMIN C 25   RIBOFLAVIN ... 15   CALCIUM 10
VITAMIN A ... 100   THIAMINE 10   NIACIN 20   IRON 10
INGREDIENTS
BEEF, CARROTS, WATER, TOMATO PUREE, GREEN PEPPERS, DRIED WHEY, MUSHROOMS, FLOUR, SALT, ROASTED BEEF AND CONCENTRATED BEEF STOCK, HYDROLYZED PLANT PROTEIN, PARTIALLY HYDROGENATED LIQUID SOYBEAN OIL, NATURAL FLAVORING, GRANULATED ONION, MONOSODIUM GLUTAMATE, MODIFIED FOOD STARCH, CORN OIL, SUGAR, CARAMEL COLOR, CAROB BEAN GUM, GUAR GUM, SPICE, XANTHAN GUM, GARLIC POWDER, GUM TRAGACANTH, ARTIFICIAL FLAVOR, BETA CAROTENE.

The average health-conscious consumer, looking at this label, will probably notice that this frozen dinner is very high in vitamin A, and moderately high in protein and vitamin C. If he or she is concerned about additives, the listing of MSG, caramel color, carob bean gum, guar gum, xanthan gum, gum tragacanth, and artificial flavor may cause some concern. But most shoppers are not well enough versed in the scientific literature to know if these particular additives are anything to worry about. And if the shopper is looking for information about the cholesterol or fiber content of this food, they will be disappointed. Chances are the dieting or weight-conscious consumer will simply add the item to the grocery cart, taking it on faith that it will make a nutritious meal on a calorie-restricted diet.

Has the shopper made a wise choice?

A glance at the *Food Book* profile of this same product quickly yields the answer.

PRODUCT: WEIGHT WATCHERS CHOPPED BEEF STEAK IN GREEN PEPPER AND MUSHROOM SAUCE
H. J. Heinz Co.

Ingredients: beef, carrots, water, tomato puree, green peppers, dried whey, mushrooms, flour, salt, roasted beef and concentrated beef stock, hydrolyzed plant protein, partially hydrogenated liquid soybean oil, natural flavoring, granulated onion, monosodium glutamate, modified food starch, corn oil, sugar, caramel color, carob bean gum, guar gum, spice, xanthan gum, garlic powder, gum tragacanth, artificial flavor, beta carotene.

Amount: approx. 9 oz			% USRDA
Calories	320	Protein	30
Protein, gm	24	Vitamin A	100
Carbohydrates, gm	12	Vitamin C	25
Fat, gm	20	Thiamine	10
Sodium, mg	1,115	Riboflavin	15
Cholesterol, mg	140e†	Niacin	20
Fiber, gm	3e†	Calcium	10
		Iron	10

Contains 4 teaspoons fat and ½ teaspoon salt.

THIS FOOD: Although Weight Watchers Chopped Beef Steak is not especially caloric, many other frozen entrées not specifically geared to dieters are

†estimated values

equally low in calories. Fat accounts for a whopping 56 percent of calories, which is substantially higher than the 30 percent recommended. This product is also high in cholesterol and saturated fat and extremely high in sodium. On the positive side, this entrée is an excellent or very good source of protein, vitamin A, vitamin C, and riboflavin, but this does not balance out its excessive fat and sodium content.

ADDITIVES: Contains monosodium glutamate (MSG), which many authorities believe should be avoided by infants and very young children; causes adverse reactions in some sensitive individuals. Also contains artificial flavor, which some studies suggest may adversely affect behavior and the ability to complete school tasks in sensitive children.

As you can see, the *Food Book* nutrition information closely follows the order of information contained on the label. But it also tells you how much fiber, cholesterol, and sodium a particular food contains. (A recent law requires manufacturers to reveal sodium content on labels, but it may take several years for full compliance to take effect.) This information is of key importance in evaluating whether a brand name food will contribute to, or help prevent heart disease and certain types of cancer, yet is very rarely provided by the manufacturer. In addition, the profile makes the existing information more meaningful by translating it into commonly understood terms. For example, like the label, the profile states that Weight Watchers Chopped Beef Steak contains 20 grams fat, but it also tells you that 56 percent of total calories come from fat (far more than the recommended 30 percent) and that that 20 grams fat is the same as 4 teaspoons of fat.

This paragraph also provides additional information on cholesterol, fiber, and saturated fat (missing altogether on the product label) as well as an overall evaluation of the nutrient content of the food. Since this frozen dinner is clearly targeted at "weight-watchers," the profile points out that its calorie content is equivalent to that of many standard frozen dinners that do not make special claims. Finally, the profile lets consumers know that two of the additives used in this product— MSG and artificial flavor—may cause adverse reactions in a small number of children and adults who are sensitive to these substances.

It's clear from this example that even when nutrition information on the label exists, it does not tell the whole story. Obviously when products don't supply any nutrient data at all, the *Food Book* profiles are even more valuable. As of 1980, more than half of all packaged foods contained no nutrient data.

Let's take a closer look at other features that make the profiles useful.

PORTIONS: When we felt the serving size provided by manufacturers was realistic, we used it. But if we felt the serving size on the product label was too large or too small, we substituted a more realistic portion. For example, Star-Kist and Bumble Bee tuna describe a full 6½-ounce can as a single serving. *The Food Book* reduces that to one-half can, or ½ cup, which reflects the amount normally eaten at one sitting. On the other hand, people very rarely eat only 3 ounces of meat or poultry as a main dish. Thus, although Victor Weaver describes a 3-ounce piece of fried chicken as a single serving, to be more realistic we have changed the amount to 6 ounces. Also, whenever possible, we have tried to keep serving sizes consistent within each category of food, to make it easier to compare individual products. The attempt was not always successful. For example, Yoplait yogurt comes in ¾-cup containers and Dannon comes in 1-cup containers. Since people most often eat a whole carton of yogurt, we have left the serving sizes provided by the manufacturers intact.

ADDED INGREDIENTS INCLUDED IN NUTRIENT DATA: Since people don't eat cake mix from the box, or Hamburger Helper without adding chopped beef, we have tried to supply nutrition data for each food as it is normally prepared. For example, if a cake mix is normally made with milk and eggs, the nutrition data in the book includes the added ingredients. Similarly, since cold cereals are usually eaten with milk, we have provided information for the combined values of milk and cereal. Whenever the nutrient values of added ingredients are included, the description of the food at the beginning of the profile will say so.

ESTIMATED VALUES: Many of the most popular brand name products are combination foods, such as soups, or frozen dinners. For many of these foods, actual laboratory analyses for cholesterol and fiber do not exist. Rather than leaving consumers with no information at all, we have looked carefully at the data which *has* been compiled, and supplied educated estimates for these important substances.

VITAMINS AND MINERALS: We've followed the standard labeling format and supplied data for eight vitamins and minerals. Clearly this information is far from complete—at least forty nutrients are considered essential to human nutrition. All of the nutrient values given are per portion. The U.S. Recommended Daily Allowances for adults is used for all products except baby foods, where the USRDA for infants has been applied.

RECOMMENDED DAILY ALLOWANCES

Nutrients which must be declared on product labels	Infants (birth to 1 year)	Adults and Children (over 4)	Pregnant or Lactating Women
Protein (g) (high quality)	20	45	45
Protein (g) (low quality)	28	65	65
Vitamin A (IU)	1,500	5,000	8,000
Vitamin C (mg)	35	60	60
Thiamine (B_1) (mg)	0.5	1.5	1.7
Riboflavin (B_2) (mg)	0.6	1.7	2.0
Niacin (mg)	8	20	20
Calcium (mg)	600	1,000	1,300
Iron (mg)	15	18	18

Nutrients which may be declared on product labels			
Vitamin D (IU)	400	400	400
Vitamin E (IU)	5	30	30
Vitamin B_6 (mg)	0.4	2.0	2.5
Folic acid (folacin) (mg)	0.1	0.4	0.8
Vitamin B_{12} (μg)	2	6	8
Phosphorus (mg)	500	1,000	1,300
Iodine (μg)	45	150	150
Magnesium (mg)	70	400	450
Zinc (mg)	5	15	15
Copper (mg)	0.6	2	2
Biotin (mg)	0.05	0.3	0.3
Pantothenic acid (mg)	3	10	10

SYMBOLS: Throughout the book, the following symbols have been used:

the letter "e" following nutrition information indicates that the data has been estimated;

< means "less than" and is generally used for small amounts of sodium or cholesterol;

na means not available and appears infrequently when nutrition data could not be obtained;

* means the food contains less than 2 percent of the USRDA for a given nutrient.

A Consistent Rating System

Throughout the book we have used consistent standards to evaluate the nutrient content of brand name foods.

FOR VITAMINS AND MINERALS:
—If a food contains 10 percent (or slightly less) of the USRDA for a given nutrient we call it only a fair source of that vitamin or mineral.
—If a food contains 10 to 20 percent of the USRDA for a given nutrient, we call it a good to very good source of that vitamin or mineral.
—If a food contains 25 percent or more of the USRDA for a given nutrient, we call it an excellent source of that vitamin or mineral.

FOR FIBER: Although there is no USRDA as such for dietary fiber, most nutrition authorities recommend that we eat thirty grams of dietary fiber per day. In the "Profile" section we use the following standards for evaluating the fiber content of brand name foods:
—If a food contains 2 to 3 grams dietary fiber, we simply note that it is a source of fiber, or provides some fiber.
—If a food contains 4 to 5 grams fiber, we call it a good source.
—If a food contains 6 to 7 grams fiber, we call it a very good source.
—If a food contains 8 grams or more of fiber (more than twenty-five percent of the amount nutritionists say we should eat each day), we call it an excellent source of fiber.

FOR SODIUM: It did not make sense to use a uniform standard throughout the book. Instead a consistent rating system was formulated for each category of food and is printed on the first page of each "Profile" section.

There is no USRDA for sodium, but a recommended "safe and adequate" range of 1,100 to 3,300 milligrams daily has been formulated by the Food and Nutrition Board of the National Academy of Sciences–National Research Council. It is not easy, but it *is* possible to stay within the upper range of these guidelines and still use brand name convenience foods regularly. Certainly the advice in this book is not intended for people on low-sodium diets, but for healthy individuals who wish to monitor their intake of sodium. When we say a food is moderate in sodium, we are comparing it with other foods in the same category, while we also take into account how it is actually eaten. In other words, a tablespoon of mustard with 150 milligrams sodium will be called "high" in sodium (because it is a concentrated source and eaten as a sandwich spread, in addition to the bread and sandwich filling) while an 8-ounce frozen entrée (which is the main part of a meal) with 475 milligrams sodium, will be called moderate in sodium.

Where We Got Our Data

Wherever possible, we used nutrition information and ingredients lists supplied by the food manufacturers in response to our written requests. We also took information directly from the labeling information on brand name foods. The USDA food tables were another important resource as well as Bowes and Church's *Food Values of Portions Commonly Used* (14th edition), especially when the label did not contain nutrient information and manufacturers failed to respond to our written and telephoned requests for information. For cholesterol and fiber values we had to go farther afield to the USDA Nutrient Data Research Group and to medical and nutrition journals, since few companies were able to provide us with their own analyses and the information in the USDA food tables was spotty, at best. Information on dietary fiber was particularly hard to come by, since only a handful of researchers have pioneered a standardized way of measuring fiber content, which includes soluble as well as insoluble forms of fiber. (Information on crude fiber, often supplied by food manufacturers, is not a useful measure for dietary assessment.)

While we have made every attempt to provide accurate data, a certain margin of error is inevitable. For instance, if a nutrition label says that a given food contains, say, 50 percent of the USRDA for vitamin A, the figure supplied may have been rounded off. In fact, it may vary as much as five percent from the true value. Since we sometimes recalculated the figures supplied by the food companies when we changed portion sizes, the error margin may also have increased.

Please remember, too, that product formulations are constantly changing. This means that by the time you read this book, it's possible, for example, that Stouffer's may be using a slightly different recipe for its French Bread Pizza. But experience tells us that the slight adjustments in product formulations that do occur rarely make a real difference in the nutritional value of brand name foods. In any event, after you have used *The Food Book* for a while, you'll learn how to make your own judgments about brand name foods, even if the ingredients and nutrition data vary somewhat from the profiles in the book.

Label Information Isn't Always Enough

Today the vast majority of packaged foods contain a disclosure of the product's ingredients, which must be listed by common name, in descending order of composition by weight. Even this simple rule has important exceptions. The Food and Drug Administration has "standards of identity," or basic recipes, for approximately 350 products. If a manufacturer follows the government's food standard for a particular product, only the optional ingredients must be spelled out on the label. Most manufacturers voluntarily include an ingredients list on products such as bread, milk, cheese, butter, noodles, mayonnaise, canned fruits and vegetables, and margarine which are covered by these food standards, but this is still not required by law. This means that a standard product such as butter need not disclose that artificial color is used in the product since this additive is part of the basic "recipe."

Right now there is no way of telling how much of a specific ingredient the product contains. Since ingredients are listed in order of their predominance by weight, we do know that the product contains more of the ingredients at the beginning of the list than at the end, and that's about it. However, existing regulations about product names are very revealing. For instance, manufacturers can only call a product "Beef with gravy" if it contains 50 percent beef; the name "Chicken with gravy" means a minimum 35 percent chicken; and "Gravy with chicken" requires a mere 15 percent chicken! Unfortunately, none of this need be stated on the label. New regulations have been proposed that would reveal this important information on the label, but as of this writing, they have not become law.

To sum up:

—Food additives must be listed, unless they are part of a standardized recipe, but the exact spice, flavor, or color used need not be specified (except for FD & C Yellow No. 5).

—The kind of vegetable shortening used does not have to be specified. Often a choice of soybean, coconut, or palm oil is given on the ingredients list. The FDA and USDA have proposed that any product containing more than 10 percent fat must specify exactly what is being used, since many consumers wish to avoid saturated fats. This regulation is not yet in effect.

Nutrition information is not required by law, with the following exceptions:

—products which contain added nutrients, such as fortified cereals

—products which make nutritional claims, such as "high-protein" or "high in vitamin C"

—products designed for special dietary uses, such as "for low-sodium diets" or baby foods

Consumers have made it clear that they are interested in nutrition information on food labels. According to a 1985 Louis Harris poll, 64 percent of shoppers avoid buying products without nutrition information, at least on occasion. Still, as of 1980, only half of all packaged foods included nutrition labeling. When food companies print statements of nutritional value, whether voluntarily or by law, they must include the following information: size of serving, number of servings per container, the number of calories, grams of protein, carbohydrates, and fat per serving; and the percentage of the U.S. Recommended Daily Allowance for protein, vitamin A, vitamin C, thiamine, riboflavin, calcium, and iron. As of July 1986, any product with nutrition labeling must also include information on milligrams of sodium per serving.

A standard label appears in the illustration below.

Using the Profiles to Shop More Healthfully

Here are some tips about specific health issues, whether you want to take off excess pounds without sacrificing good nutrition, or minimize your risk of heart disease, cancer, or osteoporosis ("thin bones").

FOR WEIGHT WATCHERS: Calories *do* count, but they are not the only, or even the most useful, way of telling whether a food will help you stay slim. You should also pay special attention to the entries for fiber and fat in each profile. Foods high in fiber tend to fill you up before you can consume too many calories. There is also some evidence that people on high-fiber diets actually absorb fewer calories than those eating the average low-fiber diet.

Watching your fat intake is another key aspect of weight control. A gram of fat contributes 9 calories, while the same amount of either protein or carbohydrate contains only 4 calories. Try to choose foods in which fat contributes 30 percent or less of total calories. Most of the profiles in *The Food Book* tell you the percentage of fat calories in each brand name food. You can also calculate this on your own by multiplying the grams of fat per serving by nine and dividing the result by the number of calories in the food.

FOR YOUR HEART: In choosing brand name foods you'll want to pay special attention to the entries for fat and cholesterol in this book and avoid foods high in those substances. Cholesterol is found only in foods of animal origin, such as meat, eggs, and cheese. Even if you have no special problem with your heart or arteries, the American Heart Association recommends eating no more than 300 milligrams a day of cholesterol. Since a single egg yolk contains 250 milligrams and a 6-ounce steak contains 160 milligrams, you'll have to choose carefully to keep your cholesterol intake down. Saturated fat should be avoided, and is often found in unexpected processed foods, such as muffins or nondairy creamers. Our profiles identify brand name foods which are high in saturated fat, but you should also know how to do this in the supermarket. Examine the ingredients list carefully for hydrogenated vegetable oils and coconut and palm oil, all of which are highly saturated.

Although you shouldn't get more than 30 percent of your total calories from fat, there are two kinds of fat that are good for you: Omega 3 fatty acid, found in fatty fish such as tuna and salmon, and monounsaturated fats, such as olive oil, are both thought to help lower cholesterol levels. Polyunsaturated fats also lower cholesterol levels, but less effectively.

You will also want to keep an eye on the fiber entry when choosing your foods. Early research studies have convinced many authorities on heart disease that foods high in soluble fiber, such as beans and oats, as well as certain fruits and vegetables, may help to lower cholesterol levels.

FOR HIGH BLOOD PRESSURE: If you already have high blood pressure, your doctor has probably told you to reduce your salt intake. Keep an eye on the sodium entry in these profiles. Even if your blood pressure is normal, if your diet is like that of most Americans, you are consuming at least twice as much salt as the recommended amount. The dietary goals of the McGovern Committee say you should limit salt intake to 5 grams, or 1 teaspoon a day, which is the equivalent of about 2,000 milligrams sodium. The 1980 guidelines of the National Academy of Sciences–National Research Council allow a higher daily sodium intake—up to 3,300 milligrams for adults. Many popular brand name foods are high in added sodium. For example, a Swanson Mexican-style frozen dinner has 1,890 milligrams sodium and a cup of Lipton's chicken rice soup has 950 milligrams sodium. Clearly you'll have to choose carefully to stay within the guidelines.

There is also growing evidence that too little potassium and calcium in the diet may be as harmful as too much sodium. New research suggests that all three factors contribute to high blood pressure.

Potassium values were simply not available for a substantial number of foods in this book, nor could they be accurately estimated. Potassium-rich foods include bananas, orange juice, dried fruits, bran, peanut butter, potatoes, and dried peas and beans.

FOR REDUCED CANCER RISK: Pay particular attention to four entries in the profiles: fat, fiber, vitamin A, and vitamin C. People who consume low-fat diets are less likely to develop breast, colon, and prostate cancer. So once again, try to choose foods that get no more than 30 percent of their calories from fat. Diets high in a variety of fibers may help protect against colon cancer. Also, it's a good idea to increase your consumption of fruits and vegetables high in vitamins A and C, especially "cruciferous" vegetables such as broccoli, cabbage, and cauliflower.

FOR ADDITIVE ALLERGIES: Pay close attention to the ingredients list for each food profile. If you know you are allergic to a par-

ticular additive, such as monosodium glutamate (MSG) or sodium sulfite, obviously you will want to avoid the brand name
foods that use it. Other additives that cause allergic reactions in
sensitive individuals include FD & C Yellow No. 5, artificial
color, and artificial flavor. If the safety of an additive or preservative included in each brand name food is still a matter of
debate, or being reinvestigated by the FDA, we have listed it
next to the "Additives" heading. The vast majority of commonly
used additives are considered safe. Also, while specific ingredients in some brand name foods may cause allergic or adverse
reactions in some sensitive consumers, we are not aware that
particular products have in fact caused such reactions; individuals
with allergies or other sensitivities should consult their physicians
for advice about the suitability of particular foods.

ESPECIALLY FOR WOMEN: Two entries are of special interest to
women: iron and calcium. Because of lost menstrual blood
each month, women need more iron than men, yet they typically get less in their diets because they consume fewer calories. Vitamin C eaten at the same meal as iron will increase the
amount of this important mineral you absorb, especially from
healthful vegetable sources such as broccoli, spinach, beans,
and grains. To help prevent osteoporosis, or "thin bones,"
women should exercise regularly as well as get more calcium in
their diets. The average woman does not get enough calcium
for her needs, which results in loss of bone density with increased age, especially after menopause. Care must be taken in
choosing a good calcium source, since many milk and cheese
products are high in fat and cholesterol. Low-fat milk, yogurt,
Lite Line Processed Cheese, and sardines and salmon (with
bones) are some excellent choices.

How to Use This Book

Let's say you want to find look up three of your favorite
foods: Celantano Pizza, Ocean Spray Cranberry Juice Drink,
and Aunt Jemima Blueberry Waffles.
Here's how to proceed:

1. Turn to the listing of "Brand Name Food Profiles" on the Contents page and look first for the category of food to which each product belongs. We've tried to avoid large, sweeping categories like "Combination Foods," "Beverages," or "Grain Products." Instead we've chosen smaller categories, in this case "Pizza," "Fruit Drinks," and "Pancakes and Waffles." Sometimes, however, we couldn't avoid using larger categories. For example, to look up Le Menu Frozen Sirloin Tips Dinner, you would glance at the Contents page until you found "Main Dishes and Dinners" and the subcategory "Frozen Dinners."
2. Turn to the page where the category begins where you'll find background information, the introduction, nutritional standards we applied in evaluating each category of food, and any relevant practical information about storing, serving, and menu planning. Then turn to the profile of the specific food you are interested in, which is arranged alphabetically within each category.
3. If you can't figure out what category a brand name food belongs in, turn to the "Index," where all products are listed individually in alphabetical order.

For Further Reading

BOOKS:

Letitia Brewster and Michael F. Jacobson, Ph.D. *The Changing American Diet.* 1983; Center for Science in the Public Interest, 1501 16th Street, NW, Washington, D.C. 20036.

Jane Brody. *Jane Brody's Nutrition Book.* New York: Bantam Books, Inc., 1981.

Cheryl Corbin. *Nutrition.* New York: Holt, Rinehart and Winston, 1980.

Jean Mayer, Ph.D. *A Diet for Living.* New York: David McKay, 1975.

Annette Natow and Jo-Ann Heslin. *Nutrition for the Prime of Your Life.* New York: McGraw-Hill, 1983.

NEWSLETTERS:

Nutrition Action Healthletter. Published 10 times a year by the Center for Science in the Public Interest, 1501 16th Street, NW, Washington, D.C. 20036.

Nutrition and Health. Bimonthly; published by the Institute of Human Nutrition, Columbia University College of Physicians and Surgeons, 701 W. 168th St. New York, N.Y. 10032.

THE

FOOD

BOOK

The
Brand Name
Food
Profiles

BABY FOOD

Baby food was introduced by Gerber in 1927. Before then mothers simply prepared their own. During your child's first year basic nutritional requirements are met by milk or formula, but after six months of age solid foods are needed as a calorie and nutrient supplement, to support growth and development. Until the late 1970s many commercially prepared baby-food items contained added salt, sugar, and even MSG, but with few exceptions today Gerber, Beech-Nut, and Heinz, the leading manufacturers, produce healthful, nutritious foods. Added starch should be avoided and high-protein and meat products (which are often high in fat) should be used in small amounts.

In 1985 Milupa introduced a line of dehydrated baby foods which contain formula, cereal, vegetables, and fruit in various combinations. The products do not contain added salt, sugar, or other additives and initial reaction from nutritionists and pediatricians has been positive. Beech-Nut also introduced a line of dehydrated products which do not contain added formula.

Please remember that although baby food comes in 3½ and 4½-ounce jars, this amount is too much for many young infants to eat at a single sitting. Leftover baby food may be capped and refrigerated in the original jar for two to three days.

Cereals

BEECH-NUT STAGE 2 OATMEAL WITH APPLESAUCE AND BANANAS

Beech-Nut Nutrition Corp.
Ingredients: water, apples, oat flour, apple juice concentrate, banana puree, citric acid, fortified with vitamin C, ferrous sulfate, niacinamide, riboflavin, thiamine hydrochloride.

Amount: 1 jar/4½ oz			% USRDA
Calories	90	Protein	8
Protein, gm	2	Vitamin A	*
Carbohydrates, gm	17	Vitamin C	45
Fat, gm	1	Thiamine	45
Sodium, mg	10	Riboflavin	45
Cholesterol, mg	0	Niacin	45
Fiber, gm	na	Calcium	2
		Iron	45

THIS FOOD: Beech-Nut Stage 2 Oatmeal with Applesauce and Bananas is low in fat and high in vitamin C, the B vitamins, and iron, with which it has been fortified. Since this product contains more apples than oat flour, its name is quite misleading.

ADDITIVES: Contains added vitamins and iron.

GERBER DRY BARLEY CEREAL
Gerber Products Co.

Ingredients: barley flour, tri- and dicalcium phosphate, soy oil–lecithin, barley malt flour, electrolytic iron, niacinamide, riboflavin, thiamine.

Amount: 4 tbsp (+ ⅓ c milk)			% USRDA
Calories	100	Protein	15
Protein, gm	4	Vitamin A	6
Carbohydrates, gm	14	Vitamin C	2
Fat, gm	3	Thiamine	50
Sodium, mg	39e	Riboflavin	70
Cholesterol, mg	10e	Niacin	25
Fiber, gm	<1e	Calcium	30
		Iron	45

THIS FOOD: Prepared with whole milk, this fortified cereal is a good source of protein and complex carbohydrates, and is especially rich in the B vitamins, calcium, and iron. Single-ingredient cereals, such as this product, are often recommended as a baby's first solid food.

ADDITIVES: Contains added vitamins and iron.

DID YOU KNOW: Most experts recommend a single-ingredient cereal, such as rice, barley, or oatmeal, as your baby's first solid food. It's best to wait until your baby weighs at least fifteen pounds, or is five or six months old, before you begin. Starting your baby too soon can sometimes trigger allergic reactions. Also, it's easy to feed a younger baby too much, since most infants cannot indicate whether they are hungry or full until they are five to six months of age.

NOTE: The letter "e" indicates that the data has been estimated; < means "less than" and is used for small amounts of sodium or cholesterol; * means food contains less than 2% of USRDA; "na" means that the information was not available and appears only when data is insufficient.

GERBER HIGH PROTEIN DRY CEREAL
Gerber Products Co.

Ingredients: soy flour, oat flour, wheat flour, soy oil–lecithin, calcium carbonate–phosphate, electrolytic iron, niacinamide, riboflavin, thiamine.

Amount: 4 tbsp (+ ⅓ cup milk)			% USRDA
Calories	100	Protein	30
Protein, gm	7	Vitamin A	6
Carbohydrates, gm	9	Vitamin C	2
Fat, gm	4	Thiamine	50
Sodium, mg	< 20	Riboflavin	70
Cholesterol, mg	10e	Niacin	25
Fiber, gm	< 2e	Calcium	30
		Iron	45

THIS FOOD: Gerber High Protein Cereal is fortified with the B vitamins, calcium, and iron. Mixed-ingredient cereals are more likely to spark allergies than ones made from single grains and are not recommended for a baby's first solid food.

ADDITIVES: Contains added vitamins and minerals.

Fruits and Fruit Juices

BEECH-NUT STAGE 1 GOLDEN DELICIOUS APPLESAUCE
Beech-Nut Nutrition Corp.

Ingredients: golden delicious apples, water (necessary for preparation), and vitamin C.

Amount: 1 jar/4½ oz			% USRDA
Calories	60	Protein	*
Protein, gm	0	Vitamin A	*
Carbohydrates, gm	14	Vitamin C	45
Fat, gm	0	Thiamine	2
Sodium, mg	< 10	Riboflavin	6
Cholesterol, mg	0	Niacin	*
Fiber, gm	2	Calcium	*
		Iron	*

THIS FOOD: Beech-Nut Stage 1 Golden Delicious Applesauce is an excellent source of vitamin C.

ADDITIVES: Contains added vitamin C.

GERBER STRAINED APPLE JUICE
Gerber Products Co.

Ingredients: apple juice and vitamin C.

Amount: 1 jar/4½ oz			% USRDA
Calories	60	Protein	*
Protein, gm	0	Vitamin A	*
Carbohydrates, gm	15	Vitamin C	120
Fat, gm	0	Thiamine	2
Sodium, mg	< 20	Riboflavin	2
Cholesterol, mg	0e	Niacin	*
Fiber, gm	0	Calcium	*
		Iron	*

THIS FOOD: Gerber Apple Juice provides natural sugar calories and is rich in vitamin C. Apple juice is often given to babies as their first liquid food other than milk.

ADDITIVES: Contains added vitamin C.

GERBER STRAINED APPLESAUCE
Gerber Products Co.

Ingredients: apples, water, and vitamin C.

Amount: 1 jar/4½ oz			% USRDA
Calories	60	Protein	*
Protein, mg	0	Vitamin A	*
Carbohydrates, gm	14	Vitamin C	45
Fat, gm	1	Thiamine	2
Sodium, mg	20	Riboflavin	4
Cholesterol, mg	0	Niacin	*
Fiber, gm	2	Calcium	*
		Iron	*

THIS FOOD: Gerber Strained Applesauce is an excellent source of vitamin C.

ADDITIVES: Contains added vitamin C.

HELPFUL HINT: Between feedings you can satisfy your baby's thirst and urge to suck with water rather than milk or juice. Many infants consume too many calories during their first year, which can contribute to a tendency toward overeating and overweight in later years.

GERBER STRAINED MIXED FRUIT JUICE
Gerber Products Co.

Ingredients: apple juice, pineapple juice, orange juice from concentrate, banana puree, vitamin C.

Amount: 1 jar/4 oz			% USRDA
Calories	60	Protein	*
Protein, mg	0	Vitamin A	2
Carbohydrates, gm	14	Vitamin C	120
Fat, gm	0	Thiamine	6
Sodium, mg	4	Riboflavin	2
Cholesterol, mg	0	Niacin	2
Fiber, gm	0	Calcium	*
		Iron	*

Contains 3½ teaspoons naturally occurring sugar.

THIS FOOD: Gerber Strained Mixed Fruit Juice provides natural sugar calories and is rich in vitamin C. Mixed juices are not recommended as a baby's first juice.

ADDITIVES: Contains vitamin C.

GERBER STRAINED ORANGE JUICE
Gerber Products Co.

Ingredients: orange juice from concentrate and vitamin C.

Amount: 1 jar/4½ oz			% USRDA
Calories	70	Protein	4
Protein, gm	1	Vitamin A	4
Carbohydrates, gm	14	Vitamin C	120
Fat, gm	1	Thiamine	15
Sodium, mg	<20	Riboflavin	8
Cholesterol, mg	na	Niacin	4
Fiber, gm	0	Calcium	2
		Iron	*

Contains 3½ teaspoons naturally occurring sugar.

THIS FOOD: Gerber Strained Orange Juice provides natural sugar calories and is rich in vitamin C.

ADDITIVES: Contains added vitamin C.

GERBER STRAINED PEACH COBBLER
Gerber Products Co.

Ingredients: peaches from concentrate, water (necessary for preparation), sugar, modified cornstarch, wheat flour, vitamin C, citric acid, and cinnamon extracts.

Amount: 1 jar/4½ oz			% USRDA
Calories	100	Protein	2
Protein, gm	1	Vitamin A	4
Carbohydrates, gm	23	Vitamin C	45
Fat, gm	1	Thiamine	*
Sodium, mg	< 20	Riboflavin	2
Cholesterol, mg	0	Niacin	2
Fiber, gm	na	Calcium	*
		Iron	*

THIS FOOD: Gerber Strained Desserts Peach Cobbler is rich in vitamin C, but it also contains modified starch and sugar, which many authorities believe should be avoided by infants less than six months old.

ADDITIVES: No questionable additives.

HEINZ BANANAS AND PINEAPPLE WITH TAPIOCA
H. J. Heinz Co.

Ingredients: water (necessary for preparation), fully ripened bananas, corn syrup, modified tapiocal starch, food starch–modified (from corn), concentrated pineapple juice, concentrated orange juice, citric acid, vitamin C.

Amount: 1 jar/4¾ oz			% USRDA
Calories	87	Protein	*
Protein, gm	<1	Vitamin A	*
Carbohydrates, gm	21	Vitamin C	39
Fat, gm	<1	Thiamine	4
Sodium, mg	20	Riboflavin	*
Cholesterol, mg	0	Niacin	*
Fiber, gm	1	Calcium	*
		Iron	3

THIS FOOD: Heinz Bananas and Pineapple with Tapioca is an excellent source of vitamin C. It contains modified starch and added sugar in the form of corn syrup, which many authorities believe should be avoided by infants less than six months old.

ADDITIVES: No questionable additives.

Meat and Vegetables

BEECH-NUT STAGE 1 CHICKEN AND CHICKEN BROTH
Beech-Nut Nutrition Corp.

Ingredients: chicken and water.

Amount: 1 jar/3½ oz			% USRDA
Calories	110	Protein	70
Protein, gm	13	Vitamin A	*
Carbohydrates, gm	1	Vitamin C	*
Fat, gm	6	Thiamine	2
Sodium, mg	70	Riboflavin	25
Cholesterol, mg	na	Niacin	35
Fiber, gm	0	Calcium	6
		Iron	8

THIS FOOD: Beech-Nut Chicken and Chicken Broth is an excellent source of protein, niacin, and riboflavin. About 50 percent of the calories in this product derive from fat.

ADDITIVES: None.

BEECH-NUT STAGE 1 MOHAWK VALLEY GREEN BEANS
Beech-Nut Nutrition Corp.

Ingredients: green beans and water (necessary for preparation).

Amount: 1 jar/4½ oz			% USRDA
Calories	40	Protein	6
Protein, gm	1	Vitamin A	45
Carbohydrates, gm	8	Vitamin C	25
Fat, gm	0	Thiamine	4
Sodium, mg	<10	Riboflavin	20
Cholesterol, mg	0	Niacin	4
Fiber, gm	2e	Calcium	10
		Iron	8

THIS FOOD: Beech-Nut Stage 1 Mohawk Valley Green Beans are rich in naturally occurring vitamins A and C and also contain some calcium and iron.

ADDITIVES: None.

BEECH-NUT STAGE 2 TURKEY DINNER SUPREME
Beech-Nut Nutrition Corp.

Ingredients: water, turkey, carrots, green beans, corn, rice starch, rice flour, onion powder, parsley flakes, basil, and garlic powder.

Amount: 1 jar/4½ oz			% USRDA
Calories	100	Protein	15
Protein, gm	4	Vitamin A	90
Carbohydrates, gm	10	Vitamin C	8
Fat, gm	5	Thiamine	2
Sodium, mg	45	Riboflavin	10
Cholesterol, mg	na	Niacin	10
Fiber, gm	1e	Calcium	10
		Iron	4

THIS FOOD: Beech-Nut Stage 2 Turkey Dinner Supreme is rich in vitamin A. Forty-five percent of its calories derive from fat. This product contains added seasonings which may appeal to adult tastes, but are not needed by babies.

ADDITIVES: None.

BEECH-NUT STAGE 2 VEGETABLE BEEF DINNER
Beech-Nut Nutrition Corp.

Ingredients: water, carrots, beef, dried potato flakes, rice flour, peas, green beans, cornstarch, pea powder, onion powder, torula yeast, and celery seed.

Amount: 1 jar/4½ oz			% USRDA
Calories	90	Protein	10
Protein, gm	2	Vitamin A	150
Carbohydrates, gm	12	Vitamin C	10
Fat, gm	3	Thiamine	4
Sodium, mg	40	Riboflavin	10
Cholesterol, mg	na	Niacin	10
Fiber, gm	1e	Calcium	2
		Iron	2

THIS FOOD: Beech-Nut Stage 2 Vegetable Beef Dinner supplies well-balanced amounts of protein, fat, and carbohydrates and is an excellent source of vitamin A (from the carrots). This product contains added seasonings which may appeal to adult tastes, but are not needed by babies.

ADDITIVES: None.

GERBER STRAINED BEEF
Gerber Products Co.

Ingredients: beef and water.

Amount: 1 jar/3½ oz			% USRDA
Calories	100	Protein	30
Protein, gm	14	Vitamin A	*
Carbohydrates, gm	1	Vitamin C	4
Fat, gm	5	Thiamine	*
Sodium, mg	80	Riboflavin	20
Cholesterol, mg	na	Niacin	35
Fiber, gm	0	Calcium	*
		Iron	10

THIS FOOD: Gerber Strained Beef is rich in protein and niacin and also provides riboflavin and iron. About 45 percent of its calories derive from fat.

ADDITIVES: None.

GERBER STRAINED MIXED VEGETABLES
Gerber Products Co.

Ingredients: water (necessary for preparation), carrots, tomato puree, wheat flour, oat flour, potato solids, and onion.

Amount: 1 jar/4½ oz			% USRDA
Calories	50	Protein	6
Protein, gm	1	Vitamin A	160
Carbohydrates, gm	10	Vitamin C	4
Fat, gm	1	Thiamine	6
Sodium, mg	30	Riboflavin	4
Cholesterol, mg	0	Niacin	4
Fiber, gm	1e	Calcium	2
		Iron	2

THIS FOOD: Gerber Strained Mixed Vegetables provide 160 percent of the USRDA for vitamin A.

ADDITIVES: None.

HELPFUL HINT: During your baby's first year, its protein requirements should be met by milk. Solid foods are important as a calorie supplement, to support rapid growth. Care must be taken not to give your baby too much protein, which can be a strain on immature kidneys.

GERBER STRAINED TURKEY WITH VEGETABLE
Gerber Products Co.

Ingredients: water, turkey, carrots, rice flour, wheat flour, tomato puree, potato solids, nonfat dry milk, and onion powder

Amount: 1 jar/4½ oz		% USRDA	
Calories	130	Protein	45
Protein, gm	8	Vitamin A	25
Carbohydrates, gm	8	Vitamin C	6
Fat, gm	7	Thiamine	2
Sodium, mg	70	Riboflavin	15
Cholesterol, mg	na	Niacin	20
Fiber, gm	< 1e	Calcium	10
		Iron	6

THIS FOOD: Gerber Strained Turkey with Vegetable is rich in protein and also supplies vitamin A, riboflavin, niacin, and calcium. About 48 percent of the calories in this product derive from fat.

ADDITIVES: None.

GERBER STRAINED VEGETABLES WITH CHICKEN
Gerber Products Co.

Ingredients: water, cooked chicken, carrots, rice flour, wheat flour, pineapple juice concentrate, potato solids, green split peas, onion powder, and celery extractives.

Amount: 1 jar/4½ oz		% USRDA	
Calories	80	Protein	10
Protein, gm	3	Vitamin A	15
Carbohydrates, gm	12	Vitamin C	2
Fat, gm	2	Thiamine	4
Sodium, mg	40	Riboflavin	4
Cholesterol, mg	na	Niacin	4
Fiber, gm	na	Calcium	4
		Iron	2

THIS FOOD: Gerber Strained Vegetables with Chicken provides a good balance of protein, fat, and carbohydrates. It contains added seasonings which may appeal to adult tastes, but are not needed by babies.

ADDITIVES: None.

HEINZ BEEF AND BEEF BROTH
H. J. Heinz Co.

Ingredients: beef, water.

Amount: 1 jar/3½ oz			% USRDA
Calories	126	Protein	30
Protein, gm	14	Vitamin A	*
Carbohydrates, gm	0	Vitamin C	*
Fat, gm	7	Thiamine	3
Sodium, mg	47	Riboflavin	14
Cholesterol, mg	na	Niacin	20
Fiber, gm	0	Calcium	*
		Iron	13

THIS FOOD: Heinz Beef and Beef Broth contains 30 percent of the USRDA for protein, 20 percent of the USRDA for riboflavin, and 13 percent for iron. About 50 percent of its calories derive from fat.

ADDITIVES: None.

HEINZ VEGETABLES, EGG NOODLES, AND CHICKEN
H. J. Heinz Co.

Ingredients: chicken broth, carrots, egg noodles, modified food starch (from corn), chicken, celery, soybean oil, defatted soy flour, nonfat dry milk, split peas, dehydrated potatoes, onion powder.

Amount: 1 jar/4½ oz			% USRDA
Calories	68	Protein	6
Protein, gm	3	Vitamin A	36
Carbohydrates, gm	10	Vitamin C	*
Fat, gm	2	Thiamine	9
Sodium, mg	31	Riboflavin	8
Cholesterol, mg	na	Niacin	8
Fiber, gm	na	Calcium	4
		Iron	5

THIS FOOD: Heinz Vegetables, Egg Noodles, and Chicken is rich in vitamin A. This product contains seasonings which may appeal to adult tastes, but are not needed by babies.

ADDITIVES: No questionable additives.

HELPFUL HINT: If your baby is prone to food allergies, most experts believe it's best to avoid mixed-ingredient foods.

BISCUITS AND BISCUIT MIXES

Biscuits and biscuit mixes are available in many varieties and provide complex carbohydrates and small amounts of dietary fiber, the B vitamins, and iron. The leading refrigerated doughs, such as Pillsbury's Butter Biscuits or Country Style Biscuits, usually contain controversial additives, such as artificial flavors and BHA. General Mills used to produce an excellent whole wheat baking mix without controversial additives as part of the Bisquick line, but this wholesome product has been taken off the market. Among the products profiled, fat content varies widely from variety to variety, supplying anywhere from 18 to 37 percent of calories, and all are moderately high in sodium.

SODIUM GUIDELINES: In evaluating the sodium content of biscuits and biscuit mixes, we have used the following standards:

350 mg to 600 mg	high in sodium
more than 600 mg	very high in sodium

Remember, these guidelines are not for people following medically restricted low-sodium diets, but for healthy individuals who wish to monitor their sodium intake.

BISQUICK BUTTERMILK BAKING MIX
General Mills, Inc.
Ingredients: enriched flour bleached (wheat flour, niacin, iron, thiamine mononitrate, riboflavin), animal and/or vegetable shortening (contains one or more of the following partially hydrogenated fats: soybean oil, cottonseed oil, palm oil, beef fat and/or nonhydrogenated lard), BHA, BHT, leavening (baking soda, sodium aluminum phosphate, monocalcium phosphate), cultured buttermilk, salt, whey.

Amount: ½ cup			% USRDA
Calories	240	Protein	6
Protein, gm	4	Vitamin A	*
Carbohydrates, gm	38	Vitamin C	*
Fat, gm	8	Thiamine	20
Sodium, mg	700	Riboflavin	15
Cholesterol, mg	<10e	Niacin	10
Fiber, gm	<1e	Calcium	8
		Iron	6

THIS FOOD: Bisquick Buttermilk Baking Mix provides protein and complex carbohydrates, and is a good source of the B vitamins. It contains 700 mg sodium per half-cup serving.

ADDITIVES: Contains BHA and BHT, whose long-term safety is currently being reexamined by FDA investigators.

HUNGRY JACK EXTRA RICH BUTTERMILK BISCUITS
The Pillsbury Co.

Ingredients: enriched bleached flour (bleached flour, niacin, iron, thiamine mononitrate, riboflavin), water, beef fat and/or hydrogenated vegetable oil (cottonseed, palm, soybean), with BHA and citric acid, dextrose, baking powder (sodium acid pyrophosphate, baking soda), cornstarch, potassium chloride, salt, artificial flavor.

Amount: 2 biscuits			% USRDA
Calories	179	Protein	8
Protein, gm	3	Vitamin A	*
Carbohydrates, gm	24	Vitamin C	*
Fat, gm	8	Thiamine	17
Sodium, mg	549	Riboflavin	8
Cholesterol, mg	<10e	Niacin	11
Fiber, gm	1e	Calcium	*
		Iron	7

THIS FOOD: Hungry Jack Extra Rich Buttermilk Biscuits provide complex carbohydrates and are a good source of the B-vitamins. Compared to other refrigerator dough biscuits, they are high in fat calories—45 percent of total. With 549 mg sodium per serving they are higher than average in this trace element. If you are concerned with your fat intake, you may want to consider Pillsbury Country Style or Butter Biscuits, which contain half the fat calories.

ADDITIVES: Contains artificial flavor, which may cause allergic reactions in sensitive individuals, and which some studies suggest may adversely affect behavior and the ability to complete school tasks in some sensitive children. Contains BHA, whose long-term safety is currently being reexamined by FDA investigators.

NOTE: The letter "e" indicates that the data has been estimated; < means "less than" and is used for small amounts of sodium or cholesterol; * means food contains less than 2% of USRDA; "na" means that the information was not available and appears only when data is insufficient.

HUNGRY JACK FLAKY BISCUITS
The Pillsbury Co.

Ingredients: enriched bleached flour (bleached flour, niacin, iron, thiamine, mononitrate, riboflavin), water, beef fat and/or hydrogenated vegetable oil (cottonseed, palm, or soybean), with BHA and citric acid, dextrose, baking powder (sodium acid pyrophosphate, baking soda), rice flour, cornstarch, xanthan gum, natural and artificial flavor.

Amount: 2 biscuits			% USRDA
Calories	171	Protein	4
Protein, gm	3	Vitamin A	*
Carbohydrates, gm	24	Vitamin C	*
Fat, gm	7	Thiamine	12
Sodium, mg	587	Riboflavin	8
Cholesterol, mg	<10e	Niacin	8
Fiber, gm	<3	Calcium	*
		Iron	8

THIS FOOD: Two Hungry Jack Flaky Biscuits provide complex carbohydrates and small amounts of the B vitamins and iron. Thirty-seven percent of their calories derive from fat, much of it saturated. With 587 mg sodium, they are higher than average in this trace element.

ADDITIVES: Contains artificial flavor, which may cause allergic reactions in sensitive individuals, and which some studies suggest may adversely affect behavior and the ability to complete school tasks in some sensitive children. Contains BHA, whose long-term safety is currently being reexamined by FDA investigators.

PILLSBURY BIG COUNTRY BUTTERMILK BISCUITS
The Pillsbury Co.

Ingredients: enriched bleached flour (bleached flour, niacin, iron, thiamine mononitrate, riboflavin), water, beef fat and/or hydrogenated vegetable oil (cottonseed, palm, soybean) with BHA and citric acid, dextrose, baking powder (sodium acid pyrophosphate, baking soda), salt, rice flour, cornstarch, potassium chloride, artificial flavor.

Amount: 2 biscuits			% USRDA
Calories	200	Protein	6
Protein, gm	4	Vitamin A	*
Carbohydrates, gm	29	Vitamin C	*
Fat, gm	8	Thiamine	15
Sodium, mg	630	Riboflavin	8
Cholesterol, mg	<10e	Niacin	10
Fiber, gm	<1e	Calcium	*
		Iron	6

THIS FOOD: Pillsbury Big Country Buttermilk Biscuits provide complex carbohydrates and are a good source of the B vitamins. Compared to other refrigerator dough biscuits, they are high in fat calories, which account for 40 percent of total calories. With 630 mg sodium per serving, they are very high in this trace element.

ADDITIVES: Contains artificial flavor, which may cause allergic reactions in sensitive individuals, and which some studies suggest may adversely affect behavior and the ability to complete school tasks in some sensitive children. Contains BHA, whose long-term safety is currently being reexamined by FDA investigators.

PILLSBURY BUTTER BISCUITS
The Pillsbury Co.

Ingredients: enriched bleached flour (bleached flour, niacin, iron, thiamine mononitrate, riboflavin), water, dextrose, beef fat and/or hydrogenated vegetable oil (cottonseed, palm, soybean), with BHA and citric acid, baking powder (sodium acid pyrophosphate, baking soda), cornstarch, potassium chloride, salt, natural and artificial flavor, artificial color, FD & C Yellow No. 5.

Amount: 2 biscuits			% USRDA
Calories	100	Protein	6
Protein, gm	3	Vitamin A	*
Carbohydrates, gm	20	Vitamin C	*
Fat, gm	2	Thiamine	10
Sodium, mg	357	Riboflavin	7
Cholesterol, mg	<10e	Niacin	6
Fiber, gm	<1e	Calcium	*
		Iron	5

THIS FOOD: Pillsbury Butter Biscuits provide complex carbohydrates. Compared to other refrigerator dough biscuits, they are relatively low in calories, only 18 percent of which come from fat. They contain less sodium than the other biscuits profiled, although they are still considered high in sodium.

ADDITIVES: Contains artificial color and flavor which some studies suggest may adversely affect behavior and the ability to complete school tasks in some sensitive children; artificial colors are inadequately tested, and artificial flavors may cause allergic reactions in some sensitive individuals. Also contains FD & C Yellow No. 5, which can cause allergic reactions, especially in aspirin-sensitive individuals.

PILLSBURY COUNTRY STYLE BISCUITS
The Pillsbury Co.

Ingredients: enriched bleached flour (bleached flour, niacin, iron, thiamine mononitrate, riboflavin), water, dextrose, beef fat and/or hydrogenated vegetable oil (cottonseed, palm, soybean), with BHA and citric acid, baking powder (sodium acid pyrophosphate, baking soda), cornstarch, potassium chloride, salt, natural and artificial flavors.

Amount: 2 biscuits			% USRDA
Calories	100	Protein	6
Protein, gm	3	Vitamin A	*
Carbohydrates, gm	20	Vitamin C	*
Fat, gm	2	Thiamine	10
Sodium, mg	356	Riboflavin	7
Cholesterol, mg	<10e	Niacin	7
Fiber, gm	< e	Calcium	*
		Iron	6

THIS FOOD: Pillsbury Country Style Biscuits provide complex carbohydrates and small amounts of the B vitamins and iron. They are relatively low in fat and, like most biscuits, high in sodium.

ADDITIVES: Contains artificial flavor, which may cause allergic reactions in sensitive individuals, and which some studies suggest may adversely affect behavior and the ability to complete school tasks in some sensitive children. Contains BHA, whose long-term safety is currently being reexamined by FDA investigators.

BREAD AND ROLLS

Bread and rolls should be an important part of everyone's diet—including people trying to lose weight. Contrary to popular myth bread is not fattening. Breads made from enriched white flour supply complex carbohydrates and small amounts of protein, the B vitamins, and iron.

Although white bread is still more popular than any other kind, consumption has declined by more than 30 percent since 1963. One explanation of this phenomenon is that there are simply fewer children today, and children are the primary consumers of white bread. At the same time rising interest in nutrition, and more sophisticated tastes, have increased the popularity of whole wheat, rye, pumpernickel, and specialty breads such as bagels and pita.

What are the nutritional facts about white bread? The Swiss government's position is clear: it actually taxes white bread and gives the proceeds to bakers of whole wheat bread! Here in this country, most nutritionists agree that whole wheat bread is better for you. When whole wheat is refined to make white flour, the bran and wheat germ are removed, along with eight vitamins and thirteen minerals. Fortification adds back thiamine, niacin, riboflavin, and iron. But white bread eaters still lose out on magnesium, zinc, copper, chromium, folic acid, vitamin B_6, vitamin K, vitamin E, and dietary fiber.

When choosing bread, be careful to read the ingredients list on the label. Many breads are packaged and named to appeal to nutrition-conscious consumers, but are actually less nutritious than they seem. For instance, Arnold Honey Wheat Berry Bread looks dark and nutty, and its name seems to promise whole grain goodness. But the ingredients list reveals that the bread contains no whole wheat flour, only cracked wheat (which is only slightly less refined than white) in combination with enriched white flour. It turns out that the dark wholesome look comes from raisin syrup and a minuscule amount of bran. For optimum nutrition, choose breads which place whole wheat flour first on the ingredients list and contain no plain wheat flour, which is the same thing as white flour. Also, for better protein quality, look for breads that contain eggs, milk, whey, or soy flour. These ingredients complement the cereal protein in bread so that the amino acid proportions better match the body's requirements.

SODIUM GUIDELINES: In evaluating the sodium content of breads, we used the following standards:

less than 200 mg	low in sodium
200 mg to 300 mg	moderate in sodium
more than 300 mg	high in sodium

Remember, these guidelines are not for people following medically restricted low-sodium diets, but for healthy individuals who wish to monitor their sodium intake.

SODIUM LOSERS

These breads and rolls are especially high in salt, with more than 400 mg sodium per serving.

Arnold Honey Wheat Berry Bread
Arnold Pumpernickel
Pepperidge Farm Brown 'n Serve French Enriched Rolls

ARNOLD BRICK OVEN WHITE BREAD
Continental Grain, Inc.

Ingredients: unbleached enriched wheat flour (flour, malted barley flour, niacin, reduced iron, thiamine mononitrate, riboflavin), water, corn syrup, partially hydrogenated soybean oil, salt, whey, yeast, nonfat milk, soy flour, mono- and diglycerides, honey, butter.

Amount: 2 slices			% USRDA
Calories	130	Protein	4
Protein, gm	4	Vitamin A	*
Carbohydrates, gm	22	Vitamin C	*
Fat, gm	2	Thiamine	8
Sodium, mg	205	Riboflavin	6
Cholesterol, mg	<5	Niacin	8
Fiber, gm	2e	Calcium	4
		Iron	6

THIS FOOD: Arnold Brick Oven White Bread supplies complex carbohydrates and average amounts of protein, B vitamins, and iron. It has fewer additives than most white breads, and no preservatives.

ADDITIVES: No questionable additives.

ARNOLD BRICK OVEN WHOLE WHEAT BREAD
Continental Grain, Inc.

Ingredients: whole wheat flour, water, corn syrup, partially hydrogenated soybean oil, molasses, salt, yeast, wheat gluten, whey, soy flour, ethoxylated mono- and diglycerides.

Amount: 2 slices			% USRDA
Calories	120	Protein	6
Protein, gm	4	Vitamin A	*
Carbohydrates, gm	19	Vitamin C	*
Fat, gm	3	Thiamine	4
Sodium, mg	190	Riboflavin	4
Cholesterol, mg	<5	Niacin	8
Fiber, gm	3e	Calcium	2
		Iron	6

NOTE: The letter "e" indicates that the data has been estimated; < means "less than" and is used for small amounts of sodium or cholesterol; * means food contains less than 2% of USRDA; "na" means that the information was not available and appears only when data is insufficient.

THIS FOOD: Arnold Brick Oven Whole Wheat Bread provides dietary fiber, complex carbohydrates, and average amounts of protein, B vitamins, and iron. Two slices supply 190 mg sodium, which is less than average for most breads.

ADDITIVES: No questionable additives.

ARNOLD HONEY WHEAT BERRY BREAD
Continental Grain, Inc.

Ingredients: cracked wheat, unbleached enriched wheat flour (flour, malted barley flour, niacin, reduced iron, thiamine mononitrate, riboflavin), water, honey, raisin syrup, partially hydrogenated soybean oil, salt, wheat bran, ground raisins, yeast, wheat gluten, wheat germ, vinegar.

Amount: 2 slices			% USRDA
Calories	180	Protein	8
Protein, gm	6	Vitamin A	*
Carbohydrates, gm	32	Vitamin C	*
Fat, gm	2	Thiamine	15
Sodium, mg	410	Riboflavin	4
Cholesterol, mg	<5	Niacin	10
Fiber, gm	2.5e	Calcium	2
		Iron	10

THIS FOOD: Arnold Honey Wheat Berry Bread is a high-protein bread and a good source of complex carbohydrates and thiamine. It also supplies a fair amount of iron. It contains fewer additives than most other commercially prepared breads and is preservative free. Because the slices are rather thick, a two-slice serving has more calories and nutrients than most other breads. A serving supplies 410 mg sodium, which is higher than average for this category.

ADDITIVES: No questionable additives.

FOR WEIGHT WATCHERS: Contrary to popular belief, bread (as well as other complex carbohydrates like pasta, grains, and starchy vegetables) is not fattening. In fact, it can actually help you to lose weight. According to a 1975 study, men who ate 12 slices of high-fiber bread with their meals lost weight effortlessly. They were simply asked to stay away from high calorie foods, but otherwise their diet was unrestricted. A comparable group of men who were given low-fiber bread also lost weight—but not as much. In choosing your bread, remember that whole wheat or whole grain breads are both richer in nutrients and better for weight control.

ARNOLD HOT DOG BUNS
Continental Grain, Inc.

Ingredients: unbleached enriched spring wheat flour (flour, malted barley flour, niacin, reduced iron, thiamine mononitrate, riboflavin), water, corn syrup, partially hydrogenated vegetable shortening (soybean oil), yeast, salt, gluten, yeast nutrients (calcium sulfate, ammonium sulfate, potassium bromate), malt, ethoxylated mono- and diglycerides, calcium propionate, spice, paprika.

Amount: 1 roll			% USRDA
Calories	110	Protein	4
Protein, gm	3	Vitamin A	*
Carbohydrates, gm	20	Vitamin C	*
Fat, gm	1	Thiamine	6
Sodium, mg	290	Riboflavin	4
Cholesterol, mg	0	Niacin	6
Fiber, gm	<1e	Calcium	2
		Iron	6

THIS FOOD: Arnold Hot Dog Buns provide complex carbohydrates as well as very small amounts of the B vitamins and iron

ADDITIVES: No questionable additives.

ARNOLD ORIGINAL BRAN'NOLA BREAD
Continental Grain, Inc.

Ingredients: unbleached enriched wheat flour (flour, malted barley flour, niacin, reduced iron, thiamine mononitrate, riboflavin), water, whole wheat flour, honey, four whole grain cereals (wheat, oats, rye, barley), unprocessed miller's bran, wheat gluten, yeast, raisin syrup, partially hydrogenated soybean oil, salt, wheat germ, whey, lecithin, coconut, soya grits, sesame seeds.

Amount: 2 slices			% USRDA
Calories	180	Protein	10
Protein, gm	7	Vitamin A	*
Carbohydrates, gm	31	Vitamin C	*
Fat, gm	3	Thiamine	15
Sodium, mg	355	Riboflavin	8
Cholesterol, mg	<5e	Niacin	15
Fiber, gm	3.5e	Calcium	2
		Iron	10

THIS FOOD: Arnold's Original Bran'nola Bread is basically white bread with added bran. It is a high-protein bread and a good source of complex carbohydrates and the B vitamins. It also supplies a fair amount of iron and fiber. Because the slices are rather thick, a two-slice serving has more calories and nutrients than most other breads.

ADDITIVES: No questionable additives.

ARNOLD PUMPERNICKEL
Continental Grain, Inc.

Ingredients: unbleached enriched wheat flour (flour, malted barley flour, niacin, reduced iron, thiamine mononitrate, riboflavin), water, light rye flour, rye sour, pumpernickel meal, caramel color, salt, yeast, partially hydrogenated vegetable shortening (soybean oil), malt, corn syrup, wheat gluten, ground caraway, calcium propionate, mono- and diglycerides, potassium bromate.

Amount: 2 slices			% USRDA
Calories	150	Protein	8
Protein, gm	5	Vitamin A	*
Carbohydrates, gm	28	Vitamin C	*
Fat, gm	1	Thiamine	2
Sodium, mg	460	Riboflavin	6
Cholesterol, mg	0	Niacin	10
Fiber, gm	3e	Calcium	*
		Iron	2

THIS FOOD: Arnold Pumpernickel supplies complex carbohydrates and protein and some dietary fiber. Compared to most other breads, it is high in sodium.

ADDITIVES: No questionable additives.

EARTH GRAINS LIGHT RYE BREAD
Campbell Taggart, Inc.

Ingredients: water, unbleached wheat flour, rye flour, wheat gluten, molasses, yeast, 2 percent or less of: salt, vegetable shortening (partially hydrogenated soybean and/or cottonseed and/or palm oils), caraway seeds, distilled vinegar, cultured sweet whey, whey solids, soy flour, yellow corn flour, garlic and onion powder, cornstarch, malted barley flour, mono- and diglycerides, malic, lactic, acetic, and phosphoric acids, yeast nutrients, (monocalcium phosphate, calcium sulfate, ammonium sulfate) potassium bromate, baking soda, iron, niacin, thiamine mononitrate, riboflavin.

Amount: 2 slices			% USRDA
Calories	150	Protein	10
Protein, gm	6	Vitamin A	*
Carbohydrates, gm	26	Vitamin C	*
Fat, gm	2	Thiamine	15
Sodium, mg	295	Riboflavin	6
Cholesterol, mg	<5e	Niacin	8
Fiber, gm	2e	Calcium	4
		Iron	6

THIS FOOD: Earth Grains Light Rye Bread is a high-protein bread which also supplies complex carbohydrates and dietary fiber. It is a good source of thiamine.

ADDITIVES: No questionable additives.

EARTH GRAINS STONE GROUND WHEAT BREAD
Campbell Taggart, Inc.

Ingredients: unbleached wheat flour, water, whole wheat flour, corn syrup, wheat bran, wheat gluten, 2 percent or less of: yeast, molasses, salt, partially hydrogenated soybean oil, whey solids, soy flour, distilled vinegar, caramel color, baking soda, cornstarch, malted barley flour, calcium and sodium stearoyl lactylate, yeast nutrients (monocalcium phosphate, calcium sulfate, ammonium sulfate), potassium bromate, iron, niacin, thiamine, mononitrate riboflavin.

Amount: 2 slices			% USRDA
Calories	140	Protein	10
Protein, gm	6	Vitamin A	*
Carbohydrates, gm	25	Vitamin C	*
Fat, gm	1	Thiamine	20
Sodium, mg	310	Riboflavin	10
Cholesterol, mg	0	Niacin	10
Fiber, gm	2.5e	Calcium	4
		Iron	10

THIS FOOD: Earth Grains Stone Ground Wheat Bread is a high-protein bread that also supplies complex carbohydrates and dietary fiber. It is a very good source of thiamine, and a fair source of riboflavin, niacin, and iron.

ADDITIVES: No questionable additives.

FRESH HORIZONS WHEAT BREAD
Ralston Purina Co.

Ingredients: water, enriched flour (barley malt, iron, niacin, thiamine mononitrate, riboflavin), powdered cellulose, wheat gluten, wheat bran, whole wheat flour, brown sugar, yeast, salt, sugar, soy flour, calcium sulfate, whey, dough conditioners (one or more of: sodium stearoyl lactylate, mono- and diglycerides, ethoxylated mono- and diglycerides, mono- or dicalcium phosphate, potassium bromate, artificial flavor, calcium propionate.

BEST BETS: Only two of the breads profiled contain less than 200 mg sodium per serving. Arnold Brick Oven Whole Wheat Bread, and Thomas' Protogen Protein Bread. The Arnold bread is the better choice because it is richer in dietary fiber.

Amount: 2 slices			% USRDA
Calories	100	Protein	8
Protein, gm	5	Vitamin A	*
Carbohydrates, gm	19	Vitamin C	*
Fat, gm	1	Thiamine	15
Sodium, mg	290	Riboflavin	8
Cholesterol, mg	0	Niacin	10
Fiber, gm	6e	Calcium	8
		Iron	10

THIS FOOD: This bread supplies complex carbohydrates, a fair amount of iron, and the B vitamins. While technically high in dietary fiber, the "powdered cellulose" which contributes the extra fiber is made from wood shavings. Many experts believe that fiber from this source is not as beneficial as fiber from more natural plant and cereal sources.

ADDITIVES: Contains artificial flavor, which may cause allergic reactions in sensitive individuals, and which some studies suggest may adversely affect behavior and the ability to complete school tasks in some sensitive children.

HOME PRIDE BUTTER TOP WHITE BREAD
Ralston Purina Co.

Ingredients: enriched flour (with barley malt, iron, niacin, thiamine mononitrate, riboflavin), water, sugar, partially hydrogenated vegetable shortening (soybean, cottonseed), yeast, salt, butter, whey, wheat gluten, soy flour, calcium sulfate, calcium caseinate, dough conditioners (calcium stearoyl lactylate, mono- and diglycerides, mono- or dicalcium phosphate, potassium bromate), skim milk.

Amount: 2 slices			% USRDA
Calories	150	Protein	8
Protein, gm	5	Vitamin A	*
Carbohydrates, gm	26	Vitamin C	*
Fat, gm	3	Thiamine	15
Sodium, mg	300	Riboflavin	10
Cholesterol, mg	<5	Niacin	10
Fiber, gm	1.5e	Calcium	6
		Iron	8

THIS FOOD: In addition to supplying complex carbohydrates, Home Pride Butter Top White Bread is a good source of the B vitamins. Made from refined white flour, it contains little fiber. There is in fact real butter in the recipe, but the fat content of this bread is no higher than average. This product is moderate in sodium.

ADDITIVES: No questionable additives.

HOME PRIDE 100% WHOLE WHEAT BREAD
Ralston Purina Co.

Ingredients: enriched flour (barley malt, iron, niacin, thiamine mononitrate, riboflavin), water, sugar, wheat bran, whole wheat flour, wheat gluten, yeast, partially hydrogenated vegetable and/or animal shortening (may contain soybean and/or cottonseed oils and/or beef fat and/or lard), salt, whey, soy flour, butter, honey, corn syrup, calcium sulfate, calcium caseinate, dough conditioners (calcium stearoyl lactylate, mono- and diglyceride, ethoxylated mono- and diglycerides, mono- or dicalcium phosphate, potassium bromate).

Amount: 2 slices			% USRDA
Calories	140	Protein	8
Protein, gm	5	Vitamin A	*
Carbohydrates, gm	24	Vitamin C	*
Fat, gm	2	Thiamine	15
Sodium, mg	280	Riboflavin	10
Cholesterol, mg	<5	Niacin	10
Fiber, gm	3e	Calcium	4
		Iron	10

THIS FOOD: Home Pride 100% Whole Wheat Bread contains protein, dietary fiber, and complex carbohydrates and is a good source of the B vitamins and iron.

ADDITIVES: No questionable additives.

HOME PRIDE 7 GRAIN BREAD
Ralston Purina Co.

Ingredients: enriched flour (barley malt, iron, niacin, thiamine mononitrate, riboflavin), water, whole wheat flour, corn syrup, brown sugar, wheat bran, honey, partially hydrogenated vegetable shortening (may contain soybean and/or cottonseed oils), yeast, wheat gluten, salt, butter, soy meal, triticale flour, rye meal, soy flour, flaxseed meal, oatmeal, cornmeal, cracked wheat, whey, calcium sulfate, dough conditioners (one or more of: sodium stearoyl lactylate, mono- and diglycerides, ethoxylated mono- and diglycerides, mono- or dicalcium phosphate, potassium bromate).

Amount: 2 slices			% USRDA
Calories	140	Protein	8
Protein, gm	5	Vitamin A	*
Carbohydrates, gm	25	Vitamin C	*
Fat, gm	2	Thiamine	15
Sodium, mg	270	Riboflavin	10
Cholesterol, mg	0	Niacin	10
Fiber, gm	3e	Calcium	4
		Iron	10

THIS FOOD: Home Pride 7 Grain Bread provides protein, dietary fiber, and complex carbohydrates and is a good source of the B vitamins and iron. Because the protein comes from several grains as well as flaxseed and soy products, it is better than average in quality.

ADDITIVES: No questionable additives.

HOME PRIDE WHEATBERRY BREAD
Ralston Purina Co.

Ingredients: whole wheat flour, water, cracked wheat, corn syrup, enriched flour (barley malt, iron, niacin, thiamine mononitrate, riboflavin), wheat gluten, whole grain wheat, salt, honey, molasses, partially hydrogenated vegetable shortening (may contain soybean and/or cottonseed oils), wheat germ, yeast, calcium sulfate, dough conditioners (calcium stearoyl lactylate, mono- and diglyceride).

Amount: 2 slices			% USRDA
Calories	140	Protein	8
Protein, gm	5	Vitamin A	*
Carbohydrates, gm	25	Vitamin C	*
Fat, gm	2	Thiamine	15
Sodium, mg	300	Riboflavin	8
Cholesterol, mg	0	Niacin	10
Fiber, gm	3e	Calcium	6
		Iron	10

THIS FOOD: Home Pride Wheatberry Bread supplies protein, dietary fiber, and complex carbohydrates and is a good source of the B vitamins and iron.

ADDITIVES: No questionable additives.

LENDER'S PLAIN BAGELS
Lender's Bagel Bakery, Inc.

Ingredients: unbleached enriched high-gluten flour, water, sugar, salt, yeast, malt. Enriched with niacin, reduced iron, thiamine mononitrate, riboflavin.

Amount: 1 bagel/2 oz			% USRDA
Calories	150	Protein	10
Protein, gm	6	Vitamin A	*
Carbohydrates, gm	30	Vitamin C	*
Fat, gm	1	Thiamine	15
Sodium, mg	352	Riboflavin	8
Cholesterol, mg	0	Niacin	8
Fiber, gm	1e	Calcium	2
		Iron	6

THIS FOOD: This high protein specialty bread provides complex carbohydrates as well as small amounts of fiber, B vitamins, and iron. It contains no preservatives and has a minimum of other additives.

ADDITIVES: No questionable additives.

LENDER'S RAISIN 'N HONEY BAGELS
Lender's Bagel Bakery, Inc.

Ingredients: unbleached enriched high-gluten flour, water, raisins, sugar, cottonseed or soya oil, yeast, honey, salt, cinnamon. Enriched with niacin, reduced iron, thiamine mononitrate, riboflavin.

Amount: 1 bagel/2½ oz			% USRDA
Calories	200	Protein	10
Protein, gm	8	Vitamin A	4
Carbohydrates, gm	40	Vitamin C	*
Fat, gm	1	Thiamine	15
Sodium, mg	385	Riboflavin	10
Cholesterol, mg	0	Niacin	10
Fiber, gm	1.5e	Calcium	2
		Iron	8

THIS FOOD: This high-protein specialty bread provides complex carbohydrates as well as average amounts of fiber and iron. It is a good source of B vitamins, contains no preservatives and has a minimum of other additives.

ADDITIVES: No questionable additives.

LEVY'S REAL UNSEEDED JEWISH RYE
Continental Grain, Inc.

Ingredients: unbleached enriched wheat flour, (flour, malted barley flour, niacin, reduced iron, thiamine mononitrate, riboflavin), water, light rye flour, rye sour, salt, yeast, partially hydrogenated vegetable shortening (soybean oil), ground caraway, malt, corn syrup, wheat gluten, calcium propionate, mono- and diglycerides, potassium bromate.

Amount: 2 slices			% USRDA
Calories	160	Protein	8
Protein, gm	6	Vitamin A	*
Carbohydrates, gm	30	Vitamin C	*
Fat, gm	2	Thiamine	15
Sodium, mg	370	Riboflavin	8
Cholesterol, mg	0	Niacin	10
Fiber, gm	2e	Calcium	2
		Iron	15

THIS FOOD: Levy's Real Unseeded Jewish Rye is a high-protein bread which also supplies complex carbohydrates, dietary fiber, iron, and is a good source of B vitamins.

ADDITIVES: No questionable additives.

MRS. WRIGHT'S BUTTER AND EGG BREAD
Safeway Stores, Inc.

Ingredients: unbleached enriched flour (flour, malted barley flour, iron [ferrous sulfate], niacin, thiamine [thiamine mononitrate or thiamine hydrochloride], riboflavin), water, whey, eggs, high-fructose corn syrup, butter, 2 percent or less of: yeast, soya flour, salt, calcium sulfate, dough conditioners (may contain one or more of: sodium stearoyl lactylate, ethoxylated mono- and diglycerides, monocalcium phosphate, calcium carbonate, potassium bromate) mono- and diglycerides, yeast nutrients (diammonium phosphate and/or ammonium chloride or ammonium sulfate), calcium propionate.

Amount: 2 slices			% USRDA
Calories	150	Protein	6
Protein, gm	4	Vitamin A	*
Carbohydrates, gm	25	Vitamin C	*
Fat, gm	3	Thiamine	15
Sodium, mg	250e	Riboflavin	8
Cholesterol, mg	<5e	Niacin	8
Fiber, gm	1.5e	Calcium	6
		Iron	8

THIS FOOD: Mrs. Wright's Butter and Egg Bread supplies complex carbohydrates as well as small amounts of the B vitamins and iron.

ADDITIVES: No questionable additives.

MRS. WRIGHT'S 100% WHOLE WHEAT BREAD
Safeway Stores, Inc.

Ingredients: whole wheat flour, water, high-fructose corn syrup, 2 percent or less of: vegetable shortening (partially hydrogenated soybean oil and/or palm oil), molasses, yeast, salt, cultured whey, soya flour, calcium sulfate, dough conditioners (may contain one or more of: sodium stearoyl lactylate, ethoxylated mono- and diglycerides, monocalcium phosphate, calcium carbonate, ascorbic acid, potassium bromate), mono- and diglycerides, malted barley flour, yeast nutrients (ammonium chloride or ammonium sulfate).

Amount: 2 slices			% USRDA
Calories	110	Protein	6
Protein, gm	4	Vitamin A	*
Carbohydrates, gm	20	Vitamin C	*
Fat, gm	2	Thiamine	10
Sodium, mg	280	Riboflavin	2
Cholesterol, mg	0	Niacin	6
Fiber, gm	3e	Calcium	8
		Iron	4

THIS FOOD: Mrs. Wright's 100% Whole Wheat Bread provides complex carbohydrates, dietary fiber, and thiamine.

ADDITIVES: No questionable additives.

MRS. WRIGHT'S SANDWICH WHITE ENRICHED BREAD
Safeway Stores, Inc.

Ingredients: unbleached enriched flour (flour, malted barley flour, iron, niacin, thiamine [thiamine mononitrate or thiamine hydrochloride], riboflavin), water, whey, high-fructose corn syrup, 2 percent or less of: vegetable shortening (partially hydrogenated soybean oil and/or palm oil), yeast, soya flour, salt, calcium sulfate, dough conditioners (may contain one or more of: sodium stearoyl lactylate, ethoxylated mono- and diglycerides, monocalcium phosphate, calcium carbonate, potassium bromate) mono- and diglycerides, yeast nutrients (diammonium phosphate and/or ammonium chloride or ammonium sulfate), calcium propionate.

Amount: 2 slices			% USRDA
Calories	120	Protein	4
Protein, gm	3	Vitamin A	*
Carbohydrates, gm	24	Vitamin C	*
Fat, gm	1	Thiamine	10
Sodium, mg	250	Riboflavin	6
Cholesterol, mg	0	Niacin	6
Fiber, gm	1.5e	Calcium	6
		Iron	6

THIS FOOD: Supplies complex carbohydrates and small amounts of the B vitamins and iron.

ADDITIVES: No questionable additives.

PEPPERIDGE FARM BROWN 'N SERVE FRENCH ENRICHED ROLLS
Pepperidge Farm, Inc.

Ingredients: unbleached enriched wheat flour (flour, niacin, reduced iron, thiamine mononitrate, riboflavin), water, yeast, salt, corn syrup, partially hydrogenated vegetable shortening (soybean, palm and/or cottonseed oils), yellow cornmeal, barley malt, calcium propionate, mono- and diglycerides (from hydrogenated vegetable oil).

Amount: ½ roll			% USRDA
Calories	180	Protein	10
Protein, gm	6	Vitamin A	*
Carbohydrates, gm	36	Vitamin C	*
Fat, gm	2	Thiamine	25
Sodium, mg	420	Riboflavin	10
Cholesterol, mg	0	Niacin	15
Fiber, gm	1e	Calcium	6
		Iron	8

THIS FOOD: Supplies complex carbohydrates, a small amount of iron, is good source of protein and vitamins. This product is high in sodium.

ADDITIVES: No questionable additives.

PEPPERIDGE FARM FAMILY RYE BREAD
Pepperidge Farm, Inc.

Ingredients: unbleached enriched wheat flour (flour, niacin, reduced iron, thiamine mononitrate, riboflavin), water, enriched rye flour (rye flour, niacin, reduced iron, thiamine mononitrate, riboflavin), natural rye sour flavor, wheat gluten, salt, partially hydrogenated vegetable shortening (soybean, palm and/ or cottonseed oils), unsulphured molasses, yeast, caraway seed, calcium propionate, onion powder, garlic powder, and mono- and diglycerides (from hydrogenated vegetable oil).

Amount: 2 slices			% USRDA
Calories	170	Protein	10
Protein, gm	6	Vitamin A	*
Carbohydrates, gm	31	Vitamin C	*
Fat, gm	2	Thiamine	20
Sodium, mg	490	Riboflavin	10
Cholesterol, mg	0	Niacin	10
Fiber, gm	2e	Calcium	4
		Iron	10

THIS FOOD: Is a high-protein bread providing complex carbohydrates and dietary fiber. It is a good source of B vitamins.

ADDITIVES: No questionable additives.

PEPPERIDGE FARM HONEY WHEAT BERRY BREAD
Pepperidge Farm, Inc.

Ingredients: unbleached enriched wheat flour (flour, niacin, reduced iron, thiamine mononitrate, riboflavin), water, cracked wheat, stone-ground 100 percent whole wheat flour, honey, unsulphured molasses, partially hydrogenated vegetable shortening (soybean, palm and/or cottonseed oils), yeast, wheat gluten, salt, vinegar, caramel color, and mono- and diglycerides (from hydrogenated vegetable oil).

Amount: 2 slices			% USRDA
Calories	140	Protein	6
Protein, gm	4	Vitamin A	*
Carbohydrates, gm	27	Vitamin C	*
Fat, gm	2	Thiamine	10
Sodium, mg	320	Riboflavin	6
Cholesterol, mg	0	Niacin	8
Fiber, gm	2e	Calcium	2
		Iron	8

THIS FOOD: Despite its wholesome-sounding name, Pepperidge Farm Honey Wheat Berry Bread is really white bread with small amounts of cracked wheat and whole wheat flour added. It is an average source of protein, dietary fiber, and complex carbohydrates and provides small amounts of the B vitamins and iron.

ADDITIVES: No questionable additives.

PEPPERIDGE FARM PETITE ALL BUTTER CROISSANTS
Pepperidge Farm, Inc.

Ingredients: unbleached enriched wheat flour (flour, niacin, reduced iron, thiamine mononitrate, riboflavin), butter, nonfat milk, sugar, yeast, salt and calcium propionate.

Amount: 1 croissant			% USRDA
Calories	130	Protein	4
Protein, gm	3	Vitamin A	6
Carbohydrates, gm	14	Vitamin C	*
Fat, gm	7	Thiamine	6
Sodium, mg	160	Riboflavin	8
Cholesterol, mg	12e	Niacin	6
Fiber, gm	< 1e	Calcium	4
		Iron	6

THIS FOOD: Contains the equivalent of 1½ teaspoons butter and 48 percent of its calories derive from fat. In addition to complex carbohydrates, a croissant supplies small amounts of the B vitamins and iron. Its sodium content is low.

ADDITIVES: No questionable additives.

PEPPERIDGE FARM SIDE-SLICED ENRICHED FRANKFURTER ROLLS
Pepperidge Farm, Inc.

Ingredients: unbleached enriched wheat flour (flour, niacin, reduced iron, thiamine mononitrate, riboflavin, nonfat milk, sugar, partially hydrogenated vegetable shortening (soybean, palm and/or cottonseed oils), yeast, wheat gluten, salt, barley malt, calcium propionate, mono- and diglycerides (from hydrogenated vegetable oil), protease, potassium bromate, and lecithin.

Amount: 1 roll			% USRDA
Calories	140	Protein	8
Protein, gm	5	Vitamin A	*
Carbohydrates, gm	23	Vitamin C	*
Fat, gm	3	Thiamine	10
Sodium, mg	320	Riboflavin	10
Cholesterol, mg	<5e	Niacin	10
Fiber, gm	< 1e	Calcium	4
		Iron	6

THIS FOOD: Provides complex carbohydrates, average amounts of protein and iron, and more of the B vitamins than most other hot dog rolls. It is high in sodium.

ADDITIVES: No questionable additives.

PEPPERIDGE FARM SPROUTED WHEAT SLICED BREAD
Pepperidge Farm, Inc.

Ingredients: stone ground 100 percent whole wheat flour, water, wheat kernels, sesame seed, wheat germ, sunflower seed, honey, partially hydrogenated soybean oil, salt, wheat gluten, brown sugar, unsulphured molasses, yeast, vinegar and lemon puree.

Amount: 2 slices			% USRDA
Calories	140	Protein	8
Protein, gm	5	Vitamin A	*
Carbohydrates, gm	23	Vitamin C	*
Fat, gm	3	Thiamine	10
Sodium, mg	220	Riboflavin	4
Cholesterol, mg	0	Niacin	8
Fiber, gm	3.5e	Calcium	2
		Iron	10

THIS FOOD: Pepperidge Farm Sprouted Wheat Sliced Bread is a source of protein, dietary fiber, and complex carbohydrates and provides small amounts of the B vitamins and iron. It has none of the preservatives, emulsifiers, stabilizers, and other additives common to other commercially prepared breads.

ADDITIVES: No questionable additives.

PEPPERIDGE FARM WHITE THIN SLICED ENRICHED BREAD
Pepperidge Farm, Inc.

Ingredients: unbleached enriched wheat flour (flour, niacin, reduced iron, thiamine mononitrate, riboflavin), nonfat milk, water, corn syrup, partially hydrogenated vegetable shortening (soybean, palm and/or cottonseed oils), salt, yeast, mono- and diglycerides (from hydrogenated vegetable oil), butter, calcium propionate, honey, and lecithin.

Amount: 2 slices			% USRDA
Calories	150	Protein	6
Protein, gm	4	Vitamin A	*
Carbohydrates, gm	25	Vitamin C	*
Fat, gm	3	Thiamine	15
Sodium, mg	270	Riboflavin	10
Cholesterol, mg	<5e	Niacin	10
Fiber, gm	1.5e	Calcium	4
		Iron	6

THIS FOOD: In addition to supplying complex carbohydrates and a small amount of iron, Pepperidge Farm White Thin Sliced Enriched Bread is a good source of the B vitamins.

ADDITIVES: No questionable additives.

PEPPERIDGE FARM WHOLE WHEAT THIN SLICED BREAD
Pepperidge Farm, Inc.

Ingredients: stone ground 100 percent whole wheat flour, water, nonfat milk, unsulphured molasses, partially hydrogenated vegetable shortening (soybean, palm and/or cottonseed oils), corn syrup, wheat gluten, yeast, salt, butter, calcium propionate, honey, mono- and diglycerides (from hydrogenated vegetable oil), and lecithin.

Amount: 2 slices			% USRDA
Calories	130	Protein	8
Protein, gm	5	Vitamin A	*
Carbohydrates, gm	24	Vitamin C	*
Fat, gm	3	Thiamine	10
Sodium, mg	250	Riboflavin	2
Cholesterol, mg	<5e	Niacin	6
Fiber, gm	3e	Calcium	4
		Iron	10

THIS FOOD: Pepperidge Farm Whole Wheat Thin Sliced Bread supplies protein, dietary fiber, and complex carbohydrates and provides small amounts of the B vitamins and iron.

ADDITIVES: No questionable additives.

PIPIN' HOT WHEAT LOAF DINNER ROLLS
The Pillsbury Co.

Ingredients: bleached bromated enriched flour (flour, potassium bromate, niacin, iron, thiamine mononitrate, riboflavin), water, cracked wheat, whole wheat flour, beef fat, and hydrogenated soybean oil with BHA and citric acid, artificial flavor, vital wheat gluten, sugar, glucono delta-lactone, salt, baking soda, xanthan gum, sodium aluminum phosphate, caramel color, ascorbic acid.

Amount: 2 rolls			% USRDA
Calories	155	Protein	11
Protein, gm	5	Vitamin A	*
Carbohydrates, gm	25	Vitamin C	*
Fat, gm	3	Thiamine	13
Sodium, mg	341	Riboflavin	8
Cholesterol, mg	<5e	Niacin	8
Fiber, gm	2e	Calcium	*
		Iron	6

THIS FOOD: Pipin' Hot Wheat Loaf Dinner Rolls provide valuable fiber, complex carbohydrates, and small amounts of B vitamins and iron.

ADDITIVES: Contains artificial flavor, which may cause allergic reactions in sensitive individuals, and which some studies suggest may adversely affect behavior and the ability to complete school tasks in some sensitive children. Contains BHA, whose long-term safety is currently being reexamined by FDA investigators.

PIPIN' HOT WHITE LOAF DINNER ROLLS
The Pillsbury Co.

Ingredients: bleached bromated enriched flour (flour, potassium bromate, niacin, iron, thiamine mononitrate, riboflavin), water, beef fat, and hydrogenated soybean oil with BHA and citric acid, artificial flavor, sugar, vital wheat gluten, glucono delta-lactone, salt, baking soda, xanthan gum, sodium aluminum phosphate, ascorbic acid.

Amount: 2 rolls			% USRDA
Calories	153	Protein	11
Protein, gm	5	Vitamin A	*
Carbohydrates, gm	26	Vitamin C	*
Fat, gm	3	Thiamine	13
Sodium, mg	336	Riboflavin	8
Cholesterol, mg	<5e	Niacin	9
Fiber, gm	1.5e	Calcium	*
		Iron	6

THIS FOOD: Pipin' Hot White Loaf Dinner Rolls supply complex carbohydrates as well as small amounts of the B vitamins and iron.

ADDITIVES: Contains artificial flavor, which may cause allergic reactions in sensitive individuals, and which some studies suggest may adversely affect behavior and the ability to complete school tasks in some sensitive children. Contains BHA, whose long-term safety is currently being reexamined by FDA investigators.

ROMAN MEAL
Ralston Purina Co.

Ingredients: wheat flour bleached, water, corn syrup, select wheat bran, whole wheat, yeast, vital wheat gluten, vegetable shortening (soybean, cottonseed, palm), whole rye, honey, molasses, salt, soy flour, whey solids, dough conditioners (ethoxylated mono- and diglycerides, sodium and/or calcium steroyl-2-lactylate, polysorbate 60, succinylated monoglycerides, malted barley flour, and potassium bromate) yeast nutrients (calcium sulfate and ammonium sulfate) defatted flaxseed meal, calcium propionate, calcium sulfate, ferrous sulfate, niacin, thiamine mononitrate, riboflavin.

Amount: 2 slices			% USRDA
Calories	140	Protein	8
Protein, gm	6	Vitamin A	0
Carbohydrates, gm	25	Vitamin C	0
Fat, gm	2	Thiamine	15
Sodium, mg	280	Riboflavin	10
Cholesterol, mg	<5	Niacin	10
Fiber, gm	3e	Calcium	6
		Iron	10

THIS FOOD: The bleached white flour in Roman Meal bread is mixed with some bran and whole grain and soy flours. As a result it is somewhat higher in protein and fiber than are true white breads. Also the protein is higher in quality than the protein found in single-grain wheat breads. This product is a good source of the B vitamins and a fair source of iron. It has a moderate amount of sodium.

ADDITIVES: No questionable additives.

THOMAS' PROTOGEN PROTEIN BREAD
S. B. Thomas, Inc.

Ingredients: water, flour (unbleached white flour and malted barley), whole wheat flour, gluten flour, soya flour, yeast, vinegar, salt, calcium propionate, and mono- and diglycerides. Enriched with niacin, iron, thiamine, and riboflavin.

Amount: 2 slices			% USRDA
Calories	93	Protein	10
Protein, gm	7	Vitamin A	*
Carbohydrates, gm	15	Vitamin C	*
Fat, gm	1	Thiamine	8
Sodium, mg	188	Riboflavin	4
Cholesterol, mg	0	Niacin	6
Fiber, gm	2e	Calcium	4
		Iron	6

THIS FOOD: Thomas' Protogen Protein Bread is low in calories and high in protein because its recipe includes soya flour. It is a source of complex carbohydrates and fiber and supplies small amounts of B vitamins and iron. One serving contains 188 mg sodium, which is low for this category. This product has fewer additives than most breads.

ADDITIVES: No questionable additives.

WONDER HOT DOG ROLLS
Ralston Purina Co.

Ingredients: enriched flour (barley malt, iron, niacin, thiamine mononitrate, riboflavin), water, corn syrup, partially hydrogenated vegetable and/or animal shortening (may contain soybean and/or cottonseed oils and/or beef fat and/or lard), yeast, salt, wheat gluten, soy flour, calcium sulfate, whey, calcium casei-nate, dough conditioners (contains one or more of: calcium stearoyl lactylate, mono- and diglycerides, mono- or dicalcium phosphate, potassium bromate), calcium propionate.

Amount: 1 roll			% USRDA
Calories	120	Protein	6
Protein, gm	4	Vitamin A	0
Carbohydrates, gm	22	Vitamin C	0
Fat, gm	3	Thiamine	10
Sodium, mg	230	Riboflavin	6
Cholesterol, mg	<5	Niacin	6
Fiber, gm	< 1e	Calcium	6
		Iron	6

THIS FOOD: Wonder Hot Dog Rolls are made from bleached flour and supply complex carbohydrates as well as small amounts of protein, the B vitamins, and iron.

ADDITIVES: No questionable additives.

OTHER BRANDS: Pepperidge Farm Enriched Frankfurter Rolls are made from unbleached flour. Although unbleached flour may contain slightly more protein, fiber, and B vitamins, the difference is not significant. It is considered preferable because the bleaching process may occasionally leave chemical residues in the flour.

WONDER WHITE BREAD
Ralston Purina Co.

Ingredients: enriched flour (barley malt, iron, niacin, thiamine mononitrate, riboflavin), water, sugar, yeast, partially hydrogenated vegetable and/or animal shortening (may contain soybean and/or cottonseed oils and/or beef fat and/or lard), salt, wheat gluten, soy flour, calcium sulfate, whey, dough conditioners (one or more of: calcium stearoyl lactylate, mono- and diglycerides, mono- or dicalcium phosphate, potassium bromate), calcium propionate.

Amount: 2 slices			% USRDA
Calories	140	Protein	8
Protein, gm	5	Vitamin A	*
Carbohydrates, gm	27	Vitamin C	*
Fat, gm	2	Thiamine	15
Sodium, mg	305	Riboflavin	8
Cholesterol, mg	<5	Niacin	10
Fiber, gm	1.5e	Calcium	6
		Iron	8

THIS FOOD: In addition to providing complex carbohydrates, Wonder White Bread supplies a fair amount of B vitamins. It is moderately high in sodium.

ADDITIVES: No questionable additives.

BREAD CRUMBS AND STUFFING MIXES

The main ingredient in these products is bread, so it's hardly surprising that like bread, bread crumbs, croutons, and stuffing mixes also supply complex carbohydrates and small amounts of the B vitamins and iron. Although there are nutritional differences among these products, they don't have much practical significance, since, with the possible exception of stuffing, most people eat them in very small amounts. Stove Top Stuffing Mixes are high in sodium, and once you add the butter called for, they are also high in saturated fat. They also contain several controversial additives. Pepperidge Farm products generally contain fewer additives and more nutritious ingredients.

SODIUM GUIDELINES: In evaluating the sodium content of stuffing mixes, we have used the following standards:

350 mg to 600 mg	high in sodium
more than 600 mg	very high in sodium

Remember, these guidelines are not for people following medically restricted low-sodium diets, but for healthy individuals who wish to monitor their sodium intake.

PEPPERIDGE FARM CHEDDAR AND ROMANO CHEESE CROUTONS
Pepperidge Farm, Inc.

Ingredients: unbleached enriched wheat flour (flour, niacin, reduced iron, thiamine mononitrate, riboflavin), coconut oil, dehydrated pasteurized process Cheddar cheese, water, corn syrup, salt, dehydrated pasteurized process Romano cheese made from cow's milk, natural sour flavor, yeast, vinegar, natural flavor, and citric acid.

Amount: ½ cup			% USRDA
Calories	120	Protein	6
Protein, gm	4	Vitamin A	*
Carbohydrates, gm	18	Vitamin C	*
Fat, gm	4	Thiamine	12
Sodium, mg	380	Riboflavin	8
Cholesterol, mg	<5e	Niacin	8
Fiber, gm	1e	Calcium	4
		Iron	4

THIS FOOD: Pepperidge Farm Cheddar and Romano Cheese Croutons contain complex carbohydrates and fair amounts of the B vitamins. This product gets 30 percent of its calories from fat, mostly from coconut oil, which is highly saturated.

ADDITIVES: No questionable additives.

PEPPERIDGE FARM HERB SEASONED STUFFING MIX
Pepperidge Farm, Inc.

Ingredients: unbleached enriched wheat flour (flour, niacin, reduced iron, thiamine mononitrate, riboflavin), stone ground 100 percent whole wheat flour, water, salt, corn syrup, yeast, partially hydrogenated vegetable shortening (soybean, palm and/or cottonseed oils), unsulphured molasses, spices, onion powder, calcium propionate, celery seed, mono- and diglycerides (from hydrogenated vegetable oil), and citric acid.

Amount: ½ cup (+ 1½ tsp butter)			% USRDA
Calories	164	Protein	6
Protein, gm	4	Vitamin A	*
Carbohydrates, gm	22	Vitamin C	*
Fat, gm	5	Thiamine	20
Sodium, mg	481	Riboflavin	12
Cholesterol, mg	15e	Niacin	16
Fiber, gm	1e	Calcium	4
		Iron	12

THIS FOOD: Pepperidge Farm Herb Seasoned Stuffing Mix lists healthful stone ground whole wheat flour as its second main ingredient and is relatively high in protein. It is a good source of the B vitamins and iron. While the mix itself contains little fat, the instructions call for 1½ teaspoons added butter or margarine, which naturally detracts from the nutritional value of this food.

ADDITIVES: No questionable additives.

HELPFUL HINT: In order to reduce fat calories, try using about half the butter or margarine called for in the instructions and replace with an equal amount of liquid.

NOTE: The letter "e" indicates that the data has been estimated; < means "less than" and is used for small amounts of sodium or cholesterol; * means food contains less than 2% of USRDA; "na" means that the information was not available and appears only when data is insufficient.

PROGRESSO PLAIN BREAD CRUMBS
Ogden Food Products Corp.

Ingredients: toasted crumbs of enriched bread (enriched flour [wheat flour, niacin, reduced iron, thiamine mononitrate, riboflavin], corn syrup, sugar, shortening [hydrogenated soybean, cottonseed, palm, butter], salt, yeast, whey, soy flour, dough conditioner, yeast nutrients, calcium propionate).

Amount: ½ cup			% USRDA
Calories	173	Protein	9
Protein, gm	6	Vitamin A	*
Carbohydrates, gm	33	Vitamin C	*
Fat, gm	2	Thiamine	6
Sodium, mg	324	Riboflavin	8
Cholesterol, mg	0	Niacin	8
Fiber, gm	1.5	Calcium	*
		Iron	9

THIS FOOD: Progresso Plain Bread Crumbs are a good source of complex carbohydrates. They contain less sodium than seasoned croutons and stuffing mixes.

ADDITIVES: No questionable additives.

STOVE TOP AMERICANA NEW ENGLAND STYLE STUFFING MIX
General Foods Corp.

Ingredients: enriched bromated flour (wheat flour, niacin, reduced iron, thiamine mononitrate, riboflavin), corn syrup, rye flour, yeast, hydrolyzed vegetable protein, onion, salt, whey (from milk), partially hydrogenated soybean, cottonseed and/or palm oils, BHA, TBHQ, and citric acid, red bell peppers with sodium bisulfite, onion powder, parsley flakes, sugar, monosodium glutamate, soy flour, spices, calcium propionate, caramel color, natural flavor.

Amount: ½ cup (+ 2 tsp butter)			% USRDA
Calories	180	Protein	6
Protein, gm	4	Vitamin A	6
Carbohydrates, gm	21	Vitamin C	*
Fat, gm	9	Thiamine	10
Sodium, mg	635	Riboflavin	6
Cholesterol, mg	<5e	Niacin	6
Fiber, gm	<1e	Calcium	4
		Iron	6

THIS FOOD: When prepared with 2 teaspoons salted butter per serving, 45 percent of the calories in Stove Top Americana New England Style Stuffing derive from fat. One half-cup serving supplies a hefty 635 mg sodium.

ADDITIVES: Contains monosodium glutamate (MSG), which many experts believe should be avoided by infants and very young children; causes adverse reactions in some sensitive individuals. Also contains sodium sulfite, which can cause severe allergic reactions, especially in individuals with asthma.

OTHER BRANDS: Pepperidge Farm Stuffing Mixes do not contain questionable additives.

STOVE TOP CORNBREAD STUFFING MIX
General Foods Corp.

Ingredients: enriched bromated flour (wheat flour, niacin, reduced iron, thiamine mononitrate, riboflavin), degerminated yellow cornmeal, corn syrup, salt, onion, yeast, dried celery with sodium sulfite, partially hydrogenated soybean, cottonseed and/or palm oils with BHA, TBHQ, and citric acid, wheat gluten, parsley flakes, monosodium glutamate, chicken fat with BHA, propyl gallate and citric acid, spices, sugar, onion powder, turmeric, calcium propionate, hydrolized vegetable protein, dehydrated chicken meat, with BHA, propyl gallate and citric acid, artificial flavor, annatto, natural flavor.

Amount: ½ cup (+ 2 tsp butter)			% USRDA
Calories	174	Protein	4
Protein, gm	3	Vitamin A	6
Carbohydrates, gm	21	Vitamin C	*
Fat, gm	9	Thiamine	8
Sodium, mg	665	Riboflavin	4
Cholesterol, mg	20e	Niacin	6
Fiber, gm	<1e	Calcium	2
		Iron	6

THIS FOOD: More than 46 percent of the calories in Stove Top Cornbread Stuffing Mix come from fat. One serving supplies a very high amount of sodium—665 mg when prepared with salted butter.

ADDITIVES: Contains BHA, whose long-term safety is currently being reexamined by FDA investigators, as well as artificial flavor, which may cause allergic reactions in sensitive individuals, and which some studies suggest may adversely affect behavior and the ability to complete school tasks in some sensitive children. Also contains monosodium glutamate (MSG), which many experts believe should be avoided by infants and very young children; causes adverse reactions in sensitive individuals.

OTHER BRANDS: Pepperidge Farm Stuffing Mixes do not contain questionable additives.

BUTTER AND MARGARINE

Up to twenty percent of the milk produced in the United States is used to manufacture butter. Margarine, the substitute spread made from partially hydrogenated vegetable oil, emulsifiers, artificial flavor, and salt is consumed in far greater amounts. The cost issue is clear—margarine is cheaper, but most Americans report they buy margarine largely for health reasons. Is margarine healthier than butter? The simple answer to a complicated question is yes. Margarine is lower in cholesterol and saturated fat, both of which tend to raise cholesterol levels in the blood—and the risk of heart disease. But some margarines contain almost as much saturated fat as butter, so it's important to choose carefully. For instance, Blue Bonnet Soft and Stick Margarines are relatively high in saturated fat compared to Mrs. Filbert's Soft Corn Oil Margarine, which has nearly twice as much polyunsaturated fat. Generally speaking, the softer margarines which list liquid vegetable oil as their first ingredient are highest in desirable polyunsaturated fats. Many nutritionists feel it is more important to cut down on all fats, than to worry about the margarine-versus-butter issue. Also see *Oils* on page 363.

The relationship between polyunsaturated and saturated fats is sometimes expressed as the p/s ratio. Margarines with the highest ratio are the most unsaturated—and most desirable. The p/s ratio is still the accepted way of gauging whether a given oil is considered "heart healthy" even though it does not take into account new evidence which shows that monounsaturated fats may be as, or even more, helpful in lowering cholesterol levels.

SODIUM GUIDELINES: In evaluating the sodium content of butter and margarine, we used the following standards:

less than 100 mg	moderate in sodium
more than 100 mg	high in sodium

Remember, these guidelines are not for people following medically restricted low-sodium diets, but for healthy individuals who wish to monitor their sodium intake.

BUTTER

LAND O' LAKES LIGHTLY SALTED SWEET BUTTER
Land O'Lakes, Inc.

Ingredients: cream, milk, salt, annatto.

Amount: 1 tbsp			% USRDA
Calories	100	Protein	*
Protein, gm	0	Vitamin A	8
Carbohydrates, gm	0	Vitamin C	*
Fat, gm	11	Thiamine	*
Sodium, mg	115	Riboflavin	*
Cholesterol, mg	30	Niacin	*
Fiber, gm	0	Calcium	*
		Iron	*

THIS FOOD: Butter is high in cholesterol and derives 100 percent of its calories from fat, most of it saturated. Too much cholesterol and saturated fat in the diet may lead to elevated levels of serum cholesterol, a major risk factor in heart disease. One tablespoon of butter provides 8 percent of the USRDA for vitamin A. This product, which is "lightly salted," contains 115 mg sodium per serving.

ADDITIVES: No questionable additives.

LAND O' LAKES UNSALTED SWEET CREAM BUTTER
Land O' Lakes, Inc.

Ingredients: butter.

Amount: 1 tbsp			% USRDA
Calories	100	Protein	*
Protein, gm	0	Vitamin A	8
Carbohydrates, gm	0	Vitamin C	*
Fat, gm	11	Thiamine	*
Sodium, mg	2	Riboflavin	*
Cholesterol, mg	30	Niacin	*
Fiber, gm	0	Calcium	*
		Iron	*

THIS FOOD: Butter is high in cholesterol and derives 100 percent of its calories from fat, most of it saturated. Too much cholesterol and saturated fat in the diet may lead to elevated levels of serum cholesterol, a major risk factor in heart disease. One tablespoon of butter provides 8 percent of the USRDA for vitamin A.

ADDITIVES: No questionable additives.

MARGARINE AND BLENDS

BLUE BONNET SOFT MARGARINE
R. J. Reynolds Industries, Inc.

Ingredients: partially hydrogenated soybean oil, water, salt, whey, vegetable mono- and diglycerides and lecithin, sodium benzoate, artificially flavored and colored, (carotene) vitamin A palmitate, vitamin D_2.

Amount: 1 tbsp			% USRDA
Calories	100	Protein	*
Protein, gm	0	Vitamin A	10
Carbohydrates, gm	0	Vitamin C	*
Fat, gm	11	Thiamine	*
Sodium, mg	95	Riboflavin	*
Cholesterol, mg	0	Niacin	*
Fiber, gm	0	Calcium	*
		Iron	*

THIS FOOD: This product is made from partially hydrogenated soybean oil. Compared to other margarines, it has a below-average p/s rating of 1.5. While "soft" margarines usually have less saturated fat than stick varieties, this is not true for the two Blue Bonnet products. Like most margarines, this product contains a moderate amount of sodium.

ADDITIVES: Contains artificial flavor, which may cause allergic reactions in sensitive individuals, and which some studies suggest may adversely affect behavior and the ability to complete school tasks in some sensitive children.

BLUE BONNET STICK MARGARINE
R. J. Reynolds Industries, Inc.

Ingredients: partially hydrogenated soybean oil, liquid soybean oil, water, salt, whey, vegetable mono- and diglycerides and lecithin, sodium benzoate, artificially flavored and colored, (carotene) vitamin A palmitate, vitamin D_2.

Amount: 1 tbsp			% USRDA
Calories	100	Protein	*
Protein, gm	0	Vitamin A	10
Carbohydrates, gm	0	Vitamin C	*
Fat, gm	11	Thiamine	*
Sodium, mg	95	Riboflavin	*
Cholesterol, mg	0	Niacin	*
Fiber, gm	0	Calcium	*
		Iron	*

THIS FOOD: Partially hydrogenated oil is the largest single ingredient in this margarine. Compared to other margarines, it has a below-average p/s ratio of 1.5. Like most margarines it contains a moderate amount of sodium.

ADDITIVES: Contains artificial flavor, which may cause allergic reactions in sensitive individuals, and which some studies suggest may adversely affect behavior and the ability to complete school tasks in some sensitive children.

CHIFFON SOFT MARGARINE
Anderson Clayton Foods, Inc.

Ingredients: liquid soybean oil, partially hydrogenated soybean oil, water, salt, nonfat dry milk, mono- and diglycerides, vegetable lecithin, sorbic acid as a preservative, artificial flavoring, calcium disodium EDTA as a preservative, artificial coloring (beta carotene), vitamin A palmitate.

Amount: 1 tbsp			% USRDA
Calories	90	Protein	*
Protein, gm	0	Vitamin A	10
Carbohydrates, gm	0	Vitamin C	*
Fat, gm	10	Thiamine	*
Sodium, mg	105	Riboflavin	*
Cholesterol, mg	<5	Niacin	*
Fiber, gm	0	Calcium	*
		Iron	*

THIS FOOD: Made primarily from liquid soybean oil, this margarine has an acceptable p/s ratio of 2. Like most margarines it contains a moderate amount of sodium.

ADDITIVES: Contains artificial flavor, which may cause allergic reactions in sensitive individuals, and which some studies suggest may adversely affect behavior and the ability to complete school tasks in some sensitive children.

NUTRITION TIP: Virtually all manufacturers use beta carotene to give margarines their yellow coloring. This substance is a precursor of vitamin A and is considered totally safe. Indeed, recent research suggests that consuming large quantities of carotenoids from natural sources may help to protect against cancer.

NOTE: The letter "e" indicates that the data has been estimated; < means "less than" and is used for small amounts of sodium or cholesterol; * means food contains less than 2% of USRDA; "na" means that the information was not available and appears only when data is insufficient.

FLEISCHMANN'S DIET MARGARINE
R. J. Reynolds Industries, Inc.

Ingredients: water, liquid corn oil, partially hydrogenated corn oil, salt, vegetable, monoglycerides and lecithin, potassium sorbate, sodium benzoate, calcium disodium EDTA, artificially flavored and colored (carotene), vitamin A palmitate, vitamin D_2.

Amount: 1 tbsp			% USRDA
Calories	50	Protein	*
Protein, gm	0	Vitamin A	10
Carbohydrates, gm	0	Vitamin C	*
Fat, gm	6	Thiamine	*
Sodium, mg	100	Riboflavin	*
Cholesterol, mg	0	Niacin	*
Fiber, gm	0	Calcium	*
		Iron	*

THIS FOOD: One tablespoon of Fleischmann's Diet Margarine has about half the fat and calories of regular Fleischmann's margarines because water, rather than oil, is the main ingredient. It has an acceptable p/s ratio of 2 and contains a moderate amount of sodium.

ADDITIVES: Contains artificial flavor, which may cause allergic reactions in sensitive individuals, and which some studies suggest may adversely affect behavior and the ability to complete school tasks in some sensitive children.

FLEISCHMANN'S STICK MARGARINE
R. J. Reynolds Industries, Inc.

Ingredients: liquid corn oil, partially hydrogenated corn oil, water, salt, whey, vegetable mono- and diglycerides and lecithin, sodium benzoate, artificially flavored and colored (carotene), vitamin A palmitate, vitamin D_2.

Amount: 1 tbsp			% USRDA
Calories	100	Protein	*
Protein, gm	0	Vitamin A	10
Carbohydrates, gm	0	Vitamin C	*
Fat, gm	11	Thiamine	*
Sodium, mg	95	Riboflavin	*
Cholesterol, mg	0	Niacin	*
Fiber, gm	0	Calcium	*
		Iron	*

THIS FOOD: Made primarily from liquid corn oil, this margarine has an acceptable p/s ratio of 2. Like most margarines this product contains a moderate amount of sodium.

ADDITIVES: Contains artificial flavor which may cause allergic reactions in sensitive individuals, and which some studies suggest may adversely affect behavior and the ability to complete school tasks in some sensitive children.

FLEISCHMANN'S UNSALTED STICK MARGARINE
R. J. Reynolds Industries, Inc.

Ingredients: liquid corn oil, partially hydrogenated corn oil, water, mono- and diglycerides and lecithin, potassium sorbate, calcium disodium EDTA, phosphoric acid, artificially flavored and colored (carotene), vitamin A palmitate, vitamin D_2.

Amount: 1 tbsp			% USRDA
Calories	100	Protein	*
Protein, gm	0	Vitamin A	10
Carbohydrates, gm	0	Vitamin C	*
Fat, gm	11	Thiamine	*
Sodium, mg	1	Riboflavin	*
Cholesterol, mg	0	Niacin	*
Fiber, gm	0	Calcium	*
		Iron	*

THIS FOOD: Made primarily from liquid corn oil, this margarine has an acceptable p/s ratio of 2 and is also low in sodium.

ADDITIVES: Contains artificial flavor, which may cause allergic reactions in sensitive individuals, and which some studies suggest may adversely affect behavior and the ability to complete school tasks in some sensitive children. Beta carotene is considered safe.

HAIN SAFFLOWER MARGARINE
Hain Pure Foods Co., Inc.

Ingredients: liquid safflower oil, partially hydrogenated soybean oil, liquid soybean oil, water, vegetable lecithin, potassium sorbate, citric acid, carotene, vitamin A palmitate.

Amount: 1 tbsp			% USRDA
Calories	101	Protein	*
Protein, gm	<1	Vitamin A	9
Carbohydrates, gm	0	Vitamin C	*
Fat, gm	11	Thiamine	*
Sodium, mg	6	Riboflavin	*
Cholesterol, mg	0	Niacin	*
Fiber, gm	0	Calcium	*
		Iron	*

THIS FOOD: Hain Safflower Margarine, made primarily with liquid safflower oil, contains less saturated fat than most other margarines. All of the calories in this product derive from fat. It has a p/s ratio of 2.5.

ADDITIVES: No questionable additives.

IMPERIAL STICK MARGARINE
Unilever United States, Inc.

Ingredients: partially hydrogenated soybean and cottonseed oils, water, salt, whey, vegetable mono- and diglycerides and lecithin, sodium benzoate, artificial flavor, colored with beta carotene, vitamin A palmitate, vitamin D calciferol.

Amount: 1 tbsp			% USRDA
Calories	100	Protein	*
Protein, gm	0	Vitamin A	10
Carbohydrates, gm	0	Vitamin C	*
Fat, gm	11	Thiamine	*
Sodium, mg	112	Riboflavin	*
Cholesterol, mg	0	Niacin	*
Fiber, gm	0	Calcium	*
		Iron	*

THIS FOOD: Imperial Stick Margarine, made from partially hydrogenated soybean and cottonseed oils, contains more saturated fat than other leading brands. As with other margarines, 100 percent of calories derive from fat. This product has a p/s ratio of slightly more than 1.

ADDITIVES: Contains artificial flavors, which may cause allergic reactions in sensitive individuals, and which some studies suggest may adversely affect behavior and the ability to complete school tasks in some sensitive chldren.

HELPFUL HINT: If you like the flavor of butter when sautéeing, but wish to cut down on saturated fat, try halving the amount of butter you normally use, then substitute a good polyunsaturated vegetable oil, such as safflower oil, for half of this reduced amount. This means if you normally use 4 tablespoons butter for sautéeing a particular dish, try using only 1 tablespoon butter mixed with 1 tablespoon polyunsaturated oil. If the food sticks to the pan, add a little water or broth.

IMPERIAL WHIPPED MARGARINE
Unilever United States, Inc.

Ingredients: partially hydrogenated soybean and cottonseed oils, water, salt, vegetable mono- and diglycerides and lecithin, potassium sorbates and calcium disodium EDTA, artificial flavor, whey colored with beta carotene, vitamin A palmitate, vitamin D calciferol.

Amount: 1 tbsp			% USRDA
Calories	50	Protein	*
Protein, gm	0	Vitamin A	6
Carbohydrates, gm	0	Vitamin C	*
Fat, gm	5	Thiamine	*
Sodium, mg	70	Riboflavin	*
Cholesterol, mg	0	Niacin	*
Fiber, gm	0	Calcium	*
		Iron	*

THIS FOOD: Whipped Imperial Margarine, made from partially hydrogenated soybean and cottonseed oils, contains more saturated fat than other leading brands. It has fewer calories than regular margarines simply because it contains more air. This product has a p/s ratio of slightly more than 1.

ADDITIVES: Contains artificial flavors, which may cause allergic reactions in sensitive individuals, and which some studies suggest may adversely affect behavior and the ability to complete school tasks in some sensitive children.

LAND O' LAKES COUNTRY BLEND LIGHTLY SALTED MARGARINE
Land O' Lakes, Inc.

Ingredients: butter (grade AA sweet cream), liquid corn oil, partially hydrogenated corn oil, skim milk, water, salt, lecithin, mono- and diglycerides, artificial flavor, beta carotene, vitamin A.

Amount: 1 tbsp			% USRDA
Calories	100	Protein	*
Protein, gm	0	Vitamin A	10
Carbohydrates, gm	0	Vitamin C	*
Fat, gm	11	Thiamine	*
Sodium, mg	115	Riboflavin	*
Cholesterol, mg	10	Niacin	*
Fiber, gm	0	Calcium	*
		Iron	*

THIS FOOD: Land O' Lakes Country Blend Lightly Salted Margarine names butter as its main ingredient and so contains more saturated fat than unblended margarines. It has a low p/s ratio of 1. Still, if you find the taste of other margarines unacceptable, this product is better than butter in terms of its cholesterol and saturated fat content.

ADDITIVES: Contains artificial flavor, which may cause allergic reactions in sensitive individuals, and which some studies suggest may adversely affect behavior and the ability to complete school tasks in some sensitive children. Beta carotene is considered safe.

LAND O' LAKES MARGARINE STICK
Land O' Lakes, Inc.

Ingredients: partially hydrogenated soybean oil, pasteurized skim milk, water, salt, lecithin, vegetable mono- and diglycerides, sodium benzoate, artificial flavor, beta carotene, vitamin A palmitate.

Amount: 1 tbsp			% USRDA
Calories	100	Protein	*
Protein, gm	0	Vitamin A	10
Carbohydrates, gm	0	Vitamin C	*
Fat, gm	11	Thiamine	*
Sodium, mg	115	Riboflavin	*
Cholesterol, mg	0	Niacin	*
Fiber, gm	0	Calcium	*
		Iron	*

THIS FOOD: Made primarily from partially hydrogenated soybean oil, this margarine has a low p/s ratio of 1. Like most margarines, it contains a moderate amount of sodium.

ADDITIVES: Contains artificial flavor, which may cause allergic reactions in sensitive individuals, and which some studies suggest may adversely affect behavior and the ability to complete school tasks in some sensitive children.

BEST BETS: Among the most popular brands, Mrs. Filbert's Soft Corn Oil Margarine has the least saturated fat and a p/s ratio of 2.5. Diet Mazola Imitation Margarine has an even more favorable p/s ratio of 3. For those who wish to restrict their sodium intake, Fleischmann's Unsalted Stick Margarine and Diet Mazola Imitation Margarine contain only 1 mg and 13 mg sodium respectively.

MAZOLA DIET IMITATION MARGARINE
CPC International, Inc.

Ingredients: water, liquid corn oil, partially hydrogenated corn oil, salt, lecithin, artificial flavor, monoglycerides, potassium sorbate, isopropyl citrate, calcium disodium EDTA, vitamin A palmitate, vitamin D_2, beta carotene.

Amount: 1 tbsp			% USRDA
Calories	50	Protein	*
Protein, gm	0	Vitamin A	10
Carbohydrates, gm	0	Vitamin C	*
Fat, gm	6	Thiamine	*
Sodium, mg	13	Riboflavin	*
Cholesterol, mg	0	Niacin	*
Fiber, gm	0	Calcium	*
		Iron	*

THIS FOOD: One tablespoon of Mazola Diet Imitation Margarine has about half the fat and calories of regular margarines because water, rather than oil, is the main ingredient. It has a better-than-average p/s ratio of 3 and is low in sodium.

ADDITIVES: Contains artificial flavor, which may cause allergic reactions in sensitive individuals, and which some studies suggest may adversely affect behavior and the ability to complete school tasks in some sensitive children. Beta carotene is considered safe.

MAZOLA MARGARINE
CPC International, Inc.

Ingredients: Mazola liquid corn oil, partially hydrogenated corn oil, skim milk, salt, natural and artificial flavors, lecithin, monoglycerides, isopropyl citrate, calcium disodium EDTA, vitamin A palmitate, vitamin D_2, beta carotene.

Amount: 1 tbsp			% USRDA
Calories	100	Protein	*
Protein, gm	0	Vitamin A	10
Carbohydrates, gm	0	Vitamin C	*
Fat, gm	11	Thiamine	*
Sodium, mg	115	Riboflavin	*
Cholesterol, mg	0	Niacin	*
Fiber, gm	0	Calcium	*
		Iron	*

THIS FOOD: Made primarily from liquid corn oil, this margarine has an acceptable p/s ratio of 2. It contains slightly more sodium per serving (115 mg) than most other brands.

ADDITIVES: Contains artificial flavor, which may cause allergic reactions in sensitive individuals, and which some studies suggest may adversely affect behavior and the ability to complete school tasks in some sensitive children.

MAZOLA UNSALTED MARGARINE
CPC International, Inc.

Ingredients: Mazola liquid corn oil, partially hydrogenated corn oil, water, artificial flavor, lecithin, monoglycerides, potassium sorbate, isopropyl citrate, vitamin A palmitate, vitamin D_2, beta carotene.

Amount: 1 tbsp			% USRDA
Calories	100	Protein	*
Protein, gm	0	Vitamin A	10
Carbohydrates, gm	0	Vitamin C	*
Fat, gm	11	Thiamine	*
Sodium, mg	.1	Riboflavin	*
Cholesterol, mg	0	Niacin	*
Fiber, gm	0	Calcium	*
		Iron	*

THIS FOOD: Made primarily from liquid corn oil, this margarine has an acceptable p/s ratio of 2. Because no salt is added to this product, it is very low in sodium.

ADDITIVES: Contains artificial flavor, which may cause allergic reactions in sensitive individuals, and which some studies suggest may adversely affect behavior and the ability to complete school tasks in some sensitive children.

MRS. FILBERT'S FAMILY SPREAD
J. H. Filbert, Inc.

Ingredients: partially hydrogenated soybean oil, water, salt, vegetable mono- and diglycerides, vegetable lecithin, artificial flavor, potassium sorbate, citric acid, calcium disodium EDTA, beta carotene, vitamin A palmitate.

Amount: 1 tbsp			% USRDA
Calories	70	Protein	*
Protein, gm	0	Vitamin A	10
Carbohydrates, gm	0	Vitamin C	*
Fat, gm	7	Thiamine	*
Sodium, mg	85	Riboflavin	*
Cholesterol, mg	0	Niacin	*
Fiber, gm	0	Calcium	*
		Iron	*

THIS FOOD: Mrs. Filbert's Family Spread has about one third the fat and calories of regular margarines because it contains more water. Made primarily from partially hydrogenated soybean oil, it has an acceptable p/s ratio of 2. With 85 mg sodium per serving, it has slightly less added salt than most brands.

ADDITIVES: Contains artificial flavor, which may cause allergic reactions in sensitive individuals, and which some studies suggest may adversely affect behavior and the ability to complete school tasks in some sensitive children. Beta carotene is considered safe.

HELPFUL HINT: To cut down on the fat calories you consume, try using nonstick pans for sautéeing with only a teaspoon or so of margarine. If foods still stick, try adding a little broth or wine.

MRS. FILBERT'S SOFT CORN OIL MARGARINE
J. H. Filbert, Inc.

Ingredients: vegetable oil blend (liquid corn oil, partially hydrogenated corn oil), water, salt, whey, vegetable lecithin, vegetable mono- and diglycerides, sodium benzoate and citric acid, artificial flavor, potassium caseinate, colored with beta carotene (a form of vitamin A), vitamin A palmitate.

Amount: 1 tbsp			% USRDA
Calories	100	Protein	*
Protein, gm	0	Vitamin A	10
Carbohydrates, gm	0	Vitamin C	*
Fat, gm	11	Thiamine	*
Sodium, mg	110	Riboflavin	*
Cholesterol, mg	0	Niacin	*
Fiber, gm	0	Calcium	*
		Iron	*

THIS FOOD: Made primarily from liquid corn oil, this product has a better-than-average p/s ratio of 2.5, the highest of all the regular popular margarines. Mrs. Filbert's Soft Corn Oil Margarine contains a moderate amount of sodium.

ADDITIVES: Contains artificial flavor, which may cause allergic reactions in sensitive individuals, and which some studies suggest may adversely affect behavior and the ability to complete school tasks in some sensitive children. Beta carotene is considered safe.

PARKAY MARGARINE
Kraft, Inc.

Ingredients: partially hydrogenated soybean oil, water, salt, whey, sodium benzoate, lecithin, potassium caseinate, artificial flavor, vitamin A palmitate, beta carotene.

Amount: 1 tbsp			% USRDA
Calories	102	Protein	*
Protein, gm	0	Vitamin A	11
Carbohydrates, gm	0	Vitamin C	*
Fat, gm	11	Thiamine	*
Sodium, mg	98	Riboflavin	*
Cholesterol, mg	0	Niacin	*
Fiber, gm	0	Calcium	*
		Iron	*

THIS FOOD: Parkay Margarine is made from partially hydrogenated soybean oil and contains more saturated fat than many popular margarines. All of the calories in this product come from fat. It has a p/s ratio of ½.

ADDITIVES: Contains artificial flavor, which may cause allergic reactions in sensitive individuals, and which some studies suggest may adversely affect behavior and the ability to complete school tasks in some sensitive children.

CAKES AND CAKE MIXES

People eat cake, not because they think it is nutritious, but because it is a treat. Cake satisfies America's enormous sweet tooth and is also traditional on celebratory occasions. Almost all cakes are high in sugar—in fact, the majority of Pillsbury, Duncan Hines, and Betty Crocker mixes contain more sugar than any other single ingredient. Many cakes are also high in fat—even before you add the icing. Pepperidge Farm and Sara Lee cakes tend to have fewer additives and artificial ingredients than the popular (and less expensive) mixes. Try to restrict your cake eating to very special occasions.

SODIUM GUIDELINES: In evaluating the sodium content of cakes and cake mixes, we used the following standards:

less than 200 mg	low in sodium
200 mg to 300 mg	moderate in sodium
more than 300 mg	high in sodium

Remember, these guidelines are not for people following medically restricted low-sodium diets, but for healthy individuals who wish to monitor their sodium intake.

Cake Mixes

BETTY CROCKER CLASSIC BOSTON CREAM PIE MIX
General Mills, Inc.

Ingredients: sugar, enriched flour bleached (wheat flour, niacin, iron, thiamine mononitrate, riboflavin), animal and/or vegetable shortening (contains one or more of: soybean oil, cottonseed oil, beef tallow, palm oil and/or lard) with BHA and BHT, dried corn syrup, wheat starch, cocoa processed with alkali, leavening (baking soda, monocalcium, phosphate, sodium aluminum phosphate, aluminum sulfate), proplyene glycol monoesters, salt, sodium alginate, dextrose, artificial flavor, calcium gluconate, tetrasodium pyrophosphate, isolated soy protein, calcium carbonate, caramel color, mono- and diglycerides, guar gum, cellulose gum, modified cornstarch, polysorbate 60, annatto and turmeric extract color, sodium caseinate, FD & C Yellow No. 5.

Amount: ⅛ recipe (1 egg, 1⅓ cups milk added to recipe)			% USRDA
Calories	260	Protein	6
Protein, gm	3	Vitamin A	2
Carbohydrates, gm	48	Vitamin C	*
Fat, gm	6	Thiamine	6
Sodium, mg	405	Riboflavin	8
Cholesterol, mg	33e	Niacin	2
Fiber, gm	<1e	Calcium	15
		Iron	2

Contains 1½ teaspoons fat.

THIS FOOD: Sugar is the main ingredient in Betty Crocker Classic Boston Cream Pie Mix. It contains much less fat than other items in the category—only 20 percent of total calories derive from fat. Although this mix doesn't contain any dairy products, it is still a good source of calcium from calcium carbonate in the mix and added milk. This product is high in sodium.

ADDITIVES: Contains artificial flavor, which may cause allergic reactions in sensitive individuals, and which some studies suggest may adversely affect behavior and the ability to complete school tasks in some sensitive children. Also contains Yellow No. 5, which can cause allergic reactions, especially in aspirin-sensitive individuals, as well as BHA and BHT, whose long-term safety is currently being reexamined by FDA investigators.

BETTY CROCKER SUPERMOIST GERMAN CHOCOLATE CAKE MIX
General Mills, Inc.

Ingredients: sugar, enriched flour bleached (wheat flour, niacin, iron, thiamine mononitrate, riboflavin), animal and/or vegetable shortening (contains one or more of: soybean oil, cottonseed oil, beef tallow, palm oil and/or lard), with BHA and BHT, modified cornstarch, leavening (baking soda, monocalcium phosphate), wheat starch, cocoa processed with alkali, cocoa, artificial flavor, salt, propylene glycol monoesters, dextrose, guar gum, mono- and di-glycerides, cellulose gum.

Amount: ¹⁄₁₂ recipe (3 eggs, ⅓ cup oil added to recipe)			% USRDA
Calories	260	Protein	6
Protein, gm	3	Vitamin A	*
Carbohydrates, gm	36	Vitamin C	*
Fat, gm	11	Thiamine	6
Sodium, mg	420	Riboflavin	4
Cholesterol, mg	65e	Niacin	4
Fiber, gm	<1e	Calcium	6
		Iron	4

Contains more than 2 teaspoons fat.

THIS FOOD: Sugar is the main ingredient in Betty Crocker Supermoist German Chocolate Cake Mix. It is high in saturated fat and contains 38 percent fat calories. This cake is high in sodium.

ADDITIVES: Contains artificial flavor, which may cause allergic reactions in sensitive individuals, and which some studies suggest may adversely affect behavior and the ability to complete school tasks in some sensitive children. Also contains BHA and BHT, whose long-term safety is currently being reexamined by FDA investigators.

FOR WEIGHT WATCHERS: Duncan Hines Angel Food Cake Mix is a good choice if you are watching calories, since it contains no fat. Low sodium content is an additional advantage. But asthma sufferers or other sulfite-sensitive individuals should be aware that this product does contain sodium bisulfite.

BETTY CROCKER WALNUT BROWNIE MIX
General Mills, Inc.

Ingredients: sugar, enriched flour bleached (wheat flour, niacin, iron, thiamine mononitrate, riboflavin), walnut pieces, cocoa processed with alkali, animal and/or vegetable shortening (contains one or more of: soybean oil, cottonseed oil, beef, tallow palm oil and/or lard), wheat starch, salt, mono- and diglycerides, artificial flavor, egg white, dried corn syrup, leavening (baking soda, monocalcium phosphate), sodium caseinate, BHA, BHT.

Amount: ¹⁄₁₆ recipe (2 eggs, 3 tbsp. oil added to recipe)			% USRDA
Calories	160	Protein	2
Protein, gm	1	Vitamin A	*
Carbohydrates, gm	22	Vitamin C	*
Fat, gm	7	Thiamine	2
Sodium, mg	100	Riboflavin	2
Cholesterol, mg	15e	Niacin	2
Fiber, gm	<1e	Calcium	*
		Iron	4

Contains 1½ teaspoons fat.

THIS FOOD: Sugar is the main ingredient in Betty Crocker Walnut Brownie Mix. It is high in saturated fat and contains 39 percent fat calories. One brownie is low in sodium compared to other items in this category.

ADDITIVES: Contains artificial flavor, which can cause allergic reactions in sensitive individuals and which some studies suggest may adversely affect behavior and the ability to complete school tasks in some sensitive children. Also contains BHA and BHT, whose long-term safety is currently being reexamined by FDA investigators.

BUNDT POUND CAKE SUPREME
The Pillsbury Co.

Ingredients: enriched bleached flour (bleached flour, niacin, iron, thiamine mononitrate, riboflavin), sugar, hydrogenated vegetable oil (cottonseed or soybean oil), dextrose, cornstarch, whey, propylene glycol monoesters, mono- and diglycerides, salt, artificial flavor, baking powder (baking soda, sodium aluminum phosphate, monocalcium phosphate), cellulose gum, lecithin, FD & C Yellow No. 5.

Amount: 1/16 cake (1/4 cup margarine, 3 eggs added to recipe)		% USRDA	
Calories	230	Protein	4
Protein, gm	3	Vitamin A	4
Carbohydrates, gm	33	Vitamin C	*
Fat, gm	9	Thiamin	8
Sodium, mg	260	Riboflavin	8
Cholesterol, mg	47e	Niacin	4
Fiber, gm	<1e	Calcium	2
		Iron	4

Contains 2 teaspoon fat.

THIS FOOD: Sugar is the primary ingredient of Bundt Pound Cake Supreme, and fat accounts for 35 percent of calories, much of it saturated.

ADDITIVES: Contains artificial color and flavor, which some studies suggest may adversely affect behavior and the ability to complete school tasks in some sensitive children; artificial colors are inadequately tested, and artificial flavor may cause allergic reactions in sensitive individuals. Also contains Yellow No. 5, which can cause allergic reactions, especially in aspirin-sensitive individuals.

DUNCAN HINES ANGEL FOOD CAKE MIX
Procter and Gamble

Ingredients: sugar, bleached wheat flour, dried egg whites, wheat starch, leavening (cream of tartar, monocalcium phosphate, and baking soda), cornstarch, dextrose, tristearin, artificial flavoring, salt, sodium bisulfite, sodium lauryl sulfate.

Amount: 1/12 cake (water only added to recipe)		% USRDA	
Calories	140	Protein	4
Protein, gm	3	Vitamin A	*
Carbohydrates, gm	30	Vitamin C	*
Fat, gm	0	Thiamine	*
Sodium, mg	130	Riboflavin	6
Cholesterol, mg	<5e	Niacin	*
Fiber, gm	<1e	Calcium	2
		Iron	*

THIS FOOD: Duncan Hines Angel Food Cake Mix lists sugar as its primary ingredient, but it is lower in calories than most cakes because it contains no fat.

ADDITIVES: Contains sodium bisulfite, which can cause severe allergic reactions, especially in individuals with asthma. Also contains artificial flavor, which some studies suggest may adversely affect behavior and the ability to complete school tasks in some sensitive children.

DUNCAN HINES DELUXE CARROT CAKE MIX
Procter and Gamble

Ingredients: sugar, enriched bleached flour (enriched with iron, niacin, thiamine mononitrate, riboflavin), vegetable shortening (partially hydrogenated soybean oil), dried carrots, modified food starch, propylene glycol monoesters, leavening (baking soda, dicalcium phosphate, sodium aluminum phosphate), spice, dextrose, salt, polyglycerol esters, cellulose gum, xanthan gum, FD & C Yellow No. 5, artificial color and flavor.

Amount: ¹⁄₁₂ recipe (3 eggs, ¹⁄₃ cup oil added to recipe)			% USRDA
Calories	250	Protein	4
Protein, gm	3	Vitamin A	20
Carbohydrates, gm	34	Vitamin C	*
Fat, gm	11	Thiamine	4
Sodium, mg	265	Riboflavin	6
Cholesterol, mg	63e	Niacin	4
Fiber, gm	<1e	Calcium	6
		Iron	6

Contains more than 2 teaspoons fat.

THIS FOOD: Sugar is the main ingredient in this carrot cake, and 40 percent of its calories derive from fat. Because of the carrots, this cake is a very good source of vitamin A. This product contains a moderate amount of sodium.

ADDITIVES: Contains artificial colors, which are inadequately tested and which some studies suggest may adversely affect behavior and the ability to complete school tasks in sensitive children; also contains Yellow No. 5, which can cause allergic reactions, especially in aspirin-sensitive individuals; and artificial flavor, which may cause allergic reactions in sensitive individuals and which may also adversely affect behavior and the ability to complete school tasks in sensitive children.

DUNCAN HINES DELUXE DEVIL'S FOOD CAKE MIX
Procter and Gamble

Ingredients: sugar, enriched bleached flour (enriched with iron, niacin, thiamine mononitrate, riboflavin), Dutched cocoa (processed with alkali), vegetable shortening (partially hydrogenated soybean oil), dextrose, leavening (baking soda, dicalcium phosphate, sodium aluminum phosphate, and monocalcium phosphate), propylene glycol monoesters, modified food starch, polyglycerol esters, salt, cellulose gum, xanthan gum, soy protein isolate, FD & C Yellow No. 5, artificial color and flavor.

Amount: ½2 cake (½ cup oil and 3 eggs added to recipe)			% USRDA
Calories	280	Protein	6
Protein, gm	4	Vitamin A	*
Carbohydrates, gm	33	Vitamin C	*
Fat, gm	15	Thiamine	*
Sodium, mg	375	Riboflavin	6
Cholesterol, mg	33e	Niacin	4
Fiber, gm	<1e	Calcium	6
		Iron	6
Contains 3 teaspoons fat.			

THIS FOOD: Sugar is the main ingredient in Duncan Hines Deluxe Devil's Food Cake Mix. It is high in saturated fat and contains 48 percent fat calories. This product is high in sodium.

ADDITIVES: Contains artificial colors, which are inadequately tested and which some studies suggest may adversely affect behavior and the ability to complete school tasks in some sensitive children; also contains Yellow No. 5, which can cause allergic reactions, especially in aspirin-sensitive individuals; and artificial flavor, which may cause allergic reactions in sensitive individuals and which may also adversely affect behavior and the ability to complete school tasks in some sensitive children.

PILLSBURY CARROT NUT BREAD MIX
The Pillsbury Co.

Ingredients: enriched bleached flour (bleached flour, malted barley flour, niacin, iron, thiamine mononitrate, riboflavin), sugar, hydrogenated soybean oil and/or animal fat (beef fat or lard) with BHA, BHT, and citric acid, dried carrots (color protected with sodium bisulfite), almonds (BHA), dextrose, toasted wheat germ, wheat starch, baking powder (baking soda, sodium acid pyrophosphate, monocalcium phosphate, salt, spices, mono- and diglycerides, artificial flavor, cornstarch, artificial color.

Amount: ½2 recipe (1 egg added to recipe)			% USRDA
Calories	150	Protein	4
Protein, gm	2	Vitamin A	30
Carbohydrates, gm	27	Vitamin C	*
Fat, gm	4	Thiamine	4
Sodium, mg	185	Riboflavin	4
Cholesterol, mg	20e	Niacin	4
Fiber, gm	<1e	Calcium	4
		Iron	4

THIS FOOD: Contains less sugar and fat than most cakes prepared from mixes. It is also an excellent source of vitamin A.

ADDITIVES: Contains artificial flavor and color, which may adversely affect behavior and the ability to complete school tasks in some sensitive children. Artificial color is inadequately tested, and artificial flavor may cause allergic reactions in sensitive individuals. Also contains BHA and BHT, whose long-term safety is currently being reviewed by FDA investigators, and sodium bisulfite, which can cause severe allergic reactions, especially in individuals with asthma.

PILLSBURY DATE BREAD MIX
The Pillsbury Co.

Ingredients: enriched bleached flour (bleached flour, malted barley flour, niacin, iron, thiamine mononitrate, riboflavin), sugar, dried dates, hydrogenated soybean oil and/or hydrogenated animal fat (beef fat or lard), with BHA, BHT, and citric acid, dextrose, wheat starch, baking powder (baking soda, sodium acid pyrophosphate, monocalcium phosphate), salt, mono- and diglycerides, cellulose gum, cornstarch, artificial color.

Amount: ¹⁄₁₂ recipe (1 egg added to recipe)			% USRDA
Calories	160	Protein	4
Protein, gm	2	Vitamin A	*
Carbohydrates, gm	31	Vitamin C	*
Fat, gm	3	Thiamine	8
Sodium, mg	155	Riboflavin	4
Cholesterol, mg	20e	Niacin	4
Fiber, gm	<1e	Calcium	*
		Iron	4

THIS FOOD: Contains slightly less fat and sugar than most cakes.

ADDITIVES: Contains artificial colors, which are inadequately tested, and which some studies suggest may adversely affect behavior and the ability to complete school tasks in some sensitive children. Also contains BHA and BHT, whose long-term safety is currently being reexamined by the FDA.

PILLSBURY DUTCH APPLE STREUSEL SWIRL CAKE MIX
The Pillsbury Co.

Ingredients: sugar, enriched bleached flour (bleached flour, niacin, iron, thiamine mononitrate, riboflavin), hydrogenated vegetable oils (soybean and coconut oil) and/or hydrogenated animal fat (beef fat or lard) with BHA, BHT, and citric acid, brown sugar, dried apples (color protected with sulfur dioxide), modified cornstarch, dextrose, propylene glycol monoesters, baking powder (baking soda, sodium aluminum phosphate, monocalcium phosphate, aluminum sulfate), cornstarch, mono- and diglycerides, salt, natural and artificial flavor, soy flour, wheat starch, cinnamon, lecithin, modified tapioca starch, xanthan gum, artificial color and FD & C Yellow No. 5, whey protein, cellulose gum, sodium phosphate, polysorbate 80.

Amount: 1/16 recipe (1/3 cup oil and 3 eggs added to recipe)		% USRDA	
Calories	260	Protein	4
Protein, gm	3	Vitamin A	2
Carbohydrates, gm	38	Vitamin C	*
Fat, gm	11	Thiamine	6
Sodium, mg	200	Riboflavin	6
Cholesterol, mg	47e	Niacin	4
Fiber, gm	<1e	Calcium	2
		Iron	6

Contains more than 2 teaspoons fat.

THIS FOOD: Sugar is the primary ingredient of this artificially flavored and colored cake, and fat accounts for 38 percent of total calories, much of it saturated.

ADDITIVES: Contains artificial color and flavor, which may adversely affect behavior and the ability to complete school tasks in some sensitive children. Artificial colors are inadequately tested; artificial flavors may cause allergic reactions in sensitive individuals. Also contains BHA and BHT, whose long-term safety is currently being reexamined by FDA investigators. and FD & C Yellow No. 5, which may cause allergic reactions, especially in aspirin-sensitive individuals.

PILLSBURY PLUS CHOCOLATE MINT CAKE
The Pillsbury Co.

Ingredients: sugar, enriched bleached flour (bleached flour, niacin, iron, thiamine mononitrate, riboflavin), hydrogenated soybean oil and/or hydrogenated animal fat (beef fat or lard) with BHA, BHT, and citric acid, dextrose, cocoa processed with alkali, modified tapioca starch, baking powder (baking soda, dicalcium phosphate, sodium aluminum phosphate, monocalcium phosphate), carob powder, propylene glycol monoesters, mono- and diglycerides, salt, artificial flavor, sodium phosphate, calcium acetate, guar gum, xanthan gum, natural peppermint flavor, cellulose gum, polysorbate 60, lecithin.

Amount: 1/12 recipe (1/3 cup oil and 3 eggs added to recipe)		% USRDA	
Calories	260	Protein	4
Protein, gm	3	Vitamin A	2
Carbohydrates, gm	35	Vitamin C	*
Fat, gm	12	Thiamine	4
Sodium, mg	340	Riboflavin	6
Cholesterol, mg	62e	Niacin	6
Fiber, gm	<1e	Calcium	10
		Iron	6

Contains more than 2 teaspoons fat.

THIS FOOD: Sugar is the primary ingredient of this artificially flavored cake, and fat accounts for 41 percent of total calories, much of it saturated.

ADDITIVES: Contains artificial flavor, which may adversely affect behavior and ability to complete school tasks in some sensitive children. Sensitve individuals may have allergic reactions.

Ready-to-Eat Cakes

PEPPERIDGE FARM BOSTON CREAM CAKE SUPREME
Pepperidge Farm, Inc.

Ingredients: nonfat milk, sugar, partially hydrogenated vegetable shortening (soybean, cottonseed, palm and palm kernel oils), corn syrup, bleached wheat flour, whole eggs, chocolate liquor, modified food starch, egg yolks, invert syrup, sweet cream butter, vanilla extract, natural flavoring, salt, wheat gluten, water, leavening (baking powder containing baking soda, sodium acid pyrophosphate, cornstarch, monocalcium phosphate, calcium sulfate), mono- and diglycerides, polyglycerol esters, gelatin, propylene glycol, monoesters, lactylic stearate.

Amount: ¼ cake/2⅞ oz			% USRDA
Calories	290	Protein	4
Protein, gm	3	Vitamin A	*
Carbohydrates, gm	39	Vitamin C	*
Fat, gm	14	Thiamine	*
Sodium, mg	190	Riboflavin	4
Cholesterol, mg	na	Niacin	*
Fiber, gm	<1e	Calcium	2
		Iron	4

Contains 3 teaspoons fat.

THIS FOOD: Like most frozen cakes, Pepperidge Farm Boston Cream Cake Supreme is high in sugar and fat calories. Forty-three percent of this product's calories derive from fat, much of it saturated.

ADDITIVES: No questionable additives.

PEPPERIDGE FARM GOLDEN LAYER CAKE
Pepperidge Farm, Inc.

Ingredients: sugar, partially hydrogenated vegetable shortening (soybean, cottonseed, palm and palm kernel oils), bleached wheat flour, water, whole eggs, corn syrup, nonfat milk, chocolate liquor, contains 2 percent or less of: cocoa processed with alkali (Dutched), dextroified food starch, leavening (baking powder containing sodium acid pyrophosphate, baking soda, cornstarch, monocalcium phosphate, calcium sulfate), mono- and diglycerides, dextrin, slat, gelatin, propylene glycol monoesters, polyglycerol esters, sodium caseinate, ethoxylated mono- and diglycerides, lactylic stearate, natural flavor, natural coloring (annatto), xanthan gum, lecithin.

Amount: ⅒ cake/1⅝ oz			% USRDA
Calories	180	Protein	2
Protein, gm	1	Vitamin A	*
Carbohydrates, gm	24	Vitamin C	*
Fat, gm	9	Thiamine	*
Sodium, mg	115	Riboflavin	2
Cholesterol, mg	20e	Niacin	*
Fiber, gm	<1e	Calcium	*
		Iron	2
Contains 2 teaspoons fat.			

THIS FOOD: Like most frozen cakes, Pepperidge Farm Golden Layer Cake is loaded with sugar and fat calories. Sugar is the largest single ingredient, and 45 percent of its calories derive from fat, much of it saturated.

ADDITIVES: No questionable additives.

SARA LEE CHOCOLATE CAKE
Consolidated Foods Corp.
Ingredients: sugar, enriched bleached flour (with niacin, iron, thiamine mononitrate, riboflavin), corn syrup, fresh whole eggs, partially hydrogenated vegetable shortening (cottonseed, soybean), skim milk, butter, cocoa, water, chocolate, mono- and diglycerides, fresh egg whites, baking powder (sodium acid pyrophosphate, baking soda, cornstarch, monocalcium phosphate, calcium sulfate), salt, natural flavors, vanilla, propylene glycol esters, lactylic stearate.

Amount: ⅛ cake			% USRDA
Calories	185	Protein	2
Protein, gm	2	Vitamin A	2
Carbohydrates, gm	24	Vitamin C	2
Fat, gm	9	Thiamine	*
Sodium, mg	135	Riboflavin	8
Cholesterol, mg	30e	Niacin	2
Fiber, gm	<1e	Calcium	*
		Iron	6
Contains 2 teaspoons fat.			

THIS FOOD: Like most frozen cakes, Sara Lee Chocolate Cake is loaded with sugar and fat calories. Forty-four percent of its calories derive from fat, which is about average for this category.

ADDITIVES: No questionable additives.

FOR FAT WATCHERS: Of the ready-to-eat cakes profiled, Sara Lee Fresh Banana Cake is lowest in fat as a percentage of calories. But Sara Lee Original Pound Cake contains the same absolute amount of fat, 1½ teaspoons, and is significantly lower in calories.

SARA LEE CHOCOLATE MOUSSE BAVARIAN
Consolidated Foods Corp.

Ingredients: whipping cream, sugar, skim milk, partially hydrogenated vegetable shortening (coconut, soybean, palm, cottonseed), whey, enriched flour (malted barley flour, niacin, iron, thiamine mononitrate, riboflavin), water, corn syrup, cocoa, modified food starch, malto-dextrin, whey protein concentrate, chocolate, rolled oats, gelatin, skim milk protein concentrate, lactated mono-diglycerides, mono- and diglycerides, salt, natural flavors, sodium stearoyl lactylate, vanilla, baking soda, carob bean gum, lecithin, propylene glycol esters, lactylic stearate.

Amount: ⅛ cake			% USRDA
Calories	285	Protein	4
Protein, gm	3	Vitamin A	6
Carbohydrates, gm	23	Vitamin C	*
Fat, gm	20	Thiamine	*
Sodium, mg	78	Riboflavin	6
Cholesterol, mg	na	Niacin	2
Fiber, gm	<1e	Calcium	4
		Iron	4

Contains 4 teaspoons fat.

THIS FOOD: Sara Lee Chocolate Mousse Bavarian lists the real thing—whipping cream—as its first ingredient, followed by sugar. This rich dessert has a higher percentage of fat calories (63 percent of total) than any other frozen cake profiled. It is also high in saturated fat and cholesterol.

ADDITIVES: No questionable additives.

SARA LEE FRESH BANANA CAKE
Consolidated Foods Corp.

Ingredients: sugar, bananas, enriched bleached flour (with niacin, iron, thiamine mononitrate, riboflavin), fresh whole eggs, partially hydrogenated vegetable shortening (cottonseed, soybean), butter, corn syrup, water, mono- and diglycerides, fresh egg whites, baking powder (sodium acid pyrophosphate, baking soda, cornstarch, monocalcium phosphate, calcium sulfate), salt, cornstarch, skim milk, propylene glycol esters, natural flavors, vanilla, carob bean gum, guar gum, lactylic stearate, annatto extract.

Amount: ⅛ cake			% USRDA
Calories	175	Protein	2
Protein, gm	1	Vitamin A	2
Carbohydrates, gm	27	Vitamin C	*
Fat, gm	7	Thiamine	2
Sodium, mg	154	Riboflavin	2
Cholesterol, mg	na	Niacin	2
Fiber, gm	<1e	Calcium	*
Contains 1½ teaspoons fat.		Iron	2

THIS FOOD: Like most frozen cakes, Sara Lee Fresh Banana Cake is loaded with sugar calories. Thirty-six percent of its calories derive from fat, which is below average for this category.

ADDITIVES: No questionable additives.

SARA LEE ORIGINAL CHEESECAKE
Consolidated Foods Corp

Ingredients: cream cheese, sugar, sour cream, baker's cheese, fresh whole eggs, enriched flour, (niacin, iron, thiamine mononitrate, riboflavin), skim milk, partially hydrogenated vegetable shortening (soybean, palm), graham flour, corn syrup, fresh egg whites, modified food starch, gum arabic, salt, vanilla, baking powder (sodium acid pyrophosphate, baking soda, cornstarch, monocalcium phosphate, calcium sulfate), molasses, carbohydrate gum, gelatin, carob bean gum, cinnamon, xanthan gum, citric acid, guar gum, carrageenan.

Amount: ⅙ cake			% USRDA
Calories	230	Protein	6
Protein, gm	5	Vitamin A	6
Carbohydrates, gm	27	Vitamin C	2
Fat, gm	11	Thiamine	2
Sodium, mg	153	Riboflavin	10
Cholesterol, mg	100e	Niacin	2
Fiber, gm	< 1e	Calcium	6
Contains more than 2 teaspoons fat.		Iron	2

THIS FOOD: The ingredients list begins just like a homemade recipe: cream cheese, sugar, sour cream, baker's cheese, fresh whole eggs, enriched flour . . . and while this rich dessert is relatively high in protein from the dairy ingredient, it has far too many fat and sugar calories for good nutrition. Forty-three percent of its calories derive from fat, much of it saturated. This product is also high in cholesterol.

ADDITIVES: No questionable additives.

SARA LEE ORIGINAL POUND CAKE
Consolidated Foods Corp.

Ingredients: enriched bleached flour (with niacin, iron, thiamine mononitrate, riboflavin), fresh whole eggs, sugar, butter, corn syrup, mono- and di-glycerides, skim milk, fresh egg whites, salt, vanilla, baking powder (sodium acid pyrophosphate, baking soda, cornstarch, monocalcium phosphate, calcium stearate).

Amount: ⅒ cake/1 oz			% USRDA
Calories	125	Protein	2
Protein, gm	2	Vitamin A	2
Carbohydrates, gm	14	Vitamin C	*
Fat, gm	7	Thiamine	4
Sodium, mg	104	Riboflavin	4
Cholesterol, mg	50e	Niacin	2
Fiber, gm	<1e	Calcium	*
		Iron	2

Contains 1½ teaspoons fat.

THIS FOOD: Like most frozen cakes Sara Lee Original Pound Cake is high in fat, which contributes 50 percent of its calories. Compared to other frozen cakes, and cakes prepared from mixes, this product is lower than average in sugar.

ADDITIVES: No questionable additives.

NOTE: The letter "e" indicates that the data has been estimated; < means "less than" and is used for small amounts of sodium or cholesterol; * means food contains less than 2% of USRDA; "na" means that the information was not available and appears only when data is insufficient.

CAKE ICINGS

Cake icings are high in sugar and saturated fat. All of the popular varieties profiled contain controversial additives and none provide any vitamins or minerals. A little icing (presumably on cake) isn't going to do any harm, as long as it's eaten infrequently—but the key word here is *infrequent*.

BETTY CROCKER COCONUT PECAN FROSTING MIX
General Mills, Inc.

Ingredients: sugar, chopped pecans, dried corn syrup, coconut, cornstarch, animal and/or vegetable shortening (contains one or more of: soybean oil, cottonseed oil, beef tallow, and/or palm oil), with BHA and BHT, wheat starch, artificial flavor, caramel color, propylene glycol, annatto, and turmeric extract.

Amount: ¹/₁₂ recipe (3 tbsp milk and 3 tbsp butter added to recipe)			% USRDA
Calories	140	Protein	*
Protein, gm	0	Vitamin A	2
Carbohydrates, gm	18	Vitamin C	*
Fat, gm	8	Thiamine	*
Sodium, mg	100	Riboflavin	*
Cholesterol, mg	<5e	Niacin	*
Fiber, gm	0	Calcium	*
		Iron	*

THIS FOOD: This product, like nearly all packaged frostings, consists of sugar, saturated fat, and a host of additives.

ADDITIVES: Contains artificial flavor, which may cause allergic reactions in sensitive individuals, and which some studies suggest may adversely affect behavior and the ability to complete school tasks in some sensitive children. Also contains BHA and BHT, whose long-term safety is currently being reexamined by FDA investigators.

BETTY CROCKER CREAMY DELUXE CHERRY FROSTING
General Mills, Inc.

Ingredients: sugar, margarine—(vegetable and/or animal shortening [contains one or more of: soybean oil, cottonseed oil, beef tallow and/or palm oil], water, sodium caseinate, vitamin A palmitate), water, corn syrup, wheat starch, butter, mono- and diglycerides, dried corn salt, polysorbate 60, artificial color, soy lecithin, sodium acid pyrophosphate, dextrose, citric acid, pectin, artificial flavor, potassium sorbate, TBHQ.

Amount: ¹⁄₁₂ container			% USRDA
Calories	160	Protein	*
Protein, gm	0	Vitamin A	⋆
Carbohydrates, gm	26	Vitamin C	*
Fat, gm	6	Thiamine	*
Sodium, mg	100	Riboflavin	*
Cholesterol, mg	<5e	Niacin	*
Fiber, gm	0	Calcium	*
		Iron	*

THIS FOOD: Is primarily sugar and saturated fat.

ADDITIVES: Contains artificial flavor, which may cause allergic reactions in sensitive individuals, and which some studies suggest may adversely affect behavior and the ability to complete school tasks in some sensitive children.

BETTY CROCKER CREAMY DELUXE CHOCOLATE CHIP FROSTING
General Mills, Inc.

Ingredients: sugar, margarine (vegetable and/or animal shortening [partially hydrogenated soybean oil/cotton seed oil/beef tallow/palm oil], water, sodium caseinate, vitamin A palmitate), semisweet chocolate chips with added emulsifier, corn syrup, cocoa processed with alkali, wheat starch, butter, mono- and diglycerides, salt, polysorbate 60, citric acid, artificial flavor, confectioner's glaze, soy lecithin, sodium acid pyrophosphate, dextrose, natural flavor, pectin, acetylated monoglycerides, potassium sorbate, TBHQ.

Amount: ¹⁄₁₂ container			% USRDA
Calories	160	Protein	*
Protein, gm	<1	Vitamin A	*
Carbohydrates, gm	24	Vitamin C	*
Fat, gm	7	Thiamine	*
Sodium, mg	100	Riboflavin	*
Cholesterol, mg	10e†	Niacin	*
Fiber, gm	0	Calcium	*
		Iron	2

†if beef tallow is used.

THIS FOOD: Like nearly all packaged frostings, this product is primarily sugar and saturated fat.

ADDITIVES: Contains artificial flavor, which may cause allergic reactions in sensitive individuals, and which some studies suggest may adversely affect behavior and the ability to complete school tasks in some sensitive children.

BETTY CROCKER CREAMY VANILLA FROSTING MIX
General Mills, Inc.

Ingredients: powdered sugar, wheat starch, dried corn syrup, partially hydroge-nated animal and/or vegetable shortening (contains one or more of: soybean oil, cottonseed oil, beef tallow and/or palm oil) with BHA and BHT, mono- and diglycerides, modified cornstarch, natural vanilla flavor, and other artificial flavors, polysorbate 60, sodium caseinate, annatto, and turmeric extract.

Amount: ½2 recipe (+ ¾ tsp butter)			% USRDA
Calories	190	Protein	*
Protein, gm	0	Vitamin A	2
Carbohydrates, gm	33	Vitamin C	*
Fat, gm	6	Thiamine	*
Sodium, mg	50	Riboflavin	*
Cholesterol, mg	10e†	Niacin	*
Fiber, gm	0	Calcium	*
		Iron	*

†if beef tallow is used.

THIS FOOD: This product, like nearly all packaged frostings, consists of sugar, saturated fat, and a host of additives.

ADDITIVES: Contains artificial flavor, which may cause allergic reactions in sensitive individuals, and which some studies suggest may adversely affect behavior and the ability to complete school tasks in some sensitive children. Also contains BHA and BHT, whose long-term safety is currently being reexamined by FDA investigators.

NOTE: The letter "e" indicates that the data has been estimated; < means "less than" and is used for small amounts of sodium or cholesterol; * means food contains less than 2% of USRDA; "na" means that the information was not available and appears only when data is insufficient.

DUNCAN HINES CREAMY CHOCOLATE FROSTING
Procter and Gamble

Ingredients: sugar, water, partially hydrogenated vegetable shortening (soybean and/or palm and/or cottonseed oil), cocoa (processed with alkali), corn syrup, modified food starch, food starch, salt, soy lecithin, potassium sorbate, citric acid, polysorbate 60, mono- and diglycerides, pectin, and artificial color and flavor.

Amount: 1/12 container			% USRDA
Calories	160	Protein	*
Protein, gm	0	Vitamin A	*
Carbohydrates, gm	24	Vitamin C	*
Fat, gm	7	Thiamine	*
Sodium, mg	80	Riboflavin	*
Cholesterol, mg	0	Niacin	*
Fiber, gm	0	Calcium	*
		Iron	*

THIS FOOD: Like nearly all packaged frostings, this product is primarily sugar and saturated fat.

ADDITIVES: Contains artificial color and flavor, which may adversely affect behavior and the ability to complete school tasks in some sensitive children. Artificial colors are inadquately tested, and artificial flavors may cause allergic reactions in sensitive individuals.

DUNCAN HINES CREAMY VANILLA FROSTING
Procter and Gamble

Ingredients: sugar, water, partially hydrogenated vegetable shortening (soybean and/or palm and/or cottonseed oil), corn syrup, modified food starch, salt, soy lecithin, nonfat milk, food starch, potassium sorbate, mono- and diglycerides, pectin, polysorbate 60, citric acid, FD & C Yellow No. 5, artificial color and flavor.

Amount: 1/12 container			% USRDA
Calories	160	Protein	*
Protein, gm	0	Vitamin A	*
Carbohydrates, gm	25	Vitamin C	*
Fat, gm	7	Thiamine	*
Sodium, mg	80	Riboflavin	*
Cholesterol, mg	0	Niacin	*
Fiber, gm	0	Calcium	*
		Iron	*

THIS FOOD: Like nearly all packaged frostings, this product is primarily sugar and saturated fat.

ADDITIVES: Contains artificial flavor and color, which may adversely affect behavior and the ability to complete school tasks in some sensitive children; artificial colors are inadequately tested and artificial flavors may cause allergic reactions in sensitive individuals.

PILLSBURY CHOCOLATE FUDGE FLAVOR FROSTING SUPREME
The Pillsbury Co.

Ingredients: sugar, water, hydrogenated vegetable oil (soybean palm or cotton-seed) with BHA and BHT, cocoa processed with alkali, corn syrup, cornstarch, salt, mono- and diglycerides, citric acid, polysorbate 60, potassium sorbate, pectin, lecithin, sodium citrate.

Amount: ⅟₁₂ container			% USRDA
Calories	150	Protein	*
Protein, gm	<1	Vitamin A	*
Carbohydrates, gm	24	Vitamin C	*
Fat, gm	6	Thiamine	*
Sodium mg	80	Riboflavin	*
Cholesterol, mg	0	Niacin	*
Fiber, gm	0	Calcium	*
		Iron	*

THIS FOOD: This product, like nearly all packaged frostings, consists of sugar, saturated fat, and a host of additives.

ADDITIVES: Contains BHA and BHT, whose long-term safety is currently being reexamined by FDA investigators.

CANDY

All nonchocolate candies are high in sugar and some (Brach Royals and Toffees) also contain a substantial amount of saturated fat. It goes without saying that candies of all kinds are without nutritional value, but if you or your child can't resist once in a while, you're best off with a simple sugar candy such as Life Savers. Since one candy contains only ten calories, it is a fairly innocuous choice. For unknown reasons people in Utah buy twice as much candy as residents of any other state—and the average consumer eats more than sixteen pounds of candy (including chocolate) a year! *Also see "Chocolate," page 145.*

BRACH ROYALS
E. J. Brach and Sons, Inc.

Ingredients: sweetened condensed skim milk, corn syrup, sugar, partially hy-drogenated blend of vegetable oils (coconut, cottonseed, palm, palm kernel, peanut, soybean) and BHA, delactosed whey, cocoa, salt, molasses, rasp-berries, modified starch, maple syrup, egg whites, soy protein, butter, soy lecithin, pectin, citric acid, sodium phosphate, sodium citrate, artificial colors, FD & C Yellow No. 5, artificial and natural flavors.

Amount: 1 oz			% USRDA
Calories	120	Protein	2
Protein, gm	1	Vitamin A	*
Carbohydrates, gm	21	Vitamin C	*
Fat, gm	3	Thiamine	*
Sodium, mg	80	Riboflavin	6
Cholesterol, mg	<5e	Niacin	*
Fiber, gm	0e	Calcium	6
		Iron	*
Contains 5 teaspoons sugar.			

THIS FOOD: Like many candies, Brach Royals are full of nutritionally worth-less sugar calories.

ADDITIVES: Contains artificial colors and flavors. which some studies sug-gest may adversely affect behavior and the ability to complete school tasks in some sensitive children. Artificial colors are inadequately tested; artificial flavors may cause allergic reactions in sensitive individuals. Also contains Yellow No. 5, which can cause allergic reactions, especially in aspirin-sen-sitive individuals.

BRACH TOFFEES
E. J. Brach and Sons, Inc.

Ingredients: sweetened condensed skim milk, corn syrup, sugar, partially hy-drogenated blend of vegetable oils (coconut, cottonseed, palm, palm kernel, peanut, soybean) and BHA, delactosed whey, cocoa, salt, molasses, butter, modified starch, soy lecithin, artificial and natural flavors.

NOTE: The letter "e" indicates that the data has been estimated; < means "less than" and is used for small amounts of sodium or cholesterol; * means food contains less than 2% of USRDA; "na" means that the information was not available and appears only when data is insufficient.

Amount: 1 oz			% USRDA
Calories	120	Protein	2
Protein, gm	2	Vitamin A	*
Carbohydrates, gm	20	Vitamin C	*
Fat, gm	3	Thiamine	*
Sodium, mg	75	Riboflavin	6
Cholesterol, mg	<5e	Niacin	*
Fiber, gm	0	Calcium	6
		Iron	*

THIS FOOD: Like many candies, Brach Toffees are full of nutritionally empty sugar calories.

ADDITIVES: Contains artificial flavors and colors, which some studies suggest may adversely affect behavior and the ability to complete school tasks in some sensitive children. Artificial colors are inadequately tested; artificial flavors may cause allergic reactions in sensitive individuals. Also contains BHA, whose long-term safety is currently being reexamined by FDA investigators.

CRACKER JACK
Borden, Inc.

Ingredients: sugar, corn syrup, popcorn, peanuts, molasses, corn oil, salt, soy lecithin.

Amount: 1 oz			% USRDA
Calories	120	Protein	2
Protein, gm	2	Vitamin A	*
Carbohydrates, gm	22	Vitamin C	*
Fat, gm	3	Thiamine	*
Sodium, mg	85	Riboflavin	2
Cholesterol, mg	0	Niacin	2
Fiber, gm	1e	Calcium	*
		Iron	4

THIS FOOD: Cracker Jack is marginally better for you than most candies because the popcorn and peanuts it contains have some food value. Still, since sugar is the main ingredient, this snack remains basically worthless food.

ADDITIVES: No questionable additives.

HUBBA BUBBA ORIGINAL FLAVOR BUBBLE GUM
William Wrigley, Jr., Co.

Ingredients: sugar, gum base, corn syrup, softeners, artificial and natural flavors, artificial colors, and BHT.

Amount: 1 piece			% USRDA
Calories	23	Protein	*
Protein, gm	0	Vitamin A	*
Carbohydrates, gm	6	Vitamin C	*
Fat, gm	<1	Thiamine	*
Sodium, mg	<1	Riboflavin	*
Cholesterol, mg	0	Niacin	*
Fiber, gm	0	Calcium	*
		Iron	*
Contains 1½ teaspoons sugar.			

THIS FOOD: Full of sugar and artificial ingredients, this bubble gum is terrible for your teeth and nutritionally worthless.

ADDITIVES: Contains artificial flavors and colors, which some studies suggest may adversely affect behavior and the ability to complete school tasks in some sensitive children. Artificial colors are inadequately tested; artificial flavors may cause allergic reactions in sensitive individuals. Also contains BHT, whose long-term safety is currently being reexamined by FDA investigators.

KRAFT JET-PUFFED MARSHMALLOWS
Kraft, Inc.

Ingredients: corn syrup, sugar, modified food starch, dextrose, water, gelatin, tetrasodium pyrophosphate, artificial and natural flavor, artificial color.

Amount: 1 piece			% USRDA
Calories	25	Protein	*
Protein, gm	0	Vitamin A	*
Carbohydrates, gm	6	Vitamin C	*
Fat, gm	0	Thiamine	*
Sodium, mg	10	Riboflavin	*
Cholesterol, mg	0	Niacin	*
Fiber, gm	0	Calcium	*
		Iron	*

THIS FOOD: Like many candies, Kraft Jet-Puffed Marshmallows are little more than artificially flavored and colored sugar.

ADDITIVES: Contains artificial flavors and colors, which some studies suggest may adversely affect behavior and the ability to complete school tasks in

HELPFUL HINT: If you can't resist candy but wish to minimize tooth decay, eat it with—rather than in between—meals.

some sensitive children. Artificial colors are inadequately tested; artificial flavors may cause allergic reactions in sensitive individuals.

LIFE SAVERS, SPEAR O MINT
Nabisco Brands, Inc.

Ingredients: sugar, corn syrup, natural flavor, stearic acid.

Amount: 1 Life Saver			% USRDA
Calories	10	Protein	*
Protein, gm	0	Vitamin A	*
Carbohydrates, gm	2	Vitamin C	*
Fat, gm	0	Thiamine	*
Sodium, mg	45	Riboflavin	*
Cholesterol, mg	0	Niacin	*
Fiber, gm	0	Calcium	*
		Iron	*
Contains about ½ teaspoon sugar.			

THIS FOOD: Spear O Mint Life Savers are basically flavored sugar. They contain no vitamins and minerals.

ADDITIVES: No questionable additives.

LIFE SAVERS, WILD CHERRY
Nabisco Brands, Inc.

Ingredients: sugar, corn syrup, artificial flavors and colors.

Amount: 1 Life Saver			% USRDA
Calories	10	Protein	*
Protein, gm	0	Vitamin A	*
Carbohydrates, gm	3	Vitamin C	*
Fat, gm	0	Thiamine	*
Sodium, mg	45	Riboflavin	*
Cholesterol, mg	0	Niacin	*
Fiber, gm	0	Calcium	*
		Iron	*
Contains about ½ teaspoon sugar.			

THIS FOOD: Wild Cherry Life Savers are basically artificially colored and flavored sugar. They contain no vitamins or minerals.

ADDITIVES: Contains artificial colors and flavors, which some studies suggest may adversely affect behavior and the ability to complete school tasks in some sensitive children. Artificial colors are inadequately tested and artificial flavors may cause allergic reactions in sensitive individuals.

WRIGLEY'S DOUBLEMINT GUM
William Wrigley, Jr., Co.

Ingredients: sugar, gum base, corn syrup, dextrose, softeners, and natural flavor.

Amount: 1 stick			% USRDA
Calories	10	Protein	*
Protein, gm	0	Vitamin A	*
Carbohydrates, gm	2	Vitamin C	*
Fat, gm	1	Thiamine	*
Sodium, mg	3	Riboflavin	*
Cholesterol, mg	0	Niacin	*
Fiber, gm	0	Calcium	*
		Iron	*

THIS FOOD: A stick of Wrigley's Doublemint Gum contains only about ½ teaspoon sugar. Although relatively low in sugar calories, chewing gum definitely contributes to tooth decay.

ADDITIVES: No questionable additives.

CEREALS

A staggering array of cereals are promoted—letters, loops and logs, pebbles, puffs, and crisps, in every imaginable color, flavor, and grain combination—with almost universal disregard for the nutritional facts. Popular cartoon characters like Sugar Bear and Tony the Tiger imply that eating sugar-loaded cereals will make kids strong. Other cereals make their appeal to the health-conscious by boldly lettering NO CHOLESTEROL on the box without bothering to mention that no cereal product on the market contains any cholesterol. Or by proclaiming NO ARTIFICIAL PRESERVATIVES. How many consumers will bother to read the fine print on the side panel which reveals this same apparently "natural" product contains Yellow No. 5 and other artificial colors?

Here are some of the facts you need in order to make an intelligent choice of breakfast cereal:

Cereal, cold or hot, can be an excellent breakfast food. Ideally, it should be a good source of fiber, complex carbohydrates, and trace minerals, all of which are in short supply in the average diet; it should also be low in sugar.

Currently Americans consume only about one half of the dietary fiber and complex carbohydrates recommended by the 1980 Surgeon General's report on preventive medicine and the 1980 guidelines of the National Academy of Sciences National Research Council. A diet high in fiber has been associated with a lower incidence of intestinal disorders including colon cancer, a major killer. Unfortunately sugar is a major component in many popular cereals. Most people know that too much sugar provides nutritionally "empty" calories, causes tooth decay and obesity. It can also contribute to diabetes and, among susceptible individuals, to elevated levels of cholesterol and tri-glycerides, both major risk factors in heart disease.

The desirable nutrients in cereal—complex carbohydrates, protein, fiber, and minerals—are naturally present in richest concentrations from whole grain sources, Yet the vast majority of popular cereals are made from highly processed grains. The refining process, which almost always removes the bran and germ layers also removes up to 80 percent of the grain's essential nutrients, including most of the fiber. Cereal manufacturers have responded to criticism by fortifying their products. This is where the confusion begins.

Typically manufacturers fortify their cereals with "nine essential nutrients." The problem is that far more than nine nutrients have been removed. With few exceptions the nutrients added back are likely to be supplied by other foods eaten during the day. To put it bluntly, in cereals made from refined grains, the nutrients you need most (fiber, trace minerals, protein from vegetable sources, and vi-tamin E) have been removed, and the nutrients most people get enough of from other foods have been added back, too often along with excess sugar. For example, Kellogg's Most, which contains 100 percent of the USRDA for eleven vitamins, also derives 29 percent of its calories from sugar, while other fortified products aimed at chil-dren contain still more sugar—up to 56 percent by weight! These examples illustrate the major danger of fortification: it is often mis-used to make foods appear nutritious.

Zinc and iron fortification are, however, a different story, since these trace minerals are generally in short supply in the American diet. Thus, in the nutritional assessments which follow, iron and zinc fortification are considered a plus, but fortification with vitamins is not. Generally speaking, low-sugar, high fiber cereals made from whole grain sources—fortified or not—are the best nutritional choices. To cut down on fat and cholesterol, try adding low-fat milk (1 percent less fat, and 60 percent less cholesterol, and 30 percent fewer calories. Whole milk contains 48 percent fat calories, compared to the 20 percent fat calories in low-fat milk. If you find it hard to get used to the taste of low-fat milk, try mixing it with whole milk, then gradually increase the proportion of low-fat to whole milk. Many nutritionists believe that, with the exception of children less than two years old, everyone is better off drinking vitamin-D-fortified low-fat milk.

Cold Cereals

Since most people eat cold cereal with ½ cup of whole milk, we have presented the combined nutrient content of the cereal and whole milk in our profiles. The milk contributes 1½ teaspoons naturally occurring sugar and 60 milligrams sodium as well as other important nutrients.

Amount: ½ cup milk			% USRDA
Calories	75	Protein	6
Protein, gm	4	Vitamin A	5
Carbohydrates, gm	6	Vitamin C	*
Fat, gm	4	Thiamine	5
Sodium, mg	60	Riboflavin	10
Cholesterol, mg	16	Niacin	*
Fiber, gm	0	Calcium	15
		Iron	*

If you wish to know the nutritional content of the cereal alone, simply subtract the above values, which are contributed by the milk.

SODIUM GUIDELINES: In evaluating the sodium content of hot and cold cereals, we used the following standards:

125 mg to 200 mg	low in sodium
200 mg to 300 mg	moderate in sodium
more than 300 mg	high in sodium

Remember, these guidelines are not for people following medically restricted low-sodium diets, but for healthy individuals who wish to monitor their sodium intake.

SODIUM WINNERS

Those on strict low-sodium diets can choose from Nabisco Shredded Wheat and Quaker 100% Natural Cereal, which are both virtually sodium free and good sources of fiber. Of the two cereals, Shredded Wheat is the better choice since it's lower in fat and sugar. All of these cold cereals contain less than 100 mg sodium without added milk:

Corn Pops
Frosted Mini-Wheats
Honey Smacks
Nabisco Shredded Wheat
Quaker 100% Natural Cereal
Smurf-Berry Crunch

SODIUM LOSERS

High sodium cereals are fairly common. The following contain more than 300 mg sodium per 1-ounce serving. A half cup of whole milk will add an additional 60 mg sodium.

All-Bran
Cheerios
Kix
Post Toasties Corn Flakes
Product 19
Total
Wheaties

FIBER WINNERS

These cereals contain at least 4 grams fiber per serving:

All-Bran
Corn Bran
Fruit and Fiber
Health Valley Sprouts 7 with Raisins
Kellogg's 40% Bran Flakes
Post 40% Bran Flakes

ALL-BRAN
Kellogg Co.

Ingredients: wheat bran, sugar, corn syrup, malt flavoring, salt, vitamin C, vitamin B_3, zinc, iron, vitamin A, vitamin B_6, vitamin B_2, vitamin B_1, folic acid, and vitamin D.

Amount: ⅓ cup (+ ½ cup milk)			% USRDA
Calories	140	Protein	6
Protein, gm	7	Vitamin A	25
Carbohydrates, gm	27	Vitamin C	25
Fat, gm	5	Thiamine	25
Sodium, mg	380	Riboflavin	25
Cholesterol, mg	16	Niacin	25
Fiber, gm	9	Calcium	2
		Iron	25
Cereal without milk contains 1 teaspoon sugar.			

THIS FOOD: Provides more dietary fiber than any other popular cereal. It is low in added sugar and fortified with both zinc and iron. It is high in sodium for this category (320 mg per serving).

ADDITIVES: No questionable additives.

ALPHA-BITS
General Foods Corp.

Ingredients: oat flour, sugar, corn flour, salt, corn syrup, hydrogenated coconut and/or palm kernel oil, vitamin A, artificial color (including FD & C Yellow No. 5), niacinamide, zinc, iron, viramin B_6, vitamin B_2, vitamin B_1, vitamin B_{12}, folic acid, vitamin D, BHA.

Amount: 1 cup (+ ½ cup milk)			% USRDA
Calories	190	Protein	8
Protein, gm	6	Vitamin A	30
Carbohydrates, gm	30	Vitamin C	*
Fat, gm	5	Thiamine	30
Sodium, mg	255	Riboflavin	35
Cholesterol, mg	16	Niacin	25
Fiber, gm	<1	Calcium	15
		Iron	10
Cereal without milk contains 2¾ teaspoons sugar.			

THIS FOOD: Like many cereals aimed at children, Alpha-Bits is high in sugar—38 percent by weight—and low in fiber. It is fortified with zinc and iron.

ADDITIVES: Contains FD & C Yellow No. 5, which can cause allergic reactions, primarily in aspirin-sensitive individuals; also contains artificial colors, which are inadequately tested and which some studies suggest may adversely affect behavior and the ability to complete school tasks in some sensitive children.

APPLE JACKS
Kellogg Co.

Ingredients: sugar, corn, wheat, and oat flour, salt, corn cereal, dried apples, corn syrup, cinnamon, partially hydrogenated vegetable oil (one or more of: cottonseed, coconut, soybean and palm), vitamin C, artificial coloring, vitamin B_3, zinc, natural apple flavoring, iron, baking soda, vitamin A, BHT, vitamin B_6, vitamin B_2, vitamin B_1, folic acid, and vitamin D.

Amount: 1 cup (+ ½ cup milk)			% USRDA
Calories	180	Protein	10
Protein, gm	6	Vitamin A	30
Carbohydrates, gm	31	Vitamin C	25
Fat, gm	4	Thiamine	30
Sodium, mg	185	Riboflavin	30
Cholesterol, mg	16	Niacin	25
Fiber, gm	<1	Calcium	15
		Iron	25
Cereal without milk contains 3½ teaspoons sugar.			

THIS FOOD: This popular cereal is little more than apple-flavored sugar. Although the added zinc and iron are useful, Apple Jacks is made from refined flours and has little fiber or nutrient content of its own.

ADDITIVES: Contains artificial colors, which are inadequately tested, and which some studies suggest may adversely affect behavior and the ability to complete school tasks in some sensitive children. Also contains BHT, whose long-term safety is currently being reexamined by FDA investigators.

NOTE: The letter "e" indicates that the data has been estimated; < means "less than" and is used for small amounts of sodium or cholesterol; * means food contains less than 2% of USRDA; "na" means that the information was not available and appears only when data is insufficient.

CAP'N CRUNCH
Quaker Oats Co.

Ingredients: corn flour, sugar, oat flour, coconut oil, brown sugar, salt, niacinamide, reduced iron, calcium pantothenate, FD & C Yellow No. 5, zinc oxide, FD & C Yellow No. 6, vitamin B_6, B_1, BHA, riboflavin, folic acid, vitamin B_{12}.

Amount: 1 cup (+ ½ cup milk)			% USRDA
Calories	201	Protein	10
Protein, gm	5	Vitamin A	5
Carbohydrates, gm	29	Vitamin C	*
Fat, gm	7	Thiamine	30
Sodium, mg	245	Riboflavin	25
Cholesterol, mg	16	Niacin	25
Fiber, gm	<1	Calcium	15
		Iron	25

Cereal without milk contains 3 teaspoons sugar.

THIS FOOD: Is artificially colored, high in sugar, low in protein and fiber. Vitamin and mineral supplementation cannot make up for these failings.

ADDITIVES: Contains FD & C Yellow No. 5, which can cause allergic reactions, primarily in aspirin-sensitive individuals, and Yellow No. 6, which appears somewhat safer, but also can cause occasional allergic reactions. Also contains BHA, whose long-term safety is currently being reexamined by FDA investigators.

CAP'N CRUNCH'S CRUNCHBERRIES
Quaker Oats Co.

Ingredients: sugar, corn flour, oat flour, coconut oil, brown sugar, salt, nonfat dry milk, natural and artificial flavors, sodium citrate, dried whey, FD & C Yellow No. 5 and other artificial colors, malic acid, mono- and diglycerides, niacin, reduced iron, calcium pantothenate, zinc oxide, vitamin B_6, thiamine, BHA, riboflavin, folic acid, vitamin B_{12}.

Amount: 1 cup (+ ½ cup milk)			% USRDA
Calories	200	Protein	10
Protein, gm	5	Vitamin A	5
Carbohydrates, gm	29	Vitamin C	*
Fat, gm	7	Thiamine	30
Sodium, mg	226	Riboflavin	25
Cholesterol, mg	16	Niacin	25
Fiber, gm	<1	Calcium	15
		Iron	25

Cereal without milk contains 3¼ teaspoons sugar.

THIS FOOD: Cap'n Crunch's Crunchberries has the nutritional faults typical of most cereals aimed at children: it is a highly refined product, artificially colored and flavored, high in sugar, and low in protein and fiber. Vitamin and mineral supplementation cannot make up for these failings.

ADDITIVES: Contains artificial colors and flavors, which some studies suggest may adversely affect behavior and the ability to complete school tasks in some sensitive children. Artificial colors are inadequately tested; artificial flavors may cause allergic reactions in sensitive individuals. Also contains BHA, whose long-term safety is currently being reexamined by FDA investigators.

CHEERIOS
General Mills, Inc.

Ingredients: whole oat flour, wheat starch, salt, sugar, calcium carbonate, trisodium phosphate, sodium ascorbate, niacin, iron, vitamin A palmitate, vitamin B_6, vitamin B_2, vitamin B_1, vitamin B_{12}, and vitamin D.

Amount: 1¼ cups (+ ½ cup milk)			% USRDA
Calories	190	Protein	15
Protein, gm	8	Vitamin A	30
Carbohydrates, gm	26	Vitamin C	25
Fat, gm	6	Thiamine	30
Sodium, mg	390	Riboflavin	35
Cholesterol, mg	16	Niacin	25
Fiber, gm	2	Calcium	20
		Iron	25
Cereal without milk contains ¼ teaspoon sugar.			

THIS FOOD: Cheers for Cheerios! Introduced as Cheeri Oats in the 1940s, this product quickly gained a following and today remains the number-one best seller. The good news is that it is nutritionally sound: it is low in sugar, a good source of protein, an excellent source of trace minerals, and provides some fiber. Cheerios is also popular with kids. A high sodium content is this cereal's sole drawback.

ADDITIVES: No questionable additives.

HELPFUL HINT: To increase your iron absorption, it's important to consume orange juice or another good source of vitamin C at the same meal as your iron-fortified cereal.

FOR SODIUM WATCHERS: Remember that the figure for sodium given in the data box includes 60 mg sodium contributed by ½ cup milk.

COCOA CRISPIES
Kellogg Co.

Ingredients: rice, sugar, cocoa, corn syrup, whey, salt, partially hydrogenated vegetable oil (one or more of: cottonseed, coconut, soybean, and palm), malt flavoring, vitamin C, vitamin B_3, artificial flavoring, zinc, iron , vitamin A, BHT, vitamin B_6, vitamin B_2, vitamin B_1, folic acid, and vitamin D.

Amount: ¾ cup (+ ½ cup milk)			% USRDA
Calories	190	Protein	10
Protein, gm	5	Vitamin A	30
Carbohydrates, gm	31	Vitamin C	25
Fat, gm	5	Thiamine	30
Sodium, mg	255	Riboflavin	35
Cholesterol, mg	16	Niacin	25
Fiber, gm	<1	Calcium	15
		Iron	25

Cereal without milk contains 3 teaspoons sugar.

THIS FOOD: Chocolate cereal? You bet! Concocted for chocolate-loving kids, Cocoa Crispies is 43 percent sugar by weight and lower than average in protein and fiber. The product is fortified with zinc and iron.

ADDITIVES: Contains artificial flavor, which may cause allergic reactions in sensitive individuals, and which some studies suggest may adversely affect behavior and the ability to complete school tasks in some sensitive children.

COCOA PEBBLES
General Foods Corp.

Ingredients: rice, sugar, hydrogenated coconut and/or palm kernel oil, cocoa, corn syrup, salt, artificial flavoring, vitamin A, niacinamide, iron, zinc oxide, vitamin B_6, vitamin B_2, vitamin B_1, vitamin B_{12}, folic acid, and vitamin D_2.

Amount: ⅞ cup (+ ½ cup milk)			% USRDA
Calories	190	Protein	8
Protein, gm	5	Vitamin A	30
Carbohydrates, gm	30	Vitamin C	*
Fat, gm	6	Thiamine	30
Sodium, mg	225	Riboflavin	35
Cholesterol, mg	16	Niacin	25
Fiber, gm	<1	Calcium	15
		Iron	10

Cereal without milk contains 3 teaspoons sugar.

THIS FOOD: Cocoa Pebbles has all of the nutritional failings typical of cereals aimed at children. In addition to being low in fiber and high in sugar, this product contains saturated fat. This zinc- and iron-fortified cereal is low in sodium.

ADDITIVES: Contains artificial flavor, which may cause allergic reactions in sensitive individuals, and which some studies suggest may adversely affect behavior and the ability to complete school tasks in some sensitive children.

COCOA PUFFS
General Mills, Inc.

Ingredients: degermed yellow cornmeal, sugar, corn syrup, cocoa puffs with alkali, salt, coconut oil, beet powder, and caramel color, trisodium phosphate, artificial flavor, vitamin C, calcium carbonate, niacin, iron, vitamin B_6, riboflavin, thiamine, vitamin B_{12}.

Amount: 1 cup (+ ½ cup milk)			% USRDA
Calories	190	• Protein	10
Protein, gm	5	Vitamin A	4
Carbohydrates, gm	31	Vitamin C	25
Fat, gm	5	Thiamine	30
Sodium, mg	265	Riboflavin	35
Cholesterol, mg	16	Niacin	25
Fiber, gm	<1	Calcium	15
		Iron	25
Cereal without milk contains 2¾ teaspoons sugar.			

THIS FOOD: Like many cereals aimed at children, Cocoa Puffs is a poor breakfast choice: high in sugar, and low in fiber and trace nutrients, since it is made from a refined grain. It contains added iron but no added zinc.

ADDITIVES: Contains artificial flavor, which may cause allergic reactions in sensitive individuals, and which some studies suggest may adversely affect behavior and the ability to complete school tasks in some sensitive children.

COOKIE CRISPS
Ralston Purina Co.

Ingredients: sugar, yellow corn flour, rice flour, wheat flour, oat flour, coconut oil, dried apples, salt, cocoa, artificial flavor, partially hydrogenated vegetable oil (contains one or more of the following: cottonseed, soybean), vitamin C, vitamin B_3, reduced iron, FD & C Yellow No. 5, artificial color, vitamin A, vitamin B_6, BHT, vitamin B_2, B_1, B_{12}, D.

Amount: 1 cup (+ ½ cup milk)			% USRDA
Calories	190	Protein	10
Protein, gm	5	Vitamin A	25
Carbohydrates, gm	31	Vitamin C	25
Fat, gm	5	Thiamine	25
Sodium, mg	260	Riboflavin	35
Cholesterol, mg	16	Niacin	25
Fiber, gm	<1	Calcium	15
		Iron	25

Cereal without milk contains 3¼ teaspoons sugar.

THIS FOOD: Contains artificial color, flavor, and saturated fat. Sugar content is high, contributing about 45 percent of total calories. It is also low in fiber.

ADDITIVES: Artificial color and flavor, some studies suggest, may adversely affect behavior and ability to complete school tasks in some sensitive children. Artificial color is inadequately tested; artificial flavor may cause allergic reactions in sensitive individuals. Contains Yellow No. 5, which causes allergic reactions, especially in aspirin-sensitive individuals. Contains BHT, whose long-term safety is now being reexamined by FDA investigators.

CORN BRAN
Quaker Oats Co.

Ingredients: corn flour, corn bran flour, sugar, oat flour, salt, coconut oil, sodium bicarbonate, calcium carbonate, reduced iron, FD & C Yellow No. 5 and other artificial colors, niacinamide, zinc oxide, calcium pantothenate, pyridoxine hydrochloride, thiamine mononitrate, riboflavin, folic acid, vitamin B_{12}.

Amount: ⅔ cup (+ ½ cup milk)			% USRDA
Calories	189	Protein	11
Protein, gm	6	Vitamin A	2
Carbohydrates, gm	29	Vitamin C	*
Fat, gm	5	Thiamine	30
Sodium, mg	305	Riboflavin	25
Cholesterol, mg	16	Niacin	25
Fiber, gm	5.5	Calcium	17
		Iron	25

Cereal without milk contains 1½ teaspoons sugar.

THIS FOOD: Relatively low in added sugar, a good source of fiber, and supplemented with iron as well as 20 percent of the USRDA for zinc. The label proclaims NO ARTIFICIAL PRESERVATIVES but it does contain artificial colors.

ADDITIVES: Contains FD & C Yellow No. 5, which can cause allergic reactions, primarily in aspirin-sensitive individuals, and artificial colors, which are inadequately tested and which some studies suggest may adversely affect behavior and the ability to complete school tasks in some sensitive children.

CORN CHEX
Ralston Purina Co.

Ingredients: milled yellow corn, sugar, salt, malted cereal syrup, leavening, vitamin C, niacinamide, reduced iron, vitamin B_1, B_6, folic acid and vitamin B_{12}, BHT.

Amount: 1 cup (+ ½ cup milk)			% USRDA
Calories	190	Protein	10
Protein, gm	6	Vitamin A	4
Carbohydrates, gm	31	Vitamin C	25
Fat, gm	4	Thiamine	25
Sodium, mg	350	Riboflavin	15
Cholesterol, mg	16	Niacin	25
Fiber, gm	<1	Calcium	15
		Iron	10

THIS FOOD: This cereal is slightly higher than average in sodium, and lower than average in fiber. It contains a substantial amount of added sugar, and is fortified with iron. Overall this cereal is not an especially good breakfast choice.

ADDITIVES: Contains BHT, whose long-term safety is currently being reexamined by FDA investigators.

CORN POPS
Kellogg Co.

Ingredients: corn, sugar, corn syrup, molasses, salt, partially hydrogenated vegetable oil (one or more of: cottonseed, coconut, soybean, and palm), annatto color, vitamin C, vitamin B_3, zinc, iron, vitamin A, BHT, vitamin B_6, vitamin B_2, vitamin B_1, folic acid, vitamin D.

Amount: 1 cup (+ ½ cup milk)			% USRDA
Calories	180	Protein	10
Protein, gm	5	Vitamin A	30
Carbohydrates, gm	32	Vitamin C	25
Fat, gm	4	Thiamine	30
Sodium, mg	155	Riboflavin	35
Cholesterol, mg	16	Niacin	25
Fiber, gm	<1	Calcium	15
		Iron	10
Cereal without milk contains 3¼ teaspoons sugar.			

THIS FOOD: Corn Pops is yet another high-sugar, low-fiber, low-protein cereal made from refined grains. Nearly 50 percent of the calories in Corn Pops derives from sugar. This cereal is fortified with iron and 10 percent of the USRDA for zinc.

ADDITIVES: Contains BHT, whose long-term safety is currently being reexamined by FDA investigators.

CRISPIX
Kellogg Co.

Ingredients: corn, rice, brown sugar, salt, malt flavoring, baking soda, turmeric color, vitamin C, vitamin B_3, zinc, iron, vitamin A, vitamin B_6, vitamin B_2, vitamin B_1, folic acid, vitamin D, BHT.

Amount: ¾ cup (+ ½ cup milk)			% USRDA
Calories	180	Protein	10
Protein, gm	6	Vitamin A	30
Carbohydrates, gm	30	Vitamin C	25
Fat, gm	4	Thiamine	30
Sodium, mg	290	Riboflavin	35
Cholesterol, mg	16	Niacin	25
Fiber, gm	<1e	Calcium	15
		Iron	10
Cereal without milk contains ½ teaspoon sugar.			

THIS FOOD: Crispix is low in sugar, moderate in sodium, and fortified with both zinc and iron. Unfortunately, this product provides little dietary fiber, which prevents it from being an especially good breakfast choice.

ADDITIVES: Contains BHT, whose long-term safety is currently being reexamined by FDA investigators.

CRISPY WHEATS 'N RAISINS
General Mills, Inc.

Ingredients: whole wheat, raisins, sugar, honey, salt, brown sugar syrup, cereal malt syrup, calcium carbonate, trisodium phosphate, niacinamide, iron, annatto extract color, vitamin A palmitate, vitamin B_6, vitamin B_1, vitamin B_2, and vitamin B_{12}.

Amount: ¾ cup (+ ½ cup milk)			% USRDA
Calories	190	Protein	10
Protein, gm	6	Vitamin A	30
Carbohydrates, gm	29	Vitamin C	*
Fat, gm	5	Thiamine	30
Sodium, mg	245	Riboflavin	35
Cholesterol, mg	16	Niacin	25
Fiber, gm	2.5e	Calcium	20
		Iron	25
Cereal without milk contains 2½ teaspoons sugar.			

THIS FOOD: Whole wheat flakes, the basic ingredient of this cereal, are a perfectly healthy food, high in trace minerals, and provide some fiber. Unfortunately the value of this product has been undermined by an overdose of added sugars and too many raisins, which are also a concentrated source of sugar.

ADDITIVES: No questionable additives.

OTHER BRANDS: Nutri-Grain, Wheat, or Wheaties are both better choices, since they are low in sugar. Crispy Wheats 'n Raisins derives 35 percent of its calories from sugar, compared to 8 percent for Nutri-Grain, Wheat, and 10 percent for Wheaties.

FROOT LOOPS
Kellogg Co.

Ingredients: corn, wheat, and oat flour, sugar, partially hydrogenated vegetable oil (one or more of: cottonseed, coconut, soybean, and palm), salt, vitamin C, color added, vitamin B_3, zinc, iron, natural orange, lemon, cherry, with other natural flavorings, vitamin A, BHT, vitamin B_6, vitamin B_2, vitamin B_1, folic acid, and vitamin D.

Amount: 1 cup (+ ½ cup milk)			% USRDA
Calories	190	Protein	10
Protein, gm	6	Vitamin A	30
Carbohydrates, gm	31	Vitamin C	100
Fat, gm	5	Thiamine	30
Sodium, mg	195	Riboflavin	25
Cholesterol, mg	16	Niacin	25
Fiber, gm	<1	Calcium	15
		Iron	25
Cereal without milk contains 3¼ teaspoons sugar.			

THIS FOOD: Made from refined grains, Froot Loops is low in fiber and naturally occurring trace minerals. Like the vast majority of products aimed at children, this cereal has a heavy dose of added sugar—48 percent by weight. It is fortified with iron and 20 percent of the USRDA for zinc.

ADDITIVES: No questionable additives.

NUTRITION TIP: To avoid digestive upsets, increase your fiber intake gradually, drawing from a variety of fiber sources, especially fruits and vegetables in addition to bran. There are at least five different types of fiber. Cellulose, which is the type of fiber found in wheat bran, is just one of them. Some studies suggest that pectins and gums from fruits and vegetables can help lower serum cholesterol levels.

FROSTED FLAKES
Kellogg Co.

Ingredients: corn, sugar, salt, malt flavoring, corn syrup, vitamin C, vitamin B_3, iron, vitamin A, BHT, vitamin B_6, vitamin B_2, vitamin B_1, folic acid, and vitamin D.

Amount: ¾ cup (+ ½ cup milk)			% USRDA
Calories	180	Protein	10
Protein, gm	5	Vitamin A	30
Carbohydrates, gm	31	Vitamin C	25
Fat, gm	4	Thiamine	30
Sodium, mg	250	Riboflavin	35
Cholesterol, mg	16	Niacin	25
Fiber, gm	<1	Calcium	15
		Iron	10

Cereal without milk contains 2½ teaspoons sugar.

THIS FOOD: Like many breakfast cereals aimed at children, Frosted Flakes is a poor breakfast choice: high in sugar, and low in fiber. Cereal without milk contains 190 mg sodium per serving, which is considered low for this category.

ADDITIVES: Contains BHT, whose long-term safety is currently being reexamined by FDA investigators.

FROSTED MINI-WHEATS
Kellogg Co.

Ingredients: whole wheat, sugar, sorbitol, gelatin, vitamin C, vitamin B_3, zinc, iron, vitamin A, vitamin B_6, vitamin B_2, vitamin B_1, folic acid, and vitamin D.

Amount: 4 biscuits (+ ½ cup milk)			% USRDA
Calories	180	Protein	15
Protein, gm	6	Vitamin A	30
Carbohydrates, gm	29	Vitamin C	25
Fat, gm	4	Thiamine	30
Sodium, mg	65	Riboflavin	35
Cholesterol, mg	16	Niacin	25
Fiber, gm	3	Calcium	15
		Iron	10

Cereal without milk contains 1½ teaspoons sugar.

THIS FOOD: Frosted Mini-Wheats is very much like Spoon Sized Shredded Wheat, only with added sugar. It provides 3 grams of fiber per serving, and valuable trace nutrients from whole wheat. With the cereal contributing only 5 mg sodium per serving, this product may be useful to people on low-sodium diets. Frosted Mini-Wheats is fortified with both iron and 10 percent of the USRDA for zinc.

ADDITIVES: No questionable additives.

FRUIT AND FIBER WITH DATES, RAISINS, AND WALNUTS
General Foods Corp.

Ingredients: whole wheat, wheat bran, sugar, dates, raisins, walnuts, salt, corn syrup, wheat flour, malted barley, dextrose (corn sugar), natural and artificial flavor, honey, vitamin A, niacinamide, iron, zinc oxide, vitamin B_6, vitamin B_2, vitamin B_1, vitamin B_{12}, folic acid, vitamin D_2, BHA.

Amount: ½ cup (+ ½ cup milk)			% USRDA
Calories	160	Protein	10
Protein, gm	7	Vitamin A	30
Carbohydrates, gm	27	Vitamin C	*
Fat, gm	5	Thiamine	30
Sodium, mg	230	Riboflavin	35
Cholesterol, mg	16	Niacin	25
Fiber, gm	4	Calcium	15
		Iron	25
Cereal without milk contains 1¾ teaspoons sugar.			

THIS FOOD: Fruit and Fiber provides a fair amount of dietary fiber but artificial flavor and too much added sugar detract from the nutritional value of this cereal. Thirty-three percent of the calories in each serving of Fruit and Fiber come from sugar. This cereal is fortified with iron and 10 percent of the USRDA for zinc.

ADDITIVES: Contains artificial flavor, which may cause allergic reactions in sensitive individuals, and which some studies suggest may adversely affect behavior and the ability to complete school tasks in some sensitive children. Also contains BHA, whose long-term safety is currently being reexamined by FDA investigators.

OTHER BRANDS: Other fiber-rich cereals that do not contain too much added sugar include Kellogg's All-Bran, Post or Kellogg's 40% Bran Flakes, and Shredded Wheat.

FRUITY PEBBLES
General Foods Corp.

Ingredients: rice, sugar, hydrogenated coconut and/or palm kernel oil, corn syrup, salt, artificial color, natural and artificial fruit flavors, and fortified with the following nutrients: vitamin A palmitate, niacinamide, iron, zinc oxide, vitamin B_6, riboflavin, vitamin B_1, vitamin B_{12}, folic acid, and vitamin D_2.

Amount: 1 cup (+ ½ cup milk)			% USRDA
Calories	190	Protein	6
Protein, gm	4	Vitamin A	30
Carbohydrates, gm	30	Vitamin C	*
Fat, gm	6	Thiamine	30
Sodium, mg	220	Riboflavin	35
Cholesterol, mg	16	Niacin	25
Fiber, gm	<1	Calcium	15
		Iron	10

Cereal without milk contains 3 teaspoons of sugar.

THIS FOOD: Fruity Pebbles is little more than candy. This artificially colored and flavored cereal is low in protein, loaded with sugar, and also contains saturated fat. It contains very little dietary fiber.

ADDITIVES: Contains artificial colors, which are inadequately tested and which some studies suggest may adversely affect behavior and the ability to complete school tasks in some sensitive children.

GOLDEN GRAHAMS
General Mills, Inc.

Ingredients: degermed yellow cornmeal, sugar, graham flour, wheat starch, brown sugar syrup, coconut oil, honey, salt, nonfat dry milk, sodium bicarbonate, dextrose, trisodium phosphate, sodium ascorbate, artificial flavor, calcium carbonate, niacin, iron, vitamin A palmitate, vitamin B_6, vitamin B_1, vitamin B_2, vitamin B_{12}, and vitamin D.

Amount: ¾ cup (+ ½ cup milk)			% USRDA
Calories	190	Protein	10
Protein, gm	6	Vitamin A	30
Carbohydrates, gm	30	Vitamin C	25
Fat, gm	5	Thiamine	30
Sodium, mg	345	Riboflavin	35
Cholesterol, mg	16	Niacin	25
Fiber, gm	<1	Calcium	15
		Iron	25

Cereal without milk contains 2¼ teaspoons sugar.

THIS FOOD: Graham flour, a form of whole wheat, is an excellent source of fiber and trace minerals. Despite its name this artificially flavored cereal has too little graham flour in it to be a good breakfast choice. Because refined cornmeal is the main ingredient, it is low in fiber. Golden Grahams is also slightly higher than average in sodium.

ADDITIVES: Contains artificial flavor, which may cause allergic reactions in sensitive individuals, and which some studies suggest may adversely affect behavior and the ability to complete school tasks in some sensitive children.

GRAPE-NUTS
General Foods Corp.

Ingredients: wheat, malted barley, salt, yeast, and fortified with the following nutrients: vitamin A palmitate, niacinamide, vitamin B_6, vitamin B_2, vitamin B_1, vitamin B_{12}, folic acid, and vitamin D_2.

Amount: ¼ cup (+ ½ cup milk)			% USRDA
Calories	180	Protein	10
Protein, gm	7	Vitamin A	30
Carbohydrates, gm	29	Vitamin C	*
Fat, gm	5	Thiamine	30
Sodium, mg	255	Riboflavin	35
Cholesterol, mg	16	Niacin	25
Fiber, gm	3.5	Calcium	15
		Iron	4

Cereal without milk contains ¾ teaspoon naturally occurring sugar.

THIS FOOD: Grape-Nuts is one of the few cereals profiled to contain no added sugar, although malted barley contributes natural sugars to serve as sweetening. This product is made from refined wheat, but is still a fairly good source of fiber. All in all, Grape-Nuts is well above average in nutrition.

ADDITIVES: No questionable additives.

HEALTH VALLEY SPROUTS 7 WITH RAISINS
Health Valley Foods

Ingredients: sprouted whole grains: wheat, barley, raisins, oats, triticale, buckwheat, rye, flaxseed, bran, yeast.

Amount: ¼ cup (+ ½ cup milk)			% USRDA
Calories	180	Protein	10
Protein, gm	7	Vitamin A	4
Carbohydrates, gm	26	Vitamin C	8
Fat, gm	5	Thiamine	10
Sodium, mg	5	Riboflavin	20
Cholesterol, mg	16	Niacin	10
Fiber, gm	4e	Calcium	15
		Iron	6

Cereal without milk contains no added sugar.

THIS FOOD: Made from whole grains, Health Valley Sprouts 7 with Raisins is a healthful alternative to most granolas, since it is a good source of fiber and contains no added sugar. The raisins, however, contain naturally occurring sugar. While this particular product may not be distributed in your area, if you enjoy granola-type cereals, choose a brand whose ingredients list reveals a similar sugarless, whole-grain recipe.

ADDITIVES: None.

HONEYCOMB
General Foods Corp.

Ingredients: corn flour, sugar, oat flour, salt, hydrogenated coconut and/or palm kernel oil, corn syrup, honey, and fortified with the following nutrients: vitamin A palmitate, niacinamide, iron, zinc oxide, vitamin B_6, vitamin B_2, vitamin B_1, vitamin B_{12}, folic acid, and vitamin D_2, BHA.

Amount: 1⅓ cups (+ ½ cup milk)			% USRDA
Calories	190	Protein	8
Protein, gm	5	Vitamin A	30
Carbohydrates, gm	31	Vitamin C	*
Fat, gm	5	Thiamine	30
Sodium, mg	255	Riboflavin	35
Cholesterol, mg	16	Niacin	25
Fiber, gm	<1	Calcium	15
		Iron	10

Cereal without milk contains 2¾ teaspoons sugar.

THIS FOOD: Honeycomb has most of the nutritional faults typical of cereals aimed at kids: it is high in sugar—37 percent by weight, low in protein, fiber, and the trace minerals present in whole grains.

ADDITIVES: Contains BHA, whose long-term safety is currently being reexamined by FDA investigators.

HONEY NUT CHEERIOS
General Mills, Inc.

Ingredients: oat flour, sugar, defatted wheat germ, wheat starch, honey, brown sugar syrup, salt, almonds, trisodium phosphate, sodium ascorbate, calcium carbonate, niacin, iron, vitamin A palmitate, vitamin B_6, vitamin B_2, vitamin B_1, vitamin B_{12}, and vitamin D.

Amount: ¾ cup (+ ½ cup milk)			% USRDA
Calories	190	Protein	15
Protein, gm	7	Vitamin A	30
Carbohydrates, gm	29	Vitamin C	25
Fat, gm	5	Thiamine	30
Sodium, mg	315	Riboflavin	35
Cholesterol, mg	16	Niacin	25
Fiber, gm	1.5	Calcium	15
		Iron	25

Cereal without milk contains 2½ teaspoons sugar.

THIS FOOD: To widen Cheerios' appeal, the manufacturers have added lots of sweetening and a tiny amount of almonds and defatted wheat germ to the basic formula. The end result is Honey Nut Cheerios, a product that has less protein, less fiber and trace minerals, and far more sugar, than its namesake. If you like Cheerios, stick to the plain kind.

ADDITIVES: No questionable additives.

HONEY NUT CRUNCH RAISIN BRAN
General Foods Corp.

Ingredients: whole wheat, raisins, wheat flour, wheat bran, sugar, honey, almonds, salt, corn syrup, flavoring, partially hydrogenated vegetable oil (coconut, soybean, cottonseed), yeast, vitamin A palmitate, niacinamide, iron, zinc oxide, vitamin B_6, vitamin B_2, vitamin B_1, vitamin B_{12}, folic acid, and vitamin D_2.

Amount: ½ cup (+½ cup milk)			% USRDA
Calories	160	Protein	10
Protein, gm	6	Vitamin A	30
Carbohydrates, gm	29	Vitamin C	*
Fat, gm	4	Thiamine	30
Sodium, mg	210	Riboflavin	35
Cholesterol, mg	16	Niacin	25
Fiber, gm	2	Calcium	15
		Iron	20
Cereal without milk contains 2 teaspoons sugar.			

THIS FOOD: Sugar—including naturally occurring sugars—accounts for 37 percent of the calories in Honey Nut Crunch Raisin Bran. This cereal provides some fiber and is fortified with both zinc and iron. It contains 150 mg sodium per serving, which is considered low for this category.

ADDITIVES: No questionable additives.

HONEY SMACKS
Kellogg Co.

Ingredients: sugar, wheat, corn syrup, honey, hydrogenated soybean oil, caramel color, salt, sodium acetate, vitamin C, vitamin B_3, iron, lecithin, vitamin A, vitamin B_6, vitamin B_2, vitamin B_1, folic acid, and vitamin D.

Amount: 1 cup (+½ cup milk)			% USRDA
Calories	190	Protein	10
Protein, gm	6	Vitamin A	30
Carbohydrates, gm	31	Vitamin C	25
Fat, gm	4	Thiamine	30
Sodium, mg	130	Riboflavin	35
Cholesterol, mg	16	Niacin	25
Fiber, gm	<1	Calcium	15
		Iron	10
Cereal without milk contains 4 teaspoons sugar.			

THIS FOOD: Kellogg's Honey Smacks is a clear example of sugar-laden food masquerading as a reasonable breakfast choice. A staggering 55 percent of its calories derive from sugar, more than for any other cereal profiled. And since it is made from refined wheat flour, the cereal is low in fiber and trace minerals. This product is low in sodium.

ADDITIVES: No questionable additives.

KELLOGG'S CORN FLAKES
Kellogg Co.

Ingredients: corn, sugar, salt, malt flavoring, corn syrup, vitamin C, vitamin B_3, iron, vitamin B_6, vitamin A, vitamin B_2, vitamin B_1, folic acid, and vitamin D, BHT.

Amount: 1¼ cups (+½ cup milk)			% USRDA
Calories	180	Protein	10
Protein, gm	6	Vitamin A	30
Carbohydrates, gm	30	Vitamin C	25
Fat, gm	4	Thiamine	40
Sodium, mg	345	Riboflavin	45
Cholesterol, mg	16	Niacin	35
Fiber, gm	2.5	Calcium	15
		Iron	10
Cereal without milk contains ¼ teaspoon sugar.			

THIS FOOD: An all-time favorite since 1907, when it was introduced by John Harvey Kellogg, a self-styled nutritionist, Kellogg's Corn Flakes is the third most popular cold cereal today. It has only a tiny amount of added sugar and provides some fiber, but because it is made from degermed, milled corn rather than whole kernels, most of the fiber and trace nutrients have been removed. Kellogg's Corn Flakes is slightly higher than average in sodium.

ADDITIVES: Contains BHT, whose long-term safety is currently being reexamined by FDA investigators.

OTHER BRANDS: If you enjoy this type of cereal, try Nutri-Grain, Corn, which is made from whole kernel corn and thus contains more fiber and naturally occurring trace nutrients.

KELLOGG'S 40% BRAN FLAKES
Kellogg Co.

Ingredients: wheat bran with other parts of wheat, sugar, corn syrup, salt, malt flavoring, iron, vitamin B_3, zinc, vitamin A, vitamin B_6, vitamin B_2, vitamin B_1, folic acid, vitamin B_{12}, and vitamin D.

Amount: ¾ cup (+½ cup milk)			% USRDA
Calories	160	Protein	15
Protein, gm	7	Vitamin A	30
Carbohydrates, gm	28	Vitamin C	2
Fat, gm	5	Thiamine	30
Sodium, mg	280	Riboflavin	35
Cholesterol, mg	16	Niacin	25
Fiber, gm	5	Calcium	15
		Iron	45

Cereal without milk contains 1 teaspoon sugar.

THIS FOOD: Among the most popular cereals, 40% Bran Flakes is also one of the very best. It is a very good source of fiber, high in protein, and moderate in added sugar, which contributes 17 percent of total calories. It is fortified with iron and 20 percent of the USRDA for zinc.

ADDITIVES: No questionable additives.

OTHER BRANDS: Post 40% Bran Flakes has a slight nutritional edge over Kellogg's 40% Bran Flakes, since it is made from whole wheat as well as wheat bran.

KELLOGG'S RAISIN BRAN
Kellogg Co.

Ingredients: wheat bran with other parts of wheat, raisins, sugar, corn syrup, salt, malt flavoring, iron, vitamin B_3, zinc, vitamin A, vitamin B_6, vitamin B_2, vitamin B_1, folic acid, vitamin B_{12}, and vitamin D.

Amount: ¾ cup (+½ cup milk)			% USRDA
Calories	190	Protein	15
Protein, gm	7	Vitamin A	30
Carbohydrates, gm	36	Vitamin C	2
Fat, gm	5	Thiamine	30
Sodium, mg	355	Riboflavin	35
Cholesterol, mg	16	Niacin	25
Fiber, gm	3	Calcium	15
		Iron	45

Cereal without milk contains 3 teaspoons sugar.

THIS FOOD: Kellogg's Raisin Bran is a good source of fiber and is fortified with zinc and iron. More than 40 percent of the calories in this product come from sugar (including the naturally occurring sugar in the raisins). This product contains 295 mg sodium, which is considered moderate for cold cereals.

ADDITIVES: No questionable additives.

KIX
General Mills, Inc.

Ingredients: degermed yellow cornmeal, oat flour, sugar, wheat starch, salt, dextrose, calcium carbonate, trisodium phosphate, vitamin C, iron, niacin, vitamin A, vitamin B_6, riboflavin, vitamin B_1, vitamin B_{12}, vitamin D.

Amount: 1½ cups (+ ½ cup milk)			% USRDA
Calories	190	Protein	10
Protein, gm	6	Vitamin A	30
Carbohydrates, gm	30	Vitamin C	25
Fat, gm	5	Thiamine	30
Sodium, mg	375	Riboflavin	35
Cholesterol, mg	16	Niacin	25
Fiber, gm	<1	Calcium	20
		Iron	45
Cereal without milk contains ½ teaspoon sugar.			

THIS FOOD: Less than 7 percent of the calories in Kix comes from sugar. While this product avoids the most common nutritional failing among breakfast cereals, it remains low in fiber and trace minerals because it is made from refined grains. Also, people concerned with their sodium intake should note that this cereal contains 315 mg sodium per serving, which is quite high for this category.

ADDITIVES: No questionable additives.

LIFE
Quaker Oats Co.

Ingredients: oat flour, sugar, soy flour, corn flour, salt, calcium carbonate, sodium phosphate, l-lysine monohydrochloride, reduced iron, niacinamide, FD & C Yellow No. 5, BHA, FD & C Yellow No. 6, riboflavin, vitamin B_1.

Amount: ⅔ cup (+ ½ cup milk)			% USRDA
Calories	185	Protein	12
Protein, gm	10	Vitamin A	2
Carbohydrates, gm	26	Vitamin C	*
Fat, gm	5	Thiamine	30
Sodium, mg	223	Riboflavin	35
Cholesterol, mg	16	Niacin	25
Fiber, gm	2.5	Calcium	25
		Iron	25
Cereal without milk contains 1¼ teaspoons sugar.			

THIS FOOD: Does this cereal live up to the healthy image its name conjures up? Life is unusually high in protein (from soy flour), a fact which is stressed in promotion and advertising. It provides some fiber, is fortified with iron, moderate in added sugar, and low in sodium. On the negative side, Life does contain several controversial additives.

ADDITIVES: Contains FD & C Yellow No. 5, which can cause allergic reactions, primarily in aspirin-sensitive individuals, and Yellow No. 6, which is inadequately tested and which some studies suggest may adversely affect behavior and the ability to complete school tasks in some sensitive children. Also contains BHA, whose long-term safety is currently being reexamined by FDA investigators.

LUCKY CHARMS
General Mills, Inc.

Ingredients: whole oat flour, sugar, corn syrup, cornstarch, dextrose, wheat starch, salt, gelatin, calcium carbonate, trisodium phosphate, sodium ascorbate, natural and artificial flavor, niacin, iron, artificial colors, vitamin A palmitate, vitamin B_6, vitamin B_2, vitamin B_1, vitamin B_{12}, and vitamin D.

Amount: 1 cup (+ ½ cup milk)			% USRDA
Calories	190	Protein	10
Protein, gm	6	Vitamin A	30
Carbohydrates, gm	30	Vitamin C	25
Fat, gm	5	Thiamine	30
Sodium, mg	245	Riboflavin	35
Cholesterol, mg	16	Niacin	25
Fiber, gm	<1	Calcium	15
		Iron	25

Cereal without milk contains 2¾ teaspoons sugar.

THIS FOOD: We honestly don't know if Lucky Charms brings good luck, but we do know that it is a poor breakfast food: artificially colored and flavored, low in fiber, and high in sugar.

ADDITIVES: Contains artificial colors, which are inadequately tested and which some studies suggest may adversely affect behavior and the ability to complete school tasks in some sensitive children.

MARSHMALLOW KRISPIES
Kellogg Co.

Ingredients: rice, marshmallows (sugar, corn syrup, modified cornstarch, gelatin, artificial and natural flavorings, and artificial colorings), sugar, salt, corn syrup, malt flavoring, vitamin C, vitamin B_3, iron, vitamin A, vitamin B_6, vitamin B_2, vitamin B_1, folic acid, vitamin D, BHT.

Amount: 1 cup (+ ½ cup milk)			% USRDA
Calories	220	Protein	10
Protein, gm	6	Vitamin A	30
Carbohydrates, gm	39	Vitamin C	25
Fat, gm	4	Thiamine	30
Sodium, mg	215	Riboflavin	35
Cholesterol, mg	16	Niacin	25
Fiber, gm	<1e	Calcium	15
		Iron	10

Cereal without milk contains 2½ teaspoons sugar.

THIS FOOD: This cereal aimed at youngsters is low in fiber and fairly high in sugar. A glance at the ingredients list explains why: the second largest ingredient is marshmallows. This cereal contains 155 mg sodium per serving, which is low for this category.

ADDITIVES: Contains artificial color and flavor, which some studies suggest may adversely affect behavior and the ability to complete school tasks in some sensitive children; artificial colors are inadequately tested, and artificial flavor may cause allergic reactions in sensitive individuals. Also contains BHT, whose long-term safety is currently being reexamined by FDA investigators.

NABISCO SHREDDED WHEAT
R. J. Reynolds Industries, Inc.

Ingredients: 100 percent natural whole wheat, BHT.

Amount: 1 biscuit (+ ½ cup milk)			% USRDA
Calories	170	Protein	10
Protein, gm	7	Vitamin A	2
Carbohydrates, gm	25	Vitamin C	*
Fat, gm	5	Thiamine	6
Sodium, mg	60	Riboflavin	10
Cholesterol, mg	16	Niacin	6
Fiber, gm	3.5e	Calcium	15
		Iron	4

Cereal contains no sugar.

THIS FOOD: Shredded Wheat is an excellent breakfast cereal. A good source of fiber, and low in sodium, fat and sugar, it contains no added nutrients, a very unusual feature among ready-to-eat cereals. The cereal itself is virtually sodium free.

ADDITIVES: Contains BHT, whose long-term safety is currently being reexamined by FDA investigators.

NUTRI-GRAIN, CORN
Kellogg Co.

Ingredients: whole corn kernels, malt flavoring, salt, baking soda, vitamin C, vitamin E, vitamin B_3, zinc, vitamin A, vitamin B_6, vitamin B_2, vitamin B_1, folic acid, vitamin B_{12}, and vitamin D.

Amount: ⅔ cup (+ ½ cup milk)			% USRDA
Calories	180	Protein	15
Protein, gm	6	Vitamin A	30
Carbohydrates, gm	30	Vitamin C	25
Fat, gm	5	Thiamine	30
Sodium, mg	260	Riboflavin	35
Cholesterol, mg	16	Niacin	25
Fiber, gm	3.5e	Calcium	15
		Iron	6
Cereal without milk contains ½ teaspoon sugar.			

THIS FOOD: Nutri-Grain, Corn, provides fiber and trace minerals from whole grains. Less than 8 percent of calories come from sugar, all of it naturally present in the grain. This cereal is fortified with zinc and contains 200 mg sodium per serving, which is considered moderate for this category.

ADDITIVES: No questionable additives.

NUTRI-GRAIN, WHEAT
Kellogg Co.

Ingredients: whole wheat kernels, malt flavoring, salt, vitamin C, vitamin E, vitamin B_3, zinc, vitamin A, vitamin B_6, vitamin B_2, vitamin B_1, folic acid, vitamin B_{12}, and vitamin D.

Amount: ¾ cup (+ ½ cup milk)			% USRDA
Calories	180	Protein	15
Protein, gm	7	Vitamin A	30
Carbohydrates, gm	30	Vitamin C	25
Fat, gm	4	Thiamine	30
Sodium, mg	255	Riboflavin	35
Cholesterol, mg	16	Niacin	25
Fiber, gm	3.5e	Calcium	15
		Iron	6
Cereal without milk contains ½ teaspoon sugar.			

THIS FOOD: Nutri-Grain, Wheat, provides fiber and trace minerals from whole grains. Less than 8 percent of calories come from sugar, all of it naturally present in the grain. This cereal is fortified with zinc and contains 195 mg sodium per serving, which is considered low for this category.

ADDITIVES: No questionable additives.

PAC-MAN
General Mills, Inc.

Ingredients: degermed yellow cornmeal, sugar, oat flour, corn syrup, cornstarch, dextrose, wheat starch, salt, gelatin, calcium carbonate, trisodium phosphate, sodium ascorbate, sodium phosphate, artificial and natural flavor, niacin, iron, artificial color, vitamin A palmitate, vitamin B_6, riboflavin, vitamin B_1, vitamin B_{12}, and vitamin D.

Amount: 1 cup (+ ½ cup milk)			% USRDA
Calories	180	Protein	10
Protein, gm	5	Vitamin A	30
Carbohydrates, gm	31	Vitamin C	25
Fat, gm	4	Thiamine	30
Sodium, mg	255	Riboflavin	35
Cholesterol, mg	16	Niacin	25
Fiber, gm	<1e	Calcium	15
		Iron	25

Cereal without milk contains 3 teaspoons sugar.

THIS FOOD: Made from refined grains, it is low in fiber and trace minerals and 46 percent of calories come from sugar. It contains 195 mg sodium per serving.

ADDITIVES: Contains artificial color and flavor, which some studies suggest may adversely affect behavior and the ability to complete school tasks in some sensitive children; artificial colors are inadequately tested, and artificial flavor may cause allergic reactions in sensitive individuals.

POST 40% BRAN FLAKES
General Foods Corp.

Ingredients: whole wheat, wheat bran, sugar, flavoring, salt, corn syrup, and fortified with the following nutrients: vitamin A palmitate, niacinamide, iron, zinc oxide, vitamin B_6, vitamin B_2, vitamin B_1, vitamin B_{12}, folic acid, vitamin D_2, BHA.

Amount: ⅔ cup (+ ½ cup milk)			% USRDA
Calories	170	Protein	10
Protein, gm	7	Vitamin A	30
Carbohydrates, gm	28	Vitamin C	*
Fat, gm	5	Thiamine	30
Sodium, mg	285	Riboflavin	35
Cholesterol, mg	16	Niacin	25
Fiber, gm	5	Calcium	15
		Iron	25

Cereal without milk contains 1 teaspoon sugar.

THIS FOOD: A good source of fiber and trace minerals, low in sugar, and fortified with zinc as well as iron. It is well above average in terms of nutrition but contains 225 mg sodium per serving.

ADDITIVES: Contains BHA, whose long-term safety is currently being reexamined by FDA investigators.

POST RAISIN BRAN
General Foods Corp.

Ingredients: whole wheat, wheat bran, raisins, sugar, flavoring, corn syrup, salt, partially hydrogenated vegetable oil (coconut, soybean, cottonseed), honey, vitamin A palmitate, niacinamide, iron, zinc oxide, vitamin B_6, vitamin B_2, vitamin B_1, vitamin B_{12}, folic acid, and vitamin D_2.

Amount: ½ cup (+ ½ cup milk)			% USRDA
Calories	160	Protein	10
Protein, gm	6	Vitamin A	30
Carbohydrates, gm	27	Vitamin C	*
Fat, gm	5	Thiamine	30
Sodium, mg	230	Riboflavin	35
Cholesterol, mg	16	Niacin	25
Fiber, gm	3	Calcium	15
		Iron	25

Cereal without milk contains 2 teaspoons sugar.

THIS FOOD: Made from whole wheat as well as wheat bran, it is rich in naturally occurring trace minerals and provides dietary fiber. About 38 percent of its calories derive from sugar, with raisins accounting for half of the sugar calories. It is low in sodium and fortified with 10 percent of the USRDA for both zinc and iron.

ADDITIVES: No questionable additives.

POST TOASTIES CORN FLAKES
General Foods Corp.

Ingredients: corn, sugar, salt, corn syrup, coconut oil, malt syrup, vitamin A, niacinamide, iron, vitamin B_6, riboflavin, thiamine, vitamin B_{12}, folic acid, annatto extract color, vitamin D_2, BHA.

Amount: 1 cup (+ ½ cup milk)			% USRDA
Calories	180	Protein	8
Protein, gm	6	Vitamin A	30
Carbohydrates, gm	30	Vitamin C	*
Fat, gm	5	Thiamine	30
Sodium, mg	365	Riboflavin	35
Cholesterol, mg	16	Niacin	25
Fiber, gm	2.5	Calcium	15
		Iron	2

Cereal without milk contains ½ teaspoon sugar.

THIS FOOD: It is low in sugar, a fair source of fiber, but high in sodium, supplying 305 mg per serving. It is made from milled, degermed corn and therefore low in naturally occurring trace minerals.

ADDITIVES: Contains BHA, whose long-term safety is currently being reexamined by FDA investigators.

OTHER BRANDS: If you enjoy this type of cereal, try Nutri-Grain, Corn, which is made from whole kernel corn and thus contains more fiber and naturally occurring trace nutrients.

PRODUCT 19
Kellogg Co.

Ingredients: corn, oat and wheat flour, sugar, rice, salt, defatted wheat germ, malt flavoring, corn syrup, annatto color, vitamin C, vitamin E, vitamin B_3, zinc, iron, calcium pantothenate, vitamin A, BHT, vitamin B_6, vitamin B_2, vitamin B_1, folic acid, vitamin D.

Amount: ¾ cup (+ ½ cup milk)			% USRDA
Calories	180	Protein	15
Protein, gm	6	Vitamin A	100
Carbohydrates, gm	30	Vitamin C	100
Fat, gm	4	Thiamine	100
Sodium, mg	380	Riboflavin	110
Cholesterol, mg	16	Niacin	100
Fiber, gm	<1	Calcium	15
		Iron	100
Cereal without milk contains ¾ teaspoon sugar.			

THIS FOOD: Are highly fortified cereals like Product 19 your best bet? Not necessarily. Although it provides a full 100 percent of the USRDA for five vitamins, most Americans get enough of these vitamins from natural food sources. Added iron and zinc, on the other hand, are nutritional assets. Because it is made from refined flours, Product 19 is low in fiber and the balanced trace nutrients provided by whole grains. Those concerned with their sodium intake should note that Product 19 is high in sodium, providing 320 mg per serving without milk. If you are interested in extra vitamins and minerals, ask your doctor to recommend a balanced supplement.

ADDITIVES: Contains BHT, whose long-term safety is currently being reexamined by FDA investigators.

QUAKER 100% NATURAL CEREAL
Quaker Oats Co.

Ingredients: rolled oats, rolled whole wheat, brown sugar, coconut oil, dried unsweetened coconut, nonfat dry milk, almonds, corn syrup, honey, natural flavors.

Amount: ¼ cup (+ ½ cup milk)			% USRDA
Calories	184	Protein	13
Protein, gm	7	Vitamin A	2
Carbohydrates, gm	28	Vitamin C	*
Fat, gm	4	Thiamine	10
Sodium, mg	61	Riboflavin	15
Cholesterol, mg	16	Niacin	7
Fiber, gm	3	Calcium	16
		Iron	5

Cereal without milk contains 1½ teaspoons sugar and 1 teaspoon fat.

THIS FOOD: Like most granolas Quaker's 100% Natural Cereal is aimed at a nutrition-conscious audience. Unfortunately this food does not deserve its healthy image. On the positive side, this product has less sugar than most granolas, and rolled oats and whole wheat, the two main ingredients, are fair sources of fiber and rich in trace minerals. But the excessive amount of fat in this cereal, most of it saturated, makes it a less than healthy choice. Also, because a normal one-ounce serving amounts only to a mere quarter cup of granola, most people tend to eat too much of it. Dieters should be wary of this and most other granolas.

ADDITIVES: No questionable additives.

◆ RICE CHEX
Ralston Purina Co.

Ingredients: milled rice, sugar, salt, malted cereal syrup, vitamin C, niacinamide, reduced iron, vitamin B_1, B_6, folic acid, vitamin B_{12}, BHT.

Amount: 1 cup (+ ½ cup milk)			% USRDA
Calories	190	Protein	10
Protein, gm	5	Vitamin A	4
Carbohydrates, gm	31	Vitamin C	25
Fat, gm	4	Thiamine	25
Sodium, mg	340	Riboflavin	10
Cholesterol, mg	16	Niacin	25
Fiber, gm	1	Calcium	15
		Iron	10

Cereal without milk contains ½ teaspoon sugar.

THIS FOOD: Although Rice Chex avoids the most common nutritional failing in this food category—too much added sugar—it is low in protein and fiber and relatively high in sodium.

ADDITIVES: Contains BHT, whose long-term safety is currently being reexamined by FDA investigators.

RICE KRISPIES
Kellogg Co.

Ingredients: rice, sugar, salt, corn syrup, malt flavoring, vitamin C, vitamin B_3, iron, vitamin A, vitamin B_6, vitamin B_2, vitamin B_1, folic acid, vitamin D, BHT.

Amount: 1 cup (+½ cup milk)			% USRDA
Calories	180	Protein	10
Protein, gm	6	Vitamin A	30
Carbohydrates, gm	30	Vitamin C	25
Fat, gm	4	Thiamine	30
Sodium, mg	345	Riboflavin	35
Cholesterol, mg	16	Niacin	25
Fiber, gm	1	Calcium	15
		Iron	10

Cereal without milk contains ½ teaspoon sugar.

THIS FOOD: Everyone knows that Rice Krispies is fun—but fans will be disappointed to learn that it is not especially good for you. While the cereal avoids the most common failing in this category—too much added sugar—it is slightly higher than average in sodium and low in fiber and trace nutrients.

ADDITIVES: Contains BHT, whose long-term safety is currently being reexamined by FDA investigators.

SMURF-BERRY CRUNCH
General Foods Corp.

Ingredients: sugar, corn flour, oat flour, wheat flour, hydrogenated coconut and/or palm kernel oil, salt, artificial flavor, artificial color, and fortified with the following nutrients: vitamin A palmitate, niacinamide, iron, zinc oxide, vitamin B_6, riboflavin, vitamin B_1, vitamin B_{12}, folic acid, vitamin D_2, BHA.

Amount: 1 cup (+½ cup milk)			% USRDA
Calories	190	Protein	8
Protein, gm	5	Vitamin A	30
Carbohydrates, gm	31	Vitamin C	*
Fat, gm	5	Thiamine	30
Sodium, mg	125	Riboflavin	35
Cholesterol, mg	16	Niacin	25
Fiber, gm	<1	Calcium	15
		Iron	25

Cereal without milk contains 3¼ teaspoons sugar.

THIS FOOD: Smurf-Berry Crunch is artificially colored and flavored, low in protein, loaded with sugar, contains saturated fat, and has no measurable dietary fiber.

ADDITIVES: Has artificial colors, which are inadequately tested and which some studies suggest may adversely affect behavior and the ability to complete school tasks in some sensitive children. Contains BHA, whose long-term use is being reexamined by the FDA.

SPECIAL K
Kellogg Co.

Ingredients: rice, wheat gluten, sugar, defatted wheat germ, salt, corn syrup, whey, malt flavoring, calcium caseinate, vitamin C, vitamin B_3, zinc, iron, vitamin B_6, vitamin A, vitamin B_2, vitamin B_1, folic acid, vitamin D, BHT.

Amount: 1⅓ cups (+ ½ cup milk)			% USRDA
Calories	180	Protein	20
Protein, gm	10	Vitamin A	30
Carbohydrates, gm	26	Vitamin C	25
Fat, gm	4	Thiamine	40
Sodium, mg	280	Riboflavin	45
Cholesterol, mg	16	Niacin	35
Fiber, gm	<1	Calcium	15
		Iron	25

Cereal without milk contains ¾ teaspoon sugar.

THIS FOOD: This moderately fortified cereal contains at least 50 percent more protein than most other brands and provides both iron and 20 percent of the USRDA for zinc. Sugar contributes only 11 percent of calories. Unfortunately Special K is a poor source of dietary fiber and trace minerals.

ADDITIVES: Contains BHT, whose long-term safety is currently being reexamined by FDA investigators.

TOTAL
General Mills, Inc.

Ingredients: degermed yellow cornmeal, sugar, salt, cereal malt syrup, tricalcium phosphate, vitamin C, vitamin E, niacinamide, iron, vitamin B_6, vitamin A palmitate, vitamin B_2, vitamin B_1, folic acid, vitamin B_{12}, BHT.

Amount: 1 cup (+ ½ cup milk)			% USRDA
Calories	190	Protein	10
Protein, gm	7	Vitamin A	100
Carbohydrates, gm	29	Vitamin C	100
Fat, gm	5	Thiamine	100
Sodium, mg	435	Riboflavin	110
Cholesterol, mg	16	Niacin	100
Fiber, gm	2.5	Calcium	20
		Iron	100

Cereal without milk contains ¾ teaspoons sugar.

THIS FOOD: Total is low in sugar and a fairly good source of fiber. Because it contains 100 percent of the USRDA for ten vitamins and iron, it is legally classified as a diet supplement rather than a cereal. As a diet supplement Total is extremely expensive, and not especially well balanced. The Center for Science in the Public Interest estimates that the added vitamins cost approximately two cents, yet customers are charged about thirty cents more for it, in comparison to similar, less fortified cereals. Total is also extremely high in sodium. At 375 mg per serving without milk, it provides more sodium than any other cereal profiled. If you are interested in a vitamin and mineral supplement, ask your doctor for a recommendation.

ADDITIVES: Contains BHT, whose long-term safety is currently being reexamined by FDA investigators.

NUTRITION TIP: According to recent studies, the soluble fiber found in oats, when eaten regularly, can help to lower serum cholesterol levels.

TRIX
General Mills, Inc.

Ingredients: degermed yellow cornmeal, sugar, corn syrup, oat flour, wheat starch, coconut oil, salt, artificial colors, sodium ascorbate, natural flavors, citric acid (for flavor), calcium carbonate, niacin, iron, vitamin B_6, vitamin A palmitate, vitamin B_2, thiamin mononitrate, vitamin B_{12}, and vitamin D.

Amount: 1 cup (+½ cup milk)			% USRDA
Calories	190	Protein	10
Protein, gm	5	Vitamin A	30
Carbohydrates, gm	31	Vitamin C	25
Fat, gm	5	Thiamine	30
Sodium, mg	230	Riboflavin	35
Cholesterol, mg	16	Niacin	25
Fiber, gm	<1	Calcium	15
		Iron	25
Cereal without milk contains 3 teaspoons sugar.			

THIS FOOD: A variation of Kix, tri-colored Trix outsells its plainer parent by more than two to one. This artificially colored cereal has almost no dietary fiber and is loaded with excess sugar.

ADDITIVES: Contains artificial colors, which are inadequately tested, and which some studies suggest may adversely affect behavior and the ability to complete school tasks in some sensitive children.

WHEAT CHEX
Ralston Purina Co.

Ingredients: whole wheat, sugar, malted cereal syrup, salt, vitamin C, niacinamide, reduced iron, vitamin B_1, B_6, BHT, folic acid, and vitamin B_{12}.

Amount: ⅔ cup (+½ cup milk)			% USRDA
Calories	180	Protein	10
Protein, gm	7	Vitamin A	4
Carbohydrates, gm	29	Vitamin C	25
Fat, gm	5	Thiamine	25
Sodium, mg	260	Riboflavin	15
Cholesterol, mg	16	Niacin	25
Fiber, gm	2.5	Calcium	15
		Iron	25

Cereal without milk contains ½ teaspoon sugar.

THIS FOOD: Wheat Chex is an excellent breakfast food. Made from whole wheat, it is higher than average in protein and trace minerals, without too much added sugar or salt. This cereal also supplies some dietary fiber.

ADDITIVES: Contains BHT, whose long-term safety is currently being reexamined by FDA investigators.

WHEATIES
General Mills, Inc.

Ingredients: whole wheat, sugar, salt, cereal malt syrup, calcium carbonate, trisodium phosphate, vitamin C, annatto extract color, niacinamide, iron, vitamin A, vitamin B_6, vitamin B_1, vitamin B_2, vitamin B_{12}, and vitamin D, BHT.

Amount: 1 cup (+½ cup milk)			% USRDA
Calories	190	Protein	10
Protein, gm	7	Vitamin A	30
Carbohydrates, gm	29	Vitamin C	25
Fat, gm	5	Thiamine	30
Sodium, mg	430	Riboflavin	35
Cholesterol, mg	16	Niacin	25
Fiber, gm	3.5e	Calcium	20
		Iron	25

Cereal without milk contains ¾ teaspoons sugar.

THIS FOOD: Wheaties, a whole wheat cereal, is higher than average in protein, low in sugar, and a fairly good source of fiber. Unfortunately it is extremely high in sodium, providing 370 mg per serving without milk.

ADDITIVES: Contains BHT, whose long-term safety is currently being reexamined by FDA investigators.

Hot Cereals

INSTANT QUAKER OATMEAL WITH APPLES AND CINNAMON
Quaker Oats Co.

Ingredients: rolled oats, sugar, dehydrated apple flakes, salt, calcium carbonate, guar gum, cinnamon, artificial flavor, vitamin A palmitate, reduced iron, niacinamide, vitamin B_6, B_1, riboflavin, folic acid.

Amount: 1 packet/1¼ oz			% USRDA
Calories	130	Protein	6
Protein, gm	4	Vitamin A	20
Carbohydrates, gm	26	Vitamin C	*
Fat, gm	2	Thiamine	20
Sodium, mg	260	Riboflavin	10
Cholesterol, mg	0	Niacin	15
Fiber, gm	2	Calcium	10
		Iron	25
Contains 2 teaspoons sugar.			

THIS FOOD: Like all oatmeals, this cereal is made from the whole grain and provides trace minerals as well as dietary fiber. Unfortunately, added sugar, which contributes 30 percent of calories, detracts from its nutritional value. This cereal contains a moderate amount of sodium and is fortified with iron.

ADDITIVES: Contains artificial flavor, which may cause allergic reactions in sensitive individuals, and which some studies suggest may adversely affect behavior and the ability to complete school tasks in some sensitive children.

INSTANT QUAKER OATMEAL WITH MAPLE AND BROWN SUGAR
Quaker Oats Co.

Ingredients: rolled oats, sugar, natural and artificial flavors, salt, calcium carbonate, guar gum, reduced iron, caramel color, vitamin A palmitate, niacinamide, vitamin B_6, B_1, riboflavin, folic acid.

HELPFUL HINT: Instead of using presweetened packets, try adding a drizzle of honey and a few currants to plain oatmeal. Chances are you'll end up eating less sugar.

Amount: 1 packet/1½ oz			% USRDA
Calories	160	Protein	6
Protein, gm	5	Vitamin A	20
Carbohydrates, gm	31	Vitamin C	*
Fat, gm	2	Thiamine	20
Sodium, mg	325	Riboflavin	10
Cholesterol, mg	0	Niacin	15
Fiber, gm	<1	Calcium	10
		Iron	45

Contains more than 3 teaspoons sugar.

THIS FOOD: Like all oatmeals, this cereal is made from the whole grain and provides trace minerals as dietary fiber. Unfortunately, added sugar, which contributes 30 percent of total calories, detracts from its nutritional value. This cereal is high in sodium and fortified with iron. The ingredients list for Instant Quaker Oatmeal with Maple and Brown Sugar contains artificial flavors, but nothing identified as maple sugar.

ADDITIVES: Contains artificial flavor, which may cause allergic reactions in sensitive individuals, and which some studies suggest may adversely affect behavior and the ability to complete school tasks in some sensitive children.

NABISCO QUICK CREAM OF WHEAT
R. J. Reynolds Industries, Inc.

Ingredients: farina, wheat germ, disodium phosphate, calcium carbonate, iron phosphate, niacin, vitamin B_1, vitamin B_2.

Amount: ¾ cup cooked			% USRDA
Calories	100	Protein	4
Protein, gm	3	Vitamin A	*
Carbohydrates, gm	22	Vitamin C	*
Fat, gm	0	Thiamine	10
Sodium, mg	130	Riboflavin	4
Cholesterol, mg	0	Niacin	6
Fiber, gm	1	Calcium	4
		Iron	45

Contains no sugar.

THIS FOOD: In addition to supplying complex carbohydrates, Nabisco Quick Cream of Wheat is rich in iron. It contains a lower than average amount of sodium. Cream of Wheat has less dietary fiber than oat-based hot cereals.

ADDITIVES: No questionable additives.

OLD FASHIONED QUAKER OATS
Quaker Oats Co.

Ingredients: 100 percent rolled oats.

Amount: ¾ cup cooked			% USRDA
Calories	110	Protein	6
Protein, gm	5	Vitamin A	*
Carbohydrates, gm	18	Vitamin C	*
Fat, gm	2	Thiamine	10
Sodium, mg	<10	Riboflavin	*
Cholesterol, mg	0	Niacin	*
Fiber, gm	3.5	Calcium	*
		Iron	4
Contains no sugar.			

THIS FOOD: In addition to providing complex carbohydrates, Old Fashioned Quaker Oats is a fairly good source of thiamine and fiber. This low-sodium product contains no added sugar or salt.

ADDITIVES: None.

QUICK QUAKER OATS
Quaker Oats Co.

Ingredients: 100 percent rolled oats.

Amount: ¾ cup cooked			% USRDA
Calories	110	Protein	6
Protein, gm	5	Vitamin A	*
Carbohydrates, gm	18	Vitamin C	*
Fat, gm	2	Thiamine	16
Sodium, mg	<10	Riboflavin	*
Cholesterol, mg	0	Niacin	*
Fiber, gm	3.5	Calcium	*
		Iron	4
Contains no sugar.			

THIS FOOD: In addition to providing complex carbohydrates and dietary fiber, Quick Quaker Oats is a fairly good source of thiamine and fiber. This naturally low-sodium product contains no added sugar or salt.

ADDITIVES: None.

CHEESE

In the United States the average person eats about ten pounds of cheese a year—far less than in Europe. This relative lack of popularity may not be a bad thing in nutritional terms since most cheeses are high in fat, cholesterol, and sodium. On the other hand, hard cheeses are an excellent source of hard-to-get calcium. Borden produces a line of processed cheeses called Lite-Line with reduced cholesterol, fat, and sodium content. But many people prefer the more distinctive taste available only in natural cheeses. Cheeses marked PART SKIM MILK are not necessarily lower in fat, because although the cheese manufacturer may start out using skim milk, additional fats are often added before the final product is ready. Most hard cheeses derive seventy to eighty percent of their calories from fat. Parmesan and part-skim-milk mozzarella generally have about half that amount. Fresh cheeses, such as cottage cheese, pot cheese, farmer cheese, and ricotta also have a moderate fat content—but a half-cup serving contains only about half the calcium of a one-ounce serving of hard cheese.

SODIUM GUIDELINES: In evaluating the sodium content of cheese, we used the following standards:

less than 250 mg moderate in sodium
250 mg to 500 mg high in sodium

Remember, these guidelines are not for people following medically restricted low-sodium diets, but for healthy individuals who wish to monitor their sodium intake.

CASINO BRAND MONTEREY JACK CHEESE
Kraft, Inc.

Ingredients: pasteurized milk, cheese culture, salt, enzymes.

Amount: 1 oz			% USRDA
Calories	110	Protein	15
Protein, gm	6	Vitamin A	6
Carbohydrates, gm	0	Vitamin C	*
Fat, gm	9	Thiamine	*
Sodium, mg	195	Riboflavin	4
Cholesterol, mg	30	Niacin	*
Fiber, gm	0	Calcium	20
		Iron	*

THIS FOOD: Hard cheese is a very good source of calcium and protein. Unfortunately it is high in fat and supplies unwanted cholesterol. This product contains 75 percent fat calories and a moderate amount of sodium.

ADDITIVES: No questionable additives.

CHEEZ-WHIZ PASTEURIZED PROCESS CHEESE SPREAD
Kraft, Inc.

Ingredients: natural cheese (American [Cheddar, Colby], Muenster), water, whey, milkfat, sodium phosphate, skim milk, salt, whey protein concentrate, Worcestershire sauce, mustard flour, lactic acid, sorbic acid, annatto, oleoresin paprika.

Amount: 1 oz			% USRDA
Calories	80	Protein	10
Protein, gm	5	Vitamin A	4
Carbohydrates, gm	2	Vitamin C	*
Fat, gm	6	Thiamine	*
Sodium, mg	370	Riboflavin	6
Cholesterol, mg	15	Niacin	*
Fiber, gm	0	Calcium	15
		Iron	*

THIS FOOD: This processed cheese is a good source of calcium and protein. It contains 67 percent fat calories and is high in sodium.

ADDITIVES: No questionable additives.

DRUG INTERACTION: Aged cheese contains tyramine, which interacts with a group of drugs called monoamine oxidase inhibitors. Some common drugs of this type are Parnate, Eutonyl, and Nardil. Check with your pharmacist or doctor before eating aged cheese if you are taking any of these drugs.

NOTE: The letter "e" indicates that the data has been estimated; < means "less than" and is used for small amounts of sodium or cholesterol; * means food contains less than 2% of USRDA; "na" means that the information was not available and appears only when data is insufficient.

CRACKER BARREL SHARP CHEDDAR CHEESE
Kraft, Inc.

Ingredients: milk, cheese culture, salt, enzymes, annatto, potassium sorbate.

Amount: 1 oz			% USRDA
Calories	110	Protein	15
Protein, gm	7	Vitamin A	4
Carbohydrates, gm	1	Vitamin C	*
Fat, gm	9	Thiamine	*
Sodium, mg	175	Riboflavin	6
Cholesterol, mg	25	Niacin	*
Fiber, gm	0	Calcium	20
		Iron	*

THIS FOOD: Hard cheese is a very good source of calcium and protein. Unfortunately it is high in fat and supplies unwanted cholesterol. This product contains 75 percent fat calories and contains a moderate amount of sodium.

ADDITIVES: No questionable additives.

KRAFT AMERICAN SINGLES PASTEURIZED PROCESS CHEESE FOOD
Kraft, Inc.

Ingredients: natural Cheddar cheese, water, whey, sodium citrate, whey protein concentrate, skim milk, milkfat, sodium phosphate, salt, sorbic acid.

Amount: 1 oz			% USRDA
Calories	90	Protein	10
Protein, gm	6	Vitamin A	4
Carbohydrates, gm	2	Vitamin C	*
Fat, gm	7	Thiamine	0
Sodium, mg	390	Riboflavin	6
Cholesterol, mg	20	Niacin	*
Fiber, gm	0	Calcium	15
		Iron	*

THIS FOOD: This processed cheese is a good source of calcium and protein. It contains 70 percent fat calories and is high in sodium.

ADDITIVES: No questionable additives.

KRAFT NATURAL COLBY CHEESE
Kraft, Inc.

Ingredients: pasteurized milk, cheese culture, salt, enzymes, annatto.

Amount: 1 oz			% USRDA
Calories	110	Protein	15
Protein, gm	7	Vitamin A	4
Carbohydrates, gm	1	Vitamin C	*
Fat, gm	9	Thiamine	*
Sodium, mg	175	Riboflavin	6
Cholesterol, mg	30	Niacin	*
Fiber, gm	0	Calcium	15
		Iron	*

THIS FOOD: Hard cheese is a very good source of calcium and protein. Unfortunately it is high in fat and supplies unwanted cholesterol. This product contains 75 percent fat calories and contains a moderate amount of sodium.

ADDITIVES: No questionable additives.

KRAFT NATURAL MILD CHEDDAR CHEESE
Kraft, Inc.

Ingredients: pasteurized milk, cheese culture, salt, enzymes, annatto.

Amount: 1 oz			% USRDA
Calories	110	Protein	15
Protein, gm	7	Vitamin A	6
Carbohydrates, gm	1	Vitamin C	*
Fat, gm	9	Thiamine	*
Sodium, mg	205	Riboflavin	6
Cholesterol, mg	25	Niacin	*
Fiber, gm	0e	Calcium	20
		Iron	*

THIS FOOD: Hard cheese is a very good source of calcium and protein. Unfortunately it is high in fat and supplies unwanted cholesterol. This product contains 75 percent fat calories and contains a moderate amount of sodium.

ADDITIVES: No questionable additives.

LITE-LINE LOW CHOLESTEROL CHEESE FOOD SUBSTITUTE
Borden, Inc.

Ingredients: whey, vegetable oils (sunflower, partially hydrogenated soybean, cottonseed), calcium caseinate, casein, American cheese, Romano cheese, sodium citrate, enzyme modified cheese, salt, sodium phosphate, citric acid, blue cheese, autolyzed yeast extract, malto-dextrin, corn syrup solids, sorbic acid, Parmesan cheese, cultured skim milk, lactic acid, artificial flavors, lipolized butterfat, artificial color, calcium hydroxide, buttermilk, vitamin A palmitate, riboflavin.

Amount: 1 oz			% USRDA
Calories	90	Protein	10
Protein, gm	5	Vitamin A	4
Carbohydrates, gm	2	Vitamin C	*
Fat, gm	7	Thiamine	*
Sodium, mg	410e	Riboflavin	6
Cholesterol, mg	5	Niacin	*
Fiber, gm	0	Calcium	15
		Iron	*

THIS FOOD: This product has less cholesterol than other processed cheeses because vegetable oils are substituted for butterfat. But if partially hydrogenated or cottonseed oil is used, the result may not be much better for you since these oils are fairly high in saturated fat. Like other processed cheese this product is a good source of calcium and protein. It is high in sodium.

ADDITIVES: Contains artificial color and flavor, which some studies suggest may adversely affect behavior and the ability to complete school tasks in some sensitive children; artificial colors are inadequately tested and artificial flavor may cause allergic reactions in sensitive individuals.

LITE-LINE PASTEURIZED PROCESS CHEESE PRODUCT
Borden, Inc.

Ingredients: skim milk cheese, water, American cheese, sodium phosphate, salt, enzyme modified cheese solids, sorbic acid, citric acid, artificial color.

Amount: 1 oz			% USRDA
Calories	50	Protein	15
Protein, gm	7	Vitamin A	*
Carbohydrates, gm	1	Vitamin C	*
Fat, gm	2	Thiamine	*
Sodium, mg	410	Riboflavin	2
Cholesterol, mg	10	Niacin	*
Fiber, gm	0	Calcium	20
		Iron	*

THIS FOOD: This processed cheese is a good source of calcium and protein. It is very low in calories, only 36 percent of which derive from fat. Compared to other cheeses it is high in sodium.

ADDITIVES: Contains artificial colors, which are inadequately tested and which some studies suggest may adversely affect behavior and the ability to complete school tasks in some sensitive children.

LITE-LINE REDUCED SODIUM PASTEURIZED PROCESS CHEESE PRODUCT
Borden, Inc.

Ingredients: American cheese, skim milk cheese, whey, potassium citrate, enzyme modified cheese, lactic acid, sorbic acid, xanthan gum, carob bean gum, citric acid, guar gum, artificial color.

Amount: 1 oz			% USRDA
Calories	70	Protein	15
Protein, gm	6	Vitamin A	4
Carbohydrates, gm	2	Vitamin C	*
Fat, gm	4	Thiamine	*
Sodium, mg	90	Riboflavin	4
Cholesterol, mg	22e	Niacin	*
Fiber, gm	0	Calcium	20
		Iron	*

THIS FOOD: This processed cheese is a very good source of calcium and protein. About half the calories in this product come from fat, which is much lower than average, and it contains a moderate amount of sodium.

ADDITIVES: Contains artificial colors, which are inadequately tested and which some studies suggest may adversely affect behavior and the ability to complete school tasks in some sensitive children.

PHILADELPHIA BRAND CREAM CHEESE
Kraft, Inc.

Ingredients: pasteurized milk and cream, cheese culture, salt, carob bean gum.

Amount: 1 oz			% USRDA
Calories	100	Protein	4
Protein, gm	2	Vitamin A	6
Carbohydrates, gm	1	Vitamin C	*
Fat, gm	10	Thiamine	*
Sodium, mg	85	Riboflavin	2
Cholesterol, mg	30	Niacin	*
Fiber, gm	0	Calcium	2
		Iron	*

THIS FOOD: Unlike most other cheeses, cream cheese is not a good source of calcium or protein, but it is still high in fat and supplies unwanted cholesterol. It contains 90 percent fat calories and a moderate amount of sodium.

ADDITIVES: No questionable additives.

SARGENTO SLICED SWISS CHEESE
Sargento Cheese Co., Inc.

Ingredients: Swiss cheese.

Amount: 1 oz			% USRDA
Calories	107	Protein	15
Protein, gm	8	Vitamin A	4
Carbohydrates, gm	1	Vitamin C	*
Fat, gm	8	Thiamine	*
Sodium, mg	74	Riboflavin	4
Cholesterol, mg	26	Niacin	*
Fiber, gm	0	Calcium	25
		Iron	*

THIS FOOD: Hard cheese is a very good source of calcium and protein. Unfortunately, it is high in fat and supplies unwanted cholesterol. This product contains 67 percent fat calories and a moderate amount of sodium.

ADDITIVES: No questionable additives.

TILLAMOOK CHEDDAR CHEESE
Tillamook County Creamery Assn.

Ingredients: milk, starter culture, natural coloring, salt, enzyme coagulant.

Amount: 1 oz			% USRDA
Calories	120	Protein	15
Protein, gm	8	Vitamin A	8
Carbohydrates, gm	.63	Vitamin C	*
Fat, gm	10	Thiamine	*
Sodium, mg	165	Riboflavin	9
Cholesterol, mg	30	Niacin	*
Fiber, gm	0	Calcium	23
		Iron	2

THIS FOOD: Hard cheese is a very good source of calcium and protein. Unfortunately, it is high in fat and supplies unwanted cholesterol. This product contains 75 percent fat calories and a moderate amount of sodium.

ADDITIVES: No questionable additives.

TILLAMOOK LOW SODIUM CHEDDAR CHEESE
Tillamook County Creamery Assn.

Ingredients: milk, starter culture, natural coloring, salt, enzyme coagulant.

Amount: 1 oz			% USRDA
Calories	120	Protein	15
Protein, gm	8	Vitamin A	8
Carbohydrates, gm	<1	Vitamin C	*
Fat, gm	10	Thiamine	*
Sodium, mg	12	Riboflavin	9
Cholesterol, mg	30	Niacin	*
Fiber, gm	0	Calcium	23
		Iron	2

THIS FOOD: Hard cheese is a very good source of calcium and protein. Unfortunately, it is high in fat and supplies unwanted cholesterol. This product contains 75 percent fat calories and is very low in sodium.

ADDITIVES: No questionable additives.

VELVEETA PASTEURIZED PROCESS CHEESE SPREAD
Kraft, Inc.

Ingredients: natural cheese, water, whey, skim milk, sodium phosphate, whey protein concentrate, milkfat, salt, annatto, apocarotenal.

Amount: 1 oz			% USRDA
Calories	80	Protein	10
Protein, gm	5	Vitamin A	4
Carbohydrates, gm	2	Vitamin C	*
Fat, gm	6	Thiamine	*
Sodium, mg	430	Riboflavin	8
Cholesterol, mg	20	Niacin	*
Fiber, gm	0	Calcium	15
		Iron	*

THIS FOOD: This processed cheese is a good source of calcium and protein. It contains 67 percent fat calories and is high in sodium.

ADDITIVES: No questionable additives.

FOR WEIGHT WATCHERS: Since cheese is a concentrated source of calories, it's important to keep track of portion size. A 1-ounce chunk is scarcely more than a mouthful, so it's easy to eat several ounces without feeling that you have overindulged.

VELVEETA PASTEURIZED PROCESS CHEESE SPREAD SLICES
Kraft, Inc.

Ingredients: natural cheese (Cheddar, Swiss), water, whey, skim milk, sodium citrate, milkfat, whey protein concentrate, salt, sodium phosphate, sorbic acid, annatto, oleoresin paprika.

Amount: 1 oz			% USRDA
Calories	90	Protein	10
Protein, gm	5	Vitamin A	6
Carbohydrates, gm	2	Vitamin C	*
Fat, gm	6	Thiamine	*
Sodium, mg	400	Riboflavin	6
Cholesterol, mg	20	Niacin	*
Fiber, gm	0	Calcium	15
		Iron	*

THIS FOOD: This processed cheese is a good source of calcium and protein. It contains 60 percent fat calories and is high in sodium.

ADDITIVES: No questionable additives.
See "Basic Foods" on page 557 for additional cheese listings.

CHOCOLATE

Chocolate bars as we know them were not mass produced until the Hershey Bar was manufactured at the end of the nineteenth century. Ever since, chocolate has been by far the most popular type of candy. Plain chocolate, as well as most candy bars made with chocolate, are high in sugar and saturated fat. Chocolate also contains a small amount of caffeine, to which young children may be sensitive. Compulsive chocolate eaters may be reassured to learn that their addiction may not be a simple matter of poor willpower. Recent studies have shown that a neurotransmitter released in the body after eating chocolate is also found in people who describe themselves as being in love. So there may actually be something to the traditional lover's gift of chocolate!

ALMOND JOY
Cadbury Schweppes, Inc.

Ingredients: corn syrup, sugar, coconut, almonds, cocoa butter, milk, chocolate, partially hydrogenated soybean and cottonseed oils, whey, cocoa, salt, lecithin, vanilla, egg whites.

Amount: 1 bar/1.6 oz			% USRDA
Calories	220	Protein	2
Protein, gm	2	Vitamin A	*
Carbohydrates, gm	26	Vitamin C	*
Fat, gm	12	Thiamine	*
Sodium, mg	90	Riboflavin	4
Cholesterol, mg	<5e	Niacin	*
Fiber, gm	<1e	Calcium	2
		Iron	2
Contains 2½ teaspoons fat.			

THIS FOOD: Like most chocolate candies, Almond Joy is high in sugar and saturated fat.

ADDITIVES: No questionable additives.

BAKER'S SEMI-SWEET CHOCOLATE
General Foods Corp.

Ingredients: chocolate liquor, sugar, cocoa butter, lecithin (from soybeans), natural flavor.

Amount: 1 oz			% USRDA
Calories	130	Protein	2
Protein, gm	2	Vitamin A	*
Carbohydrates, gm	17	Vitamin C	*
Fat, gm	9	Thiamine	*
Sodium, mg	1	Riboflavin	*
Cholesterol, mg	0	Niacin	*
Fiber, gm	<1	Calcium	*
		Iron	6
Contains 2 teaspoons fat and 4 teaspoons sugar.			

THIS FOOD: Baker's Semi-Sweet Chocolate contains 62 percent highly saturated fat calories. Sugar is the second largest ingredient in this product.

ADDITIVES: No questionable additives.

NOTE: The letter "e" indicates that the data has been estimated; < means "less than" and is used for small amounts of sodium or cholesterol; * means food contains less than 2% of USRDA; "na" means that the information was not available and appears only when data is insufficient.

BAKER'S UNSWEETENED CHOCOLATE
General Foods Corp.

Ingredients: chocolate.

Amount: 1 oz			% USRDA
Calories	140	Protein	4
Protein, gm	3	Vitamin A	*
Carbohydrates, gm	9	Vitamin C	*
Fat, gm	15	Thiamine	*
Sodium, mg	1	Riboflavin	4
Cholesterol, mg	0	Niacin	2
Fiber, gm	1	Calcium	2
		Iron	10
Contains 3 teaspoons fat.			

THIS FOOD: Baker's Unsweetened Chocolate contains 95 percent highly saturated fat calories from naturally occurring cocoa butter. Surprisingly, chocolate in this form is a fairly good source of iron.

ADDITIVES: None.

BUTTERFINGER
R. J. Reynolds Industries, Inc.

Ingredients: sugar, corn syrup, ground roasted peanuts, hydrogenated vegetable oil (palm kernel, coconut, soybean, palm, cottonseed or safflower oil), cocoa, soy flour, whey, molasses, confectioner's corn flakes, salt, lecithin, artificial flavor and color.

Amount: 1 bar/1.6 oz			% USRDA
Calories	220	Protein	6
Protein, gm	4	Vitamin A	*
Carbohydrates, gm	28	Vitamin C	*
Fat, gm	10	Thiamine	*
Sodium, mg	70	Riboflavin	4
Cholesterol, mg	0	Niacin	4
Fiber, gm	<1e	Calcium	2
		Iron	4
Contains 2 teaspoons fat.			

THIS FOOD: Like most chocolate candy bars, Butterfinger is high in sugar and saturated fat.

ADDITIVES: Contains artificial color and flavor which some studies suggest may adversely affect behavior and the ability to complete school tasks in some sensitive children; artificial colors are inadequately tested and artificial flavor may cause allergic reactions in sensitive individuals.

HERSHEY'S KISSES
Hershey Food Corp.

Ingredients: milk chocolate (sugar, cocoa butter, milk, chocolate, soy lecithin).

Amount: 6 kisses/approx. 1 oz			% USRDA
Calories	150	Protein	2
Protein, gm	2	Vitamin A	*
Carbohydrates, gm	16	Vitamin C	*
Fat, gm	9	Thiamine	*
Sodium, mg	25	Riboflavin	6
Cholesterol, mg	<5e	Niacin	*
Fiber, gm	<1e	Calcium	6
		Iron	2

Contains 2 teaspoons fat and 4 teaspoons sugar.

THIS FOOD: Hershey's Kisses, like other forms of milk chocolate, are high in sugar and saturated fat.

ADDITIVES: No questionable additives.

HERSHEY'S MILK CHOCOLATE WITH ALMONDS
Hershey Food Corp.

Ingredients: milk chocolate (sugar, cocoa butter, chocolate, soya lecithin, vanillin), almonds.

Amount: 1 bar/1.45 oz			% USRDA
Calories	230	Protein	6
Protein, gm	4	Vitamin A	*
Carbohydrates, gm	22	Vitamin C	*
Fat, gm	14	Thiamine	*
Sodium, mg	35	Riboflavin	10
Cholesterol, mg	<5e	Niacin	*
Fiber, gm	<1e	Calcium	8
		Iron	2

Contains 3 teaspoons fat and 5 teaspoons sugar.

THIS FOOD: Hershey's Milk Chocolate with Almonds is high in sugar and saturated fat.

ADDITIVES: No questionable additives.

KIT KAT
Hershey Food Corp.

Ingredients: sugar, milk, flour, cocoa butter, chocolate, refined palm kernel oil, dairy butter, soya lecithin, yeast, sodium bicarbonate, vanillin.

Amount: 1 bar/1½ oz.			% USRDA
Calories	210	Protein	4
Protein, gm	3	Vitamin A	*
Carbohydrates, gm	25	Vitamin C	*
Fat, gm	11	Thiamine	*
Sodium, mg	40	Riboflavin	6
Cholesterol, mg	<5e	Niacin	*
Fiber, gm	<1e	Calcium	6
		Iron	2

Contains 2 teaspoons fat and 5 teaspoons sugar.

THIS FOOD: Like most chocolate candy bars Kit Kat is high in sugar and saturated fat.

ADDITIVES No questionable additives.

MILKY WAY BAR
Mars, Inc.

Ingredients: milk chocolate (sugar, milk, cocoa butter, chocolate, lecithin, artificial and natural flavors), corn syrup, sugar, milk, partially hydrogenated vegetable oil (soybean and/or cottonseed), malted milk (malted barley, flour, milk, baking soda, salt), butter, cocoa, salt, egg whites, soy protein, artificial flavor.

Amount: 1 bar/2.1 oz			% USRDA
Calories	270	Protein	4
Protein, gm	3	Vitamin A	*
Carbohydrates, gm	41	Vitamin C	*
Fat, gm	10	Thiamine	*
Sodium, mg	na	Riboflavin	6
Cholesterol, mg	<5e	Niacin	*
Fiber, gm	<1e	Calcium	6
		Iron	2

Contains 2 teaspoons fat.

THIS FOOD: Like most chocolate candy bars Milky Way is high in sugar and saturated fat.

ADDITIVES: Contains artificial flavor, which may cause allergic reactions in sensitive individuals, and which some studies suggest may adversely affect behavior and the ability to complete school tasks in some sensitive children.

M & M'S PEANUT CHOCOLATE CANDIES
Mars, Inc.

Ingredients: milk chocolate (sugar, milk, chocolate, cocoa butter, peanuts, lecithin, salt, artificial flavors), sugar, peanuts, cornstarch, corn syrup, gum acacia, artificial colors (includes FD & C Yellow No. 5), dextrin.

Amount: 1 bag/1.67 oz			% USRDA
Calories	240	Protein	8
Protein, gm	5	Vitamin A	*
Carbohydrates, gm	28	Vitamin C	*
Fat, gm	12	Thiamine	*
Sodium, mg	na	Riboflavin	4
Cholesterol, mg	<5e	Niacin	6
Fiber, gm	1e	Calcium	4
		Iron	2
Contains 2½ teaspoons fat.			

THIS FOOD: Like most chocolate candies M & M's Peanut Chocolate Candies are high in sugar and saturated fat.

ADDITIVES: Contains artificial color and flavor which some studies suggest may adversely affect behavior and the ability to complete school tasks in some sensitive children; artificial colors are inadequately tested and artificial flavor may cause allergic reactions in sensitive individuals. Also contains Yellow No. 5, which can cause allergic reactions, especially in aspirin-sensitive individuals.

M & M'S PLAIN CHOCOLATE CANDIES
Mars, Inc.

Ingredients: milk chocolate (sugar, milk, chocolate, cocoa butter, peanuts, lecithin, salt, artificial flavors), sugar, cornstarch, corn syrup, gum acacia, artificial colors (includes FD & C Yellow No. 5), dextrin.

Amount: 1 bag/1.69 oz			% USRDA
Calories	240	Protein	6
Protein, gm	3	Vitamin A	*
Carbohydrates, gm	33	Vitamin C	*
Fat, gm	10	Thiamine	*
Sodium, mg	na	Riboflavin	6
Cholesterol, mg	<5e	Niacin	*
Fiber, gm	<1e	Calcium	8
		Iron	4
Contains 2 teaspoons fat.			

THIS FOOD: Like most chocolate candies M & M's Plain Chocolate Candies are high in sugar and saturated fat.

ADDITIVES: Contains artificial color and flavor which some studies suggest may adversely affect behavior and the ability to complete school tasks in some sensitive children; artificial colors are inadequately tested and artificial flavor may cause allergic reactions in sensitive individuals. Also contains Yellow No. 5, which can cause allergic reactions, especially in aspirin-sensitive individuals.

NESTLÉ CHOCO-BAKE
Nestlé, S.A.

Ingredients: cocoa, coconut oil, hydrogenated cottonseed oil and soy oils, BHA.

Amount: 1 oz			% USRDA
Calories	170	Protein	2
Protein, gm	2	Vitamin A	*
Carbohydrates, gm	12	Vitamin C	*
Fat, gm	14	Thiamine	*
Sodium, mg	<5	Riboflavin	*
Cholesterol, mg	0	Niacin	*
Fiber, gm	na	Calcium	2
		Iron	10
Contains 3 teaspoons fat.			

THIS FOOD: Nestlé Choco-Bake contains 75 percent highly saturated fat calories. Surprisingly, chocolate in this form is a good source of iron.

ADDITIVES: Contains BHA, whose long-term safety is currently being reexamined by FDA investigators.

NESTLÉ CRUNCH
Nestlé, S.A.

Ingredients: milk chocolate (sugar, fresh whole milk, cocoa butter, chocolate, lecithin, vanillin), crisped rice.

Amount: 1 bar/1¹⁄₁₆ oz			% USRDA
Calories	160	Protein	2
Protein, gm	2	Vitamin A	*
Carbohydrates, gm	19	Vitamin C	*
Fat, gm	8	Thiamine	*
Sodium, mg	50	Riboflavin	4
Cholesterol, mg	5	Niacin	*
Fiber, gm	na	Calcium	6
		Iron	*
Contains nearly 2 teaspoons fat.			

THIS FOOD: Like most chocolate candy bars Nestlé Crunch is high in sugar and saturated fat.

ADDITIVES: No questionable additives.

NESTLÉ SEMI-SWEET MORSELS
Nestlé, S.A.

Ingredients: semisweet chocolate (sugar, chocolate, cocoa butter, lecithin, vanillin, natural flavoring).

Amount: 1 oz			% USRDA
Calories	150	Protein	2
Protein, gm	2	Vitamin A	*
Carbohydrates, gm	18	Vitamin C	*
Fat, gm	8	Thiamine	*
Sodium, mg	<5	Riboflavin	*
Cholesterol, mg	0e	Niacin	*
Fiber, gm	<1e	Calcium	*
		Iron	4

Contains nearly 2 teaspoons fat.

THIS FOOD: Nestle Semi-Sweet Morsels contains 48 percent highly saturated fat calories. Sugar is the single largest ingredient in this product.

ADDITIVES: No questionable additives.

REESE'S PEANUT BUTTER CUPS
Hershey Food Corp.

Ingredients: milk chocolate (sugar, cocoa butter, milk, chocolate, soy lecithin), peanuts, sugar, dextrose, salt.

Amount: 2 large peanut butter cups/1.6 oz			% USRDA
Calories	240	Protein	10
Protein, gm	6	Vitamin A	*
Carbohydrates, gm	23	Vitamin C	*
Fat, gm	14	Thiamine	*
Sodium, mg	140	Riboflavin	4
Cholesterol, mg	na	Niacin	10
Fiber, gm	1e	Calcium	4
		Iron	2

Contains 3 teaspoons fat and 5 teaspoons sugar.

THIS FOOD: Like most chocolate candies Reese's Peanut Butter Cups are high in sugar and saturated fat. Because of their peanut butter content this candy provides 10 percent of the USRDA for protein and niacin. Compared to other chocolate candy bars this product is moderately high in sodium.

ADDITIVES: No questionable additives.

SNICKERS BAR
Mars, Inc.

Ingredients: milk chocolate, peanuts, corn syrup, sugar, milk, butter, salt, flour, egg white, soy protein, artificial flavor (milk chocolate contains sugar, milk, cocoa butter, chocolate, lecithin, vanillin).

Amount: 1 bar/2 oz			% USRDA
Calories	270	Protein	8
Protein, gm	6	Vitamin A	*
Carbohydrates, gm	33	Vitamin C	*
Fat, gm	13	Thiamine	*
Sodium, mg	na	Riboflavin	4
Cholesterol, mg	<5e	Niacin	8
Fiber, gm	1e	Calcium	6
		Iron	2
Contains nearly 3 teaspoons fat.			

THIS FOOD: Like most chocolate candy bars, Snickers is high in sugar and saturated fat.

ADDITIVES: Contains artificial flavor which may cause allergic reactions in sensitive individuals, and which some studies suggest may adversely affect behavior and the ability to complete school tasks in some sensitive children.

THREE MUSKETEERS BAR
Mars, Inc.

Ingredients: milk chocolate (sugar, milk, cocoa butter, chocolate, lecithin, artificial and natural flavors), sugar, corn syrup, partially hydrogenated vegetable oil (soybean and/or cottonseed), cocoa, salt, egg whites, soy protein, artificial flavor.

Amount: 1 bar/2.28 oz			% USRDA
Calories	280	Protein	2
Protein, gm	2	Vitamin A	*
Carbohydrates, gm	49	Vitamin C	*
Fat, gm	8	Thiamine	*
Sodium, mg	na	Riboflavin	4
Cholesterol, mg	<5e	Niacin	*
Fiber, gm	<1e	Calcium	4
		Iron	2
Contains nearly 2 teaspoons fat.			

THIS FOOD: Like most chocolate candy bars, Three Musketeers is high in sugar and saturated fat.

ADDITIVES: Contains artificial flavor, which may cause allergic reactions in sensitive individuals, and which some studies suggest may adversely affect behavior and the ability to complete school tasks in some sensitive children.

TWIX CARAMEL COOKIE BARS
Mars, Inc.

Ingredients: milk chocolate (sugar, milk, cocoa butter, chocolate, lecithin, vanillin), sugar, flour, corn syrup, partially hydrogenated vegetable oil (soybean and/or cottonseed), skim milk, salt, cocoa, baking soda, artificial flavor.

Amount: 1 bar/.93 oz			% USRDA
Calories	130	Protein	2
Protein, gm	1	Vitamin A	*
Carbohydrates, gm	17	Vitamin C	*
Fat, gm	2	Thiamine	*
Sodium, mg	na	Riboflavin	2
Cholesterol, mg	<5e	Niacin	*
Fiber, gm	<1e	Calcium	2
		Iron	*
Contains less than ½ teaspoon fat.			

THIS FOOD: Twix Caramel Cookie Bars are just as sugary as most other chocolate candy bars, but they contain less fat.

ADDITIVES: Contains artificial flavor, which may cause allergic reactions in sensitive individuals, and which some studies suggest may adversely affect behavior and the ability to complete school tasks in some sensitive children.

NOTE: The letter "e" indicates that the data has been estimated; < means "less than" and is used for small amounts of sodium or cholesterol; * means food contains less than 2% of USRDA; "na" means that the information was not available and appears only when data is insufficient.

COFFEE CREAMERS

Coffee creamers are added to coffee instead of milk or cream. This ersatz food contains more calories than an equal volume of the real thing, and because a major ingredient is hydrogenated vegetable oil, it contains highly saturated fat. The two most popular brands, Carnation Coffee-Mate and Cremora Non-Dairy Creamer, both contain sodium caseinate, a milk protein, which makes this product unsuitable for anyone trying to avoid milk products. These products do not require refrigeration.

CARNATION COFFEE-MATE
Carnation Co.

Ingredients: corn syrup solids, partially hydrogenated vegetable oil (coconut, cottonseed, palm, palm kernel, safflower or soybean), sodium caseinate, mono- and diglycerides, dipotassium phosphate, artificial flavor, and annatto.

Amount: 1 tsp			% USRDA
Calories	11	Protein	*
Protein, gm	0	Vitamin A	*
Carbohydrates, gm	1	Vitamin C	*
Fat, gm	<1	Thiamine	*
Sodium, mg	4	Riboflavin	*
Cholesterol, mg	<1	Niacin	*
Fiber, gm	0	Calcium	*
		Iron	*

THIS FOOD: Carnation Coffee-Mate offers no nutritional advantage over the real thing. It contains more calories than milk or even light cream; and for anyone who has milk allergies or trouble digesting milk products, it contains sodium caseinate, a milk protein. Because a major ingredient is hydrogenated vegetable oil, this product contains highly saturated fat.

ADDITIVES: Contains artificial flavor, which may cause allergic reactions in sensitive individuals, and which some studies suggest may adversely affect behavior and the ability to complete school tasks in some sensitive children.

CREMORA NON-DAIRY CREAMER
Borden, Inc.

Ingredients: corn syrup solids, partially hydrogenated vegetable oils (coconut, cottonseed, palm, palm kernel, peanut or soybean), sodium caseinate, dipotassium phosphate, monoglycerides, sodium silico aluminate, sodium tri-polyphosphate, diacetyl tartaric acid ester of mono- and diglycerides, artificial flavors, beta carotene, and riboflavin.

Amount: 1 tsp			% USRDA
Calories	12	Protein	*
Protein, gm	0	Vitamin A	*
Carbohydrates, gm	1	Vitamin C	*
Fat, gm	1	Thiamine	*
Sodium, mg	5	Riboflavin	*
Cholesterol, mg	0	Niacin	*
Fiber, gm	0	Calcium	*
		Iron	*

THIS FOOD: Cremora Non-Dairy Creamer offers no nutritional advantage over the real thing. It contains more calories than milk or even light cream; and for anyone who has milk allergies or trouble digesting milk products, it contains sodium caseinate, a milk protein. Because a major ingredient is hydrogenated vegetable oil, this product contains highly saturated fat.

ADDITIVES: Contains artificial flavor, which may cause allergic reactions in sensitive individuals, and which some studies suggest may adversely affect behavior and the ability to complete school tasks in some sensitive children.

HELPFUL HINT: If refrigeration is a problem, try using a little dry whole milk instead of nondairy creamers.

COOKIES AND GRANOLA BARS

The Dutch popularized cookies in colonial America, calling them *koekjes,* or "little cakes." The term is nutritionally, as well as descriptively, apt. Both cookies and cakes are high in sugar, and the vast majority are also high in fat. The main difference between the two sweets is size. You are better off eating two cookies than a slice of cake, which is generally two to three times as big. Try to serve your children plain cookies, such as Honey Maid Graham Crackers, which provide some fiber and are fairly low in fat.

Despite their healthy image, granola bars are really cookies. They may have slightly more food value than the average cookie because oats contain more nutrients than white flour, but they are still high in saturated fat and sugar. The average bar contains 5 to 6 teaspoons sugar and 1 teaspoon of fat. Both of the leading brands, Nature Valley and Quaker, sometimes include questionable additives in their granola bars.

SODIUM GUIDELINES: In evaluating the sodium content of cookies and granola bars, we used the following standards:

less than 100 mg	low in sodium
more than 100 mg to 250 mg	moderate in sodium

Remember, these guidelines are not for people following medically restricted low-sodium diets, but for healthy individuals who wish to monitor their sodium intake.

BARNUM'S ANIMAL CRACKERS
R. J. Reynolds Industries, Inc.

Ingredients: enriched wheat flour (niacin, reduced iron, thiamine mononitrate, riboflavin), sugar, corn sweetener, vegetable and animal shortening (partially hydrogenated soybean, palm or lard), corn flour, whey, salt, sodium bicarbonate, artificial flavor.

Amount: 11 crackers/1 oz			% USRDA
Calories	130	Protein	2
Protein, gm	2	Vitamin A	*
Carbohydrates, gm	21	Vitamin C	*
Fat, gm	4	Thiamine	4
Sodium, mg	120	Riboflavin	4
Cholesterol, mg	<5	Niacin	4
Fiber, gm	<1e	Calcium	*
		Iron	2

THIS FOOD: More a cookie than a cracker, Barnum's Animal Crackers are somewhat less sweet and fatty than the average cookie. About 36 percent of their calories derive from fat, most of it saturated.

ADDITIVES: Contains artificial flavor, which may cause allergic reactions in sensitive individuals, and which some studies suggest may adversely affect behavior and the ability to complete school tasks in some sensitive children.

DUNCAN HINES CHOCOLATE CHIP COOKIES
Procter and Gamble

Ingredients: bleached flour, corn syrup, sugar, partially hydrogenated vegetable shortening (soybean and/or palm and/or cottonseed oil), real semisweet chocolate chips (lecithin and artificial vanilla flavor), water, modified food starch, molasses, whey, salt, baking soda, and artificial flavors.

Amount: 2 cookies/1 oz			% USRDA
Calories	110	Protein	*
Protein, gm	1	Vitamin A	*
Carbohydrates, gm	14	Vitamin C	*
Fat, gm	5	Thiamine	*
Sodium, mg	70	Riboflavin	*
Cholesterol, mg	e	Niacin	*
Fiber, gm	<1e	Calcium	*
		Iron	*

THIS FOOD: Because Duncan Hines Chocolate Chip Cookies contain too much sugar and saturated fat, they should only be eaten occasionally. About 40 percent of their calories derive from fat.

ADDITIVES: Contains artificial flavor, which may cause allergic reactions in sensitive individuals, and which some studies suggest may adversely affect behavior and the ability to complete school tasks in some sensitive children.

DUNCAN HINES PEANUT BUTTER 'N FUDGE COOKIES
Procter and Gamble

Ingredients: bleached flour, sugar, corn syrup, partially hydrogenated vegetable shortening (soybean and/or palm and/or cottonseed oil), peanut butter chips (peanuts, sugar, palm kernel and soybean oil, nonfat milk, dextrose, salt, lecithin, and artificial vanilla flavor), real semisweet chocolate chips (lecithin and artificial vanilla flavor), cocoa, water, modified food starch, baking soda.

Amount: 2 cookies/1 oz			% USRDA
Calories	110	Protein	*
Protein, gm	1	Vitamin A	*
Carbohydrates, gm	14	Vitamin C	*
Fat, gm	5	Thiamine	*
Sodium, mg	90	Riboflavin	*
Cholesterol, mg	<5e	Niacin	*
Fiber, gm	1e	Calcium	*
		Iron	*

THIS FOOD: Because Duncan Hines Peanut Butter 'n Fudge Cookies contain too much sugar and saturated fat, they should only be eaten occasionally. About 40 percent of their calories derive from fat.

ADDITIVES: Contains artificial flavor, which may cause allergic reactions in sensitive individuals, and which some studies suggest may adversely affect behavior and the ability to complete school tasks in some sensitive children.

FIG NEWTONS
R. J. Reynolds Industries, Inc.

Ingredients: figs, sugar, enriched wheat flour (niacin, iron, thiamine mononitrate, riboflavin), animal and/or vegetable shortening (lard, partially hydrogenated soybean, palm) corn sweetener, water, whey, salt, sodium bicarbonate, yellow corn flour, artificial flavor.

Amount: 2 cookies/1 oz			% USRDA
Calories	120	Protein	2
Protein, gm	1	Vitamin A	*
Carbohydrates, gm	22	Vitamin C	*
Fat, gm	2	Thiamine	2
Sodium, mg	na	Riboflavin	2
Cholesterol, mg	<5e	Niacin	2
Fiber, gm	2e	Calcium	2
		Iron	4

THIS FOOD: Fig Newtons contain less than half the fat calories of most packaged cookies and twice the dietary fiber. Even so, they should only be eaten occasionally because of their high sugar content.

ADDITIVES: Contains artificial flavor, which may cause allergic reactions in sensitive individuals and which some studies suggest may adversely affect behavior and the ability to complete school tasks in some sensitive children.

HONEY MAID GRAHAM CRACKERS
R. J. Reynolds Industries, Inc.

Ingredients: enriched wheat flour (niacin, iron, thiamine mononitrate, riboflavin), sugar, animal and vegetable shortening (lard, partially hydrogenated soybean, palm), graham flour, honey, corn sweetener, salt, sodium bicarbonate, artificial flavor.

Amount: 4 crackers/1 oz			% USRDA
Calories	120	Protein	2
Protein, gm	2	Vitamin A	*
Carbohydrates, gm	22	Vitamin C	*
Fat, gm	3	Thiamine	2
Sodium, mg	180	Riboflavin	4
Cholesterol, mg	<10	Niacin	6
Fiber, gm	2.5e	Calcium	*
		Iron	4

THIS FOOD: Honey Maid Graham Crackers are relatively low in fat and supply complex carbohydrates and fiber. Compared to most cookies, graham crackers are low in sugar. Only 23 percent of their calories derive from fat.

ADDITIVES: Contains artificial flavor, which may cause allergic reactions in sensitive individuals, and which some studies suggest may adversely affect behavior and the ability to complete school tasks in some sensitive children.

KEEBLER CHIPS DELUXE COOKIES
Keebler Co., Inc.

Ingredients: enriched wheat flour (containing niacin, reduced iron, thiamine mononitrate, riboflavin), animal and/or vegetable shortening (beef fat and/or partially hydrogenated soybean, coconut, palm kernel and/or palm oils), sugar, sweet chocolate (with lecithin and artificial flavor), brown sugar, eggs, cocoa, salt, leavening (sodium bicarbonate), natural and artificial flavor, whey, cocoa.

Amount: 2 cookies/1 oz			% USRDA
Calories	180	Protein	*e
Protein, gm	1e	Vitamin A	*
Carbohydrates, gm	20	Vitamin C	*
Fat, gm	8	Thiamine	*e
Sodium, mg	150	Riboflavin	4
Cholesterol, mg	<10e	Niacin	4
Fiber, gm	<1e	Calcium	*
		Iron	4

Contains nearly 2 teaspoons fat.

THIS FOOD: Because Keebler Chips Deluxe Cookies contain too much sugar and saturated fat, they should only be eaten occasionally. About 40 percent of calories come from fat.

ADDITIVES: Contains artificial flavor, which may cause allergic reactions in sensitive individuals, and which some studies suggest may adversely affect behavior and the ability to complete school tasks in some sensitive children.

KEEBLER OATMEAL CREMES SANDWICH COOKIES
Keebler Co., Inc.

Ingredients: enriched wheat flour (containing niacin, reduced iron, thiamine mononitrate, riboflavin), sugar, animal and/or vegetable shortening (lard, partially hydrogenated soybean, coconut, palm kernel and palm oils), oatmeal, cornstarch, corn syrup, salt, leavening (sodium bicarbonate), cinnamon, lecithin, artificial color (caramel color), natural and artificial flavor.

Amount: 2 cookies/1 oz			% USRDA
Calories	160	Protein	*e
Protein, gm	1e	Vitamin A	*
Carbohydrates, gm	22	Vitamin C	*
Fat, gm	6	Thiamine	4
Sodium, mg	120	Riboflavin	8
Cholesterol, mg	<10e	Niacin	4
Fiber, gm	<1e	Calcium	*
		Iron	*e

THIS FOOD: Because Keebler Oatmeal Cremes Sandwich Cookies contain too much sugar and saturated fat, they should only be eaten occasionally. About 34 percent of calories derive from fat, which makes these cookies slightly less fatty than average.

ADDITIVES: Contains artificial color and flavor, which may cause allergic reactions in sensitive individuals, and which some studies suggest may adversely affect behavior and the ability to complete school tasks in sensitive children; artificial colors are inadequately tested and artificial flavors may cause allergic reactions in sensitive individuals.

LORNA DOONE SHORTBREAD
R. J. Reynolds Industries, Inc.

Ingredients: enriched wheat flour (niacin, reduced iron, thiamine mononitrate, riboflavin), vegetable shortening (partially hydrogenated soybean, hydrogenated cottonseed, palm), sugar, corn flour, eggs, egg whites, salt, whey, cornstarch, sodium bicarbonate, calcium phosphate, artificial flavor.

Amount: 3 cookies/1 oz			% USRDA
Calories	140	Protein	2
Protein, gm	2	Vitamin A	*
Carbohydrates, gm	18	Vitamin C	*
Fat, gm	7	Thiamine	6
Sodium, mg	135	Riboflavin	4
Cholesterol, mg	10	Niacin	4
Fiber, gm	<1e	Calcium	*
		Iron	2

THIS FOOD: Because Lorna Doone Shortbread is high in sugar and saturated fat, it should only be eaten on occasion. About 45 percent of calories come from fat.

ADDITIVES: Contains artificial flavor, which may cause allergic reactions in sensitive individuals, and which some studies suggest may adversely affect behavior and the ability to complete school tasks in some sensitive children.

MYSTIC MINT SANDWICH COOKIES
R. J. Reynolds Industries, Inc.

Ingredients: sugar, animal and/or vegetable shortening (hydrogenated palm kernel, soybean and palm oils, lard and/or partially hydrogenated soybean oil and palm oil), enriched wheat flour (contains niacin, reduced iron, thiamine mononitrate, riboflavin), cocoa (processed with alkali), whey, dextrose, corn flour, corn sweetener, cornstarch, caramel color, chocolate, sodium bicarbonate, sorbitan.

Amount: 2 cookies/1 oz			% USRDA
Calories	150	Protein	*
Protein, gm	1	Vitamin A	*
Carbohydrates, gm	19	Vitamin C	*
Fat, gm	8	Thiamine	2
Sodium, mg	95	Riboflavin	2
Cholesterol, mg	<5e	Niacin	2
Fiber, gm	<1e	Calcium	*
		Iron	4

Contains nearly 2 teaspoons fat.

THIS FOOD: Because Mystic Mint Sandwich Cookies are high in sugar and saturated fat, they should only be eaten on occasion. About 48 percent of calories derive from fat.

ADDITIVES: No questionable additives.

NATURE VALLEY GRANOLA BARS WITH ROASTED ALMONDS
General Mills, Inc.

Ingredients: rolled oats, brown sugar, coconut oil, almond pieces, salt, sesame seeds, soy lecithin, natural flavoring.

Amount: 1 bar/0.8 oz			% USRDA
Calories	120	Protein	4
Protein, gm	2	Vitamin A	*
Carbohydrates, gm	16	Vitamin C	*
Fat, gm	5	Thiamine	4
Sodium, mg	85	Riboflavin	2
Cholesterol, mg	0	Niacin	*
Fiber, gm	1e	Calcium	*
		Iron	4

THIS FOOD: Granola bars of all types are basically cookies. As cookies, they may be marginally better for you than average because they contain some dietary fiber and protein (from the oats)—but they are still full of empty sugar calories and saturated fat. Nature Valley Granola Bars with Roasted Almonds are low in sodium for this category.

ADDITIVES: No questionable additives.

NATURE VALLEY OATS 'N HONEY GRANOLA BARS
General Mills, Inc.

Ingredients: rolled oats, brown sugar, coconut oil and/or fractionated palm oil, honey, salt, sesame seeds, soy lecithin, natural flavoring.

Amount: 1 bar/0.8 oz			% USRDA
Calories	110	Protein	4
Protein, gm	2	Vitamin A	*
Carbohydrates, gm	17	Vitamin C	*
Fat, gm	4	Thiamine	4
Sodium, mg	70	Riboflavin	*
Cholesterol, mg	0	Niacin	*
Fiber, gm	1e	Calcium	*
		Iron	4

THIS FOOD: Granola bars of all types are basically cookies. As cookies, they may be marginally better for you than average because they contain some dietary fiber and protein (from the oats)—but they are still full of empty sugar calories and saturated fat. Nature Valley Oats 'n Honey Granola Bars are low in sodium for this category.

ADDITIVES: No questionable additives.

NILLA WAFERS
R. J. Reynolds Industries, Inc.

Ingredients: enriched wheat flour (contains niacin, reduced iron, thiamine mononitrate, riboflavin), sugar, animal or vegetable shortening (lard or partially hydrogenated soybean oil with hydrogenated cottonseed, soybean, or palm oil), high-fructose corn syrup, whey, butter, eggs, leavening (baking soda and calcium phosphate), salt, mono- and diglycerides, and artificial flavor.

Amount: 7 cookies/1 oz			% USRDA
Calories	130	Protein	2
Protein, gm	1	Vitamin A	*
Carbohydrates, gm	21	Vitamin C	*
Fat, gm	4	Thiamine	4
Sodium, mg	na	Riboflavin	4
Cholesterol, mg	<10e	Niacin	4
Fiber, gm	<1e	Calcium	*
		Iron	2

THIS FOOD: Although Nilla Wafers are high in sugar, they contain only 27% fat calories, which makes these cookies less fatty—and caloric—than most.

ADDITIVES: Contains artificial flavor, which may cause allergic reactions in sensitive individuals, and which some studies suggest may adversely affect behavior and the ability to complete school tasks in some sensitive children.

OREO CHOCOLATE SANDWICH COOKIES
R. J. Reynolds Industries, Inc.

Ingredients: sugar, enriched wheat flour (niacin, reduced iron, thiamine mononitrate, riboflavin), vegetable and animal shortening (partially hydrogenated soy and hydrogenated cottonseed, soy, palm, lard), cocoa processed with alkali, high-fructose corn syrup, corn flour, leavening (baking soda, sodium acid pyrophosphate), whey, chocolate, salt, lecithin, vanilla.

Amount: 3 cookies/1 oz			% USRDA
Calories	140	Protein	2
Protein, gm	1	Vitamin A	*
Carbohydrates, gm	20	Vitamin C	*
Fat, gm	6	Thiamine	*
Sodium, mg	170	Riboflavin	2
Cholesterol, mg	<5e	Niacin	2
Fiber, gm	<1e	Calcium	*
		Iron	4

THIS FOOD: Because Oreo Chocolate Sandwich Cookies are high in sugar and saturated fat, they should only be eaten on occasion. About 38 percent of calories come from fat.

ADDITIVES: No questionable additives.

PEPPERIDGE FARM CHOCOLATE-LACED PIROUETTES
Pepperidge Farm, Inc.

Ingredients: unbleached wheat flour, sugar, partially hydrogenated vegetable shortening (soybean and/or cottonseed and coconut oils), sweet chocolate (with lecithin), egg whites, lecithin, nonfat milk, salt, and vanilla extract.

Amount: 3 cookies			% USRDA
Calories	110	Protein	*
Protein, gm	0	Vitamin A	*
Carbohydrates, gm	13	Vitamin C	*
Fat, gm	7	Thiamine	*
Sodium, mg	45	Riboflavin	*
Cholesterol, mg	0e	Niacin	*
Fiber, gm	<1e	Calcium	*
		Iron	*

THIS FOOD: Because Pepperidge Farm Chocolate-Laced Pirouettes are high in sugar and saturated fat, they should only be eaten on occasion. With 57 percent fat calories, this is the fattiest cookie in the book!

ADDITIVES: No questionable additives.

PEPPERIDGE FARM LARGE OLD FASHIONED GRANOLA COOKIES

Pepperidge Farm, Inc.

Ingredients: unbleached wheat flour, partially hydrogenated vegetable shortening (soybean and/or cottonseed and coconut oils), brown sugar, sugar, oatmeal, whole eggs, almonds, coconut, raisins, butter, dates, honey, leavening (ammonium bicarbonate, baking soda), vanilla extract, and salt.

Amount: 1 cookie			% USRDA
Calories	120	Protein	2
Protein, gm	1	Vitamin A	*
Carbohydrates, gm	15	Vitamin C	*
Fat, gm	6	Thiamine	2
Sodium, mg	85	Riboflavin	*
Cholesterol, mg	<5e	Niacin	*
Fiber, gm	<1e	Calcium	*
		Iron	2

THIS FOOD: Despite its healthful image a Pepperidge Farm Large Old Fashioned Granola Cookie is not much better for you than any other cookie. True, it is made from unbleached flour and doesn't contain any questionable additives, but it is still very high in sugar and saturated fat. About 45 percent of calories derive from fat.

ADDITIVES: No questionable additives.

PEPPERIDGE FARM MILANO DISTINCTIVE COOKIES

Pepperidge Farm, Inc.

Ingredients: unbleached wheat flour, sweet chocolate, sugar, partially hydrogenated vegetable shortening (soybean and/or cottonseed and coconut oils), nonfat milk, whole eggs, cornstarch, egg whites, salt, vanilla extract, and baking soda.

Amount: 3 cookies			% USRDA
Calories	110	Protein	2
Protein, gm	1	Vitamin A	*
Carbohydrates, gm	16	Vitamin C	*
Fat, gm	5	Thiamine	*
Sodium, mg	80	Riboflavin	*
Cholesterol, mg	<5e	Niacin	*
Fiber, gm	<1e	Calcium	*
		Iron	*

THIS FOOD: Because Pepperidge Farm Milano Distinctive Cookies are high in sugar and saturated fat, they should only be eaten on occasion. About 40 percent of calories come from fat.

ADDITIVES: No questionable additives.

PILLSBURY CHOCOLATE CHIP COOKIE DOUGH
The Pillsbury Co.

Ingredients: sugar, enriched bleached flour (niacin, iron, thiamine mononitrate, riboflavin), beef fat and/or hydrogenated vegetable oil (cottonseed, palm, soybean), with BHA and citric acid, water, cocoa, molasses, egg yolks, baking soda, soy protein isolate, salt, soy flour, nonfat milk, monoglycerides, lecithin, glycerin, carrageenan, natural and artificial flavor.

Amount: 2 cookies/1 oz			% USRDA
Calories	129	Protein	3
Protein, gm	1	Vitamin A	*
Carbohydrates, gm	17	Vitamin C	*
Fat, gm	6	Thiamine	6
Sodium, mg	87	Riboflavin	3
Cholesterol, mg	<10e	Niacin	3
Fiber, gm	<1e	Calcium	*
		Iron	5

THIS FOOD: Like packaged cookies, Pillsbury Chocolate Chip Cookies made from refrigerated dough are high in sugar and saturated fat. About 42 percent of calories come from fat. Although a cookie or two on occasion won't do anybody any harm, it's especially hard to resist warm cookies fresh from the oven.

ADDITIVES: Contains artificial flavor, which may cause allergic reactions in sensitive individuals, and which some studies suggest may adversely affect behavior and the ability to complete school tasks in some sensitive children. Also contains BHA, whose long-term safety is currently being reexamined by FDA investigators.

PILLSBURY CHOCOLATE CHIP OATMEAL FUDGE JUMBLES
The Pillsbury Co.

Ingredients: sugar, enriched bleached flour (bleached flour, niacin, iron, thiamine mononitrate, riboflavin), brown sugar, chocolate chips (sugar, chocolate liquor, cocoa butter, dextrose, lecithin, salt, artificial flavor), rolled oats, whey, wheat starch, natural and artificial flavor, cocoa processed with alkali, hydrogenated vegetable oils (soybean and cottonseed oil), cocoa, calcium and sodium caseinate, salt, baking soda, carob powder, cornstarch, egg whites, artificial color.

Amount: ⅟₃₆ recipe/1 bar (½ cup oil and 2 eggs added to recipe)		% USRDA	
Calories	100	Protein	*
Protein, gm	1	Vitamin A	*
Carbohydrates, gm	14	Vitamin C	*
Fat, gm	4	Thiamine	*
Sodium, mg	60	Riboflavin	*
Cholesterol, mg	<5e	Niacin	*
Fiber, gm	<1e	Calcium	*
		Iron	*

THIS FOOD: Sugar is the primary ingredient of this artificially flavored and colored cake, and fat accounts for 36 percent of total calories, much of it saturated.

ADDITIVES: Contains artificial color and flavor, which may adversely affect behavior and the ability to complete school tasks in some sensitive children. Artificial colors are inadequately tested; and artificial flavors may cause allergic reactions in sensitive individuals.

QUAKER CHEWY CHOCOLATE CHIP GRANOLA BARS
Quaker Oats Co.

Ingredients: rolled oats, brown sugar, semisweet chocolate chips (with added emulsifier vanilla), corn syrup, rolled whole wheat, partially hydrogenated vegetable oil (soybean, palm and/or cottonseed oil), crisp rice (rice, sugar, salt, malt), invert sugar, corn syrup solids, glycerin, nonfat dry milk, dried unsweetened coconut, almonds, sorbitol, honey, salt, natural and artificial flavors, BHA, citric acid.

Amount: 1 bar/1 oz		% USRDA	
Calories	129	Protein	3
Protein, gm	2	Vitamin A	*
Carbohydrates, gm	· 19	Vitamin C	*
Fat, gm	5	Thiamine	5
Sodium, mg	79	Riboflavin	8
Cholesterol, mg	<5e	Niacin	*
Fiber, gm	1e	Calcium	2
		Iron	2

THIS FOOD: Granola bars of all types should be considered candy. As candy, they may be marginally better for you than average because they contain some dietary fiber and protein (from the oats)—but they are still full of empty calories, saturated fat, and too much sugar.

ADDITIVES: Contains artificial flavor, which may cause allergic reactions in sensitive individuals, and which some studies suggest may adversely affect behavior and the ability to complete school tasks in some sensitive children; and BHA, whose long-term safety is currently being reexamined by FDA investigators.

QUAKER CHEWY HONEY AND OATS GRANOLA BARS
Quaker Oats Co.

Ingredients: rolled oats, brown sugar, corn syrup, rolled whole wheat, partially hydrogenated vegetable oil (soybean and/or palm and/or cottonseed oil), crisp rice (rice, sugar, salt, malt), corn syrup solids, honey, glycerin, nonfat dry milk, dried unsweetened coconut, almonds, sorbitol, salt, natural and artificial flavors, BHA, citric acid.

Amount: 1 bar/1 oz			% USRDA
Calories	125	Protein	3
Protein, gm	2	Vitamin A	*
Carbohydrates, gm	19	Vitamin C	*
Fat, gm	4	Thiamine	5
Sodium, mg	93	Riboflavin	9
Cholesterol, mg	<5e	Niacin	*
Fiber, gm	1e	Calcium	3
		Iron	3

THIS FOOD: Granola bars of all types should be considered candy—not food. As candy, they may be marginally better for you than average because they contain some dietary fiber and protein (from the oats). Overall, though, they remain a poor food choice, full of empty calories, saturated fat, and too much sugar.

ADDITIVES: Contains artificial flavor, which may cause allergic reactions in sensitive individuals, and which some studies suggest may adversely affect behavior and the ability to complete school tasks in some sensitive children; also contains BHA, whose long-term safety is currently being reexamined by FDA investigators.

CRACKERS

Crackers are a bread product and provide complex carbohydrates and small amounts of protein, the B vitamins, iron, and dietary fiber. Many crackers, including Keebler Harvest Wheat Crackers, Pepperidge Farm Salted Tiny Goldfish, and the ever-popular Ritz Crackers, are generally higher in saturated fat and sodium than most commercially baked breads and should not be eaten as a bread substitute.

SODIUM GUIDELINES: In evaluating the sodium content of crackers, we have used the following standards:

less than 200 mg	low in sodium
200 mg to 300 mg	moderate in sodium
more than 300 mg	high in sodium

Remember, these guidelines are not for people following medically restricted low sodium diets, but for healthy individuals who wish to monitor their sodium intake.

KEEBLER HARVEST WHEAT CRACKERS
Keebler Co., Inc.

Ingredients: enriched wheat flour (wheat flour, niacin, reduced iron, thiamine mononitrate, riboflavin), vegetable shortening (coconut, partially hydrogenated soybean), steamed crushed wheat, corn syrup, malt, salt, defatted wheat germ, leavening (sodium bicarbonate), spices, onion powder, toasted sesame meal, garlic powder.

Amount: 6 crackers/1 oz			% USRDA
Calories	140	Protein	4
Protein, gm	2	Vitamin A	*
Carbohydrates, gm	16	Vitamin C	*
Fat, gm	8	Thiamine	4
Sodium, mg	230	Riboflavin	4
Cholesterol, mg	0e	Niacin	4
Fiber, gm	2e	Calcium	*
		Iron	4
Contains nearly 2 teaspoons fat.			

THIS FOOD: Keebler Harvest Wheat Crackers are a good source of complex carbohydrates. Unfortunately they are moderately high in saturated fat. About 50 percent of their calories derive from fat. They contain a moderate amount of sodium.

ADDITIVES: No questionable additives.

BEST BET: Wasa Lite Rye Crispbread is a low-calorie, fat-free product made from whole grain flour, yeast, salt, and nothing else. This cracker would make a healthy snack to munch just about anytime, and it's suitable for dieters as well. Although this particular brand may not be available in all regions, other crispbreads made from whole grains without added oil undoubtedly are. Be sure to check the ingredients list before you buy.

PEPPERIDGE FARM SALTED TINY GOLDFISH
Pepperidge Farm, Inc.

Ingredients: unbleached wheat flour, nonfat milk, coconut oil, partially hydrogenated vegetable shortening (soybean and/or cottonseed and coconut oils), salt, yeast, leavening (ammonium bicarbonate, baking soda, cream of tartar), butter, sugar, spices, celery seed, and onion powder.

Amount: 45 crackers/1 oz			% USRDA
Calories	140	Protein	2
Protein	2	Vitamin A	*
Carbohydrates, gm	18	Vitamin C	*
Fat, gm	7	Thiamine	4
Sodium, mg	180	Riboflavin	2
Cholesterol, mg	<5e	Niacin	2
Fiber, gm	<1e	Calcium	*
		Iron	*

Contains 1½ teaspoons fat.

THIS FOOD: Rich in complex carbohydrates, unfortunately they are moderately high in saturated fat. About 45 percent of the calories in these crackers derive from fat. They are low in sodium for this category.

ADDITIVES: No questionable additives.

PREMIUM SALTINE CRACKERS
R. J. Reynolds Industries, Inc.

Ingredients: enriched wheat flour (niacin, iron, thiamine mononitrate, riboflavin), vegetable and animal shortening (lard, partially hydrogenated soy, hydrogenated cottonseed), salt, baking soda, yeast, malted barley flour, calcium carbonate.

Amount: 10 crackers/1 oz			% USRDA
Calories	120	Protein	4
Protein, gm	3	Vitamin A	*
Carbohydrates, gm	20	Vitamin C	*
Fat, gm	4	Thiamine	8
Sodium, mg	360	Riboflavin	8
Cholesterol, mg	<10	Niacin	8
Fiber, gm	1e	Calcium	4
		Iron	6

Contains nearly 1 teaspoon fat.

NOTE: The letter "e" indicates that the data has been estimated; < means "less than" and is used for small amounts of sodium or cholesterol; * means food contains less than 2% of USRDA; "na" means that the information was not available and appears only when data is insufficient.

THIS FOOD: Premium Saltine Crackers are rich in complex carbohydrates and relatively low in fat. Only 30 percent of the calories in this product derive from fat, though too much of it is saturated. Unfortunately Saltines are indeed salty and provide a hefty 360 mg sodium per serving.

ADDITIVES: No questionable additives.

RITZ CRACKERS
R. J. Reynolds Industries, Inc.

Ingredients: enriched wheat flour (niacin, iron, thiamine mononitrate, riboflavin), vegetable and animal shortening (partially hydrogenated soybean, hydrogenated cottonseed, lard), sugar, high-fructose corn syrup, salt, leavening (baking soda and calcium phosphate), malted barley flour, lecithin.

Amount: 9 crackers/1 oz			% USRDA
Calories	150	Protein	2
Protein, gm	2	Vitamin A	*
Carbohydrates, gm	18	Vitamin C	*
Fat, gm	8	Thiamine	6
Sodium, mg	240	Riboflavin	6
Cholesterol, mg	<10	Niacin	6
Fiber, gm	<1e	Calcium	4
		Iron	4
Contains nearly 2 teaspoons fat.			

THIS FOOD: Like most crackers, Ritz Crackers supply complex carbohydrates, but they contain more fat and sugar than average. About 48 percent of their calories derive from fat, most of it saturated.

ADDITIVES: No questionable additives.

TRISCUIT WAFERS
R. J. Reynolds Industries, Inc.

Ingredients: whole wheat, vegetable oil (partially hydrogenated soybean, palm, or hydrogenated coconut oils), salt, TBHQ, citric acid.

Amount: 6 wafers/approx. 1 oz.			% USRDA
Calories	140	Protein	4
Protein, gm	2	Vitamin A	*
Carbohydrates, gm	16	Vitamin C	*
Fat, gm	8	Thiamine	*
Sodium, mg	180	Riboflavin	*
Cholesterol, mg	0	Niacin	4
Fiber, gm	2e	Calcium	4
		Iron	4
Contains nearly 2 teaspoons fat.			

THIS FOOD: Like most crackers, Triscuit Wafers are a good source of complex carbohydrates. Because they are made from whole wheat, they contain more fiber than the average product in this category. About 50 percent of their calories derive from fat, much of it saturated. This product contains a moderate amount of sodium.

ADDITIVES: No questionable additives.

WHEAT THINS
R. J. Reynolds Industries, Inc.

Ingredients: whole wheat flour, enriched wheat flour (with niacin, reduced iron, thiamine mononitrate, riboflavin), vegetable shortening (partially hydrogenated soybean oil with hydrogenated cottonseed oil), sugar, salt, high-fructose corn syrup, malted barley flour, turmeric oleoresin, annatto extract.

Amount: 16 Wheat Thins/1 oz			% USRDA
Calories	140	Protein	*
Protein, gm	2	Vitamin A	*
Carbohydrates, gm	18	Vitamin C	*
Fat, gm	6	Thiamine	8
Sodium, mg	240	Riboflavin	4
Cholesterol, mg	0	Niacin	4
Fiber, gm	1e	Calcium	*
Contains more than 1 teaspoon fat.		Iron	4

THIS FOOD: Nabisco Wheat Thins are a good source of complex carbohydrates. About 38 percent of their calories derive from fat, much of it saturated. These crackers contain a moderate amount of sodium.

ADDITIVES: No questionable additives.

UNEEDA BISCUITS
R. J. Reynolds Industries, Inc.

Ingredients: enriched wheat flour (with niacin, reduced iron, thiamine mononitrate, riboflavin), vegetable shortening (partially hydrogenated soybean and hydrogenated cottonseed, palm), salt, sodium bicarbonate, malted barley flour, yeast.

Amount: 6 biscuits/approx. 1 oz			% USRDA
Calories	130	Protein	4
Protein, gm	3	Vitamin A	*
Carbohydrates, gm	22	Vitamin C	*
Fat, gm	4	Thiamine	8
Sodium, mg	100	Riboflavin	8
Cholesterol, mg	0	Niacin	8
Fiber, gm	1e	Calcium	*
Contains nearly 1 teaspoon fat.		Iron	8

THIS FOOD: Uneeda Biscuits are a good source of complex carbohydrates. Although they are lower in fat than average, with only 27 percent fat calories, too much of the fat they do contain is saturated. This product is low in sodium.

ADDITIVES: No questionable additives.

WASA LITE RYE CRISPBREAD
Schaeffer, Clarke Co.

Ingredients: whole rye flour, yeast, salt.

Amount: 3 pieces/approx. 1 oz			% USRDA
Calories	90	Protein	3
Protein, gm	3	Vitamin A	*
Carbohydrates, gm	18	Vitamin C	*
Fat, gm	0	Thiamine	3
Sodium, mg	250	Riboflavin	3
Cholesterol, mg	0	Niacin	*
Fiber, gm	2e	Calcium	*
		Iron	6
Contains no fat.			

THIS FOOD: Made from whole grain flour and with a minimum of additives, Wasa Lite Rye Crispbread is higher than average in fiber, contains no added oil, and is virtually fat free. This product is low in calories and moderate in sodium.

ADDITIVES: No questionable additives.

DESSERT TOPPINGS

Dairy and nondairy products such as Cool Whip and La Creme are high in saturated fat. Ice cream sauces, such as Smucker's line of toppings, contain concentrated sugars. Both typically contain controversial additives. If you eat dessert toppings as an occasional treat, they certainly aren't going to do any harm, but you should avoid including them often in your diet.

BIRDS EYE COOL WHIP EXTRA CREAMY DAIRY WHIPPED TOPPING
General Foods Corp.

Ingredients: skim milk, hydrogenated coconut and palm kernel oils, water, sugar, corn syrup, light cream, sodium caseinate, dextrose, natural and artificial flavors, polysorbate 60 and sorbitan monostearate, xanthan gum, sodium phosphates, guar gum, artificial color.

Amount: 1 tbsp			% USRDA
Calories	16	Protein	*
Protein, gm	0	Vitamin A	*
Carbohydrates, gm	1	Vitamin C	*
Fat, gm	1	Thiamine	*
Sodium, mg	<5	Riboflavin	*
Cholesterol, mg	<5	Niacin	*
Fiber, gm	0	Calcium	*
		Iron	*

THIS FOOD: Actually contains a tiny amount of cream, stabilizers and other additives. It supplies 56% fat calories and is high in saturated fat.

ADDITIVES: Contains artificial color and flavor, which some studies suggest may adversely affect behavior and the ability to complete school tasks in some sensitive children; artificial colors are inadequately tested, and artificial flavor may cause allergic reactions in sensitive individuals.

BIRDS EYE COOL WHIP NON-DAIRY WHIPPED TOPPING
General Foods Corp.

Ingredients: water, hydrogenated coconut, palm kernel oils, corn syrup, sugar, sodium caseinate, dextrose, natural and artificial flavors, polysorbate 60, sorbitan monostearate, xanthan gum and guar gum, artificial color.

Amount: 1 tbsp			% USRDA
Calories	14	Protein	*
Protein, gm	0	Vitamin A	*
Carbohydrates, gm	1	Vitamin C	*
Fat, gm	1	Thiamine	*
Sodium, mg	<5	Riboflavin	*
Cholesterol, mg	<5	Niacin	*
Fiber, gm	0	Calcium	*
		Iron	*

NOTE: The letter "e" indicates that the data has been estimated; < means "less than" and is used for small amounts of sodium or cholesterol; * means food contains less than 2% of USRDA; "na" means that the information was not available and appears only when data is insufficient.

THIS FOOD: Birds Eye Cool Whip Non-Dairy Whipped Topping contains 64 percent fat calories and is high in saturated fat. Although it contains no actual dairy products, it does contain sodium caseinate, a milk protein.

ADDITIVES: Contains artificial color and flavor, which some studies suggest may adversely affect behavior and the ability to complete school tasks in some sensitive children; artificial colors are inadequately tested and artificial flavor may cause allergic reactions in sensitive individuals.

LA CREME WHIPPED TOPPING
Kraft, Inc.

Ingredients: skim milk, partially hydrogenated coconut oil, cream, corn syrup, sugar, milk, water, sodium caseinate, egg yolks, xanthan gum, polysorbate 60, sodium phosphate, potassium phosphate, propylene glycol monostearate, natural and artificial flavor, starter culture, glyceryl monostearate, salt, lecithin, guar gum, sorbitan monostearate, sodium stearoyl lactylate, calcium carrageenan, carob bean gum, beta carotene.

Amount: 1 tbsp			% USRDA
Calories	12	Protein	*
Protein, gm	0	Vitamin A	*
Carbohydrates, gm	1	Vitamin C	*
Fat, gm	1	Thiamine	*
Sodium, mg	5	Riboflavin	*
Cholesterol, mg	0	Niacin	*
Fiber, gm	0	Calcium	*
		Iron	*

THIS FOOD: La Creme Whipped Topping actually does contain cream, along with a host of stabilizers and other additives. It supplies 75 percent fat calories and is high in saturated fat.

ADDITIVES: Contains artificial flavor, which may cause allergic reactions in sensitive individuals, and which some studies suggest may adversely affect behavior and the ability to complete school tasks in some sensitive children.

SMUCKER'S BUTTERSCOTCH FLAVORED TOPPING
The J. M. Smucker Co.

Ingredients: nonfat milk, corn syrup, high-fructose corn syrup, sugar, partially hydrogenated vegetable oil (soybean and palm oils), salt, natural flavors, pectin, sodium citrate, disodium phosphate, vanillin, caramel color, FD & C Yellow No. 5, and artificial color.

Amount: 1 tbsp			% USRDA
Calories	70	Protein	*
Protein, gm	0	Vitamin A	*
Carbohydrates, gm	17	Vitamin C	*
Fat, gm	0	Thiamine	*
Sodium, mg	38	Riboflavin	*
Cholesterol, mg	<5e	Niacin	*
Fiber, gm	0	Calcium	*
		Iron	*

Contains 3 teaspoons sugar.

THIS FOOD: No one will be surprised to learn that Smucker's Butterscotch Flavored Topping has no useful nutrients. Nearly all of its calories derive from sugar.

ADDITIVES: Contains artificial colors, which are inadequately tested and which some studies suggest may adversely affect behavior and the ability to complete school tasks in some sensitive children. Also contains Yellow No. 5, which can cause allergic reactions, especially in aspirin-sensitive individuals.

SMUCKER'S STRAWBERRY TOPPING
The J. M. Smucker Co.

Ingredients: strawberries, corn syrup, high-fructose corn syrup, water, sugar, citric acid, pectin, artificial color.

Amount: 1 tbsp			% USRDA
Calories	60	Protein	*
Protein, gm	0	Vitamin A	*
Carbohydrates, gm	15	Vitamin C	*
Fat, gm	0	Thiamine	*
Sodium, mg	<5	Riboflavin	*
Cholesterol, mg	0	Niacin	*
Fiber, gm	<1	Calcium	*
		Iron	*

Contains 3 teaspoons sugar.

THIS FOOD: No one will be surprised to learn that Smucker's Strawberry

Topping contains no useful nutrients. Nearly all of its calories derive from sugar.

ADDITIVES: Contains artificial colors, which are inadequately tested and which some studies suggest may adversely affect behavior and the ability to complete school tasks in some sensitive children.

FISH

All types of fish are rich in protein and make a nutritious substitute for red meats. Most fish are either low in fat, or the fat they do contain is largely unsaturated. The cholesterol issue is a little more complicated. According to current measurements, some fish, such as salmon, are high in cholesterol. But recent studies suggest that the presence of a fatty acid, Omega 3, in fatty fin fish, may actually protect against heart disease.

The most popular canned fish is tuna, a rich source of niacin and significant source of iron. All of the major brands, including Bumble Bee, Star-Kist, and Chicken of the Sea, offer tuna packed in water (with about 10 percent fat calories), as well as the standard oil-packed product (with more than 55 percent fat calories, or 35 percent fat calories with the oil drained).

All canned tuna, except for the hard-to-find low-sodium packs, are high in salt. Canned salmon is an excellent nondairy source of calcium if you crush up and eat the bones.

Frozen fish vary widely in their fat content. Plain fish such as Gorton's Perch and Sole Fillets are rich in protein and low in saturated fat and overall fat. But most of the popular prepared dishes produced by Mrs. Paul, Gorton's, and Taste O' Sea are breaded and contain 40 percent or more fat calories. Among the breaded fish dishes only Gorton's Light Recipe Fish Fillets (cod) and Taste O' Sea Batter Dipt Scallops keep close to the recommended maximum of 30 percent fat calories.

SODIUM GUIDELINES: In evaluating the sodium content of a ½-cup serving of canned fish, we used the following standard:

less than 300 mg	low in sodium
300 mg to 400 mg	moderate in sodium
more than 400 mg	high in sodium

Remember, these guidelines are not for people following medically restricted low-sodium diets, but for healthy individuals who wish to monitor their sodium intake.

Canned Fish

BUMBLE BEE CHUNK LIGHT TUNA IN WATER
Castle and Cooke, Inc.

Ingredients: chunk light tuna in water, seasoned with vegetable broth, salt.

Amount: ½ cup			% USRDA
Calories	117	Protein	53
Protein, gm	26	Vitamin A	2
Carbohydrates, gm	0	Vitamin C	*
Fat, gm	1	Thiamine	3
Sodium, mg	311	Riboflavin	6
Cholesterol, mg	58	Niacin	66
Fiber, gm	0	Calcium	*
		Iron	8

THIS FOOD: Tuna packed in water is a low-fat food that is rich in protein and niacin and also provides a fair amount of iron. While tuna is moderately high in cholesterol, recent research suggests that a fatty acid found in cold-water fish, Omega 3, may actually help protect against heart disease. This product contains a moderate amount of sodium.

ADDITIVES: No questionable additives.

DID YOU KNOW: the iron content of canned tuna may vary significantly according to the sex of the fish, whether or not it is spawning, and what body of water it is in? The species used for most canned tuna is albacore.

HELPFUL HINT: The soft bones in canned salmon contain most of the valuable calcium. Instead of discarding, mash them up before preparing a salad or other salmon dish.

NOTE: The letter "e" indicates that the data has been estimated; < means "less than" and is used for small amounts of sodium or cholesterol; * means food contains less than 2% of USRDA; "na" means that the information was not available and appears only when data is insufficient.

BUMBLE BEE PINK SALMON
Castle and Cooke, Inc.

Ingredients: pink salmon, salt.

Amount: ½ cup			% USRDA
Calories	155	Protein	50
Protein, gm	23	Vitamin A	*
Carbohydrates, gm	0	Vitamin C	*
Fat, gm	7	Thiamine	3
Sodium, mg	542	Riboflavin	12
Cholesterol, mg	30	Niacin	44
Fiber, gm	0	Calcium	22
		Iron	5

THIS FOOD: Bumble Bee Pink Salmon is an excellent source of protein, niacin, and calcium and also provides a good amount of riboflavin and iron. Although salmon is moderately high in fat and cholesterol, recent research suggests that this food is still a good choice for people interested in lowering their risk of heart disease, since most of the fat is unsaturated and it also contains Omega 3, a fatty acid that may actually help protect against heart disease. Bumble Bee Pink Salmon is high in sodium.

ADDITIVES: No questionable additives.

BUMBLE BEE RED SOCKEYE SALMON
Castle and Cooke, Inc.

Ingredients: red sockeye salmon, salt.

Amount: ½ cup			% USRDA
Calories	188	Protein	50
Protein, gm	23	Vitamin A	5
Carbohydrates, gm	0	Vitamin C	*
Fat, gm	11	Thiamine	4
Sodium, mg	455	Riboflavin	11
Cholesterol, mg	40	Niacin	40
Fiber, gm	0	Calcium	29
		Iron	7

THIS FOOD: Bumble Bee Red Sockeye Salmon is an excellent source of protein, niacin, and calcium and also provides some riboflavin and iron. Although red sockeye salmon is high in fat and cholesterol, recent research suggests that this food is still a good choice for people interested in lowering their risk of heart disease since it also contains Omega 3, a fatty acid which may actually help protect against heart disease. This product is high in sodium.

ADDITIVES: No questionable additives.

BUMBLE BEE SOLID WHITE TUNA IN WATER
Castle and Cooke, Inc.

Ingredients: albacore in water, seasoned with vegetable broth, salt.

Amount: ½ cup			% USRDA
Calories	126	Protein	62
Protein, gm	28	Vitamin A	2
Carbohydrates, gm	0	Vitamin C	*
Fat, gm	1	Thiamine	3
Sodium, mg	333	Riboflavin	6
Cholesterol, mg	58	Niacin	66
Fiber, gm	0	Calcium	*
		Iron	9

THIS FOOD: Tuna packed in water is a low-fat food that is rich in protein and niacin. While tuna is moderately high in cholesterol, recent research suggests that a fatty acid found in cold-water fish, Omega 3, may actually help protect against heart disease. This product contains a moderate amount of sodium.

ADDITIVES: No questionable additives.

CHICKEN OF THE SEA CHUNK LIGHT TUNA IN WATER
Ralston Purina Co.

Ingredients: chunk light tuna, water, hydrolyzed protein, salt.

Amount: ½ cup			% USRDA
Calories	100	Protein	50
Protein, gm	23	Vitamin A	*
Carbohydrates, gm	0	Vitamin C	*
Fat, gm	1	Thiamine	*
Sodium, mg	373	Riboflavin	4
Cholesterol, mg	56	Niacin	50
Fiber, gm	0	Calcium	*
		Iron	5

THIS FOOD: Tuna packed in water is a low-fat food that is an excellent source of protein and niacin. While tuna is moderately high in cholesterol, recent research suggests that a fatty acid found in cold-water fish, Omega 3, actually helps protect against heart disease. This product contains a moderate amount of sodium.

ADDITIVES: No questionable additives.

CHICKEN OF THE SEA LOW SODIUM CHUNK WHITE TUNA IN WATER
Ralston Purina Co.

Ingredients: chunk white tuna, water, vegetable broth.

Amount: ½ cup			% USRDA
Calories	110	Protein	50
Protein, gm	23	Vitamin A	*
Carbohydrates, gm	0	Vitamin C	*
Fat, gm	3	Thiamine	2
Sodium, mg	48	Riboflavin	2
Cholesterol, mg	32	Niacin	55
Fiber, gm	0	Calcium	*
		Iron	2

THIS FOOD: This water-packed tuna is low in fat and sodium and high in protein and niacin. While tuna contains some cholesterol, recent research suggests that a fatty acid found in cold-water fish, Omega 3, actually helps protect against heart disease.

ADDITIVES: No questionable additives.

CHICKEN OF THE SEA SOLID WHITE TUNA IN OIL
Ralston Purina Co.

Ingredients: solid white tuna, soybean oil, hydrolyzed protein, salt, sodium pyrophosphate.

Amount: ½ cup			% USRDA
Calories	225	Protein	55
Protein, gm	25	Vitamin A	*
Carbohydrates, gm	0	Vitamin C	*
Fat, gm	14	Thiamine	2
Sodium, mg	596	Riboflavin	4
Cholesterol, mg	23	Niacin	55
Fiber, gm	0	Calcium	*
		Iron	3

THIS FOOD: Tuna packed in oil is rich in protein and niacin. If served with the packing oil, about 55 percent of its calories derive from fat. Drained, the fat calories reduce to a reasonable 35 percent. While tuna contains some cholesterol, recent research suggests that a fatty acid found in cold-water fish, Omega 3, actually helps protect against heart disease. This product is high in sodium.

ADDITIVES: No questionable additives.

STAR-KIST CHUNK LIGHT TUNA IN OIL
H. J. Heinz Co.

Ingredients: light tuna, soybean oil, vegetable broth, salt.

Amount: ½ cup			% USRDA
Calories	225	Protein	50
Protein, gm	23	Vitamin A	*
Carbohydrates, gm	0	Vitamin C	*
Fat, gm	15	Thiamine	*
Sodium, mg	500e	Riboflavin	5
Cholesterol, mg	50	Niacin	60
Fiber, gm	0	Calcium	*
		Iron	5

THIS FOOD: Tuna packed in oil is rich in protein and niacin. If served with the packing oil, about 55 percent of its calories derive from fat. Drained, the fat calories reduce to a reasonable 35 percent. While tuna is moderately high in cholesterol, recent research suggests that a fatty acid found in cold-water fish, Omega 3, may actually protect against heart disease. This product is high in sodium.

ADDITIVES: No questionable additives.

STAR-KIST SOLID WHITE TUNA IN WATER
H. J. Heinz Co.

Ingredients: white tuna, spring water, vegetable broth, salt, pyrophosphate.

Amount: ½ cup			% USRDA
Calories	110	Protein	50
Protein, gm	23	Vitamin A	*
Carbohydrates, gm	0	Vitamin C	*
Fat, gm	2	Thiamine	*
Sodium, mg	350e	Riboflavin	3
Cholesterol, mg	58	Niacin	55
Fiber, gm	0e	Calcium	*
		Iron	2

THIS FOOD: Tuna packed in water is a low-fat food that is rich in protein and niacin. While tuna is moderately high in cholesterol, recent research suggests that a fatty acid found in cold-water fish, Omega 3, may actually help protect against heart disease. This product contains a moderate amount of sodium.

ADDITIVES: No questionable additives.

HELPFUL HINT: For healthier tuna salad, try cutting the amount of mayonnaise you usually use in half and add plain yogurt if the resulting mixture is too dry.

HELPFUL HINT: Always drain oil from canned tuna before preparing salads or casseroles. To remove even more fat calories, rinse away extra oil with water. Of course, you can avoid the need to remove the oil by using water-packed tuna in the first place.

Frozen Fish

GORTON'S FISHMARKET FRESH OCEAN PERCH FILLETS
General Mills, Inc.
Ingredients: premium ocean perch fillets.

Amount: 4 oz			% USRDA
Calories	130	Protein	45
Protein, gm	20	Vitamin A	*
Carbohydrates, gm	2	Vitamin C	*
Fat, gm	5	Thiamine	6
Sodium, mg	80e	Riboflavin	8
Cholesterol, mg	70e	Niacin	10
Fiber, gm	0	Calcium	8
		Iron	*
Contains 1 teaspoon fat.			

THIS FOOD: Gorton's Fishmarket Fresh Ocean Perch Fillets are a low-calorie, low-sodium, high-protein food. They contain 37 percent fat calories. Although perch contain about 70 mg cholesterol per serving, they also contain Omega 3, a fatty acid, which new research suggests may actually help protect against heart disease. Overall, this fish is an excellent nutritional choice.

ADDITIVES: None.

GORTON'S FISHMARKET FRESH SOLE FILLETS
General Mills, Inc.
Ingredients: premium sole fillets.

Amount: 4 oz			% USRDA
Calories	100	Protein	40
Protein, gm	19	Vitamin A	*
Carbohydrates, gm	0	Vitamin C	*
Fat, gm	3	Thiamine	2
Sodium, mg	260	Riboflavin	2
Cholesterol, mg	70e	Niacin	8
Fiber, gm	0	Calcium	*
		Iron	*

Contains less than ¾ teaspoon fat.

THIS FOOD: Gorton's Fishmarket Fresh Sole Fillets are low in fat and calories and high in protein. Although moderately high in cholesterol, sole is low in saturated fat and also contains Omega 3, a fatty acid, which new research suggests may actually help protect against heart disease. A 4-oz serving of this fish contains a moderate 260 mg naturally occurring sodium.

ADDITIVES: None.

GORTON'S LIGHT RECIPE BAKED STUFFED SCROD
General Mills, Inc.

Ingredients: haddock, butter, wheat flour bromated, lemon juice, water, salt, parsley, sugar, partially hydrogenated soybean oil with TBHQ, yeast, calcium propionate.

Amount: 1 fillet/4 oz			% USRDA
Calories	240	Protein	40
Protein, gm	25	Vitamin A	4
Carbohydrates, gm	11	Vitamin C	*
Fat, gm	11	Thiamine	4
Sodium, mg	470	Riboflavin	6
Cholesterol, mg	100e	Niacin	15
Fiber, gm	<1	Calcium	2
		Iron	*

Contains 2½ teaspoons fat.

THIS FOOD: Gorton's Light Recipe Baked Stuffed Scrod provides lots of protein and small amounts of the B vitamins. About 41 percent of the calories in this product derive from fat, most of it from added butter, which is highly saturated. Although moderately high in cholesterol, scrod also contains Omega 3, a fatty acid which early studies suggest tends to protect against heart disease. This product contains a moderate amount of sodium.

ADDITIVES: No questionable additives.

GORTON'S LIGHT RECIPE ENTRÉE-SIZE FISH FILLETS
General Mills, Inc.

Ingredients: cod, wheat flour, cottonseed oil, water, yellow corn flour, dextrose, whey, cornstarch, salt, soybean oil, eggs, yeast, natural flavors.

Amount: 1 fillet/4 oz			% USRDA
Calories	270	Protein	40
Protein, gm	20	Vitamin A	*
Carbohydrates, gm	25	Vitamin C	*
Fat, gm	10	Thiamine	10
Sodium, mg	500	Riboflavin	10
Cholesterol, mg	65e	Niacin	10
Fiber, gm	<1e	Calcium	2
		Iron	4
Contains more than 2 teaspoons fat.			

THIS FOOD: Provides a good balance of nutrients, is high in protein and provides 10 percent of USRDA for the B vitamins. Gorton's is the only brand that keeps its fat content down to 30 percent of total calories—the recommended proportion. Although moderately high in cholesterol, cod also contains Omega 3. Early research suggests this tends to protect against heart disease. This product is high in sodium.

ADDITIVES: No questionable additives.

MRS. PAUL'S CRISPY CRUNCHY FISH STICKS
Campbell Soup Co.

Ingredients: select pollock fillets, bread crumbs (bromated wheat flour, sugar, partially hydrogenated soybean oil, salt, yeast, calcium propionate), enriched flour (flour, niacin, reduced iron, thiamine mononitrate or thiamine hydrochloride, riboflavin), partially hydrogenated soybean oil, corn flour, whey, modified food starch, dextrose, salt, whole egg solids, baking powder (sodium acid pyrophosphate, sodium bicarbonate, cornstarch, monocalcium phosphate), wheat gluten. *Sauce mix:* pickle relish, onions, salt, spices.

Amount: 5 sticks/3¾ oz			% USRDA
Calories	250	Protein	19
Protein, gm	14	Vitamin A	*
Carbohydrates, gm	21	Vitamin C	*
Fat, gm	13	Thiamine	8
Sodium, mg	569	Riboflavin	10
Cholesterol, mg	50e	Niacin	10
Fiber, gm	<1e	Calcium	3
		Iron	3
Contains nearly 3 teaspoons fat.			

THIS FOOD: Mrs. Paul's Crispy Crunchy Fish Sticks are a very good source of protein and provide small amounts of the B vitamins. About 45 percent of the calories in this product derive from fat. Although pollock is moderately high in cholesterol it also contains Omega 3, a fatty acid believed to protect against heart disease. Like most prepared foods this product is high in sodium.

ADDITIVES: No questionable additives.

MRS. PAUL'S FRIED CLAMS IN A LIGHT BATTER
Campbell Soup Co.

Ingredients: select ocean clams, enriched flour (flour, niacin, reduced iron, thiamine mononitrate or thiamine hydrochloride, riboflavin), cornmeal, nonfat dry milk, partially hydrogenated soybean oil, dextrose, salt, baking powder (sodium acid pyrophosphate, sodium bicarbonate, cornstarch, monocalcium phosphate), spices. *Sauce mix:* pickle relish, onions, salt, spices.

Amount: 4 oz			% USRDA
Calories	368	Protein	24
Protein, gm	14	Vitamin A	*
Carbohydrates, gm	32	Vitamin C	*
Fat, gm	21	Thiamine	16
Sodium, mg	616	Riboflavin	16
Cholesterol, mg	48e	Niacin	16
Fiber, gm	<1e	Calcium	*
		Iron	10
Contains 4½ teaspoons fat.			

THIS FOOD: Mrs. Paul's Fried Clams in a Light Batter derive more than 50 percent of their calories from fat. The clams themselves are high in protein and are a good source of the B vitamins and iron, but the recipe adds too many fat calories for good nutrition. While clams are moderately high in cholesterol, they also contain Omega 3, a fatty acid believed to protect against heart disease. Like most prepared foods this product is high in sodium.

ADDITIVES: No questionable additives.

MRS. PAUL'S LIGHT AND NATURAL FLOUNDER FILLETS
Campbell Soup Co.

Ingredients: select flounder fillets, bread crumbs (bromated wheat flour, sugar, partially hydrogenated soybean oil, salt, yeast, calcium propionate), enriched flour (flour, niacin, reduced iron, thiamine mononitrate or thiamine hydrochloride, riboflavin), partially hydrogenated soybean oil, corn flour, whey, modified food starch, dextrose, salt, whole egg solids, leavening (sodium aluminum phosphate, sodium bicarbonate), wheat gluten.

Amount: 1 fillet			% USRDA
Calories	280	Protein	30
Protein, gm	21	Vitamin A	*
Carbohydrates, gm	19	Vitamin C	*
Fat, gm	13	Thiamine	8
Sodium, mg	na	Riboflavin	8
Cholesterol, mg	70e	Niacin	15
Fiber, gm	<1e	Calcium	4
		Iron	6

Contains nearly 3 teaspoons fat.

THIS FOOD: Mrs. Paul's Light and Natural Flounder Fillets are high in protein and provide small amounts of the B vitamins. About 42 percent of the calories in this product derive from fat. Although flounder is moderately high in cholesterol, it also contains Omega 3, a fatty acid believed to protect against heart disease. Sodium values are not available, but it's safe to assume that this product is high in sodium.

ADDITIVES: No questionable additives.

HELPFUL HINT: If you like fried foods but wish to cut down on your fat intake, choose large fillets rather than fried clams or "nuggets." The greater surface area on the small pieces of fish are likely to absorb more oil when fried.

MRS. PAUL'S LIGHT AND NATURAL SOLE FILLETS
Campbell Soup Co.

Ingredients: select sole fillets, bread crumbs (bromated wheat flour, sugar, partially hydrogenated soybean oil, salt, yeast, calcium propionate), enriched flour (flour, niacin, reduced iron, thiamine mononitrate or thiamine hydrochloride, riboflavin), partially hydrogenated soybean oil, corn flour, whey, modified food starch, dextrose, salt, whole egg solids, leavening (sodium aluminum phosphate, sodium bicarbonate), wheat gluten.

Amount: 1 fillet			% USRDA
Calories	280	Protein	30
Protein, gm	21	Vitamin A	*
Carbohydrates, gm	19	Vitamin C	*
Fat, gm	13	Thiamine	8
Sodium, mg	na	Riboflavin	8
Cholesterol, mg	80e	Niacin	15
Fiber, gm	<1e	Calcium	4
		Iron	6

Contains nearly 3 teaspoons fat.

THIS FOOD: Mrs. Paul's Light and Natural Sole Fillets are high in protein and provide small amounts of the B vitamins. About 42 percent of the calories in this product derive from fat. Although flounder is moderately high in cholesterol, it also contains Omega 3, a fatty acid believed to protect against heart disease. Sodium values are not available, but it's safe to assume that this product is high in sodium.

ADDITIVES: No questionable additives.

TASTE O'SEA BATTER DIPT SCALLOPS
O'Donnell-Usen Fisheries Corp.

Ingredients: sea scallops, bleached wheat flour, water, vegetable oil (partially hydrogenated soybean, and/or cottonseed, and/or palm), modified food starch, whey, salt, leavening (sodium bicarbonate, sodium aluminum phosphate), nonfat milk, sugar, monosodium glutamate, egg whites, egg yolks, natural flavor.

Amount: 3.5 oz			% USRDA
Calories	190	Protein	30
Protein, gm	13	Vitamin A	*
Carbohydrates, gm	20	Vitamin C	*
Fat, gm	7	Thiamine	8
Sodium, mg	450	Riboflavin	10
Cholesterol, mg	50e	Niacin	8
Fiber, gm	<1e	Calcium	*
		Iron	6
Contains 1½ teaspoons fat.			

THIS FOOD: Taste O'Sea Batter Dipt Scallops are one of the better nutritional choices among breaded, frozen fish dishes. It is an excellent source of protein and provides small amounts of the B vitamins; only 33 percent of its calories derive from fat. Although scallops are moderately high in cholesterol, they also contain Omega 3, a fatty acid which is thought to protect against heart disease. This product contains a moderate amount of sodium.

ADDITIVES: Contains monosodium glutamate (MSG), which many experts believe should be avoided by infants and very young children; causes adverse reactions in some sensitive individuals.

TASTE O'SEA FLOUNDER FILLETS
O'Donnell-Usen Fisheries Corp.

Ingredients: flounder fillets, sodium tripolyphosphate.

Amount: 4 oz			% USRDA
Calories	90	Protein	40
Protein, gm	18	Vitamin A	*
Carbohydrates, gm	0	Vitamin C	*
Fat, gm	1	Thiamine	4
Sodium, mg	150	Riboflavin	2
Cholesterol, mg	55e	Niacin	4
Fiber, gm	0	Calcium	*
		Iron	4
Contains less than ¼ teaspoon fat.			

THIS FOOD: Taste O'Sea Flounder Fillets are a low-fat, low-calorie, high-protein food. Although flounder contains a moderate amount of cholesterol it also provides Omega 3, a fatty acid which early research suggests may protect against heart disease. This fish contains a moderately low amount of sodium.

ADDITIVES: No questionable additives.

See "Basic Foods" on page 557 for additional fish listing.

BEST BETS FOR FAT WATCHERS: Only two of the prepared fish entrées profiled stay close to the dietary guidelines that advise getting no more than 30 percent of daily calories from fat: Gorton's Light Recipe Entrée-Size Fish Fillets derive only 30 percent of their calories from fat, most of it unsaturated. Taste O'Sea Batter Dipt Scallops are also moderate in fat, with only 33 percent fat calories.

FLOUR AND BAKING NEEDS

Flour is the main ingredient in bread and all kinds of baked goods. Most flours are produced by grinding various grains, primarily wheat, rye, and corn. All are high in complex carbohydrates, low in fat, and provide small amounts of B vitamins and iron. Nearly all white flours, like Gold Medal All-Purpose Flour and Pillsbury Best All-Purpose

Enriched Flour, are enriched because most of the naturally occurring nutrients are taken out when the bran and germ of the wheat kernel are removed during processing. General Mills recently added calcium to its Gold Medal All-Purpose Flour recipe even though calcium is not present in significant quantities in unrefined grains. It is too soon to say whether calcium fortification in flour is the coming trend. In 1986 opinion was divided among nutritionists for and against calcium fortification.

Whole wheat flour contains substantially more protein, fiber, and vitamin E than refined white flour. In general, darker flours are less refined than white flours and contain more fiber and naturally occurring nutrients. (For a fuller discussion of fortification see *Bread* on page 40.)

ARGO CORN STARCH
CPC International, Inc.

Ingredients: cornstarch.

Amount: 1 tbsp			% USRDA
Calories	30	Protein	*
Protein, gm	<1	Vitamin A	*
Carbohydrates, gm	7	Vitamin C	*
Fat, gm	<1	Thiamine	*
Sodium, mg	na	Riboflavin	*
Cholesterol, mg	0	Niacin	*
Fiber, gm	0e	Calcium	*
		Iron	*

THIS FOOD: Used as a thickening agent, cornstarch supplies carbohydrates without any other useful nutrients.

ADDITIVES: none.

NOTE: The letter "e" indicates that the data has been estimated; < means "less than" and is used for small amounts of sodium or cholesterol; * means food contains less than 2% of USRDA; "na" means that the information was not available and appears only when data is insufficient.

ARM & HAMMER BAKING SODA
Church and Dwight Company, Inc.
Ingredients: sodium bicarbonate.

Amount: 1 tsp			% USRDA
Calories	0	Protein	*
Protein, gm	0	Vitamin A	*
Carbohydrates, gm	0	Vitamin C	*
Fat, gm	0	Thiamine	*
Sodium, mg	2700	Riboflavin	*
Cholesterol, mg	0	Niacin	*
Fiber, gm	0	Calcium	*
		Iron	*

THIS FOOD: Really an additive rather than a food, baking soda is widely used in home baking and commercially prepared foods. Baking soda adds sodium to many processed foods.

ADDITIVES: No questionable additives.

AUNT JEMIMA'S ENRICHED YELLOW CORN MEAL
Quaker Oats Co.
Ingredients: yellow cornmeal enriched with niacin, reduced iron, thiamine mononitrate, riboflavin.

Amount: 1 cup			% USRDA
Calories	544	Protein	20
Protein, gm	13	Vitamin A	*
Carbohydrates, gm	118	Vitamin C	*
Fat, gm	3	Thiamine	42
Sodium, mg	1	Riboflavin	22
Cholesterol, mg	0	Niacin	27
Fiber, gm	9	Calcium	*
		Iron	24

THIS FOOD: Aunt Jemima's Enriched Yellow Corn Meal provides valuable protein and complex carbohydrates along with B vitamins and iron, mostly from fortification. Most degermed cornmeal is enriched because many of the naturally occurring nutrients are lost when the germ of the corn kernels are removed during processing. It is also an excellent source of dietary fiber.

ADDITIVES: Contains added vitamins and iron.

CALUMET BAKING POWDER
General Foods Corp.

Ingredients: baking soda and sodium aluminum sulfate, cornstarch, calcium sulfate, calcium acid phosphate, calcium silicate.

Amount: 1 tbsp			% USRDA
Calories	2	Protein	*
Protein, gm	0	Vitamin A	*
Carbohydrates, gm	1	Vitamin C	*
Fat, gm	0	Thiamine	*
Sodium, mg	405	Riboflavin	*
Cholesterol, mg	0	Niacin	*
Fiber, gm	0	Calcium	25
		Iron	4

THIS FOOD: Really an additive rather than a food, baking powder is widely used in home baking and commercially prepared foods. Baking powder is high in sodium, and adds "hidden" amounts of this too abundant mineral to many processed foods.

ADDITIVES: No questionable additives.

FLEISCHMANN'S ACTIVE DRY YEAST
R. J. Reynolds Industries, Inc.

Ingredients: active dry yeast.

Amount: ¼ oz			% USRDA
Calories	20	Protein	4
Protein, gm	3	Vitamin A	*
Carbohydrates, gm	3	Vitamin C	*
Fat, gm	0	Thiamine	*
Sodium, mg	10	Riboflavin	*
Cholesterol, mg	0	Niacin	*
Fiber, gm	<1e	Calcium	*
		Iron	*

THIS FOOD: Yeast in this form is used as a leavening agent. Really a group of microscopic fungi, during bread baking it causes carbon dioxide to be released from the dough, which makes the bread rise.

ADDITIVES: None.

GOLD MEDAL ALL-PURPOSE FLOUR
General Mills, Inc.

Ingredients: wheat flour, calcium sulfate, malted barley flour, niacin, iron, thiamine mononitrate, riboflavin.

Amount: 1 cup			% USRDA
Calories	400	Protein	15
Protein, gm	11	Vitamin A	*
Carbohydrates, gm	87	Vitamin C	*
Fat, gm	1	Thiamine	45
Sodium, mg	<5	Riboflavin	25
Cholesterol, mg	0	Niacin	30
Fiber, gm	3	Calcium	20
		Iron	25

THIS FOOD: Gold Medal All-Purpose Flour provides valuable protein and complex carbohydrates along with B vitamins, calcium, and iron, mostly from fortification. Nearly all white flours are enriched because most of the naturally occurring nutrients are taken out when the bran and germ of the wheat kernel are removed during processing.

ADDITIVES: Contains added vitamins, calcium, and iron.

GOLD MEDAL WHOLE WHEAT FLOUR
General Mills, Inc.

Ingredients: whole wheat flour, malted barley flour.

Amount: 1 cup			% USRDA
Calories	390	Protein	25
Protein, gm	16	Vitamin A	*
Carbohydrates, gm	78	Vitamin C	*
Fat, gm	2	Thiamine	35
Sodium, mg	<5	Riboflavin	8
Cholesterol, mg	0	Niacin	30
Fiber, gm	8	Calcium	2
		Iron	25

THIS FOOD: Gold Medal Whole Wheat Flour is naturally rich in protein, complex carbohydrates, fiber, thiamine, niacin, vitamin E, and trace minerals.

ADDITIVES: None.

MARTHA WHITE ALL-PURPOSE PLAIN FLOUR
Beatrice Foods Co.

Ingredients: bleached wheat flour, monocalcium phosphate, niacin, reduced iron, thiamine mononitrate, riboflavin.

Amount: 1 cup			% USRDA
Calories	390	Protein	10
Protein, gm	9	Vitamin A	*
Carbohydrates, gm	86	Vitamin C	*
Fat, gm	1	Thiamine	45
Sodium, mg	<5	Riboflavin	25
Cholesterol, mg	0	Niacin	30
Fiber, gm	3	Calcium	2
		Iron	25

THIS FOOD: Martha White All-Purpose Plain Flour provides valuable protein and complex carbohydrates, along with B vitamins and iron, mostly from fortification. Nearly all white flours are enriched, because most of the naturally occurring nutrients are taken out when the bran and germ of the wheat kernel are removed during processing.

ADDITIVES: Contains added vitamins and iron.

PILLSBURY'S BEST ALL-PURPOSE ENRICHED FLOUR
The Pillsbury Co.

Ingredients: bleached wheat flour, malted barley flour, niacin, iron, thiamine mononitrate, riboflavin.

Amount: 1 cup			% USRDA
Calories	400	Protein	15
Protein, gm	11	Vitamin A	*
Carbohydrates, gm	87	Vitamin C	*
Fat, gm	1	Thiamine	45
Sodium, mg	5	Riboflavin	25
Cholesterol, mg	0	Niacin	30
Fiber, gm	3	Calcium	*
		Iron	25

THIS FOOD: Pillsbury's Best All-Purpose Enriched Flour provides valuable protein and complex carbohydrates along with B vitamins and iron, mostly from fortification. Nearly all white flours are enriched because most of the naturally occurring nutrients are taken out when the bran and germ of the wheat kernel are removed during processing.

ADDITIVES: Contains added vitamins and iron.

PILLSBURY'S BEST MEDIUM RYE FLOUR
The Pillsbury Co.

Ingredients: medium rye flour.

Amount: 1 cup			% USRDA
Calories	400	Protein	20
Protein, gm	12	Vitamin A	*
Carbohydrates, gm	83	Vitamin C	*
Fat, gm	2	Thiamine	20
Sodium, mg	<5	Riboflavin	8
Cholesterol, mg	0	Niacin	15
Fiber, gm	4	Calcium	2
		Iron	15

THIS FOOD: Pillsbury's Best Medium Rye Flour is a refined product which provides valuable protein, complex carbohydrates, and fiber. As in white flour, most of the bran and germ have been removed from the grain. While this product also contains thiamine, niacin, and iron, it has less of these nutrients than whole wheat flour or enriched white flour.

ADDITIVES: None.

PILLSBURY'S BEST WHOLE WHEAT FLOUR
The Pillsbury Co.

Ingredients: whole wheat flour.

Amount: 1 cup			% USRDA
Calories	400	Protein	25
Protein, gm	15	Vitamin A	*
Carbohydrates, gm	80	Vitamin C	*
Fat, gm	2	Thiamine	30
Sodium, mg	10	Riboflavin	8
Cholesterol, mg	0	Niacin	25
Fiber, gm	9	Calcium	2
		Iron	20

THIS FOOD: Pillsbury's Best Whole Wheat Flour is naturally rich in protein, complex carbohydrates, fiber, thiamine, niacin, vitamin E, and trace minerals.

ADDITIVES: None.

HELPFUL HINT: When using white flour, it's better to choose the unbleached variety because the bleaching process may sometimes leave chemical residues. Unbleached flour may also contain slightly more vitamin E, but the difference is not nutritionally significant.

FRUIT

An apple a day keeps the doctor away . . . well, maybe. But there's no doubt that fruit is a low-calorie, low-fat food that contains valuable vitamins and dietary fiber. Perhaps most important, fruits contain natural sugars and are a healthful way to satisfy your craving for sweets.

Applesauce is simply a puree of peeled, cooked apples. A four-ounce serving contains about 2½ teaspoons naturally occurring sugar, but best-selling brands, such as Mott's, typically add four teaspoons more. Unsweetened applesauces are the best choice, and are now also available under the Mott and Musselman labels. Yellow-fleshed fruits such as apricots and melons are a good source of vitamin A, and many fruits provide vitamin C. Dried fruits are generally a good source of iron, but should be consumed in moderation since they contain concentrated sugar calories and promote tooth decay. Recent studies suggest that the type of fiber found in fruit, primarily pectins, and gums may be helpful in lowering cholesterol levels.

The most popular manufacturers of canned fruits, Del Monte, Dole, and Libby, all offer fruits packed in their own unsweetened juice. These are a far superior choice to fruits packed in heavy syrups. Compared to canned fruits, the frozen varieties produced by Birds Eye retain significantly more naturally occurring vitamins and minerals.

BIRDS EYE FROZEN STRAWBERRIES IN SYRUP
General Foods Corp.

Ingredients: strawberries, water, sugar.

Amount: ½ cup			% USRDA
Calories	160	Protein	*
Protein, gm	1	Vitamin A	*
Carbohydrates, gm	40	Vitamin C	150
Fat, gm	0	Thiamine	e
Sodium, mg	7	Riboflavin	5
Cholesterol, mg	0	Niacin	3
Fiber, gm	2e	Calcium	*
		Iron	8

THIS FOOD: A serving of Birds Eye Frozen Strawberries in Syrup provides 150 percent of the USRDA for vitamin C. Unfortunately this product, like most other brands, is very high in added sugar: a half-cup serving of frozen berries with syrup contains a whopping five teaspoons of sugar. It would be smart to eat strawberries in this form as a garnish—not a dessert.

ADDITIVES: None.

DEL MONTE BARTLETT PEAR HALVES
R. J. Reynolds Industries, Inc.

Ingredients: pears, water, sugar, corn sweetener.

Amount: ½ cup			% USRDA
Calories	80	Protein	*
Protein, gm	0	Vitamin A	*
Carbohydrates, gm	22	Vitamin C	2
Fat, gm	0	Thiamine	*
Sodium, mg	<10	Riboflavin	*
Cholesterol, mg	0	Niacin	*
Fiber, gm	2	Calcium	*
		Iron	*

THIS FOOD: Provides some valuable dietary fiber, but adds about 1 teaspoon sugar to each serving. Even so, this food is nutritionally superior to most commercially baked and processed desserts, which usually contain huge amounts of empty calories, fat, and additives. It is low in sodium.

ADDITIVES: No questionable additives.

DEL MONTE FRUIT COCKTAIL
R. J. Reynolds Industries, Inc.

Ingredients: diced peaches, water, diced pears, grapes, sugar, pineapple tidbits, corn sweetener, halved cherries artificially colored and flavored.

Amount: ½ cup			% USRDA
Calories	80	Protein	*
Protein, gm	0	Vitamin A	4
Carbohydrates, gm	23	Vitamin C	4
Fat, gm	0	Thiamine	*
Sodium, mg	<10	Riboflavin	*
Cholesterol, mg	0	Niacin	2
Fiber, gm	1e	Calcium	*
		Iron	2

NOTE: The letter "e" indicates that the data has been estimated; < means "less than" and is used for small amounts of sodium or cholesterol; * means food contains less than 2% of USRDA; "na" means that the information was not available and appears only when data is insufficient.

THIS FOOD: Artificial color, flavor, and a hefty dose of sugar detract from the value of Del Monte Fruit Cocktail. Almost any other canned fruit is a better nutritional choice.

ADDITIVES: Contains artificial color and flavor, which some studies suggest may adversely affect behavior and the ability to complete school tasks in some sensitive children; artificial colors are inadequately tested, and artificial flavor may cause allergic reactions in sensitive individuals.

OTHER BRANDS: Libby's Fruit Cocktail also contains artificially colored cherries, but has no artificial flavoring.

DEL MONTE PINEAPPLE CHUNKS IN PINEAPPLE JUICE
R. J. Reynolds Industries, Inc.
Ingredients: pineapple, clarified pineapple juice, sugar.

Amount: ½ cup			% USRDA
Calories	70	Protein	*
Protein, gm	0	Vitamin A	*
Carbohydrates, gm	22	Vitamin C	6
Fat, gm	0	Thiamine	6
Sodium, mg	<10	Riboflavin	*
Cholesterol, mg	0	Niacin	*
Fiber, gm	1	Calcium	*
		Iron	*

THIS FOOD: Del Monte Pineapple Chunks in Pineapple Juice provides small amounts of vitamin C and thiamine. Naturally occurring sugars in this food will satisfy most sweet tooths, without the huge amounts of empty calories, fat, and additives that are present in most processed desserts. Like most canned fruits this product is low in sodium.

ADDITIVES: No questionable additives.

HELPFUL HINT: Always rinse or brush your teeth after eating raisins or prunes. Research has shown that dried fruit, which sticks to your teeth, is one of the most potent causes of tooth decay.

BEST BET: Prunes are a far more healthful snack than raisins. Prunes contain about 65 percent fewer sugar calories, provide more than twice the fiber, and 25 percent of the USRDA for vitamin A per 2-ounce serving.

DEL MONTE SLICED PINEAPPLE IN PINEAPPLE JUICE
R. J. Reynolds Industries, Inc.

Ingredients: pineapple, clarified pineapple juice, sugar.

Amount: ½ cup			% USRDA
Calories	70	Protein	*
Protein, gm	0	Vitamin A	*
Carbohydrates, gm	22	Vitamin C	6
Fat, gm	0	Thiamine	6
Sodium, mg	<10	Riboflavin	*
Cholesterol, mg	0	Niacin	*
Fiber, gm	1	Calcium	*
		Iron	*

THIS FOOD: Naturally occurring sugars in Del Monte Sliced Pineapple in Pineapple Juice will satisfy most sweet tooths, without the huge amounts of empty calories, fat, and additives that are present in most processed desserts.

ADDITIVES: No questionable additives.

OTHER BRANDS: Dole Sliced Pineapple in Pineapple Juice has no added sugar and contains 1 teaspoon less sugar per serving than the Del Monte brand.

DEL MONTE YELLOW CLING PEACH HALVES
R. J. Reynolds Industries, Inc.

Ingredients: Peaches, water, sugar, corn sweetener.

Amount: ½ cup			% USRDA
Calories	50	Protein	*
Protein, gm	0	Vitamin A	6
Carbohydrates, gm	13	Vitamin C	4
Fat, gm	0	Thiamine	*
Sodium, mg	<10	Riboflavin	*
Cholesterol, mg	0	Niacin	4
Fiber, gm	2	Calcium	*
		Iron	*

THIS FOOD: Del Monte Yellow Cling Peach Halves are low in calories and contribute 6 percent of the USRDA for vitamin A. They are packed in syrup, which contributes about 1 teaspoon added sugar to each serving. Even so, this food is nutritionally superior to most commercially baked and processed desserts, which usually contain huge amounts of empty calories, fat, and additives.

ADDITIVES: No questionable additives.

OTHER BRANDS: Libby's Lite Yellow Cling Peaches Packed in Fruit Juice do not contain added sugar—but they are artificially flavored.

DOLE SLICED PINEAPPLE
Castle and Cooke, Inc.

Ingredients: rings cut from pineapple packed in heavy syrup.

Amount: ½ cup			% USRDA
Calories	95	Protein	*
Protein, gm	<1	Vitamin A	*
Carbohydrates, gm	25	Vitamin C	15
Fat, gm	0	Thiamine	7
Sodium, mg	1.5	Riboflavin	2
Cholesterol, mg	0	Niacin	*
Fiber, gm	1	Calcium	*
		Iron	2

THIS FOOD: Dole Sliced Pineapple in heavy syrup contains 1¾ teaspoons more sugar per serving than Dole's Pineapple packed in juice. Both varieties provide 1 gram dietary fiber. Although this product is nutritionally superior to most baked or processed desserts, it contains too much added sugar.

ADDITIVES: No questionable additives.

DOLE SLICED PINEAPPLE IN PINEAPPLE JUICE
Castle and Cooke, Inc.

Ingredients: pineapple, pineapple juice.

Amount: ½ cup			% USRDA
Calories	70	Protein	*
Protein, gm	<1	Vitamin A	*
Carbohydrates, gm	18	Vitamin C	5
Fat, gm	<1	Thiamine	5
Sodium, mg	1	Riboflavin	*
Cholesterol, mg	0	Niacin	*
Fiber, gm	1	Calcium	*
		Iron	2

THIS FOOD: Dole Sliced Pineapple in Pineapple Juice provides dietary fiber and small amounts of vitamin C and thiamine. Naturally occurring sugars in this food will satisfy most sweet tooths, without the huge amounts of empty calories, fat, and additives that are present in most processed desserts and baked goods.

ADDITIVES: None.

LIBBY'S FRUIT COCKTAIL
California Canners and Growers, Inc.

Ingredients: peaches, pears, water, corn syrup, Thompson seedless grapes, pineapple, sugar syrup, cherries artificially colored red.

Amount: ½ cup			% USRDA
Calories	85	Protein	*
Protein, gm	<1	Vitamin A	4
Carbohydrates, gm	23	Vitamin C	4
Fat, gm	0	Thiamine	*
Sodium, mg	<10	Riboflavin	*
Cholesterol, mg	0	Niacin	*
Fiber, gm	1	Calcium	*
		Iron	*

THIS FOOD: Artificial coloring and a hefty dose of sugar detract from the value of Libby's Fruit Cocktail. Almost any other canned fruit is a better nutritional choice.

ADDITIVES: Contains artificial colors, which are inadequately tested and which some studies suggest may adversely affect behavior and the ability to complete school tasks in some sensitive children.

LIBBY'S LITE YELLOW CLING PEACHES PACKED IN FRUIT JUICE
California Canners and Growers, Inc.

Ingredients: yellow cling peaches, fruit juices from concentrates (water, pineapple, apple), artificial flavor.

Amount: ½ cup			% USRDA
Calories	50	Protein	*
Protein, gm	0	Vitamin A	10
Carbohydrates, gm	13	Vitamin C	6
Fat, gm	0	Thiamine	*
Sodium, mg	10	Riboflavin	*
Cholesterol, mg	0	Niacin	2
Fiber, gm	2e	Calcium	*
		Iron	*

THIS FOOD: Libby's Lite Yellow Cling Peaches is low in calories, and contains no added sugar (extra sweetening comes from concentrated fruit juices). It also provides 10 percent of the USRDA for vitamin A.

ADDITIVES: Contains artificial flavor, which may cause allergic reactions in some sensitive individuals, and which some studies suggest may adversely affect behavior and the ability to complete school tasks in some sensitive children.

MOTT'S APPLE SAUCE
Duffy-Mott Co., Inc.

Ingredients: apples, corn sweetener, water.

Amount: ½ cup			% USRDA
Calories	115	Protein	*
Protein, gm	0	Vitamin A	*
Carbohydrates, gm	28	Vitamin C	5
Fat, gm	0	Thiamine	*
Sodium, mg	2	Riboflavin	2
Cholesterol, mg	0	Niacin	*
Fiber, gm	2	Calcium	*
		Iron	*

THIS FOOD: This product provides dietary fiber, but contains far too much sugar. A 4-ounce serving of Mott's Apple Sauce contains more than 4 teaspoons added sugar. Unsweetened applesauce contains about 2½ teaspoons naturally occurring sugar.

ADDITIVES: None.

OTHER BRANDS: Mott's Natural Style Apple Sauce, and Musselman Applesauce, have 50 percent fewer calories and no added sugar.

MOTT'S NATURAL STYLE APPLE SAUCE
Duffy-Mott Co., Inc.

Ingredients: apples, water.

Amount: ½ cup			% USRDA
Calories	50	Protein	*
Protein, gm	0	Vitamin A	*
Carbohydrates, gm	11	Vitamin C	5
Fat, gm	0	Thiamine	*
Sodium, mg	2	Riboflavin	2
Cholesterol, mg	0	Niacin	*
Fiber, gm	2	Calcium	*
		Iron	*

THIS FOOD: Mott's Natural Style Apple Sauce provides some dietary fiber. It contains about 2½ teaspoons of naturally occurring sugar per half-cup serving which should be enough to satisfy most sweet tooths healthfully.

ADDITIVES: None.

MUSSELMAN UNSWEETENED APPLESAUCE
Knouse Foods Cooperative, Inc.

Ingredients: apples, water.

Amount: ½ cup/4 oz			% USRDA
Calories	50	Protein	*
Protein, gm	0	Vitamin A	*
Carbohydrates, gm	13	Vitamin C	*
Fat, gm	0	Thiamine	*
Sodium, mg	0	Riboflavin	*
Cholesterol, mg	0	Niacin	*
Fiber, gm	2	Calcium	*
		Iron	*

THIS FOOD: Musselman Unsweetened Applesauce is a source of dietary fiber. It contains about 2½ teaspoons of naturally occurring sugar per half-cup serving, which should be enough to satisfy most sweet tooths healthfully.

ADDITIVES: None.

OCEAN SPRAY WHOLE BERRY CRANBERRY SAUCE
Ocean Spray Cranberries, Inc.

Ingredients: cranberries, high-fructose corn syrup, corn syrup, water.

Amount: ½ cup			% USRDA
Calories	200	Protein	*
Protein, gm	<1	Vitamin A	*
Carbohydrates, gm	50e	Vitamin C	*
Fat, gm	3.5e	Thiamine	*
Sodium, mg	30	Riboflavin	*
Cholesterol, mg	0	Niacin	*
Fiber, gm	2e	Calcium	*
		Iron	*

Contains 12 teaspoons sugar per serving.

THIS FOOD: Ocean Spray Whole Berry Cranberry Sauce provides some dietary fiber. One hundred percent of calories come from naturally occurring and added sugar.

ADDITIVES: No questionable additives.

NUTRITION TIP: Most of the fiber found in apples is made up of gums and pectins, which are soluble. If eaten regularly, recent studies suggest that this type of fiber may help to lower cholesterol levels.

SUN-MAID NATURAL THOMPSON SEEDLESS RAISINS
Sun-Diamond Growers of California
Ingredients: Thompson seedless raisins.

Amount: approx. ⅓ cup/2 oz			% USRDA
Calories	192	Protein	*
Protein, gm	0	Vitamin A	*
Carbohydrates, gm	46	Vitamin C	2
Fat, gm	0	Thiamine	*
Sodium, mg	>5	Riboflavin	2
Cholesterol, mg	0	Niacin	*
Fiber, gm	4	Calcium	*
		Iron	4
Contains 11 teaspoons sugar.			

THIS FOOD: Raisins are a natural sweet. But don't make the mistake of thinking that if something is natural, it can be eaten in unlimited quantities. While raisins contain valuable fiber and some iron, ounce for ounce they supply as much or more sugar than the average candy bar. Enjoy them occasionally as a candy substitute.

ADDITIVES: None.

SUNSWEET WHOLE PRUNES
Sun-Diamond Growers of California
Ingredients: whole prunes.

Amount: 5 to 6 prunes/approx. 2 oz			% USRDA
Calories	120	Protein	*
Protein, gm	1	Vitamin A	25
Carbohydrates, gm	31	Vitamin C	*
Fat, gm	0	Thiamine	2
Sodium, mg	<10	Riboflavin	4
Cholesterol, mg	0	Niacin	4
Fiber, gm	9	Calcium	2
		Iron	4
Contains 7¾ teaspoons sugar.			

THIS FOOD: Prunes are extremely high in fiber, an excellent source of vitamin A, and also supply small amounts of iron. Even though they are high in naturally occurring sugar, the sugar calories are far from nutritionally "empty." All in all this food can be considered a healthful natural sweet.

ADDITIVES: None.

See "Basic Foods" on pages 551, 552, 555, 556, 558, 559, 561, 562, 563, 564, 566, 567 for fresh fruit listings.

FRUIT DRINKS

Fruit drinks come in many varieties: canned, frozen, and dry mixes. Canned fruit drinks and frozen concentrates must contain 10 percent real fruit juice; only a few popular brands, such as Ocean Spray Cranberry Juice Cocktail, Ocean Spray Pink Grapefruit Juice Cocktail, and Welch's Frozen Cranberry Juice Cocktail, contain more juice than sugar. Obviously, artificially sweetened brands have little or no sugar. Apart from sugar calories, most fruit drinks also supply vitamin C, from fortification; Sunny Delight Florida Citrus Punch also adds vitamins A and D to its formula.

CAPRI SUN FRUIT PUNCH NATURAL FRUIT DRINK
Consolidated Foods, Inc.

Ingredients: water, high-fructose corn sweetener, fruit juices (concentrated orange, pineapple, and lemon juices), citric acid, natural fruit flavors, natural vitamin C.

Amount: 1 container/6¾ fl oz			% USRDA
Calories	102	Protein	*
Protein, gm	0	Vitamin A	*
Carbohydrates, gm	26	Vitamin C	*
Fat, gm	0	Thiamine	*
Sodium, mg	1	Riboflavin	*
Cholesterol, mg	0	Niacin	*
Fiber, gm	0	Calcium	*
		Iron	*

THIS FOOD: Capri Sun Fruit Punch Natural Fruit Drink provides no nutrients at all other than the calories supplied from 6½ teaspoons sugar per serving.

ADDITIVES: No questionable additives.

NOTE: The letter "e" indicates that the data has been estimated; < means "less than" and is used for small amounts of sodium or cholesterol; * means food contains less than 2% of·USRDA; "na" means that the information was not available and appears only when data is insufficient.

CAPRI SUN ORANGE NATURAL FRUIT DRINK
Consolidated Foods, Inc.

Ingredients: water, high-fructose corn sweetener, concentrated orange juice, citric acid, natural orange flavor.

Amount: 1 container/6¾ fl oz			% USRDA
Calories	103	Protein	*
Protein, gm	0	Vitamin A	*
Carbohydrates, gm	26	Vitamin C	*
Fat, gm	0	Thiamine	*
Sodium, mg	2	Riboflavin	*
Cholesterol, mg	0	Niacin	*
Fiber, gm	0	Calcium	*
		Iron	*

THIS FOOD: Capri Sun Orange Natural Fruit Drink provides no nutrients at all other than the calories supplied from 6½ teaspoons sugar per serving.

ADDITIVES: No questionable additives.

HAWAIIAN PUNCH, FRUIT JUICY RED
R. J. Reynolds Industries, Inc.

Ingredients: water, sugar and corn syrups, fruit juices and purees (concentrated pineapple, orange, and grapefruit juices, passion-fruit juice, apricot, papaya, and guava purees), citric acid, natural fruit flavors, vitamin C, dextrin, artificial color, ethyl maltol.

Amount: 6 fl oz			% USRDA
Calories	84	Protein	*
Protein, gm	0	Vitamin A	*
Carbohydrates, gm	21	Vitamin C	100
Fat, gm	0	Thiamine	*
Sodium, mg	na	Riboflavin	*
Cholesterol, mg	0	Niacin	*
Fiber, gm	0	Calcium	*
		Iron	*

THIS FOOD: Hawaiian Punch, Fruit Juicy Red provides over 100 percent of the USRDA for vitamin C, and no other nutrients. A serving contains about 5 teaspoons sugar.

ADDITIVES: Contains artificial colors, which are inadequately tested, and which some studies suggest may adversely affect behavior and the ability to complete school tasks in some sensitive children.

HI-C GRAPE DRINK
The Coca-Cola Co.

Ingredients: water, high-fructose corn syrup, concentrated grape juice, sugar, fumaric, citric, and malic acids, vitamin C, natural flavor, artificial colors.

Amount: 6 fl oz			% USRDA
Calories	100	Protein	*
Protein, gm	0	Vitamin A	*
Carbohydrates, gm	24	Vitamin C	100
Fat, gm	0	Thiamine	*
Sodium, mg	<5e	Riboflavin	*
Cholesterol, mg	0	Niacin	*
Fiber, gm	0	Calcium	*
		Iron	*

THIS FOOD: Hi-C Grape Drink provides 100 percent of the USRDA for vitamin C, and no other nutrients. A serving contains about 5 teaspoons sugar.

ADDITIVES: Contains artificial colors, which are inadequately tested, and which some studies suggest may adversely affect behavior and the ability to complete school tasks in some sensitive children.

MINUTE MAID LEMONADE
The Coca-Cola Co.

Ingredients: sugar, corn sweeteners, water, concentrated lemon juice, lemon pulp, lemon oil.

Amount: 6 fl oz			% USRDA
Calories	75	Protein	*
Protein, gm	0	Vitamin A	*
Carbohydrates, gm	20	Vitamin C	15
Fat, gm	0	Thiamine	*
Sodium, mg	1	Riboflavin	*
Cholesterol, mg	0	Niacin	*
Fiber, gm	0	Calcium	*
		Iron	*

THIS FOOD: A serving of Minute Maid Lemonade supplies 15 percent of the USRDA for vitamin C. Six ounces supply 75 calories, all from 5 teaspoons sugar, most of it added.

ADDITIVES: No questionable additives.

OCEAN SPRAY CRANAPPLE JUICE DRINK
Ocean Spray Cranberries, Inc.

Ingredients: filtered water, cranberry juice, high-fructose corn syrup, apple juice from concentrate, natural apple flavor, fumaric acid, vitamin C.

Amount: 6 fl oz			% USRDA
Calories	130	Protein	*
Protein, gm	0	Vitamin A	*
Carbohydrates, gm	32	Vitamin C	100
Fat, gm	0	Thiamine	*
Sodium, mg	<10	Riboflavin	*
Cholesterol, mg	0	Niacin	*
Fiber, gm	0	Calcium	*
		Iron	*

THIS FOOD: Ocean Spray Cranapple Juice Drink provides 100 percent of the USRDA for vitamin C, and no other nutrients. It is high in calories, all of which derive from simple sugars. A 6-ounce glass of this drink contains about 8 teaspoons sugar, substantially more than any other drink profiled.

ADDITIVES: No questionable additives.

OCEAN SPRAY CRANBERRY JUICE COCKTAIL
Ocean Spray Cranberries, Inc.

Ingredients: filtered water, cranberry juice, high-fructose corn syrup, vitamin C.

Amount: 6 fl oz			% USRDA
Calories	110	Protein	*
Protein, gm	0	Vitamin A	*
Carbohydrates, gm	26	Vitamin C	100
Fat, gm	0	Thiamine	*
Sodium, mg	<10	Riboflavin	*
Cholesterol, mg	0	Niacin	*
Fiber, gm	0	Calcium	*
		Iron	*

THIS FOOD: Ocean Spray Cranberry Juice Cocktail provides 100 percent of the USRDA for vitamin C, and no other nutrients. It contains more than 6 teaspoons sugar per serving.

ADDITIVES: No questionable additives.

OCEAN SPRAY LOW CALORIE CRANBERRY JUICE COCKTAIL
Ocean Spray Cranberries, Inc.

Ingredients: filtered water, cranberry juice, high-fructose corn syrup, vitamin C, calcium saccharin.

Amount: 6 fl oz			% USRDA
Calories	35	Protein	*
Protein, gm	0	Vitamin A	*
Carbohydrates, gm	9	Vitamin C	100
Fat, gm	0	Thiamine	*
Sodium, mg	<10	Riboflavin	*
Cholesterol, mg	0	Niacin	*
Fiber, gm	0	Calcium	*
		Iron	*

THIS FOOD: Ocean Spray Low Calorie Cranberry Juice Cocktail provides 100 percent of the USRDA for vitamin C, and no other nutrients. It contains about 2 teaspoons sugar plus calcium saccharin for added sweetening.

ADDITIVES: Contains calcium saccharin, which causes cancer in laboratory animals. This additive is currently being investigated and should only be used in small amounts by healthy adults.

OCEAN SPRAY PINK GRAPEFRUIT JUICE COCKTAIL
Ocean Spray Cranberries, Inc.

Ingredients: pink grapefruit juice from concentrate, filtered water, high-fructose corn syrup, pectin, citric acid, natural grapefruit flavor, gum arabic, vitamin C, ester gum, canthaxathine (natural color).

Amount: 6 fl oz			% USRDA
Calories	80	Protein	*
Protein, gm	0	Vitamin A	*
Carbohydrates, gm	20	Vitamin C	100
Fat, gm	0	Thiamine	*
Sodium, mg	15	Riboflavin	*
Cholesterol, mg	0	Niacin	*
Fiber, gm	0	Calcium	*
		Iron	*

THIS FOOD: Ocean Spray Pink Grapefruit Juice Cocktail provides 100 percent of the USRDA for vitamin C. Juice is the single largest ingredient in this product—unusual for juice drinks, which by law must contain only 10 percent fruit juice. It contains 5 teaspoons sugar per serving.

ADDITIVES: No questionable additives.

SUNNY DELIGHT FLORIDA CITRUS PUNCH
Doric Foods, Inc.

Ingredients: water, sugar and corn syrups, concentrated orange, tangerine, and lime juices, citric acid, starch, cottonseed oil, algin, sodium citrate, ascorbic acid, natural and artificial flavors, sodium phosphate, FD & C Yellow No. 5, carotene, vitamin B_1, sorbic acid, color.

Amount: 6 fl oz			% USRDA
Calories	90	Protein	*
Protein, gm	0	Vitamin A	20
Carbohydrates, gm	20	Vitamin C	100
Fat, gm	0	Thiamine	20
Sodium, mg	na	Riboflavin	*
Cholesterol, mg	0	Niacin	*
Fiber, gm	0	Calcium	*
		Iron	*

THIS FOOD: Sunny Delight Florida Citrus Punch provides 100 percent of the USRDA for vitamin C and is also fortified with vitamin A and thiamine. It contains about 5 teaspoons sugar per serving and more additives than most other fruit drinks.

ADDITIVES: Contains artificial flavor, which may cause allergic reactions in sensitive individuals, and which some studies suggest may adversely affect behavior and the ability to complete school tasks in some sensitive children. Also contains Yellow No. 5, which can cause allergic reactions, especially in aspirin-sensitive individuals.

BEST BETS: Among the popular juice drinks profiled here, the following do not contain questionable additives: Ocean Spray Pink Grapefruit Juice Cocktail, Ocean Spray Cranapple Juice, Ocean Spray Cranberry Juice Cocktail, Welch's Frozen Cranberry Juice Cocktail, Capri Sun Natural Fruit Drink (Orange and Fruit Punch). Of course all of these products contain added sugar or sweeteners, but Ocean Spray Pink Grapefruit Juice Cocktail contains more juice and less sugar than other canned juice drinks.

DID YOU KNOW: According to federal regulations, fruit drinks must contain only 10 percent fruit juice. They are typically high in added sugar and often contain controversial additives such as artificial color and flavor. Although fruit juices are also high in sugar (albeit natural) they are richer in nutrients and additive free.

WELCHADE FROZEN GRAPE DRINK CONCENTRATE
Welch Foods, Inc.

Ingredients: water, corn sweetener, sugar, concentrated grape juice, citric acid, ascorbic acid, natural and artificial flavors.

Amount: 6 fl oz			% USRDA
Calories	90	Protein	*
Protein, gm	0	Vitamin A	*
Carbohydrates, gm	23	Vitamin C	45
Fat, gm	0	Thiamine	*
Sodium, mg	<10e	Riboflavin	*
Cholesterol, mg	0	Niacin	*
Fiber, gm	0	Calcium	*
		Iron	*

THIS FOOD: Welchade Frozen Grape Drink Concentrate is little more than artificially flavored sugar water. This drink supplies empty calories without any nutrients other than vitamin C, which has been added.

ADDITIVES: Contains artificial flavor, which may cause allergic reactions in sensitive individuals, and which some studies suggest may adversely affect behavior and the ability to complete school tasks in some sensitive children.

WELCH'S FROZEN CRANBERRY JUICE COCKTAIL
Welch Foods, Inc.

Ingredients: cranberry juice concentrate, high-fructose corn syrup, sugar, citric acid, ascorbic acid.

Amount: 6 fl oz			% USRDA
Calories	100	Protein	*
Protein, gm	0	Vitamin A	*
Carbohydrates, gm	26	Vitamin C	45
Fat, gm	0	Thiamine	*
Sodium, mg	<10e	Riboflavin	*
Cholesterol, mg	0	Niacin	*
Fiber, gm	0	Calcium	*
		Iron	*

THIS FOOD: Welch's Frozen Cranberry Juice Cocktail is little more than sugar water. This drink supplies empty calories without any nutrients other than vitamin C, which has been added.

ADDITIVES: No questionable additives.

FRUIT JUICE

Fruit juice, by law, is a relatively pure, natural product, which never contains questionable additives. In order to call their products "juice," manufacturers have to follow detailed federal standards. For example, prune juice must contain not less than 18.5 percent prune solids by weight. None of the popular brands, including Welch's, Tropicana, Sunsweet, and Tree Top, add sugar to the juices profiled— though federal standards do allow sweetening (as long as it is so labeled). Natural sugar content varies widely, from 4 teaspoons sugar per 6-ounce serving for Ocean Spray Grapefruit Juice to about 8 teaspoons sugar per serving for Welch's Grape Juice and Sunsweet Prune Juice. Citrus juices are naturally high in vitamin C, and pineapple, grape, and prune juices may be supplemented with vitamin C (prune juice also contains some riboflavin and iron). The apple juices profiled are not supplemented and are not a good source of naturally occurring vitamins or minerals.

DOLE PINEAPPLE JUICE
Castle and Cooke, Inc.

Ingredients: pineapple juice with added vitamin C.

Amount: 6 fl oz			% USRDA
Calories	103	Protein	*
Protein, gm	.8	Vitamin A	*
Carbohydrates, gm	25	Vitamin C	60
Fat, gm	.2	Thiamine	6
Sodium, mg	2	Riboflavin	2
Cholesterol, mg	0	Niacin	2
Fiber, gm	0	Calcium	3
		Iron	3

THIS FOOD: Dole Pineapple Juice is rich in added vitamin C and provides 103 calories from 6 teaspoons naturally occurring sugar.

ADDITIVES: None.

NOTE: The letter "e" indicates that the data has been estimated; < means "less than" and is used for small amounts of sodium or cholesterol; * means food contains less than 2% of USRDA; "na" means that the information was not available and appears only when data is insufficient.

LUCKY LEAF APPLE JUICE
Knouse Foods Cooperative, Inc.

Ingredients: apple juice.

Amount: 6 fl oz			% USRDA
Calories	90	Protein	*
Protein, gm	0	Vitamin A	*
Carbohydrates, gm	21	Vitamin C	*
Fat, gm	0	Thiamine	*
Sodium, mg	<5	Riboflavin	*
Cholesterol, mg	0	Niacin	*
Fiber, gm	0	Calcium	*
		Iron	*

THIS FOOD: Lucky Leaf Apple Juice is not a significant source of nutrients. A 6-ounce glass supplies 90 calories from 5 teaspoons naturally occurring sugar.

ADDITIVES: None.

MINUTE MAID FROZEN ORANGE JUICE
The Coca-Cola Co.

Ingredients: frozen concentrated orange juice.

Amount: 6 fl oz, diluted			% USRDA
Calories	85	Protein	*
Protein, gm	1	Vitamin A	3
Carbohydrates, gm	20	Vitamin C	122
Fat, gm	<1	Thiamine	10
Sodium, mg	<5	Riboflavin	2
Cholesterol, mg	0	Niacin	2
Fiber, gm	<1	Calcium	*
		Iron	*

THIS FOOD: Like other popular brands, Minute Maid Frozen Orange Juice supplies a whopping 122 percent of the USRDA for vitamin C—without any fortification. Six ounces of juice supply 85 calories, all from 5 teaspoons naturally occurring sugar.

ADDITIVES: None.

MOTT'S APPLE JUICE
Duffy-Mott Co., Inc.

Ingredients: apple juice from concentrate.

Amount: 6 fl oz			% USRDA
Calories	80	Protein	*
Protein, gm	0	Vitamin A	*
Carbohydrates, gm	19	Vitamin C	6
Fat, gm	0	Thiamine	2
Sodium, mg	6	Riboflavin	6
Cholesterol, mg	0	Niacin	*
Fiber, gm	0	Calcium	*
		Iron	2

THIS FOOD: Mott's Apple Juice is not a significant source of nutrients. It supplies 80 calories, all from 5 teaspoons naturally occurring sugar.

ADDITIVES: None.

OCEAN SPRAY GRAPEFRUIT JUICE
Ocean Spray Cranberries, Inc.

Ingredients: grapefruit juice from concentrate.

Amount: 6 fl oz			% USRDA
Calories	70	Protein	*
Protein, gm	1	Vitamin A	*
Carbohydrates, gm	16	Vitamin C	70
Fat, gm	0	Thiamine	*
Sodium, mg	10	Riboflavin	*
Cholesterol, mg	0	Niacin	*
Fiber, gm	0	Calcium	*
		Iron	*

THIS FOOD: Ocean Spray Grapefruit Juice is an excellent source of vitamin C. It supplies 70 calories from 4 teaspoons naturally occurring sugar.

ADDITIVES: None.

HELPFUL HINT: Try diluting 2 or 3 ounces of real juice with water for a healthier alternative to sugary canned juice drinks and additive-laden softdrink mixes. If needed, a small amount of sugar can be added for extra sweetening.

REALEMON BRAND NATURAL STRENGTH LEMON JUICE FROM CONCENTRATE
Borden, Inc.
Ingredients: lemon juice from concentrate.

Amount: 2 tbsp			% USRDA
Calories	6	Protein	*
Protein, gm	0	Vitamin A	*
Carbohydrates, gm	2	Vitamin C	15
Fat, gm	0	Thiamine	*
Sodium, mg	10	Riboflavin	*
Cholesterol, mg	0	Niacin	*
Fiber, gm	0	Calcium	*
		Iron	*

THIS FOOD: Realemon Brand Natural Strength Lemon Juice supplies some vitamin C. Lemon juice may taste sour, but a mere 2 tablespoons contain nearly ½ teaspoon naturally occurring sugar.

ADDITIVES: None.

SENECA FROZEN APPLE JUICE
S. S. Pierce Co.
Ingredients: frozen apple juice concentrate, vitamin C.

Amount: 6 fl oz			% USRDA
Calories	90	Protein	*
Protein, gm	<1	Vitamin A	*
Carbohydrates, gm	22	Vitamin C	60
Fat, gm	<1	Thiamine	*
Sodium, mg	8	Riboflavin	*
Cholesterol, mg	0	Niacin	*
Fiber, gm	0	Calcium	*
		Iron	*

THIS FOOD: Seneca Frozen Apple Juice supplies 60 percent of the USRDA for vitamin C per serving and no-other nutrients. Six ounces of juice supply 90 calories, all from 5½ teaspoons naturally occurring sugar.

ADDITIVES: No questionable additives.

SUNSWEET PRUNE JUICE
Sun Diamond Growers of California
Ingredients: prune juice.

Amount: 6 fl oz			% USRDA
Calories	120	Protein	*
Protein, gm	2	Vitamin A	*
Carbohydrates, gm	33	Vitamin C	15
Fat, gm	0	Thiamine	2
Sodium, mg	<5e	Riboflavin	15
Cholesterol, mg	0	Niacin	6
Fiber, gm	na	Calcium	*
		Iron	10

THIS FOOD: Sunsweet Prune Juice is a good source of vitamin C, riboflavin, and iron. It is relatively high in calories and contains 8 teaspoons naturally occurring sugar per serving. Prune juice helps promote regularity.

ADDITIVES: None.

TREE TOP APPLE JUICE FROM CONCENTRATE
Tree Top, Inc.
Ingredients: pure apple juice from concentrate and pure apple juice.

Amount: 6 fl oz			% USRDA
Calories	88	Protein	*
Protein, gm	0	Vitamin A	*
Carbohydrates, gm	22	Vitamin C	2
Fat, gm	0	Thiamine	2
Sodium, mg	6	Riboflavin	*
Cholesterol, mg	0	Niacin	*
Fiber, gm	0	Calcium	*
		Iron	4

THIS FOOD: Tree Top Apple Juice from Concentrate is not a significant source of nutrients. All of the 88 calories it supplies come from 4½ teaspoons naturally occurring sugar.

ADDITIVES: None.

TREE TOP FROZEN APPLE JUICE CONCENTRATE
Tree Top, Inc.
Ingredients: apple juice concentrate.

Amount: 6 fl oz			% USRDA
Calories	88	Protein	*
Protein, gm	0	Vitamin A	*
Carbohydrates, gm	22	Vitamin C	2
Fat, gm	0	Thiamine	2
Sodium, mg	6	Riboflavin	*
Cholesterol, mg	0	Niacin	*
Fiber, gm	0	Calcium	*
		Iron	4

THIS FOOD: Tree Top Frozen Apple Juice Concentrate is unsupplemented and provides only tiny amounts of vitamin C. Six ounces of juice supply 88 calories, all from 5½ teaspoons naturally occurring sugar.

ADDITIVES: No questionable additives.

TROPICANA ORANGE JUICE
Beatrice Foods Co.
Ingredients: orange juice or orange juice from concentrate.

Amount: 6 fl oz			% USRDA
Calories	90	Protein	*
Protein, gm	1	Vitamin A	8
Carbohydrates, gm	21	Vitamin C	125
Fat, gm	0	Thiamine	8
Sodium, mg	<5	Riboflavin	*
Cholesterol, mg	0	Niacin	*
Fiber, gm	<1	Calcium	*
		Iron	*

THIS FOOD: Orange juice is a terrific source of vitamin C. A 6-ounce glass supplies 90 calories from 5 teaspoons naturally occurring sugar.

ADDITIVES: None.

WELCH'S FROZEN SWEETENED GRAPE JUICE
Welch Foods, Inc.

Ingredients: grape juice and grape juice concentrate, sugar, corn sweetener, citric acid, ascorbic acid (vitamin C).

Amount: 6 fl oz			% USRDA
Calories	100	Protein	*
Protein, gm	0	Vitamin A	*
Carbohydrates, gm	25	Vitamin C	45
Fat, gm	0	Thiamine	*
Sodium, mg	<10	Riboflavin	*
Cholesterol, mg	0	Niacin	*
Fiber, gm	0	Calcium	*
		Iron	*

THIS FOOD: Welch's Frozen Sweetened Grape Juice supplies 45 percent of the USRDA for vitamin C and no other nutrients. A serving supplies 100 calories, all from the 6 teaspoons natural and added sugars it contains.

ADDITIVES: No questionable additives.

WELCH'S PURPLE GRAPE JUICE
Welch Foods, Inc.

Ingredients: grape juice, grape juice from concentrate, ascorbic acid (vitamin C).

Amount: 6 fl oz			% USRDA
Calories	120	Protein	*
Protein, gm	0	Vitamin A	*
Carbohydrates, gm	30	Vitamin C	45
Fat, gm	0	Thiamine	2
Sodium, mg	<10	Riboflavin	2
Cholesterol, mg	0	Niacin	2
Fiber, gm	0	Calcium	*
		Iron	*

THIS FOOD: Welch's Purple Grape Juice provides 45 percent of the USRDA for vitamin C. All of its 120 calories come from 7½ teaspoons naturally occurring sugar.

ADDITIVES: Contains added vitamin C.

WELCH'S RED GRAPE JUICE
Welch Foods, Inc.

Ingredients: grape juice, grape juice from concentrate, ascorbic acid (vitamin C).

Amount: 6 fl oz			% USRDA
Calories	120	Protein	*
Protein, gm	0	Vitamin A	*
Carbohydrates, gm	30	Vitamin C	45
Fat, gm	0	Thiamine	2
Sodium, mg	<10	Riboflavin	*
Cholesterol, mg	0	Niacin	2
Fiber, gm	0	Calcium	2
		Iron	2

THIS FOOD: Welch's Red Grape Juice provides 45 percent of the USRDA for vitamin C. All of its 120 calories come from 7½ teaspoons naturally occurring sugar.

ADDITIVES: Contains added vitamin C.

GELATIN DESSERTS

Gelatin is a protein derived from animal bones and hoofs and used as a thickening agent in desserts. It is a main ingredient in Jell-O, the most popular brand of gelatin dessert. Jell-O, which comes in a huge assortment of fake fruit flavors, supplies sugar calories from 4 teaspoons sugar per half-cup serving. As desserts go, gelatin is a low-fat, low-calorie choice, but Jell-O and other major brands invariably contain artificial colors and/or flavors. Incidentally, the popular myth which holds that gelatin will help fingernails to grow strong is simply an old wives' tale.

JELL-O BRAND CHERRY FLAVOR GELATIN
General Foods Corp.

Ingredients: sugar, gelatin, adipic acid, disodium phosphate, fumaric acid, artificial color, artificial flavor.

Amount: ½ cup			% USRDA
Calories	80	Protein	*
Protein, gm	2	Vitamin A	*
Carbohydrates, gm	19	Vitamin C	*
Fat, gm	0	Thiamine	*
Sodium, mg	50	Riboflavin	*
Cholesterol, mg	0	Niacin	*
Fiber, gm	0	Calcium	*
		Iron	*

THIS FOOD: Packaged gelatin desserts are little more than artificially flavored and colored sugar. Jell-O Brand Orange Flavor Gelatin contains nearly 5 teaspoons sugar per serving.

ADDITIVES: Contains artificial color and flavor, which some studies suggest may adversely affect behavior and the ability to complete school tasks in some sensitive children; artificial colors are inadequately tested, and artificial flavor may cause allergic reactions in sensitive individuals.

JELL-O SUGAR-FREE CHERRY FLAVOR GELATIN
General Foods Corp

Ingredients: gelatin, adipic acid, disodium phosphate, maltodextrin, aspartame (contains phenylalanine), fumaric acid, artificial color, salt, artificial flavor.

Amount: ½ cup			% USRDA
Calories	8	Protein	*
Protein, gm	1	Vitamin A	*
Carbohydrates, gm	0	Vitamin C	*
Fat, gm	0	Thiamine	*
Sodium, mg	80	Riboflavin	*
Cholesterol, mg	0	Niacin	*
Fiber, gm	0	Calcium	*
		Iron	*

THIS FOOD: Like most sugar-free gelatin desserts, Jell-O Sugar-Free Cherry Flavor Gelatin is a totally fake food, artificially colored, flavored, and sweetened. Not surprisingly, it has no real nutritional value.

NOTE: The letter "e" indicates that the data has been estimated; < means "less than" and is used for small amounts of sodium or cholesterol; * means food contains less than 2% of USRDA; "na" means that the information was not available and appears only when data is insufficient.

ADDITIVES: Contains aspartame (with phenylalanine), which should be avoided by people with PKU (a rare genetic disease) and which many experts believe has been inadequately tested for long-term safety. Contains artificial color and flavor, which some studies suggest may adversely affect behavior and the ability to complete school tasks in some sensitive children; artificial colors are inadequately tested and artificial flavor may cause allergic reactions in sensitive individuals.

ROYAL STRAWBERRY-BANANA FLAVOR GELATIN
R. J. Reynolds Industries, Inc.

Ingredients: sugar, gelatin, fumaric acid, sodium citrate, salt, artificial flavor, ascorbic acid, artificial color.

Amount: ½ cup			% USRDA
Calories	80	Protein	*
Protein, gm	2	Vitamin A	*
Carbohydrates, gm	19	Vitamin C	15
Fat, gm	0	Thiamine	*
Sodium, mg	90	Riboflavin	*
Cholesterol, mg	0	Niacin	*
Fiber, gm	0	Calcium	*
		Iron	*

THIS FOOD: Packaged gelatin desserts are little more than artificially flavored and colored sugar. Royal Gelatin brand fortifies its product with 15 percent of the USRDA for vitamin C. One serving contains nearly 5 teaspoons of sugar.

ADDITIVES: Contains artificial color and flavor, which some studies suggest may adversely affect behavior and the ability to complete school tasks in some sensitive children; artificial colors are inadequately tested, and artificial flavor may cause allergic reactions in sensitive individuals.

HELPFUL HINT: Contrary to myth, plain gelatin has no special health properties, but it is still useful in making low-fat, low-calorie desserts. Instead of using additive-laden sugary Jell-Os, make your own gelatin desserts with a packet of plain gelatin and two cups of fruit juice.

GRAVY AND GRAVY MIXES

The FDA requires canned gravy to contain at least 25 percent meat stock or broth or at least 6 percent meat. Franco-American gravies, the most popular brand, are generally high in sodium and fat (except for the mushroom variety, which contains a moderate 36 percent fat calories). Most dry mixes are also high in sodium and fat. All of the gravies profiled contain questionable additives.

SODIUM GUIDELINES: In evaluating the sodium content of gravy and gravy mixes, we used the following standards:

less than 100 mg	moderate in sodium
100 mg to 200 mg	high in sodium
more than 200 mg	very high in sodium

Remember, these guidelines are not for people on medically restricted low-sodium diets, but for healthy individuals who wish to monitor their sodium intake.

FRANCO-AMERICAN CHICKEN GRAVY
Campbell Soup Co.

Ingredients: chicken stock, chicken fat, modified food starch, chicken, yeast extract and hydrolyzed plant protein, wheat flour, salt, water, dried dairy blend (whey, calcium caseinate), margarine (partially hydrogenated soybean oil, water, and beta carotene), whey, monosodium glutamate, cornstarch, soy protein isolate, natural flavoring, and spice.

Amount: ¼ cup			% USRDA
Calories	50	Protein	*
Protein, gm	0	Vitamin A	2
Carbohydrates, gm	3	Vitamin C	*
Fat, gm	4	Thiamine	*
Sodium, mg	320	Riboflavin	*
Cholesterol, mg	8e	Niacin	*
Fiber, gm	0	Calcium	*
		Iron	*

NOTE: The letter "e" indicates that the data has been estimated; < means "less than" and is used for small amounts of sodium or cholesterol; * means food contains less than 2% of USRDA; "na" means that the information was not available and appears only when data is insufficient.

THIS FOOD: Franco-American Chicken Gravy derives 72 percent of its calories from fat. Like most canned gravies, it is very high in sodium.

ADDITIVES: Contains monosodium glutamate (MSG), which many experts believe should be avoided by infants and very young children; causes adverse reactions in some sensitive individuals.

FRANCO-AMERICAN MUSHROOM GRAVY
Campbell Soup Co.

Ingredients: water, mushrooms, wheat flour, modified food starch, partially hydrogenated vegetable oils (soybean or cottonseed oil), salt, yeast extract and hydrolyzed plant protein, caramel color, monosodium glutamate, natural flavoring, and dehydrated garlic.

Amount: ¼ cup			% USRDA
Calories	25	Protein	*
Protein, gm	0	Vitamin A	*
Carbohydrates, gm	3	Vitamin C	*
Fat, gm	1	Thiamine	*
Sodium, mg	320	Riboflavin	*
Cholesterol, mg	8e	Niacin	*
Fiber, gm	<1e	Calcium	*
		Iron	*

THIS FOOD: Compared to most canned gravies, Franco-American Mushroom Gravy is low in fat. Like most other products in this category, it is very high in sodium.

ADDITIVES: Contains monosodium glutamate (MSG), which many experts believe should be avoided by infants and very young children; causes adverse reactions in some sensitive individuals.

FRENCH'S BROWN GRAVY MIX
The R. T. French Co.

Ingredients: cornstarch, whey, salt, natural flavor, beef fat, caramel color, corn syrup, lactic acid, onion, xanthan gum, beet powder, black pepper, citric acid, BHA, propyl gallate.

HELPFUL HINT: To make your own additive-free, low-calorie gravy, thicken chicken stock (or canned chicken broth) with a little cornstarch and season with a dash of Worcestershire.

Amount: ¼ cup, prepared with water			% USRDA
Calories	20	Protein	*
Protein, gm	1	Vitamin A	*
Carbohydrates, gm	3	Vitamin C	*
Fat, gm	1	Thiamine	*
Sodium, mg	280	Riboflavin	*
Cholesterol, mg	<5e	Niacin	*
Fiber, gm	0	Calcium	*
		Iron	*

THIS FOOD: French's Brown Gravy Mix contains 45 percent fat calories and is not a significant source of nutrients. It is very high in sodium.

ADDITIVES: Contains BHA, whose long-term safety is currently being reexamined by FDA investigators.

FRENCH'S MUSHROOM GRAVY MIX
The R. T. French Co.

Ingredients: cornstarch, whey, salt, beef fat, natural flavor, mushroom, caramel color, corn syrup, lactic acid, onion, xanthan gum, beet powder, black pepper, citric acid, BHA, propyl gallate.

Amount: ¼ cup, prepared with water			% USRDA
Calories	20	Protein	*
Protein, gm	1	Vitamin A	*
Carbohydrates, gm	3	Vitamin C	*
Fat, gm	1	Thiamine	*
Sodium, mg	305	Riboflavin	*
Cholesterol, mg	<5e	Niacin	*
Fiber, gm	0	Calcium	*
		Iron	*

THIS FOOD: French's Mushroom Gravy Mix contains 45 percent fat calories and is not a significant source of nutrients. It is very high in sodium.

ADDITIVES: Contains BHA, whose long-term safety is currently being reexamined by FDA investigators.

McCORMICK'S CHICKEN GRAVY MIX
McCormick and Co., Inc.

Ingredients: wheat starch and flour, lactose, salt, monosodium glutamate, yeast solids, blended milk solids, chicken, chicken fat, onion, spice and spice extractives, paprika, FD & C Yellow No. 5 and FD & C Yellow No. 6, disodium inosinate, and guanylate.

Amount: ¼ package			% USRDA
Calories	20	Protein	*
Protein, gm	.71	Vitamin A	*
Carbohydrates, gm	3	Vitamin C	*
Fat, gm	.55	Thiamine	*
Sodium, mg	348	Riboflavin	*
Cholesterol, mg	<5e	Niacin	*
Fiber, gm	0	Calcium	*
		Iron	*

THIS FOOD: McCormick's Chicken Gravy Mix is very high in sodium and does not supply any vitamins or minerals.

ADDITIVES: Contains monosodium glutamate (MSG), which many experts believe should be avoided by infants and very young children; causes adverse reactions in sensitive individuals. Also contains Yellow No. 5, which can cause allergic reactions, especially in aspirin-sensitive individuals; and Yellow No. 6, which is inadequately tested and which some studies suggest may adversely affect behavior and the ability to complete school tasks in some sensitive children.

ICE CREAM AND FROZEN DESSERTS

Since 1972, enough ice cream has been produced in the United States each year to fill the Grand Canyon! Fifteen gallons of the stuff, in every imaginable flavor, color, and shape, are consumed by the average American each year. Obviously ice cream is high in sugar and saturated fat. But compared to other desserts, such as rich cakes or pies, it is far from a nutritional disaster. Because of its milk or cream content, it provides calcium, riboflavin, and protein in varying amounts. Unfortunately it's almost impossible for consumers to make an informed choice, since very few manufacturers supply nutrition labeling. Calorie count, fat content, and vitamins and minerals supplied by different brands vary widely. For instance, among the samples we profiled, Louis Sherry Vanilla Ice Cream, with 130 calories per half-cup serving, has about one third the fat of Häagen-Dazs Coffee Ice Cream, which contains 273 calories per serving. Yet there is a trade-off involved, since the richer confection is also significantly higher in protein, vitamin A, riboflavin, and calcium. The ingredients used in different ice creams also vary widely. Some brands, such as Meadow Gold and Knudsen Party Time, contain a host of additives, some of them controversial, and no cream at all (the 10 percent butterfat required by federal standards is supplied by milk). In contrast, the ingredients list in Häagen-Dazs and other expensive premium brands reads exactly like a home recipe.

FROZFRUIT, PINEAPPLE
The Frozfruit Corp.

Ingredients: pineapple, water, fructose, sucrose, natural vegetable stabilizers (cellulose gum, guar gum, carrageenan), turmeric.

Amount: 1 bar/4 oz			% USRDA
Calories	68	Protein	*
Protein, gm	<1	Vitamin A	*
Carbohydrates, gm	17	Vitamin C	12
Fat, gm	0	Thiamine	2
Sodium, mg	<10e	Riboflavin	*
Cholesterol, mg	0	Niacin	*
Fiber, gm	<1	Calcium	*
		Iron	*
Contains 4 teaspoons natural and added sugar.			

THIS FOOD: Pineapple Frozfruit—which basically consists of frozen fruit with added sugar on a stick—is a relatively healthful frozen dessert bar. This product is low in calories and a good source of vitamin C.

ADDITIVES: No questionable additives.

GOOD HUMOR CHOCOLATE ECLAIR
Unilever United States, Inc.

Ingredients: *Ice cream:* milkfat and nonfat milk, sugar, corn syrup, whey, vanilla extract, mono- and diglycerides, guar gum, locust bean gum, calcium carrageenan, fudge (water, corn syrup, sugar, cocoa, guar gum, locust bean gum, carrageenan). *Cake crunch coating:* enriched bleached flour, sugar, vegetable shortening (partially hydrogenated soybean, palm, cottonseed, hydrogenated palm), corn syrup, salt, baking soda, lecithin, artificial flavor, vegetable oil (coconut, corn, peanut and/or soybean), sugar, cocoa.

NOTE: The letter "e" indicates that the data has been estimated; < means "less than" and is used for small amounts of sodium or cholesterol; * means food contains less than 2% of USRDA; "na" means that the information was not available and appears only when data is insufficient.

Amount: 1 bar/3 oz			% USRDA
Calories	220	Protein	2
Protein, gm	1	Vitamin A	*
Carbohydrates, gm	25	Vitamin C	*
Fat, gm	13	Thiamine	*
Sodium, mg	na	Riboflavin	2
Cholesterol, mg	25e	Niacin	*
Fiber, gm	0	Calcium	2
		Iron	*

THIS FOOD: A Good Humor Chocolate Eclair is not a significant source of nutrients. It is high in calories, saturated fat, and overall fat, which accounts for 53 percent of calories.

ADDITIVES: Contains artificial flavor, which may cause allergic reactions in sensitive individuals, and which some studies suggest may adversely affect behavior and the ability to complete school tasks in some sensitive children.

GOOD HUMOR ICE CREAM SANDWICH
Unilever United States, Inc.

Ingredients: *Ice cream:* milkfat and nonfat milk, sugar, corn syrup, whey, vanilla extract, mono- and diglycerides, guar gum, locust bean gum, calcium carrageenan. *Wafer:* enriched bleached flour, sugar, vegetable shortening (partially hydrogenated soybean, palm, cottonseed, hydrogenated palm), corn syrup, artificial color, cocoa, baking soda, salt, lecithin, artificial flavors.

Amount: 1 sandwich/2½ oz			% USRDA
Calories	200	Protein	4
Protein, gm	3	Vitamin A	*
Carbohydrates, gm	34	Vitamin C	*
Fat, gm	6	Thiamine	*
Sodium, mg	92e	Riboflavin	6
Cholesterol, mg	15e	Niacin	*
Fiber, gm	0	Calcium	6
		Iron	*

THIS FOOD: A Good Humor Ice Cream Sandwich is not a significant source of nutrients. With 27 percent fat calories, it is relatively low in fat. This product contains a moderate amount of sodium.

ADDITIVES: Contains artificial color and flavor, which some studies suggest may adversely affect behavior and the ability to complete school tasks in some sensitive children; artificial colors are inadequately tested, and artificial flavor may cause allergic reactions in sensitive individuals.

HÄAGEN-DAZS COFFEE ICE CREAM
The Pillsbury Co.

Ingredients: fresh cream, skim milk, cane sugar, yolk of egg, pure coffee.

Amount: ½ cup			% USRDA
Calories	273	Protein	13
Protein, gm	6	Vitamin A	10
Carbohydrates, gm	24	Vitamin C	*
Fat, gm	17	Thiamine	4
Sodium, mg	50e	Riboflavin	16
Cholesterol, mg	50e	Niacin	*
Fiber, gm	0	Calcium	18
		Iron	*

THIS FOOD: Because Häagen-Dazs, a premium brand, whips less air into its product than most other manufacturers, the ice cream is denser. It has significantly more nutrients—and fat and calories—than the other profiled brands. A serving of coffee ice cream is a good source of protein, calcium, and riboflavin and a fair source of vitamin A. This product is high in calories, 56 percent of which derive from fat. It contains no added salt.

ADDITIVES: No questionable additives.

JELL-O BANANA FLAVOR PUDDING POPS
General Foods Corp.

Ingredients: skim milk (vitamin A added), sugar, water, nonfat dry milk, hydrogenated coconut and palm kernel oils, corn syrup, modified tapioca starch, dextrin (from tapioca), sodium caseinate, dextrose, salt, sodium stearoyl lactylate and polysorbate 60, microcrystalline cellulose, sorbitan monostearate, xanthan gum and carrageenan, artificial flavor, cellulose gum and guar gum, artificial color, including FD & C Yellow No. 5.

Amount: 1 bar			% USRDA
Calories	90	Protein	6
Protein, gm	2	Vitamin A	*
Carbohydrates, gm	16	Vitamin C	*
Fat, gm	3	Thiamine	*
Sodium, mg	65	Riboflavin	6
Cholesterol, mg	<10e	Niacin	*
Fiber, gm	0	Calcium	8
		Iron	*

THIS FOOD: Because the single largest ingredient in a Jell-O Pudding Pop is skim milk, it supplies 8 percent of the USRDA for calcium. Like almost all prepared desserts, it is high in sugar. About 30 percent of the calories in this product derive from fat, most of it saturated.

ADDITIVES: Contains artificial color and flavor, which some studies suggest may adversely affect behavior and the ability to complete school tasks in some sensitive children; artificial colors are inadequately tested, and artificial flavor may cause allergic reactions in sensitive individuals. Also contains Yellow No. 5, which can cause allergic reactions, especially in aspirin-sensitive individuals.

JELL-O CHOCOLATE FLAVOR PUDDING POPS
General Foods Corp.

Ingredients: skim milk (vitamin A added), sugar, water, nonfat dry milk, hydrogenated coconut and palm kernel oils, cocoa processed with alkali, corn syrup, modified tapioca starch, dextrin (from tapioca), sodium caseinate, salt, artificial flavor, dextrose, sodium stearoyl lactylate and polysorbate 60, microcrystalline cellulose, sorbitan monostearate, xanthan gum, carrageenan, cellulose gum and guar gum.

Amount: 1 bar			% USRDA
Calories	100	Protein	6
Protein, gm	3	Vitamin A	*
Carbohydrates, gm	16	Vitamin C	*
Fat, gm	3	Thiamine	*
Sodium, mg	100	Riboflavin	6
Cholesterol, mg	<5e	Niacin	*
Fiber, gm	0	Calcium	8
		Iron	*

THIS FOOD: Because the single largest ingredient in a Jell-O Pudding Pop is skim milk, it supplies 8 percent of the USRDA for calcium. Like almost all prepared desserts, it is high in sugar. About 30 percent of the calories in this product derive from fat, most of it saturated.

ADDITIVES: Contains artificial flavor, which some studies suggest may adversely affect behavior and the ability to complete school tasks in some sensitive children; artificial flavor may cause allergic reactions in sensitive individuals.

BEST BET: Louis Sherry Vanilla Ice Cream contains about a third of the fat of Häagen-Dazs, and is relatively low in calories yet still supplies a significant amount of calcium and riboflavin. It contains no questionable additives.

KNUDSEN PARTY TIME VANILLA ICE CREAM
Knudsen Corp.

Ingredients: milk and nonfat milk, buttermilk, sugar, corn sweeteners, whey, artificial flavor, cellulose gum, locust bean gum, vegetable mono- and di-glycerides, polysorbate 80, artificial color, carrageenan.

Amount: ½ cup			% USRDA
Calories	122	Protein	4
Protein, gm	2	Vitamin A	3
Carbohydrates, gm	14	Vitamin C	*
Fat, gm	6	Thiamine	*
Sodium, mg	50	Riboflavin	7
Cholesterol, mg	30e	Niacin	*
Fiber, gm	0	Calcium	7
		Iron	*

THIS FOOD: Knudsen Party Time Vanilla Ice Cream is not a significant source of nutrients. It is fairly low in calories, 44 percent of which derive from fat. Like most ice creams, this product is low in sodium.

ADDITIVES: Contains artificial color and flavor, which some studies suggest may adversely affect behavior and the ability to complete school tasks in some sensitive children; artificial colors are inadequately tested, and artificial flavors may cause allergic reactions in sensitive individuals.

LOUIS SHERRY VANILLA ICE CREAM
Atlantic Processing, Inc.

Ingredients: milk, cream, nonfat milk, sugar, corn sweetener, vanilla, guar gum, locust bean gum, and carrageenan.

Amount: ½ cup			% USRDA
Calories	130	Protein	6
Proteins, gm	3	Vitamin A	6
Carbohydrates, gm	16	Vitamin C	*
Fat, gm	6	Thiamine	2
Sodium, mg	56	Riboflavin	10
Cholesterol, mg	30e	Niacin	*
Fiber, gm	0	Calcium	10
		Iron	*

THIS FOOD: Louis Sherry Vanilla Ice Cream is a fair source of calcium and riboflavin. It is relatively low in calories, 41 percent of which derive from fat. Like most ice creams, this product is low in sodium.

ADDITIVES: No questionable additives.

MEADOW GOLD BUTTER PECAN ICE CREAM
Beatrice Foods Co.

Ingredients: milkfat and nonfat milk, corn sweeteners, sugar, roasted salted pecans, whey, mono- and diglycerides, guar gum, calcium sulfate, carob bean gum, polysorbate 80, carrageenan, natural flavor, and artificial color.

Amount: ½ cup			% USRDA
Calories	150	Protein	4
Protein, gm	2	Vitamin A	6
Carbohydrates, gm	16	Vitamin C	*
Fat, gm	9	Thiamine	2
Sodium, mg	50e	Riboflavin	10
Cholesterol, mg	30e	Niacin	*
Fiber, gm	0	Calcium	10
		Iron	*

THIS FOOD: Meadow Gold Butter Pecan Ice Cream is relatively low in calories, 54 percent of which derive from fat. It is a fair source of riboflavin and calcium.

ADDITIVES: Contains artificial colors, which are inadequately tested, and which some studies suggest may adversely affect behavior and the ability to complete school tasks in some sensitive children.

MEADOW GOLD FRENCH VANILLA ICE CREAM
Beatrice Foods Co.

Ingredients: milkfat and nonfat milk, corn sweeteners, sugar, whey, egg yolks, mono- and diglycerides, guar gum, calcium sulfate, carob bean gum, polysorbate 80, carrageenan, vanilla extract, and artificial color.

Amount: ½ cup			% USRDA
Calories	140	Protein	6
Protein, gm	2	Vitamin A	6
Carbohydrates, gm	16	Vitamin C	*
Fat, gm	7	Thiamine	2
Sodium, mg	50e	Riboflavin	10
Cholesterol, mg	40e	Niacin	*
Fiber, gm	0	Calcium	10
		Iron	*

THIS FOOD: Meadow Gold French Vanilla Ice Cream is relatively low in calories, 45 percent of which come from fat. It is a fair source of calcium and riboflavin.

ADDITIVES: Contains artificial colors, which are inadequately tested, and which some studies suggest may adversely affect behavior and the ability to complete school tasks in some sensitive children.

SCHRAFFT'S CHOCOLATE ICE CREAM
Schrafft's Ice Cream Co.

Ingredients: cream, milk, chocolate liquor, natural vanilla, carob bean, guar, lecithin.

Amount: ½ cup			% USRDA
Calories	205	Protein	5
Protein, gm	3	Vitamin A	9e
Carbohydrates, gm	15	Vitamin C	*
Fat, gm	13	Thiamine	*
Sodium, mg	54e	Riboflavin	8e
Cholesterol, mg	40e	Niacin	*
Fiber, gm	0	Calcium	8e
		Iron	*

THIS FOOD: Schrafft's Chocolate Ice Cream is high in calories and overall fat, which contributes 57 percent of calories. It is not a significant source of nutrients.

ADDITIVES: No questionable additives.

TUSCAN POPS LOWFAT CHOCOLATE FROZEN YOGURT
Tuscan Foods, Inc.

Ingredients: *Yogurt:* cultured pasturized milk, cane sugar, skim milk, water, fructose, corn syrup solids, cocoa, enzyme-modified soy protein, microcrystalline cellulose, mono- and diglycerides, carob gum, carrageenan. *Coating:* coconut oil, chocolate liquor, sugar, nonfat dry milk, soya lecithin, natural vanilla flavor.

Amount: 1 bar			% USRDA
Calories	150	Protein	6
Protein, gm	2	Vitamin A	*
Carbohydrates, gm	17	Vitamin C	*
Fat, gm	8	Thiamine	*
Sodium, mg	65	Riboflavin	6
Cholesterol, mg	na	Niacin	4
Fiber, gm	0e	Calcium	20
		Iron	*

THIS FOOD: Tuscan Pops Lowfat Chocolate Frozen Yogurt contains 48 percent fat calories and is no lower in fat than many ice cream bars. Nevertheless, compared to many desserts and sweet snack foods, this product is a good choice. It is a good source of calcium and fairly low in calories.

ADDITIVES: No questionable additives.

INSTANT BREAKFASTS AND DIET BARS

Instant breakfast drinks and diet bars supply a range of vitamins and minerals from supplementation, but they are still a far cry from being a balanced meal. The popular Carnation Breakfast Bars profiled are much more nutritious than granola bars, but their primary ingredient is still sugar and about 50 percent of their calories come from fat. Carnation Instant Breakfast is really a milk flavoring with vitamins and minerals. It is low in fat, but high in sugar. The vanilla flavor, for example, contains a full 6 teaspoons of sugar.

CARNATION CHOCOLATE BREAKFAST BAR
Carnation Co.

Ingredients: sugar, partially hydrogenated vegetable oil (cottonseed, soybean, palm), chocolate, calcium caseinate, flour, soy protein isolate, dried corn syrup, peanuts, glycerin, water, cocoa, nonfat milk, salt, sodium ascorbate, magnesium hydroxide, lecithin, artificial flavors, sodium stearoyl-2-lactylate, monosodium glutamate, polysorbate 60, sorbitan monoste.

Amount: 1 bar			% USRDA
Calories	200	Protein	10
Protein, gm	6	Vitamin A	35
Carbohydrates, gm	20	Vitamin C	45
Fat, gm	11	Thiamine	20
Sodium, mg	180	Riboflavin	2
Cholesterol, mg	<1	Niacin	25
Fiber, gm	<1e	Calcium	2
		Iron	25

Contains 3 teaspoons sugar and 2 teaspoons fat.

THIS FOOD: Carnation Breakfast Bars could be described as vitamins and iron mixed with sugar and saturated fat. The vitamins are important, to be sure, and the bar does provide some protein, but it contains too many fat calories—50 percent of total—to be considered a well-balanced meal. On the other hand, because of the supplementation, it's a lot more nutritious than most candy bars or granola bars.

NOTE: The letter "e" indicates that the data has been estimated; < means "less than" and is used for small amounts of sodium or cholesterol; * means food contains less than 2% of USRDA; "na" means that the information was not available and appears only when data is insufficient.

ADDITIVES: Contains artificial flavor, which may cause allergic reactions in sensitive individuals, and which some studies suggest may adversely affect behavior and the ability to complete school tasks in some sensitive children; and monosodium glutamate (MSG), which many experts believe should be avoided by infants and very young children; causes adverse reactions in sensitive individuals.

CARNATION HONEY NUT BREAKFAST BAR
Carnation Co.

Ingredients: sugar, partially hydrogenated vegetable oil (cottonseed soybean, palm), soy protein isolate, almonds, peanuts, clover honey, dried corn syrup, flour, calcium caseinate, toasted oats (rolled oats, brown sugar, honey, coconut oil), glycerin, cocoa, nonfat milk and high-fructose corn syrup, sodium ascorbate, salt, magnesium hydroxide, sodium stearoyl-2-lactylate, artificial flavors, lecithin, polysorbate 60, sorbitan monostearate, ferrous fumarate, vitamin E, niacinamide, zinc ozide, copper gluconate, vitamin A palmitate, calcium pantothenate, thiamine mononitrate, pyridoxine hydrochloride, folic acid, vitamin B_{12}.

Amount: 1 bar			% USRDA
Calories	190	Protein	10
Protein, gm	6	Vitamin A	35
Carbohydrates, gm	18	Vitamin C	45
Fat, gm	11	Thiamine	20
Sodium, mg	155	Riboflavin	2
Cholesterol, mg	<1	Niacin	25
Fiber, gm	<1e	Calcium	2
		Iron	25
Contains 3 teaspoons sugar and 2 teaspoons fat.			

THIS FOOD: Carnation Breakfast Bars could be described as vitamins and iron mixed with sugar and saturated fat. The vitamins are important, to be sure, and the bar does provide some protein, but it contains too many fat calories—52 percent of total—to be considered a well-balanced meal. On the other hand, because of the supplementation, it's a lot more nutritious than most candy bars or granola bars.

ADDITIVES: Contains artificial flavor, which may cause allergic reactions in sensitive individuals, and which some studies suggest may adversely affect behavior and the ability to complete school tasks in some sensitive children.

CARNATION VANILLA INSTANT BREAKFAST
Carnation Co.

Ingredients: nonfat dry milk, sugar, sweet dairy whey, corn syrup solids, calcium caseinate, lactose, magnesium hydroxide, carrageenan, artificial vanilla flavors, sodium ascorbate, ferric orthophosphate, vitamin E acetate, vitamin A palmitate, niacinamide, copper gluconate, zinc oxide, calcium pantothenate, thiamine mononitrate, pyridoxine hydrochloride, folic acid.

Amount: 1 packet (+ 1 cup milk)			% USRDA
Calories	280	Protein	35
Protein, gm	15	Vitamin A	40
Carbohydrates, gm	35	Vitamin C	50
Fat, gm	8	Thiamine	25
Sodium, mg	257	Riboflavin	30
Cholesterol, mg	38	Niacin	25
Fiber, gm	0	Calcium	40
		Iron	25

THIS FOOD: Carnation Vanilla Instant Breakfast is really a milk supplement which supplies a wide range of important vitamins and minerals. Unfortunately the mix adds a full 6 teaspoons of sugar to the 1½ teaspoons naturally occurring in the milk. What you end up with is *very* sweet milk and a vitamin pill.

ADDITIVES: Contains artificial vanilla flavors, which may cause allergic reactions in sensitive individuals, and which some studies suggest may adversely affect behavior and the ability to complete school tasks in some sensitive children.

JAMS, JELLIES, AND PRESERVES

All of the calories in these products come from sugar. According to federal law, the fruit ingredient must weigh 45 percent of the total, while the sweetening may weigh up to 55 percent. It isn't obvious from most labels that there is more sugar than fruit, since major manufacturers like Smucker's and Kraft often list two or three different forms of sweetener. For instance, strawberries are listed first on the label of Kraft Strawberry Preserves even though, collectively, there is more sugar in the form of corn syrup, sugar, and high-fructose corn syrup. Artificially sweetened jams and jellies are also available and Smucker's has also introduced fruit spreads, which contain about half the sugar of the standard commercial recipes. To compensate for the missing sugar (which also acts as a preservative), these products also contain potassium sorbate, a preservative regarded as safe by consumer health advocates.

KRAFT STRAWBERRY PRESERVES
Kraft, Inc.

Ingredients: strawberries, corn syrup, sugar, high-fructose corn syrup, citric acid, fruit pectin.

Amount: 2 tsp			% USRDA
Calories	32	Protein	*
Protein, gm	0	Vitamin A	*
Carbohydrates, gm	8	Vitamin C	*
Fat, gm	0	Thiamine	*
Sodium, mg	0	Riboflavin	*
Cholesterol, mg	0	Niacin	*
Fiber, gm	<1e	Calcium	*
		Iron	*

THIS FOOD: All of the calories in this product come from sugar.

ADDITIVES: No questionable additives.

SMUCKER'S BLACKBERRY SPREAD
The J. M. Smucker Co.

Ingredients: blackberries, sugar, water, pectin, citric acid, potassium sorbate.

Amount: 2 tsp			% USRDA
Calories	16	Protein	*
Protein, gm	0	Vitamin A	*
Carbohydrates, gm	4	Vitamin C	*
Fat, gm	0	Thiamine	*
Sodium, mg	<10	Riboflavin	*
Cholesterol, mg	0	Niacin	*
Fiber, gm	<1e	Calcium	*
		Iron	*

THIS FOOD: This product has about half the sugar calories of regular jams and jellies.

ADDITIVES: No questionable additives.

NOTE: The letter "e" indicates that the data has been estimated; < means "less than" and is used for small amounts of sodium or cholesterol; * means food contains less than 2% of USRDA; "na" means that the information was not available and appears only when data is insufficient.

SMUCKER'S CONCORD GRAPE JELLY
The J. M. Smucker Co.

Ingredients: concord grape juice, high-fructose corn syrup, corn syrup, pectin, citric acid.

Amount: 2 tsp			% USRDA
Calories	35	Protein	*
Protein, gm	0	Vitamin A	*
Carbohydrates, gm	9	Vitamin C	*
Fat, gm	0	Thiamine	*
Sodium, mg	<10	Riboflavin	*
Cholesterol, mg	0	Niacin	*
Fiber, gm	<1e	Calcium	*
		Iron	*

THIS FOOD: All of the calories in this product come from sugar.

ADDITIVES: No questionable additives.

SMUCKER'S IMITATION GRAPE JELLY
The J. M. Smucker Co.

Ingredients: grape juice, water, carrageenan, natural flavor, citric acid, potassium sorbate, sodium saccharin.

Amount: 2 tsp			% USRDA
Calories	4	Protein	*
Protein, gm	0	Vitamin A	*
Carbohydrates, gm	1	Vitamin C	*
Fat, gm	0	Thiamine	*
Sodium, mg	<10	Riboflavin	*
Cholesterol, mg	0	Niacin	*
Fiber, gm	<1e	Calcium	*
		Iron	*

THIS FOOD: This artificially sweetened jelly still contains sugar calories from grape juice, which is the single largest ingredient. It does not provide any vitamins or minerals.

ADDITIVES: Contains sodium saccharin, which causes cancer in laboratory animals. This additive is currently being investigated and should only be used in small amounts by healthy adults.

SMUCKER'S ORANGE MARMALADE
The J. M. Smucker Co.

Ingredients: corn syrup, high-fructose corn syrup, orange peel, orange juice, fruit pectin, citric acid, natural orange flavor.

Amount: 2 tsp			% USRDA
Calories	35	Protein	*
Protein, gm	0	Vitamin A	*
Carbohydrates, gm	9	Vitamin C	*
Fat, gm	0	Thiamine	*
Sodium, mg	<10	Riboflavin	*
Cholesterol, mg	0	Niacin	*
Fiber, gm	<1e	Calcium	*
		Iron	*

THIS FOOD: All of the calories in this product come from sugar.

ADDITIVES: No questionable additives.

SMUCKER'S RASPBERRY PRESERVES
The J. M. Smucker Co.

Ingredients: red raspberries, high-fructose corn syrup, corn syrup, pectin, citric acid.

Amount: 2 tsp			% USRDA
Calories	35	Protein	*
Protein, gm	0	Vitamin A	*
Carbohydrates, gm	9	Vitamin C	*
Fat, gm	0	Thiamine	*
Sodium, mg	<10	Riboflavin	*
Cholesterol, mg	0	Niacin	*
Fiber, gm	<1e	Calcium	*
		Iron	*

THIS FOOD: All of the calories in this product come from sugar.

ADDITIVES: No questionable additives.

SMUCKER'S STRAWBERRY JAM
The J. M. Smucker Co.

Ingredients: strawberries, high-fructose corn syrup, corn syrup, sugar, pectin, citric acid.

Amount: 2 tsp			% USRDA
Calories	35	Protein	*
Protein, gm	0	Vitamin A	*
Carbohydrates, gm	9	Vitamin C	*
Fat, gm	0	Thiamine	*
Sodium, mg	<10	Riboflavin	*
Cholesterol, mg	0	Niacin	*
Fiber, gm	<1e	Calcium	*
		Iron	*

THIS FOOD: All of the calories in this product come from sugar.

ADDITIVES: No questionable additives.

WELCH'S GRAPE JAM
Welch Foods, Inc.

Ingredients: grapes, corn syrup, high-fructose corn syrup, sugar, fruit pectin, citric acid.

Amount: 2 tsp			% USRDA
Calories	35	Protein	*
Protein, gm	0	Vitamin A	*
Carbohydrates, gm	9	Vitamin C	*
Fat, gm	0	Thiamine	*
Sodium, mg	na	Riboflavin	*
Cholesterol, mg	0	Niacin	*
Fiber, gm	<1e	Calcium	*
		Iron	*

THIS FOOD: All of the calories in this product come from sugar.

ADDITIVES: No questionable additives.

BEST BET: Try Smucker's Fruit Spreads or Welch's Lite Fruit Spreads, which contain half the sugar calories of regular jellies and jams without artificial sweeteners.

WELCH'S GRAPE JELLY
Welch Foods, Inc.

Ingredients: grapes, corn syrup, high-fructose corn syrup, sugar, fruit pectin, citric acid.

Amount: 2 tsp			% USRDA
Calories	35	Protein	*
Protein, gm	0	Vitamin A	*
Carbohydrates, gm	9	Vitamin C	*
Fat, gm	0	Thiamine	*
Sodium, mg	na	Riboflavin	*
Cholesterol, mg	0	Niacin	*
Fiber, gm	<1e	Calcium	*
		Iron	*

THIS FOOD: All of the calories in Welch's Grape Jelly derive from sugar. This product does not supply any vitamins or minerals.

ADDITIVES: No questionable additives.

KETCHUP

Ketchup is the ultimate American condiment. While not too many Americans share Richard Nixon's passion for cottage cheese with ketchup (the former president's favorite lunch), hamburgers without ketchup are utterly unthinkable. Del Monte and Heinz produce the best-selling brands, and both list tomatoes as the main ingredient. There is no way for consumers to figure out that these products are one-third sugar by volume. All popular ketchups are high in sodium. A low-sodium variety is available from Heinz, which also contains about half the sugar in the standard item.

NOTE: The letter "e" indicates that the data has been estimated; < means "less than" and is used for small amounts of sodium or cholesterol; * means food contains less than 2% of USRDA; "na" means that the information was not available and appears only when data is insufficient.

DEL MONTE TOMATO CATSUP
R. J. Reynolds Industries, Inc.

Ingredients: tomatoes, corn sweetener, vinegar, salt, natural flavorings.

Amount: 1 tbsp			% USRDA
Calories	15	Protein	*
Protein, gm	<1	Vitamin A	3
Carbohydrates, gm	4	Vitamin C	4
Fat, gm	0	Thiamine	*
Sodium, mg	169	Riboflavin	*
Cholesterol, mg	0	Niacin	*
Fiber, gm	<1e	Calcium	*
		Iron	*
Contains 1 teaspoon sugar.			

THIS FOOD: Del Monte Tomato Catsup is high in sodium and is one-third sugar by volume.

ADDITIVES: No questionable additives.

HEINZ KETCHUP
H. J. Heinz Co.

Ingredients: red ripe tomatoes, distilled vinegar, corn sweetener, salt, onion powder, spice, natural flavoring.

Amount: 1 tbsp			% USRDA
Calories	18	Protein	*e
Protein, gm	<1	Vitamin A	4e
Carbohydrates, gm	4	Vitamin C	4e
Fat, gm	<1	Thiamine	*e
Sodium, mg	180	Riboflavin	*e
Cholesterol, mg	0	Niacin	*e
Fiber, gm	<1e	Calcium	*
		Iron	*
Contains 1 teaspoon sugar.			

THIS FOOD: Heinz Ketchup is high in sodium and is one-third sugar by volume.

ADDITIVES: No questionable additives.

HEINZ LOW SODIUM LITE KETCHUP
H. J. Heinz Co.

Ingredients: red ripe tomatoes, distilled vinegar, corn sweetener, salt, onion powder, spice, natural flavoring.

Amount: 1 tbsp			% USRDA
Calories	8	Protein	*e
Protein, gm	<1	Vitamin A	4e
Carbohydrates, gm	2	Vitamin C	4e
Fat, gm	<1	Thiamine	*e
Sodium, mg	90	Riboflavin	*e
Cholesterol, mg	0	Niacin	*e
Fiber, gm	<1e	Calcium	*
		Iron	*

Contains ½ teaspoons sugar.

THIS FOOD: Heinz Low Sodium Lite Ketchup contains half the sugar and salt of most regular ketchups. According to FDA sodium labeling regulations, this product can be called "low-sodium" because it has less than 140 mg sodium per serving. But we consider this product moderate in sodium, rather than low, since ketchup is only a condiment. Anyone using this product on a sodium-restricted diet would have to watch his or her other food choices carefully. As of this writing, there is no official definition of *lite*.

ADDITIVES: No questionable additives.

MAIN DISHES AND DINNERS

Prepared main dishes and frozen dinners are quintessential convenience foods. All consumers have to do is pop an aluminum tray in the oven, or open a can, heat, and serve. The enormous popularity of these foods is hardly surprising. More people are living alone than ever before, and more married women work, leaving less time for shopping and food preparation. TV dinners, already popular in the fifties, have come of age along with the postwar generation. The fastest-growing product lines, such as Armour Lite Dinners, Le Menu Dinners, and Stouffer Entrées, are all upscale and make their appeal to more sophisticated, health- (and calorie-) conscious consumers. There is nothing wrong with eating these foods now and then.

In fact, increased and more imaginative use of vegetables, more fish, and leaner cuts of chicken and meat have improved the nutritional quality of these products significantly. But if you tend to rely on frozen dinners and entrées for your main meal of the day, you must choose *very carefully* if you wish to avoid the two main nutritional drawbacks found in these foods: too much fat and sodium. Products clearly aimed at dieters are not always the most nutritious choices, since manufacturers sometimes use high-fat recipes and simply cut down on portion size (and thus on nutrients) in order to cut calories.

Canned Prepared Dishes

SODIUM GUIDELINES: In evaluating the sodium content of canned entrées, we used the following standards:

900 mg to 1,200 mg   high in sodium
more than 1,200 mg   very high in sodium

Remember, these guidelines are not for people following medically restricted low-sodium diets, but for healthy individuals who wish to monitor their sodium intake.

CHEF BOY-AR-DEE BEEF RAVIOLI IN TOMATO AND MEAT SAUCE
American Home Products, Inc.

Ingredients: tomatoes, water, enriched wheat flour, beef, cracker meal, salt, high-fructose corn syrup, modified food starch, carrots, rendered beef fat, textured vegetable protein (soy flour, caramel coloring), onions, monosodium glutamate, caramel coloring, flavorings, enzyme-modified Cheddar cheese.

Amount: ½ can/7½ oz			% USRDA
Calories	180	Protein	10
Protein, gm	6	Vitamin A	6
Carbohydrates, gm	27	Vitamin C	*
Fat, gm	5	Thiamine	10
Sodium, mg	1,000e	Riboflavin	10
Cholesterol, mg	25e	Niacin	10
Fiber, gm	1e	Calcium	*
		Iron	10

THIS FOOD: Chef Boy-Ar-Dee Beef Ravioli in Tomato and Meat Sauce provides complex carbohydrates and is a fair source of protein, vitamin A, the B vitamins, and iron. This product contains only 25 percent fat calories, but, like many canned foods, is high in sodium.

ADDITIVES: Contains monosodium glutamate (MSG), which many experts believe should be avoided by infants and very young children; causes adverse reactions in some sensitive individuals.

CHEF BOY-AR-DEE LASAGNA
American Home Products, Inc.

Ingredients: tomatoes, water, beef, enriched lasagna macaroni product, high-fructose corn syrup, salt, modified food starch, enzyme modified cheese, onions, flavorings.

Amount: ½ can/7½ oz			% USRDA
Calories	220	Protein	15
Protein, gm	8	Vitamin A	6
Carbohydrates, gm	28	Vitamin C	*
Fat, gm	9	Thiamine	6
Sodium, mg	1,000e	Riboflavin	10
Cholesterol, mg	50e	Niacin	10
Fiber, gm	1e	Calcium	2
		Iron	10

THIS FOOD: Chef Boy-Ar-Dee Lasagna provides complex carbohydrates, a good source of protein, a fair source of riboflavin, niacin and iron. About 37 percent of calories derive from fat. This product is high in sodium.

ADDITIVES: No questionable additives.

DINTY MOORE BEEF STEW
George A. Hormel and Co.

Ingredients: beef broth, beef, potatoes, carrots, corn flour, beef fat, salt, tomato paste, modified food starch, sugar, caramel coloring, flavoring.

Amount: ½ can/7½ oz			% USRDA
Calories	180	Protein	27e
Protein, gm	12	Vitamin A	41e
Carbohydrates, gm	14	Vitamin C	10e
Fat, gm	9	Thiamine	4e
Sodium, mg	939	Riboflavin	6e
Cholesterol, mg	60e	Niacin	11e
Fiber, gm	1.5e	Calcium	2e
		Iron	10e

NOTE: The letter "e" indicates that the data has been estimated; < means "less than" and is used for small amounts of sodium or cholesterol; * means food contains less than 2% of USRDA; "na" means that the information was not available and appears only when data is insufficient.

THIS FOOD: Dinty Moore Beef Stew is an excellent source of protein and vitamin A and a good source of niacin. It contains 45 percent fat calories and is high in saturated fat. This product is high in sodium.

ADDITIVES: No questionable additives.

FRANCO-AMERICAN BEEF RAVIOLIOS IN MEAT SAUCE
Campbell Soup Co.

Ingredients: tomatoes, water, enriched wheat flour, beef, corn syrup, carrots, cooked beef, cornstarch, cracker meal, modified food starch, salt, soy protein concentrate, enzyme-modified Cheddar cheese, textured vegetable protein (soy flour, soy protein isolate, caramel color), yeast extract and hydrolyzed plant protein, dehydrated onions, caramel color, citric acid, natural flavor, oleoresin paprika.

Amount: ½ can/7½ oz			% USRDA
Calories	210	Protein	15
Protein, gm	8	Vitamin A	30
Carbohydrates, gm	34	Vitamin C	2
Fat, gm	5	Thiamine	10
Sodium, mg	1,030	Riboflavin	8
Cholesterol, mg	35e	Niacin	10
Fiber, gm	1.5e	Calcium	2
		Iron	10

THIS FOOD: Franco-American Beef RavioliOs in Meat Sauce provides complex carbohydrates and is a very good source of protein and vitamin A. Only 21 percent of the calories in this product derive from fat. Except for its high sodium content, this product provides excellent nutritional value.

ADDITIVES: No questionable additives.

BEST BET: Parents can breathe a sigh of relief. There's absolutely no reason to feel guilty about serving Franco-American Beef RavioliOs in Meat Sauce to your kids (or yourself). With only 21 percent fat calories, this convenience food provides an excellent balance of nutrients, without questionable additives.

FRANCO-AMERICAN SPAGHETTI WITH MEATBALLS IN TOMATO SAUCE
Campbell Soup Co.

Ingredients: tomatoes, water, beef, enriched spaghetti, high-fructose corn syrup, salt, bread crumbs, beef fat, dehydrated onions, Romano cheese (made from cow's milk), dehydrated garlic, monosodium glutamate, spice, citric acid, yeast extract, and natural flavoring.

Amount: ½ can/7½ oz			% USRDA
Calories	220	Protein	15
Protein, gm	9	Vitamin A	10
Carbohydrates, gm	27	Vitamin C	6
Fat, gm	8	Thiamine	10
Sodium, mg	950	Riboflavin	10
Cholesterol, mg	80e	Niacin	15
Fiber, gm	1.5e	Calcium	2
		Iron	10

Contains 2½ teaspoons sugar, nearly 2 teaspoons fat and ½ teaspoon salt.

THIS FOOD: Provides complex carbohydrates, a good source of protein, niacin, and a fair source of vitamin A, the B vitamins, and iron. About 33 percent of its calories derive from fat. It is moderate in sodium.

ADDITIVES: Contains monosodium glutamate (MSG), which many experts believe should be avoided by infants and very young children; causes adverse reactions in some sensitive individuals.

FRANCO-AMERICAN SPAGHETTIOS WITH SLICED BEEF FRANKS IN TOMATO SAUCE
Campbell Soup Co.

Ingredients: tomatoes, water, frankfurters, (beef, water, salt, natural flavoring, spice, sodium nitrite, and oleoresin paprika), enriched macaroni product, high-fructose corn syrup, salt, enzyme-modified Cheddar cheese, potato starch, spice, vinegar, natural flavoring, citric acid, and dehydrated garlic.

Amount: ½ can/7½ oz			% USRDA
Calories	220	Protein	15
Protein, gm	7	Vitamin A	8
Carbohydrates, gm	26	Vitamin C	4
Fat, gm	9	Thiamine	10
Sodium, mg	1,070	Riboflavin	10
Cholesterol, mg	40e	Niacin	15
Fiber, gm	1.5e	Calcium	2
		Iron	10

Contains 2 teaspoons sugar, 2 teaspoons fat and ½ teaspoon salt.

THIS FOOD: SpaghettiOs with Sliced Beef Franks in Tomato Sauce provides complex carbohydrates and is a good source of protein, and the B vitamins. About 37 percent of its calories derive from fat. Like most canned foods, this product is high in sodium.

ADDITIVES: Contains sodium nitrite, which can lead to the formation of cancer-causing nitrosamines.

MARY KITCHEN CORNED BEEF HASH
George A. Hormel and Co.

Ingredients: beef, rehydrated potatoes, water, salt, sodium nitrite.

Amount: ½ can/7½ oz			% USRDA
Calories	360	Protein	44
Protein, gm	20	Vitamin A	*
Carbohydrates, gm	17	Vitamin C	0
Fat, gm	24	Thiamine	3e
Sodium, mg	1,368	Riboflavin	28e
Cholesterol, mg	80e	Niacin	36e
Fiber, gm	1.5e	Calcium	4e
		Iron	50e
Contains more than 5 teaspoons fat and ½ teaspoon salt.			

THIS FOOD: Mary Kitchen Corned Beef Hash is high in sodium, saturated fat, and overall fat. Altogether fats account for 60 percent of calories. This product is an excellent source of protein, niacin, riboflavin, and iron.

ADDITIVES: Contains sodium nitrite, which can be converted into cancer-causing substances called nitrosamines.

Dry Prepared Dishes

SODIUM GUIDELINES: In evaluating the sodium content of a dry packaged entree, we used the following standards:

650 mg to 900 mg	moderate in sodium
900 mg to 1,200 mg	high in sodium
more than 1,200 mg	very high in sodium

Remember, these guidelines are not for people following medically restricted low-sodium diets, but for healthy individuals who wish to monitor their sodium intake.

BETTY CROCKER HAMBURGER HELPER FOR CHEESEBURGER MACARONI
General Mills, Inc.

Ingredients: enriched macaroni, dried Cheddar cheese, cornstarch, partially hydrogenated soybean oil, dried tomato, salt, buttermilk, sugar, hydrolyzed vegetable protein and other natural flavoring, dried onion, dried corn syrup, disodium phosphate, dried garlic, sodium caseinate, citric acid, dipotassium phosphate, FD & C Yellow No. 5, artificial color, sodium sulfite, and BHA.

Amount: ⅕ recipe (1 lb ground beef added to recipe)			% USRDA
Calories	360	Protein	40
Protein, gm	21	Vitamin A	4
Carbohydrates, gm	28	Vitamin C	*
Fat, gm	18	Thiamine	20
Sodium, mg	1,025	Riboflavin	20
Cholesterol, mg	80e	Niacin	25
Fiber, gm	<1e	Calcium	6
		Iron	15
Contains ½ teaspoon salt and nearly 4 teaspoons fat.			

THIS FOOD: As prepared with ground beef, Betty Crocker Hamburger Helper for Cheeseburger Macaroni is an excellent source of protein and complex carbohydrates and a very good source of the B vitamins and iron. About 45 percent of the calories in this product derive from fat. Like most foods prepared from mixes, this product is high in sodium.

ADDITIVES: Contains sodium sulfite, which can cause severe allergic reactions, especially in individuals with asthma; and artificial colors which are inadequately tested and which some studies suggest may adversely affect behavior and the ability to complete school tasks in some sensitive children; also contains Yellow No. 5, which can cause allergic reactions, especially in aspirin-sensitive individuals. Also contains BHA, whose long-term safety is currently being reexamined by FDA investigators.

BETTY CROCKER HAMBURGER HELPER FOR CHILI TOMATO
General Mills, Inc.

Ingredients: enriched macaroni, cornstarch, dried onion, salt, dried tomato, sugar, dried chili pepper, spice, beet powder color, partially hydrogenated soybean oil, dried garlic, natural flavor, monosodium glutamate, yellow corn lour, sodium sulfite, and BHA.

Amount: ⅕ recipe (1 lb ground beef added to recipe)			% USRDA
Calories	330	Protein	40
Protein, gm	19	Vitamin A	4
Carbohydrates, gm	32	Vitamin C	*
Fat, gm	14	Thiamine	20
Sodium, mg	1,310	Riboflavin	15
Cholesterol, mg	80e	Niacin	25
Fiber, gm	<1e	Calcium	2
		Iron	15

Contains ⅔ teaspoon salt and 3 teaspoons fat.

THIS FOOD: Is a good source of complex carbohydrates, protein, the B vitamins, and iron. About 38 percent of the calories in this product derive from fat. Sodium watchers beware—1,310 mg sodium per serving!

ADDITIVES: Contains monosodium glutamate (MSG), which many experts believe should be avoided by infants and very young children; MSG causes adverse reactions in some sensitive individuals. It also contains sodium sulfite, which can cause severe allergic reactions, especially in individuals with asthma, and BHA, whose long-term safety is currently being reexamined by FDA investigators.

GOLDEN GRAIN MACARONI AND CHEDDAR
Golden Grain Macaroni Co.

Ingredients: enriched macaroni with niacin, iron, thiamine mononitrate, riboflavin, whey, aged Cheddar cheese, salt, dried butter, nonfat milk, natural flavor, disodium phosphate, partially hydrogenated vegetable oil (cottonseed oil, palm oil, soybean oil), lactic acid, artificial color, FD & C Yellow No. 5, citric acid.

Amount: ¾ cup (+ ½ tbsp butter and 1 tbsp milk)			% USRDA
Calories	245	Protein	11
Protein, gm	9	Vitamin A	3
Carbohydrates, gm	39	Vitamin C	*
Fat, gm	8	Thiamine	30
Sodium, mg	na	Riboflavin	15
Cholesterol, mg	45e	Niacin	10
Fiber, gm	1.5e	Calcium	10
		Iron	8

THIS FOOD: Is high in complex carbohydrates, a fair source of protein, and a good source of the B vitamins. This product is low in fat—only 29 percent of its calories derive from fat. Sodium figures are not available.

ADDITIVES: Contains artificial colors, which are inadequately tested and which some studies suggest can adversely affect behavior and the ability to complete school tasks in some sensitive children; and Yellow No. 5, which can cause allergic reactions, especially in aspirin-sensitive individuals.

KRAFT EGG NOODLE WITH CHICKEN DINNER
Kraft, Inc.

Ingredients: enriched egg noodles, chicken sauce mix (wheat starch, dehydrated chicken, monosodium glutamate, salt, nonfat dry milk, chicken fat, dextrose, partially hydrogenated soybean oil, red bell pepper, onion, celery powder, turmeric, spice, natural flavor).

Amount: ¾ cup (¼ tsp salt and ½ tsp margarine added)			% USRDA
Calories	240	Protein	10
Protein, gm	8	Vitamin A	4
Carbohydrates, gm	30	Vitamin C	*
Fat, gm	10	Thiamine	8
Sodium, mg	960	Riboflavin	6
Cholesterol, mg	35	Niacin	8
Fiber, gm	1.5e	Calcium	4
		Iron	8

Contains 2 teaspoons fat and nearly ½ teaspoon salt.

THIS FOOD: Kraft Egg Noodle with Chicken Dinner provides complex carbohydrates, some protein, and little else of nutritional value. About 37 percent of its calories derive from fat. This product is high in sodium.

ADDITIVES: Contains monosodium glutamate (MSG), which many experts believe should be avoided by infants and very young children; causes adverse reactions in some sensitive individuals.

KRAFT MACARONI AND CHEESE DINNER
Kraft, Inc.

Ingredients: enriched macaroni, cheese sauce mix (whey, dehydrated cheese [granular Cheddar (milk, cheese culture, salt, enzymes)], whey protein concentrate, skim milk, salt, buttermilk, sodium tripolyphosphate, sodium phosphate, citric acid, Yellow No. 5, artificial color, lactic acid).

Amount: ¾ cup (¼ tsp salt, 1 tbsp milk, and 1 tsp margarine added)			% USRDA
Calories	300	Protein	15
Protein, gm	8	Vitamin A	10
Carbohydrates, gm	34	Vitamin C	*
Fat, gm	14	Thiamine	15
Sodium, mg	655	Riboflavin	15
Cholesterol, mg	5	Niacin	8
Fiber, gm	1.5e	Calcium	8
		Iron	10

THIS FOOD: Kraft Macaroni and Cheese Dinner is high in complex carbohydrates and a very good source of protein, thiamine, and riboflavin. About 42 percent of its calories derive from fat. Compared to other brands of macaroni and cheese, this product is moderate in sodium.

ADDITIVES: Contains artificial colors, which are inadequately tested and which some studies suggest can adversely affect behavior and the ability to complete school tasks in some sensitive children; and Yellow No. 5, which can cause allergic reactions, especially in aspirin-sensitive individuals.

KRAFT TANGY ITALIAN STYLE SPAGHETTI DINNER
Kraft, Inc.

Ingredients: enriched spaghetti, grated Parmesan cheese, spice mix (dehydrated onion, salt, modified food starch, monosodium glutamate, hydrolyzed vegetable protein, sugar, spice, dehydrated garlic, dehydrated celery, artificial color).

Amount: 1 cup (½ tsp salt, 1½ oz tomato paste, and ¼ tsp margarine added)			% USRDA
Calories	270	Protein	15
Protein, gm	10	Vitamin A	15
Carbohydrates, gm	42	Vitamin C	2
Fat, gm	7	Thiamine	20
Sodium, mg	780	Riboflavin	8
Cholesterol, mg	5	Niacin	15
Fiber, gm	2e	Calcium	6
		Iron	8

THIS FOOD: Kraft Tangy Italian Style Spaghetti Dinner is a good source of protein, complex carbohydrates, vitamin A, thiamine, and niacin. Only 23 percent of its calories derive from fat. It is moderate in sodium for this category.

ADDITIVES: Contains monosodium glutamate (MSG), which many experts believe should be avoided by infants and very young children and which causes adverse reactions in some sensitive individuals. Also contains artificial colors, which are inadequately tested and which some studies suggest can adversely affect behavior and the ability to complete school tasks in some sensitive children.

LIPTON EGG NOODLES AND SAUCE, BEEF FLAVOR
Unilever United States, Inc.

Ingredients: enriched egg noodles, natural flavorings, cornstarch, beef fat, dried corn syrup, dehydrated onions, dehydrated beef extract, salt, monosodium glutamate, caramel color, dehydrated tomatoes, dehydrated green onions, dehydrated garlic, disodium inosinate, disodium guanylate.

Amount: 1 cup as prepared			% USRDA
Calories	380	Protein	16
Protein, gm	10	Vitamin A	8
Carbohydrates, gm	52	Vitamin C	*
Fat, gm	14	Thiamine	30
Sodium, mg	1,110	Riboflavin	8
Cholesterol, mg	50e	Niacin	20
Fiber, gm	2e	Calcium	*
		Iron	8

THIS FOOD: Lipton Egg Noodles and Sauce, Beef Flavor, provides complex carbohydrates, and is a good source of thiamine. About 33 percent of its calories derive from fat. This product is moderate in sodium for this category.

ADDITIVES: Contains monosodium glutamate (MSG), which many experts believe should be avoided by infants and very young children; causes adverse reactions in sensitive individuals.

LIPTON EGG NOODLES AND SAUCE, CHICKEN FLAVOR
Unilever United States, Inc.

Ingredients: enriched egg noodles, cornstarch, dried corn syrup, natural flavorings, salt, spray-dried partially hydrogenated soybean oil, dehydrated chicken, monosodium glutamate, dehydrated onions, chicken fat, dehydrated red bell pepper, dehydrated garlic, sodium caseinate, spices, dehydrated parsley, turmeric oleoresin, disodium inosinate, and disodium guanylate.

Amount: 1 cup as prepared			% USRDA
Calories	380	Protein	12
Protein, gm	10	Vitamin A	8
Carbohydrates, gm	50	Vitamin C	*
Fat, gm	18	Thiamine	30
Sodium, mg	930	Riboflavin	12
Cholesterol, mg	50e	Niacin	16
Fiber, gm	2e	Calcium	*
		Iron	8

THIS FOOD: Lipton Egg Noodles and Sauce, Chicken Flavor, provides complex carbohydrates and thiamine. About 43 percent of its calories derive from fat. This product is moderate in sodium for this category.

ADDITIVES: Contains monosodium glutamate (MSG), which many experts believe should be avoided by infants and very young children; causes adverse reactions in some sensitive individuals.

Prepared Frozen Dinners

SODIUM GUIDELINES: In evaluating the sodium content of a frozen dinner, we used the following standards:

1,000 mg to 1,500 mg	high in sodium
more than 1,500 mg	very high in sodium

Remember, these guidelines are not for people following medically restricted low-sodium diets, but for healthy individuals who wish to monitor their sodium intake.

DO FROZEN DINNERS DELIVER GOOD NUTRITION? According to our sampling, not many of them do. To be judged excellent, a dinner should supply at least 30 percent of the USRDA for three nutrients and protein while containing less than 35 percent fat calories. Using this standard, only two regular-sized (11-to-12-ounce) dinners and one extra large (18½-ounce) dinner make the grade. Not surprisingly, they are all high in sodium.

Armour Chicken Fricassee Dinner Classic (contains monosodium glutamate)
Morton Fried Chicken (contains artificial color and flavors)
Swanson Hungry-Man Turkey Dinner (contains monosodium glutamate)

SUPER SOURCES OF VITAMIN A

These frozen dinners contain more than 85 percent of the USRDA for vitamin A:

Armour Chicken Burgundy Classic Lite Dinner
Banquet American Favorites Beans and Franks Dinner
Banquet American Favorites Fish Dinner
Le Menu Yankee Pot Roast Dinner
Morton Fried Chicken Dinner
Morton Turkey Dinner

SUPER SOURCES OF FIBER

These frozen dinners contain at least 6 grams of fiber:

Banquet American Favorites Beans and Franks Dinner
Patio Mexican Style Combination Dinner
Swanson Macaroni and Cheese Dinner
Swanson Turkey Dinner

FAT WINNERS

Less than 30 percent of the calories in these frozen dinners come from fat:

Armour Chicken Burgundy Classic Lite Dinner
Armour Seafood Natural Herbs Classic Lite Dinner
Armour Sliced Beef with Broccoli Classic Lite Dinner
Morton Fried Chicken Dinner
Morton Veal Parmiagiana Dinner
Swanson Hungry-Man Turkey Dinner
Swanson Turkey Dinner

SODIUM LOSERS

These popular foods contain approximately 1 teaspoon salt per dinner:

Armour Sliced Beef with Broccoli Classic Lite Dinner
Morton Fried Chicken Dinner
Swanson Hungry-Man Chopped Beef Steak Dinner
Swanson Hungry-Man Turkey Dinner
Swanson Mexican Style Combination Dinner

FOR CHOLESTEROL WATCHERS

These frozen dinners contain more than 100 mg cholesterol:

Armour Sliced Beef with Broccoli Classic Lite Dinner
Le Menu Beef Sirloin Tips Dinner
Le Menu Yankee Pot Roast Dinner
Swanson Hungry-Man Chopped Beef Steak Dinner
Swanson Hungry-Man Turkey Dinner
Swanson Loin of Pork Dinner

ARMOUR CHICKEN BURGUNDY CLASSIC LITE DINNER
The Greyhound Corp.

Ingredients: cooked chicken breast meat, cooked rice, broccoli, cauliflower, carrots, mushrooms, water, tomatoes, burgundy wine, onions, butter, modified food starch, tomato paste, chicken base (chicken meat including natural chicken juices, salt, chicken fat, monosodium glutamate, sugar, dried whey flavoring, and turmeric), salt, sugar, beef base (beef [roasted beef and concentrated beef stock], salt, hydrolyzed plant protein, monosodium glutamate, sugar, flavoring, corn oil, chicken fat), spices, mono- and diglycerides, cellulose gum, monosodium glutamate, mushroom powder, caramel color, artificial butter flavor (soybean oil, dried whey, artificial flavors), lemon juice.

Amount: 11¼ oz			% USRDA
Calories	240	Protein	50
Protein, gm	23	Vitamin A	90
Carbohydrates, gm	24	Vitamin C	25
Fat, gm	5	Thiamine	8
Sodium, mg	1,060	Riboflavin	15
Cholesterol, mg	70e	Niacin	40
Fiber, gm	5e	Calcium	8
		Iron	8

THIS FOOD: Armour Chicken Burgundy Classic Lite Dinner is a reasonably well-balanced meal. It provides complex carbohydrates and is an excellent source of protein, vitamin A, vitamin C, and niacin. It is also a good source of riboflavin and fiber. A dinner contains only 240 calories, 19 percent of which derive from fat. Like most frozen dinners, this product is high in sodium.

ADDITIVES: Contains monosodium glutamate (MSG), which many authorities believe should be avoided by infants and very young children; causes adverse reactions in sensitive individuals. Also contains artificial flavor, which may cause allergic reactions in sensitive individuals, and which some studies suggest may adversely affect behavior and the ability to complete school tasks in some sensitive children.

ARMOUR CHICKEN FRICASSEE DINNER CLASSIC
The Greyhound Corp.

Ingredients: chicken broth, broccoli, cooked chicken meat, cooked rice, water, peas, carrots, butter, modified food starch, chicken fat, nonfat dry milk, rice flour, salt, lemon juice, monosodium glutamate, mono- and diglycerides, cellulose gum, flavorings, annatto color, onion powder, spice.

Amount: 11¾ oz			% USRDA
Calories	330	Protein	45
Protein, gm	23	Vitamin A	50
Carbohydrates, gm	32	Vitamin C	80
Fat, gm	12	Thiamine	10
Sodium, mg	1,190	Riboflavin	20
Cholesterol, mg	70	Niacin	30
Fiber, gm	5e	Calcium	15
		Iron	10

THIS FOOD: Armour Chicken Fricassee Dinner Classic is nutritionally superior to most items in this category. It supplies complex carbohydrates and is a good source of fiber. It is also an excellent source of protein, vitamins A, C and niacin, and a good source of the other B vitamins, calcium and iron. It contains only 330 calories, about 33 percent of which derive from fat. Like all frozen dinners, it is high in sodium.

ADDITIVES: Contains monosodium glutamate (MSG), which many authorities believe should be avoided by infants and very young children; causes adverse reactions in sensitive individuals.

ARMOUR SEAFOOD NATURAL HERBS CLASSIC LITE DINNER
The Greyhound Corp.

Ingredients: broccoli, seafood blend (pollock, snow crabmeat, turbot, wheat starch, egg white, salt, hydrolyzed vegetable protein, artificial color), water, cooked rice, cooked wild rice, mushrooms, butter, modified food starch, chicken base (chicken meat including natural chicken juices, salt, chicken fat, monosodium glutamate, sugar, dried whey, flavoring, and turmeric), onions, chives, salt, tomato paste, red peppers, Worcestershire sauce, lemon juice, spices, mono- and diglycerides, cellulose gum, monosodium glutamate, dry garlic, onion powder, caramel color.

Amount: 11½ oz			% USRDA
Calories	230	Protein	20
Protein, gm	12	Vitamin A	*
Carbohydrates, gm	33	Vitamin C	*
Fat, gm	5	Thiamine	6
Sodium, mg	1,410	Riboflavin	15
Cholesterol, mg	50e	Niacin	*
Fiber, gm	4e	Calcium	10
		Iron	6

THIS FOOD: Armour Seafood Natural Herbs Classic Lite Dinner is certainly low in fat and calories, but it is also far lower than average in nutrients. Apart from a good amount of dietary fiber and complex carbohydrates, this frozen dinner supplies a mere 20 percent of the USRDA for protein, 10 percent for calcium, 15 percent for riboflavin, and insignificant amounts of a few other nutrients. Like most frozen dinners, it is high in sodium. It all adds up to a nutritionally inadequate meal.

ADDITIVES: Contains monosodium glutamate (MSG), which many authorities believe should be avoided by infants and very young children; causes adverse reactions in sensitive individuals; also contains artificial colors which are inadequately tested and which some studies suggest may adversely affect behavior and the ability to complete school tasks in some sensitive children.

ARMOUR SEAFOOD NEWBURG DINNER CLASSIC
The Greyhound Corp.

Ingredients: green beans, water, cooked rice, seafood sticks (pollock, snow crabmeat, turbot, wheat starch, egg white, salt, hydrolyzed vegetable protein, artificial color), cooked shrimp, mushrooms, sherry wine, sweet cream, butter, peas, modified food starch, lobster base (cooked lobster, monosodium glutamate, salt, butter, flavoring, tomato paste, vegetable gum), salt, margarine (partially hydrogenated soybean oil, water, salt, whey, sodium benzoate, lecithin, potassium caseinate, artificial flavor and color, vitamin A palmitate), lemon juice, monoglycerides, monosodium glutamate, diglycerides, cellulose gum, paprika, spice, oleoresin paprika.

Amount: 10½ oz			% USRDA
Calories	270	Protein	25
Protein, gm	13	Vitamin A	2
Carbohydrates, gm	33	Vitamin C	10
Fat, gm	10	Thiamine	8
Sodium, mg	1,385	Riboflavin	10
Cholesterol, mg	90	Niacin	10
Fiber, gm	2e	Calcium	20
		Iron	10

THIS FOOD: In addition to complex carbohydrates, Armour Seafood Newburg Dinner Classic is a good source of vitamin C, niacin, riboflavin, and iron. But compared to other items in this category, it provides relatively low amounts of these nutrients. This product is low in calories, about 33 percent of which derive from fat. Like most frozen dinners, it is high in sodium.

ADDITIVES: Contains artificial color and flavor, which some studies suggest may adversely affect behavior and the ability to complete school tasks in some sensitive children; artificial colors are inadequately tested, and artificial flavor may cause allergic reactions in sensitive individuals; also contains monosodium glutamate (MSG), which many authorities believe should be avoided by infants and very young children; causes adverse reactions in sensitive individuals.

ARMOUR SLICED BEEF WITH BROCCOLI CLASSIC LITE DINNER
The Greyhound Corp.

Ingredients: water, cooked beef, cooked rice, broccoli, soy sauce, oyster sauce (oyster extractives, water, salt, starch, acetic acid, sodium benzoate, diluted with water, colored with caramel), modified food starch, red peppers, beef base (beef [roasted beef and concentrated beef stock], salt, hydrolyzed plant protein, monosodium glutamate, sugar, flavoring, corn oil and chicken fat), butter, salt, spices, granulated garlic, mono- and diglycerides, cellulose gum, monosodium glutamate, lemon juice.

Amount: 10¼ oz			% USRDA
Calories	290	Protein	60
Protein, gm	29	Vitamin A	4
Carbohydrates, gm	30	Vitamin C	*
Fat, gm	7	Thiamine	4
Sodium, mg	2,120	Riboflavin	20
Cholesterol, mg	120e	Niacin	15
Fiber, gm	4e	Calcium	4
		Iron	25
Contains more than 1 teaspoon salt.			

THIS FOOD: Armour Sliced Beef with Broccoli Classic Lite Dinner is great for dieters and those who want to restrict their intake of fat, and terrible for anyone at all concerned with sodium intake. It contains only 22 percent fat calories, which is highly desirable, but an astonishing 2,120 mg sodium per serving gives this product nearly double the average salt content of the average dinner in this high-sodium category of foods. In addition to providing fiber and complex carbohydrates, this product is a significant source of protein and iron, and a very good source of riboflavin and niacin.

ADDITIVES: Contains monosodium glutamate (MSG), which many authorities believe should be avoided by infants and very young children; causes adverse reactions in sensitive individuals.

BANQUET AMERICAN FAVORITES BEANS AND FRANKS DINNER
ConAgra, Inc.

Ingredients: water, cooked beans, carrots and peas, beef and pork, wheat flour, cornmeal, sugar, margarine, eggs, salt, corn syrup, tomato paste, nonfat dry milk (dry skim milk), starch, sodium aluminum phosphate, sodium bicarbonate, dextrose, paprika, spices, sodium erythorbate, garlic powder, sodium citrate, sodium nitrite, artificial butter flavor.

Amount: 10 oz			% USRDA
Calories	500	Protein	42
Protein, gm	19	Vitamin A	95
Carbohydrates, gm	64	Vitamin C	33
Fat, gm	19	Thiamine	22
Sodium, mg	1,377	Riboflavin	14
Cholesterol, mg	50e	Niacin	15
Fiber, gm	11e	Calcium	15
		Iron	28

THIS FOOD: Moderately high in calories and comparatively rich in important nutrients, it is high in fiber, complex carbohydrates, vitamin A, vitamin C, iron, B vitamins, and calcium. About 34 percent of calories derive from fat. Like most frozen dinners it is high in sodium.

ADDITIVES: Contains artificial flavor, which may cause allergic reactions in sensitive individuals, and which some studies suggest may adversely affect behavior and the ability to complete school tasks in some sensitive children. Also contains sodium nitrite, which can be converted into cancer-causing substances called nitrosamines.

BANQUET AMERICAN FAVORITES FISH DINNER
ConAgra, Inc.

Ingredients: fish (pollock/perch) battered with water, bleached wheat flour, corn flour, partially hydrogenated soybean oil, modified cornstarch, whey, nonfat milk, salt, dextrose, sugar, leavening (sodium acid pyrophosphate, sodium bicarbonate, sodium aluminum phosphate), spice and natural flavor, partially hydrogenated soybean oil, carrots, peas, potatoes, hydrogenated soybean and palm oil, margarine (one or more of: partially hydrogenated soybean and/or cottonseed oils, liquid soybean oil), water, salt, nonfat dry milk (dry skim milk) soybean lecithin, vegetable mono- and diglycerides, sodium benzoate, artificial color, artificial flavor, vitamin A palmitate, water, sugar, salt.

Amount: approx. 9 oz			% USRDA
Calories	553	Protein	40
Protein, gm	18	Vitamin A	106
Carbohydrates, gm	45	Vitamin C	30
Fat, gm	33	Thiamine	23
Sodium, mg	927	Riboflavin	15
Cholesterol, mg	100e	Niacin	18
Fiber, gm	3e	Calcium	6
		Iron	33

Contains nearly 5 teaspoons fat.

THIS FOOD: Weighs 20 percent less than most other frozen dinners, yet is higher than most in fat and calories. It contains more added fat by weight than carrots, peas, or potatoes! Not surprisingly, 54 percent of the calories in this product derive from fat (the fish itself contains only ten percent naturally occurring fat calories). In addition to complex carbohydrates and some fiber, it supplies more than 30 percent of the USRDA for protein, vitamin A, vitamin C, and iron. It is also a very good source of the B vitamins. It is high in sodium.

ADDITIVES: Contains artificial color and flavor, which some studies suggest may adversely affect behavior and the ability to complete school tasks in some sensitive children; artificial colors are inadequately tested, and artificial flavor may cause allergic reactions in sensitive individuals.

LE MENU BEEF SIRLOIN TIPS DINNER
Campbell Soup Co.

Ingredients: cooked choice sirloin beef, broccoli, fried potatoes, beef stock, water, mushrooms, burgundy wine, onions, sweet peppers, reconstituted skim milk, Cheddar cheese, margarine, sherry wine, modified food starch, wheat flour, tomato paste, salt, monosodium glutamate, dehydrated onions, sugar, caramel color, dehydrated garlic, dehyrated parsley, spice, and natural flavoring.

Amount: 11½ oz			% USRDA
Calories	390	Protein	50
Protein, gm	32	Vitamin A	8
Carbohydrates, gm	24	Vitamin C	40
Fat, gm	18	Thiamine	10
Sodium, mg	1,100	Riboflavin	25
Cholesterol, mg	140e	Niacin	25
Fiber, gm	5e	Calcium	10
		Iron	25

THIS FOOD: In addition to complex carbohydrates and fiber, Le Menu Beef Sirloin Tips Dinner is an excellent source of protein, vitamin C, riboflavin, niacin, and iron. It contains 41 percent fat calories and is high in saturated fat and cholesterol. Like most frozen dinners, this product is high in sodium.

ADDITIVES: Contains monosodium glutamate (MSG), which many authorities believe should be avoided by infants and very young children; causes adverse reactions in some sensitive individuals.

LE MENU BREAST OF CHICKEN PARMIGIANA DINNER
Campbell Soup Co.

Ingredients: breaded chicken breast (cooked chicken breast meat, bread crumbs, water, soy flour, cornstarch, eggs), Italian green beans, cooked enriched egg noodles, water, tomatoes, cream, margarine, mozzarella cheese, sweet red peppers, Parmesan cheese, modified food starch, salt, butter, Romano cheese made from cow's milk, sugar, wheat flour, onions, monosodium glutamate, spice, natural flavoring, dehydrated garlic, dehydrated onions, ascorbic acid.

Amount: 11½ oz			% USRDA
Calories	410	Protein	40
Protein, gm	28	Vitamin A	15
Carbohydrates, gm	26	Vitamin C	35
Fat, gm	21	Thiamine	10
Sodium, mg	950	Riboflavin	15
Cholesterol, mg	100e	Niacin	35
Fiber, gm	3e	Calcium	15
		Iron	15

THIS FOOD: Provides complex carbohydrates; some dietary fiber; and is an excellent source of protein, vitamin A and the other B vitamins, calcium, iron, vitamin C, and niacin. It contains 46 percent fat calories and is high in saturated fat. This product provides a good range of important nutrients. However, other chicken dinners deliver equivalent nutritional value without the high fat content. This product is moderate in sodium.

ADDITIVES: Contains monosodium glutamate (MSG), which many authorities believe should be avoided by infants and very young children; causes adverse reactions in some sensitive individuals.

LE MENU YANKEE POT ROAST DINNER
Campbell Soup Co.

Ingredients: cooked choice beef, fried potatoes, carrots, beef stock, water, Sauterne wine, margarine, pearl onions, mushrooms, modified food starch, tomato paste, salt, wheat flour, sugar, dehydrated onions, monosodium glutamate, butter, dehydrated garlic, dehydrated parsley, caramel color, spice, and natural flavoring.

Amount: 11 oz			% USRDA
Calories	360	Protein	50
Protein, gm	27	Vitamin A	130
Carbohydrates, gm	29	Vitamin C	15
Fat, gm	15	Thiamine	8
Sodium, mg	830	Riboflavin	15
Cholesterol, mg	140e	Niacin	25
Fiber, gm	5e	Calcium	4
		Iron	25

Contains ⅓ teaspoon salt and 1 teaspoon sugar.

THIS FOOD: One of the best beef dinners profiled. It provides complex carbohydrates, dietary fiber, is an excellent source of protein, vitamin A, niacin, and iron. It is moderate in calories, about 37 percent of which derive from fat. At 830 mg sodium per serving, this dinner is moderate in sodium.

ADDITIVES: Contains monosodium glutamate (MSG), which many authorities believe should be avoided by infants and very young children; causes adverse reactions in some sensitive individuals.

BEST CHICKEN DINNER FOR WEIGHT WATCHERS: Armour Chicken Fricassee Dinner Classic is a nutritional bonanza. To begin with, it's relatively low in fat calories (33 percent) and overall calories (330). While Armour Chicken Burgundy Classic Lite Dinner with only 19 percent fat calories and 240 overall calories is even leaner, it has fewer nutrients and contains artificial flavors. Drawbacks: contains monosodium glutamate and 1,190 milligrams sodium per serving.

MORTON FRIED CHICKEN DINNER
R. J. Reynolds Industries, Inc.

Ingredients: fried chicken (assorted white and dark chicken parts, flour, water, salt, spice, dextrose, paprika fried in shortening), rehydrated potato flakes, carrots, water, salt, food starch modified, vegetable oil, whey solids, maltodextrin, mono- and diglycerides, butter, artificial color, natural and artificial flavors.

Amount: 11 oz			% USRDA
Calories	460	Protein	80
Protein, gm	36	Vitamin A	100
Carbohydrates, gm	49	Vitamin C	30
Fat, gm	13	Thiamine	25
Sodium, mg	1,865	Riboflavin	35
Cholesterol, mg	84	Niacin	60
Fiber, gm	3e	Calcium	6
		Iron	20

Contains more than ¾ teaspoon salt.

THIS FOOD: Morton Fried Chicken Dinner provides complex carbohydrates and fiber and is an excellent source of protein, vitamin A, vitamin C, and the B vitamins, and a good source of iron. Only 25 percent of calories derive from fat. This dinner contains a whopping 1,865 mg sodium per serving.

ADDITIVES: Contains artificial color and flavor, which some studies suggest may adversely affect behavior and the ability to complete school tasks in some sensitive children; artificial colors are inadequately tested, and artificial flavor may cause allergic reactions in sensitive individuals.

MORTON TURKEY DINNER
R. J. Reynolds Industries, Inc.

Ingredients: water, rehydrated potato flakes, turkey loaf (turkey meat, water, salt, sodium phosphates), carrots, flour, cornmeal, vegetable oil, food starch modified, salt, dextrose, whey, leavening, sodium bicarbonate, maltodextrin, monosodium glutamate, sugar, hydrolyzed vegetable protein, spices, onion powder, caramel color, annatto color, mono- and diglycerides, butter, natural and artificial flavors.

Amount: 11 oz			% USRDA
Calories	340	Protein	45
Protein, gm	22	Vitamin A	100
Carbohydrates, gm	35	Vitamin C	30
Fat, gm	12	Thiamine	15
Sodium, mg	1,260	Riboflavin	15
Cholesterol, mg	66	Niacin	25
Fiber, gm	4e	Calcium	4
		Iron	15

THIS FOOD: Morton Turkey Dinner supplies complex carbohydrates and fiber, and is an excellent source of protein, vitamins A and C, and niacin. It is relatively low in calories, about 32 percent of which derive from fat. Like most frozen dinners, this product is high in sodium.

ADDITIVES: Contains monosodium glutamate (MSG), which many authorities believe should be avoided by infants and very young children; causes adverse reactions in sensitive individuals. Also contains artificial flavor, which may cause allergic reactions in sensitive individuals, and which some studies suggest may adversely affect behavior and the ability to complete school tasks in some sensitive children.

MORTON VEAL PARMIGIANA DINNER
R. J. Reynolds Industries, Inc.

Ingredients: water, breaded veal patty [beef added] (veal, bread crumbs, water, beef, textured vegetable protein, soy flour, caramel color), soy protein concentrate, flour, salt, whey solids, dextrose, hydrolyzed vegetable protein, flavoring, fried in vegetable oil, peas, rehydrated potato flakes, tomato paste, food starch modified, salt, mozzarella cheese, pasteurized process American cheese, Paramesan cheese, textured vegetable protein (soy flour, caramel coloring), sugar, whey solids, vegetable oil, maltodextrin, onion powder, dehydrated tomato, natural and artificial flavors, spices, malic acid, beet powder, monosodium glutamate, dried green pepper, garlic powder, parsley, mono- and diglycerides, butter annatto, flavoring.

Amount: 11 oz			% USRDA
Calories	250	Protein	30
Protein, gm	18	Vitamin A	15
Carbohydrates, gm	27	Vitamin C	25
Fat, gm	8	Thiamine	20
Sodium, mg	1,450	Riboflavin	15
Cholesterol, mg	36	Niacin	25
Fiber, gm	4e	Calcium	15
		Iron	20

THIS FOOD: In addition to providing fiber and complex carbohydrates, Morton Veal Parmigiana Dinner is an excellent source of protein, vitamin C, and niacin, and is a very good source of the other B vitamins, calcium, and iron. While it is not rich enough in vitamins and minerals to be judged "excellent," this frozen dinner is well above average in nutritional value. It is low in calories, only 29 percent of which derive from fat, and low in cholesterol. Its only real failing is too much sodium.

ADDITIVES: Contains monosodium glutamate (MSG), which many authorities believe should be avoided by infants and very young children; causes adverse reactions in some sensitive individuals.

SWANSON FRIED CHICKEN BREAST DINNER
Campbell Soup Co.

Ingredients: chicken breast portions with back portion (fried in vegetable oil), reconstituted dehydrated potatoes, corn, chicken broth, water, enriched wheat flour, sugar, margarine, eggs, salt, cocoa, soy flour, walnuts, dried whey, sodium phosphates, monosodium glutamate, butter, modified food starch, vanilla extract, onions, and spice.

Amount: 10¾ oz			% USRDA
Calories	650	Protein	50
Protein, gm	29	Vitamin A	*
Carbohydrates, gm	62	Vitamin C	15
Fat, gm	32	Thiamine	20
Sodium, mg	1,425	Riboflavin	15
Cholesterol, mg	80e	Niacin	35
Fiber, gm	3e	Calcium	4
		Iron	15

Contains 2 teaspoons natural and added sugar, and nearly 7 teaspoons fat.

THIS FOOD: Swanson Fried Chicken Breast Dinner is an excellent source of protein and niacin and a very good source of vitamin C, thiamin, riboflavin, and niacin. About 44 percent of calories come from fat, much of it saturated. Like most frozen dinners, this product is high in sodium. Other chicken dinners provide better nutrition.

ADDITIVES: Contains monosodium glutamate (MSG), which many experts believe should be avoided by infants and very young children; causes adverse reactions in some sensitive individuals.

SWANSON HUNGRY-MAN CHOPPED BEEF STEAK DINNER
Campbell Soup Co.

Ingredients: chopped beef steak (beef, reconstituted onions, salt, spice natural flavoring), reconstituted dehydrated potatoes, beef stock, green beans, water, graham cracker crumbs (graham cracker meal [enriched wheat flour, graham flour, sugar, partially hydrogenated vegetable oil, corn syrup, brown sugar, salt, malt, and baking soda], brown sugar, vegetable shortening and natural flavoring), dehydrated apples, margarine, black raspberries, blueberries, modified food starch, sugar, sherry wine, salt, vegetable oil, wheat flour, tomato paste, dried whey, onion powder, butter, dry garlic, caramel color, natural flavoring, spice.

Amount: 17¼ oz			% USRDA
Calories	620	Protein	60
Protein, gm	30	Vitamin A	30
Carbohydrates, gm	42	Vitamin C	30
Fat, gm	37	Thiamine	6
Sodium, mg	2,030	Riboflavin	25
Cholesterol, mg	150e	Niacin	45
Fiber, gm	4e	Calcium	6
		Iron	35
Contains 1 teaspoon salt and 8 teaspoons fat.			

THIS FOOD: Swanson Hungry-Man Chopped Beef Steak Dinner provides more than a pound of food and is therefore higher than average in fat, calories, cholesterol, and sodium. On the positive side it does provide more than 30 percent of the USRDA for protein, vitamin A, vitamin C, niacin, and iron, and is an excellent source of riboflavin. But too much fat—54 percent fat calories—make this dinner a poor choice.

ADDITIVES: Contains monosodium glutamate (MSG), which many authorities believe should be avoided by infants and very young children; causes adverse reactions in sensitive individuals.

SWANSON HUNGRY-MAN TURKEY DINNER
Campbell Soup Co.

Ingredients: cooked turkey meat (mostly white), turkey and chicken broth, reconstituted dehydrated potatoes, peas, water, stuffing (unbleached enriched wheat flour, water, corn syrup, salt, yeast, vegetable shortening, spice, onion powder, and celery seed), rehydrated apples, margarine, sugar, cranberries, onions, modified food starch, cooked turkey, salt, tomato puree, chicken fat, wheat flour, monosodium glutamate, apple powder, dried whey, carrots, celery, butter, dehydrated onions, sodium phosphates, natural flavoring, citric acid, orange peel, caramel color, spice, vanilla extract.

Amount: 18½ oz			% USRDA
Calories	630	Protein	80
Protein, gm	38	Vitamin A	10
Carbohydrates, gm	80	Vitamin C	20
Fat, gm	17	Thiamine	25
Sodium, mg	2,110	Riboflavin	30
Cholesterol, mg	125e	Niacin	70
Fiber, gm	7e	Calcium	8
		Iron	30
Contains 1 teaspoon salt.			

THIS FOOD: Since the portion of Swanson Hungry-Man Turkey Dinner is about one third larger than many other frozen dinners, it's not surprising to find that it is higher than average in calories and very high in sodium. Still, this product does deliver many important nutrients. In addition to providing complex carbohydrates, it is a very good source of fiber and vitamin C and an excellent source of protein, the B vitamins, and iron. Best of all, only 24 percent of calories come from fat.

ADDITIVES: Contains monosodium glutamate (MSG), which many authorities believe should be avoided by infants and very young children; causes adverse reactions in sensitive individuals.

SWANSON LOIN OF PORK DINNER
Campbell Soup Co.

Ingredients: cooked pork, reconstituted dehydrated potatoes, carrots, pork stock, water, apples, sugar, margarine, modified food starch, tomato puree, salt, wheat flour, apple powder, dried whey, vegetable oil, yeast extract and hydrolyzed plant protein, monosodium glutamate, spice, butter, onion powder, citric acid, caramel color, dehydrated garlic, natural flavoring and dehydrated parsley.

Amount: 11¼ oz			% USRDA
Calories	310	Protein	40
Protein, gm	21	Vitamin A	50
Carbohydrates, gm	26	Vitamin C	20
Fat, gm	13	Thiamine	35
Sodium, mg	635	Riboflavin	8
Cholesterol, mg	125e	Niacin	25
Fiber, gm	5e	Calcium	2
		Iron	10

THIS FOOD: Most people assume that pork of any kind is high in fat, but loin of pork is actually fairly lean. In addition to providing fiber and complex carbohydrates, Swanson Loin of Pork Dinner is an excellent source of protein, vitamin A, thiamine, and niacin. It is fairly low in calories, 38 percent of which derive from fat, and fairly high in cholesterol. It contains a moderate amount of sodium—less than half the salt in many other frozen dinners.

ADDITIVES: Contains monosodium glutamate (MSG), which many authorities believe should be avoided by infants and very young children; causes adverse reactions in some sensitive individuals.

SWANSON MACARONI AND BEEF DINNER
Campbell Soup Co.

Ingredients: cooked enriched elbow macaroni, tomatoes, corn, reconstituted skim milk, water, beef, sugar, vegetable oil, modified food starch, Cheddar cheese, salt, eggs, cocoa, carob, dehydrated onions, natural flavoring, vanilla extract, chili peppers, caramel color, hydrolyzed plant protein, garlic, spice, ascorbic acid, oleoresin paprika.

Amount: 12 oz			% USRDA
Calories	370	Protein	20
Protein, gm	12	Vitamin A	8
Carbohydrates, gm	46	Vitamin C	15
Fat, gm	15	Thiamine	4
Sodium, mg	925	Riboflavin	10
Cholesterol, mg	20e	Niacin	15
Fiber, gm	5e	Calcium	10
		Iron	15

THIS FOOD: In addition to supplying carbohydrates and fiber, Swanson Macaroni and Beef Dinner is a very good source of protein, vitamin C, niacin, and iron and a good source of riboflavin and calcium. It is moderate in calories, 36 percent of which come from fat. Compared to other frozen dinners it is moderate in sodium. This is one of the few dinners profiled that does not contain questionable additives.

ADDITIVES: No questionable additives.

SWANSON MACARONI AND CHEESE DINNER
Campbell Soup Co.

Ingredients: cooked enriched elbow macaroni (wheat flour enriched with niacin, ferrous sulfate, thiamine mononitrate, riboflavin), water, apples, Cheddar cheese, peas, carrots, sugar, skim milk, modified food starch, partially hydrogenated vegetable oils (soybean, palm, or cottonseed), salt, dextrose, wheat flour, apple powder, margarine (partially hydrogenated vegetable oils (soybean, palm or cottonseed oil), water, mono- and diglycerides, colored with beta carotene), spice, natural flavoring, lactic acid, and oleoresin paprika.

Amount: 12¼ oz			% USRDA
Calories	380	Protein	15
Protein, gm	12	Vitamin A	60
Carbohydrates, gm	48	Vitamin C	10
Fat, gm	15	Thiamine	10
Sodium, mg	970	Riboflavin	10
Cholesterol, mg	25e	Niacin	6
Fiber, gm	7e	Calcium	20
		Iron	10

THIS FOOD: Swanson Macaroni and Cheese Dinner is rich in complex carbohydrates, fiber, and vitamin A and is a good source of protein, vitamin C, thiamine, riboflavin, calcium, and iron. About 35 percent of calories derive from fat. This product is slightly lower than average in sodium. It is one of the few dinners profiled that does not contain questionable additives.

ADDITIVES: No questionable additives.

SWANSON TURKEY DINNER
Campbell Soup Co.

Ingredients: reconstituted dehydrated potatoes, turkey and chicken broth, cooked turkey meat (mostly white), peas, water, rehydrated apples, stuffing (unbleached enriched wheat flour, water, corn syrup, salt, yeast, vegetable shortening, spice, onion powder and celery seed), sugar, margarine, cranberries, pearl onions, modified food starch, salt, cooked turkey, tomato puree, chicken fat, wheat flour, apple powder, monosodium glutamate, dried whey, carrots, celery, butter, dehydrated onions, sodium phosphates, orange peel, natural flavorings, caramel color, spice, vanilla extract, and citric acid.

Amount: 11½ oz			% USRDA
Calories	340	Protein	40
Protein, gm	20	Vitamin A	6
Carbohydrates, gm	42	Vitamin C	10
Fat, gm	10	Thiamine	15
Sodium, mg	1,295	Riboflavin	10
Cholesterol, mg	95e	Niacin	35
Fiber, gm	6e	Calcium	4
		Iron	15

THIS FOOD: Although Swanson Turkey Dinner contains less turkey than either potatoes or broth, it is still an excellent source of protein. In addition it is a very good source of thiamine, niacin, iron, and dietary fiber. It is relatively low in calories, only 26 percent of which derive from fat. Like most frozen dinners, this product is high in sodium.

ADDITIVES: Contains monosodium glutamate (MSG), which many authorities believe should be avoided by infants and very young children; causes adverse reactions in some sensitive individuals.

WEIGHT WATCHERS CHOPPED BEEF STEAK AND GREEN PEPPER IN MUSHROOM SAUCE
H. J. Heinz Co.

Ingredients: beef, carrots, water, tomato puree, green peppers, dried whey, mushrooms, flour, salt, roasted beef and concentrated beef stock, hydrolyzed plant protein, partially hydrogenated liquid soybean oil, natural flavoring, granulated onion, monosodium glutamate, modified food starch, corn oil, sugar, caramel color, carob bean gum, guar gum, spice, xanthan gum, garlic powder, gum tragacanth, artificial flavor, beta carotene.

Amount: approx. 9 oz			% USRDA
Calories	320	Protein	30
Protein, gm	24	Vitamin A	100
Carbohydrates, gm	12	Vitamin C	25
Fat, gm	20	Thiamine	10
Sodium, mg	1,115	Riboflavin	15
Cholesterol, mg	140e	Niacin	20
Fiber, gm	3e	Calcium	10
		Iron	10

Contains 4 teaspoons fat and ½ teaspoon salt.

THIS FOOD: Although Weight Watchers Chopped Beef Steak and Green Pepper in Mushroom Sauce is not especially caloric, it is no lower in calories than an equal sized serving of many other frozen entrées not specifically geared to dieters. Fat accounts for a whopping 56 percent of calories, which is substantially higher than the 30 percent recommended. This product is also high in cholesterol and saturated fat and extremely high in sodium. On the positive side, this entree is an excellent or very good source of protein, vitamin A, vitamin C, and riboflavin, but this does not balance out its excessive fat and sodium content.

ADDITIVES: Contains monosodium glutamate (MSG), which many authorities believe should be avoided by infants and very young children; causes adverse reactions in sensitive individuals. Also contains artificial flavor, which some studies suggest may adversely affect behavior and the ability to complete school tasks in some sensitive children.

WEIGHT WATCHERS LASAGNA WITH MEAT, TOMATO SAUCE AND CHEESE

H. J. Heinz Co.

Ingredients: tomato puree, cooked enriched macaroni, part skim ricotta cheese, veal, water, salt, sugar, olive oil, Romano cheese (made from cow's milk), onion flakes, spices, hydrolyzed vegetable proteins, garlic powder, carob bean gum, guar gum, xanthan gum, gum tragacanth, furcelleran.

Amount: 12 oz			% USRDA
Calories	360	Protein	35
Protein, gm	22	Vitamin A	20
Carbohydrates, gm	38	Vitamin C	20
Fat, gm	13	Thiamine	20
Sodium, mg	1,345	Riboflavin	30
Cholesterol, mg	40e	Niacin	15
Fiber, gm	2e	Calcium	20
		Iron	10

THIS FOOD: Weight Watchers Lasagna with Meat, Tomato Sauce and Cheese is moderate in calories, only 32 percent of which derive from fat. It is rich in complex carbohydrates, protein, and riboflavin and a very good source of vitamin A, vitamin C, thiamine, and niacin. Like most frozen prepared foods, it is high in sodium.

ADDITIVES: No questionable additives.

Prepared Frozen Entrées

SODIUM GUIDELINES: In evaluating the sodium content of a frozen entrée we used the following standards:

11 to 12 ounce serving:
less than 1,000 mg	moderate in sodium
1,000 mg to 1,500 mg	high in sodium
more than 1,500 mg	very high in sodium

5 to 8 ounce serving:
less than 500 mg	moderate in sodium
500 mg to 1,200 mg	high in sodium
more than 1,200 mg	very high in sodium

Remember, these guidelines are not for people on medically restricted low-sodium diets, but for healthy individuals who wish to monitor their sodium intake.

BANQUET BUFFET SUPPER GRAVY AND SLICED BEEF
ConAgra, Inc.

Ingredients: water, cooked beef, beef fat, starch, flavoring, salt, flour, caramel color, sugar.

Amount: 8 oz			% USRDA
Calories	344	Protein	29
Protein, gm	13	Vitamin A	*
Carbohydrates, gm	6	Vitamin C	*
Fat, gm	29	Thiamine	*
Sodium, mg	890	Riboflavin	6
Cholesterol, mg	50e	Niacin	10
Fiber, gm	0e	Calcium	*
		Iron	11

Contains more than 6 teaspoons fat.

THIS FOOD: This product contains more gravy than beef and is moderate in calories, 75 percent of them from fat. Although Banquet Buffet Supper Gravy and Sliced Beef is an excellent source of protein and a fair source of niacin and iron, it contains too much saturated fat and cholesterol. Like most frozen entrées, this product is high in sodium.

ADDITIVES: No questionable additives.

FAT WINNERS

Less than 30 percent of the calories in these frozen entrées come from fat:

Stouffer's Glazed Chicken with Vegetable Rice Lean Cuisine
Stouffer's Spaghetti with Beef and Mushroom Sauce Lean Cuisine
Swanson Hungry-Man Sliced Beef

BANQUET BUFFET SUPPER GRAVY & SLICED TURKEY MAIN DISH
ConAgra, Inc.

Ingredients: chicken and turkey broth, turkey roll (turkey, natural juices, soy protein concentrate, salt, sodium phosphate), water, turkey skin, chicken and turkey fat, starch, flour, turkey giblets, salt, flavoring, monosodium glutamate, caramel color, sugar, paprika, oleoresin of turmeric, corn sugar.

Amount: 5⅓ oz			% USRDA
Calories	134	Protein	24
Protein, gm	11	Vitamin A	*
Carbohydrates, gm	4	Vitamin C	*
Fat, gm	8	Thiamine	2
Sodium, mg	576	Riboflavin	4
Cholesterol, mg	55e	Niacin	10
Fiber, gm	0e	Calcium	*
		Iron	6

THIS FOOD: A good source of protein and a fair source of niacin. It is low in calories. About 54 percent of calories come from fat. It is high in sodium.

ADDITIVES: Contains monosodium glutamate (MSG), 'which many authorities believe should be avoided by infants and very young children; causes adverse reactions in sensitive individuals.

BANQUET CHICKEN PIE
ConAgra, Inc.

Ingredients: *Filling:* chicken broth, chicken roll (binders added), chicken meat, soy protein concentrate, salt, water, sodium phosphate, cellulose gum, water, chicken meat, chicken skin, starch, potatoes, flour, carrots, peas, salt, flavorings, vegetable oil, monosodium glutamate, beta carotene, paprika, oleoresin of turmeric, dextrose, disodium inosinate, disodium guanylate. *Crust:* enriched flour (wheat flour, niacin, ferrous sulfate, thiamine hydrochloride, riboflavin), shortening, water, dextrose, salt, sodium bicarbonate, sodium aluminum phosphate, nonfat dry milk, artificial color, FD & C Yellow No. 5.

Amount: 8 oz			% USRDA
Calories	520	Protein	35
Protein, gm	16	Vitamin A	8
Carbohydrates, gm	45	Vitamin C	3
Fat, gm	30	Thiamine	5
Sodium, mg	1,027	Riboflavin	7
Cholesterol, mg	70e	Niacin	14
Fiber, gm	1e	Calcium	4
		Iron	6
Contains ½ teaspoon salt and 6½ teaspoons fat.			

THIS FOOD: Banquet Chicken Pie is high in calories, 52 percent of them from fat. Yet apart from supplying complex carbohydrates, it is a good or excellent source only of protein and niacin, which makes it below average in nutritional value, compared to the other entrées profiled. Like most prepared foods, this product is very high in sodium.

ADDITIVES: Contains monosodium glutamate (MSG), which many experts believe should be avoided by infants and very young children; causes adverse reactions in sensitive individuals. Contains artificial colors, which are inadequately tested and which some studies suggest may adversely affect behavior and the ability to complete school tasks in some sensitive children. Contains Yellow No. 5, which can cause allergic reactions, especially in aspirin-sensitive individuals.

OTHER BRANDS: Swanson Chicken Pie is nutritionally superior for several reasons. It contains 20 percent fewer calories (though about the same percentage of them derive from fat), four times more vitamin A, and significantly greater amounts of the B vitamins and iron.

BANQUET COOKIN' BAG CHICKEN À LA KING ENTRÉE
ConAgra, Inc.
Ingredients: chicken broth, water, chicken meat, chicken roll (chicken, soy protein concentrate, salt, sodium phosphate), dry whole milk, peas, nonfat dry milk (dry skim milk), flour, starch, mushrooms, red peppers, margarine, chicken fat, salt, hydrolyzed plant protein, onion powder, monosodium glutamate, paprika, and spice.

Amount: 5 oz			% USRDA
Calories	159	Protein	32
Protein, gm	14	Vitamin A	4
Carbohydrates, gm	10	Vitamin C	10
Fat, gm	7	Thiamine	6
Sodium, mg	645	Riboflavin	15
Cholesterol, mg	45e	Niacin	15
Fiber, gm	<1e	Calcium	12
		Iron	6

THIS FOOD: Banquet Cookin' Bag Chicken à la King Entrée is an excellent source of protein and a good source of vitamin C, riboflavin, niacin, and calcium. Since this product contains more chicken broth and water than chicken meat, it is not surprising that it is fairly low in calories. With 39 percent fat calories, it is moderately high in fat. Like most frozen entrées, this product is high in sodium.

ADDITIVES: Contains monosodium glutamate (MSG), which many experts believe should be avoided by infants and very young children; causes adverse reactions in some sensitive individuals.

BANQUET COOKIN' BAG SALISBURY STEAK ENTRÉE
ConAgra, Inc.

Ingredients: Salisbury steak (beef, water, onions, textured soy flour [caramel colored], soy protein concentrate, bread crumbs, salt, flavoring, caramel color, sodium phosphate, cellulose gum, disodium inosinate, disodium guanylate, gravy (water, wheat flour, cornstarch, salt, onion powder, flavoring, caramel color, sugar).

Amount: 5 oz			% USRDA
Calories	251	Protein	29
Protein, gm	13	Vitamin A	*
Carbohydrates, gm	5	Vitamin C	*
Fat, gm	20	Thiamine	2
Sodium, mg	729	Riboflavin	5
Cholesterol, mg	75e	Niacin	9
Fiber, gm	<1e	Calcium	*
		Iron	6

Contains 4½ teaspoons fat.

THIS FOOD: Banquet Cookin' Bag Salisbury Steak Entrée is not a significant source of any nutrient besides protein. Seventy-two percent of its calories derive from fat, and it is high in saturated fat. Compared to the other brands profiled, this entrée is well below average in nutritional value. Like most frozen prepared foods, this product is high in sodium.

ADDITIVES: No questionable additives.

BANQUET INTERNATIONAL FAVORITES VEAL PARMIGIANA BUFFET SUPPER
ConAgra, Inc.

Ingredients: breaded veal patty (veal, beef, water, soy protein concentrate, cereal, bread crumbs, onions, sugar, salt, monosodium glutamate, spice, garlic powder, *in a batter of:* water, corn flour, wheat flour, starch, salt, dextrose, sodium acid pyrophosphate, baking soda. Breaded with wheat flour, dextrose, sugar, salt, soybean oil, oleoresin paprika, natural flavor), water, reconstituted dehydrated potatoes, peas, tomato paste, margarine, starch, imitation Parmesan cheese, (water, sodium caseinate, hydrogenated soybean oil, tapioca flour, salt, tricalcium phosphate, adipic acid, artificial colors and flavors, monosodium glutamate, potassium sorbate), cheese (Parmesan, mozzarella), sugar, salt, dried whey, hydrolyzed plant protein, enzyme-modified cheese (Parmesan, Romano made from cow's milk), dehydrated onions, nonfat dry milk (dry skim milk), monosodium glutamate, flour, onion powder, spices, garlic powder, carboxymethyl cellulose, vegetable oil base (partially hydrogenated vegetable oil, lactose, sodium caseinate, dipotassium phosphate, sodium aluminosilicate, tricalcium phosphate, BHA), beet powder, citric acid, paprika, artificial butter flavor.

Amount: 6½ oz			% USRDA
Calories	277	Protein	20
Protein, gm	9	Vitamin A	9
Carbohydrates, gm	25	Vitamin C	10
Fat, gm	16	Thiamine	5
Sodium, mg	842	Riboflavin	6
Cholesterol, mg	85	Niacin	9
Fiber, gm	1e	Calcium	6
		Iron	6

THIS FOOD: Banquet International Favorites Veal Parmigiana is high in fat and calories and low in vitamins and minerals. Apart from complex carbohydrates, and protein, it is not a good source of nutrients. About 52 percent of its calories derive from fat. Like most frozen prepared foods, this product is high in sodium.

ADDITIVES: Contains monosodium glutamate (MSG), which many authorities believe should be avoided by infants and very young children; causes adverse reactions in sensitive individuals. Also contains artificial color and flavor, which some studies suggest may adversely affect behavior and the ability to complete school tasks in some sensitive children; artificial colors are inadequately tested, and artificial flavor may cause allergic reactions in sensitive individuals. Contains BHA, whose long-term safety is currently being reexamined by FDA investigators.

BANQUET MACARONI AND CHEESE CASSEROLE
ConAgra, Inc.

Ingredients: cooked macaroni in a sauce containing water, Cheddar cheese, margarine (partially hydrogenated soybean oil, liquid soybean oil, water, salt, nonfat dry milk, soybean lecithin, vegetable mono- and diglycerides, sodium benzoate, artificial color, artificial flavor, vitamin A palmitate), cornstarch, wheat flour, salt, whey, sodium caseinate, Cheddar cheese, flavoring, and coloring.

Amount: 8 oz			% USRDA
Calories	344	Protein	24
Protein, gm	11	Vitamin A	12
Carbohydrates, gm	36	Vitamin C	*
Fat, gm	17	Thiamine	3
Sodium, mg	930	Riboflavin	8
Cholesterol, mg	30e	Niacin	4
Fiber, gm	1.5e	Calcium	21
		Iron	6

THIS FOOD: Banquet Macaroni and Cheese Casserole supplies a lot of calories—44 percent from fat—but is relatively low in nutrients. In addition to providing complex carbohydrates, it is a very good source of protein and calcium. Like most frozen prepared foods, it is high in sodium.

ADDITIVES: Contains artificial color and flavor, which some studies suggest may adversely affect behavior and the ability to complete school tasks in some sensitive children; artificial colors are inadequately tested and artificial flavor may cause allergic reactions in sensitive individuals.

CELENTANO EGGPLANT PARMIGIANA
Celentano Bros., Inc.

Ingredients: crushed California tomatoes, eggplant, mozzarella, eggs, bread crumbs, unbleached enriched flour, imported Romano cheese, peanut oil, garlic, onion, oregano, basil, parsley, salt, pepper.

Amount: 7 oz			% USRDA
Calories	349	Protein	29
Protein, gm	13	Vitamin A	37
Carbohydrates, gm	20	Vitamin C	14
Fat, gm	24	Thiamine	na
Sodium, mg	555	Riboflavin	na
Cholesterol, mg	20e	Niacin	34
Fiber, gm	2e	Calcium	13
		Iron	16
Contains more than 5 teaspoons fat.			

THIS FOOD: Celentano Eggplant Parmigiana is very high in fat and fat calories, which account for 62 percent of the total. It is rich in protein, vitamin A, and niacin and a good source of calcium and iron. Like most frozen prepared foods, it is high in sodium.

ADDITIVES: No questionable additives.

CELENTANO LASAGNA
Celentano Bros., Inc.

Ingredients: crushed California tomatoes, whole milk ricotta, unbleached enriched fancy durum wheat flour, mozzarella, eggs, water, imported Romano cheese, peanut oil, garlic, onion, oregano, basil, parsley, salt, pepper.

Amount: 7 oz			% USRDA
Calories	288	Protein	30
Protein, gm	14	Vitamin A	30
Carbohydrates, gm	31	Vitamin C	15
Fat, gm	12	Thiamine	na
Sodium, mg	600	Riboflavin	na
Cholesterol, mg	30e	Niacin	12
Fiber, gm	2e	Calcium	16
		Iron	13

THIS FOOD: Celentano Lasagna is rich in complex carbohydrates, protein, and vitamin A and is a very good source of vitamin C and calcium (data for thiamine and riboflavin could not be obtained). About 37 percent of its calories derive from fat. Like most frozen prepared foods, this product is high in sodium.

ADDITIVES: No questionable additives.

CELENTANO STUFFED SHELLS
Celentano Bros., Inc.

Ingredients: crushed California tomatoes, whole milk ricotta, fancy durum wheat semolina flour, mozzarella, eggs, water, imported Romano cheese, peanut oil, garlic, onion, oregano, basil, parsley, salt, pepper.

Amount: 8 oz			% USRDA
Calories	310	Protein	39
Protein, gm	18	Vitamin A	35
Carbohydrates, gm	26	Vitamin C	15
Fat, gm	15	Thiamine	na
Sodium, mg	730	Riboflavin	na
Cholesterol, mg	25e	Niacin	13
Fiber, gm	2e	Calcium	21
		Iron	19

THIS FOOD: Celentano Stuffed Shells are fairly moderate in calories—43 percent of them from fat—and they are also a very good source of hard-to-find calcium and iron, as well as a good source of vitamin C and niacin. In addition, they are rich in protein and vitamin A.

ADDITIVES: No questionable additives.

MORTON BEEF PATTY BOIL-IN-BAG ENTRÉE
R. J. Reynolds Industries, Inc.

Ingredients: water, beef, partially defatted beef fatty tissues, mushroom pieces, textured vegetable protein (soy flour, caramel color), modified food starch, bread crumbs, flour, salt, dried whey, natural flavorings, onions, soy protein concentrate, monosodium glutamate, Worcestershire sauce, caramel color.

Amount: 5 oz			% USRDA
Calories	200	Protein	20
Protein, gm	10	Vitamin A	*
Carbohydrates, gm	8	Vitamin C	*
Fat, gm	15	Thiamine	4
Sodium, mg	660	Riboflavin	8
Cholesterol, mg	35	Niacin	10
Fiber, gm	<1e	Calcium	6
		Iron	8

THIS FOOD: Although the label claims it contains "partially defatted beef fatty tissue" (whatever that means), Morton Beef Patty Boil-in-Bag Entrée still contains 67 percent fat calories and is high in saturated fat. In addition to providing protein, it is only a fair source of one other nutrient: niacin. Compared to the other items profiled, this entrée is well below average in nutritional value. Like most frozen prepared foods, it is high in sodium.

ADDITIVES: Contains monosodium glutamate (MSG), which many authorities believe should be avoided by infants and very young children; causes adverse reactions in some sensitive individuals.

MORTON BEEF POT PIE
R. J. Reynolds Industries, Inc.

Ingredients: water, cooked beef, enriched flour, shortening, food starch modified, carrots, salt, peas, dehydrated potatoes, corn syrup, hydrolyzed vegetable protein, caramel color, monosodium glutamate, beef tallow, spices, onion powder, autolyzed yeast, dextrose, and thiamine hydrochloride.

Amount: 8 oz		% USRDA	
Calories	320	Protein	25
Protein, gm	11	Vitamin A	15
Carbohydrates, gm	31	Vitamin C	2
Fat, gm	16	Thiamine	15
Sodium, mg	1,040	Riboflavin	10
Cholesterol, mg	40	Niacin	15
Fiber, gm	1e	Calcium	2
		Iron	15
Contains ½ teaspoon salt.			

THIS FOOD: Moderate in calories, 45 percent of them from fat. It supplies complex carbohydrates, protein, and is a good source of vitamin A, B vitamins, and iron. It is high in sodium.

ADDITIVES: Contains monosodium glutamate (MSG), which many authorities believe should be avoided by infants and very young children; causes adverse reactions in some sensitive individuals.

MORTON CREAMED CHIPPED BEEF BOIL-IN-BAG ENTRÉE

R. J. Reynolds Industries, Inc.

Ingredients: water, dried beef (cured with salt, dextrose, sodium nitrite), margarine, modified food starch, flour, nonfat dry milk, dried whey, vegetable oil, salt, lecithin, natural flavorings, monosodium glutamate.

Amount: 5 oz		% USRDA	
Calories	160	Protein	25
Protein, gm	11	Vitamin A	4
Carbohydrates, gm	9	Vitamin C	*
Fat, gm	9	Thiamine	4
Sodium, mg	1,370	Riboflavin	15
Cholesterol, mg	17	Niacin	6
Fiber, gm	0	Calcium	6
		Iron	8
Contains ⅔ teaspoon salt.			

THIS FOOD: Derives 50 percent of calories from fat. It is an excellent source of protein and a good source of riboflavin. It is low in nutritional value and very high in sodium.

ADDITIVES: Contains monosodium glutamate (MSG), which many authorities believe should be avoided by infants and very young children; causes adverse reactions in some sensitive individuals. Also contains sodium nitrite, which can be converted to cancer-causing substances called nitrosamines.

MORTON SLOPPY JOE BOIL-IN-BAG ENTRÉE

R. J. Reynolds Industries, Inc.

Ingredients: water, beef, tomato paste, textured vegetable protein (soy flour, caramel color), onions, green peppers, sugar, flavorings, salt.

Amount: 5 oz		% USRDA	
Calories	210	Protein	25
Protein, gm	12	Vitamin A	15
Carbohydrates, gm	12	Vitamin C	25
Fat, gm	13	Thiamine	8
Sodium, mg	730	Riboflavin	8
Cholesterol, mg	33	Niacin	15
Fiber, gm	<1e	Calcium	4
		Iron	15

THIS FOOD: Contains 56 percent fat calories and is high in saturated fat. It provides protein, and is a good source of vitamin A, vitamin C, niacin, and iron. It is high in sodium.

ADDITIVES: No questionable additives.

MORTON TURKEY POT PIE
R. J. Reynolds Industries, Inc.

Ingredients: water, turkey, and structured soy protein roll with broth (turkey meat, water, structured soy protein isolate, salt, soy protein concentrate, sodium phosphates, hydrolyzed vegetable protein, monosodium glutamate, onion powder, vegetable oil, spice, BHA), enriched flour, shortening, carrots, food starch modified, whey solids, turkey loaf (turkey meat, water, salt, sodium phosphates), turkey meat, peas, salt, dehydrated potatoes, corn syrup, onion powder, hydrolyzed vegetable protein, monosodium glutamate, annatto, spices, turmeric oleoresin.

Amount: 8 oz		% USRDA	
Calories	340	Protein	35
Protein, gm	16	Vitamin A	15
Carbohydrates, gm	31	Vitamin C	2
Fat, gm	17	Thiamine	15
Sodium, mg	1,115	Riboflavin	15
Cholesterol, mg	45	Niacin	15
Fiber, gm	<1e	Calcium	2
		Iron	10

Contains ½ teaspoon salt.

THIS FOOD: Moderate in calories—45 percent of them from fat. One pie is a good source of vitamin A, B vitamins, complex carbohydrates, and protein. This product is high in sodium.

ADDITIVES: Contains monosodium glutamate (MSG), which many authorities believe should be avoided by infants and very young children; causes adverse reactions in some sensitive individuals. Also contains BHA, whose long-term safety is currently being reexamined by FDA investigators.

STOUFFER'S CHICKEN DIVAN
Nestlé, S. A.

Ingredients: milk, chicken, broccoli, sherry wine, Cheddar cheese, chicken fat, enriched wheat flour, modified cornstarch, Parmesan cheese, salt, monosodium glutamate, turmeric.

Amount: 8½ oz			% USRDA
Calories	335	Protein	30
Protein, gm	21	Vitamin A	35
Carbohydrates, gm	14	Vitamin C	15
Fat, gm	22	Thiamine	10
Sodium, mg	830	Riboflavin	15
Cholesterol, mg	80e	Niacin	20
Fiber, gm	3e	Calcium	20
		Iron	6

THIS FOOD: High in fat calories—59 percent of total—and cholesterol. Still, it is an excellent source of protein and vitamin A, a good source of B vitamins and calcium. It is high in sodium.

ADDITIVES: Contains monosodium glutamate (MSG), which many authorities believe should be avoided by infants and very young children; causes adverse reactions in some sensitive individuals.

STOUFFER'S GLAZED CHICKEN WITH VEGETABLE RICE LEAN CUISINE
Nestlé, S. A.

Ingredients: *Chicken pouch:* chicken, water, mushrooms, soybean oil, corn syrup, lemon juice, modified cornstarch, salt, enriched wheat flour, monosodium glutamate, chicken fat, caramel coloring, sugar, dehydrated onions, spices, dehydrated garlic, paprika, chicken broth, turmeric, natural flavorings. *Rice pouch:* cooked white rice, green beans, onions, cooked wild rice, salt, chicken, monosodium glutamate, chicken fat, sugar, dehydrated onions, chicken broth, turmeric, natural flavorings.

Amount: 8½ oz			% USRDA
Calories	270	Protein	40
Protein, gm	26	Vitamin A	2
Carbohydrates, gm	23	Vitamin C	6
Fat, gm	8	Thiamine	10
Sodium, mg	840	Riboflavin	8
Cholesterol, mg	75e	Niacin	50
Fiber, gm	2e	Calcium	2
		Iron	4

THIS FOOD: Stouffer's Glazed Chicken with Vegetable Rice Lean Cuisine is great for dieters—low in fat calories (23 percent of total) as well as overall calories. In addition to providing protein and complex carbohydrates, this frozen entrée is rich in niacin. Like other frozen prepared foods, it is high in sodium.

ADDITIVES: Contains monosodium glutamate (MSG), which many authorities believe should be avoided by infants and very young children; causes adverse reactions in some sensitive individuals.

STOUFFER'S SPAGHETTI WITH BEEF AND MUSHROOM SAUCE LEAN CUISINE

Nestlé, S. A.

Ingredients: *Meat sauce:* tomatoes, beef, mushrooms, onions, tomato paste, enriched wheat flour, modified cornstarch, sugar, salt, Parmesan cheese, natural flavorings, monosodium glutamate, spices, corn oil, dehydrated garlic, chicken fat, dehydrated onion, caramel coloring, erythorbic acid, dried beef stock. *Spaghetti pouch:* cooked spaghetti, corn oil, salt.

Amount: 11½ oz			% USRDA
Calories	280	Protein	25
Protein, gm	15	Vitamin A	10
Carbohydrates, gm	38	Vitamin C	10
Fat, gm	7	Thiamine	10
Sodium, mg	1,400	Riboflavin	10
Cholesterol, mg	75e	Niacin	20
Fiber, gm	2e	Calcium	6
		Iron	5

Contains ⅔ teaspoon salt.

THIS FOOD: True to its advertising, Stouffer's Spaghetti with Beef and Mushroom Sauce Lean Cuisine is indeed good for dieters and anyone interested in low-fat eating. It is rich in complex carbohydrates and protein and is a good source of vitamin A, vitamin C, and the B vitamins. Only 23 percent of calories derive from fat. Like most frozen prepared foods, this product is high in sodium. All in all, this product is well ahead of the pack in nutritional terms.

ADDITIVES: Contains monosodium glutamate (MSG), which many authorities believe should be avoided by infants and very young children; causes adverse reactions in some sensitive individuals.

STOUFFER'S SWEDISH MEATBALLS WITH PARSLEY NOODLES
Nestlé, S. A.

Ingredients: *Meatball pouch:* water, beef, pork, drhydrated sour cream mix (dehydrated sour cream, cultured nonfat milk solids, and citric acid), modified cornstarch, bread crumbs, butter, margarine, tomato puree, dehydrated onions, salt, wheat flour, natural flavorings, Worcestershire sauce, monosodium glutamate, spices, corn oil, sugar, chicken fat, caramel coloring, dehydrated garlic, paprika, dried beef stock. *Noodle pouch:* cooked noodles, margarine, salt, parsley.

Amount: 11 oz			% USRDA
Calories	475	Protein	35
Protein, gm	25	Vitamin A	10
Carbohydrates, gm	33	Vitamin C	*
Fat, gm	27	Thiamine	15
Sodium, mg	1,620	Riboflavin	20
Cholesterol, mg	100e	Niacin	25
Fiber, gm	1e	Calcium	8
		Iron	25

Contains nearly 6 teaspoons fat and more than ¾ teaspoon salt.

THIS FOOD: Stouffer's Swedish Meatballs with Parsley Noodles is moderately high in calories—51 percent of them from fat—as well as in cholesterol, and saturated fat. In addition to providing protein and complex carbohydrates, it is a very good source of the B vitamins and iron. This product is very high in sodium.

ADDITIVES: Contains monosodium glutamate (MSG), which many authorities believe should be avoided by infants and very young children; causes adverse reactions in some sensitive individuals.

STOUFFER'S VEGETABLE LASAGNA
Nestlé, S. A.

Ingredients: milk, cooked lasagna noodles, ricotta cheese, low-moisture part-skim mozzarella cheese, spinach, carrots, Parmesan cheese, onions, margarine (partially hydrogenated soybean oil, skim milk, salt, vegetable lecithin, vegetable mono- and diglycerides, sodium benzoate and citric acid, artificially flavored, colored with beta carotene, vitamin A palmitate), bread crumbs (unbleached enriched flour [malted barley flour, niacin, iron, thiamine mononitrate, riboflavin], water, corn syrup, partially hydrogenated vegetable shortening [soy bean oil], salt, yeast, nonfat dry milk, mono- and diglycerides, butter, honey, calcium propionate), modified cornstarch, enriched bleached flour (wheat flour, niacin, reduced iron, thiamine mononitrate, riboflavin), nonfat dry milk, butter, Romano cheese (made from cow's milk), salt, monosodium glutamate, mushroom base (sautéed mushrooms, salt, monosodium glutamate, butter, hydrolyzed plant protein, sugar flavoring), sugar, spices, dehydrated garlic, celery salt.

Amount: 11½ oz			% USRDA
Calories	440	Protein	35
Protein, gm	24	Vitamin A	70
Carbohydrates, gm	35	Vitamin C	8
Fat, gm	23	Thiamine	10
Sodium, mg	950	Riboflavin	20
Cholesterol, mg	50e	Niacin	40
Fiber, gm	3e	Calcium	60
		Iron	4

Contains 5 teaspoons fat and nearly ½ teaspoon salt.

THIS FOOD: Stouffer's Vegetable Lasagna is moderate in calories—47 percent of them from fat—and it is also high in nutrients. In addition to providing complex carbohydrates and protein, it is an excellent source of niacin, vitamin A, and hard-to-get calcium. It is also a very good source of thiamine. Like most frozen prepared foods, it is high in sodium.

ADDITIVES: Contains monosodium glutamate (MSG), which many authorities believe should be avoided by infants and very young children; causes adverse reactions in some sensitive individuals.

SWANSON CHICKEN PIE
Campbell Soup Co.

Ingredients: chicken broth, enriched wheat flour, cooked chicken meat, shortening, water, carrots, rehydrated potatoes, chicken, chicken skins, wheat flour, chicken fat, modified food starch, margarine, peas, salt, dextrose, whey powder, sweet peppers, monosodium glutamate, dehydrated onions, lactic acid, spice, and celery seeds.

Amount: 8 oz			% USRDA
Calories	420	Protein	25
Protein, gm	13	Vitamin A	40
Carbohydrates, gm	39	Vitamin C	4
Fat, gm	24	Thiamine	20
Sodium, mg	850	Riboflavin	15
Cholesterol, mg	40e	Niacin	20
Fiber, gm	2e	Calcium	2
		Iron	10

Contains 5 teaspoons fat.

THIS FOOD: Swanson Chicken Pie derives more than half its calories from fat, much of it saturated. Still, if you love chicken pot pie, this product delivers much better nutrition than the Banquet version. Both are excellent sources of protein, but the Swanson pie contains fewer calories yet supplies four times more vitamin A, and more of the B vitamins and iron. Like most frozen entrées, this product is high in sodium.

ADDITIVES: Contains monosodium glutamate (MSG), which many authorities believe should be avoided by infants and very young children; causes adverse reactions in sensitive individuals.

SWANSON FISH 'N' CHIPS ENTRÉE
Campbell Soup Co.

Ingredients: fried potatoes (potatoes, partially hydrogenated vegetable shortening [palm and/or soybean oil], salt, dextrose), cod, partially hydrogenated vegetable oils (palm and soybean), bleached wheat flour, corn flour, skim milk, water, salt, modified food starch, leavening (sodium aluminum phosphate, sodium bicarbonate), guar gum, whey, sugar, sodium alginate, eggs, dextrose, monosodium glutamate, spices, natural flavoring.

Amount: 5½ oz			% USRDA
Calories	310	Protein	15
Protein, gm	11	Vitamin A	*
Carbohydrates, gm	31	Vitamin C	4
Fat, gm	16	Thiamine	10
Sodium, mg	585	Riboflavin	8
Cholesterol, mg	35e	Niacin	10
Fiber, gm	2e	Calcium	2
		Iron	10

THIS FOOD: Swanson Fish 'n' Chips Entrée contains more potatoes than fish, and is moderately high in calories, relative to the amount of nutrients it supplies. In addition to supplying complex carbohydrates, it provides a fair amount of protein, thiamine, niacin, and iron. About 46 percent of its calories derive from fat. Like most frozen entrées, this product is high in sodium.

ADDITIVES: Contains monosodium glutamate (MSG), which many authorities believe should be avoided by infants and very young children; causes adverse reactions in sensitive individuals.

TO AVOID ADDITIVES: Celentano products are truly "natural" while the ingredients lists of most frozen entrees and dinners are peppered with emulsifiers, stabilizers, preservatives, and flavorings like dextrose, modified food starch, sodium benzoate, erthorbic acid, which home cooks rarely use. The ingredients used to make Celentano frozen products actually read like a home recipe.

SWANSON FRIED CHICKEN ENTRÉE
Campbell Soup Co.

Ingredients: chicken portions (fried in vegetable oil), reconstituted dehydrated potatoes, water, chicken broth, enriched wheat flour, margarine, salt, dried whey, sodium phosphates, monosodium glutamate, and butter.

Amount: 7¼ oz			% USRDA
Calories	390	Protein	40
Protein, gm	19	Vitamin A	*
Carbohydrates, gm	30	Vitamin C	8
Fat, gm	21	Thiamine	10
Sodium, mg	1,075	Riboflavin	10
Cholesterol, mg	95e	Niacin	35
Fiber, gm	2e	Calcium	4
		Iron	15

Contains ½ teaspoon salt and 4½ teaspoons fat.

THIS FOOD: Swanson Fried Chicken Entrée is high in fat calories—48 percent of total—and cholesterol. In addition to providing complex carbohydrates and protein, it is a good source of the B vitamins and iron. Like most frozen prepared foods, this product is high in sodium.

ADDITIVES: Contains monosodium glutamate (MSG), which many authorities believe should be avoided by infants and very young children; causes adverse reactions in sensitive individuals.

SWANSON HUNGRY-MAN SLICED BEEF
Campbell Soup Co.

Ingredients: cooked beef, reconstituted dehydrated potatoes, beef stock, water, margarine, modified food starch, salt, tomato paste, wheat flour, dried whey, yeast extract, and hydrolyzed plant protein, onion powder, monosodium glutamate, butter, caramel color, natural flavoring, dehydrated garlic.

Amount: 12¼ oz			% USRDA
Calories	330	Protein	80
Protein, gm	40	Vitamin A	*
Carbohydrates, gm	24	Vitamin C	20
Fat, gm	8	Thiamine	10
Sodium, mg	1,045	Riboflavin	10
Cholesterol, mg	130e	Niacin	45
Fiber, gm	3e	Calcium	2
		Iron	25

THIS FOOD: For a three-quarter pound serving, Swanson Hungry-Man Sliced Beef is relatively low in calories—only 22 percent of them from fat—and moderately high in cholesterol. In addition to providing a great deal of protein and complex carbohydrates, it is an excellent source of niacin and iron and a good source of vitamin C. Like most frozen prepared foods, this product is high in sodium.

ADDITIVES: Contains monosodium glutamate (MSG), which many authorities believe should be avoided by infants and very young children; causes adverse reactions in sensitive individuals.

SWANSON MEATBALLS WITH BROWN GRAVY ENTRÉE
Campbell Soup Co.

Ingredients: meatballs (beef, reconstituted onions, water, soy protein concentrate, cornstarch, soy protein isolate, salt, hydrolyzed plant protein, caramel color, dehydrated garlic, spice, and natural flavoring), reconstituted dehydrated potatoes, beef stock, water, margarine, modified food starch, sherry wine, salt, wheat flour, dried whey, tomato paste, onion powder, monosodium glutamate, sugar, butter, dehydrated garlic, natural flavoring.

Amount: 8½ oz			% USRDA
Calories	280	Protein	25
Protein, gm	13	Vitamin A	*
Carbohydrates, gm	20	Vitamin C	8
Fat, gm	17	Thiamine	4
Sodium, mg	885	Riboflavin	8
Cholesterol, mg	100e	Niacin	25
Fiber, gm	2e	Calcium	4
		Iron	15

THIS FOOD: Swanson Meatballs with Brown Gravy Entrée contains 55 percent fat calories and is high in cholesterol and saturated fat. In addition to protein and complex carbohydrates, this product is an excellent source of niacin, and a very good supplier of iron. Like most frozen prepared foods, it is high in sodium.

ADDITIVES: Contains monosodium glutamate (MSG), which many authorities believe should be avoided by infants and very young children; causes adverse reactions in sensitive individuals.

SWANSON SPAGHETTI IN TOMATO SAUCE WITH BREADED VEAL ENTRÉE
Campbell Soup Co.

Ingredients: tomatoes, cooked enriched spaghetti, breaded veal patty (veal, bread crumbs, water, soy flour, cornstarch, eggs, salt, spice), sugar, vegetable oil, modified food starch, Cheddar cheese, salt, onion powder, natural flavoring, dehydrated garlic, spice, and ascorbic acid.

Amount: 8¼ oz			% USRDA
Calories	270	Protein	30
Protein, gm	14	Vitamin A	10
Carbohydrates, gm	29	Vitamin C	15
Fat, gm	11	Thiamine	15
Sodium, mg	915	Riboflavin	10
Cholesterol, mg	50e	Niacin	25
Fiber, gm	1.5e	Calcium	2
		Iron	15

THIS FOOD: Moderate in calories, 36 percent of which come from fat, it supplies complex carbohydrates and protein, is a good source of vitamins A, C, B vitamins, and iron. It is high in sodium.

ADDITIVES: No questionable additives.

TASTE O'SEA PERCH DINNER
O'Donnell-Usen Fisheries Corp.

Ingredients: fish: ocean perch, bleached bromated wheat flour, water, vegetable oil (cottonseed and/or partially hydrogenated soybean), yellow corn flour, modified food starch, sugar, salt, monosodium glutamate, mono- and diglycerides, spices, leavening (sodium acid pyrophosphate, sodium bicarbonate), yeast, natural flavors, calcium propionate, sodium tripolyphosphate. Peas: peas, salt. Potato puffs: potatoes, vegetable oil (palm, and/or partially hydrogenated soybean), potato flour, salt, dextrose, disodium dihydrogen pyrophosphate.

Amount: 9 oz			% USRDA
Calories	540	Protein	50
Protein, gm	22	Vitamin A	4
Carbohydrates, gm	57	Vitamin C	4
Fat, gm	25	Thiamine	15
Sodium, mg	890	Riboflavin	15
Cholesterol, mg	80e	Niacin	15
Fiber, gm	1e	Calcium	4
		Iron	15

THIS FOOD: An excellent source of protein, a good source of vitamins and iron. About 41 percent of the calories come from fat, much of it saturated. It is high in sodium.

ADDITIVES: Contains monosodium glutamate (MSG), which many authorities believe should be avoided by infants and very young children; causes adverse reactions in some sensitive individuals.

TYSON CHICK'N QUICK THICK & CRISPY DINNER PATTIES
Tyson Foods, Inc.

Ingredients: boneless chicken breasts with rib meat, water, sodium phosphates; breaded with bleached wheat flour, partially hydrogenated soybean oil, salt, monosodium glutamate, nonfat milk, leavening (sodium acid pyrophosphate, sodium bicarbonate, monocalcium phosphate), yeast, dextrose, malt syrup, lecithin, sugar, dried whey, mono- and diglycerides, and natural flavoring; battered with water, modified food starch, corn flour, salt, leavening (sodium aluminum phosphate, sodium bicarbonate), monosodium glutamate. Fried in vegetable oil.

Amount: 7 oz			% USRDA
Calories	560	Protein	76
Protein, gm	34	Vitamin A	*
Carbohydrates, gm	20	Vitamin C	*
Fat, gm	36	Thiamine	8
Sodium, mg	662	Riboflavin	18
Cholesterol, mg	106	Niacin	52
Fiber, gm	1e	Calcium	*
		Iron	10
Contains nearly 8 teaspoons fat.			

THIS FOOD: Tyson Chick'n Quick Thick & Crispy Dinner Patties is moderately high in calories, 58 percent of them from fat. One serving is rich in protein and an excellent source of niacin. Like most frozen foods, this product is high in sodium.

ADDITIVES: Contains monosodium glutamate (MSG), which many authorities believe should be avoided by infants and very young children; causes adverse reactions in some sensitive individuals.

TYSON HEAT 'N SERVE OVEN READY FULLY COOKED CHICKEN
Tyson Foods, Inc.

Ingredients: chicken parts, water, sodium phosphates, salt; battered and breaded with bleached wheat flour, water, wheat gluten, salt, monosodium glutamate, dried egg white, leavening (sodium acid pyrophosphate, sodium bicarbonate, monocalcium phosphate), spices, natural flavor, soybean oil.

Amount: 7 oz			% USRDA
Calories	540	Protein	80
Protein, gm	36	Vitamin A	*
Carbohydrates, gm	23	Vitamin C	*
Fat, gm	33	Thiamine	10
Sodium, mg	1,176	Riboflavin	30
Cholesterol, mg	148	Niacin	44
Fiber, gm	<1e	Calcium	*
		Iron	13

Contains more than 7 teaspoons fat and ½ teaspoon salt.

THIS FOOD: Moderately high in calories, 56 percent of them from fat. It provides complex carbohydrates and protein, is a significant source of riboflavin and niacin, and is high in sodium.

ADDITIVES: Contains monosodium glutamate (MSG), which many authorities believe should be avoided by infants and very young children; causes adverse reactions in sensitive individuals.

WEAVER GOOD 'N WHOLESOME WHOLE WHEAT RECIPE FRIED CHICKEN
Victor F. Weaver, Inc.

Ingredients: skinless chicken breasts (pieces with ribs), thighs, and drumsticks, whole wheat bread crumbs, cereal flours, bran, salt, natural seasonings (spices), natural flavorings, vegetable oil.

Amount: 6 oz			% USRDA
Calories	380	Protein	62
Protein, gm	28	Vitamin A	*e
Carbohydrates, gm	22	Vitamin C	*e
Fat, gm	20	Thiamine	7e
Sodium, mg	560	Riboflavin	18e
Cholesterol, mg	100e	Niacin	44e
Fiber, gm	2e	Calcium	*e
		Iron	8e

THIS FOOD: Contains 47 percent fat calories. It provides complex carbohydrates, is an excellent source of niacin and protein, and a good source of riboflavin. It is high in sodium.

ADDITIVES: No questionable additives.

WEAVER ITALIAN STYLE CHICKEN RONDOLETS
Victor F. Weaver, Inc.

Ingredients: chicken, bread crumbs, chicken broth, water, cereal flours, hydrated soy protein isolate, egg white solids, dehydrated Parmesan cheese and dehydrated Romano cheese (made from cow's milk), salt, natural flavorings, sodium phosphates, paprika, guar gum, oleoresin of paprika, vegetable oil.

Amount: 2 patties/6 oz			% USRDA
Calories	440	Protein	58
Protein, gm	26	Vitamin A	*e
Carbohydrates, gm	18	Vitamin C	*e
Fat, gm	30	Thiamine	7e
Sodium, mg	na	Riboflavin	18e
Cholesterol, mg	100e	Niacin	44e
Fiber, gm	1e	Calcium	*e
		Iron	8e

Contains 6½ teaspoons fat.

THIS FOOD: Moderately high in calories, 61 percent of them from fat. Apart from providing protein, one serving is an excellent source of niacin and a good source of riboflavin. Although data for sodium is not available, it is probably high in salt.

ADDITIVES: No questionable additives.

WEIGHT WATCHERS SOUTHERN FRIED CHICKEN PATTY, VEGETABLE MEDLEY
H. J. Heinz Co.

Ingredients: chicken (chicken meat, water, salt, disodium phosphate), broccoli, water, carrots, cauliflower, breading (enriched wheat flour, yellow corn flour, salt, leavening [sodium acid pyrophosphate, sodium bicarbonate], monosodium glutamate, spices, sodium alginate, natural flavor, soybean oil, soya flour), batter (water, enriched wheat flour, salt, leavening [monocalcium phosphate, sodium bicarbonate], buttermilk, spice), chicken base (chicken meat, salt, chicken fat, monosodium glutamate, sugar, dried whey, natural flavorings, turmeric), modified cornstarch, natural flavor, locust bean gum, salt, spice.

Amount: 1 patty/6¾ oz			% USRDA
Calories	260	Protein	30
Protein, gm	20	Vitamin A	30
Carbohydrates, gm	11	Vitamin C	15
Fat, gm	15	Thiamine	6
Sodium, mg	785	Riboflavin	8
Cholesterol, mg	75e	Niacin	25
Fiber, gm	3e	Calcium	4
		Iron	6

Contains 3 teaspoons fat and ⅓ teaspoon salt.

THIS FOOD: Fairly low in calories relative to the nutrients it provides. Over 50 percent of its calories come from fat. It is a good source of protein, fiber, vitamin C, and an excellent source of vitamin A, and niacin. It is high in sodium.

ADDITIVES: Contains monosodium glutamate (MSG), which many authorities believe should be avoided by infants and very young children; causes adverse reactions in some sensitive individuals.

WEIGHT WATCHERS VEAL PATTY PARMIGIANA ZUCCHINI IN TOMATO SAUCE

H. J. Heinz Co.

Ingredients: tomato puree, veal patty (veal, bread crumbs, salt, hydrolyzed vegetable protein, spices, garlic powder), zucchini, low-moisture part skim mozzarella cheese, corn oil, granulated onion, salt, spices, Romano cheese (made from cow's milk), garlic powder, carob bean gum, guar gum, xanthan gum, gum tragacanth.

Amount: 9 oz			% USRDA
Calories	250	Protein	35
Protein, gm	24	Vitamin A	45
Carbohydrates, gm	12	Vitamin C	4
Fat, gm	11	Thiamine	10
Sodium, mg	1,081	Riboflavin	20
Cholesterol, mg	80e	Niacin	20
Fiber, gm	3e	Calcium	25
		Iron	8
Contains ½ teaspoon salt.			

THIS FOOD: Considering the limited number of calories in Weight Watchers Veal Patty Parmigiana, it is a fairly nutritious entrée. Unfortunately, it contains 40 percent fat calories, which is higher than the recommended guidelines. This entrée is rich in protein and vitamin A and a very good source of the B vitamins and calcium. Like most frozen prepared foods, it is high in sodium.

ADDITIVES: No questionable additives.

OTHER BRANDS: Morton Veal Parmigiana Dinner, although not specifically aimed at dieters, is just as low in calories and has other advantages as well: the portion size is 2 ounces larger, and it contains only 29 percent fat calories.

MAYONNAISE

Mayonnaise, an emulsion of oil, egg yolks, lemon juice, and seasonings—used as a sandwich spread or salad dressing. Nearly all of the calories in mayonnaise come from fat. The effect mayonnaise has on cholesterol levels depends on the kind of oil used. Kraft and Hellmann's (Best Foods) use soybean oil, which contains about three times more polyunsaturated than saturated fat; a good ratio. Other brands, such as Blue Plate, may contain cottonseed oil, which has more saturated fat. According to federal standards, mayonnaise must contain at least 65 percent vegetable oil. Products called salad dressing, such as Miracle Whip, must contain not less than 30 percent vegetable oil.

The relationship between polyunsaturated and saturated fats is sometimes expressed as the p/s ratio. The highest ratios are the most unsaturated—and most desirable. The p/s ratio is the accepted way of gauging whether an oil is considered "heart-healthy" even though it does not take into account new evidence which shows that monounsaturated fats may be as helpful in lowering cholesterol levels. Most mayonnaise has an acceptable p/s ratio of between 2 and 3, meaning 2 to 3 times as much polyunsaturated oil as compared to saturated oil.

BEST FOODS REAL MAYONNAISE
CPC International, Inc.
Ingredients: soybean oil, partially hydrogenated soybean oil, whole eggs, vinegar, water, egg yolks, salt, sugar, lemon juice and natural flavors, calcium disodium EDTA added to protect flavor.

Amount: 1 tbsp			% USRDA
Calories	100	Protein	*
Protein, gm	<1	Vitamin A	*
Carbohydrates, gm	<1	Vitamin C	*
Fat, gm	11	Thiamine	*
Sodium, mg	80	Riboflavin	*
Cholesterol, mg	7	Niacin	*
Fiber, gm	0	Calcium	*
		Iron	*

THIS FOOD: Best Foods Real Mayonnaise, like other brands, is an emulsion made from oil, egg yolks, seasonings, and various additives. Nearly 100 percent of its calories derive from fat, and it has no other nutrients. This product has a reasonably good p/s ratio of 3.

ADDITIVES: No questionable additives.

BLUE PLATE MAYONNAISE
William B. Reilly and Co.

Ingredients: soybean oil and/or cottonseed oil, distilled vinegar, egg yolks, water, sugar, salt, natural flavorings.

Amount: 1 tbsp			% USRDA
Calories	110	Protein	*
Protein, gm	0	Vitamin A	*
Carbohydrates, gm	1	Vitamin C	*
Fat, gm	12	Thiamine	*
Sodium, mg	85	Riboflavin	*
Cholesterol, mg	10	Niacin	*
Fiber, gm	0	Calcium	*
		Iron	*

THIS FOOD: Is made from oil, egg yolks, seasonings, and various additives. Nearly 100 percent of its calories derive from fat. It has no other nutrients. This product may contain cottonseed oil, which is more saturated than soybean oil. It may have a less acceptable p/s ratio of less than 2.

ADDITIVES: No questionable additives.

HELLMANN'S REAL MAYONNAISE
CPC International, Inc.

Ingredients: soybean oil, partially hydrogenated soybean oil, whole eggs, vinegar, water, egg yolks, salt, sugar, lemon juice and natural flavors, calcium disodium EDTA added to protect flavor.

Amount: 1 tbsp			% USRDA
Calories	100	Protein	*
Protein, gm	<1	Vitamin A	*
Carbohydrates, gm	<1	Vitamin C	*
Fat, gm	11	Thiamine	*
Sodium, mg	80	Riboflavin	*
Cholesterol, mg	7	Niacin	*
Fiber, gm	0	Calcium	*
		Iron	*

NOTE: The letter "e" indicates that the data has been estimated; < means "less than" and is used for small amounts of sodium or cholesterol; * means food contains less than 2% of USRDA; "na" means that the information was not available and appears only when data is insufficient.

THIS FOOD: Hellmann's Real Mayonnaise, like other brands, is an emulsion made from oil, egg yolks, seasonings, and various additives. Nearly 100 percent of its calories derive from fat and it has no other nutrients. This product has a reasonably good p/s ratio of 3.

ADDITIVES: No questionable additives.

KRAFT REAL MAYONNAISE
Kraft, Inc.

Ingredients: soybean oil, eggs, water, vinegar, egg yolks, salt, sugar, lemon juice, paprika, dehydrated garlic, dehydrated onion, calcium disodium EDTA

Amount: 1 tbsp			% USRDA
Calories	100	Protein	*
Protein, gm	0	Vitamin A	*
Carbohydrates, gm	0	Vitamin C	*
Fat, gm	11	Thiamine	*
Sodium, mg	70	Riboflavin	*
Cholesterol, mg	5	Niacin	*
Fiber, gm	0	Calcium	*
		Iron	*

THIS FOOD: Is an emulsion made from oil, egg yolks, seasonings, and various additives. Nearly 100 percent of its calories derive from fat, and it has no other nutrients. This product has a reasonably good p/s ratio of 3.

ADDITIVES: No questionable additives.

LIGHT N' LIVELY REDUCED CALORIE MAYONNAISE
Kraft, Inc.

Ingredients: water, soybean oil, modified food starch, egg yolks, vinegar, salt, eggs, mustard flour, phosphoric acid, dl-a-tocopheryl acetate (vitamin E), calcium disodium EDTA, natural and artificial flavor, oleoresin paprika, beta carotene.

Amount: 1 tbsp			% USRDA
Calories	40	Protein	*
Protein, gm	0	Vitamin A	*
Carbohydrates, gm	2	Vitamin C	*
Fat, gm	7	Thiamine	*
Sodium, mg	85	Riboflavin	*
Cholesterol, mg	5	Niacin	*
Fiber, gm	0e	Calcium	*
		Iron	*

THIS FOOD: Light n' Lively Reduced Calorie Mayonnaise has less than half the calories of regular mayonnaise because water and thickeners are substituted for much of the oil. It is made from soybean oil, which has a p/s ratio of 3.

ADDITIVES: Contains artificial flavor, which may cause allergic reactions in sensitive individuals, and which some studies suggest may adversely affect behavior and the ability to complete school tasks in some sensitive children.

MIRACLE WHIP SALAD DRESSING
Kraft, Inc.

Ingredients: soybean oil, water, vinegar, sugar, egg yolks, starch, modified food starch, salt, mustard, flour, spice, paprika, natural flavor.

Amount: 1 tbsp			% USRDA
Calories	70	Protein	*
Protein, gm	0	Vitamin A	*
Carbohydrates, gm	2	Vitamin C	*
Fat, gm	7	Thiamine	*
Sodium, mg	85	Riboflavin	*
Cholesterol, mg	5	Niacin	*
Fiber, gm	0	Calcium	*
		Iron	*

THIS FOOD: Miracle Whip Salad Dressing cannot describe itself as mayonnaise, since it uses starches and flour as thickeners. It is almost a third lower in calories than real mayonnaise, but 90 percent of them come from fat. Like most mayonnaise made from soybean oil, it has an acceptable p/s ratio of 3.

ADDITIVES: No questionable additives.

HELPFUL HINT: To cut down on your fat intake, try using half the mayonnaise called for in recipes. If the resulting mixture is too dry, add a little yogurt.

HELPFUL HINT: Try spreading mustard on your sandwiches instead of mayonnaise—you'll save lots of fat calories.

MEAT AND POULTRY PRODUCTS

Bacon

Bacon is a popular breakfast food made from cured, fatty pork. All popular brands are high in saturated fat and sodium. They also contain sodium nitrite, which is one of the most controversial additives in use today. There are no significant nutritional differences among the popular brands of regular bacon. And the substitute bacons profiled (Swift's Premium Sizzlean, Oscar Mayer Lean 'n Tasty Beef Breakfast Strips) are not really any better. On the other hand Oscar Mayer Canadian Bacon (which is cut from the lean loin portion of the pig) contains nearly 50 percent less fat than regular bacon and substantially less sodium.

SODIUM GUIDELINES: In evaluating the sodium content of bacon, we have used the following standards:

less than 250 mg	moderate in sodium
250 mg to 500 mg	high in sodium
more than 500 mg	very high in sodium

Remember, these guidelines are not for people following medically restricted low-sodium diets, but for healthy individuals who wish to monitor their sodium intake.

FARMLAND SLICED BACON
Farmland Foods, Inc.

Ingredients: bacon, cured with water, salt, sugar, sodium phosphate, sodium erythorbate, and sodium nitrite.

Amount: 3 to 4 slices/1 oz (cooked)			% USRDA
Calories	160	Protein	20
Protein, gm	9	Vitamin A	*
Carbohydrates, gm	1	Vitamin C	*
Fat, gm	13	Thiamine	10
Sodium, mg	626	Riboflavin	5
Cholesterol, mg	17	Niacin	10
Fiber, gm	0	Calcium	*
		Iron	3

THIS FOOD: Farmland Sliced Bacon is typical of most ordinary breakfast bacons: very high in fat and sodium and low in other nutrients. About 75 percent of the calories in this product come from fat.

ADDITIVES: Contains sodium nitrite, which can be converted into cancer-causing substances called nitrosamines.

HYGRADE'S WEST VIRGINIA BRAND BACON
Hygrade Food Products Corp.

Ingredients: bacon cured with water, salt, sugar, sodium phosphates, sodium erythorbate, sodium nitrite.

Amount: 3 to 4 slices/1 oz (cooked)			% USRDA
Calories	154	Protein	20
Protein, gm	9	Vitamin A	*
Carbohydrates, gm	<1	Vitamin C	*
Fat, gm	13	Thiamine	13
Sodium, mg	414	Riboflavin	5
Cholesterol, mg	19	Niacin	10
Fiber,gm	0	Calcium	*
		Iron	3

THIS FOOD: Hygrade's West Virginia Brand Bacon is typical of most ordinary breakfast bacons: high in fat and sodium and low in other nutrients. About 75 percent of the calories in this product come from fat.

ADDITIVES: Contains sodium nitrite, which can be converted into cancer-causing substances called nitrosamines.

OSCAR MAYER BACON
Oscar Mayer and Co.

Ingredients: bacon, cured with water, salt, sugar, sodium phosphate, sodium ascorbate (vitamin C), sodium nitrite.

Amount: 3 to 4 slices/1 oz (cooked)			% USRDA
Calories	166	Protein	17
Protein, gm	8	Vitamin A	*
Carbohydrates, gm	<1	Vitamin C	16
Fat, gm	15	Thiamine	13
Sodium, mg	542	Riboflavin	5
Cholesterol, mg	24	Niacin	10
Fiber, gm	0	Calcium	*
		Iron	3

NOTE: The letter "e" indicates that the data has been estimated; < means "less than" and is used for small amounts of sodium or cholesterol; * means food contains less than 2% of USRDA; "na" means that the information was not available and appears only when data is insufficient.

THIS FOOD: Oscar Mayer Bacon is typical of most ordinary breakfast bacons: very high in fat and sodium and low in other nutrients. About 80 percent of the calories in this product come from fat.

ADDITIVES: Contains sodium nitrite, which can be converted into cancer-causing substances called nitrosamines.

OSCAR MAYER CANADIAN STYLE BACON
Oscar Mayer and Co.

Ingredients: Canadian-style bacon, cured with water, salt, sugar, sodium phosphate, sodium ascorbate (vitamin C), sodium nitrite.

Amount: one 1-oz slice (cooked)			% USRDA
Calories	40	Protein	12
Protein, gm	6	Vitamin A	*
Carbohydrates, gm	0	Vitamin C	12
Fat, gm	2	Thiamine	13
Sodium, mg	393	Riboflavin	2
Cholesterol, mg	12	Niacin	7
Fiber, gm	0	Calcium	*
		Iron	*

THIS FOOD: Oscar Mayer Canadian Style Bacon is much leaner and lower in calories than conventional bacons. About 45 percent of the calories in this product derive from fat, a great improvement over the 75 to 80 percent average in the usual fat-streaked variety. While it contains a substantial amount of sodium, 393 mg per serving, this is lower than that of most of the other bacons profiled.

ADDITIVES: Contains sodium nitrite, which can be converted into cancer-causing substances called nitrosamines.

NUTRITION TIP: According to some studies, nitrites are much less likely to form cancer-causing nitrosamines in the presence of excess vitamin C.

OSCAR MAYER LEAN 'N TASTY BEEF BREAKFAST STRIPS
Oscar Mayer and Co.

Ingredients: cured, chopped, formed beef, cured with water, salt, sugar, smoke flavoring, monosodium glutamate, sodium ascorbate (vitamin C), sodium nitrite.

Amount: 3 to 4 slices/1 oz (cooked)			% USRDA
Calories	126	Protein	20
Protein, gm	9	Vitamin A	*
Carbohydrates, gm	.6	Vitamin C	16
Fat, gm	9	Thiamine	2
Sodium, mg	636	Riboflavin	4
Cholesterol, mg	35	Niacin	9
Fiber, gm	0	Calcium	*
		Iron	5

THIS FOOD: Oscar Mayer Lean 'n Tasty Beef Breakfast Strips are in fact much leaner than regular bacon, with 50 percent of their calories deriving from fat instead of the standard 80 percent. They contain a whopping 636 mg sodium per serving, which is very high for this food.

ADDITIVES: Contains sodium nitrite, which can be converted into cancer-causing substances called nitrosamines; and monosodium glutamate (MSG), which many experts believe should be avoided by infants and very young children, and which causes adverse reactions in some sensitive individuals.

SWIFT PREMIUM SIZZLEAN
Swift and Co.

Ingredients: pork, water, salt, natural flavoring, sugar, sodium phosphate, monosodium glutamate, natural smoke flavor, sodium erythorbate, sodium nitrite.

Amount: 3–4 slices/1 oz (cooked)			% USRDA
Calories	123	Protein	16
Protein, gm	7	Vitamin A	*
Carbohydrates, gm	0	Vitamin C	*
Fat, gm	11	Thiamine	14
Sodium, mg	669	Riboflavin	6
Cholesterol, mg	35	Niacin	11
Fiber, gm	0	Calcium	*
		Iron	3

THIS FOOD: Its name implies that Swift Premium Sizzlean is less fatty than the regular bacon for which it substitutes, but the label tells a different story. With 80 percent of its calories deriving from fat, this product is certainly no leaner than real bacon. A serving of these breakfast strips, which are formed from chopped pork, contains a whopping 669 mg sodium—more than any other brand profiled.

ADDITIVES: Contains sodium nitrite, which can be converted into cancer-causing substances called nitrosamines; and monosodium glutamate (MSG), which many experts believe should be avoided by infants and young children, and which causes adverse reactions in some sensitive individuals.

Bologna

Most kids like bologna, and a sandwich containing a slice or two with a little mustard or mayonnaise is certainly easy to prepare. Bologna is a good source of protein, and eating it once in a while won't do you much harm. But the key phrase here is "once in a while." Like other packaged sandwich meats, bologna is high in saturated fat, cholesterol, and sodium. Armour, Eckrich, and Oscar Mayer make beef or beef-and-pork bolognas which contain about 80 percent fat calories and 580 milligrams sodium per 2-ounce serving. Louis Rich Turkey Bologna, is significantly lower in fat and calories than traditional meat bolognas, but it is still high in sodium. All of the bolognas profiled contain sodium nitrite, a controversial additive which causes cancer in laboratory animals.

ARMOUR BEEF BOLOGNA
The Greyhound Corp.

Ingredients: beef, water, dextrose, salt, corn syrup, spices, flavorings, sodium erythorbate, sodium nitrite and oleoresin of paprika.

Amount: two 1-oz slices			% USRDA
Calories	180	Protein	13
Protein, gm	6	Vitamin A	*
Carbohydrates, gm	11e	Vitamin C	17e
Fat, gm	16	Thiamine	*
Sodium, mg	570	Riboflavin	2e
Cholesterol, mg	30	Niacin	7e
Fiber, gm	0	Calcium	*
		Iron	2e

THIS FOOD: Armour Beef Bologna is a good source of protein and added vitamin C. Although people think of bologna as inexpensive, the protein it contains (which is its sole nutritional asset) actually costs twice as much as the protein in tuna fish, or four times as much as the protein in peanut butter. This bologna contains 80 percent fat calories and is high in saturated fat and very high in sodium.

ADDITIVES: Contains sodium nitrite, which can be converted into cancer-causing substances called nitrosamines.

NOTE: The letter "e" indicates that the data has been estimated; < means "less than" and is used for small amounts of sodium or cholesterol; * means food contains less than 2% of USRDA; "na" means that the information was not available and appears only when data is insufficient.

ECKRICH BOLOGNA
Beatrice Foods Co.

Ingredients: beef and pork, water, dextrose, corn syrup, salt, flavorings, smoke flavoring, ascorbic acid, sodium nitrite, extract of paprika.

Amount: two 1-oz slices			% USRDA
Calories	180	Protein	12
Protein, gm	6	Vitamin A	*
Carbohydrates, gm	4	Vitamin C	20
Fat, gm	16	Thiamine	8
Sodium, mg	580	Riboflavin	4
Cholesterol, mg	32e	Niacin	4
Fiber, gm	0e	Calcium	*
		Iron	4
Contains 3 teaspoons fat.			

THIS FOOD: A good source of protein and added vitamin C, although the protein it contains (its sole nutritional asset) costs twice as much as the protein in tuna fish, or four times as much as the protein in peanut butter. It has 80 percent fat calories, is high in saturated fat and very high in sodium.

ADDITIVES: Contains sodium nitrite, which can be converted into cancer-causing substances called nitrosamines.

ECKRICH GARLIC BOLOGNA
Beatrice Foods Co.

Ingredients: beef and pork, water, dextrose, corn syrup, salt, flavorings, garlic, smoke flavoring, ascorbic acid, sodium nitrite, extract of paprika.

Amount: two 1-oz slices			% USRDA
Calories	180	Protein	12
Protein, gm	6	Vitamin A	*
Carbohydrates, gm	4	Vitamin C	20
Fat, gm	16	Thiamine	8
Sodium, mg	580	Riboflavin	4
Cholesterol, mg	32e	Niacin	4
Fiber, gm	0e	Calcium	*
		Iron	4
Contains 3 teaspoons fat.			

THIS FOOD: A good source of protein and added vitamin C, although the protein it contains (its sole nutritional asset) actually costs twice as much as the protein in tuna fish, or four times as much as the protein in peanut butter. It has 80 percent fat calories, is high in saturated fat, and very high in sodium.

ADDITIVES: Contains sodium nitrite, which can be converted into cancer-causing substances called nitrosamines.

LOUIS RICH TURKEY BOLOGNA
Oscar Mayer and Co.

Ingredients: turkey, water, corn syrup solids, salt, spices, garlic powder, sodium erythorbate, and sodium nitrite.

Amount: two 1-oz slices			% USRDA
Calories	120	Protein	16
Protein, gm	7	Vitamin A	*
Carbohydrates, gm	1	Vitamin C	*
Fat, gm	9	Thiamine	*
Sodium, mg	428	Riboflavin	4
Cholesterol, mg	40	Niacin	10
Fiber, gm	0	Calcium	6
		Iron	4
Contains 2 teaspoons fat.			

THIS FOOD: Louis Rich Turkey Bologna contains significantly less fat than the standard beef or beef and pork bolognas. This product is a good source of protein and niacin. It is high in sodium and contains 67 percent fat calories, which is below average for this category.

ADDITIVES: Contains sodium nitrite, which can be converted into cancer-causing substances called nitrosamines.

OSCAR MAYER BEEF BOLOGNA
Oscar Mayer and Co.

Ingredients: beef, water, corn syrup, salt, flavoring, dextrose, paprika, ascorbic acid (vitamin C), sodium nitrite.

Amount: two 1-oz slices			% USRDA
Calories	183	Protein	12
Protein, gm	6	Vitamin A	*
Carbohydrates, gm	1	Vitamin C	15
Fat, gm	16	Thiamine	*
Sodium, mg	581	Riboflavin	3
Cholesterol, mg	32	Niacin	7
Fiber, gm	0	Calcium	*
		Iron	4
Contains 3 teaspoons fat.			

THIS FOOD: Oscar Mayer Beef Bologna is a good source of protein and added vitamin C. Although people think of bologna as inexpensive, the protein it contains (which is its sole nutritional asset) actually costs twice as much as the protein in tuna fish, or four times as much as the protein in peanut butter. This bologna contains 78 percent fat calories and is high in saturated fat and very high in sodium.

ADDITIVES: Contains sodium nitrite, which can be converted into cancer-causing substances called nitrosamines.

OSCAR MAYER BOLOGNA
Oscar Mayer and Co.

Ingredients: pork, water, beef, corn syrup, salt, flavoring, dextrose, paprika, ascorbic acid (vitamin C), sodium nitrite.

Amount: two 1-oz slices			% USRDA
Calories	183	Protein	12
Protein, gm	6	Vitamin A	0
Carbohydrates, gm	1	Vitamin C	15
Fat, gm	17	Thiamine	7
Sodium, mg	587	Riboflavin	2
Cholesterol, mg	32	Niacin	5
Fiber, gm	0	Calcium	*
		Iron	*
Contains more than 3 teaspoons fat.			

THIS FOOD: Oscar Mayer Bologna is a good source of protein and added vitamin C. Although people think of bologna as inexpensive, the protein it contains (which is its sole nutritional asset) actually costs twice as much as the protein in tuna fish, or four times as much as the protein in peanut butter. This bologna contains 84 percent fat calories and is high in saturated fat and very high in sodium.

ADDITIVES: Contains sodium nitrite, which can be converted into cancer-causing substances called nitrosamines.

BEST BET: If you love bologna, try Louis Rich Turkey Bologna, which is lower in fat and calories than standard meat bolognas.

Canned Meat and Poultry

Canned meat and poultry products have a bad reputation—and for good reason. The vast majority are high in overall fat and saturated fat—and extremely high in sodium. In addition these products typically contain sodium nitrate, a controversial additive which causes cancer in laboratory animals.

All of the canned meat products profiled, including Libby's Corned Beef, Spam, Underwood Deviled Ham, and Treet have these drawbacks. Swanson Premium Chunk White Chicken offers much better nutrition, since it is low in overall fat and saturated fat and contains no controversial additives.

SODIUM GUIDELINES: In evaluating the sodium content of canned meat and poultry products, we used the following standards:

less than 250 mg	moderate in sodium
250 mg to 500 mg	high in sodium
more than 500 mg	very high in sodium

Remember, these guidelines are not for people following medically restricted low-sodium diets, but for healthy individuals who wish to monitor their sodium intake.

LIBBY'S CORNED BEEF
Carnation Co.
Ingredients: cooked beef, beef, salt, sugar, water, sodium nitrite.

Amount: 2.3 oz			% USRDA
Calories	160	Protein	35
Protein, gm	17	Vitamin A	*
Carbohydrates, gm	2	Vitamin C	*
Fat, gm	9	Thiamine	*
Sodium, mg	720	Riboflavin	6
Cholesterol, mg	25e	Niacin	6
Fiber, gm	0	Calcium	*
		Iron	8

Contains 2 teaspoons fat and more than ⅓ teaspoon salt.

THIS FOOD: Libby's Corned Beef is moderately high in saturated fat and overall fat, which contributes 50 percent of calories. It is an excellent source of protein. This product is extremely high in sodium.

ADDITIVES: Contains sodium nitrite, which can be converted into cancer-causing substances called nitrosamines.

SPAM
George A. Hormel and Co.

Ingredients: chopped pork shoulder meat with ham meat added and salt, water, sugar, sodium nitrite.

Amount: 2 oz			% USRDA
Calories	174	Protein	15
Protein, gm	8	Vitamin A	*
Carbohydrates, gm	2	Vitamin C	*
Fat, gm	15	Thiamine	14
Sodium, mg	772	Riboflavin	6
Cholesterol, mg	36e	Niacin	9
Fiber, gm	0	Calcium	*
		Iron	2
Contains 3 teaspoons fat and more than ⅓ teaspoon salt.			

THIS FOOD: Spam is extremely high in sodium, saturated fat, and overall fat, which accounts for a full 79 percent of calories. It is a good source of protein and thiamine.

ADDITIVES: Contains sodium nitrite, which can be converted into cancer-causing substances called nitrosamines.

SWANSON PREMIUM CHUNK WHITE CHICKEN
Campbell Soup Co.

Ingredients: white chicken meat, water, salt, natural flavorings.

Amount: 2½ oz			% USRDA
Calories	90	Protein	35
Protein, gm	17	Vitamin A	*
Carbohydrates, gm	0	Vitamin C	*
Fat, gm	2	Thiamine	*
Sodium, mg	230	Riboflavin	2
Cholesterol, mg	35e	Niacin	30
Fiber, gm	0	Calcium	*
		Iron	2
Contains less than ½ teaspoon fat.			

NOTE: The letter "e" indicates that the data has been estimated; < means "less than" and is used for small amounts of sodium or cholesterol; * means food contains less than 2% of USRDA; "na" means that the information was not available and appears only when data is insufficient.

THIS FOOD: Swanson Premium Chunk White Chicken is fairly low in calories, and only 20 percent of them come from fat. In addition to providing protein, this product is a good source of niacin. It contains a moderate amount of sodium.

ADDITIVES: No questionable additives.

TREET
The Greyhound Corp.

Ingredients: pork, chicken, beef, salt, water, corn syrup, sugar, brown sugar, hydrolyzed vegetable protein, smoke flavoring, paprika, spices, flavoring, sodium nitrite.

Amount: 2 oz			% USRDA
Calories	193	Protein	15
Protein, gm	7	Vitamin A	*
Carbohydrates, gm	2	Vitamin C	*
Fat, gm	17	Thiamine	5
Sodium, mg	793	Riboflavin	5
Cholesterol, mg	36e	Niacin	7
Fiber, gm	0	Calcium	*
		Iron	3

Contains 3½ teaspoons fat and more than ⅓ teaspoon salt.

THIS FOOD: Treet is extremely high in sodium, saturated fat, and overall fat, which accounts for 79 percent of calories. It is a good source of protein and no other nutrients.

ADDITIVES: Contains sodium nitrite, which can be converted into cancer-causing substances called nitrosamines.

UNDERWOOD DEVILED HAM
IC Industries, Inc.

Ingredients: unsmoked ham (cured with water, salt, sugar, sodium nitrite), natural spices.

Amount: 2 oz			% USRDA
Calories	198	Protein	18
Protein, gm	8	Vitamin A	*
Carbohydrates, gm	1	Vitamin C	*
Fat, gm	18	Thiamine	16e
Sodium, mg	576	Riboflavin	4e
Cholesterol, mg	20e	Niacin	6e
Fiber, gm	0	Calcium	*e
		Iron	*e

Contains nearly 4 teaspoons fat and ¼ teaspoon salt.

THIS FOOD: Underwood Deviled Ham is very high in sodium, saturated fat, and overall fat, which accounts for 82 percent of calories. It is a very good source of protein and thiamine.

ADDITIVES: Contains sodium nitrite, which can be converted into cancer-causing substances called nitrosamines.

See "Basic Foods" on pages 553, 554, 556, 559, 560, 563, 564, 566, 567 for fresh meat listings.

FOR SODIUM WATCHERS: You'll want to avoid Spam and Treet, which contain more than 750 mg sodium, or about ⅓ teaspoon salt, in a small 2-ounce serving.

BEST BET: Swanson Premium Chunk White Chicken is the only food profiled in this section that is low in calories and fat, moderate in sodium, and free of controversial additives.

Ham

All of the canned and packaged hams profiled are high in sodium, but two popular brands, Oscar Mayer Jubilee Ham Slice and Armour Golden Star Canned Ham, are actually quite lean—only 30 percent of calories derive from fat. Unfortunately consumers are forced to take pot luck when choosing their hams, since Oscar Mayer is the only major brand to include nutrition information on the label. Like the pork from which it is made, ham is moderately high in cholesterol. All of the popular hams and turkey hams profiled are very high in sodium, but it should be noted that Louis Rich Turkey Ham, with 524 milligrams sodium per serving, contains 20 to 40 percent less sodium than the other brands.

SODIUM GUIDELINES: In evaluating the sodium content of a 2-ounce serving of ham, we used the following standards:

less than 250 mg	moderate in sodium
250 mg to 500 mg	high in sodium
more than 500 mg	very high in sodium

Remember, these guidelines are not for people on medically restricted low-sodium diets, but for healthy individuals who wish to monitor their sodium intake.

ARMOUR GOLDEN STAR CANNED HAM
Con Agra, Inc.

Ingredients: ham, sectioned and formed, with natural juices and gelatin, cured with water, salt, sodium phosphates, and sodium nitrite.

Amount: 2 oz			% USRDA
Calories	60	Protein	22
Protein, gm	10	Vitamin A	*
Carbohydrates, gm	1	Vitamin C	*
Fat, gm	2	Thiamine	35
Sodium, mg	647	Riboflavin	7
Cholesterol, mg	33	Niacin	14
Fiber, gm	0	Calcium	*
		Iron	2
Contains ⅓ teaspoon salt.			

THIS FOOD: Armour Golden Star Canned Ham is low in calories, only 30 percent of which come from fat. It is a very good source of protein, thiamine, and niacin, but contains cholesterol and is very high in sodium.

ADDITIVES: Contains sodium nitrite, which can be converted into cancer-causing substances called nitrosamines.

LAND O' FROST HAM
Land O' Frost of Arkansas, Inc.

Ingredients: ham, water, salt, corn syrup, dextrose, sodium phosphates, hydrolyzed plant protein, monosodium glutamate, flavorings, sodium erythorbate, sodium nitrite.

Amount: 2 oz			% USRDA
Calories	100	Protein	10
Protein, gm	10	Vitamin A	*
Carbohydrates, gm	2	Vitamin C	*
Fat, gm	6	Thiamine	8
Sodium, mg	800	Riboflavin	4
Cholesterol, mg	33	Niacin	6
Fiber, gm	0	Calcium	0*
		Iron	2
Contains more than ⅓ teaspoon salt.			

NOTE: The letter "e" indicates that the data has been estimated; < means "less than" and is used for small amounts of sodium or cholesterol; * means food contains less than 2% of USRDA; "na" means that the information was not available and appears only when data is insufficient.

THIS FOOD: Land O' Frost Ham is lower in protein and B vitamins than the other brands profiled. It contains 54 percent fat calories and unwanted cholesterol and is extremely high in sodium.

ADDITIVES: Contains sodium nitrite, which can be converted into cancer-causing substances called nitrosamines.

LOUIS RICH TURKEY HAM
Oscar Mayer and Co.

Ingredients: turkey thigh meat, water, salt, sugar, sodium phosphates, sodium erythorbate, and sodium nitrite.

Amount: 2 oz			% USRDA
Calories	70	Protein, gm	22
Protein, gm	11	Vitamin A	*
Carbohydrates, gm	<1	Vitamin C	0
Fat, gm	2	Thiamine	2
Sodium, mg	524	Riboflavin	8
Cholesterol, mg	34	Niacin	16
Fiber, gm	0	Calcium	*
		Iron	*

THIS FOOD: Louis Rich Turkey Ham is one of the rare luncheon meats to contain fewer than 30 percent fat calories. In fact, only 26 percent of calories come from fat. It is also very low in overall calories. This product is an excellent source of protein and a good source of niacin. It is very high in sodium.

ADDITIVES: Contains sodium nitrite, which can be converted into cancer-causing substances called nitrosamines.

MR. TURKEY TURKEY HAM
Bil Mar Foods, Inc.

Ingredients: turkey thigh meat, water, salt, sugar, sodium phosphate, monosodium glutamate, ascorbic acid, citric acid, sodium nitrite.

Amount: 2 oz			% USRDA
Calories	72	Protein	22
Protein, gm	10	Vitamin A	*
Carbohydrates, gm	1	Vitamin C	*
Fat, gm	3	Thiamine	*
Sodium, mg	843	Riboflavin	11
Cholesterol, mg	34e	Niacin	10
Fiber, gm	0	Calcium	*
		Iron	7

Contains more than ⅓ teaspoon salt.

THIS FOOD: Mr. Turkey Turkey Ham is a very good source of protein and a fairly good source of riboflavin and niacin. It contains unwanted cholesterol and is moderate in fat with 37 percent fat calories. This product is extremely high in sodium.

ADDITIVES: Contains monosodium glutamate (MSG), which many experts believe should be avoided by infants and very young children; causes adverse reactions in sensitive individuals. It also contains sodium nitrite, which can be converted into cancer-causing substances called nitrosamines.

OSCAR MAYER JUBILEE HAM SLICE
Oscar Mayer and Co.

Ingredients: ham, cured with water, salt, sugar, sodium phosphate, sodium ascorbate (vitamin C), sodium nitrite.

Amount: 2 oz			% USRDA
Calories	60	Protein	24
Protein, gm	11	Vitamin A	*
Carbohydrates, gm	0	Vitamin C	28
Fat, gm	2	Thiamine	32
Sodium, mg	746	Riboflavin	6
Cholesterol, mg	28	Niacin	12
Fiber, gm	0	Calcium	*
		Iron	2

Contains more than ⅓ teaspoon salt.

THIS FOOD: Oscar Mayer Jubilee Ham Slice is low in calories, only 30 percent of which come from fat. It is a very good source of protein, thiamine, and niacin. It contains unwanted cholesterol and is very high in sodium.

ADDITIVES: Contains sodium nitrite, which can be converted into cancer-causing substances called nitrosamines.

See "Basic Foods" on pages 553, 554, 556, 559, 560, 563, 564, 566, 567 for fresh meat listings.

BEST BETS: Despite its fatty reputation, some brands of ham are actually very lean. Only 30 percent of calories in Armour Golden Star Canned Ham and Oscar Mayer Jubilee Ham Slice derive from fat. Louis Rich Turkey Ham is even leaner, with only 26 percent fat calories.

Hot Dogs

Hot dogs, also called franks, wieners, and red hots, are as American as apple pie, despite their German ancestry. In 1913 the Coney Island Chamber of Commerce banned the term "hot dog" because they feared people would believe the sausage was actually made from ground canine! Beef and/or pork are used, which contain about 45 percent water and 28 percent fat by weight. An additional 10 percent water is added to the mix during manufacturing. Consumers who believe that if beef is listed first, there is more of it than pork, are mistaken. According to the "70/30" rule, the beef and pork together must account for 70 percent of the frank's meat content and can be added in *any proportion*, as long as neither meat accounts for less than 30 percent of the total meat used.

In 1984 Americans ate 17 billion hot dogs or more than seventy-five hot dogs per person. This perfect fast food has serious nutritional failings. About 80 percent of its calories come from fat, much of it saturated. It is high in sodium and cholesterol. Although hot dogs seem inexpensive, the protein costs $14.97 a pound, compared to $8.72 a pound for hamburger, $5.90 for chicken, or $2.95 for dried beans.

SODIUM GUIDELINES: In evaluating the sodium content of hot dogs, we used the following standards:

less than 250 mg	moderate in sodium
250 mg to 500 mg	high in sodium
more than 500 mg	very high in sodium

Remember, these guidelines are not for people following medically restricted low-sodium diets, but for healthy individuals who wish to monitor their sodium intake.

ARMOUR BEEF HOT DOGS
The Greyhound Corp.

Ingredients: beef, water, dextrose, salt, corn syrup, spices, flavorings, sodium erythorbate, sodium nitrite, oleoresin of paprika.

NOTE: The letter "e" indicates that the data has been estimated; < means "less than" and is used for small amounts of sodium or cholesterol; * means food contains less than 2% of USRDA; "na" means that the information was not available and appears only when data is insufficient.

Amount: 1 hot dog			% USRDA
Calories	150	Protein	7
Protein, gm	3	Vitamin A	*e
Carbohydrates, gm	1e	Vitamin C	*e
Fat, gm	13	Thiamine	*e
Sodium, mg	455	Riboflavin	2e
Cholesterol, mg	20	Niacin	5e
Fiber, gm	0e	Calcium	*e
		Iron	3e

THIS FOOD: Armour Beef Franks are relatively low in protein and other nutrients, while 80 percent of their calories derive from fat. Ounce for ounce, these hot dogs are a more expensive source of protein than sirloin steak. This product is not recommended for those who wish to restrict their intake of sodium, cholesterol, or saturated fat.

ADDITIVES: Contains sodium nitrite, which can be converted into cancer-causing substances called nitrosamines.

BALL PARK BEEF FRANKS
Hygrade Food Products Corp.

Ingredients: beef, water, salt, flavoring, sodium erythorbate, sodium nitrite, oleoresin paprika.

Amount: 1 hot dog/2 oz			% USRDA
Calories	167	Protein	15e
Protein, gm	7	Vitamin A	*e
Carbohydrates, gm	0	Vitamin C	*e
Fat, gm	16	Thiamine	2e
Sodium, mg	535	Riboflavin	3e
Cholesterol, mg	29e	Niacin	7e
Fiber, gm	0	Calcium	*e
		Iron	4e

THIS FOOD: Ball Park Beef Franks are relatively low in protein and other nutrients, while 86 percent of their calories derive from fat. Ounce for ounce, hot dogs are a more expensive source of protein than sirloin steak. This product is not recommended for those who wish to restrict their intake of sodium, cholesterol, or saturated fat.

ADDITIVES: Contains sodium nitrite, which can be converted into cancer-causing substances called nitrosamines.

BALL PARK FRANKS
Hygrade Food Products Corp.

Ingredients: beef and pork, water, salt, flavorings, sodium erythorbate, sodium nitrite, oleoresin paprika.

Amount: 1 hot dog/2 oz			% USRDA
Calories	174	Protein	14e
Protein, gm	7	Vitamin A	*e
Carbohydrates, gm	0	Vitamin C	*e
Fat, gm	17	Thiamine	8e
Sodium, mg	535	Riboflavin	4e
Cholesterol, mg	29e	Niacin	8e
Fiber, gm	0	Calcium	*e
		Iron	4e

THIS FOOD: Ball Park Franks are relatively low in protein and other nutrients, while 88 percent of their calories derive from fat. Ounce for ounce, hot dogs are a more expensive source of protein than sirloin steak. This product is not recommended for those who wish to restrict their intake of sodium, cholesterol, or saturated fat.

ADDITIVES: Contains sodium nitrite, which can be converted into cancer-causing substances called nitrosamines.

ECKRICH BEEF FRANKS
Beatrice Foods Co.

Ingredients: beef, water, corn syrup, salt, dextrose, flavorings, ascorbic acid, sodium nitrite, extract of paprika.

Amount: 1 hot dog/1¼ oz			% USRDA
Calories	110	Protein	10
Protein, gm	4	Vitamin A	*
Carbohydrates, gm	2	Vitamin C	10
Fat, gm	10	Thiamine	*
Sodium, mg	380	Riboflavin	2
Cholesterol, mg	18e	Niacin	4
Fiber, gm	0	Calcium	*
		Iron	2

THIS FOOD: Eckrich Beef Franks are relatively low in protein and other nutrients, while 80 percent of their calories derive from fat. Ounce for ounce, hot dogs are a more expensive source of protein than sirloin steak. This product is not recommended for those who wish to restrict their intake of sodium, cholesterol, or saturated fat.

ADDITIVES: Contains sodium nitrite, which can be converted nito cancer-causing substances called nitrosamines.

ECKRICH FRANKS
Beatrice Foods Co.

Ingredients: beef and pork, water, corn syrup, salt, dextrose, flavorings, ascorbic acid, sodium nitrite, extract of paprika.

Amount: 1 hot dog/1¼ oz			% USRDA
Calories	120	Protein	8
Protein, gm	3	Vitamin A	*
Carbohydrates, gm	2	Vitamin C	6
Fat, gm	11	Thiamine	2
Sodium, mg	360	Riboflavin	2
Cholesterol, mg	18e	Niacin	4
Fiber, gm	0	Calcium	*
		Iron	2

THIS FOOD: Eckrich Franks are relatively low in protein and other nutrients, while 80 percent of their calories derive from fat. Ounce for ounce, hot dogs are a more expensive source of protein than sirloin steak. This product is not recommended for those who wish to restrict their intake of sodium, cholesterol, or saturated fat.

ADDITIVES: Contains sodium nitrite, which can be converted into cancer-causing substances called nitrosamines.

FARMER JOHN WIENERS
Clougherty Packing Co.

Ingredients: beef and pork, water, salt, corn syrup, dextrose, flavoring, hydrolyzed vegetable protein, monosodium glutamate, ascorbic acid, oleoresin paprika, sodium nitrite.

Amount: 1 hot dog/1½ oz			% USRDA
Calories	143	Protein	13e
Protein, gm	6	Vitamin A	*e
Carbohydrates, gm	<1	Vitamin C	20e
Fat, gm	11	Thiamine	6e
Sodium, mg	793	Riboflavin	3e
Cholesterol, mg	22e	Niacin	6e
Fiber, gm	0	Calcium	*e
		Iron	3e

THIS FOOD: Farmer John Wieners are relatively low in protein and other nutrients, while 70 percent of their calories derive from fat. Ounce for ounce, hot dogs are a more expensive source of protein than sirloin steak. Each hot dog contains a whopping 793 mg sodium—higher than any other popular brand. This product is not recommended for those who wish to restrict their intake of saturated fat and cholesterol.

ADDITIVES: Contains sodium nitrite, which can be converted into cancer-causing substances called nitrosamines.

OSCAR MAYER BEEF FRANKS
Oscar Mayer and Co.

Ingredients: beef, water, corn syrup, salt, flavoring, dextrose, sodium ascorbate (vitamin C), sodium nitrite.

Amount: 1 hot dog/1½ oz			% USRDA
Calories	145	Protein	11
Protein, gm	5	Vitamin A	*
Carbohydrates, gm	<1	Vitamin C	18
Fat, gm	14	Thiamine	*
Sodium, mg	466	Riboflavin	2
Cholesterol, mg	27	Niacin	5
Fiber, gm	0	Calcium	*
		Iron	3

THIS FOOD: Oscar Mayer Beef Franks are relatively low in protein and other nutrients while 87 percent of their calories derive from fat. Ounce for ounce, these hot dogs are a more expensive source of protein than sirloin steak. This product is not recommended for people who wish to restrict their intake of sodium, cholesterol, or saturated fat.

ADDITIVES: Contains sodium nitrite, which can be converted into cancer-causing substances called nitrosamines.

OSCAR MAYER WIENERS
Oscar Mayer and Co.

Ingredients: beef and pork, water, salt, corn syrup, flavoring, dextrose, sodium ascorbate (vitamin C), sodium nitrite.

Amount: 1 hot dog/1½ oz			% USRDA
Calories	145	Protein	11
Protein, gm	5	Vitamin A	*
Carbohydrates, gm	<1	Vitamin C	19
Fat, gm	14	Thiamine	6
Sodium, mg	459	Riboflavin	2
Cholesterol, mg	24	Niacin	5
Fiber, gm	0	Calcium	*
		Iron	2

THIS FOOD: Oscar Mayer Wieners are relatively low in protein and other nutrients while 87 percent of their calories derive from fat. Ounce for ounce, these hot dogs are a more expensive source of protein than sirloin steak. This product is not recommended for those who wish to restrict their intake of sodium, cholesterol, or saturated fat.

ADDITIVES: Contains sodium nitrite, which can be converted into cancer-causing substances called nitrosamines.

OSCAR MAYER WIENERS WITH CHEESE
Oscar Mayer and Co.

Ingredients: pork, water, beef, pasteurized process American cheese, salt, corn syrup, flavoring, dextrose, sodium ascorbate (vitamin C), sodium nitrite.

Amount: 1 hot dog/1½ oz			% USRDA
Calories	145	Protein	12
Protein, gm	5	Vitamin A	*
Carbohydrates, gm	<1	Vitamin C	15
Fat, gm	14	Thiamine	5
Sodium, mg	10	Riboflavin	3
Cholesterol, mg	31	Niacin	4
Fiber, gm	0	Calcium	2
		Iron	2

THIS FOOD: Oscar Mayer Wieners with Cheese are no more nutritious than plain franks, since the cheese contributes very little besides extra fat and cholesterol. Like most franks. they are relatively low in protein and other nutrients, while 87 percent of their calories derive from fat. Ounce for ounce these hot dogs are a more expensive source of protein than sirloin steak. This product is not recommended for those who wish to restrict their intake of sodium, cholesterol, or saturated fat.

ADDITIVES: Contains sodium nitrite, which can be converted into cancer-causing substances called nitrosamines.

TYSON CHICKEN FRANKS
Tyson Foods, Inc.

Ingredients: chicken, salt, flavorings, water, sodium phosphates, paprika, sodium erythorbate, smoke flavoring, onion powder, garlic, sodium nitrite.

Amount: 1 hot dog/1½ oz			% USRDA
Calories	122	Protein	12
Protein, gm	5	Vitamin A	*
Carbohydrates, gm	1	Vitamin C	*
Fat, gm	11	Thiamine	4
Sodium, mg	505	Riboflavin	5
Cholesterol, mg	29	Niacin	7
Fiber, gm	0	Calcium	*
		Iron	4

THIS FOOD: Tyson Chicken Franks are no more nutritious than other hot dogs. They are relatively low in protein and other nutrients, while 81 percent of their calories derive from fat. Ounce for ounce, these hot dogs are a more expensive source of protein than sirloin steak. This product is not recommended for those who want to restrict their intake of sodium or saturated fat.

ADDITIVES: Contains sodium nitrite, which can be converted into cancer-causing substances called nitrosamines.

See "Basic Foods" on pages 553, 554, 556, 559, 560, 563, 564, 566, 567 for fresh meat listings.

Salami

Salami contains slightly more protein and B vitamins than most other packaged lunch meats, but it still exhibits all the nutritional failings typical of this convenience food: too much fat, cholesterol, and sodium. Two of the brands profiled, Eckrich Hard Salami and Oscar Mayer Hard Salami, each contain a very large amount of sodium, the equivalent of ½ teaspoon salt per 2-ounce serving. Louis Rich Turkey Cotto Salami and Oscar Mayer Cotto Salami contain about 50 percent less sodium. The popular meat salami profiled contain 70 to 80 percent fat calories, much of it saturated. Louis Rich's Turkey Salami is high in overall fat, but less of it is saturated. All of the salami profiled contain sodium nitrite, a controversial additive.

SODIUM GUIDELINES: In evaluating the sodium content of salami, we used the following standards:

less than 250 mg	moderate in sodium
250 mg to 500 mg	high in sodium
more than 500 mg	very high in sodium

Remember, these guidelines are not for people following medically restricted low-sodium diets, but for healthy individuals who wish to monitor their sodium intake.

ARMOUR COOKED SALAMI
The Greyhound Corp.

Ingredients: beef, beef hearts, water, pork, salt, dextrose, corn syrup, spices, garlic powder, sodium erythorbate, sodium nitrite, flavorings.

NOTE: The letter "e" indicates that the data has been estimated; < means "less than" and is used for small amounts of sodium or cholesterol; * means food contains less than 2% of USRDA; "na" means that the information was not available and appears only when data is insufficient.

Amount: two 1-oz slices			% USRDA
Calories	160	Protein	13
Protein, gm	6e	Vitamin A	*
Carbohydrates, gm	1e	Vitamin C	*
Fat, gm	14	Thiamine	8
Sodium, mg	600	Riboflavin	11
Cholesterol, mg	40	Niacin	8
Fiber, gm	0	Calcium	*
		Iron	7

THIS FOOD: Armour Cooked Salami is a good source of protein and riboflavin. Compared to other salamis, it is moderate in calories, but a full 78 percent of them come from fat, much of it saturated. This product is very high in sodium.

ADDITIVES: Contains sodium nitrite, which can be converted into cancer-causing substances called nitrosamines.

ECKRICH HARD SALAMI
Beatrice Foods Co.

Ingredients: beef and pork, salt, dextrose, natural smoke flavor, spices, dehydrated garlic, sodium nitrite, BHA, BHT, citric acid.

Amount: two 1-oz slices			% USRDA
Calories	260	Protein	20
Protein, gm	10	Vitamin A	*
Carbohydrates, gm	2	Vitamin C	*
Fat, gm	24	Thiamine	8
Sodium, mg	1,200	Riboflavin	8
Cholesterol, mg	44e	Niacin	12
Fiber, gm	0	Calcium	*
		Iron	4
Contains more than ½ teaspoon salt and 5 teaspoons fat			

THIS FOOD: Eckrich Hard Salami is especially high in calories, 83 percent of which derive from fat. It is a very good source of protein, and a good source of niacin. Like other salamis, it is high in cholesterol, and it is higher in sodium than any other salami profiled.

ADDITIVES: Contains sodium nitrite, which can be converted into cancer-causing substances called nitrosamines. Also contains BHA and BHT, whose long-term safety is currently being reexamined by FDA investigators.

GALLO PEPPERONI
Consolidated Foods, Inc.

Ingredients: pork, beef, salt, dextrose, paprika, spices, smoked flavoring, lactic acid starter culture, garlic powder, sodium nitrite, sodium nitrate.

Amount: two 1-oz slices			% USRDA
Calories	278e	Protein	27e
Protein, gm	12e	Vitamin A	*
Carbohydrates, gm	2e	Vitamin C	*
Fat, gm	25e	Thiamine	12e
Sodium, mg	1,142e	Riboflavin	8e
Cholesterol, mg	na	Niacin	14e
Fiber, gm	0	Calcium	*
		Iron	4e

Contains more than ½ teaspoon salt and 5 teaspoons fat.

THIS FOOD: Gallo Pepperoni is high in calories, saturated fat, and overall fat, which contributes 80 percent of calories. It is an excellent source of protein, and a good source of thiamine and niacin. This product is extremely high in sodium.

ADDITIVES: Contains sodium nitrite, which can be converted into cancer-causing substances called nitrosamines.

LOUIS RICH TURKEY COTTO SALAMI
Oscar Mayer and Co.

Ingredients: turkey, turkey hearts, water, salt, spices, sugar, sodium erythorbate, garlic powder, and sodium nitrite.

Amount: two 1-oz slices			% USRDA
Calories	100	Protein	18
Protein, gm	8	Vitamin A	*
Carbohydrates, gm	<1	Vitamin C	*
Fat, gm	8	Thiamine	2
Sodium, mg	502	Riboflavin	10
Cholesterol, mg	46	Niacin	12
Fiber, gm	0	Calcium	*
		Iron	4

Contains ¼ teaspoon salt and nearly 2 teaspoons fat.

THIS FOOD: Louis Rich Turkey Cotto Salami gets 80 percent of its calories from fat, which is a little higher than average for salami. It still has an advantage over regular pork and beef salamis, though: a lower proportion of saturated fat. This product is a good source of protein and niacin. Like most salamis, it is high in cholesterol and sodium.

ADDITIVES: Contains sodium nitrite, which can be converted into cancer-causing substances called nitrosamines.

OSCAR MAYER COTTO SALAMI
Oscar Mayer and Co.

Ingredients: pork, beef, water, salt, corn syrup, flavoring, dextrose, ascorbic acid (vitamin C), sodium nitrite.

Amount: two 1-oz slices			% USRDA
Calories	126	Protein	17
Protein, gm	8	Vitamin A	*
Carbohydrates, gm	1	Vitamin C	15
Fat, gm	10	Thiamine	10
Sodium, mg	597	Riboflavin	12
Cholesterol, mg	35	Niacin	10
Fiber, gm	0	Calcium	*
		Iron	7

Contains 2 teaspoons fat and more than ¼ teaspoon salt.

THIS FOOD: Oscar Mayer Cotto Salami is a very good source of protein and added vitamin C, and a good source of the B vitamins. About 71 percent of calories come from fat. This product is also high in saturated fat and cholesterol and very high in sodium.

ADDITIVES: Contains sodium nitrite, which can be converted into cancer-causing substances called nitrosamines.

OSCAR MAYER HARD SALAMI
Oscar Mayer and Co.

Ingredients: pork, beef, salt, sugar, lactic acid starter culture, flavoring, sodium ascorbate (vitamin C), sodium nitrite.

Amount: two 1-oz slices			% USRDA
Calories	207	Protein	27
Protein, gm	12	Vitamin A	*
Carbohydrates, gm	1	Vitamin C	21
Fat, gm	17	Thiamine	20
Sodium, mg	1,038	Riboflavin	7
Cholesterol, mg	45	Niacin	14
Fiber, gm	0	Calcium	*
		Iron	5

Contains ½ teaspoon salt and 3½ teaspoons fat.

THIS FOOD: Oscar Mayer Hard Salami is a very good source of protein, vitamin C, thiamine, and niacin. About 74 percent of calories come from fat. This product is also high in saturated fat and cholesterol and extremely high in sodium.

ADDITIVES: Contains sodium nitrite, which can be converted into cancer-causing substances called nitrosamines.

See "Basic Foods" on pages 553, 554, 556, 559, 560, 563, 564, 566, 567 for fresh meat listings.

Sandwich Meats

Packaged sandwich meats are more popular than canned and offer more options for the nutrition conscious. Most of the products profiled, including Eckrich Bologna, Gallo Salami, Eckrich Olive Loaf, Land O' Frost Chicken, Oscar Mayer Olive Loaf, and Oscar Mayer Picnic Loaf, have the typical faults already described. But the presence of several turkey products presents a real alternative to the usual fat-and-sodium-laden offerings. Louis Rich Turkey Breast Slices, with only 11 percent fat calories, and Mr. Turkey No Sodium Added Turkey Breast, with 23 percent fat calories, are both superior sandwich meats. In addition to being low in sodium, they contain no additives at all.

SODIUM LOSERS

These sandwich meats contain over 750 mg sodium (about ⅓ teaspoon salt) per 2-ounce serving:

Buddig Smoked Sliced Beef
Buddig Smoked Sliced Corned Beef
Land O' Frost Beef
Land O' Frost Chicken
Oscar Mayer Olive Loaf

BUDDIG SMOKED SLICED BEEF
Carl Buddig and Co.

Ingredients: beef, water, salt, sugar, monosodium glutamate, maple sugar, flavorings, sodium erythorbate, sodium nitrite.

Amount: two 1-oz slices			% USRDA
Calories	90	Protein	20
Protein, gm	12	Vitamin A	*
Carbohydrates, gm	2	Vitamin C	*
Fat, gm	4	Thiamine	*
Sodium, mg	850	Riboflavin	4
Cholesterol, mg	32	Niacin	12
Fiber, gm	0	Calcium	*
		Iron	8

THIS FOOD: Buddig Smoked Sliced Beef is a very good source of protein and a good source of niacin. About 40 percent of its calories come from fat, which is moderate for this category. This product is extremely high in sodium.

ADDITIVES: Contains sodium nitrite, which can be converted into cancer-causing substances called nitrosamines. Also contains monosodium glutamate (MSG), which many experts believe should be avoided by infants and very young children; causes adverse reactions in some sensitive individuals.

BUDDIG SMOKED SLICED CHICKEN
Carl Buddig and Co.

Ingredients: chicken, water, modified food starch, salt, monosodium glutamate, sugar, flavorings, hydrolyzed vegetable protein, turmeric.

Amount: two 1-oz slices			% USRDA
Calories	100	Protein	20
Protein, gm	10	Vitamin A	*
Carbohydrates, gm	2	Vitamin C	*
Fat, gm	6	Thiamine	*
Sodium, mg	680	Riboflavin	4
Cholesterol, mg	24	Niacin	12
Fiber, gm	0	Calcium	4
		Iron	4

THIS FOOD: Buddig Smoked Sliced Chicken is a very good source of protein and a good source of niacin. About 54 percent of its calories come from fat. This product is very high in sodium.

ADDITIVES: Contains monosodium glutamate (MSG), which many experts believe should be avoided by infants and very young children; causes adverse reactions in some sensitive individuals.

BUDDIG SMOKED SLICED CORNED BEEF
Carl Buddig and Co.

Ingredients: beef, water, salt, sugar, monosodium glutamate, maple sugar, hydrolyzed vegetable protein, sodium erythorbate, garlic, sodium nitrite, flavorings.

Amount: two 1-oz slices			% USRDA
Calories	90	Protein	20
Protein, gm	12	Vitamin A	*
Carbohydrates, gm	2	Vitamin C	*
Fat, gm	4	Thiamine	*
Sodium, mg	760	Riboflavin	4
Cholesterol, mg	32	Niacin	12
Fiber, gm	0	Calcium	*
		Iron	8

THIS FOOD: Buddig Smoked Sliced Corned Beef is a very good source of protein and a good source of niacin. About 40 percent of its calories come from fat, which is moderate for this category. This product is very high in sodium.

ADDITIVES: Contains monosodium glutamate (MSG), which many experts believe should be avoided by infants and very young children; causes adverse reactions in some sensitive individuals. Also contains sodium nitrite, which can be converted into cancer-causing substances called nitrosamines.

NITRITE FREE SANDWICH MEATS are not always easy to find. The following products are free of sodium nitrite, a controversial additive that causes cancer in laboratory animals.

Buddig Smoked Sliced Chicken
Louis Rich Turkey Breast Slices
Mr. Turkey Cooked White Turkey Roll
Mr. Turkey No Sodium Added Roasted Turkey Breast
Mr. Turkey Sliced Turkey Breast
Steam-Um Frozen Steak Sandwich Meat

ECKRICH OLIVE LOAF
Beatrice Foods Co.

Ingredients: beef and pork, water, olives, nonfat dry milk, sweet red peppers, salt, flavorings, dextrose, ascorbic acid, sodium nitrite.

Amount: two 1-oz slices			% USRDA
Calories	160	Protein	12
Protein, gm	6	Vitamin A	*
Carbohydrates, gm	4	Vitamin C	20
Fat, gm	14	Thiamine	4
Sodium, mg	740	Riboflavin	8
Cholesterol, mg	22e	Niacin	4
Fiber, gm	0	Calcium	4
		Iron	4

THIS FOOD: Eckrich Olive Loaf is very high in sodium, saturated fat, and overall fat, which accounts for 79 percent of its calories. It is a good source of protein and a very good source of added vitamin C.

ADDITIVES: Contains sodium nitrite, which can be converted into cancer-causing substances called nitrosamines.

JONES ORIGINAL LIVERWURST
Jones Dairy Farm, Inc.

Ingredients: pork livers, pork, bacon, salt, spices, dehydrated onions, water, sugar, sodium phosphate, sodium nitrite, sodium ascorbate.

Amount: two 1-oz slices			% USRDA
Calories	184	Protein	18
Protein, gm	08	Vitamin A	*
Carbohydrates, gm	1	Vitamin C	na
Fat, gm	16	Thiamine	10
Sodium, mg	na	Riboflavin	34
Cholesterol, mg	90	Niacin	na
Fiber, gm	0	Calcium	*
		Iron	20

THIS FOOD: Like many luncheon meats, Jones Original Liverwurst is high in fat and cholesterol, but it is also unusually high in nutrients: a good source of protein and thiamine and an excellent source of iron and riboflavin. While data on sodium could not be obtained, it is safe to assume that this product is high in sodium.

ADDITIVES: Contains sodium nitrite, which can be converted into cancer-causing substances called nitrosamines.

LAND O' FROST BEEF
Land O' Frost of Arkansas, Inc.

Ingredients: beef, water, salt, corn syrup, sugar, monosodium glutamate, flavorings, sodium erythorbate, sodium nitrite.

Amount: 2 oz			% USRDA
Calories	80	Protein	20
Protein, gm	12	Vitamin A	*
Carbohydrates, gm	2	Vitamin C	*
Fat, gm	4	Thiamine	*
Sodium, mg	850	Riboflavin	4
Cholesterol, mg	24	Niacin	12
Fiber, gm	0	Calcium	*
		Iron	8

THIS FOOD: Land O' Frost Beef is a very good source of protein and niacin. About 45 percent of calories come from fat, which is below average for sandwich meats. This product is extremely high in sodium.

ADDITIVES: Contains monosodium glutamate (MSG), which many experts believe should be avoided by infants and very young children; causes adverse reactions in some sensitive individuals. Also contains sodium nitrite, which can be converted into cancer-causing substances called nitrosamines.

LAND O' FROST CHICKEN
Land O' Frost of Arkansas, Inc.

Ingredients: chicken, water, salt, soy protein concentrate, dextrose, sodium tripolyphosphate, hydrolyzed plant protein, monosodium glutamate, flavorings, sodium erythorbate, sodium nitrite.

Amount: 2 oz			% USRDA
Calories	120	Protein	20
Protein, gm	10	Vitamin A	0
Carbohydrates, gm	2	Vitamin C	0
Fat, gm	9	Thiamine	0
Sodium, mg	800	Riboflavin	4
Cholesterol, mg	76	Niacin	16
Fiber, gm	0	Calcium	0
		Iron	4

THIS FOOD: Land O' Frost Chicken is moderately high in cholesterol and fat, which accounts for 67 percent of calories. It is a very good source of protein and niacin. This product is extremely high in sodium.

ADDITIVES: Contains monosodium glutamate (MSG), which many experts believe should be avoided by infants and very young children; causes adverse reactions in some sensitive individuals. Also contains sodium nitrite, which can be converted into cancer-causing substances called nitrosamines.

OTHER BRANDS: Buddig Smoked Sliced Chicken is lower in fat, calories and sodium. It is also one of the few sandwich meats with no added sodium nitrite.

LAND O' FROST PASTRAMI
Land O' Frost of Arkansas, Inc.

Ingredients: beef, water, salt, corn syrup, flavorings, sodium erythorbate, sodium nitrite, garlic powder.

Amount: 2 oz			% USRDA
Calories	80	Protein	20
Protein, gm	12	Vitamin A	*
Carbohydrates, gm	2	Vitamin C	*
Fat, gm	4	Thiamine	*
Sodium, mg	740	Riboflavin	4
Cholesterol, mg	24	Niacin	12
Fiber, gm	0	Calcium	*
		Iron	8

THIS FOOD: Land O' Frost Pastrami is a very good source of protein and a good source of niacin. About 45 percent of calories come from fat, which is moderate for this category. This product is very high in sodium.

ADDITIVES: Contains sodium nitrite, which can be converted into cancer-causing substances called nitrosamines.

LOUIS RICH TURKEY BREAST SLICES
Oscar Mayer and Co.

Ingredients: turkey breast slices.

Amount: two 1-oz slices			% USRDA
Calories	80	Protein	38
Protein, gm	17	Vitamin A	0
Carbohydrates, gm	0	Vitamin C	0
Fat, gm	1	Thiamine	*
Sodium, mg	48	Riboflavin	4
Cholesterol, mg	24	Niacin	20
Fiber, gm	0	Calcium	0
		Iron	2

THIS FOOD: Eureka—a luncheon meat that is low in sodium, fat, calories, and has absolutely no additives! Only 11 percent of calories in Louis Rich

Turkey Breast Slices come from fat. This product is rich in protein and is a very good source of niacin. A glance at the ingredients list explains the unusual nutritional bonanza—the manufacturer has simply left the turkey breast alone! Like cooked turkey, this product will stay fresh for about five days in the refrigerator if it is kept well wrapped.

ADDITIVES: None.

LOUIS RICH TURKEY LUNCHEON LOAF
Oscar Mayer and Co.

Ingredients: turkey, water, salt, sugar, sodium phosphates, spice, sodium erythorbate, natural flavorings, sodium nitrite, paprika, and garlic powder.

Amount: two 1-oz slices			% USRDA
Calories	80	Protein	20
Protein, gm	9	Vitamin A	*
Carbohydrates, gm	<1	Vitamin C	0
Fat, gm	5	Thiamine	*
Sodium, mg	574	Riboflavin	2
Cholesterol, mg	26	Niacin	14
Fiber, gm	0	Calcium	*
		Iron	*

THIS FOOD: Louis Rich Turkey Luncheon Loaf is relatively low in calories, 56 percent of which come from fat. It is a very good source of protein and niacin. This product is very high in sodium.

ADDITIVES: Contains sodium nitrite, which can be converted into cancer-causing substances called nitrosamines.

MR. TURKEY COOKED WHITE TURKEY ROLL
Bil Mar Foods, Inc.

Ingredients: turkey, water, salt, sugar, sodium phosphates, onion powder, gelatin, flavorings.

Amount: two 1-oz slices			% USRDA
Calories	79	Protein	28
Protein, gm	13	Vitamin A	*
Carbohydrates, gm	<1	Vitamin C	*
Fat, gm	3	Thiamine	3e
Sodium, mg	280	Riboflavin	8e
Cholesterol, mg	48e	Niacin	20e
Fiber, gm	0	Calcium	2e
		Iron	4e

THIS FOOD: Mr. Turkey Cooked White Turkey Roll is a very good source of protein and niacin. About 34 percent of calories derive from fat, which makes this sandwich meat leaner than average. This product is high in sodium.

ADDITIVES: No questionable additives.

MR. TURKEY NO SODIUM ADDED ROASTED TURKEY BREAST

Bil Mar Foods, Inc.

Ingredients: turkey breast.

Amount: two 1-oz slices			% USRDA
Calories	80	Protein	24
Protein, gm	11	Vitamin A	*
Carbohydrates, gm	0	Vitamin C	*
Fat, gm	2	Thiamine	*
Sodium, mg	23	Riboflavin	4
Cholesterol, mg	23	Niacin	23
Fiber, gm	0	Calcium	*
		Iron	*

THIS FOOD: Low in fat, sodium, and calories, Mr. Turkey No Sodium Added Roasted Turkey is an excellent nutritional value. It is rich in protein, and a very good source of niacin—all without additives of any kind. Only 23 percent of calories come from fat, which makes this product leaner than all the lunch meats profiled, except for Louis Rich Turkey Breast Slices.

ADDITIVES: None.

MR. TURKEY SLICED TURKEY BREAST

Bil Mar Foods, Inc.

Ingredients: turkey, turkey broth, salt, sugar, sodium phosphates.

Amount: two 1-oz slices			% USRDA
Calories	79	Protein	33
Protein, gm	15	Vitamin A	*
Carbohydrates, gm	<1	Vitamin C	*
Fat, gm	2	Thiamine	*
Sodium, mg	248	Riboflavin	3
Cholesterol, mg	24e	Niacin	23
Fiber, gm	0	Calcium	*
		Iron	*

THIS FOOD: Mr. Turkey Sliced Turkey Breast is low in calories, only 23 percent of which come from fat. It is an excellent source of protein and a very good source of niacin. This product contains a moderate amount of sodium.

ADDITIVES: No questionable additives.

OSCAR MAYER LUNCHEON MEAT
Oscar Mayer and Co.

Ingredients: pork, beef, salt, water, corn syrup, dextrose, flavoring, ascorbic acid (vitamin C), sodium nitrite.

Amount: two 1-oz slices			% USRDA
Calories	190	Protein	16
Protein, gm	7	Vitamin A	0
Carbohydrates, gm	.8	Vitamin C	12
Fat, gm	18	Thiamine	10
Sodium, mg	716	Riboflavin	4
Cholesterol, mg	32	Niacin	8
Fiber, gm	0	Calcium	*
		Iron	2
Contains more than 3½ teaspoons fat.			

THIS FOOD: Oscar Mayer Luncheon Meat is very high in sodium, saturated fat, and overall fat, which accounts for a whopping 85 percent of calories. This product is a good source of protein, vitamin C, and thiamine.

ADDITIVES: Contains sodium nitrite, which can be converted into cancer-causing substances called nitrosamines.

OSCAR MAYER OLIVE LOAF
Oscar Mayer and Co.

Ingredients: pork, water, partially defatted pork fatty tissue, olives, whey, corn syrup, calcium caseinate, red sweet peppers, salt, flavoring, ascorbic acid (vitamin C), sodium nitrite.

Amount: two 1-oz slices			% USRDA
Calories	130	Protein	14
Protein, gm	7	Vitamin A	*
Carbohydrates, gm	5	Vitamin C	8
Fat, gm	9	Thiamine	10
Sodium, mg	800	Riboflavin	8
Cholesterol, mg	22	Niacin	4
Fiber, gm	0	Calcium	6
		Iron	2

BEST BETS: Louis Rich Turkey Breast Slices, with only 11 percent fat calories, and Mr. Turkey No Sodium Added Turkey Breast, with 23 percent fat calories, are both superior sandwich meats. They are also low in sodium and additive free.

THIS FOOD: Oscar Mayer Olive Loaf is moderately high in saturated fat and overall fat, which accounts for 62 percent of calories. This product is a good source of protein and thiamine. It is extremely high in sodium.

ADDITIVES: Contains sodium nitrite, which can be converted into cancer-causing substances called nitrosamines.

OSCAR MAYER PICNIC LOAF
Oscar Mayer and Co.

Ingredients: pork, water, partially defatted pork fatty tissue, beef, corn syrup, whey, salt, flavoring, calcium caseinate, ascorbic acid (vitamin C), sodium nitrite.

Amount: two 1-oz slices			% USRDA
Calories	130	Protein	18
Protein, gm	8	Vitamin A	6
Carbohydrates, gm	3	Vitamin C	14
Fat, gm	9	Thiamine	14
Sodium, mg	640	Riboflavin	6
Cholesterol, mg	22	Niacin	6
Fiber, gm	0	Calcium	3
		Iron	3

THIS FOOD: Oscar Mayer Picnic Loaf is moderately high in saturated fat and overall fat, which accounts for 62 percent of its calories. In addition to supplying protein, it is a good source of thiamine and added vitamin C. This product is very high in sodium.

ADDITIVES: Contains sodium nitrite, which can be converted into cancer-causing substances called nitrosamines.

STEAK-UM FROZEN STEAK SANDWICH MEAT
H. J. Heinz, Inc.

Ingredients: beef.

Amount: 2 oz			% USRDA
Calories	180	Protein	20
Protein, gm	9	Vitamin A	*
Carbohydrates, gm	0	Vitamin C	*
Fat, gm	15	Thiamine	2
Sodium, mg	35	Riboflavin	4
Cholesterol, mg	35	Niacin	8
Fiber, gm	0	Calcium	*
		Iron	4
Contains 3 teaspoons fat.			

THIS FOOD: Steak-Um Frozen Steak Sandwich Meat is high in saturated fat and overall fat, which accounts for 75 percent of calories. It is a very good source of protein. It contains no added salt and is low in sodium.

ADDITIVES: None.

See "Basic Foods" on pages 553, 554, 556, 559, 560, 563, 564, 566, 567 for fresh meat listings.

NUTRITION TIP: According to some studies, nitrites are much less likely to form cancer-causing nitrosamines in the presence of excess vitamin C.

Sausages

This popular breakfast food has many of the same nutritional failings as hot dogs, which are also a type of sausage. Typical breakfast sausages, such as those produced by Swift, Jones, Oscar Mayer, and Jimmy Dean, are high in fat, saturated fat, cholesterol, and sodium and often contain additives of questionable safety. If you eat a single egg, along with sausages for breakfast, you'll be consuming your full cholesterol quota for the day—with your first meal. Of the popular brands profiled, Swift Original Brown 'n Serve Links contain significantly less sodium and fat than the other brands.

SODIUM GUIDELINES: In evaluating the sodium content of sausage, we used the following standards:

less than 250 mg	moderate in sodium
250 mg to 500 mg	high in sodium
more than 500 mg	very high in sodium

Remember, these guidelines are not for people following medically restricted low-sodium diets, but for healthy individuals who wish to monitor their sodium intake.

JIMMY DEAN PORK SAUSAGES
Jimmy Dean Companies
Ingredients: pork, ham loins, water, salt, spices, sugar, monosodium glutamate.

Amount: 1 link/approx. 2 oz cooked			% USRDA
Calories	200	Protein	27
Protein, gm	12	Vitamin A	*
Carbohydrates, gm	<1e	Vitamin C	*
Fat, gm	16e	Thiamine	19
Sodium, mg	539	Riboflavin	13
Cholesterol, mg	58	Niacin	*
Fiber, gm	0	Calcium	*
		Iron	7

THIS FOOD: Jimmy Dean Pork Sausages derive 72 percent of their calories from fat, most of it saturated. They are very high in sodium.

ADDITIVES: Contains monosodium glutamate (MSG), which many authorities believe should be avoided by infants and very young children; causes adverse reactions in some sensitive individuals.

JONES LITTLE SAUSAGES
Jones Dairy Farm, Inc.

Ingredients: pork, salt, spices.

Amount: 1 link/approx. 2 oz cooked			% USRDA
Calories	221	Protein	28
Protein, gm	13	Vitamin A	*
Carbohydrates, gm	<1	Vitamin C	*
Fat, gm	18	Thiamine	27
Sodium, mg	850	Riboflavin	9
Cholesterol, mg	38	Niacin	13
Fiber, gm	0	Calcium	*
		Iron	2

THIS FOOD: Jones Little Sausages derive 73 percent of their calories from fat, most of it saturated. This product contains significantly more sodium than most other brands of breakfast sausages.

ADDITIVES: No questionable additives.

SWIFT ORIGINAL BROWN 'N SERVE BEEF LINKS
Swift and Co.

Ingredients: beef, water, salt, sugar, spices, monosodium glutamate, BHA, BHT, citric acid.

NOTE: The letter "e" indicates that the data has been estimated; < means "less than" and is used for small amounts of sodium or cholesterol; * means food contains less than 2% of USRDA; "na" means that the information was not available and appears only when data is insufficient.

Amount: 1 link/approx. 2 oz cooked			% USRDA
Calories	113	Protein	7
Protein, gm	3	Vitamin A	*
Carbohydrates, gm	<1	Vitamin C	*
Fat, gm	10	Thiamine	13
Sodium, mg	254	Riboflavin	5
Cholesterol, mg	17	Niacin	10
Fiber, gm	0	Calcium	0*
		Iron	4

THIS FOOD: Swift Original Brown 'n Serve Beef Links derive 79 percent of their calories from fat, most of it saturated. While the percentage of fat calories per serving is about the same as that of other brands, there is significantly less fat and protein by weight. As a result, this product is relatively low in calories. It contains less sodium than most other sausages.

ADDITIVES: Contains monosodium glutamate (MSG), which many authorities believe should be avoided by infants and very young children; causes adverse reactions in some sensitive individuals. Also contains BHA and BHT, whose long-term safety is currently being reexamined by FDA investigators.

SWIFT ORIGINAL BROWN 'N SERVE PORK LINKS
Swift and Co.

Ingredients: pork, beef, water, salt, sugar, spices, monosodium glutamate, BHA, BHT, citric acid.

Amount: 1 link/approx. 2 oz cooked			% USRDA
Calories	130	Protein	7
Protein, gm	3	Vitamin A	*
Carbohydrates, gm	<1	Vitamin C	*
Fat, gm	12	Thiamine	13
Sodium, mg	254	Riboflavin	5
Cholesterol, mg	20	Niacin	10
Fiber, gm	0	Calcium	*
		Iron	*

THIS FOOD: Swift Original Brown 'n Serve Pork Links derive 83 percent of their calories from fat, most of it saturated. While the percentage of fat calories per serving is about the same as that of other brands, there is significantly less fat and protein by weight. As a result, this product is relatively low in calories. It contains less sodium than most other sausages.

ADDITIVES: Contains monosodium glutamate (MSG), which many authorities believe should be avoided by infants and very young children; causes adverse reactions in some sensitive individuals. Also contains BHA and BHT, whose long-term safety is currently being reexamined by FDA investigators.

MEXICAN FOOD

Between 1974 and 1984, Americans increased their consumption of ethnic foods in the home by 50 percent. Mexican foods, geared both to the growing Hispanic population and adventurous yuppie tastes, are an important element in this growth spurt. On the positive side, Mexican combination foods and dinners tend to be higher than average in complex carbohydrates and fiber, because of their traditional use of beans, rice, and corn-flour tortillas. But most of the foods profiled are far from ideal because they tend to be moderately high in saturated fat and overall fat as well as in sodium. One outstanding exception, Old El Paso Refried Beans, with only 9 percent fat calories, is also a good source of vegetable protein and iron.

OLD EL PASO REFRIED BEANS
IC Industries, Inc.

Ingredients: cooked beans, water, salt, lard, onion powder.

Amount: 1 cup			% USRDA
Calories	200	Protein	21
Protein, gm	14	Vitamin A	*
Carbohydrates, gm	34	Vitamin C	*
Fat, gm	2	Thiamine	4
Sodium, mg	600e	Riboflavin	4
Cholesterol, mg	<5e	Niacin	4
Fiber, gm	12e	Calcium	12
		Iron	20

THIS FOOD: Old El Paso Refried Beans is a nutritional bonanza. One serving provides more than one third of the 30 grams of dietary fiber which nutritionists recommend for daily intake. In addition, this food is a very good source of protein and iron, a good source of calcium, and contains only 9 percent fat calories. Although it contains lard, which is high in saturated fat and cholesterol, there isn't enough for it to have any nutritional impact. Like most canned foods, it is high in sodium.

ADDITIVES: No questionable additives.

OLD EL PASO REFRIED BEANS WITH SAUSAGE
IC Industries, Inc.

Ingredients: cooked pinto beans, water, pork, beef, salt, chili powder, cumin, red pepper powder, lard, garlic powder, onion powder, oregano.

Amount: 1 cup			% USRDA
Calories	388	Protein	21
Protein, gm	14	Vitamin A	*
Carbohydrates, gm	26	Vitamin C	4
Fat, gm	26	Thiamine	8
Sodium, mg	624	Riboflavin	4
Cholesterol, mg	na	Niacin	*
Fiber, gm	12e	Calcium	8
		Iron	20

THIS FOOD: Old El Paso Refried Beans with Sausage provides complex carbohydrates, is a good source of iron and an excellent source of dietary fiber. It contains 32 percent fat calories and is high in saturated fat. Like most canned foods, it is high in sodium.

ADDITIVES: No questionable additives.

OLD EL PASO TAMALES IN CHILI SAUCE
IC Industries, Inc.

Ingredients: water, corn flour, beef, pork, chili powder, wheat flour, tomato paste, salt, oatmeal flakes, cumin, sugar, red pepper powder, oregano, onion powder, garlic powder, sage.

Amount: 2 tamales			% USRDA
Calories	232	Protein	3
Protein, gm	6	Vitamin A	2
Carbohydrates, gm	23	Vitamin C	*
Fat, gm	13	Thiamine	*
Sodium, mg	na	Riboflavin	8
Cholesterol, mg	10e	Niacin	8
Fiber, gm	2e	Calcium	3
		Iron	25

NOTE: The letter "e" indicates that the data has been estimated; < means "less than" and is used for small amounts of sodium or cholesterol; * means food contains less than 2% of USRDA; "na" means that the information was not available and appears only when data is insufficient.

THIS FOOD: Old El Paso Tamales in Chili Sauce provides complex carbohydrates and a full 25 percent of the USRDA for iron. Unfortunately it contains about 50 percent fat calories and is high in saturated fat. Although sodium figures could not be obtained, this product is undoubtedly high in salt.

ADDITIVES: No questionable additives.

PATIO BEEF AND BEAN BURRITO
R. J. Reynolds Industries, Inc.

Ingredients: flour tortilla (enriched flour, water, lard, salt, baking powder), cooked beans, beef, water, onions, sweet red peppers, tomato paste, textured soy flour (caramel colored), spices, modified food starch, salt, sugar, monosodium glutamate, garlic powder.

Amount: 1 burrito/5 oz			% USRDA
Calories	190	Protein	8
Protein, gm	5	Vitamin A	8
Carbohydrates, gm	21	Vitamin C	*
Fat, gm	9	Thiamine	10
Sodium, mg	na	Riboflavin	6
Cholesterol, mg	15e	Niacin	4
Fiber, gm	3e	Calcium	4
		Iron	6

THIS FOOD: Provides complex carbohydrates, and a fair amount of fiber and thiamine. About 43 percent of its calories derive from fat, and is relatively low in nutrients. While data for sodium is not available, it's safe to assume that this product is high in salt.

ADDITIVES: Contains monosodium glutamate (MSG), which many experts believe should be avoided by infants and very young children; causes adverse reactions in some sensitive individuals.

PATIO MEXICAN STYLE COMBINATION DINNER
R. J. Reynolds Industries, Inc.

Ingredients: water, cooked beans, cooked rice, masa, flour, beef, lard, tomato paste, pork, red and green peppers, salt, modified food starch, partially hydrogenated soybean and/or coconut and/or palm oil, spices, sodium caseinate, flour, hydrolyzed plant protein, textured soy flour (caramel colored), garlic powder, sugar, dehydrated onion, monosodium glutamate, caramel color, tapioca flour, tricalcium phosphate, adipicacid, artificial flavor and color, turmeric.

Amount: 11¼ oz			% USRDA
Calories	590	Protein	30
Protein, gm	19	Vitamin A	45
Carbohydrates, gm	66	Vitamin C	*
Fat, gm	28	Thiamine	25
Sodium, mg	na	Riboflavin	15
Cholesterol, mg	20e	Niacin	6
Fiber, gm	7e	Calcium	15
		Iron	25
Contains 6 teaspoons fat.			

THIS FOOD: Provides complex carbohydrates, is an excellent source of protein, vitamin A, thiamine, and iron; a very good source of fiber, calcium, and riboflavin. This product is fairly high in calories, about 43 percent of which derive from fat. Although sodium data could not be obtained, it's safe to assume that this dinner is high in salt.

ADDITIVES: Contains monosodium glutamate (MSG), which many experts believe should be avoided by infants and very young children; causes adverse reactions in sensitive individuals. Also contains artificial color and flavor, which some studies suggest may adversely affect behavior and the ability to complete school tasks in some sensitive children; artificial colors are inadequately tested and artificial flavor may cause allergic reactions in sensitive individuals.

SWANSON MEXICAN STYLE COMBINATION DINNER
Campbell Soup Co.

Ingredients: tomatoes, cooked beans, water, masa, beef, cooked rice, beef stock, beef fat, reconstituted onions, sweet peppers, Cheddar cheese, vegetable oil, enriched wheat flour, salt, textured vegetable protein (soy flour, caramel color), modified food starch, chili peppers, carrots, hydrolyzed plant protein, sugar, natural flavoring, gelatin, dehydrated garlic, dehydrated onions, spice, and turmeric.

Amount: 16 oz			% USRDA
Calories	590	Protein	30
Protein, gm	17	Vitamin A	30
Carbohydrates, gm	64	Vitamin C	15
Fat, gm	29	Thiamine	15
Sodium, mg	1,865	Riboflavin	6
Cholesterol, mg	80e	Niacin	15
Fiber, gm	8e	Calcium	10
		Iron	15
Contains more than ¾ teaspoon salt and 6 teaspoons fat.			

THIS FOOD: Swanson Mexican Style Combination Dinner is rich in complex carbohydrates, and is an excellent source of fiber, protein, and vitamin A. It is also a very good source of vitamin C, thiamine, niacin, and iron. About 44 percent of calories derive from fat. For a full one-pound portion, 590 calories is not especially high. This dinner is very high in sodium.

ADDITIVES: No questionable additives.

VAN DE KAMP'S CHEESE ENCHILADAS RANCHERO
The Pillsbury Co.

Ingredients: water, yellow and white Cheddar cheeses, onions, corn flour (treated with lime, cellulose gum, mono- and diglycerides), beans, chicken broth, rice, tomato paste, bell peppers, ripe olives, soybean oil, tomatoes, modified food starch, salt, whey solids, calcium/sodium caseinate, spices, Cheddar and blue cheese solids, dehydrated onion, skim milk solids, corn syrup solids, monosodium glutamate, garlic powder, sour cream solids, natural flavor, lactose, caramel color, xanthan gum.

Amount: 14¾ oz			% USRDA
Calories	620	Protein	36
Protein, gm	24	Vitamin A	8
Carbohydrates, gm	60	Vitamin C	10
Fat, gm	31	Thiamine	19
Sodium, mg	1,460	Riboflavin	16
Cholesterol, mg	100e	Niacin	20
Fiber, gm	3e	Calcium	50
		Iron	16

Contains nearly 7 teaspoons fat and ¾ teaspoon salt.

THIS FOOD: Van de Kamp's Cheese Enchiladas Ranchero contains a rich array of nutrients, but it is also relatively high in calories and saturated fat. Specifically, it provides complex carbohydrates and a fair amount of fiber, is an excellent source of protein and calcium, and a very good source of vitamin C, the B vitamins, and iron. This product is high in cholesterol and sodium.

ADDITIVES: Contains monosodium glutamate (MSG), which many experts believe should be avoided by infants and very young children; causes adverse reactions in some sensitive individuals.

VAN DE KAMP'S CHICKEN ENCHILADAS SUIZA
The Pillsbury Co.

Ingredients: water, white Cheddar cheese, chicken, corn flour (treated with lime, cellulose gum, mono- and diglycerides), tomatillos (green tomatoes), beans, onions, chilies, rice, bell peppers, chicken broth, Monterey Jack jalapeño cheese, tomatoes, sour cream powder, vegetable oil, sour cream, whey solids, modified food starch, tomato paste, salt, Parmesan cheese, natural flavors, calcium/sodium caseinate, Cheddar and blue cheese solids, skim milk solids, corn syrup solids, monosodium glutamate, spices, caramel color, lactose, garlic powder.

Amount: 14¾ oz			% USRDA
Calories	490	Protein	45
Protein, gm	28	Vitamin A	10
Carbohydrates, gm	64	Vitamin C	10
Fat, gm	20	Thiamine	27
Soidum, mg	1,210	Riboflavin	25
Cholesterol, mg	200e	Niacin	20
Fiber, gm	3e	Calcium	45
		Iron	12

Contains more than 4 teaspoons fat and ½ teaspoon salt.

THIS FOOD: Van de Kamp's Chicken Enchiladas Suiza provides protein and complex carbohydrates, and is a fair source of dietary fiber. At 490 calories for a serving of nearly one pound, this frozen dinner also packs in a lot of vitamins and minerals: it is a fair source of vitamin A and C, a very good source of B vitamins, and an excellent provider of calcium and protein. This product contains 37 percent fat calories and is high in cholesterol and saturated fat. Like many frozen dishes, this product is high in sodium.

ADDITIVES: Contains monosodium glutamate (MSG), which many experts believe should be avoided by infants and very young children; causes adverse reactions in some sensitive individuals.

VAN DE KAMP'S SHREDDED BEEF ENCHILADAS
The Pillsbury Co.

Ingredients: water, cooked beef, corn flour (treated with lime cellulose gum, mono- and diglycerides), onions, white and yellow Cheddar cheese, chilies, tomato paste, vegetable oil, bell peppers, modified food starch, spices, garlic puree, salt, natural flavor, dextrose, monosodium glutamate.

Amount: 5½ oz			% USRDA
Calories	180	Protein	20
Protein, gm	11	Vitamin A	12
Carbohydrates, gm	16	Vitamin C	*
Fat, gm	8	Thiamine	4
Sodium, mg	930	Riboflavin	4
Cholesterol, mg	80e	Niacin	4
Fiber, gm	1e	Calcium	18
		Iron	8

Contains nearly 2 teaspoons fat and ½ teaspoon salt.

THIS FOOD: A very good source of protein and calcium, contains about 40 percent fat calories and is very high in sodium.

ADDITIVES: Contains monosodium glutamate (MSG), which many experts believe should be avoided by infants and very young children; causes adverse reactions in some sensitive individuals.

MILK PRODUCTS AND FLAVORINGS

Milk is one of nature's most nutritious foods. It is an important source of protein and, a major dietary source of calcium, riboflavin and vitamin D. Many nutritionists believe that, except for infants less than two years old, everyone is better off drinking low-fat milk rather than whole milk to avoid unwanted saturated fat and cholesterol. The same rule applies to the popular Carnation and Eagle Brand condensed and dry-milk products profiled, since these items have exactly the same food values—and nutritional liabilities—of regular milk.

Milk flavorings are most often used to entice kids to drink more milk. Not surprisingly, the lure used by manufacturers is sweetness, either from sugar or artificial sweeteners. Carnation, Swiss Miss, Nestlé, and Ovaltine products all contain about 4 to 5 teaspoons added sugar per serving (in addition to the 2½ teaspoons naturally occurring sugar in milk). Many of these products contain artificial colors and/or flavors. Only Ovaltine contains added vitamins and minerals, which compensate for milk's lack of vitamin C and iron, while supplementing its vitamin A and B vitamin content.

Milk Flavorings

CARNATION INSTANT NATURAL MALTED MILK
Carnation Co.

Ingredients: wheat flour and malted barley extracts, dry whole milk, lecithin, salt, bicarbonate of soda.

Amount: 3 heaping tsp (+ 1 cup milk)			% USRDA
Calories	240	Protein	24
Protein, gm	11	Vitamin A	10
Carbohydrates, gm	28	Vitamin C	*
Fat, gm	10	Thiamine	18
Sodium, mg	218	Riboflavin	30
Cholesterol, mg	38	Niacin	4
Fiber, gm	0	Calcium	36
		Iron	*

THIS FOOD: Carnation Instant Natural Malted Milk is sweetened with malted barley extract rather than sugar. The mix is a significant source of thiamine, but the milk you add provides most of the protein, riboflavin, and calcium, along with 3 teaspoons naturally occurring milk sugar. Compared to other milk modifiers, this product is moderately high in sodium.

ADDITIVES: No questionable additives.

CARNATION 70 CALORIE HOT COCOA MIX
Carnation Co.

Ingredients: sugar, nonfat dry milk, cocoa, salt, cellulose gum, artificial vanilla flavor.

Amount: 3 heaping tsp (+ ¾ cup water)			% USRDA
Calories	70	Protein	6
Protein, gm	3	Vitamin A	*
Carbohydrates, gm	15	Vitamin C	*
Fat, gm	0	Thiamine	*
Sodium, mg	125	Riboflavin	8
Cholesterol, mg	2	Niacin	*
Fiber, gm	0	Calcium	10
		Iron	*
Contains about 4 teaspoons sugar.			

NOTE: The letter "e" indicates that the data has been estimated; < means "less than" and is used for small amounts of sodium or cholesterol; * means food contains less than 2% of USRDA; "na" means that the information was not available and appears only when data is insufficient.

THIS FOOD: Carnation 70 Calorie Hot Cocoa Mix is a fair source of calcium (from nonfat dry milk). About 85 percent of the calories in this product derive from sugar.

ADDITIVES: No questionable additives.

CARNATION SUGAR FREE HOT COCOA MIX
Carnation Co.

Ingredients: nonfat dry milk, whey, cocoa, sodium caseinate, salt, guar gum, aspartame, artificial vanilla flavor.

Amount: 4 heaping tsp (+ ¾ cup water)			% USRDA
Calories	50	Protein	8e
Protein, gm	4	Vitamin A	*
Carbohydrates, gm	8	Vitamin C	*
Fat, gm	<1	Thiamine	2
Sodium, mg	160	Riboflavin	10
Cholesterol, mg	2	Niacin	*
Fiber, gm	0	Calcium	10
		Iron	4

Contains 2 teaspoons naturally occurring sugar.

THIS FOOD: Carnation Sugar Free Hot Cocoa Mix is a fair source of calcium and riboflavin, mostly from nonfat dry milk.

ADDITIVES: Contains aspartame (with phenylalanine), which should be avoided by people with PKU, a rare genetic disease, and which many experts believe has been inadequately tested for long-term safety.

DID YOU KNOW: Most cocoa drinks and chocolate-flavored milk modifiers contain about 10 milligrams caffeine per serving. In addition cocoa contains theobromine, a compound that also has a stimulant effect on the body. One or two cups of cocoa or chocolate milk a day is probably nothing to worry about, but if your child *only* drinks flavored milk, then he or she may be getting too much caffeine and theobromine for good health. Younger children are most likely to be negatively affected by these components. Also, cocoa and most chocolate-flavored milk modifiers contain oxalic acid, a compound which may interfere with calcium absorption. Research indicates that as much as 30 percent of the calcium in milk may not be absorbed in the presence of oxalic acid.

NESTLÉ CHOCOLATE FLAVOR QUIK
Nestlé, S.A.

Ingredients: sugar, cocoa processed with alkali, lecithin, salt, artificial and natural flavors.

Amount: 3½ tsp (+ 1 cup milk)			% USRDA
Calories	240	Protein	18
Protein, gm	9	Vitamin A	6
Carbohydrates, gm	30	Vitamin C	4
Fat, gm	9	Thiamine	6
Sodium, mg	155	Riboflavin	23
Cholesterol, mg	33	Niacin	*
Fiber, gm	0	Calcium	29
		Iron	2

Contains about 4 teaspoons added sugar.

THIS FOOD: Nestlé's Chocolate Flavor Quik is mostly sugar. Nearly all of the valuable nutrients in this product—protein, riboflavin, and calcium—come from the added milk.

ADDITIVES: Contains artificial flavor, which may cause allergic reactions in sensitive individuals, and which some studies suggest may adversely affect behavior and the ability to complete school tasks in some sensitive children.

NESTLÉ STRAWBERRY FLAVOR QUIK
Nestlé, S.A.

Ingredients: sugar, maltodextrin, citric acid, artificial flavors, artificial colors, salt.

Amount: 3½ tsp (+ 1 cup milk)			% USRDA
Calories	240	Protein	12
Protein, gm	8	Vitamin A	6
Carbohydrates, gm	33	Vitamin C	2
Fat, gm	8	Thiamine	6
Sodium, mg	160	Riboflavin	25
Cholesterol, mg	33	Niacin	*
Fiber, gm	0	Calcium	29
		Iron	*

Contains about 5 teaspoons added sugar.

THIS FOOD: Nestlé Strawberry Flavor Quik is basically artificially colored and flavored sugar. It contributes no nutrients at all to the milk it is used to flavor.

ADDITIVES: Contains artificial color and flavor, which some studies suggest may adversely affect behavior and the ability to complete school tasks in some sensitive children; artificial colors are inadequately tested and artificial flavor may cause allergic reactions in sensitive individuals.

OVALTINE, CHOCOLATE FLAVOR
Sandoz Nutrition, Inc.

Ingredients: sugar, whey, cocoa processed with alkali, barley malt syrup, tricalcium phosphate, salt, mono- and diglycerides, vitamin C, ferric sodium pyrophosphate, vanillin, niacin, riboflavin, vitamin B_6, thiamine hydrocholoride, vitamin A, vitamin D.

Amount: ¾ oz (+ 1 cup milk)			% USRDA
Calories	230	Protein	20
Protein, gm	9	Vitamin A	55
Carbohydrates, gm	27	Vitamin C	45
Fat, gm	8	Thiamine	51
Sodium, mg	150	Riboflavin	68
Cholesterol, mg	33	Niacin	45
Fiber, gm	0	Calcium	37
		Iron	15
Contains about 4 teaspoons added sugar.			

THIS FOOD: Drinking a cup of Ovaltine is like having a multivitamin pill with your milk—along with 4 teaspoons added sugar. This heavily fortified product is a very significant source of vitamins A and C, the B vitamins, calcium, and iron.

ADDITIVES: No questionable additives.

REGULAR SWISS MISS
Beatrice Foods Co.

Ingredients: sugar, corn syrup solids, cocoa (processed with alkali), partially hydrogenated coconut and/or soybean oil, nonfat dry milk, whey, salt, mono- and diglycerides, cellulose gum, sodium caseinate, sodium citrate, dipotassium phosphate, artificial flavor, carrageenan.

Amount: 1 oz (+ ¾ cup water)			% USRDA
Calories	110	Protein	4
Protein, gm	2	Vitamin A	*
Carbohydrates, gm	23	Vitamin C	2
Fat, gm	2	Thiamine	2
Sodium, mg	na	Riboflavin	8
Cholesterol, mg	0	Niacin	*
Fiber, gm	0	Calcium	6
		Iron	2
Contains about 3 teaspoons added sugar.			

THIS FOOD: Regular Swiss Miss, made with water, is not a significant source of nutrients. More than 80 percent of the calories in this product derive from sugar.

ADDITIVES: Contains artificial flavor, which may cause allergic reactions in sensitive individuals, and which some studies suggest may adversely affect behavior and the ability to complete school tasks in some sensitive children.

HELPFUL HINT: If you like hot cocoa, it only takes seconds more to make it from scratch. Chances are you'll add far less sugar than is usually found in presweetened cocoa mixes.

Milk Products

CARNATION EVAPORATED MILK
Carnation Co.

Ingredients: milk, disodium phosphate, carrageenan, and vitamin D_3.

Amount: ½ cup			% USRDA
Calories	170	Protein	20
Protein, gm	8	Vitamin A	4
Carbohydrates, gm	12	Vitamin C	*
Fat, gm	10	Thiamine	2
Sodium, mg	133	Riboflavin	20
Cholesterol, mg	37	Niacin	*
Fiber, gm	0	Calcium	30
		Iron	*

THIS FOOD: Evaporated milk has all the nutritional values and liabilities of whole milk. It is a terrific source of calcium, riboflavin, and protein, but is relatively high in saturated fat and cholesterol.

ADDITIVES: No questionable additives.

CARNATION EVAPORATED SKIMMED MILK
Carnation Co.

Ingredients: skimmed milk, vitamin A palmitate, vitamin D_3.

Amount: ½ cup			% USRDA
Calories	100	Protein	20
Protein, gm	9	Vitamin A	10
Carbohydrates, gm	14	Vitamin C	*
Fat, gm	<1	Thiamine	2
Sodium, mg	15	Riboflavin	20
Cholesterol, mg	5e	Niacin	*
Fiber, gm	0	Calcium	30
		Iron	*

THIS FOOD: Carnation Evaporated Skimmed Milk contains almost no fat. It is a good source of protein, vitamin A, and riboflavin and an excellent source of calcium. It can be substituted for whole milk in many recipes and, when chilled, can even be whipped like heavy cream.

ADDITIVES: No questionable additives.

CARNATION INSTANT NONFAT DRY MILK
Carnation Co.
Ingredients: nonfat dry milk.

Amount: 1 tbsp (+1 cup water)			% USRDA
Calories	80	Protein	20
Protein, gm	8	Vitamin A	10
Carbohyrates, gm	12	Vitamin C	2
Fat, gm	<1	Thiamine	6
Sodium, mg	125	Riboflavin	25
Cholesterol, mg	4	Niacin	*
Fiber, gm	0	Calcium	30
		Iron	*

THIS FOOD: Nonfat dry milk is a terrific source of protein, calcium, and riboflavin. It has all the advantages of whole milk without unwanted fat and cholesterol.

ADDITIVES: None.

DID YOU KNOW: Condensed milk was developed by Gail Borden in 1856. The innovation made Borden's fortune, but his success was bittersweet at best since it came after years of failed attempts at marketing condensed meats and vegetables—his true passion. Apparently the dried meats and vegetables tasted just awful.

CARNATION SWEETENED CONDENSED MILK
Carnation Co.

Ingredients: condensed milk, sugar.

Amount: ½ cup			% USRDA
Calories	490	Protein	25
Protein, gm	12	Vitamin A	10
Carbohydrates, gm	83	Vitamin C	6
Fat, gm	13	Thiamine	8
Sodium, mg	196	Riboflavin	35
Cholesterol, mg	33	Niacin	*
Fiber, gm	0	Calcium	40
		Iron	*

Contains 17½ teaspoons added sugar.

THIS FOOD: Like whole milk, sweetened condensed milk is a terrific source of calcium, riboflavin, and protein, and moderately high in cholesterol and saturated fat. It's also loaded with added sugar, which supplies more than 50 percent of this product's calories. Most people use sweetened condensed milk to make desserts. Because of its extremely high sugar content, it should not be used as a beverage.

ADDITIVES: None.

EAGLE BRAND SWEETENED CONDENSED MILK
Borden, Inc.

Ingredients: concentrated whole milk, sugar.

Amount: ⅓ cup			% USRDA
Calories	320	Protein	15
Protein, gm	7	Vitamin A	4
Carbohydrates, gm	52	Vitamin C	*
Fat, gm	9	Thiamine	4
Sodium, mg	120	Riboflavin	25
Cholesterol, mg	35	Niacin	*
Fiber, gm	0	Calcium	30
		Iron	*

Contains about 10 teaspoons added sugar.

THIS FOOD: Like whole milk, sweetened condensed milk is a terrific source of calcium, riboflavin, and protein, and moderately high in cholesterol and saturated fat. It's also loaded with added sugar, which supplies about 50 percent of this product's calories. Most people use sweetened condensed milk to make desserts. Because of its extremely high sugar content, it should not be used as a beverage.

ADDITIVES: None.

See "Basic Foods" on pages 560, 561 for fresh milk listings.

MUFFINS AND MUFFIN MIXES

We have profiled a sampling of products by Arnold, Betty Crocker, Duncan Hines, Jiffy, Pepperidge Farm, and Thomas', which vary widely in nutrient content. All provide complex carbohydrates and some fiber, but fat, sodium, and sugar content vary widely. For example, a Betty Crocker Wild Blueberry Muffin contains 150 milligrams sodium, while a Betty Crocker Corn Muffin contains more than twice that amount! Similarly, fat content may vary more than fivefold, from a low of 6 percent fat calories for Arnold Extra Crisp Muffins, to a high of 35 percent fat calories for Pepperidge Farm Hot Frozen Old Fashioned Corn Muffins. Since most manufacturers use animal shortening and/or partially hydrogenated vegetable shortening, many prepared muffins are high in saturated fat.

SODIUM GUIDELINES: In evaluating the sodium content of muffins, we used the following standards:

less than 200 mg	low in sodium
200 mg to 300 mg	moderate in sodium
more than 300 mg	high in sodium

Remember, these guidelines are not for people following medically restricted low-sodium diets, but for healthy individuals who wish to monitor their sodium intake.

ARNOLD EXTRA CRISP MUFFINS
Continental Grain, Inc.

Ingredients: unbleached enriched wheat flour (flour, malted barley flour, niacin, reduced iron, thiamine mononitrate, riboflavin), water, yeast, corn syrup, salt, partially hydrogenated vegetable shortening (soy), calcium propionate, whey, soya flour, nonfat milk, cornmeal, farina, potassium sorbate, calcium sulfate, monocalcium phosphate, potassium bromate, potassium iodate.

Amount: 1 muffin			% USRDA
Calories	150	Protein	6
Protein, gm	5	Vitamin A	*
Carbohydrates, gm	30	Vitamin C	*
Fat, gm	1	Thiamine	25
Sodium, mg	310	Riboflavin	15
Cholesterol, mg	<5	Niacin	10
Fiber, gm	1e	Calcium	2
		Iron	10

THIS FOOD: Arnold Extra Crisp Muffins are a significant source of complex carbohydrates, and a very good source of B vitamins. Compared to most muffins, they are very low in fat, with only 6 percent fat calories. They contain a moderate amount of sodium.

ADDITIVES: No questionable additives.

BETTY CROCKER CORN MUFFIN MIX
General Mills, Inc.

Ingredients: enriched flour bleached (wheat flour, niacin, iron, thiamine mononitrate, riboflavin), enriched degermed yellow cornmeal (with niacin, iron, thiamine mononitrate, riboflavin), animal and/or vegetable shortening (contains one or more of the following partially hydrogenated fats: soybean oil, cottonseed oil, beef tallow, palm oil and/or lard), with BHA and BHT, dextrose, sugar, leavening (baking soda, sodium aluminum phosphate, monocalcium phosphate), salt, wheat starch.

Amount: 1 muffin/ ½₂ recipe (1 egg and 1 cup milk added to recipe)			% USRDA
Calories	160	Protein	4
Protein, gm	3	Vitamin A	*
Carbohydrates, gm	25	Vitamin C	*
Fat, gm	5	Thiamine	8
Sodium, mg	315	Riboflavin	6
Cholesterol, mg	20e	Niacin	4
Fiber, gm	1e	Calcium	4
		Iron	4

NOTE: The letter "e" indicates that the data has been estimated; < means "less than" and is used for small amounts of sodium or cholesterol; * means food contains less than 2% of USRDA; "na" means that the information was not available and appears only when data is insufficient.

THIS FOOD: A Betty Crocker Corn Muffin provides complex carbohydrates. About 28 percent of its calories derive from fat. Compared to other muffins, this product is slightly higher than average in sodium.

ADDITIVES: Contains BHA and BHT, whose long-term safety is currently being reexamined by FDA investigators.

BETTY CROCKER WILD BLUEBERRY MUFFIN MIX
General Mills, Inc.

Ingredients: enriched flour bleached (wheat flour, malted barley flour, niacin, iron, thiamine mononitrate, riboflavin), blueberries canned in water, sugar, animal and/or vegetable shortening (contains one or more of the following partially hydrogenated fats: soybean oil, cottonseed oil, beef tallow, palm oil and/or lard), with BHA and BHT, dextrose, leavening (baking soda, sodium aluminum phosphate, monocalcium phosphate), modified cornstarch, salt, wheat starch, artificial flavor.

Amount: 1 muffin/ 1⁄12 recipe (1 egg and 1 cup milk added to recipe)			% USRDA
Calories	120	Protein	4
Protein, gm	2	Vitamin A	*
Carbohydrates, gm	18	Vitamin C	*
Fat, gm	4	Thiamine	4
Sodium, mg	150	Riboflavin	4
Cholesterol, mg	20e	Niacin	2
Fiber, gm	<1e	Calcium	4
		Iron	2

THIS FOOD: A Betty Crocker Wild Blueberry Muffin provides complex carbohydrates. About 30 percent of its calories derive from fat. Compared to other muffins, this product is low in sodium.

ADDITIVES: Contains artificial flavor which may cause allergic reactions in sensitive individuals, and which some studies suggest may adversely affect behavior and the ability to complete school tasks in some sensitive children. Also contains BHA and BHT, whose long-term safety is currently being reexamined by FDA investigators.

BEST BET: Arnold Crisp Muffins are low in fat and have more B vitamins and iron than the other muffins profiled. Unfortunately they are high in sodium.

DUNCAN HINES WILD BLUEBERRY MUFFIN MIX
Procter and Gamble

Ingredients: enriched unbleached flour (enriched with iron, niacin, thiamine mononitrate, riboflavin), blueberries packed in extra-light syrup, sugar, vegetable shortening (partially hydrogenated soybean and palm oils), leavening (baking soda and sodium aluminum phosphate), dextrose, salt, artificial flavor.

Amount: 1 muffin (1 egg added to recipe)			% USRDA
Calories	110	Protein	2
Protein, gm	2	Vitamin A	*
Carbohydrates, gm	17	Vitamin C	*
Fat, gm	3	Thiamine	4
Sodium, mg	155	Riboflavin	4
Cholesterol, mg	20e	Niacin	4
Fiber, gm	<1e	Calcium	*
		Iron	2

THIS FOOD: A Duncan Hines Wild Blueberry Muffin provides complex carbohydrates. About 25 percent of its calories derive from fat. Compared to other muffins, this product is low in sodium.

ADDITIVES: Contains artificial flavor, which may cause allergic reactions in sensitive individuals, and which some studies suggest may adversely affect behavior and the ability to complete school tasks in some sensitive children.

JIFFY BRAN DATE MUFFIN MIX
Chelsea Milling Co.

Ingredients: enriched flour (flour, niacin, iron, thiamine mononitrate, riboflavin), sugar, shortening (partially hydrogenated soybean, cottonseed oil, lard or tallow and tallow or lard, BHA, BHT), wheat bran, dates, leavening (sodium aluminum phosphate, baking soda), salt, spice.

Amount: 1 muffin (1 egg and ½ cup milk added to recipe)			% USRDA
Calories	110	Protein	4
Protein, gm	3	Vitamin A	*
Carbohydrates, gm	17	Vitamin C	*
Fat, gm	4	Thiamine	5
Sodium, mg	190	Riboflavin	8
Cholesterol, mg	10e	Niacin	5
Fiber, gm	1.5e	Calcium	*
		Iron	8

THIS FOOD: A Jiffy Bran Date Muffin provides complex carbohydrates. About 32 percent of its calories derive from fat, and it is fairly low in sodium.

ADDITIVES: Contains BHA and BHT, whose long-term safety is currently being reexamined by FDA investigators.

JIFFY CORN MUFFIN MIX
Chelsea Milling Co.

Ingredients: enriched flour (flour, niacin, iron, thiamine mononitrate, riboflavin), cornmeal, sugar, shortening, partially hydrogenated soybean oil, cottonseed oil, lard or tallow, and tallow or lard, with BHA and BHT, leavening (baking soda, sodium acid pyrophosphate, monocalcium phosphate), salt.

Amount: 1 muffin (1 egg and ⅓ cup milk added to recipe)			% USRDA
Calories	115	Protein	4
Protein, gm	3	Vitamin A	*
Carbohydrates, gm	17	Vitamin C	*
Fat, gm	4	Thiamine	8
Sodium, mg	240	Riboflavin	5
Cholesterol, mg	10e	Niacin	5
Fiber, gm	1e	Calcium	*
		Iron	*

THIS FOOD: A Jiffy Corn Muffin provides complex carbohydrates. About 31 percent of its calories derive from fat, which is higher than average, and it contains a moderate amount of sodium.

ADDITIVES: Contains BHA and BHT, whose long-term safety is currently being reexamined by FDA investigators.

PEPPERIDGE FARM ENGLISH MUFFINS
Pepperidge Farm, Inc.

Ingredients: unbleached enriched wheat flour (flour, niacin, reduced iron, thiamine mononitrate, riboflavin), water, cultured buttermilk, whey, yeast, vinegar, wheat gluten, yellow cornmeal, sugar, partially hydrogenated vegetable shortening (soybean, palm, and/or cottonseed oils), salt, potassium sorbate, mono- and diglycerides (from hydrogenated vegetable oil), and lecithin.

Amount: 1 muffin/2 oz			% USRDA
Calories	135	Protein	8
Protein, gm	5	Vitamin A	*
Carbohydrates, gm	26	Vitamin C	*
Fat, gm	1	Thiamine	15
Sodium, mg	220	Riboflavin	10
Cholesterol, mg	<5e	Niacin	10
Fiber, gm	1.5e	Calcium	2
		Iron	6

THIS FOOD: Pepperidge Farm English Muffins provide complex carbohydrates and the B vitamins. They are low in fat (7 percent fat calories) and moderate in sodium.

ADDITIVES: No questionable additives.

PEPPERIDGE FARM HOT FROZEN OLD FASHIONED CORN MUFFIN MIX
Pepperidge Farm, Inc.

Ingredients: unbleached enriched wheat flour (flour, niacin, reduced iron, thiamine mononitrate, riboflavin), nonfat milk, yellow cornmeal, sugar, whole eggs, partially hydrogenated soybean oil, leavening (sodium aluminum phosphate, baking soda), modified food starch, and salt.

Amount: 1 muffin/2 oz			% USRDA
Calories	180	Protein	4
Protein, gm	3	Vitamin A	*
Carbohydrates, gm	27	Vitamin C	*
Fat, gm	7	Thiamine	4
Sodium, mg	259	Riboflavin	6
Cholesterol, mg	<5e	Niacin	4
Fiber, gm	2e	Calcium	2
		Iron	2

THIS FOOD: A Pepperidge Farm Hot Frozen Old Fashioned Corn Muffin provides complex carbohydrates and dietary fiber. It contains about 35 percent fat calories, which is higher than average, and a moderate amount of sodium.

ADDITIVES: No questionable additives.

THOMAS' HONEY WHEAT ENGLISH MUFFINS
S. B. Thomas, Inc.

Ingredients: enriched wheat flour (unbleached wheat flour, malted barley, niacin, reduced iron, thiamine mononitrate, riboflavin), whole wheat flour, water, farina, wheat gluten, honey, corn syrup, yeast, vinegar, corn bran, salt, calcium propionate, and partially hydrogenated soybean oil with mono- and diglycerides.

Amount: 1 muffin/2 oz			% USRDA
Calories	129	Protein	6
Protein, gm	4	Vitamin A	*
Carbohydrates, gm	27	Vitamin C	*
Fat, gm	1	Thiamine	15
Sodium, mg	228	Riboflavin	2
Cholesterol, mg	0	Niacin	10
Fiber, gm	2e	Calcium	2
		Iron	6

THIS FOOD: A Thomas' Honey Wheat English Muffin provides complex carbohydrates, dietary fiber, niacin, and thiamine. A mere 7 percent of its calories derive from fat, and it contains a moderate amount of sodium.

ADDITIVES: No questionable additives.

THOMAS' REGULAR ENGLISH MUFFINS
S. B. Thomas, Inc.

Ingredients: enriched wheat flour (unbleached wheat flour, malted barley, niacin, reduced iron, thiamine mononitrate, riboflavin), water, farina, corn syrup, yeast, salt, partially hydrogenated soybean oil with mono- and di-glycerides, vinegar, calcium propionate, soya flour, nonfat dry milk, and whey solids.

Amount: 1 muffin/2 oz			% USRDA
Calories	130	Protein	6
Protein, gm	4	Vitamin A	*
Carbohydrates, gm	26	Vitamin C	*
Fat, gm	1	Thiamine	10
Sodium, mg	208	Riboflavin	8
Cholesterol, mg	0	Niacin	6
Fiber, gm	1.5e	Calcium	8
		Iron	10

THIS FOOD: A Thomas' English Muffin provides complex carbohydrates and a fair amount of thiamine and iron. Only 7 percent of its calories derive from fat, and it contains a moderate amount of sodium.

ADDITIVES: No questionable additives.

DID YOU KNOW: Many prepared muffins and muffin mixes are high in saturated fat. As much as 35 percent of the calories in the muffins profiled come from fat. And if you eat it with a pat of butter, you'll be consuming 60 percent fat calories!

HELPFUL HINT: If you want to cut down on fat calories, beware of butter. A mere teaspoon of butter on your English muffin raises fat calories from 7 percent to 34 percent!

MUSTARD

Mustard is prepared from ground mustard seeds, vinegar, salt, and spices, and is used as a condiment and sandwich spread. It is low in fat and high in sodium. French's prepared mustards dominate the American market.

SODIUM GUIDELINES: In evaluating the sodium content of mustard we used the following standards:

less than 100 mg	moderate in sodium
100 mg to 200 mg	high in sodium
more than 200 mg	very high in sodium

Remember, these guidelines are not for people following medically restricted low-sodium diets, but for healthy individuals who wish to monitor their sodium intake.

FRENCH'S BOLD 'N SPICY MUSTARD
The R. T. French Co.

Ingredients: distilled vinegar and water, mustard seed, salt, spices, turmeric, natural flavor.

Amount: 1 tbsp			% USRDA
Calories	16	Protein	*
Protein, gm	1	Vitamin A	*
Carbohydrates, gm	1	Vitamin C	*
Fat, gm	1	Thiamine	*
Sodium, mg	145	Riboflavin	*
Cholesterol, mg	0	Niacin	*
Fiber, gm	0	Calcium	*
		Iron	*

THIS FOOD: Mustard has no real nutritional value, and it is high in sodium. However, it is an excellent low-fat condiment when used as a replacement for oil, butter, mayonnaise, or other fatty spreads.

ADDITIVES: No questionable additives.

NOTE: The letter "e" indicates that the data has been estimated; < means "less than" and is used for small amounts of sodium or cholesterol; * means food contains less than 2% of USRDA; "na" means that the information was not available and appears only when data is insufficient.

FRENCH'S MUSTARD WITH HORSERADISH
The R. T. French Co.

Ingredients: vinegar and water, mustard seed, salt, horseradish, turmeric, spices.

Amount: 1 tbsp			% USRDA
Calories	16	Protein	*
Protein, gm	1	Vitamin A	*
Carbohydrates, gm	1	Vitamin C	*
Fat, gm	1	Thiamine	*
Sodium, mg	265	Riboflavin	*
Cholesterol, mg	0	Niacin	*
Fiber, gm	0	Calcium	*
		Iron	*

THIS FOOD: Mustard has no real nutritional value, and it is very high in sodium. However, it is an excellent low-fat condiment when used as a replacement for oil, butter, mayonnaise, or other fatty spreads.

ADDITIVES: No questionable additives.

FRENCH'S PREPARED YELLOW MUSTARD
The R. T. French Co.

Ingredients: distilled vinegar and water, no. 1 grade mustard seed, salt, turmeric spices, natural flavor.

Amount: 1 tbsp			% USRDA
Calories	10	Protein	*
Protein, gm	1	Vitamin A	*
Carbohydrates, gm	1	Vitamin C	*
Fat, gm	1	Thiamine	*
Sodium, mg	180	Riboflavin	*
Cholesterol, mg	0	Niacin	*
Fiber, gm	0	Calcium	*
		Iron	*

THIS FOOD: Mustard has no real nutritional value, and it is high in sodium. However it is an excellent low-fat condiment when used as a replacement for oil, butter, mayonnaise, or other fatty spread.

ADDITIVES: No questionable additives.

NUTS AND COCONUT

Peanuts, almonds, walnuts, and cashews are popular snack foods and are used in baking and candies. All contain valuable dietary fiber and vegetable protein, but are also high in fat (most of which is unsaturated). A quarter-cup serving of nuts (whether "dry roasted" or roasted in vegetable oil) contains approximately 1 tablespoon of oil. Most nuts are high in sodium, but Planter's offers unsalted nuts.

Most coconut eaten by Americans is found in cakes, icings, and candies. Although coconut is high in saturated fat, the average person doesn't consume enough of it to have much nutritional impact. Coconut oil, which is widely used in many processed foods, is far more harmful (see entry for "Oils").

SODIUM GUIDELINES: In evaluating the sodium content of nuts, we used the following standards:

less than 200 mg	moderate in sodium
more than 200 mg	high in sodium

Remember, these guidelines are not for people on medically restricted low-sodium diets, but for healthy individuals who wish to monitor their sodium intake.

BAKER'S PREMIUM SHRED COCONUT
General Foods Corp.
Ingredients: coconut, sugar, water, glycerine, propylene glycol, creamed coconut, glycerol monostearate, salt.

Amount: ⅓ cup			% USRDA
Calories	140	Protein	*
Protein, gm	1	Vitamin A	*
Carbohydrates, gm	12	Vitamin C	*
Fat, gm	9	Thiamine	*
Sodium, mg	75	Riboflavin	*
Cholesterol, mg	0	Niacin	*
Fiber, gm	3e	Calcium	*
		Iron	2

Contains nearly 2 teaspoons fat.

THIS FOOD: Shredded coconut contains too much saturated fat to be considered a healthful food. About 65 percent of its calories derive from fat, nearly all of it highly saturated. On the positive side, this product is a good source of fiber.

ADDITIVES: No questionable additives.

BLUE DIAMOND BLANCHED ALMONDS
California Almond Growers' Exchange

Ingredients: blanched almonds roasted in vegetable oil (almond, safflower), salt.

Amount: 25/approx. 1 oz			% USRDA
Calories	150	Protein	10
Protein, gm	7	Vitamin A	*
Carbohydrates, gm	4	Vitamin C	*
Fat, gm	14	Thiamine	*
Sodium, mg	80	Riboflavin	25
Cholesterol, mg	0	Niacin	4
Fiber, gm	4	Calcium	6
		Iron	4
Contains about 3 teaspoons fat.			

THIS FOOD: Blue Diamond Blanched Almonds are a fair source of dietary fiber and protein. Because of their high fat content, they should only be eaten occasionally. About 85 percent of calories in these nuts come from fat. Compared to other salted nuts, they contain a moderate amount of sodium.

ADDITIVES: No questionable additives.

NOTE: The letter "e" indicates that the data has been estimated; < means "less than" and is used for small amounts of sodium or cholesterol; * means food contains less than 2% of USRDA; "na" means that the information was not available and appears only when data is insufficient.

DIAMOND BAKING WALNUTS
Sun Diamond Growers of California
Ingredients: walnuts.

Amount: ¼ cup/1 oz			% USRDA
Calories	170	Protein	9
Protein, gm	4	Vitamin A	*
Carbohydrates, gm	3	Vitamin C	2
Fat, gm	17	Thiamine	5
Sodium, mg	110e	Riboflavin	3
Cholesterol, mg	0	Niacin	*
Fiber, gm	1	Calcium	9
		Iron	4
Contains about 4 teaspoons fat.			

THIS FOOD: Diamond Baking Walnuts derive 90 percent of their calories from fat, most of it unsaturated. One serving also supplies 9 percent of the USRDA for calcium and protein. Because of their high fat content, these walnuts should be eaten only on occasion.

ADDITIVES: None.

PLANTER'S COCKTAIL PEANUTS
R. J. Reynolds Industries, Inc.
Ingredients: peanuts roasted in coconut and/or peanut oil, salt.

Amount: approx. ⅛ cup/1 oz			% USRDA
Calories	170	Protein	10
Protein, gm	7	Vitamin A	*
Carbohydrates	5	Vitamin C	*
Fat, gm	15	Thiamine	*
Sodium, mg	220	Riboflavin	2
Cholesterol, mg	0	Niacin	20
Fiber, gm	3	Calcium	*
		Iron	2
Contains about 3 teaspoons fat.			

THIS FOOD: Planter's Cocktail Peanuts are a fair source of protein and dietary fiber, and a very good source of niacin. About 80 percent of their calories come from fat. They should be eaten only occasionally, because of their high fat content. They are high in sodium.

ADDITIVES: No questionable additives.

PLANTER'S DRY ROASTED PEANUTS
R. J. Reynolds Industries, Inc.

Ingredients: peanuts with added salt, modified food starch, monosodium gluta-mate, gum arabic, yeast, dried corn syrup, paprika and other spices, natural flavor, garlic, onion powder.

Amount: approx. ⅛ cup/1 oz			% USRDA
Calories	160	Protein	10
Protein, gm	7	Vitamin A	*
Carbohydrates, gm	6	Vitamin C	*
Fat, gm	14	Thiamine	*
Sodium, mg	220	Riboflavin	2
Cholesterol, mg	0	Niacin	20
Fiber, gm	3	Calcium	*
		Iron	2
Contains about 1 tablespoon fat.			

THIS FOOD: Planter's Dry Roasted Peanuts are a fair source of dietary fiber and protein, and a very good source of niacin. About 78 percent of their calories derive from mostly unsaturated fat. Like other salted nuts, they are high in sodium.

ADDITIVES: Contains monosodium glutamate (MSG), which many authorities believe should be avoided by infants and very young children; causes adverse reactions in some sensitive individuals.

PLANTER'S SNACKNUTS, MIXED NUTS WITH PEANUTS
R. J. Reynolds Industries, Inc.

Ingredients: peanuts, cashews, almonds, brazils, filberts, roasted in coconut and/or peanut oil, salt.

Amount: approx. ⅛ cup/1 oz			% USRDA
Calories	180	Protein	8
Protein, gm	5	Vitamin A	*
Carbohydrates, gm	6	Vitamin C	*
Fat, gm	16	Thiamine	2
Sodium, mg	220	Riboflavin	2
Cholesterol, mg	0	Niacin	8
Fiber, gm	3	Calcium	2
		Iron	4
Contains more than 3 teaspoons fat.			

THIS FOOD: Planter's SnackNuts, Mixed Nuts with Peanuts, provide dietary fiber but should be eaten only occasionally because of their high fat content. About 80 percent of their calories derive from fat. Like most salted nuts, this product is high in sodium.

ADDITIVES: No questionable additives.

PLANTER'S SPANISH PEANUTS
R. J. Reynolds Industries, Inc.

Ingredients: redskin Spanish peanuts roasted in coconut and/or peanut oil, salt.

Amount: approx. ⅛ cup/1 oz			% USRDA
Calories	170	Protein	10
Protein, gm	7	Vitamin A	8
Carbohydrates, gm	5	Vitamin C	*
Fat, gm	15	Thiamine	4
Sodium, mg	220	Riboflavin	*
Cholesterol, mg	0	Niacin	15
Fiber, gm	3	Calcium	*
		Iron	2
Contains 3 teaspoons fat.			

THIS FOOD: Planter's Spanish Peanuts are a fair source of protein and dietary fiber and a good source of niacin. About 80 percent of calories come from fat. They should be eaten only occasionally, because of their high fat content. They are high in sodium.

ADDITIVES: No questionable additives.

PLANTER'S UNSALTED CASHEWS
R. J. Reynolds Industries, Inc.

Ingredients: cashews.

Amount: 12–15 nuts/1 oz			% USRDA
Calories	160	Protein	8
Protein, gm	5	Vitamin A	*
Carbohydrates, gm	9	Vitamin C	*
Fat, gm	13	Thiamine	2
Sodium, mg	<10	Riboflavin	4
Cholesterol, mg	0	Niacin	*
Fiber, gm	2	Calcium	*
		Iron	10
Contains nearly 3 teaspoons fat.			

THIS FOOD: Cashews are a fair source of iron but should be eaten only occasionally because of their high fat content. About 73 percent of calories come from fat. These nuts contain no added salt and are very low in sodium.

ADDITIVES: None.

PLANTER'S UNSALTED PEANUTS
R. J. Reynolds Industries, Inc.
Ingredients: peanuts roasted in peanut and/or coconut oil.

Amount: approx. ⅛ cup/1 oz			% USRDA
Calories	170	Protein	10
Protein, gm	7	Vitamin A	*
Carbohydrates, gm	5	Vitamin C	*
Fat, gm	15	Thiamine	*
Sodium, mg	<10	Riboflavin	2
Cholesterol, mg	0	Niacin	20
Fiber, gm	3	Calcium	*
		Iron	2
Contains 3 teaspoons fat.			

THIS FOOD: Planter's Unsalted Peanuts are a fair source of protein and dietary fiber and a very good source of niacin. About 80 percent of calories come from fat. Because of their high fat content, nuts should be eaten only occasionally. This product is very low in sodium.

ADDITIVES: No questionable additives.

OILS AND VINEGAR

Oil

How much fat or oil you eat, and what kind, is considered crucial to your health. High fat intake of any kind, saturated or unsaturated, is associated with a greater risk of colon, breast, uterine, and prostate cancer, while too much saturated fat in the diet is associated with increased incidence of atherosclerosis.

Most Americans get 42 percent of their calories from fat, up ten percentage points from the early twentieth century. This means the average person consumes 6 to 8 tablespoons of fat daily, far in excess of the body's needs. Current American Heart Association guidelines advise a general reduction of fat intake to 30 percent of calories. But for the more than fifty percent of the population who have serum cholesterol readings of 210 milligrams per deciliter or more, the

American Heart Association recommends restricting fat intake to only 20 percent of calories—a full fifty percent reduction from the average current intake.

Reducing your consumption of all fats is one of the most important things you do for your health. Polyunsaturated fats tend to reduce cholesterol levels in the blood, while saturated fats tend to raise them. Recent but convincing research indicates that monounsaturated oils (such as olive and peanut oils), previously thought to have no effect on cholesterol levels, also help to lower them and may actually be superior to polyunsaturated fats because they cause no reduction of HDL cholesterol, the "good" kind.

Obviously you should avoid saturated oils whenever possible. But even when you are cooking with the most healthful oil, it's important to use as little as possible.

All vegetable oils contain 120 calories per tablespoon and 14 grams of fat, and that's it. Vegetable oil contains no other nutrients. The most healthful oils contain the greatest proportion of polyunsaturated and monounsaturated fats. Brands which list the oil used as "partially hydrogenated" always have more saturated fat than other brands. These brands will also usually contain an additive or two, generally emulsifiers. The additives are not harmful in themselves, but are another sign that the less desirable "partially hydrogenated" oils have been used.

The relationship between polyunsaturated and saturated fats is sometimes expressed as the p/s ratio. The oils with the highest ratio are the most unsaturated—and most desirable. The p/s ratio is still the accepted way of gauging whether a given oil is considered "heart healthy" even though it does not take into account new evidence which shows that monounsaturated fats may be as, or even more, helpful in lowering cholesterol levels.

BERTOLLI OLIVE OIL
Alivar S. p. A.
Ingredients: olive oil.

Amount: 1 tbsp			% USRDA
Calories	120	Protein	*
Protein, gm	0	Vitamin A	*
Carbohydrates, gm	0	Vitamin C	*
Fat, gm	14	Thiamine	*
Sodium, mg	<1	Riboflavin	*
Cholesterol, mg	0	Niacin	*
Fiber, gm	0	Calcium	*
		Iron	*

THIS FOOD: Bertolli Olive Oil contains 120 calories, all of them from fat. Like other olive oils, Bertolli contains monounsaturated fat. Recent evidence suggests that monounsaturated oils may be more effective than polyunsaturated oils in helping to lower cholesterol levels. This oil has a p/s ratio of ½.

ADDITIVES: None.

CRISCO OIL
Procter and Gamble

Ingredients: vegetable oil (partially hydrogenated soybean oil), polysorbate 80, polyglycerol esters.

Amount: 1 tbsp			% USRDA
Calories	120	Protein	*
Protein, gm	0	Vitamin A	*
Carbohydrates, gm	0	Vitamin C	*
Fat, gm	14	Thiamine	*
Sodium, mg	0	Riboflavin	*
Cholesterol, mg	0	Niacin	*
Fiber, gm	0	Calcium	*
		Iron	*

THIS FOOD: Crisco Oil is made from partially hydrogenated soybean oil and has a p/s ratio of 2.5.

ADDITIVES: No questionable additives.

CRISCO SHORTENING
Procter and Gamble

Ingredients: partially hydrogenated vegetable oils (soybean, palm and sunflower), mono- and diglycerides.

Amount: 1 tbsp			% USRDA
Calories	110	Protein	*
Protein, gm	0	Vitamin A	4
Carbohydrates, gm	0	Vitamin C	*
Fat, gm	12	Thiamine	*
Sodium, mg	0	Riboflavin	*
Cholesterol, mg	0	Niacin	*
Fiber, gm	0	Calcium	*
		Iron	*

NOTE: The letter "e" indicates that the data has been estimated; < means "less than" and is used for small amounts of sodium or cholesterol; * means food contains less than 2% of USRDA; "na" means that the information was not available and appears only when data is insufficient.

THIS FOOD: Crisco is solid at room temperature. This always indicates a high proportion of saturated fat. Because the manufacturing process adds some air to the hardened oils, it contains slightly less fat and calories per serving than liquid oils. The p/s ratio of this very popular product is 1.

ADDITIVES: No questionable additives.

HOLLYWOOD SAFFLOWER OIL
Hollywood Health Foods, Inc.
Ingredients: safflower oil.

Amount: 1 tbsp			% USRDA
Calories	120	Protein	*
Protein, gm	0	Vitamin A	*
Carbohydrates, gm	0	Vitamin C	*
Fat, gm	14	Thiamine	*
Sodium, mg	0	Riboflavin	*
Cholesterol, mg	0	Niacin	*
Fiber, gm	0	Calcium	*
		Iron	*

THIS FOOD: Like other oils, Hollywood Safflower Oil contains 120 calories, all of them from fat. Compared to all the oils profiled, this product, with a p/s ratio of 11, contains the highest proportion of polyunsaturated fat.

ADDITIVES: None.

MAZOLA CORN OIL
CPC International, Inc.
Ingredients: corn oil.

Amount: 1 tbsp			% USRDA
Calories	125	Protein	*
Protein, gm	0	Vitamin A	*
Carbohydrates, gm	0	Vitamin C	*
Fat, gm	14	Thiamine	*
Sodium, mg	0	Riboflavin	*
Cholesterol, mg	0	Niacin	*
Fiber, gm	0	Calcium	*
		Iron	*

THIS FOOD: Mazola Corn Oil is made from corn oil and nothing else. It has a good p/s ratio of 4.5.

ADDITIVES: None.

PAM
American Home Products, Inc.

Ingredients: partially hydrogenated vegetable oil (soybean), alcohol, lecithin, propellant.

Amount: 1 spray/.3 gm			% USRDA
Calories	2	Protein	*
Protein, gm	0	Vitamin A	*
Carbohydrates, gm	0	Vitamin C	*
Fat, gm	1	Thiamine	*
Sodium, mg	<10	Riboflavin	*
Cholesterol, mg	0	Niacin	*
Fiber, gm	0	Calcium	*
		Iron	*

THIS FOOD: Because the lecithin in this product has antistick properties, you no longer need a full teaspoon of butter to fry an egg—a mere 2-calorie spray will do the job! Pam and similar vegetable-oil sprays offer an easy way to drastically reduce fat calories when you cook. Because this product is made from partially hydrogenated vegetable oil, its p/s ratio is 2.5, but you use such a tiny amount of oil that the amount of fat and its degree of saturation become unimportant. Pam should be considered by anyone seriously interested in reducing his or her intake of fat.

ADDITIVES: No questionable additives.

PURITAN OIL
Procter and Gamble

Ingredients: sunflower and soybean oils.

Amount: 1 tbsp			% USRDA
Calories	120	Protein	*
Protein, gm	0	Vitamin A	*
Carbohydrates, gm	0	Vitamin C	*
Fat, gm	14	Thiamine	*
Sodium, mg	0	Riboflavin	*
Cholesterol, mg	0	Niacin	*
Fiber, gm	0	Calcium	*
		Iron	*

THIS FOOD: Puritan Oil combines sunflower and soybean oils, and has a good p/s ratio of 4.5.

ADDITIVES: None.

SUNLITE OIL
Hunt-Wesson Foods, Inc.

Ingredients: liquid sunflower oil.

Amount: 1 tbsp			% USRDA
Calories	120	Protein	*
Protein, gm	0	Vitamin A	*
Carbohydrates, gm	0	Vitamin C	*
Fat, gm	14	Thiamine	*
Sodium, mg	0	Riboflavin	*
Cholesterol, mg	0	Niacin	*
Fiber, gm	0	Calcium	*
		Iron	*

THIS FOOD: Made from liquid sunflower oil and nothing else, this oil has an excellent p/s ratio of 5.

ADDITIVES: None.

WESSON OIL
Hunt-Wesson Foods, Inc.

Ingredients: partially hydrogenated soybean oil and polyglycerides (made from vegetable oils).

Amount: 1 tbsp			% USRDA
Calories	120	Protein	*
Protein, gm	0	Vitamin A	*
Carbohydrates, gm	0	Vitamin C	*
Fat, gm	14	Thiamine	*
Sodium, mg	0	Riboflavin	*
Cholesterol, mg	0	Niacin	*
Fiber, gm	0	Calcium	*
		Iron	*

THIS FOOD: Wesson Oil is made from partially hydrogenated soybean oil, which gives it a p/s ratio of 2. It also contains polyglycerides, an emulsifier which is regarded as a safe additive.

ADDITIVES: No questionable additives.

Vinegar

Vinegar is made from fermented wine or cider and used most often in salad dressings, and as a condiment and preservative. It contains no fat, practically no calories, and a small amount of potassium. While it does not contain enough nutrients to be considered nutritious in its own right, vinegar has many healthful uses. For example, to reduce fat calories, vinegar can be used to thin bottled salad dressings or dressings served in restaurants. A dash or two of vinegar can be substituted for salt in soups, stews, sauces, and many other recipes. Try experimenting with specialty vinegars, such as balsamic or rice vinegar, until you find one that appeals to your taste.

HEINZ CIDER VINEGAR
H. J. Heinz Co.

Ingredients: cider vinegar.

Amount: 1 tbsp			% USRDA
Calories	<1	Protein	*
Protein, gm	<1	Vitamin A	*
Carbohydrates, gm	<1	Vitamin C	*
Fat, gm	0	Thiamine	*
Sodium, mg	0	Riboflavin	*
Cholesterol, mg	0	Niacin	*
Fiber, gm	0	Calcium	*
		Iron	*

THIS FOOD: Vinegar is not a significant source of nutrients.

ADDITIVES: None.

NOTE: The letter "e" indicates that the data has been estimated; < means "less than" and is used for small amounts of sodium or cholesterol; * means food contains less than 2% of USRDA; "na" means that the information was not available and appears only when data is insufficient.

OLIVES

Most of the calories in olives (about 5 to 10 calories each, depending on size) come from naturally occurring olive oil. Because they are pickled in brine, most popular brands, including Lindsay and S & W, are very high in sodium. Most olives consumed in the United States are grown in California, where the fruit is picked green and given a lye cure. Although black olives are called "ripe," in this country they are usually picked green and then oxidized in a ferrous gluconate solution, which turns them black. In Europe, black olives are usually left to ripen on the trees. Recent studies suggest that olive oil, which is a monounsaturated fat, may help to lower blood cholesterol levels.

SODIUM GUIDELINES: In evaluating the sodium content of olives, we used the following standards:

less than 100 mg	moderate in sodium
100 mg to 200 mg	high in sodium
more than 200 mg	very high in sodium

Remember, these guidelines are not for people on medically restricted low-sodium diets, but for healthy individuals who wish to monitor their sodium intake.

LINDSAY RIPE OLIVES*
Lindsay International, Inc.

Ingredients: ripe olives, water, salt, ferrous gluconate.

Amount: 3 small or 2 large			% USRDA
Calories	18	Protein	*
Protein, gm	<1	Vitamin A	*
Carbohydrates, gm	1	Vitamin C	*
Fat, gm	2	Thiamine	*
Sodium, mg	82	Riboflavin	*
Cholesterol, mg	0	Niacin	*
Fiber, gm	<1	Calcium	2
		Iron	2

THIS FOOD: Ripe olives derive most of their calories from naturally occurring olive oil. A serving of Lindsay Ripe Olives contains only one fourth the sodium of most brands of green olives.

ADDITIVES: No questionable additives.

NOTE: The letter "e" indicates that the data has been estimated; < means "less than" and is used for small amounts of sodium or cholesterol; * means food contains less than 2% of USRDA; "na" means that the information was not available and appears only when data is insufficient.

S & W MAMMOTH QUEEN OLIVES, MEDIUM*
S & W Fine Foods, Inc.

Ingredients: olives, water, salt, lactic acid.

Amount: 4			% USRDA
Calories	20	Protein	*
Protein, gm	<1	Vitamin A	*
Carbohydrates, gm	1	Vitamin C	*
Fat, gm	2	Thiamine	*
Sodium, mg	360	Riboflavin	*
Cholesterol, mg	0	Niacin	*
Fiber, gm	<1	Calcium	*
		Iron	2

THIS FOOD: Green olives derive most of their calories from naturally occurring olive oil, a monounsaturated fat. Because salt is added during pickling, they are very high in sodium.

ADDITIVES: No questionable additives.

*Nutrition information could not be obtained from the manufacturer and has been taken from *Church's Food Values of Portions Commonly Used* (Fourteenth Edition).

DID YOU KNOW: Processed olives are soaked in a weak brine solution to remove bitterness. Green olives are soaked in brine from two to seven months, while black olives are soaked for only a week or two. Thus the difference in sodium content is due solely to processing—not to any intrinsic difference in the olives themselves.

ORIENTAL FOOD

Retail sales of Oriental foods are expected to double between 1985 and 1990. Because most Oriental foods are relatively low in calories and fat, industry analysts believe they appeal to health- and diet-conscious consumers.

Does Chinese and Japanese food deserve its healthy reputation? Relative to other prepared entrées, the answer is yes. Because of its reliance on vegetables, these foods tend to have more fiber and less fat and cholesterol. Out of the eleven La Choy, Chun King, and Stouffer products profiled, only three contain more than 35 percent fat calories (Chun King Egg Foo Yung Stir Fry Dinner, Chun King Sweet and Sour Pork Pouch, and Stouffer's Chicken Chow Mein). The news is not all good, however. Like most prepared foods, these products are generally very high in sodium and many contain MSG, a controversial additive.

CHUN KING BEEF PEPPER ORIENTAL DIVIDER PAK
R. J. Reynolds Industries, Inc.

Ingredients: *Sauce:* water, beef, modified food starch, salt, sugar, hydrolyzed plant protein, monosodium glutamate, onion powder, natural flavorings, garlic powder, caramel color, spice, disodium inosinate, disodium guanylate. *Vegetables:* Water, bean sprouts, green bell peppers, sweet red peppers, carrots, citric acid.

Amount: 10½ oz			% USRDA
Calories	70	Protein	10
Protein, gm	8	Vitamin A	70
Carbohydrates, gm	8	Vitamin C	10
Fat, gm	1	Thiamine	30
Sodium, mg	na	Riboflavin	6
Cholesterol, mg	20e	Niacin	4
Fiber, gm	4e	Calcium	*
		Iron	4

THIS FOOD: A serving of Chun King Beef Pepper Oriental Divider Pak supplies 70 calories, only 13 percent of which come from fat. Considering that it supplies so little unwanted fat and calories, it is an excellent source of vitamin A, and thiamine.

ADDITIVES: Contains monosodium glutamate (MSG), which many authorities believe should be avoided by infants and very young children; causes adverse reactions in some sensitive individuals.

NOTE: The letter "e" indicates that the data has been estimated; < means "less than" and is used for small amounts of sodium or cholesterol; * means food contains less than 2% of USRDA; "na" means that the information was not available and appears only when data is insufficient.

CHUN KING CHICKEN CHOW MEIN DIVIDER PAK
R. J. Reynolds Industries, Inc.

Ingredients: *Sauce:* water, chicken, modified food starch, chicken fat, salt, chicken broth, hydrolyzed plant protein, sugar, dried egg whites, monosodium glutamate, onion powder, extract of turmeric and paprika, caramel color, natural flavorings, garlic powder, citric acid, disodium inosinate, disodium guanylate. *Vegetables:* water, bean sprouts, celery, bamboo shoots, sweet red peppers, carrots, water chestnuts, calcium lactate, citric acid.

Amount: 10½ oz			% USRDA
Calories	80	Protein	8
Protein, gm	6	Vitamin A	15
Carbohydrates, gm	9	Vitamin C	*
Fat, gm	3	Thiamine	10
Sodium, mg	1,200e	Riboflavin	6
Cholesterol, mg	15e	Niacin	4
Fiber, gm	4e	Calcium	*
		Iron	4

THIS FOOD: Chun King Chicken Chow Mein Divider Pak is relatively low in protein and other nutrients—especially if it is being served as the primary dish at lunch or dinner. It is a good source of vitamin A and thiamine. A moderate 34 percent of calories come from fat. Like most other canned Oriental foods, this product is high in sodium.

ADDITIVES: Contains monosodium glutamate (MSG), which many authorities believe should be avoided by infants and very young children; causes adverse reactions in some sensitive individuals.

CHUN KING CHICKEN CHOW MEIN POUCH
Con Agra, Inc.

Ingredients: water, bean sprouts, celery, chicken meat, water chestnuts, carrots, bamboo shoots, modified food starch, pea pods, mushrooms, sweet red peppers, chicken fat, salt, sugar, hydrolyzed plant protein, monosodium glutamate, natural flavorings, caramel coloring.

Amount: 6 oz			% USRDA
Calories	90	Protein	6
Protein, gm	5	Vitamin A	15
Carbohydrates, gm	12	Vitamin C	2
Fat, gm	2	Thiamine	200
Sodium, mg	700e	Riboflavin	4
Cholesterol, mg	13e	Niacin	6
Fiber, gm	3e	Calcium	2
		Iron	4

THIS FOOD: Chun King Chicken Chow Mein Pouch is a great source of thiamine and also provides 15 percent of the USRDA for vitamin A. It is low in calories, only 20 percent of which come from fat. Like most frozen Oriental foods, this product in high in sodium.

ADDITIVES: Contains monosodium glutamate (MSG), which many authorities believe should be avoided by infants and very young children; causes adverse reactions in some sensitive individuals.

CHUN KING EGG FOO YUNG STIR FRY DINNER
R. J. Reynolds Industries, Inc.

Ingredients: *Sauce mix:* modified food starch, hydrolyzed plant protein, sugar, natural flavorings, onion powder, garlic powder, partially hydrogenated soybean and/or cottonseed oil. *Patty seasoning mix:* dried egg whites, modified food starch, salt, onion powder, hydrolyzed plant protein, monosodium glutamate, partially hydrogenated soybean and/or cottonseed oil, natural flavoring, garlic powder. *Oriental vegetables:* water, bean sprouts, celery, bamboo shoots, sweet red peppers, carrots, water chestnuts, calcium lactate, citric acid.

Amount: ¾ cup/10½ oz (1 egg added)			% USRDA
Calories	210	Protein	17
Protein, gm	13	Vitamin A	21
Carbohydrates, gm	13	Vitamin C	*
Fat, gm	11	Thiamine	13
Sodium, mg	na	Riboflavin	21
Cholesterol, mg	250e	Niacin	4
Fiber, gm	1e	Calcium	13
		Iron	8

THIS FOOD: Chun King Egg Foo Yung Stir Fry Dinner is a very good source of protein, vitamin A, thiamine, riboflavin, and calcium. Although it is fairly low in calories, 47 percent of them derive from fat, which is quite high compared to other canned Oriental foods. Although sodium data could not be obtained, this product is probably high in salt.

ADDITIVES: Contains monosodium glutamate (MSG), which many authorities believe should be avoided by infants and very young children; causes adverse reactions in some sensitive individuals.

CHUN KING SWEET AND SOUR PORK POUCH
Con Agra, Inc.

Ingredients: cooked pork rolls (pork, water, salt), water, green bell peppers, pineapple, peaches, sugar, onions, sweet red peppers, carrots, tomato paste, vinegar, sweet pickles, modified food starch, salt, hydrolyzed plant protein, monosodium glutamate, spice, garlic powder, natural flavoring.

Amount: 6 oz			% USRDA
Calories	200	Protein	10
Protein, gm	8	Vitamin A	30
Carbohydrates, gm	22	Vitamin C	10
Fat, gm	9	Thiamine	590
Sodium, mg	1,100e	Riboflavin	8
Cholesterol, mg	50e	Niacin	2
Fiber, gm	<1e	Calcium	2
		Iron	4

THIS FOOD: Chun King Sweet and Sour Pork Pouch is an excellent source of vitamin A and thiamine. It is high in sugar and contains 40 percent fat calories. Like most frozen Oriental foods, this product is high in sodium.

ADDITIVES: Contains monosodium glutamate (MSG), which many authorities believe should be avoided by infants and very young children; causes adverse reactions in some sensitive individuals.

LA CHOY CHINESE STYLE FRIED RICE

Beatrice Foods Co.

Ingredients: water, rice, sweet red peppers, sugar, salt, dehydrated onions, partially hydrogenated vegetable oil (soybean, cottonseed), monosodium glutamate, caramel color, flavorings.

Amount: ¾ cup			% USRDA
Calories	140	Protein	6
Protein, gm	4	Vitamin A	*
Carbohydrates, gm	40	Vitamin C	*
Fat, gm	2	Thiamine	6
Sodium, mg	960	Riboflavin	*
Cholesterol, mg	0	Niacin	6
Fiber, gm	1e	Calcium	*
		Iron	4

THIS FOOD: La Choy Chinese Style Fried Rice is rich in complex carbohydrates but otherwise low in nutrients since it is made from unenriched white rice. Like most frozen prepared foods, this product is high in sodium.

ADDITIVES: Contains monosodium glutamate (MSG), which many authorities believe should be avoided by infants and very young children; causes adverse reactions in some sensitive individuals.

LA CHOY FANCY CHINESE MIXED VEGETABLES
Beatrice Foods Co.

Ingredients: water, bean sprouts, bamboo shoots, water chestnuts, mushrooms, sweet red peppers, salt.

Amount: ½ cup drained			% USRDA
Calories	12	Protein	*
Protein, gm	<1	Vitamin A	*
Carbohydrates, gm	2	Vitamin C	*
Fat, gm	<1	Thiamine	*
Sodium, mg	35	Riboflavin	*
Cholesterol, mg	0e	Niacin	*
Fiber, gm	2e	Calcium	*
		Iron	*

THIS FOOD: La Choy Fancy Chinese Mixed Vegetables is a low-fat, low-sodium, low-calorie food. Although it doesn't provide nutrients other than dietary fiber, this product could be used to fill out a low-calorie meal—as long as more nutritious foods are eaten at the same time.

ADDITIVES: None.

LA CHOY SHRIMP CHOW MEIN
Beatrice Foods Co.

Ingredients: water, bean sprouts, cooked shrimp, water chestnuts, celery, bamboo shoots, carrots, onion, pea pods, sweet red peppers, modified food starch, salt, sugar, brown sugar, hydrolyzed vegetable protein, dextrose, tomato powder, garlic, pepper.

Amount: ¾ cup			% USRDA
Calories	60	Protein	6
Protein, gm	4	Vitamin A	4
Carbohydrates, gm	4	Vitamin C	*
Fat, gm	3	Thiamine	*
Sodium, mg	855	Riboflavin	2
Cholesterol, mg	48e	Niacin	*
Fiber, gm	1e	Calcium	8
		Iron	2

THIS FOOD: La Choy Shrimp Chow Mein is very low in calories—and nutritional value. Since it doesn't provide significant amounts of any vitamin or mineral, it should be served as a side dish, rather than the main attraction, at lunch or dinner.

ADDITIVES: No questionable additives.

LA CHOY SUKIYAKI
Beatrice Foods Co.

Ingredients: *Sauce-and-beef can:* water, cooked beef, cornstarch, onions, sugar, cooking sherry, hydrolyzed plant protein, soy sauce, salt, flavorings, dextrin, beef extract, caramel color. *Vegetable-and-seasonings can:* water, bean sprouts, celery, water chestnuts, bamboo shoots, carrots, sweet red peppers, green peppers, green beans, onions, salt, sugar, monosodium glutamate, flavorings.

Amount: ¾ cup/10½ oz			% USRDA
Calories	70	Protein	8
Protein, gm	6	Vitamin A	10
Carbohydrates, gm	8	Vitamin C	2
Fat, gm	2	Thiamine	*
Sodium, mg	910	Riboflavin	4
Cholesterol, mg	75e	Niacin	6
Fiber, gm	3e	Calcium	2
		Iron	6

THIS FOOD: La Choy Sukiyaki is low in calories, only 25 percent of which derive from fat. Compared to other Oriental main dishes, it is fairly low in nutrients. A serving of Sukiyaki provides a fair amount of dietary fiber and 10 percent of the USRDA for vitamin A. This product is moderate in sodium for this category.

ADDITIVES: Contains monosodium glutamate (MSG), which many authorities believe should be avoided by infants and very young children; causes adverse reactions in some sensitive individuals.

STOUFFER'S CHICKEN CHOW MEIN WITHOUT NOODLES
Nestlé, S.A.

Ingredients: water, chicken, bean sprouts, celery, onions, water chestnuts, soy sauce, green peppers, mushrooms, red peppers, modified cornstarch, bok choy, chicken fat, sugar, salt, monosodium glutamate, caramel coloring, dehydrated onions, celery salt, chicken broth, spice, turmeric, natural flavorings.

Amount: 8 oz			% USRDA
Calories	145	Protein	20
Protein, gm	13	Vitamin A	6
Carbohydrates, gm	10	Vitamin C	*
Fat, gm	6	Thiamine	8
Sodium, mg	1,115	Riboflavin	10
Cholesterol, mg	80e	Niacin	15
Fiber, gm	1e	Calcium	4
		Iron	10

THIS FOOD: Stouffer's Chicken Chow Mein Without Noodles is a very good source of protein and niacin. It is relatively low in calories, about 37 percent of which come from fat. Like most frozen Oriental foods, this product is high in sodium.

ADDITIVES: Contains monosodium glutamate (MSG), which many authorities believe should be avoided by infants and very young children; causes adverse reactions in some sensitive individuals.

STOUFFER'S CHINESE GREEN PEPPER STEAK
Nestlé, S.A.

Ingredients: *Green pepper steak pouch:* beef, water, tomatoes with puree, green peppers, soy sauce, modified cornstarch, margarine, dehydrated onions, salt, sugar, natural flavorings, monosodium glutamate, corn oil, chicken fat, caramel coloring, erythorbic acid, dried beef stock, dehydrated garlic, spice, algin. *Rice pouch:* cooked rice, salt, soybean oil.

Amount: 10½ oz			% USRDA
Calories	350	Protein	35
Protein, gm	25	Vitamin A	8
Carbohydrates, gm	35	Vitamin C	*
Fat, gm	13	Thiamine	4
Sodium, mg	1,500	Riboflavin	15
Cholesterol, mg	na	Niacin	25
Fiber, gm	1e	Calcium	2
		Iron	15

THIS FOOD: Compared to the other items profiled, this entrée offers above average nutritional value. In addition to supplying complex carbohydrates and protein, Stouffer's Chinese Style Green Pepper Steak is a very good source of riboflavin, niacin, and iron. A moderate 33 percent of calories derive from fat. This product is very high in sodium.

ADDITIVES: Contains monosodium glutamate (MSG), which many authorities believe should be avoided by infants and very young children; causes adverse reactions in some sensitive individuals.

PANCAKES AND WAFFLES

Pancakes and waffles are an American passion. The homemade recipe is concocted from flour, milk, eggs, baking powder, salt, and a little melted butter. Needless to say, many commercially prepared mixes contain a variety of additives, some of them controversial. In terms of nutrition, all of the products profiled provide complex carbohydrates, some protein, the B vitamins, and iron. Aunt Jemima Complete Buttermilk Pancake Mix is also a terrific source of calcium. Pancakes and waffles would be nutritious breakfast foods, if only they weren't eaten slathered with butter and syrup. A stack of three average pancakes, eaten with three pats of margarine or butter and five tablespoons syrup, contains more than twice the fat, sodium, and calories of a breakfast of one poached egg with two slices buttered toast, and more than three times the fat, sodium, and calories of a breakfast of Cheerios and one-half cup whole milk.

SODIUM GUIDELINES: In evaluating the sodium content of pancakes and waffles, we used the following standards:

less than 500 mg	high in sodium
more than 500 mg	very high in sodium

Remember, these guidelines are not for people following medically restricted low-sodium diets, but for healthy individuals who wish to monitor their sodium intake.

AUNT JEMIMA BLUEBERRY WAFFLES
Quaker Oats Co.

Ingredients: enriched flour (flour, niacin, reduced iron, thiamine mononitrate, riboflavin), whey, water, artificially flavored blueberry buds (sugar, dextrose, partially hydrogenated cottonseed oil, artificial flavor, salt, citric acid, modified soy protein flour, cellulose gum, corn syrup solids, silicon dioxide, FD & C, Blue No. 2, malic acid, FD & C Red No. 40), partially hydrogenated vegetable oil (soybean, palm, cottonseed), lecithin, sugar, leavening (monocalcium phosphate, sodium bicarbonate), whole egg, soy flour, salt, ferrous fumarate, niacin, FD & C Yellow No. 5, pyridoxine hydrochloride, FD & C Yellow No. 6, riboflavin, thiamine mononitrate, B_{12}.

Amount: 2 waffles			% USRDA
Calories	172	Protein	5
Protein, gm	4	Vitamin A	*
Carbohydrates, gm	30	Vitamin C	*
Fat, gm	4	Thiamine	20
Sodium, mg	486	Riboflavin	20
Cholesterol, mg	<5e	Niacin	20
Fiber, gm	<1e	Calcium	15
		Iron	20

THIS FOOD: Aunt Jemima Blueberry Waffles do not, alas, contain any real blueberries. Even so they provide complex carbohydrates and are a very good source of the B vitamins, calcium, and iron. If you limit yourself to 2 teaspoons of butter, you'll be consuming 33 percent fat calories. Like most frozen waffles, this product is high in sodium.

ADDITIVES: Contains artificial color and flavor, which some studies suggest may adversely affect behavior and the ability to complete school tasks in some sensitive children; artificial colors are inadequately tested and artificial flavors may cause allergic reactions in sensitive individuals. Also contains Yellow No. 5, which can cause allergic reactions, especially in aspirin-sensitive individuals.

AUNT JEMIMA COMPLETE BUTTERMILK PANCAKE MIX
Quaker Oats Co.

Ingredients: enriched unbleached flour (flour, niacin, iron, thiamine mononitrate, riboflavin), corn flour, sugar, dried buttermilk, dried whey, leavening (monocalcium phosphate, sodium bicarbonate), partially hydrogenated vegetable shortening (soybean) with mono- and diglycerides, salt, egg extender (soy flour, wheat flour, lecithin, partially hydrogenated cottonseed, soybean oils, glycerin, carrageenan), dried whole eggs, nonfat dry milk.

Amount: three 4-inch pancakes (water only added to recipe)			% USRDA
Calories	260	Protein	10
Protein, gm	8	Vitamin A	*
Carbohydrates, gm	51	Vitamin C	*
Fat, gm	3	Thiamine	25
Sodium, mg	960	Riboflavin	20
Cholesterol, mg	<5e	Niacin	10
Fiber, gm	<1e	Calcium	40
		Iron	10

NOTE: The letter "e" indicates that the data has been estimated; < means "less than" and is used for small amounts of sodium or cholesterol; * means food contains less than 2% of USRDA; "na" means that the information was not available and appears only when data is insufficient.

THIS FOOD: Aunt Jemima Complete Buttermilk Pancake Mix provides valuable complex carbohydrates and is a very good source of the B vitamins and iron, and an excellent source of calcium. If you can go easy on the syrup, these pancakes will provide an extremely nutritious meal. If you add one pat of butter, you'll be consuming only 25 percent fat calories; if you add two pats, the fat calories will increase to 35 percent. This pancake mix is extremely high in sodium.

ADDITIVES: No questionable additives.

AUNT JEMIMA ORIGINAL PANCAKE MIX
Quaker Oats Co.

Ingredients: enriched unbleached flour (flour, niacin, iron, thiamine mononitrate, riboflavin), corn flour, oat flour, leavening (monocalcium phosphate, sodium bicarbonate), rye flour, dextrose, salt.

Amount: three 4-inch pancakes (+ ¼ cup milk, ½ tbsp oil, and ½ egg)			% USRDA
Calories	200	Protein	10
Protein, gm	7	Vitamin A	4
Carbohydrates, gm	26	Vitamin C	*
Fat, gm	8	Thiamine	10
Sodium, mg	550	Riboflavin	10
Cholesterol, mg	175e	Niacin	4
Fiber, gm	<1e	Calcium	20
		Iron	8

THIS FOOD: Aunt Jemima Original Pancake Mix provides valuable complex carbohydrates and is a fair source of protein, thiamine, riboflavin, and a very good source of calcium. If you add one pat of butter, you'll be consuming 48 percent fat calories; if you add two pats, the fat calories will increase to 57 percent. This product is very high in sodium and cholesterol (from added eggs and milk).

ADDITIVES: No questionable additives.

AUNT JEMIMA ORIGINAL WAFFLES
Quaker Oats Co.

Ingredients: enriched flour (flour, niacin, reduced iron, thiamine mononitrate, riboflavin), whey, water, partially hydrogenated vegetable oil (soybean, palm, cottonseed), with lecithin, sugar, leavening (monocalcium phosphate, sodium bicarbonate), whole eggs, soy flour, salt, ferrous fumarate, niacin, FD & C Yellow No. 5, pyridoxine hydrochloride, FD & C Yellow No. 6, riboflavin, thiamine mononitrate, B_{12}.

Amount: 2 waffles			% USRDA
Calories	160	Protein	6
Protein, gm	5	Vitamin A	*
Carbohydrates, gm	28	Vitamin C	*
Fat, gm	3	Thiamine	20
Sodium, mg	650	Riboflavin	15
Cholesterol, mg	<10	Niacin	15
Fiber, gm	<1e	Calcium	10
		Iron	15

THIS FOOD: Aunt Jemima Original Waffles provide complex carbohydrates and are a fair source of calcium and a very good source of the B vitamins and iron. If you limit yourself to 2 teaspoons of butter, you'll be consuming 41 percent fat calories. Like most frozen waffles, this product is very high in sodium.

ADDITIVES: Contains Yellow 6, which some studies suggest may adversely affect behavior and the ability to complete school tasks in some sensitive children; artificial colors are inadequately tested and artificial flavor may cause allergic reactions in sensitive individuals. Also contains Yellow No. 5, which can cause allergic reactions, especially in aspirin-sensitive individuals.

DOWNYFLAKE BUTTERMILK WAFFLES
IC Industries, Inc.

Ingredients: wheat, water, corn flour, buttermilk, vegetable oil shortening (palm, partially hydrogenated soybean, hydrogenated palm, cottonseed), dextrose, sodium acid pyrophosphate, salt, baking soda, eggs, niacin, iron, thiamine mononitrate, riboflavin, artificial flavor, artificial color, FD & C Yellow No. 5.

Amount: 2 waffles			% USRDA
Calories	170	Protein	6
Protein, gm	4	Vitamin A	*
Carbohydrates, gm	30	Vitamin C	*
Fat, gm	4	Thiamine	20
Sodium, mg	450e	Riboflavin	10
Cholesterol, mg	20e	Niacin	10
Fiber, gm	<1e	Calcium	*
		Iron	15

THIS FOOD: DownyFlake Buttermilk Waffles provide complex carbohydrates and are a good source of the B vitamins and iron. If you limit yourself to 2 teaspoons of butter, you'll be consuming 37 percent fat calories. Like most frozen waffles, this product is high in sodium.

ADDITIVES: Contains artificial color and flavor, which some studies suggest may adversely affect behavior and the ability to complete school tasks in some sensitive children; artificial colors are inadequately tested and artificial flavor may cause allergic reactions in sensitive individuals. Also contains Yellow No. 5, which can cause allergic reactions, especially in aspirin-sensitive individuals.

EGGO HOMESTYLE WAFFLES
Kellogg Co.

Ingredients: enriched wheat flour, water, partially hydrogenated soybean oil, eggs, sugar, whey, baking soda, sodium aluminum phosphate, salt, monocalcium phosphate, vitamin A palmitate, niacinamide, reduced iron, FD & C Yellow No. 5, FD & C Yellow No. 6, thiamine hydrochloride, riboflavin.

Amount: 2 waffles			% USRDA
Calories	240	Protein	8
Protein, gm	6	Vitamin A	20
Carbohydrates, gm	32	Vitamin C	*
Fat, gm	10	Thiamine	20
Sodium, mg	600	Riboflavin	20
Cholesterol, mg	40e	Niacin	20
Fiber, gm	1e	Calcium	24
		Iron	20

THIS FOOD: Eggo Homestyle Waffles provide complex carbohydrates and are a very good source of the B vitamins and iron. If you limit yourself to 2 teaspoons of butter, you'll be consuming 43 percent fat calories. Like most frozen waffles, this product is very high in sodium.

ADDITIVES: Contains artificial colors which some studies suggest can negatively affect behavior and the ability to complete school tasks in some sensitive children; also contains Yellow No. 5, which can cause allergic reactions, especially in aspirin-sensitive individuals.

BEST BET: Among the pancake mixes profiled, Aunt Jemima Complete Buttermilk Pancake Mix is the clear winner. It has much less fat and cholesterol than the other brands, at least twice as much calcium, and more valuable iron. Unfortunately, it is extremely high in sodium.

HUNGRY JACK BUTTERMILK PANCAKE AND WAFFLE MIX
The Pillsbury Co.

Ingredients: enriched flour (flour, niacin, iron, thiamine mononitrate, riboflavin), sugar, rice flour, baking powder (baking soda, sodium aluminum phosphate), buttermilk, salt.

Amount: three 4-inch pancakes (+ ⅙ cup milk, ½ tbsp oil, and ½ egg)			% USRDA
Calories	240	Protein	10
Protein, gm	7	Vitamin A	4
Carbohydrates, gm	29	Vitamin C	*
Fat, gm	11	Thiamine	15
Sodium, mg	570	Riboflavin	20
Cholesterol, mg	60e	Niacin	10
Fiber, gm	<1e	Calcium	6
		Iron	6

THIS FOOD: Hungry Jack Buttermilk Pancake and Waffle Mix provides valuable complex carbohydrates and is a good source of the B vitamins. If you add one pat of butter, you'll be consuming 51 percent fat calories; if you add two pats, the fat calories will increase to 58 percent. Like most pancake mixes, this product is very high in sodium.

ADDITIVES: No questionable additives.

HUNGRY JACK EXTRA LIGHTS PANCAKE AND WAFFLE MIX
The Pillsbury Co.

Ingredients: enriched flour (flour, niacin, iron, thiamine mononitrate, riboflavin), yellow corn flour, sugar, baking powder (baking soda, monocalcium phosphate, sodium aluminum phosphate), salt.

Amount: three 4-inch pancakes (+ ⅙ cup milk, ½ tbsp oil, and ½ egg)			% USRDA
Calories	210	Protein	10
Protein, gm	6	Vitamin A	4
Carbohydrates, gm	30	Vitamin C	*
Fat, gm	7	Thiamine	15
Sodium, mg	485	Riboflavin	10
Cholesterol, mg	50e	Niacin	6
Fiber, gm	<1e	Calcium	15
		Iron	8

THIS FOOD: Hungry Jack Extra Lights Pancake and Waffle Mix provides valuable complex carbohydrates and is a good source of protein, thiamine, riboflavin, and calcium. If you add one pat of butter, you'll be consuming 43 percent fat calories; if you add two pats, the fat calories will increase to 53 percent. Like most pancake mixes, this product is high in sodium.

ADDITIVES: No questionable additives.

HELPFUL HINT: To cut down on empty sugar calories, try topping pancakes and waffles with lightly sweetened fresh fruit instead of syrup. Try skipping the butter, or at least limit yourself to a single pat. Eaten in this way, pancakes or waffles are healthful and reasonably low in calories.

PASTA

Pasta is available in a staggering array of shapes and sizes, from spirals and bows to tubes, ribbons, and shells. But whether it's called spaghetti, macaroni, vermicelli, or ziti, pasta is a simple flour-based food which provides complex carbohydrates as well as protein, the B vitamins, and iron. Plain pasta is naturally low in fat, cholesterol, and sodium, but nobody eats pasta plain. Most sauces—especially commercially prepared products—are fairly high in sodium, and many cream- or butter-based sauces are extremely high in fat. But eaten with a carefully chosen, low-fat sauce, pasta can make a healthful meal for nutrition and calorie-conscious consumers. Tomato sauces are a good choice because they are generally low or moderate in fat and also supply vitamin A and vitamin C, which are lacking in the pasta itself.

BUITONI HIGH-PROTEIN SPINACH LINGUINE
Buitoni Foods Corp.

Ingredients: unbleached wheat flour, spinach, partially defatted wheat germ, dried yeast, niacin, reduced iron, thiamine mononitrate, riboflavin.

Amount: 1 cup cooked/2 oz dry			% USRDA
Calories	210	Protein	15
Protein, gm	12	Vitamin A	*
Carbohydrates, gm	37	Vitamin C	*
Fat, gm	1	Thiamine	35
Sodium, mg	<5	Riboflavin	15
Cholesterol, mg	0	Niacin	15
Fiber, gm	2.5	Calcium	*
		Iron	10

THIS FOOD: True to its name, Buitoni High-Protein Spinach Linguine is especially high in protein in addition to supplying the iron, B vitamins, and complex carbohydrates found in other pastas.

ADDITIVES: No questionable additives.

MUELLER'S EGG NOODLES
CPC International, Inc.

Ingredients: fancy flour, selected eggs.

Amount: 1 cup cooked/2 oz dry			% USRDA
Calories	210	Protein	12e
Protein, gm	7e	Vitamin A	*e
Carbohydrates, gm	41	Vitamin C	*e
Fat, gm	2	Thiamine	16e
Sodium, mg	22	Riboflavin	8e
Cholesterol, mg	63	Niacin	10e
Fiber, gm	1.5	Calcium	*e
		Iron	8e

THIS FOOD: Mueller's Egg Noodles are high in complex carbohydrates and low in sodium and fat. They are a good source of protein, thiamine, and niacin. Because of their egg content, these noodles contain some cholesterol.

ADDITIVES: None.

MUELLER'S MACARONI (ALL SHAPES)
CPC International, Inc.

Ingredients: semolina and farina (enriched).

Amount: 1 cup cooked/2 oz dry			% USRDA
Calories	210	Protein	12e
Protein, gm	8e	Vitamin A	*e
Carbohydrates, gm	44	Vitamin C	*e
Fat, gm	1	Thiamine	25e
Sodium, mg	7	Riboflavin	12e
Cholesterol, mg	0	Niacin	15e
Fiber, gm	2	Calcium	*e
		Iron	10e

NOTE: The letter "e" indicates that the data has been estimated; < means "less than" and is used for small amounts of sodium or cholesterol; * means food contains less than 2% of USRDA; "na" means that the information was not available and appears only when data is insufficient.

THIS FOOD: Mueller's Macaroni is a nutritionally valuable food: low in fat and sodium, high in complex carbohydrates. At the same time it is a good source of protein, the B vitamins, and iron, and also provides some fiber.

ADDITIVES: None.

PRINCE ENRICHED MACARONI AND SPAGHETTI
Prince Macaroni Manufacturing Co.

Ingredients: semolina, niacinamide, ferrous sulfate, thiamine mononitrate, riboflavin.

Amount: 1 cup cooked/2 oz dry			% USRDA
Calories	204	Protein	16
Protein, gm	7	Vitamin A	*
Carbohydrates, gm	40	Vitamin C	*
Fat, gm	2	Thiamine	43
Sodium, mg	5	Riboflavin	9
Cholesterol, mg	0	Niacin	24
Fiber, gm	2	Calcium	*
		Iron	17

THIS FOOD: Prince Enriched Macaroni and Spaghetti is a nutritionally valuable food: low in fat and sodium, high in complex carbohydrates. Like other pastas, it supplies protein and fiber, but it also has significantly more iron and B vitamins than most other brands.

ADDITIVES: No questionable additives.

PRINCE SUPERONI
Prince Macaroni Manufacturing Co.

Ingredients: semolina, whey protein concentrate, wheat gluten, niacinamide, ferrous sulfate, thiamine mononitrate, riboflavin.

Amount: 1 cup cooked/2 oz dry			% USRDA
Calories	210	Protein	25
Protein, gm	13	Vitamin A	*
Carbohydrates, gm	40	Vitamin C	*
Fat, gm	1	Thiamine	25
Sodium, mg	70	Riboflavin	15
Cholesterol, mg	0	Niacin	20
Fiber, gm	2	Calcium	*
		Iron	10

THIS FOOD: Like other pastas, Prince Superoni is high in complex carbohydrates and low in sodium and fat. But additional enrichment gives this product a nutritional boost. It is an excellent source of thiamine and provides twice the protein of, and one third more riboflavin and niacin than, most other brands.

ADDITIVES: No questionable additives.

RONZONI EGG NOODLES
Ronzoni Macaroni Co., Inc.

Ingredients: durum wheat, no. 1 semolina, pasteurized egg yolks.

Amount: 1 cup cooked/2 oz dry			% USRDA
Calories	220	Protein	12
Protein, gm	8	Vitamin A	*e
Carbohydrates, gm	40	Vitamin C	*e
Fat, gm	3	Thiamine	16e
Sodium, mg	15	Riboflavin	8e
Cholesterol, mg	80	Niacin	10e
Fiber, gm	1.5	Calcium	*e
		Iron	8e

THIS FOOD: Ronzoni Egg Noodles are high in complex carbohydrates and low in sodium and fat. They are a good source of protein, thiamine, and niacin. Because of their egg content, these noodles contain some cholesterol.

ADDITIVES: No questionable additives.

RONZONI SPAGHETTI
Ronzoni Macaroni Co, Inc.

Ingredients: durum wheat, no. 1 semolina.

Amount: 1 cup cooked/2 oz dry			% USRDA
Calories	210	Protein	11e
Protein, gm	7	Vitamin A	*e
Carbohydrates, gm	41	Vitamin C	*e
Fat, gm	1	Thiamine	25e
Sodium, mg	<5	Riboflavin	12e
Cholesterol, mg	0	Niacin	15e
Fiber, gm	2	Calcium	*
		Iron	10e

THIS FOOD: Ronzoni Spaghetti is almost an ideal food: low in fat and sodium, high in complex carbohydrates. At the same time it is a good source of protein, the B vitamins, iron, and provides some fiber.

ADDITIVES: None.

SAN GIORGIO SPAGHETTI
Hershey Food Corp.

Ingredients: durum wheat, semolina.

Amount: 1 cup cooked/2 oz dry			% USRDA
Calories	210	Protein	10
Protein, gm	7	Vitamin A	*
Carbohydrates, gm	42	Vitamin C	*
Fat, gm	1	Thiamine	30
Sodium, mg	<5e	Riboflavin	10
Cholesterol, mg	0	Niacin	15
Fiber, gm	2	Calcium	*
		Iron	10

THIS FOOD: This spaghetti is a nutritionally valuable food: low in fat and sodium, high in complex carbohydrates. At the same time it is a good source of protein, the B vitamins, and iron, and provides some fiber.

ADDITIVES: None.

FOR WEIGHT WATCHERS: Pasta itself is not a fattening food, but cream, oil, or butter-based sauces can raise the percentage of fat calories alarmingly. Eat your spaghetti with tomato or other low-fat sauces and you can enjoy your pasta and still lose or maintain your weight.

PEANUT BUTTER

More than half the peanut crop in the United States is used for peanut butter, most of which goes into peanut-butter-and-jelly sandwiches consumed by youngsters. Parents who are concerned that their kids' favorite lunch is under par in terms of nutrition need not worry. Peanuts are actually a kind of legume and a good, inexpensive source of fiber, protein, niacin, and magnesium. Eaten with bread (preferably whole wheat), a glass of milk (preferably low fat), and a teaspoon of jelly, peanut butter makes a well balanced meal. According to federal standards, peanut butter must contain at least 90 percent ground nuts by weight, leaving 10 percent for "seasoning and stabilizing" ingredients, such as sugar, salt, and hydrogenated vegetable oils (which tend to raise cholesterol levels). Jif, Peter Pan, and Skippy, which together account for 60 percent of all sales, use these optional ingredients. Of the brands profiled, only Smucker's Natural No Salt Added Peanut Butter contains ground peanuts and nothing else.

JIF CREAMY PEANUT BUTTER
Procter and Gamble

Ingredients: choice roasted peanuts with sugar, hardened vegetable oil, salt, molasses, mono- and diglycerides.

Amount: 2 tbsp			% USRDA
Calories	190	Protein	15
Protein, gm	9	Vitamin A	*
Carbohydrates, gm	6	Vitamin C	*
Fat, gm	16	Thiamine	*
Sodium, mg	155	Riboflavin	2
Cholesterol, mg	0	Niacin	20
Fiber, gm	2	Calcium	*
		Iron	2

THIS FOOD: Peanut butter is a very good source of protein and niacin and provides some fiber. About 75 percent of calories come from fat. This inexpensive source of protein should not be eaten too often, because of its fat content. This product contains added sugar and salt.

ADDITIVES: Contains hardened vegetable oil, another term for hydrogenated vegetable oil. Hydrogenated vegetable oil is highly saturated and has an adverse effect on cholesterol levels.

BEST BETS: Smucker's Natural No Salt Added brand is made of ground peanuts and nothing else. Smucker's Natural Peanut Butter is also an excellent choice since it contains no hydrogenated oil or sugar.

NOTE: The letter "e" indicates that the data has been estimated; < means "less than" and is used for small amounts of sodium or cholesterol; * means food contains less than 2% of USRDA; "na" means that the information was not available and appears only when data is insufficient.

PETER PAN CRUNCHY PEANUT BUTTER
Swift and Co.

Ingredients: golden roasted peanuts, sucrose, hydrogenated vegetable oil, salt.

Amount: 2 tbsp			% USRDA
Calories	190	Protein	15
Protein, gm	9	Vitamin A	*
Carbohydrates, gm	6	Vitamin C	*
Fat, gm	16	Thiamine	2
Sodium, mg	190	Riboflavin	2
Cholesterol, mg	0	Niacin	15
Fiber, gm	2	Calcium	*
		Iron	2

THIS FOOD: Peanut butter is a very good source of protein and niacin and provides some fiber. A 2-tablespoon serving of this product contains more than 1 tablespoon of fat. This food is an inexpensive source of protein but should not be eaten too often, because of its fat content. This peanut butter contains added sugar and salt.

ADDITIVES: Contains hydrogenated vegetable oil, a highly saturated fat which has an adverse effect on cholesterol levels.

SKIPPY CREAMY PEANUT BUTTER
CPC International, Inc.

Ingredients: U.S. grade no. 1 peanuts, dextrose, partially hydrogenated vegetable oil, salt, sugar.

Amount: 2 tbsp			% USRDA
Calories	190	Protein	15
Protein, gm	9	Vitamin A	*
Carbohydrates, gm	4	Vitamin C	*
Fat, gm	16	Thiamine	*
Sodium, mg	150	Riboflavin	*
Cholesterol, mg	0	Niacin	20
Fiber, gm	2	Calcium	*
		Iron	2

THIS FOOD: Peanut butter is a very good source of protein and niacin and provides some fiber, but is very high in fat. A 2-tablespoon serving of this product contains more than 1 tablespoon of fat! This food is an inexpensive source of protein but should not be eaten too often, because of its fat content. This peanut butter contains added sugar and salt.

ADDITIVES: No questionable additives.

SKIPPY SUPER CHUNK PEANUT BUTTER
CPC International, Inc.

Ingredients: U.S. grade no. 1 peanuts, dextrose, partially hydrogenated vegetable oil, salt, sugar.

Amount: 2 tbsp			% USRDA
Calories	190	Protein	15
Protein, gm	9	Vitamin A	*
Carbohydrates, gm	4	Vitamin C	*
Fat, gm	17	Thiamine	*
Sodium, mg	130	Riboflavin	*
Cholesterol, mg	0	Niacin	20
Fiber, gm	2	Calcium	*
		Iron	2

THIS FOOD: Peanut butter is a very good source of protein and niacin and provides some fiber, but is very high in fat. A 2-tablespoon serving of this product contains more than 1 tablespoon of fat! This food is an inexpensive source of protein but should not be eaten too often, because of its fat content. This peanut butter contains added sugar and salt.

ADDITIVES: No questionable additives.

SMUCKER'S NATURAL NO SALT ADDED PEANUT BUTTER
J. M. Smucker, Inc.

Ingredients: peanuts.

Amount: 2 tbsp			% USRDA
Calories	200	Protein	10
Protein, gm	8	Vitamin A	*
Carbohydrates, gm	6	Vitamin C	*
Fat, gm	17	Thiamine	*
Sodium, mg	<10	Riboflavin	*
Cholesterol, mg	0	Niacin	25
Fiber, gm	2e	Calcium	*
		Iron	4

THIS FOOD: This product is one of the few widely distributed brands of peanut butter that contain no added sugar, hydrogenated oil, or salt. Although this means it has less saturated fat than Skippy, Peter Pan, or other popular brands, it is still naturally high in fat which accounts for 75 percent of calories. Peanut butter is an inexpensive source of protein, fiber, and niacin, but should not be eaten too often, because of its fat content.

ADDITIVES: None.

SMUCKER'S NATURAL PEANUT BUTTER
J. M. Smucker, Inc.

Ingredients: peanuts, salt.

Amount: 2 tbsp			% USRDA
Calories	200	Protein	10
Protein, gm	8	Vitamin A	*
Carbohydrates, gm	6	Vitamin C	*
Fat, gm	16	Thiamine	*
Sodium, mg	125	Riboflavin	*
Cholesterol, mg	0	Niacin	25
Fiber, gm	2e	Calcium	*
		Iron	4

THIS FOOD: Smucker's Natural Peanut Butter is one of the few widely distributed brands to contain no added sugar or hydrogenated oil. Although it does contain added salt, its sodium content is lower than average. Peanut butter is an inexpensive source of protein and niacin, but should not be eaten too often, because of its naturally high fat content.

ADDITIVES: None.

HELPFUL HINT: The oil in all natural peanut butters will separate. If you mix the product by hand and then refrigerate, separation will be kept to a minimum.

PICKLES AND RELISH

Pickles and relish are usually quite high in sodium and many popular brands contain Yellow No. 5 and other artificial colorings, which are of questionable safety. Hot dog relishes, including Heinz and Vlasic, contain lots of hidden sugar—two full teaspoons per 1-ounce serving. Of the popular brands profiled, Claussen Sweet 'n Sour Pickles contains the least sodium (100 mg per 1-ounce serving). All of these products are low in calories—and nutrients.

SODIUM GUIDELINES: In evaluating the sodium intake of pickles and relish, we used the following standards:

less than 100 mg	moderate in sodium
100 mg to 200 mg	high in sodium
less than 200 mg	very high in sodium

Remember, these guidelines are not for people following a medically restricted low-sodium diet, but for healthy individuals who wish to monitor their sodium intake.

CLAUSSEN KOSHER PICKLES
Oscar Mayer and Co.

Ingredients: cucumbers, water, salt, vinegar, garlic, spices, benzoate of soda (preservative), natural flavorings, polysorbate 80.

Amount: 1 oz/¼ large pickle			% USRDA
Calories	4	Protein	*
Protein, gm	<1	Vitamin A	*
Carbohydrates, gm	<1	Vitamin C	*
Fat, gm	<1	Thiamine	*
Sodium, mg	290	Riboflavin	*
Cholesterol, mg	0	Niacin	*
Fiber, gm	<1	Calcium	*
		Iron	*

THIS FOOD: Like most pickles, Claussen Kosher Pickles are not a significant source of nutrients. This product is low in calories and very high in sodium.

ADDITIVES: No questionable additives.

NOTE: The letter "e" indicates that the data has been estimated; < means "less than" and is used for small amounts of sodium or cholesterol; * means food contains less than 2% of USRDA; "na" means that the information was not available and appears only when data is insufficient.

CLAUSSEN SWEET 'N SOUR PICKLES
Oscar Mayer and Co.

Ingredients: cucumbers, water, corn syrup, vinegar, salt, spices, calcium chloride, benzoate of soda, onion, turmeric.

Amount: 1 oz/¼ large pickle			% USRDA
Calories	12	Protein	*
Protein, gm	<1	Vitamin A	*
Carbohydrates, gm	<1	Vitamin C	2
Fat, gm	<1	Thiamine	*
Sodium, mg	100	Riboflavin	*
Cholesterol, mg	0	Niacin	*
Fiber, gm	<1	Calcium	*
		Iron	*

THIS FOOD: Like most pickles Claussen Sweet 'n Sour Pickles are not a significant source of nutrients. This product is low in calories and contains a moderate amount of sodium.

ADDITIVES: No questionable additives.

HEINZ BREAD 'N BUTTER CUCUMBER SLICES
H. J. Heinz Co.

Ingredients: cucumbers, distilled vinegar, corn syrup, salt, dehydrated onions, spices, calcium chloride, natural flavoring, FD & C Yellow No. 5, polysorbate 80.

Amount: 1 oz/5 slices			% USRDA
Calories	25	Protein	*e
Protein, gm	0	Vitamin A	*e
Carbohydrates, gm	6	Vitamin C	5e
Fat, gm	0	Thiamine	*e
Sodium, mg	170	Riboflavin	*e
Cholesterol, mg	0	Niacin	*e
Fiber, gm	<1	Calcium	*e
		Iron	*e

THIS FOOD: Like most pickles, Heinz Bread 'n Butter Cucumber Slices are not a significant source of nutrients. They are low in calories and high in sodium.

ADDITIVES: Contains Yellow No. 5, which can cause allergic reactions, especially in aspirin-sensitive individuals.

HEINZ SWEET GHERKINS
H. J. Heinz Co.

Ingredients: pickles, corn syrup, distilled vinegar, salt, alum, natural flavoring, polysorbate 80, turmeric oleoresin.

Amount: 1 oz/½ pickle			% USRDA
Calories	35	Protein	*e
Protein, gm	0	Vitamin A	*e
Carbohydrates, gm	8	Vitamin C	2e
Fat, gm	0	Thiamine	*e
Sodium, mg	210	Riboflavin	*e
Cholesterol, mg	0	Niacin	*e
Fiber, gm	<1	Calcium	*e
		Iron	*e

THIS FOOD: Like other pickles, Heinz Sweet Gherkins are not a significant source of nutrients. They are relatively low in calories and very high in sodium.

ADDITIVES: No questionable additives.

HEINZ SWEET RELISH
H. J. Heinz Co.

Ingredients: pickles, corn syrup, cabbage, distilled vinegar, salt, dextrose, alum, xanthan gum, natural flavoring, dehydrated red peppers, polysorbate 80, turmeric oleoresin, artificial colors (including FD & C Yellow No. 5).

Amount: 2 tbsp			% USRDA
Calories	35	Protein	*e
Protein, gm	0	Vitamin A	*e
Carbohydrates, gm	9	Vitamin C	2e
Fat, gm	0	Thiamine	*e
Sodium, mg	205	Riboflavin	*e
Cholesterol, mg	0	Niacin	*e
Fiber, gm	<1	Calcium	*e
		Iron	*e

THIS FOOD: Heinz Sweet Relish is high in sodium and does not provide a significant amount of other nutrients.

ADDITIVES: Contains artificial colors, which are inadequately tested and which some studies suggest may adversely affect behavior and the ability to complete school tasks in some sensitive children. Also contains Yellow No. 5, which can cause allergic reactions, especially in aspirin-sensitive individuals.

VLASIC HALF THE SALT KOSHER CRUNCHY DILLS
Campbell Soup Co.

Ingredients: fresh cucumbers, water, vinegar, salt, potassium chloride, calcium chloride, natural flavors, garlic extract, polysorbate 80, FD & C Yellow No. 5.

Amount: 1 oz/¼ large pickle			% USRDA
Calories	4	Protein	*
Protein, gm	0	Vitamin A	*
Carbohydrates, gm	1	Vitamin C	*
Fat, gm	0	Thiamine	*
Sodium, mg	125	Riboflavin	*
Cholesterol, mg	0	Niacin	*
Fiber, gm	<1	Calcium	*
		Iron	*

THIS FOOD: Like most pickles, Vlasic Half the Salt Kosher Crunchy Dills are not a significant source of nutrients. They are low in calories and high in sodium. The product name is more than a little misleading: these pickles have 50 percent less salt than *some* other pickles, but several other brands have still less salt, without calling attention to the fact.

ADDITIVES: Contains Yellow No. 5, which can cause allergic reactions, especially in aspirin-sensitive individuals.

VLASIC HOT DOG RELISH
Campbell Soup Co.

Ingredients: cucumbers, corn syrup, salad mustard, water, salt, vinegar, starch, spice, natural flavors, alum, polysorbate 80, FD & C Yellow No. 5.

Amount: 2 tbsp			% USRDA
Calories	40	Protein	*
Protein, gm	0	Vitamin A	*
Carbohydrates, gm	8	Vitamin C	2
Fat, gm	1	Thiamine	*
Sodium, mg	255	Riboflavin	*
Cholesterol, mg	0	Niacin	*
Fiber, gm	<1	Calcium	*
		Iron	2

THIS FOOD: Vlasic Hot Dog Relish is very high in sodium and does not provide a significant amount of other nutrients.

ADDITIVES: Contains Yellow No. 5, which can cause allergic reactions, especially in aspirin-sensitive individuals.

VLASIC KOSHER DILL SPEARS
Campbell Soup Co.

Ingredients: fresh cucumbers, water, salt, vinegar, calcium chloride, natural flavors, polysorbate 80, FD & C Yellow No. 5.

Amount: 1 oz/½ spear			% USRDA
Calories	4	Protein	*
Protein, gm	0	Vitamin A	*
Carbohydrates, gm	1	Vitamin C	*
Fat, gm	0	Thiamine	*
Sodium, mg	175	Riboflavin	*
Cholesterol, mg	0	Niacin	*
Fiber, gm	<1	Calcium	*
		Iron	*

THIS FOOD: Like most pickles, Vlasic Kosher Dill Spears are not a significant source of nutrients. This product is low in calories and high in sodium.

ADDITIVES: Contains Yellow No. 5, which can cause allergic reactions, especially in aspirin-sensitive individuals.

PIES AND PASTRIES

Virtually all commercially prepared pies and pastries are high in sugar, saturated fat, sodium, and calories, about half of which come from the crust. Many also contain additives of questionable safety. Most people treat themselves to a piece of pie with the full knowledge that it is not a nutritious food. Of the popular brands profiled, only Mrs. Smith's Pumpkin Custard Pie provides more than empty calories. It contains significant amounts of nutrients: protein, vitamin A, calcium, and riboflavin along with a moderate 32 percent fat calories.

SODIUM GUIDELINES: In evaluating the sodium content of pies, we used the following standards:

less than 200 mg	low in sodium
200 mg to 300 mg	moderate in sodium
more than 300 mg	high in sodium

Remember, these guidelines are not for people following medically restricted low-sodium diets, but for healthy individuals who wish to monitor their sodium intake.

BETTY CROCKER PIECRUST MIX
General Mills, Inc.

Ingredients: enriched flour (bleached flour, malted barley flour, niacin, iron, thiamine mononitrate, riboflavin), animal and/or vegetable shortening (partially hydrogenated soybean, cottonseed oils, beef tallow, palm oil, lard), with BHA and BHT, modified cornstarch, salt, dried corn syrup, mono- and diglycerides, sodium caseinate, annatto, turmeric extract.

Amount: ⅛ piecrust			% USRDA
Calories	120	Protein	*
Protein, gm	1	Vitamin A	*
Carbohydrates, gm	10	Vitamin C	*
Fat, gm	8	Thiamine	*
Sodium, mg	140	Riboflavin	2
Cholesterol, mg	10e	Niacin	2
Fiber, gm	<1	Calcium	*
		Iron	*

THIS FOOD: Betty Crocker Piecrust Mix is not a significant source of nutrients. It contains 60 percent fat calories and is high in saturated fat. Piecrust generally contributes one-half to one-third of the calories in dessert pies.

ADDITIVES: Contains BHA and BHT whose long-term safety is currently being reexamined by FDA investigators.

MRS. SMITH'S PEACH PIE
Kellogg Co.

Ingredients: peaches, wheat flour, water, corn syrup, lard, sugar, margarine (partially hydrogenated soybean oil and/or lard, soybean oil, water, salt, [may contain nonfat dry milk, lecithin, mono- and diglycerides; may contain sodium benzoate, BHA or citric acid], artificial color and flavor, vitamin A palmitate), modified food starch, salt, dextrose, natural flavoring, baking soda, sodium bisulfite, citric acid.

NOTE: The letter "e" indicates that the data has been estimated; < means "less than" and is used for small amounts of sodium or cholesterol; * means food contains less than 2% of USRDA; "na" means that the information was not available and appears only when data is insufficient.

Amount: ⅙ pie			% USRDA
Calories	365	Protein	6
Protein, gm	4	Vitamin A	3
Carbohydrates, gm	53	Vitamin C	*
Fat, gm	16	Thiamine	4
Sodium, mg	435	Riboflavin	*
Cholesterol, mg	10	Niacin	*
Fiber, gm	2e	Calcium	*
		Iron	4

THIS FOOD: Mrs. Smith's Peach Pie is not a significant source of any nutrient. It is high in saturated fat, and overall fat, which contributes 39 percent of calories. It is also high in sodium and sugar.

ADDITIVES: Contains artificial color and flavor, which some studies suggest may adversely affect behavior and the ability to complete school tasks in some sensitive children; artificial colors are inadequately tested, and artificial flavor may cause allergic reactions in some sensitive individuals. Also contains sodium bisulfite, which can cause severe allergic reactions, especially in individuals with asthma. May also contain BHA, whose long-term safety is currently being reexamined by FDA investigators.

MRS. SMITH'S PUMPKIN CUSTARD PIE
Kellogg Co.

Ingredients: pumpkin, milk, skim milk, sugar, wheat flour, eggs, water, lard, margarine (partially hydrogenated soybean oil and/or lard, soybean oil, water, salt, may contain nonfat dry milk, lecithin, mono- and diglycerides; [may contain sodium benzoate, BHA or citric acid], artificial color and flavor, vitamin A palmitate), cornstarch, salt, spice, dextrose, modified food starch, locust bean gum, calcium carrageenan, sodium propionate, baking soda, sodium carboxymethylcellulose.

Amount: ⅛ pie			% USRDA
Calories	310	Protein	9
Protein, gm	6	Vitamin A	31
Carbohydrates, gm	46	Vitamin C	*
Fat, gm	11	Thiamine	4
Sodium, mg	495	Riboflavin	15
Cholesterol, mg	30	Niacin	*
Fiber, gm	1e	Calcium	10
		Iron	4

THIS FOOD: Among the pies profiled, this product offers the best nutrition. The first three ingredients in Mrs. Smith's Pumpkin Custard Pie—pumpkin, milk, and skim milk—are all healthful foods. This pie is rich in vitamin A and is also a good source of calcium and riboflavin. Compared to other pies, it is relatively high in protein. A moderate 32 percent of calories come from fat. This product is very high in sodium.

ADDITIVES: Contains artificial color and flavor, which some studies suggest may adversely affect behavior and the ability to complete school tasks in some sensitive children; artificial colors are inadequately tested and artificial flavor may cause allergic reactions in sensitive individuals. Also contains BHA, whose long-term safety is currently being reexamined by FDA investigators.

PEPPERIDGE FARM FROZEN BLUEBERRY TURNOVERS
Pepperidge Farm, Inc.

Ingredients: unbleached wheat flour, water, partially hydrogenated vegetable shortening (soybean, cottonseed, and palm oils), blueberries, corn syrup, sugar, modified food starch, salt, apple powder, dextrin, and citric acid.

Amount: 1 turnover			% USRDA
Calories	320	Protein	4
Protein, gm	3	Vitamin A	*
Carbohydrates, gm	32	Vitamin C	10
Fat, gm	19	Thiamine	2
Sodium, mg	240	Riboflavin	2
Cholesterol, mg	<5e	Niacin	2
Fiber, gm	<1e	Calcium	*
		Iron	4

THIS FOOD: Pepperidge Farm Frozen Blueberry Turnovers are high in sugar, saturated fat, and overall fat. Altogether, fat contributes 53 percent of calories. One turnover supplies 10 percent of the USRDA for vitamin C but is not a significant source of other nutrients. This product contains a moderate amount of sodium.

ADDITIVES: No questionable additives.

PEPPERIDGE FARM FROZEN CHEESE DANISH
Pepperidge Farm, Inc.

Ingredients: sugar, unbleached enriched wheat flour (flour, niacin, reduced iron, thiamine mononitrate, riboflavin), dry curd cottage cheese, margarine (partially hydrogenated soybean and cottonseed oils, skim milk, cultured skim milk, salt, mono- and diglycerides, lecithin, colored with beta carotene, vitamin A), nonfat milk, whole eggs, egg whites, walnuts, butter, bleached wheat flour, water, corn syrup, inverted syrup, defatted soy flour, modified food starch, partially hydrogenated vegetable shortening (cottonseed, soybean, palm, corn), yeast, salt, lemon puree, leavening (baking powder containing sodium acid pyrophosphate, baking soda, cornstarch, monocalcium phosphate, calcium sulfate), vanilla extract, degermed yellow corn flour, mono- and diglycerides (from hydrogenated vegetable oil), natural flavors, agar, lecithin, potassium bromate.

Amount: 1 danish			% USRDA
Calories	280	Protein	8
Protein, gm	5	Vitamin A	*
Carbohydrates, gm	35	Vitamin C	2
Fat, gm	13	Thiamine	6
Sodium, mg	310	Riboflavin	8
Cholesterol, mg	<5e	Niacin	6
Fiber, gm	<1e	Calcium	2
		Iron	6

THIS FOOD: Is not a significant source of nutrients. It is high in sugar, sodium, saturated fat, and overall fat. Fat contributes 42 percent of calories.

ADDITIVES: No questionable additives.

PET RITZ PIE CRUST
IC Industries, Inc.

Ingredients: flour, animal fat and/or vegetable oil shortening (lard, hydrogenated palm oil, hydrogenated soybean oil, beef fat with BHA, BHT, propyl gallate, citric acid), water, corn syrup, salt, whey solids, baking soda, sodium bisulfite, artificial color, FD & C Yellow No. 5.

Amount: 1/8 crust			% USRDA
Calories	107	Protein	3
Protein, gm	2	Vitamin A	*
Carbohydrates, gm	9	Vitamin C	*
Fat, gm	7	Thiamine	*
Sodium, mg	130	Riboflavin	*
Cholesterol, mg	8	Niacin	*
Fiber, gm	<1	Calcium	*
		Iron	*

THIS FOOD: Pet Ritz Pie Crust is not a significant source of nutrients. It contains 57 percent fat calories and is high in saturated fat. Pie crust generally contributes one-half to one-third of the calories in dessert pies.

ADDITIVES: Contains sodium bisulfite, which can cause severe allergic reactions, especially in individuals with asthma; and artificial colors, which some studies suggest may adversely affect behavior and the ability to complete school tasks in some sensitive children. Also contains Yellow No. 5, which can cause allergic reactions, especially in aspirin-sensitive individuals, as well as BHA, whose long-term safety is currently being reexamined by FDA investigators.

OTHER BRANDS: Betty Crocker Piecrust Mix does not contain any questionable additives.

PILLSBURY'S BEST APPLE DANISH
The Pillsbury Co.

Ingredients: *Roll:* enriched bleached flour (bleached flour, niacin, iron, thiamine mononitrate, riboflavin), water, beef fat and/or hydrogenated vegetable oil (coconut, cottonseed, palm, soybean) with BHA and citric acid, sugar, dextrose, artificial flavor, mono- and diglycerides, cornstarch, baking powder (baking soda, sodium acid pyrophosphate, sodium aluminum phosphate), cinnamon, vital wheat gluten, salt, egg yolks, glucono delta-lactone, sodium stearoyl lactylate, polysorbate 60, xanthan gum, artificial color. *Icing:* sugar, water, corn syrup solids, propylene glycol alginate, potassium sorbate, calcium gluconate, sodium phosphate, natural and artificial flavor, citric acid.

Amount: 1 roll			% USRDA
Calories	240	Protein	4
Protein, gm	3	Vitamin A	*
Carbohydrates, gm	33	Vitamin C	*
Fat, gm	11	Thiamine	8
Sodium, mg	260	Riboflavin	6
Cholesterol, mg	10e	Niacin	6
Fiber, gm	<1e	Calcium	*
		Iron	6

THIS FOOD: Pillsbury's Best Apple Danish does not provide significant amounts of any nutrient. It is high in sugar, saturated fat, and overall fat, which contributes about 41 percent of calories. This product is moderate in sodium.

ADDITIVES: Contains artificial color and flavor, which some studies suggest may adversely affect behavior and the ability to complete school tasks in some sensitive children; artificial colors are inadequately tested and artificial flavor may cause allergic reactions in sensitive individuals. Also, contains BHA, whose long-term safety is currently being reexamined by FDA investigators.

THANK YOU APPLE PIE FILLING
Curtice-Burns, Inc.

Ingredients: apples, water, corn sweetener, modified food starch, spice flavoring and coloring, salt, calcium lactate, citric acid, erythorbic acid.

Amount: 3⅓ oz			% USRDA
Calories	100	Protein	*
Protein, gm	0	Vitamin A	*
Carbohydrates, gm	25	Vitamin C	*
Fat, gm	0	Thiamine	*
Sodium, mg	95	Riboflavin	*
Cholesterol, mg	0	Niacin	*
Fiber, gm	2e	Calcium	2
		Iron	*
Contains about 6 teaspoons sugar.			

THIS FOOD: About three quarters of the calories in this product derive from added sugar. Apart from providing some dietary fiber, Thank You Apple Pie Filling is not a significant source of nutrients.

ADDITIVES: No questionable additives.

THANK YOU CHERRY PIE FILLING
Curtice-Burns, Inc.

Ingredients: red tart cherries, water, corn sweetener, modified food starch, erythorbic acid.

Amount: 3⅓ oz			% USRDA
Calories	120	Protein	*
Protein, gm	0	Vitamin A	*
Carbohydrates, gm	30	Vitamin C	*
Fat, gm	0	Thiamine	*
Sodium, mg	20	Riboflavin	*
Cholesterol, mg	0	Niacin	*
Fiber, gm	<1e	Calcium	*
		Iron	2
Contains 7½ teaspoons sugar.			

THIS FOOD: Nearly all of the calories in this product derive from added sugar. Thank You Cherry Pie Filling is not a significant source of nutrients.

ADDITIVES: No questionable additives.

THANK YOU LITE APPLE PIE FILLING
Curtice-Burns, Inc.

Ingredients: apples, water, corn sweetener, modified food starch, spice flavoring and coloring, salt, calcium lactate, citric acid, erythorbic acid.

Amount: 3¼ oz			% USRDA
Calories	60	Protein	*
Protein, gm	0	Vitamin A	*
Carbohydrates, gm	15	Vitamin C	*
Fat, gm	0	Thiamine	*
Sodium, mg	100	Riboflavin	*
Cholesterol, mg	0	Niacin	*
Fiber, gm	2e	Calcium	*
		Iron	*
Contains nearly 4 teaspoons sugar.			

THIS FOOD: Nearly all of the calories in this product derive from sugar, about half of it naturally occurring. Other than some fiber, Thank You Lite Apple Pie Filling is not a significant source of nutrients.

ADDITIVES: No questionable additives.

BEST BETS: Thank You Lite Apple Pie Filling contains 2½ teaspoons less sugar per serving than the regular Apple flavor and nearly 4 teaspoons less sugar than Thank You Cherry Pie Filling.

PIZZA

This popular fast food is the snack of choice among consumers between the ages of twenty-one and forty-three. A nutritional disaster? Not at all. It is far superior to hot dogs, hamburgers, fried chicken, or other fast food choices. Pizza contains protein, carbohydrate, and fat in proportions very close to those recommended by the McGovern Committee nutritional guidelines. A typical pizza slice has 15 percent protein, 27 percent fat, and 58 percent carbohydrate. Does that mean it's all right if your teenaged son seems to eat pizza for breakfast, lunch, and dinner five days a week? Most certainly not. While pizza is a reasonably well-balanced food, it is low in Vitamin C and iron, and high in sodium. But eaten as an occasional snack or meal, both kids and adults could do much, much worse.

SODIUM GUIDELINES: In evaluating the sodium content of frozen pizzas, we used the following standards:

less than 500 mg	moderate in sodium
500 mg to 1,000 mg	high in sodium
more than 1,000 mg	very high in sodium

Remember, these guidelines are not for people following medically restricted low-sodium diets, but for healthy individuals who wish to monitor their sodium intake.

FAT WINNERS

Less than 30 percent of the calories in these frozen pizzas come from fat:

Celentano 9 Slice Pizza
Celentano Thick Crust Pizza
Tree Tavern Frozen Cheese Pizza

SODIUM LOSERS

These pizzas contain more than ½ teaspoon salt per serving:

Celeste Deluxe Pizza
Celeste Pepperoni Pizza
Elio's Pepperoni Pizza
Stouffer's French Bread Pepperoni Pizza

CELENTANO 9 SLICE PIZZA
Celentano Brothers
Ingredients: *Topping:* crushed tomatoes, mozzarella cheese, peanut oil, salt, oregano, onion, garlic, parsley, basil, pepper. *Crust:* unbleached enriched flour, water, vegetable shortening, yeast.

Amount: 2 slices/5⅓ oz			% USRDA
Calories	314	Protein	38
Protein, gm	18	Vitamin A	16
Carbohydrates, gm	40	Vitamin C	6
Fat, gm	10	Thiamine	18
Sodium, mg	332	Riboflavin	22
Cholesterol, mg	40e	Niacin	14
Fiber, gm	2e	Calcium	12
		Iron	8

THIS FOOD: Celentano 9 Slice Pizza offers a healthful balance of nutrients. To start off, it is relatively low in fat and contains a moderate amount of sodium. In addition to supplying complex carbohydrates and protein, it is a very good source of the B vitamins and a good source of hard-to-get calcium. Only 28 percent of the calories in this product come from fat.

ADDITIVES: No questionable additives.

CELENTANO THICK CRUST PIZZA
Celentano Brothers

Ingredients: *Topping:* crushed tomatoes, mozzarella cheese, peanut oil, salt, oregano, onion, garlic, parsley, basil, pepper. *Crust:* unbleached enriched flour, water, vegetable shortening, yeast.

Amount: ⅓ pie/approx. 4.3 oz			% USRDA
Calories	238	Protein	29
Protein, gm	13	Vitamin A	12
Carbohydrates, gm	31	Vitamin C	5
Fat, gm	7	Thiamine	14
Sodium, mg	252	Riboflavin	16
Cholesterol, mg	25e	Niacin	11
Fiber, gm	1.5e	Calcium	9
		Iron	7

THIS FOOD: Celentano Thick Crust Pizza offers a healthful balance of nutrients. To start off, it contains a moderate amount of sodium and fat. In addition to supplying complex carbohydrates and protein, it is a good source of the B vitamins. Only 26 percent of the calories in this product come from fat.

ADDITIVES: No questionable additives.

NOTE: The letter "e" indicates that the data has been estimated; < means "less than," and is used for small amounts of sodium or cholesterol; * means food contains less than 2% of USRDA; "na" means that the information was not available and appears only when data is insufficient.

CELESTE CHEESE PIZZA
Quaker Oats Co.

Ingredients: low-moisture mozzarella cheese, tomato puree, flour, water, soybean oil, salt, green peppers, yeast, sugar, modified food starch, Romano cheese (made from cow's milk), spices, leavening (sodium bicarbonate, sodium aluminum phosphate), corn oil, calcium propionate, xanthan gum, dough conditioner (sodium metabisulfite), garlic powder.

Amount: ¼ pizza/approx. 4½ oz			% USRDA
Calories	309	Protein	36
Protein, gm	16	Vitamin A	8
Carbohydrates, gm	32	Vitamin C	*
Fat, gm	13	Thiamine	7
Sodium, mg	803	Riboflavin	21
Cholesterol, mg	35e	Niacin	7
Fiber, gm	1.5e	Calcium	36
		Iron	8

THIS FOOD: Celeste Cheese Pizza supplies complex carbohydrates, protein, and riboflavin and is an excellent source of calcium. About 38 percent of the calories in this product come from fat. Like most pizzas, it is high in sodium.

ADDITIVES: Contains sodium metabisulfite, which can cause severe allergic reactions, especially in individuals with asthma.

ELIO'S PEPPERONI PIZZA
The Greyhound Corp.

Ingredients: enriched flour (bleached with malted barley flour, niacin, reduced iron, potassium bromate, thiamine mononitrate, riboflavin), water, Cheddar cheese, tomato paste, pepperoni (pork and beef, salt, dextrose, spices, oleoresin of paprika, garlic powder, sodium nitrite, BHA, BHT, citric acid), vegetable oil (soybean and olive oils), sugar, salt, yeast, modified food starch, hydrolyzed vegetable protein, leavening (sodium bicarbonate, monocalcium phosphate), dough conditioners (sodium metabisulfite, protease), spices, garlic powder.

Amount: 2 slices/approx. 6 oz			% USRDA
Calories	481	Protein	38
Protein, gm	20	Vitamin A	11
Carbohydrates, gm	49	Vitamin C	20
Fat, gm	22	Thiamine	16
Sodium, mg	1,019	Riboflavin	20
Cholesterol, mg	38e	Niacin	30
Fiber, gm	3.5e	Calcium	30
		Iron	8

Contains nearly 5 teaspoons fat and ½ teaspoon salt.

THIS FOOD: An excellent source of protein, complex carbohydrates, hard-to-get calcium, and a very good source of vitamin C and the B vitamins. It contains 40 percent fat calories. Like most pizzas, it is high in sodium.

ADDITIVES: Contains sodium nitrite, which can be converted into cancer-causing substances called nitrosamines, and sodium metabisulfite, which can cause severe allergic reactions in sensitive individuals, especially those with asthma.

ELIO'S ROUND FAMILY STYLE CHEESE PIZZA
The Greyhound Corp.

Ingredients: enriched flour (bleached, malted barley flour, niacin, reduced iron, potassium bromate, thiamine mononitrate, riboflavin), water, Cheddar cheese, tomato paste, vegetable oil (soybean and olive oils), sugar, salt, yeast, modified food starch, hydrolyzed vegetable protein, leavening (sodium bicarbonate, monocalcium phosphate), dough conditioners (sodium metabisulfite, protease), spices, garlic powder.

Amount: 2 slices/approx. 4 oz			% USRDA
Calories	240	Protein	24
Protein, gm	12	Vitamin A	8
Carbohydrates, gm	32	Vitamin C	8
Fat, gm	12	Thiamine	4
Sodium, mg	540	Riboflavin	12
Cholesterol, mg	24e	Niacin	12
Fiber, gm	1.5e	Calcium	20
		Iron	8

THIS FOOD: Supplies protein, complex carbohydrates, calcium, riboflavin, niacin, and iron. With 45 percent fat calories, it contains a higher proportion of fat than other pizzas. It is high in sodium.

ADDITIVES: Contains sodium metabisulfite, which can cause severe allergic reactions in sensitive individuals, especially those with asthma.

STOUFFER'S FRENCH BREAD CHEESE PIZZA
Nestlé,S.A.

Ingredients: French bread: (bleached enriched flour [wheat flour, niacin, iron, thiamine mononitrate, riboflavin], water, corn syrup, salt, yeast, vegetable shortening [partially hydrogenated soybean, cottonseed and/or palm oil], corn sugar, dough conditioners [vegetable mono- and diglycerides, vegetable calcium stearoyl-2-lactylate, monocalcium phosphate, calcium sulfate, ammonium sulfate, potassium bromate], calcium propionate, cornstarch, soy flour, acetic acid, lactic acid) tomatoes, low-moisture part-skim mozzarella cheese, tomato puree, brick cheese, margarine (partially hydrogenated soybean oil, skim milk, salt, vegetable lecithin, vegetable mono- and diglycerides, sodium benzoate and citric acid, artificial flavor, beta carotene, vitamin A palmitate), tomato paste, Parmesan cheese, corn oil, sugar, modified cornstarch, Romano cheese (made from cow's milk), salt, dehydrated onions, spices, beef, erythorbic acid, dehydrated garlic, natural flavors, monosodium glutamate, caramel coloring, dried beef stock.

Amount: 1 slice/approx. 5¼ oz			% USRDA
Calories	330	Protein	15
Protein, gm	10	Vitamin A	10
Carbohydrates, gm	43	Vitamin C	*
Fat, gm	13	Thiamine	25
Sodium, mg	850	Riboflavin	10
Cholesterol, mg	30e	Niacin	15
Fiber, gm	2e	Calcium	25
		Iron	15

THIS FOOD: A very good source of protein, complex carbohydrates, hard-to-get calcium, vitamin A, the B vitamins, and iron. It contains a moderate 35 percent fat calories, and is high in sodium.

ADDITIVES: Contains monosodium glutamate (MSG), which many authorities believe should be avoided by infants and very young children; causes adverse reactions in sensitive individuals. Also contains artificial flavor, which may cause allergic reactions in sensitive individuals, and which some studies suggest may adversely affect behavior and the ability to complete school tasks in some sensitive children.

STOUFFER'S FRENCH BREAD PEPPERONI PIZZA
Nestlé, S.A.

Ingredients: French bread, tomatoes, pepperoni (pork and beef, salt, water, dextrose, natural spices, lactic acid starter culture, oleoresin of paprika, dehydrated garlic, sodium nitrite, BHA, BHT, citric acid), low-moisture part skim mozzarella cheese, tomato puree, margarine, brick cheese, tomato paste, corn oil, sugar, modified cornstarch, Romano cheese (made from cow's milk), salt, dehydrated onions, spices, beef, erythorbic acid, dehydrated garlic, natural flavors, monosodium glutamate, caramel coloring, dried beef stock.

Amount: 1 slice/approx. 5½ oz			% USRDA
Calories	410	Protein	15
Protein, gm	12	Vitamin A	15
Carbohydrates, gm	44	Vitamin C	*
Fat, gm	20	Thiamine	25
Sodium, mg	1,190	Riboflavin	20
Cholesterol, mg	35e	Niacin	15
Fiber, gm	2e	Calcium	20
		Iron	15

Contains more than 4 teaspoons fat and ½ teaspoon salt.

THIS FOOD: Supplies protein, complex carbohydrates, hard-to-get calcium, vitamin A, the B vitamins, and iron. It is high in calories, 44 percent of which derive from fat, and is especially high in sodium.

ADDITIVES: Contains monosodium glutamate (MSG), which many authorities believe should be avoided by infants and very young children; causes adverse reactions in some sensitive individuals; sodium nitrite, which can be converted into cancer-causing nitrosamines. Also contains BHA and BHT, whose long-term safety is currently being reexamined by FDA investigators.

TOTINO'S MY CLASSIC DELUXE CHEESE PIZZA
The Pillsbury Co.

Ingredients: *Crust:* enriched flour (flour, niacin, iron, thiamine mononitrate, riboflavin), water, hydrogenated soybean oil, yeast, salt, dough conditioner (sodium stearoyl lactylate, calcium sulfate, sodium sulfite). *Sauce:* water, tomato paste, hydrogenated vegetable oil (soybean, cottonseed), sugar, salt, dried onion, modified cornstarch, spice, natural flavor, Romano cheese (made from cow's milk), xanthan gum, hydrolyzed plant protein, artificial color, topping: Cheddar cheese, low-moisture part skim mozzarella cheese, dried parsley.

Amount: ⅓ pizza/7 oz			% USRDA
Calories	350	Protein	26e
Protein, gm	16	Vitamin A	11
Carbohydrates, gm	36	Vitamin C	6
Fat, gm	16	Thiamine	14
Sodium, mg	686	Riboflavin	18
Cholesterol, mg	30e	Niacin	11
Fiber, gm	2.5e	Calcium	32
		Iron	7

THIS FOOD: In addition to supplying protein and complex carbohydrates, Totino's My Classic Deluxe Cheese Pizza is especially rich in hard-to-get calcium and also provides B vitamins. About 41 percent of the calories in this product come from fat. Like most frozen pizzas, it is high in sodium.

ADDITIVES: Contains sodium sulfite, which can cause severe allergic reactions, especially in individuals with asthma.

TOTINO'S PARTY CHEESE PIZZA
The Pillsbury Co.

Ingredients: *Crust:* enriched flour (flour, sugar, niacin, reduced iron, thiamine mononitrate, riboflavin), water, hydrogenated soybean oil, yeast, salt, dough conditioner (sodium stearoyl lactylate, calcium sulfate, sodium sulfite). *Sauce:* tomato concentrate, water, sugar, soybean oil, modified cornstarch, salt, spice, coloring, Romano cheese (made from cow's milk), natural flavor, beet powder, xanthan gum. *Topping:* low-moisture part-skim mozzarella cheese, provolone cheese, dried parsley.

Amount: ½ pizza/approx. 5½ oz			% USRDA
Calories	350	Protein	25
Protein, gm	15	Vitamin A	8
Carbohydrates, gm	41	Vitamin C	4
Fat, gm	16	Thiamine	15
Sodium, mg	635	Riboflavin	20
Cholesterol, mg	35e	Niacin	10
Fiber, gm	2.5e	Calcium	25
		Iron	8

THIS FOOD: In addition to supplying protein, complex carbohydrates, and hard-to-get calcium, Totino's Party Cheese Pizza is a very good source of the B vitamins. About 41 percent of the calories in this product come from fat. Like most frozen pizzas, it is high in sodium.

ADDITIVES: Contains sodium metabisulfite, which can cause severe allergic reactions, especially in individuals with asthma.

TREE TAVERN FROZEN CHEESE PIZZA
Tree Tavern Products, Inc.

Ingredients: enriched flour, tomatoes, whole milk, mozzarella cheese, water, salt, blend of peanut and olive oil, yeast, salt, Romano cheese, spices, garlic powder.

Amount: 1 slice/4 oz			% USRDA
Calories	240	Protein	15
Protein, gm	11	Vitamin A	6
Carbohydrates, gm	32	Vitamin C	2
Fat, gm	8	Thiamine	25
Sodium, mg	546	Riboflavin	10
Cholesterol, mg	25e	Niacin	10
Fiber, gm	1.5e	Calcium	10
		Iron	15

THIS FOOD: Tree Tavern Frozen Cheese Pizza is relatively low in fat and moderately high in sodium. In addition to supplying complex carbohydrates and protein, it is a good source of calcium, the B vitamins, and iron. Only 30 percent of calories come from fat.

ADDITIVES: No questionable additives.

WEIGHT WATCHERS CHEESE PIZZA
H. J. Heinz, Inc.

Ingredients: low-moisture part-skim mozzarella cheese, enriched crust (enriched wheat flour [wheat flour, malted barley flour, niacin, iron, thiamine mononitrate, riboflavin], water, yeast, salt, sugar, soybean oil, L-cysteine), water, tomato paste, sugar, green peppers, salt, corn oil, modified food starch, dextrose, Romano cheese (made from cow's milk), flavorings, paprika, citric acid, beet powder, garlic powder.

Amount: One 6-oz package			% USRDA
Calories	350	Protein	40
Protein, gm	20	Vitamin A	15
Carbohydrates, gm	37	Vitamin C	6
Fat, gm	14	Thiamine	10
Sodium, mg	740	Riboflavin	15
Cholesterol, mg	45e	Niacin	10
Fiber, gm	3e	Calcium	35
		Iron	10

THIS FOOD: In addition to being an excellent source of protein, complex carbohydrates, and calcium, Weight Watchers Cheese Pizza is a good source of vitamin A, the B vitamins, and iron. It contains a moderate 36 percent fat calories and, like most frozen pizzas, is high in sodium.

ADDITIVES: No questionable additives.

POTATOES

Today potatoes are a staple food and eaten in many guises—puffed, scalloped, mashed, hashed-brown, and fried—but it wasn't always this way. They were spurned as possibly poisonous and fit only for the poor until well into the nineteenth century; but Americans soon changed their minds. By the turn of the century, they were eating 200 pounds of the humble tuber each year, and today consumption stands at about 125 pounds—more than half of them processed. A plain potato is a nutritionist's delight. A five-ounce, 100 calorie potato is a low-fat, low-sodium source of complex carbohydrates and dietary fiber, an excellent source of vitamin C, and a good source of niacin, vitamin B_6, potassium, iron, and various trace minerals. In contrast, most brand name products are high in sodium and fat. Of the popular foods profiled, only Ore-Ida Golden Crinkles (frozen french fries) do not contain added sodium. About 38 percent of the calories in this product come from fat, which is below average for this category of prepared foods. A plain 100-calorie baked potato, topped with 1 teaspoon of butter, contains only 33 percent fat calories.

BETTY CROCKER AU GRATIN POTATOES
General Mills, Inc.

Ingredients: dried potatoes (with sodium bisulfite), cornstarch, whey, salt, dried Cheddar cheese, partially hydrogenated soybean oil, maltodextrin, buttermilk, enriched flour (wheat flour, niacin, iron, thiamine mononitrate, and riboflavin), dried onion, monosodium glutamate, monocalcium phosphate, natural flavor, baking soda, wheat starch, dried garlic, dried blue cheese, disodium phosphate, FD & C Yellow No. 5 and other artificial colors, disodium inosinate, disodium guanylate.

Amount: ½ cup (+ 2 tbsp butter and ⅔ cup milk)			% USRDA
Calories	150	Protein	4
Protein, gm	3	Vitamin A	4
Carbohydrates, gm	21	Vitamin C	2
Fat, gm	6	Thiamine	*
Sodium, mg	605	Riboflavin	6
Cholesterol, mg	<5e	Niacin	4
Fiber, gm	1e	Calcium	8
		Iron	2

Contains nearly ⅓ teaspoon salt.

THIS FOOD: Potatoes in this form are a good source of complex carbohydrates, but have lost most of the vitamin C and B vitamins that are present in the unprocessed vegetable. Prepared according to package instructions, 36 percent of the calories in this product derive from fat. Betty Crocker Au Gratin Potatoes are very high in sodium.

ADDITIVES: Contains sodium bisulfite, which can cause allergic reactions, especially in individuals with asthma; also contains artificial colors, which are inadequately tested and which some studies suggest may adversely affect behavior and the ability to complete school tasks in some sensitive children, and Yellow No. 5, which can cause allergic reactions, especially in aspirin-sensitive individuals.

BETTY CROCKER POTATO BUDS
General Mills, Inc.

Ingredients: dried potato (with sodium bisulfite and BHT), mono- and di-glycerides.

Amount: ½ cup (+½ tsp butter, 4 tsp milk, and ⅛ tsp salt)			% USRDA
Calories	130	Protein	4
Protein, gm	3	Vitamin A	4
Carbohydrates, gm	15	Vitamin C	2
Fat, gm	6	Thiamine	*
Sodium, mg	355	Riboflavin	2
Cholesterol, mg	0e	Niacin	6
Fiber, gm	1e	Calcium	2
		Iron	*

THIS FOOD: Potatoes in this form are a good source of complex carbohydrates, but have lost most of the vitamin C and B vitamins that are present in unprocessed potatoes. If the product is prepared according to package instructions, 42 percent of the calories in it derive from fat. Betty Crocker Potato Buds are high in sodium.

ADDITIVES: Contains sodium bisulfite, which can cause allergic reactions, especially in individuals with asthma; and BHT, whose long-term safety is currently being reexamined by FDA investigators.

HUNGRY JACK INSTANT MASHED POTATOES
The Pillsbury Co.

Ingredients: potato flakes, monoglycerides, natural and artificial flavor, sodium bisulfite, calcium stearoyl lactylate, BHA and BHT, sodium acid pyrophosphate, citric acid.

Amount: ½ cup (+1½ tsp butter, 2 tbsp milk, and ⅛ tsp salt)			% USRDA
Calories	140	Protein	4
Protein, gm	3	Vitamin A	6
Carbohydrates, gm	17	Vitamin C	8
Fat, gm	7	Thiamine	2
Sodium, mg	380	Riboflavin	6
Cholesterol, mg	10e	Niacin	2
Fiber, gm	2e	Calcium	4
		Iron	*

NOTE: The letter "e" indicates that the data has been estimated; < means "less than," and is used for small amounts of sodium or cholesterol; * means food contains less than 2% of USRDA; "na" means that the information was not available and appears only when data is insufficient.

THIS FOOD: Potatoes in this form are a good source of complex carbohydrates and provide some dietary fiber. If the product is prepared according to package instructions, 45 percent of the calories in it derive from fat. Hungry Jack Instant Mashed Potatoes are high in sodium.

ADDITIVES: Contains sodium bisulfite, which can cause severe allergic reactions, especially in individuals with asthma. Also contains BHA and BHT, whose long-term safety is currently being reexamined by FDA investigators, as well as artificial flavors, which may cause allergic reaction in sensitive individuals; and which some studies suggest may adversely affect behavior and the ability to complete school tasks in some sensitive children.

ORE-IDA GOLDEN CRINKLES

H. J. Heinz, Inc.

Ingredients: potatoes, vegetable oil, shortening (palm oil, partially hydrogenated soybean), dextrose, disodium dihydrogen pyrophosphate.

Amount: ⅔ cup			% USRDA
Calories	120	Protein	4
Protein, gm	2	Vitamin A	*
Carbohydrates, gm	20	Vitamin C	6
Fat, gm	5	Thiamine	2
Sodium, mg	40	Riboflavin	*
Cholesterol, mg	0	Niacin	4
Fiber, gm	2	Calcium	*
		Iron	2

THIS FOOD: Ore-Ida Golden Crinkles are a good source of complex carbohydrates and provide some dietary fiber, but they have lost most of the vitamin C and B vitamins that are present in the unprocessed vegetable. About 38 percent of the calories in this product derive from fat, most of it saturated. These french fries are low in sodium.

ADDITIVES: No questionable additives.

ORE-IDA TATER TOTS

H. J. Heinz, Inc.

Ingredients: potatoes vegetable oil, shortening (palm, partially hydrogenated soybean), salt, enriched wheat flour (niacin, iron thiamine mononitrate, riboflavin), rice flour, monosodium glutamate, hydrolyzed vegetable protein, dehydrated onions, natural flavor, dextrose, disodium dihydrogen pyrophosphate.

Amount: ½ cup			% USRDA
Calories	160	Protein	2
Protein, gm	2	Vitamin A	*
Carbohydrates, gm	21	Vitamin C	4
Fat, gm	8	Thiamine	2
Sodium, mg	550	Riboflavin	*
Cholesterol, mg	0	Niacin	4
Fiber, gm	2e	Calcium	*
		Iron	2

Contains ½ teaspoon salt.

THIS FOOD: Ore-Ida Tater Tots are a good source of complex carbohydrates and provide some dietary fiber, but they have lost most of the vitamin C and B vitamins that are present in the unprocessed vegetable. About 45 percent of the calories in this product derive from fat. These potato puffs are high in sodium.

ADDITIVES: Contains monosodium glutamate (MSG), which many authorities believe should be avoided by infants and very young children; causes adverse reactions in sensitive individuals.

See "Basic Foods" on page 564 for fresh potato listing.

POTATO CHIPS, POPCORN, AND SNACKS

It really is hard to eat just one. Many of us, when faced with a bag of potato chips, corn chips, or pretzels, turn into instant addicts. Unfortunately, it's not a good idea to munch at will—even if you're not concerned about extra calories, since all of these snacks are very high in sodium and most are also high in saturated fat. Popcorn, on the other hand, has all the virtues of plain corn. It is low in calories, fat, sodium, high in fiber, and complex carbohydrates—as long as you refrain from adding butter and salt.

SODIUM GUIDELINES: Here are the standards we applied in evaluating the sodium content of potato chips and snacks:

less than 200 mg	moderate in sodium
200 mg to 450 mg	high in sodium
more than 450 mg	very high in sodium

All of the products profiled, with the exception of plain popcorn, are high or very high in sodium. These guidelines are not for people following medically restricted low-sodium diets, but for healthy individuals who wish to monitor their sodium intake.

FRITOS CORN CHIPS
PepsiCo, Inc.

Ingredients: corn, vegetable oil (corn, peanut, soybean, sunflower, partially hydrogenated sunflower), salt.

Amount: 15 chips/1 oz			% USRDA
Calories	150	Protein	2
Protein, gm	2	Vitamin A	*
Carbohydrates, gm	16	Vitamin C	*
Fat, gm	10	Thiamine	*
Sodium, mg	220	Riboflavin	*
Cholesterol, mg	0	Niacin	*
Fiber, gm	1e	Calcium	2
		Iron	2

THIS FOOD: Like most chips, this product is high in saturated fat and sodium. It provides complex carbohydrates and 60 percent fat calories. Although the basic ingredient—corn—is a nutritious grain, during deep frying most of the water is replaced with fat.

ADDITIVES: No questionable additives.

ORVILLE REDENBACHER GOURMET MICROWAVE POPCORN
Hunt-Wesson Foods, Inc.

Ingredients: gourmet yellow popping corn, partially hydrogenated vegetable oils (soybean, cottonseed, palm), salt, natural flavors.

Amount: 4 cups popped			% USRDA
Calories	140	Protein	4
Protein, gm	2	Vitamin A	*
Carbohydrates, gm	17	Vitamin C	*
Fat, gm	7	Thiamine	*
Sodium, mg	210	Riboflavin	2
Cholesterol, mg	0	Niacin	2
Fiber, gm	4	Calcium	*
		Iron	4

THIS FOOD: Popcorn is a good snack food, low in sodium and calories, and a good source of complex carbohydrates and fiber. About 45 percent of the calories in this product derive from fat, most of it saturated.

ADDITIVES: No questionable additives.

ORVILLE REDENBACHER GOURMET POPCORN
Hunt-Wesson Foods, Inc.

Ingredients: yellow popping corn.

Amount: 4 cups popped, plain			% USRDA
Calories	90	Protein	4
Protein, gm	3	Vitamin A	*
Carbohydrates, gm	18	Vitamin C	*
Fat, gm	1	Thiamine	*
Sodium, mg	<1	Riboflavin	2
Cholesterol, mg	0	Niacin	2
Fiber, gm	4	Calcium	*
		Iron	4

THIS FOOD: Plain popcorn is a good snack food, low in calories, fat, and sodium and a good supplier of complex carbohydrates and fiber.

ADDITIVES: None.

PIZZA FLAVOR COMBOS
Mars, Inc.

Ingredients: enriched flour (with niacin, reduced iron, thiamine mononitrate, and riboflavin), starch, partially hydrogenated soybean oil, salt, dextrose, baking soda, sodium stearoyl lactylate, sodium acid pyrophosphate, monocalcium phosphate. *Filling:* whey, partially hydrogenated soybean oil, cheese (Cheddar, Parmesan, and blue), tomato, salt, onion and garlic powder, spices, lecithin, natural cheese flavor, monosodium glutamate, yeast, nonfat milk, citric acid, buttermilk, lactic acid, coloring.

Amount: 1 oz			% USRDA
Calories	130	Protein	4
Protein, gm	3	Vitamin A	*
Carbohydrates, gm	19	Vitamin C	*
Fat, gm	5	Thiamine	6
Sodium, mg	330	Riboflavin	8
Cholesterol, mg	<5e	Niacin	4
Fiber, gm	<1	Calcium	4
		Iron	4

THIS FOOD: Basically pretzel nuggets stuffed with processed cheese, Pizza Flavor Combos are high in saturated fat and sodium. They provide complex carbohydrates and 65 percent fat calories.

ADDITIVES: Contains monosodium glutamate (MSG), which many experts believe should be avoided by infants and very young children; causes adverse reactions in some sensitive individuals.

ROLD GOLD PRETZEL TWISTS
PepsiCo, Inc.

Ingredients: enriched flour (wheat flour, niacin, reduced iron, thiamine mononitrate, riboflavin), corn syrup, salt, vegetable oil (partially hydrogenated cottonseed, partially hydrogenated soybean), baking soda, malt extract, yeast, artificial flavor.

Amount: 1 oz			% USRDA
Calories	110	Protein	4
Protein, gm	2	Vitamin A	*
Carbohydrates, gm	23	Vitamin C	*
Fat, gm	1	Thiamine	6
Sodium, mg	500	Riboflavin	6
Cholesterol, mg	0	Niacin	6
Fiber, gm	<1	Calcium	*
		Iron	4

THIS FOOD: Like most pretzels, Rold Gold Pretzel Twists are low in fat and very high in sodium. They provide complex carbohydrates and only 8 percent fat calories.

ADDITIVES: Contains artificial flavor, which may cause allergic reactions in sensitive individuals and which some studies suggest may adversely affect behavior and the ability to complete school tasks in some sensitive children.

HELPFUL HINT: Try sprinkling your popcorn with a tablespoon of grated low-fat Parmesan and herbs.

WISE REGULAR POTATO CHIPS
Borden, Inc.

Ingredients: potatoes, vegetable oil (cottonseed, palm, corn, partially hydrogenated soymeal, partially hydrogenated cottonseed), salt.

Amount: 15 chips/1 oz			% USRDA
Calories	160	Protein	2
Protein	2	Vitamin A	*
Carbohydrates, gm	14	Vitamin C	10
Fat, gm	11	Thiamine	2
Sodium, mg	190	Riboflavin	*
Cholesterol, mg	0	Niacin	6
Fiber, gm	<1e	Calcium	*
		Iron	2

THIS FOOD: Like most chips, Wise Regular Potato Chips are high in saturated fat and sodium. They provide complex carbohydrates and some vitamin C—along with 62 percent fat calories. Although the basic ingredient—potatoes—is certainly nutritious, during deep frying, nearly all of the water in the potato is replaced with fat.

ADDITIVES: No questionable additives.

PUDDING

All packaged puddings and pudding mixes are high in sugar. But if you prepare a mix with milk, the resulting dessert will be a good source of calcium and riboflavin. Obviously, using low-fat milk will also reduce fat calories. In general, pudding mixes will yield more nutritious results than ready-to-eat puddings. For example, Hunt's ready-to-eat Snack Pack puddings contain about 40 percent fat calories and are high in saturated fat. Jell-O pudding mixes, prepared with whole milk, contain three times as much calcium and only half the fat calories. Both types of pudding contain controversial additives.

HUNT'S CHOCOLATE FLAVOR SNACK PACK
Hunt-Wesson Foods, Inc.

Ingredients: water, skim milk, sugar, partially hydrogenated soybean oil, modified food starch, cocoa processed with alkali, salt, sodium stearoyl lactylate, artificial flavors.

Amount: 5 oz			% USRDA
Calories	210	Protein	4
Protein, gm	2	Vitamin A	*
Carbohydrates, gm	30	Vitamin C	*
Fat, gm	9	Thiamine	*
Sodium, mg	160	Riboflavin	4
Cholesterol, mg	10e	Niacin	*
Fiber, gm	<1e	Calcium	4
		Iron	2

THIS FOOD: Hunt's Chocolate Flavor Snack Pack pudding is high in sugar and saturated fat. It does not contribute significant amounts of any nutrient.

ADDITIVES: Contains artificial flavor, which may cause allergic reactions in sensitive individuals, and which some studies suggest may adversely affect behavior and the ability to complete school tasks in some sensitive children.

HUNT'S VANILLA FLAVOR SNACK PACK
Hunt-Wesson Foods, Inc.

Ingredients: skim milk, water, sugar, partially hydrogenated soybean oil, modified food starch, salt, sodium, stearoyl lactylate, disodium phosphate, artificial flavor, FD & C Yellow No. 5, color added.

Amount: 5 oz			% USRDA
Calories	210	Protein	4
Protein, gm	2	Vitamin A	*
Carbohydrates, gm	31	Vitamin C	*
Fat, gm	9	Thiamine	*
Sodium, mg	195	Riboflavin	6
Cholesterol, mg	10e	Niacin	*
Fiber, gm	<1e	Calcium	4
		Iron	*

THIS FOOD: Hunt's Vanilla Flavor Snack Pack pudding is high in sugar and saturated fat. It does not contribute significant amounts of any nutrient.

ADDITIVES: Contains Yellow No. 5, which may cause allergic reactions, especially in aspirin-sensitive individuals, also contains artificial flavor, which may cause allergic reactions in sensitive individuals, and which some studies suggest may adversely affect behavior and the ability to complete school tasks in some sensitive children.

JELL-O AMERICANA TAPIOCA PUDDING MIX
General Foods Corp.

Ingredients: sugar, tapioca, cornstarch, dextrose, salt, coconut oil with BHA, artificial flavor, artificial color (including FD & C Yellow No. 5), natural flavor.

Amount: ½ cup (includes ½ cup milk)			% USRDA
Calories	160	Protein	8
Protein, gm	4	Vitamin A	2
Carbohydrates, gm	27	Vitamin C	*
Fat, gm	4	Thiamine	2
Sodium, mg	170	Riboflavin	10
Cholesterol, mg	75e	Niacin	*
Fiber, gm	e	Calcium	15
		Iron	*

THIS FOOD: Compared to other pudding mixes, Jell-O Americana Tapioca Pudding Mix is high in calories. Because it is prepared with milk, this dessert is a good source of riboflavin and calcium.

ADDITIVES: Contains artificial color and flavor, which some studies suggest may adversely affect behavior and the ability to complete school tasks in some sensitive children; artificial colors are inadequately tested, and artificial flavor may cause allergic reactions in sensitive individuals; colored with FD & C Yellow No. 5, which can cause allergic reactions, especially in aspirin-sensitive individuals. Also contains BHA, whose long-term safety is currently being reexamined by FDA investigators.

JELL-O VANILLA PUDDING MIX
General Foods Corp.

Ingredients: sugar, dextrose, cornstarch, modified cornstarch, salt, polysorbate 60, calcium carrageenan, artificial flavor, artificial color (including FD & C Yellow No. 5), natural flavor.

Amount: ½ cup (includes ½ cup milk)			% USRDA
Calories	110	Protein	8
Protein, gm	4	Vitamin A	2
Carbohydrates, gm	27	Vitamin C	*
Fat, gm	4	Thiamine	2
Sodium, mg	200	Riboflavin	10
Cholesterol, mg	15e	Niacin	*
Fiber, gm	e	Calcium	15
		Iron	*

THIS FOOD: Because milk is added to Jell-O Vanilla Pudding Mix, this dessert is a good source of calcium and riboflavin.

ADDITIVES: Contains artificial color and flavor, which some studies suggest may adversely affect behavior and the ability to complete school tasks in some sensitive children; artificial colors are inadequately tested, and artificial flavor may cause allergic reactions in sensitive individuals; also contains Yellow No. 5, which can cause allergic reactions, especially in aspirin-sensitive individuals.

NOTE: The letter "e" indicates that the data has been estimated; < means "less than," and is used for small amounts of sodium or cholesterol; * means food contains less than 2% of USRDA; "na" means that the information was not available and appears only when data is insufficient.

JELL-O VANILLA SUGAR-FREE INSTANT PUDDING MIX
General Foods Corp.

Ingredients: modified tapioca starch, tapiocal dextrin, sodium phosphates, aspartame, salt, microcrystalline cellulose, artificial flavor, artificial color (including FD & C Yellow No. 5), mono- and diglycerides, nonfat milk, natural flavor.

Amount: ½ cup (includes ½ cup milk)			% USRDA
Calories	105	Protein	8
Protein, gm	4	Vitamin A	2
Carbohydrates, gm	12	Vitamin C	*
Fat, gm	4	Thiamine	2
Sodium, mg	420	Riboflavin	10
Cholesterol, mg	16e	Niacin	*
Fiber, gm	e	Calcium	15
		Iron	*

THIS FOOD: Because milk is added to Jell-O Vanilla Sugar-Free Instant Pudding Mix, this dessert is a good source of calcium and riboflavin. Compared to other pudding mixes, it is high in sodium.

ADDITIVES: Contains aspartame (with phenylalanine), which should be avoided by people with PKU, a rare genetic disease and which many experts believe has been inadequately tested for long-term safety. Contains artificial color and flavor, which some studies suggest may adversely affect behavior and the ability to complete school tasks in some sensitive children; artificial colors are inadequately tested, and artificial flavor may cause allergic reactions in sensitive individuals; also contains Yellow No. 5, which can cause allergic reactions, especially in aspirin-sensitive individuals.

RICE

For more than a billion and a half people worldwide, rice makes up fully one half of the daily food. In America, rice is not especially popular—we eat only about 10 pounds per person each year, compared with 400 pounds per capita in Asia. What does rice have to recommend it—and should we be eating more? Rice is low in sodium, rich in complex carbohydrates, and very easy to digest. Brown rice, which retains most of the bran and all of the germ, is richer in B vitamins, protein, and fiber than refined white rice. If you prefer the taste of white rice, make sure the brand you choose is enriched (most popular brands are), and preferably "converted" as well. This means that the grains are subjected to high pressure steam that pushes some of the nutrients into the center of the grain before milling so that fewer vitamins and minerals will be lost. Most prepared rice mixes, such as Rice-A-Roni, are high in sodium.

CAROLINA EXTRA LONG GRAIN ENRICHED RICE
Riviana Foods, Inc.

Ingredients: long grain rice enriched with niacin, iron, thiamine.

Amount: 1 cup			% USRDA
Calories	200	Protein	4
Protein, gm	4	Vitamin A	*
Carbohydrates, gm	44	Vitamin C	*
Fat, gm	0	Thiamine	16
Sodium, mg	<10	Riboflavin	*
Cholesterol, mg	0	Niacin	12
Fiber, gm	1.5e	Calcium	*
		Iron	8

THIS FOOD: Carolina Extra Long Grain Enriched Rice is a good source of thiamine, niacin, and complex carbohydrates and also supplies small amounts of protein, fiber, and iron.

ADDITIVES: No questionable additives.

NOTE: The letter "e" indicates that the data has been estimated; < means "less than," and is used for small amounts of sodium or cholesterol; * means food contains less than 2% of USRDA; "na" means that the information was not available and appears only when data is insufficient.

CHICKEN RICE-A-RONI
Golden Grain Macaroni Co.

Ingredients: enriched rice, enriched vermicelli, salt, dried corn syrup, chicken fat, monosodium glutamate, dextrose, potato starch, dried onion, dried chicken meat, partially hydrogenated vegetable oil (cottonseed oil, palm oil, soybean oil), enriched flour (with niacin, iron, thiamine mononitrate, and riboflavin), turmeric, dried parsley, dried garlic, natural flavors, BHA, propyl gallate, citric acid.

Amount: ¾ cup cooked (1 tsp butter added per serving)			% USRDA
Calories	196	Protein	4
Protein, gm	3	Vitamin A	3
Carbohydrates, gm	33	Vitamin C	*
Fat, gm	5	Thiamine	20
Sodium, mg	na	Riboflavin	6
Cholesterol, mg	11	Niacin	6
Fiber, gm	1e	Calcium	*
		Iron	8

THIS FOOD: Chicken Rice-A-Roni is high in valuable complex carbohydrates and thiamine. About 23 percent of its calories derive from fat. Although data for sodium could not be obtained, salt is listed as the third largest ingredient so there is undoubtedly lots of it in this product.

ADDITIVES: Contains monosodium glutamate (MSG), which many authorities believe should be avoided by infants and very young children; causes adverse reactions in some sensitive individuals.

MAHATMA LONG GRAIN ENRICHED RICE
Riviana Foods, Inc.

Ingredients: long grain rice enriched with niacin, iron, thiamine.

Amount: 1 cup			% USRDA
Calories	200	Protein	4
Protein, gm	4	Vitamin A	*
Carbohydrates, gm	44	Vitamin C	*
Fat, gm	0	Thiamine	16
Sodium, mg	<10	Riboflavin	*
Cholesterol, mg	0	Niacin	12
Fiber, gm	1.5e	Calcium	*
		Iron	8

THIS FOOD: Mahatma Long Grain Enriched Rice is a good source of thiamine, niacin, and complex carbohydrates and also supplies small amounts of protein, fiber, and iron.

ADDITIVES: No questionable additives.

MAHATMA NATURAL LONG GRAIN BROWN RICE
Riviana Foods, Inc.

Ingredients: natural long grain brown rice.

Amount: 1 cup			% USRDA
Calories	220	Protein	8
Protein, gm	4	Vitamin A	*
Carbohydrates, gm	46	Vitamin C	*
Fat, gm	0	Thiamine	12
Sodium, mg	<10	Riboflavin	*
Cholesterol, mg	0	Niacin	16
Fiber, gm	5e	Calcium	*
		Iron	4

THIS FOOD: Mahatma Natural Long Grain Brown Rice is a good source of naturally occurring thiamine, niacin, complex carbohydrates, and fiber. It contains at least three times more dietary fiber than white rice and also provides small amounts of protein and iron.

ADDITIVES: None.

MINUTE RICE
General Foods Corp.

Ingredients: precooked, long grain rice, niacin, iron, thiamine.

Amount: 1 cup			% USRDA
Calories	180	Protein	6
Protein, gm	5	Vitamin A	*
Carbohydrates, gm	41	Vitamin C	*
Fat, gm	0	Thiamine	15
Sodium, mg	3	Riboflavin	*
Cholesterol, mg	0	Niacin	9
Fiber, gm	1e	Calcium	*
		Iron	9

THIS FOOD: Minute Rice is a good source of thiamine and complex carbohydrates and also supplies small amounts of protein, fiber, and iron.

ADDITIVES: No questionable additives.

HELPFUL HINT: For nutritious low-cost, low-fat meals, try combining leftover rice with bits of meat or poultry and vegetables. Brown rice will supply more fiber and naturally occurring vitamins than white rice.

SPANISH RICE-A-RONI
Golden Grain Macaroni Co.

Ingredients: enriched rice, enriched vermicelli, dried onion, salt, hydrolyzed vegetable protein, dried green bell pepper, monosodium glutamate, dextrose, paprika, partially hydrogenated vegetable oil (cottonseed oil, palm oil, soybean oil), spices, natural flavors, niacin, iron (ferrous sulfate, reduced iron, ferric orthophosphate), thiamine mononitrate, riboflavin.

Amount: ¾ cup cooked (1 tsp butter and ⅓ cup canned tomatoes added) % USRDA

Calories	172	Protein	5
Protein, gm	4	Vitamin A	13
Carbohydrates, gm	30	Vitamin C	21
Fat, gm	5	Thiamine	18
Sodium, mg	na	Riboflavin	7
Cholesterol, mg	11	Niacin	13
Fiber, gm	2e	Calcium	*
		Iron	8

THIS FOOD: Spanish Rice-A-Roni is high in complex carbohydrates and a good source of niacin and thiamine. About 26 percent of the calories in this product derive from fat. Although data on sodium could not be obtained, this product is undoubtedly high in salt.

ADDITIVES: Contains monosodium glutamate (MSG), which many authorities believe should be avoided by infants and very young children; causes adverse reactions in some sensitive individuals.

UNCLE BEN'S CONVERTED RICE
Mars, Inc.

Ingredients: long grain, parboiled rice, ferric orthophosphate, thiamine mononitrate.

Amount: 1 cup % USRDA

Calories	194	Protein	7
Protein, gm	5	Vitamin A	*
Carbohydrates, gm	43	Vitamin C	*
Fat, gm	<1	Thiamine	16
Sodium, mg	3	Riboflavin	*
Cholesterol, mg	0	Niacin	11
Fiber, gm	1e	Calcium	6
		Iron	9

THIS FOOD: Uncle Ben's Converted Rice is a good source of thiamine, niacin, and complex carbohydrates and also supplies small amounts of protein, fiber, and iron.

ADDITIVES: No questionable additives.

NUTRITION TIP: White rice contains substantially fewer B vitamins and much less fiber than brown rice because the bran and germ have been removed. In the United States, the vitamins and iron lost during processing are generally added back, but the dietary fiber is not replaced.

SALAD DRESSING

As everyone knows, salad dressings are mainly used to coat and season nutritious, low-calorie greens and vegetables. After the greens are tossed with most brand name dressings, the percentage of fat calories in the salad rises to more than half of total calories. Since the typical dressing is based on oil or mayonnaise, it's hard to keep fat calories low unless you use a diet dressing. Food manufacturers produce these in abundance, but they are often especially high in sodium. Of all the Kraft, Wish-Bone, Roka, and Marie's dressings profiled, only Wish-Bone Lite-Line French Style Salad Dressing is both low in fat calories and moderate in sodium.

SODIUM GUIDELINES: In evaluating the sodium content of salad dressings we used the following standards:

less than 100 mg	moderate in sodium
100 mg to 200 mg	high in sodium
more than 200 mg	very high in sodium

Remember, these guidelines are not for people following medically restricted low-sodium diets, but for healthy individuals who wish to monitor their sodium intake.

HIDDEN VALLEY RANCH GARDEN HERB SALAD DRESSING
The Clorox Co.

Ingredients: maltodextrin, salt, buttermilk solids, sugar, dehydrated onion, lactic acid, monosodium glutamate, modified cornstarch, natural and artificial flavors, whey solids, spices, citric acid, casein, hydroxypropyl methylcellulose, dehydrated garlic, calcium stearate, and soybean oil.

Amount: 1 tbsp			% USRDA
Calories	70	Protein	*
Protein, gm	<1	Vitamin A	*
Carbohydrates, gm	2	Vitamin C	*
Fat, gm	7	Thiamine	*
Sodium, mg	125	Riboflavin	*
Cholesterol, mg	<5e	Niacin	*
Fiber, gm	0	Calcium	*
		Iron	*

THIS FOOD: Hidden Valley Ranch Garden Herb Salad Dressing contains 90 percent fat calories and no vitamins or minerals. Compared to other items in this category, sodium content is high.

ADDITIVES: Contains monosodium glutamate (MSG), which many authorities believe should be avoided by infants and very young children; causes adverse reactions in some sensitive individuals. Also contains artificial flavor, which may cause allergic reactions in sensitive individuals, and which some studies suggest may adversely affect behavior and the ability to complete school tasks in some sensitive children.

HIDDEN VALLEY RANCH ORIGINAL RANCH SALAD DRESSING
The Clorox Co.

Ingredients: maltodextrin, salt, buttermilk solids, monosodium glutamate, whey solids, dehydrated garlic, dehydrated onion, lactic acid, modified food starch, citric acid, casein, calcium lactate, carbohydrate gum, spices, dehydrated parsley, artificial flavor, soybean oil, guar gum, calcium stearate.

Amount: 1 tbsp			% USRDA
Calories	70	Protein	*
Protein, gm	<1	Vitamin A	*
Carbohydrates, gm	2	Vitamin C	*
Fat, gm	7	Thiamine	*
Sodium, mg	125	Riboflavin	*
Cholesterol, mg	<5e	Niacin	*
Fiber, gm	0	Calcium	*
		Iron	*

THIS FOOD: Hidden Valley Ranch Original Ranch Salad Dressing contains 90 percent fat calories and no vitamins or minerals. Compared to other items in this category, sodium content is high.

ADDITIVES: Contains monosodium glutamate (MSG), which many authorities believe should be avoided by infants and very young children; causes adverse reactions in sensitive individuals. Also contains artificial flavor, which may cause allergic reactions in sensitive individuals, and which some studies suggest may adversely affect behavior and the ability to complete school tasks in some sensitive children.

KRAFT BACON AND TOMATO DRESSING
Kraft, Inc.

Ingredients: soybean oil, water, tomato, sugar, tomato juice, vinegar, dehydrated sour cream, tomato paste, salt, bacon bits with added hickory smoke flavor, dehydrated cultured skim milk, natural flavor, xanthan gum, phosphoric acid, polysorbate 60, propylene glycol alginate, with sodium benzoate and calcium disodium EDTA.

Amount: 1 tbsp			% USRDA
Calories	70	Protein	*
Protein, gm	0	Vitamin A	*
Carbohydrates, gm	1	Vitamin C	*
Fat, gm	7	Thiamine	*
Sodium, mg	130	Riboflavin	*
Cholesterol, mg	0	Niacin	*
Fiber, gm	0	Calcium	*
		Iron	*

THIS FOOD: Kraft Bacon and Tomato Dressing does not supply any vitamins and minerals and derives 90 percent of its calories from fat. Like most bottled dressings, this product is high in sodium.

ADDITIVES: No questionable additives.

KRAFT CREAMY CUCUMBER REDUCED CALORIE DRESSING
Kraft, Inc.

Ingredients: soybean oil, water, vinegar, cucumber juice, sugar, salt, dehydrated sour cream, dehydrated onion, dehydrated cultured skim milk, xanthan gum, natural flavor, polysorbate 60, propylene glycol alginate, spice, calcium disodium EDTA.

NOTE: The letter "e" indicates that the data has been estimated; < means "less than," and is used for small amounts of sodium or cholesterol; * means food contains less than 2% of USRDA; "na" means that the information was not available and appears only when data is insufficient.

Amount: 1 tbsp			% USRDA
Calories	30	Protein	*
Protein, gm	0	Vitamin A	*
Carbohydrates, gm	1	Vitamin C	*
Fat, gm	3	Thiamine	*
Sodium, mg	230	Riboflavin	*
Cholesterol, mg	0	Niacin	*
Fiber, gm	0	Calcium	*
		Iron	*

THIS FOOD: Kraft Creamy Cucumber Reduced Calorie Dressing is really a condiment rather than a food since it doesn't supply any vitamins and minerals. It contains about half the oil of most regular dressings, but 90 percent of its calories still derive from fat. This product is very high in sodium.

ADDITIVES: No questionable additives.

KRAFT FRENCH DRESSING
Kraft, Inc.

Ingredients: soybean oil, water, sugar, vinegar, salt, mustard flour, paprika, xanthan gum, propylene glycol alginate, natural flavor, calcium disodium EDTA, apocarotenal.

Amount: 1 tbsp			% USRDA
Calories	60	Protein	*
Protein, gm	0	Vitamin A	*
Carbohydrates, gm	2	Vitamin C	*
Fat, gm	6	Thiamine	*
Sodium, mg	125	Riboflavin	*
Cholesterol, mg	0	Niacin	*
Fiber, gm	0	Calcium	*
		Iron	*

THIS FOOD: Kraft French Dressing does not supply any vitamins or minerals and derives 90 percent of its calories from fat. Compared to most bottled dressings, this product is high in sodium.

ADDITIVES: No questionable additives.

HELPFUL HINT: Try thinning thick bottled dressings with vinegar or lemon juice. You'll save calories two ways, since you need less of a thinner dressing to coat salad leaves and vegetables, and the dressing itself will be less fattening.

KRAFT FRENCH REDUCED CALORIE DRESSING
Kraft, Inc.

Ingredients: water, vinegar, sugar, soybean oil, salt, paprika, mustard flour, propylene glycol alginate, xanthan gum, dehydrated garlic, natural flavor, calcium disodium EDTA, apocarotenal.

Amount: 1 tbsp			% USRDA
Calories	20	Protein	*
Protein, gm	0	Vitamin A	2
Carbohydrates, gm	2	Vitamin C	*
Fat, gm	2	Thiamine	*
Sodium, mg	145	Riboflavin	*
Cholesterol, mg	0	Niacin	*
Fiber, gm	0	Calcium	*
		Iron	*

THIS FOOD: Kraft French Reduced Calorie Dressing is really a condiment rather than a food since it doesn't supply any vitamins and minerals. It is low in calories, but 90 percent of them derive from fat. Like most dressings, it is high in sodium.

ADDITIVES: No questionable additives.

KRAFT ITALIAN REDUCED CALORIE DRESSING
Kraft, Inc.

Ingredients: water, vinegar, salt, sugar, soybean oil, dehydrated garlic, garlic, xanthan gum, spice, dehydrated onion, dehydrated red bell pepper, calcium disodium EDTA, natural flavor, artificial color, FD & C Yellow No. 5.

Amount: 1 tbsp			% USRDA
Calories	6	Protein	*
Protein, gm	0	Vitamin A	*
Carbohydrates, gm	1	Vitamin C	*
Fat, gm	0	Thiamine	*
Sodium, mg	210	Riboflavin	*
Cholesterol, mg	0	Niacin	*
Fiber, gm	0	Calcium	*
		Iron	*

THIS FOOD: Kraft Italian Reduced Calorie Dressing is really a condiment rather than a food since it doesn't supply any vitamins and minerals. It contains only a minuscule amount of oil, and most of its calories derive from sugar. This product is very high in sodium.

ADDITIVES: Contains artificial colors, which are inadequately tested and which some studies suggest may adversely affect behavior and the ability to complete school tasks in some sensitive children; and Yellow No. 5, which can cause allergic reactions, especially in aspirin-sensitive individuals.

KRAFT OIL-FREE ITALIAN DRESSING
Kraft, Inc.

Ingredients: water, vinegar, salt, sugar, dehydrated garlic, garlic, xanthan gum, propylene glycol, propylene glycol alginate, phosphoric acid, spice, dehydrated onion, dehydrated red bell peppers, natural flavor.

Amount: 1 tbsp			% USRDA
Calories	4	Protein	*
Protein, gm	0	Vitamin A	*
Carbohydrates, gm	1	Vitamin C	*
Fat, gm	0	Thiamine	*
Sodium, mg	215	Riboflavin	*
Cholesterol, mg	0	Niacin	*
Fiber, gm	0	Calcium	*
		Iron	*

THIS FOOD: True to its name, Kraft Oil-Free Italian Dressing contains no fat at all—the few calories supplied per serving all derive from sugar. Like most dressings, this product does not supply any vitamins or minerals. It is very high in sodium.

ADDITIVES: No questionable additives.

MARIE'S BLUE CHEESE REFRIGERATED DRESSING
United Biscuits Holdings, Ltd.

Ingredients: soybean oil, buttermilk, blue cheese, eggs, sour cream, vinegar distilled, salt, dehydrated spices, dehydrated garlic.

Amount: 1 tbsp			% USRDA
Calories	100	Protein	*
Protein, gm	<1	Vitamin A	*
Carbohydrates, gm	1	Vitamin C	*
Fat, gm	10	Thiamine	*
Sodium, mg	64	Riboflavin	*
Cholesterol, mg	<5e	Niacin	*
Fiber, gm	0	Calcium	*
		Iron	*

THIS FOOD: Marie's Blue Cheese Refrigerated Dressing does not supply any vitamins and minerals and derives 90 percent of its calories from fat. It has fewer additives and less sodium than most bottled dressings.

ADDITIVES: No questionable additives.

MARIE'S ITALIAN REFRIGERATED DRESSING
United Biscuits Holdings, Ltd.

Ingredients: soybean oil, buttermilk, eggs, sour cream, vinegar distilled, salt, dehydrated garlic, dehydrated spices, dehydrated onion.

Amount: 1 tbsp			% USRDA
Calories	100	Protein	*
Protein, gm	<1	Vitamin A	*
Carbohydrates, gm	1	Vitamin C	*
Fat, gm	11	Thiamine	*
Sodium, mg	108	Riboflavin	*
Cholesterol, mg	<5e	Niacin	*
Fiber, gm	0	Calcium	*
		Iron	*

THIS FOOD: Marie's Italian Refrigerated Dressing does not supply any vitamins and minerals and derives 90 percent of its calories from fat. It has fewer additives than most bottled dressings.

ADDITIVES: No questionable additives.

MARIE'S THOUSAND ISLAND REFRIGERATED DRESSING
United Biscuits Holdings, Ltd.

Ingredients: soybean oil, sweet pickle relish, sugar, vinegar distilled, sour cream, tomatoes, egg yolk, salt, lactic acid, natural flavoring, oleoresin paprika.

Amount: 1 tbsp			% USRDA
Calories	88	Protein	*
Protein, gm	0	Vitamin A	*
Carbohydrates, gm	2	Vitamin C	*
Fat, gm	9	Thiamine	*
Sodium, mg	103	Riboflavin	*
Cholesterol, mg	<5e	Niacin	*
Fiber, gm	<1	Calcium	*
		Iron	*

HELPFUL HINT: Most reduced calorie dressings are relatively high in sodium. To make your own low-sodium dressing, mix ½ cup yogurt, ¼ cup vinegar, ¼ cup oil, 2 tablespoons Dijon mustard, ½ teaspoon sugar with garlic, and seasonings to taste. A 1-tablespoon serving of this delicious dressing has only 30 calories and 30 milligrams sodium.

THIS FOOD: Marie's Thousand Island Refrigerated Dressing does not supply any vitamins and minerals and derives 90 percent of its calories from fat. It has fewer additives than most bottled dressings.

ADDITIVES: No questionable additives.

ROKA BRAND BLUE CHEESE DRESSING
Kraft, Inc.

Ingredients: soybean oil, blue cheese, water, vinegar, egg yolks, sugar, salt, mustard flour, propylene glycol alginate with sodium benzoate and calcium disodium EDTA, natural flavor.

Amount: 1 tbsp			% USRDA
Calories	60	Protein	*
Protein, gm	1	Vitamin A	*
Carbohydrates, gm	1	Vitamin C	*
Fat, gm	6	Thiamine	*
Sodium, mg	175	Riboflavin	*
Cholesterol, mg	10	Niacin	*
Fiber, gm	0	Calcium	2
		Iron	*

THIS FOOD: Roka Brand Blue Cheese Dressing does not supply any vitamins and minerals and derives 90 percent of its calories from fat. Like most bottled dressings, this product is high in sodium.

ADDITIVES: No questionable additives.

WISH-BONE ITALIAN SALAD DRESSING
Unilever United States, Inc.

Ingredients: soybean oil, water, vinegar, high-fructose corn syrup, salt, dehydrated garlic, sugar, xanthan gum, spice, colored with annatto and caramel, lemon juice, calcium disodium EDTA.

Amount: 1 tbsp			% USRDA
Calories	80	Protein	*
Protein, gm	0	Vitamin A	*
Carbohydrates, gm	1	Vitamin C	*
Fat, gm	8	Thiamine	*
Sodium, mg	285	Riboflavin	*
Cholesterol, mg	0	Niacin	*
Fiber, gm	0	Calcium	*
		Iron	*

THIS FOOD: Wish-Bone Italian Salad Dressing doesn't supply vitamins and minerals and derives 90 percent of its calories from fat. It is very high in sodium.

ADDITIVES: No questionable additives.

WISH-BONE LITE-LINE CHUNKY BLUE CHEESE SALAD DRESSING
Unilever United States, Inc.

Ingredients: water, soybean oil, distilled vinegar, blue cheese flavored bits, blue cheese, sugar, salt, algin derivative, cellulose gum, xanthan gum, polysorbate 60 and glyceryl monostearate, natural flavorings, lactic acid, spice, potassium sorbate and sodium benzoate, onion powder, artificial flavor, disodium guanylate, and disodium inosinate.

Amount: 1 tbsp			% USRDA
Calories	40	Protein	*
Protein, gm	0	Vitamin A	*
Carbohydrates, gm	3	Vitamin C	*
Fat, gm	3	Thiamine	*
Sodium, mg	195	Riboflavin	*
Cholesterol, mg	0	Niacin	*
Fiber, gm	0	Calcium	*
		Iron	*

THIS FOOD: Wish-Bone Lite-Line Chunky Blue Cheese Salad Dressing is low in calories because it contains more water than oil. About 68 percent of calories derive from fat. It is high in sodium.

ADDITIVES: Contains artificial flavor, which may cause allergic reactions in sensitive individuals, and which some studies suggest may adversely affect behavior and the ability to complete school tasks in some sensitive children.

HELPFUL HINT: If you are watching your fat calories, always order salad dressings on the side in restaurants and dilute with plain vinegar or lemon juice. This way you can control the serving size.

WISH-BONE LITE-LINE FRENCH STYLE SALAD DRESSING
Unilever United States, Inc.

Ingredients: water, vinegar, soybean oil, sugar, tomato paste, xanthan gum, algin derivative and polysorbate 60, salt, spice, dehydrated garlic, dehydrated onion, oleoresin paprika, potassium sorbate, sodium benzoate, calcium disodium EDTA.

Amount: 1 tbsp			% USRDA
Calories	30	Protein	*
Protein, gm	0	Vitamin A	*
Carbohydrates, gm	2	Vitamin C	*
Fat, gm	2	Thiamine	*
Sodium, mg	70	Riboflavin	*
Cholesterol, mg	0	Niacin	*
Fiber, gm	0	Calcium	*
		Iron	*

THIS FOOD: Wish-Bone Lite-Line French Style Salad Dressing is low in calories because it contains more water and vinegar than oil. About 60 percent of calories derive from fat. It contains a moderate amount of sodium.

ADDITIVES: No questionable additives.

WISH-BONE LITE-LINE THOUSAND ISLAND SALAD DRESSING
Unilever United States, Inc.

Ingredients: water, vinegar, pickle relish, sugar, soybean oil, tomato paste, salt, egg yolk solids, algin derivative, xanthan gum and polysorbate 60, spice, dehydrated bell peppers, dehydrated onions, lactic acid, potassium sorbate, calcium disodium EDTA, natural flavor.

Amount: 1 tbsp			% USRDA
Calories	25	Protein	*
Protein, gm	0	Vitamin A	*
Carbohydrates, gm	3	Vitamin C	*
Fat, gm	2	Thiamine	*
Sodium, mg	160	Riboflavin	*
Cholesterol, mg	5	Niacin	*
Fiber, gm	<1	Calcium	*
		Iron	*

THIS FOOD: Wish-Bone Lite-Line Thousand Island Salad Dressing is low in calories because it contains more water, vinegar, pickle relish, and sugar than oil. About 72 percent of its calories derive from fat. It is high in sodium.

ADDITIVES: No questionable additives.

WISH-BONE RUSSIAN SALAD DRESSING
Unilever United States, Inc.

Ingredients: corn syrup, soybean oil, water, tomato paste, sugar, vinegar, salt, steak sauce, beet juice, dehydrated lemon juice, spices, dehydrated garlic, dehydrated onion, natural flavor, potassium sorbate, and calcium disodium EDTA.

Amount: 1 tbsp			% USRDA
Calories	50	Protein	*
Protein, gm	0	Vitamin A	*
Carbohydrates, gm	7	Vitamin C	*
Fat, gm	2	Thiamine	*
Sodium, mg	145	Riboflavin	*
Cholesterol, mg	0	Niacin	*
Fiber, gm	<1	Calcium	*
		Iron	*

THIS FOOD: Like most prepared dressings, this product does not supply any vitamins or minerals. It actually contains more sugar than oil; as a result, only 36 percent of its calories derive from fat. Compared to other dressings, this product is high in sodium.

ADDITIVES: No questionable additives.

WISH-BONE THOUSAND ISLAND SALAD DRESSING
Unilever United States, Inc.

Ingredients: soybean oil, high-fructose corn syrup, water, pickle relish, vinegar, tomato paste, salt, egg yolk solids, spice, algin derivative, xanthan gum, hydroxypropyl methylcellulose and polysorbate 60, dehydrated onions, dehydrated bell peppers, natural flavor, calcium disodium EDTA.

Amount: 1 tbsp			% USRDA
Calories	70	Protein	*
Protein, gm	0	Vitamin A	*
Carbohydrates, gm	3	Vitamin C	*
Fat, gm	6	Thiamine	*
Sodium, mg	135	Riboflavin	*
Cholesterol, mg	5	Niacin	*
Fiber, gm	<1	Calcium	*
		Iron	*

THIS FOOD: Wish-Bone Thousand Island Salad Dressing doesn't supply vitamins and minerals and derives 77 percent of its calories from fat. It is high in sodium.

ADDITIVES: No questionable additives.

SAUCES AND SEASONINGS

It is difficult to generalize about the products in this category, since a variety of condiments, dry seasoning mixes, barbecue sauces, as well as salt are included. For the most part these products are used to add zest and savor to foods. Obviously salt is a concentrated source of sodium. Unfortunately all of the other products are also high in sodium. If you are concerned with your sodium intake, you can make your own saltless seasoning mix by combining your favorite herbs and spices. Or add onion, garlic, lemon juice, or vinegar to your favorite recipes instead of salt or high-sodium seasonings. Using a dash or two of wine will also help perk up bland foods without unwanted sodium. Avoid cooking wine, which usually contains added salt.

SODIUM GUIDELINES: In evaluating the sodium content of sauces and seasonings, we used the following standards:

less than 100 mg	moderate in sodium
100 to 200 mg	high in sodium
more than 200 mg	very high in sodium

Remember, these guidelines are not for people following medically restricted low-sodium diets, but for healthy individuals who wish to monitor their sodium intake.

HEINZ 57 SAUCE
H. J. Heinz Co.

Ingredients: tomatoes, malt and distilled vinegar, sugar, salt, spices, natural flavoring, apples, soy oil, turmeric, guar gum, onion powder, caramel coloring, garlic powder.

Amount: 1 tbsp			% USRDA
Calories	15	Protein	*
Protein, gm	<1	Vitamin A	*
Carbohydrates, gm	3	Vitamin C	*
Fat, gm	<1	Thiamine	*
Sodium, mg	265	Riboflavin	*
Cholesterol, mg	0	Niacin	*
Fiber, gm	0	Calcium	*
		Iron	*

Contains ¾ teaspoon sugar.

THIS FOOD: Heinz 57 Sauce is high in sugar and very high in sodium.

ADDITIVES: No questionable additives.

HUNT'S ALL-NATURAL HOT AND ZESTY BARBECUE SAUCE
Hunt-Wesson Foods, Inc.

Ingredients: tomatoes, sugar, distilled vinegar, corn syrup, water, salt, dehydrated onions, hickory smoke flavor, spices, dehydrated carrots, pectin, xanthan gum, dehydrated celery, dehydrated green bell peppers, garlic powder, dehydrated tomato flakes, natural flavors.

Amount: 1 tbsp			% USRDA
Calories	25	Protein	*
Protein, gm	0	Vitamin A	4
Carbohydrates, gm	6	Vitamin C	4
Fat, gm	0	Thiamine	*
Sodium, mg	195	Riboflavin	*
Cholesterol, mg	0	Niacin	*
Fiber, gm	0	Calcium	*
		Iron	*

Contains 1½ teaspoons sugar.

THIS FOOD: Hunt's All-Natural Hot and Zesty Barbecue Sauce is high in sugar and sodium.

ADDITIVES: No questionable additives.

HUNT'S ALL-NATURAL ORIGINAL FLAVOR BARBECUE SAUCE
Hunt-Wesson Foods, Inc.

Ingredients: tomatoes, sugar, distilled vinegar, corn syrup, water, salt, dehydrated onions, dehydrated carrots, pectin, dehydrated celery, dehydrated green bell pepper, xanthan gum, dehydrated tomatoes, garlic powder, natural flavors.

Amount: 1 tbsp			% USRDA
Calories	20	Protein	*
Protein, gm	0	Vitamin A	4
Carbohydrates, gm	5	Vitamin C	4
Fat, gm	0	Thiamine	*
Sodium, mg	195	Riboflavin	*
Cholesterol, mg	0	Niacin	*
Fiber, gm	<1	Calcium	*
		Iron	*

Contains 1 teaspoon sugar.

THIS FOOD: Hunt's All-Natural Original Flavor Barbecue Sauce is high in sugar and sodium.

ADDITIVES: No questionable additives.

HUNT'S ORIGINAL MANWICH
Hunt-Wesson Foods, Inc.

Ingredients: tomatoes, water, sugar, vinegar, salt, modified food starch, dehydrated onions, spices, dehydrated peppers, garlic powder, natural flavors.

Amount: 2½ oz/5 tbsp			% USRDA
Calories	40	Protein	2
Protein, gm	1	Vitamin A	20
Carbohydrates, gm	10	Vitamin C	25
Fat, gm	0	Thiamine	2
Sodium, mg	405	Riboflavin	*
Cholesterol, mg	0	Niacin	4
Fiber, gm	0	Calcium	*
		Iron	6
Contains 2½ teaspoons sugar.			

THIS FOOD: Hunt's Original Manwich contains 80 percent sugar calories and is a very good source of vitamins A and C. It is very high in sodium.

ADDITIVES: No questionable additives.

KIKKOMAN SOY SAUCE
Kikkoman International, Inc.

Ingredients: water, wheat, soybeans, salt, sodium benzoate.

Amount: 1 tsp			% USRDA
Calories	4	Protein	*
Protein, gm	>1	Vitamin A	*
Carbohydrates, gm	0	Vitamin C	*
Fat, gm	0	Thiamine	*
Sodium, mg	320	Riboflavin	*
Cholesterol, mg	0	Niacin	*
Fiber, gm	0	Calcium	*
		Iron	*

THIS FOOD: Kikkoman Soy Sauce is used as seasoning in place of salt. Not surprisingly, this product is very high in sodium. If you are watching your sodium intake, don't make the mistake of using soy sauce at will!

ADDITIVES: No questionable additives.

KRAFT BARBECUE SAUCE
Kraft, Inc.

Ingredients: vinegar, water, sugar, tomato paste, salt, paprika, modified food starch, soybean oil, liquid brown sugar, spice, dehydrated garlic, hickory smoke flavor, mustard flour, dehydrated onion, natural and artificial flavors, xanthan gum, sodium benzoate.

Amount: 1 tbsp			% USRDA
Calories	23	Protein	*
Protein, gm	0	Vitamin A	4
Carbohydrates, gm	5	Vitamin C	*
Fat, gm	5	Thiamine	*
Sodium, mg	248	Riboflavin	*
Cholesterol, mg	0	Niacin	*
Fiber, gm	0	Calcium	*
		Iron	*

THIS FOOD: Like most bottled barbecue sauces, Kraft Barbecue Sauce is high in sugar and very high in sodium.

ADDITIVES: Contains artificial flavor, which may cause allergic reactions in sensitive individuals, and which some studies suggest may adversely affect behavior and the ability to complete school tasks in some sensitive children.

OTHER BRANDS: Hunt's All-Natural Barbecue Sauces do not contain questionable additives.

KRAFT ONION BITS BARBECUE SAUCE
Kraft, Inc.

Ingredients: vinegar, water, sugar, tomato paste, salt, dehydrated onion, soybean oil, modified food starch, spice, dehydrated garlic, mustard flour, natural and artificial flavor, dehydrated lemon juice, sodium benzoate, xanthan gum.

Amount: 1 tbsp			% USRDA
Calories	25	Protein	*
Protein, gm	0	Vitamin A	2
Carbohydrates, gm	6	Vitamin C	*
Fat, gm	<1	Thiamine	*
Sodium, mg	215	Riboflavin	*
Cholesterol, mg	0	Niacin	*
Fiber, gm	0	Calcium	*
		Iron	*

THIS FOOD: Like most bottled barbecue sauces, Kraft Onion Bits Barbecue Sauce is high in sugar and sodium.

ADDITIVES: Contains artificial flavor, which some studies suggest may adversely affect behavior and the ability to complete school tasks in some sensitive children; may cause allergic reactions in sensitive individuals.

OTHER BRANDS: Hunt's All-Natural Barbecue Sauces do not contain questionable additives.

KRAFT TARTAR SAUCE
Kraft, Inc.

Ingredients: soybean oil, onions, water, chopped pickle, vinegar, egg yolk, sugar, salt, olives, artificial and natural flavor, ground mustard seed, xanthan gum, calcium disodium EDTA, spice.

Amount: 1 tbsp			% USRDA
Calories	70	Protein	*
Protein, gm	0	Vitamin A	*
Carbohydrates, gm	1	Vitamin C	*
Fat, gm	8	Thiamine	*
Sodium, mg	160	Riboflavin	*
Cholesterol, mg	5	Niacin	*
Fiber, gm	0	Calcium	*
		Iron	*

THIS FOOD: Kraft Tartar Sauce is high in sodium, and almost all of its calories derive from fat.

ADDITIVES: Contains artificial flavor, which can cause allergic reactions in sensitive individuals and which some studies suggest may adversely affect behavior and the ability to complete school tasks in some sensitive children.

McCORMICK'S CHILI SEASONING MIX
McCormick and Co., Inc.

Ingredients: chili pepper and other spices, wheat flour, onion salt, and garlic.

Amount: 1/16 package			% USRDA
Calories	18	Protein	*
Protein, gm	<1	Vitamin A	16
Carbohydrates, gm	3	Vitamin C	*
Fat, gm	<1	Thiamine	*
Sodium, mg	193	Riboflavin	*
Cholesterol, mg	0	Niacin	*
Fiber, gm	0	Calcium	*
		Iron	*

THIS FOOD: McCormick's Chili Seasoning Mix is a good source of vitamin A.

ADDITIVES: No questionable additives.

MORTON IODIZED SALT
Morton Thiokol, Inc.

Ingredients: salt, sodium silicoaluminate, dextrose, potassium iodide.

Amount: 1 tsp			% USRDA
Calories	0	Protein	*
Protein, gm	0	Vitamin A	*
Carbohydrates, gm	0	Vitamin C	*
Fat, gm	0	Thiamine	*
Sodium, mg	2,400	Riboflavin	*
Cholesterol, mg	0	Niacin	*
Fiber, gm	0	Calcium	*
		Iron	*

THIS FOOD: There is no nutritional need for salt, or sodium chloride, added to food for seasoning. The average American diet contains 1,200 mg of naturally occurring sodium per day, which is the equivalent of ½ teaspoon salt. This is well in excess of your body's physiological needs. Yet an additional 1,600 to 2,400 mg sodium are eaten on average from added salt in prepared foods, topped off by still more salt added by consumers. The grand total is an average intake of 4,000 to 4,800 mg sodium—far in excess of the safe and adequate dietary intake recommended. Among susceptible individuals, excessive sodium intake is associated with an increased risk of developing high blood pressure. Most experts agree that infants should not be given added salt in their food.

ADDITIVES: No questionable additives.

MORTON SALT
Morton Thiokol, Inc.

Ingredients: salt, sodium silicoaluminate.

Amount: 1 tsp			% USRDA
Calories	0	Protein	*
Protein, gm	0	Vitamin A	*
Carbohydrates, gm	0	Vitamin C	*
Fat, gm	0	Thiamine	*
Sodium, mg	2,400	Riboflavin	*
Cholesterol, mg	0	Niacin	*
Fiber, gm	0	Calcium	*
		Iron	*

THIS FOOD: There is no nutritional need for salt, or sodium chloride, added to food for seasoning. The average American diet contains 1,200 mg of naturally occurring sodium, which is the equivalent of ½ teaspoon salt. This is all you need for proper nutrition. Yet an additional 1,600 to 2,400 mg sodium are eaten on average from added salt in prepared foods, topped off by still more salt added by consumers. The grand total is an average intake of 4,000 to 4,800 mg sodium—far in excess of the safe and adequate dietary intake recommended. Among susceptible individuals, excessive sodium intake is associated with an increased risk of developing high blood pressure. Most experts agree that infants should not be given added salt in their food.

ADDITIVES: No questionable additives.

OPEN PIT HICKORY SMOKE FLAVOR BARBECUE SAUCE
General Foods Corp.

Ingredients: distilled vinegar, corn syrup, tomato puree, salt, modified starch (cornstarch, tapioca, potato starch), natural hickory smoke flavor, water, soybean oil, hydrolyzed soy protein, spice, cellulose powder, onion powder, garlic powder, artificial color, natural flavor, caramel color, artificial flavor.

Amount: 1 tbsp			% USRDA
Calories	23	Protein	*
Protein, gm	0	Vitamin A	*
Carbohydrates, gm	5	Vitamin C	*
Fat, gm	<1	Thiamine	*
Sodium, mg	232	Riboflavin	*
Cholesterol, mg	e	Niacin	*
Fiber, gm	e	Calcium	*
		Iron	*
Contains 1 teaspoon sugar.			

THIS FOOD: Like most bottled barbecue sauces, Open Pit Hickory Smoke Flavor Barbecue Sauce is high in sugar and sodium.

ADDITIVES: Contains artificial flavor, which may cause allergic reactions in some sensitive individuals, and which some studies suggest may adversely affect behavior and the ability to complete school tasks in some sensitive children.

DID YOU KNOW: Most experts believe that adding iodine to salt is no longer necessary. The average American consumes four to thirteen times the RDA for iodine.

OPEN PIT ORIGINAL FLAVOR BARBECUE SAUCE
General Foods Corp.

Ingredients: distilled vinegar, corn syrup, tomato puree, salt, modified starch (cornstarch, tapioca, potato starch), water, soybean oil, hydrolyzed soy protein, spice, cellulose powder, artificial color, caramel color, natural flavor, artificial flavor.

Amount: 1 tbsp			% USRDA
Calories	23	Protein	*
Protein, gm	<1	Vitamin A	2
Carbohydrates, gm	6	Vitamin C	3
Fat, gm	<1	Thiamine	*
Sodium, mg	255	Riboflavin	*
Cholesterol, mg	0	Niacin	*
Fiber, gm	<1	Calcium	*
		Iron	*
Contains 1½ teaspoons sugar.			

THIS FOOD: Like most bottled barbecue sauces, Open Pit Original Flavor Barbecue Sauce is very high in sugar and sodium.

ADDITIVES: Contains artificial color and flavor, which some studies suggest may adversely affect behavior and the ability to complete school tasks in some sensitive children; artificial colors are inadequately tested and artificial flavor may cause allergic reactions in sensitive individuals.

SHAKE 'N BAKE ORIGINAL CHICKEN
General Foods Corp.

Ingredients: wheat flour, partially hydrogenated vegetable oils (soybean, cottonseed, palm), salt, malted barley, sugar, spices (mustard flour, celery seed, chili pepper, thyme, basil, red pepper, cloves, oregano, rosemary), paprika, yeast, cornstarch, garlic powder, monosodium glutamate, natural hickory smoke flavor, artificial color, onion powder.

Amount: ¼ envelope			% USRDA
Calories	78	Protein	4
Protein, gm	3	Vitamin A	8
Carbohydrates, gm	12	Vitamin C	*
Fat, gm	2	Thiamine	5
Sodium, mg	445	Riboflavin	4
Cholesterol, mg	0	Niacin	4
Fiber, gm	<1	Calcium	*
		Iron	3

THIS FOOD: Shake 'n Bake Original Chicken seasoning mix is not a significant source of vitamins or minerals. Like most products of this kind, it is very high in sodium.

ADDITIVES: Contains monosodium glutamate (MSG), which many authorities believe should be avoided by infants and very young children; causes adverse reactions in some sensitive individuals.

SHAKE 'N BAKE FOR PORK
General Foods Corp.

Ingredients: milled and flaked corn, wheat flour, modified cornstarch, salt, partially hydrogenated soybean, cottonseed, and palm oils, sugar, monosodium glutamate, corn syrup, spices, onion powder, natural flavor, caramel color, disodium inosinate and disodium guanylate, artificial color.

Amount: ¼ envelope			% USRDA
Calories	81	Protein	2
Protein, gm	1	Vitamin A	5
Carbohydrates, gm	17	Vitamin C	*
Fat, gm	1	Thiamine	2
Sodium, mg	624	Riboflavin	*
Cholesterol, mg	0	Niacin	*
Fiber, gm	<1	Calcium	*
		Iron	2

THIS FOOD: Shake 'n Bake for Pork seasoning mix is not a significant source of vitamins or minerals. Compared to other products in this category, it is extremely high in sodium.

ADDITIVES: Contains monosodium glutamate (MSG), which many authorities believe should be avoided by infants and very young children; causes adverse reactions in some sensitive individuals.

SNACK CAKES AND PIES

There is little if any nutritional difference between individually packaged cakes and pies and the full-sized version. All are high in empty sugar calories, and often high in saturated fat, but the convenience and availability of the individually wrapped miniatures encourage people to eat more of them. Unfortunately, most advertising for popular snack cakes and pies is aimed at children. For example, Hostess Twinkies, with sales of almost a billion each year, are the largest selling cake product on earth. Compared to snack pies and most of the popular chocolate-covered snack cakes, such as Drake's Ring Dings and Devil Dogs, Twinkies are moderate in fat, but they are still high in sugar calories and contain questionable additives. More than 25 billion have been sold since 1930, when this product was launched (without filling) as "Little Short Cake Fingers."

SODIUM GUIDELINES: In evaluating the sodium content of snack cakes and pies, we used the following standards:

less than 200 mg	low in sodium
200 mg to 300 mg	moderate in sodium
more than 300 mg	high in sodium

Remember, these guidelines are not for people following medically restricted low-sodium diets, but for healthy individuals who wish to monitor their sodium intake.

DRAKE'S DEVIL DOGS
Borden, Inc.

Ingredients: corn syrup, partially hydrogenated vegetable shortening (contains one or more of: soybean oil, cottonseed oil, palm oil), enriched bleached flour (wheat flour, niacin, reduced iron, thiamine mononitrate, riboflavin), water, whey, sugar, dextrose, cocoa, skim milk. Contains 2 percent or less of: soya flour, eggs, baking soda, salt, sodium caseinate, sodium propionate, buttermilk, mono- and diglycerides, vanillin, sodium aluminium phosphate with aluminum sulfate, isolated soy protein, calcium caseinate, sorbitan monostearate and polysorbate 60, cellulose gum, xanthan gum, vanilla.

Amount: 1 piece			% USRDA
Calories	170	Protein	2
Protein, gm	2	Vitamin A	*
Carbohydrates, gm	22	Vitamin C	*
Fat, gm	8	Thiamine	2
Sodium, mg	165	Riboflavin	4
Cholesterol, mg	na	Niacin	2
Fiber, gm	<1e	Calcium	*
		Iron	4

THIS FOOD: Drake's Devil Dogs are full of sugar and fat calories without compensating nutrients. Forty-two percent of the calories in this snack cake derive from fat, nearly all of it saturated.

ADDITIVES: No questionable additives.

DRAKE'S RING DING JR.
Borden, Inc.

Ingredients: corn syrup, partially hydrogenated vegetable shortening (contains one or more of: soybean oil, cottonseed oil, palm oil), sugar, whey, enriched bleached flour (wheat flour, niacin, reduced iron, thiamine mononitrate, riboflavin), dextrose, cocoa. Contains 2 percent or less of: carob powder, skim milk, Dutch process cocoa (alkalized), soya flour, salt, baking soda, buttermilk, sodium caseinate, mono- and diglycerides, isolated soy protein, sodium aluminum phosphate with aluminum sulfate, calcium caseinate, eggs, vanilla, vanillin, lecithin, egg whites, whole milk, sorbitan monostearate and polysorbate 60, sodium propionate.

Amount: 1 piece			% USRDA
Calories	160	Protein	2
Protein, gm	1	Vitamin A	*
Carbohydrates, gm	20	Vitamin C	*
Fat, gm	9	Thiamine	*
Sodium, mg	120	Riboflavin	2
Cholesterol, mg	<5e	Niacin	*
Fiber, gm	<1e	Calcium	*
		Iron	4

THIS FOOD: A glance at the ingredients list tells all: corn syrup and partially hydrogenated vegetable oil are the two main ingredients in this snack cake, which does not contain significant amounts of any nutrient. More than 50 percent of the calories in this product derive from fat, most of it saturated.

ADDITIVES: No questionable additives.

EARTH GRAINS DEVIL'S FOOD DOUGHNUTS
Campbell Taggart, Inc.

Ingredients: sugar, wheat flour, partially hydrogenated vegetable and animal shortening (soybean oil and/or cottonseed oil and/or palm oil and/or beef fat and/or lard), water, cocoa, egg yolks, invert sugar. Contains 2 percent or less of: cocoa processed with alkali, corn syrup, whey solids, soy flour, salt, baking powder (baking soda, sodium acid pyrophosphate), wheat starch, cornstarch, corn dextrin, tapioca dextrin, agar, sodium carboxymethyl cellulose, dough conditioners (one or more of: lecithin, mono- and diglycerides, polysorbate 60, sorbitan monostearate), natural and artificial flavors, annatto and turmeric extracts, sorbic acid, niacin, iron, thiamine mononitrate, riboflavin.

NOTE: The letter "e" indicates that the data has been estimated; < means "less than" and is used for small amounts of sodium or cholesterol; * means food contains less than 2% of USRDA; "na" means that the information was not available and appears only when data is insufficient.

Amount: 1 doughnut			% USRDA
Calories	350	Protein	4
Protein, gm	3	Vitamin A	*
Carbohydrates, gm	36	Vitamin C	*
Fat, gm	21	Thiamine	6
Sodium, mg	505	Riboflavin	6
Cholesterol, mg	na	Niacin	4
Fiber, gm	<1e	Calcium	2
		Iron	4

Contains 4½ teaspoons fat.

THIS FOOD: The brand name, Earth Grains, which seems to promise natural, wholesome food, is totally misleading. This artificially flavored doughnut is higher in fat, sugar, and sodium than most other snack cakes profiled. A whopping 54 percent of the calories in this product derive from fat, most of it saturated. One doughnut contributes an extraordinary 505 mg sodium.

ADDITIVES: Contains artificial flavors, which may cause allergic reactions in sensitive individuals, and which some studies suggest may adversely affect behavior and the ability to complete school tasks in some sensitive children.

EARTH GRAINS OLD FASHIONED GLAZED DOUGHNUTS
Campbell Taggart, Inc.

Ingredients: wheat flour, sugar, partially hydrogenated vegetable and animal shortening (soybean oil and/or cottonseed oil and/or palm oil and/or beef fat and/or lard), water, egg yolks, invert sugar, corn syrup. Contains 2 percent or less of: whey solids, soy flour, salt, baking powder (baking soda, sodium acid pyrophosphate), cornstarch, wheat starch, corn dextrin, tapioca dextrin, agar, sodium carboxymethyl cellulose, dough conditioners (one or more of: lecithin, mono- and diglycerides, polysorbate 60, sorbitan monostearate), natural and artificial flavors, annatto and turmeric extracts, sorbic acid, niacin, iron, thiamine mononitrate, riboflavin.

Amount: 1 doughnut			% USRDA
Calories	360	Protein	4
Protein, gm	3	Vitamin A	*
Carbohydrates, gm	34	Vitamin C	*
Fat, gm	24	Thiamine	8
Sodium, mg	485	Riboflavin	4
Cholesterol, mg	na	Niacin	4
Fiber, gm	1e	Calcium	2
		Iron	4

Contains 5 teaspoons fat.

THIS FOOD: The brand name, Earth Grains, which seems to promise natural, wholesome food, is totally misleading. This artificially flavored glazed doughnut is higher in fat and sugar than any other snack cake profiled. A whopping 60 percent of the calories in this product derive from fat, most of it saturated. One doughnut contributes 485 mg sodium, which is extremely high for this category.

ADDITIVES: Contains artificial flavors, which may cause allergic reactions in some sensitive individuals, and which may adversely affect behavior and the ability to complete school tasks in some sensitive children.

HOSTESS BLUEBERRY PIE
Ralston Purina Co.

Ingredients: blueberries, enriched flour, niacin, iron, thiamine mononitrate, riboflavin, water, partially hydrogenated vegetable and/or animal shortening (contains one or more of the following: soybean oil, cottonseed oil, palm oil, beef fat, lard), sugar, corn syrup, apples, modified food starch, skim milk, salt, cornstarch, calcium sulfate, citric acid, agar, locust bean gum, sodium phosphate, mono- and diglycerides, natural and artificial flavors, artificial colors (FD & C Yellow No. 5), sodium benzoate and propionate.

Amount: 1 pie			% USRDA
Calories	390	Protein	4
Protein, gm	3	Vitamin A	*
Carbohydrates, gm	49	Vitamin C	4
Fat, gm	20	Thiamine	10
Sodium, mg	450	Riboflavin	8
Cholesterol, mg	18	Niacin	8
Fiber, gm	<1e	Calcium	2
		Iron	8
Contains 4 teaspoons fat.			

THIS FOOD: Hostess Blueberry Pie is high in sugar, sodium, saturated fat, and overall fat. Fat contributes 46 percent of calories. It is a fair source of thiamine.

ADDITIVES: Contains Yellow No. 5, which can cause allergic reactions, especially in aspirin-sensitive individuals; and artificial color and flavor, which some studies suggest may adversely affect behavior and the ability to complete school tasks in some sensitive children. Artificial colors are inadequately tested and artificial flavor may cause allergic reactions in sensitive individuals.

HOSTESS CHERRY PIE
Ralston Purina Co.

Ingredients: cherries, enriched flour, (niacin, iron, thiamine mononitrate, riboflavin), water, partially hydrogenated vegetable and/or animal shortening (contains one or more of the following: soybean oil, cottonseed oil, palm oil, beef fat, lard), sugar, corn syrup, modified food starch, skim milk, salt, corn-starch, calcium sulfate, citric acid, agar, locust bean gum, sodium phosphate, mono- and diglycerides, natural and artificial flavors, artificial colors (FD & C Yellow No. 5), sodium benzoate and propionate.

Amount: 1 pie			% USRDA
Calories	390	Protein	6
Protein, gm	5	Vitamin A	*
Carbohydrates, gm	55	Vitamin C	2
Fat, gm	20	Thiamine	10
Sodium, mg	530	Riboflavin	8
Cholesterol, mg	18	Niacin	8
Fiber, gm	<1e	Calcium	2
		Iron	8
Contains 4 teaspoons fat.			

THIS FOOD: Hostess Cherry Pie is high in sugar, sodium, saturated fat, and overall fat. Fat contributes 46 percent of calories. It is a fair source of thiamine.

ADDITIVES: Contains artificial color and flavor, which some studies suggest may adversely affect behavior and the ability to complete school tasks in some sensitive children; artificial colors are inadequately tested and artificial flavor may cause allergic reactions in sensitive individuals. Also contains Yellow No. 5, which can cause allergic reactions, especially in aspirin-sensitive individuals.

HOSTESS CHOCOLATE CUPCAKES
Ralston Purina Co.

Ingredients: sugar, water, enriched flour (niacin, iron, thiamine mononitrate, riboflavin), partially hydrogenated vegetable and/or animal shortening (contains one or more of: soybean oil, cottonseed oil, palm oil, beef fat, lard), corn syrup, skim milk, cocoa, whey, starch, leavening (sodium acid pyrophosphate, baking soda, monocalcium phosphate), salt, chocolate liquor, mono- and di-glycerides, gelatin, sodium caseinate, sodium phosphate, polysorbate 60, agar, lecithin, natural and artificial flavors, artificial color, sorbic acid.

Amount: 1 cupcake			% USRDA
Calories	170	Protein	2
Protein, gm	2	Vitamin A	*
Carbohydrates, gm	29	Vitamin C	*
Fat, gm	6	Thiamine	4
Sodium, mg	250	Riboflavin	4
Cholesterol, mg	3	Niacin	2
Fiber, gm	<1e	Calcium	2
		Iron	4

THIS FOOD: Hostess Chocolate Cupcakes, a familiar item in all too many childhood diets, are filled with nutritionally empty sugar and fat calories. This snack cake contains 250 mg sodium per serving.

ADDITIVES: Contains artificial color and flavor, which some studies suggest may adversely affect behavior and the ability to complete school tasks in some sensitive children; artificial colors are inadequately tested, and artificial flavors may cause allergic reactions in sensitive individuals.

HOSTESS CRUMB CAKES
Ralston Purina Co.

Ingredients: enriched flour (niacin, iron, thiamine mononitrate, riboflavin), sugar, skim milk, brown sugar, partially hydrogenated vegetable and/or animal shortening (contains one or more of: soybean oil, cottonseed oil, palm oil, beef fat, lard), corn syrup, eggs, egg whites, water, invert sugar, egg yolks, cinnamon, leavening (sodium acid pyrophosphate, baking soda, monocalcium phosphate), salt, mono- and diglycerides, tapioca starch, starch, cellulose gum, xanthan gum, artificial and natural flavors, artificial colors (FD & C Yellow No. 5), sodium propionate.

Amount: 1 crumb cake			% USRDA
Calories	130	Protein	2
Protein, gm	1	Vitamin A	*
Carbohydrates, gm	22	Vitamin C	*
Fat, gm	4	Thiamine	4
Sodium, mg	95	Riboflavin	4
Cholesterol, mg	10	Niacin	2
Fiber, gm	na	Calcium	2
		Iron	4

THIS FOOD: Hostess Crumb Cakes contain less fat than the chocolate covered snack foods, but are still high in nutritionally empty sugar calories. This product is low in sodium.

ADDITIVES: Contains artificial color and flavor, which some studies suggest may adversely affect behavior and the ability to complete school tasks in some sensitive children; artificial colors are inadequately tested, and artificial flavors may cause allergic reactions in sensitive individuals. Also contains Yellow No. 5, which may cause allergic reactions, especially in aspirin-sensitive individuals.

HOSTESS DING DONGS
Ralston Purina Co.

Ingredients: sugar, partially hydrogenated vegetable and/or animal shortening (may contain one or more of: soybean oil, cottonseed oil, palm oil, beef fat, lard), enriched flour (niacin, iron, thiamine mononitrate, riboflavin), water, cocoa, skim milk, corn syrup, eggs, mono- and diglycerides, starch, whey, leavening (baking soda, sodium acid pyrophosphate, monocalcium phosphate), salt, sodium caseinate, lecithin, cellulose gum, polysorbate 60, artificial color, artificial and natural flavors, sorbic acid.

Amount: 1 Ding Dong			% USRDA
Calories	170	Protein	2
Protein, gm	1	Vitamin A	*
Carbohydrates, gm	21	Vitamin C	*
Fat, gm	9	Thiamine	*
Sodium, mg	130	Riboflavin	2
Cholesterol, mg	6	Niacin	2
Fiber, gm	<1	Calcium	2
		Iron	2
Contains 4½ teaspoons fat.			

THIS FOOD: Hostess Ding Dongs are full of sugar and fat calories without compensating nutrients. Forty-two percent of the calories in this snack cake derive from fat, nearly all of it saturated. Incidentally, a Hostess Big Wheel is the same as a Ding Dong, but marketed under a different name.

ADDITIVES: Contains artificial colors and flavors, which some studies suggest may adversely affect behavior and the ability to complete school tasks in some sensitive children; artificial colors are inadequately tested and artificial flavors may cause allergic reactions in sensitive individuals.

HOSTESS TWINKIES
Ralston Purina Co.
Ingredients: sugar, enriched flour (niacin, iron, thiamine mononitrate, riboflavin), corn syrup, water, partially hydrogenated vegetable and/or animal shortening (contains one or more of: soybean oil, cottonseed oil, palm oil, beef fat, lard), eggs, skim milk, leavening (sodium acid pyrophosphate, baking soda, monocalcium phosphate), whey, starch, salt, mono- and diglycerides, sodium caseinate, polysorbate 60, lecithin, xanthan gum, natural and artificial flavors, artificial color, FD & C Yellow No. 5, sorbic acid.

Amount: 1 Twinkie			% USRDA
Calories	160	Protein	2
Protein, gm	1	Vitamin A	*
Carbohydrates, gm	26	Vitamin C	*
Fat, gm	5	Thiamine	4
Sodium, mg	150	Riboflavin	4
Cholesterol, mg	20	Niacin	2
Fiber, gm	<1e	Calcium	2
		Iron	2

THIS FOOD: Twinkies contain slightly less fat than the chocolate-covered snack foods, but are still high in nutritionally empty sugar calories.

ADDITIVES: Contains artificial colors and flavors, which some studies suggest may adversely affect behavior and the ability to perform school tasks in some sensitive children; artificial colors are inadequately tested, and artificial flavors may cause allergic reactions in sensitive individuals. Also contains Yellow No. 5, which can cause allergic reactions, especially in aspirin-sensitive individuals.

KELLOGG'S BLUEBERRY POP-TARTS
Kellogg Co.

Ingredients: enriched wheat flour, blueberry filling (corn syrup, dextrose, blueberries, grapes, cracker meal, wheat starch, partially hydrogenated soybean oil, citric acid, artificial coloring), partially hydrogenated soybean oil, corn syrup, sugar, whey, dextrose, salt, baking powder, baking soda, niacinamide, iron, vitamin A palmitate, pyridoxine hydrochloride, riboflavin, thiamine hydrochloride, folic acid.

Amount: 1 Pop-Tart			% USRDA
Calories	210	Protein	4
Protein, gm	3	Vitamin A	10
Carbohydrates, gm	36	Vitamin C	*
Fat, gm	5	Thiamine	10
Sodium, mg	220	Riboflavin	10
Cholesterol, mg	0	Niacin	10
Fiber, gm	<1e	Calcium	*
		Iron	10

THIS FOOD: Vitamin-supplemented Kellogg's Blueberry Pop-Tarts are a fair source of vitamin A, the B vitamins, and iron. About 21 percent of calories come from fat. This product is moderately high in sodium.

ADDITIVES: Contains artificial coloring, which is inadequately tested, and which some studies suggest can adversely affect behavior and the ability to complete school tasks in some sensitive children.

KELLOGG'S FROSTED STRAWBERRY POP-TARTS
Kellogg Co.

Ingredients: enriched wheat flour, strawberry filling (corn syrup, dextrose, strawberries, cracker meal, wheat starch, partially hydrogenated soybean oil, apples, citric acid, artificial color), sugar, partially hydrogenated soybean oil, corn syrup, whey, dextrose, salt, baking powder, corn, baking soda, gelatin, artificial coloring, niacinamide, iron, vitamin A palmitate, pyridoxine hydrochloride, riboflavin, thiamine hydrochloride, folic acid.

Amount: 1 Pop-Tart			% USRDA
Calories	200	Protein	4
Protein, gm	3	Vitamin A	10
Carbohydrates, gm	38	Vitamin C	*
Fat, gm	5	Thiamine	10
Sodium, mg	210	Riboflavin	10
Cholesterol, mg	0	Niacin	10
Fiber, gm	<1e	Calcium	*
		Iron	10

THIS FOOD: Vitamin supplemented Kellogg's Frosted Strawberry Pop-Tarts are a fair source of vitamin A, the B vitamins, and iron. About 21 percent of their calories come from fat. This product is moderately high in sodium.

ADDITIVES: Contains artificial coloring, which is inadequately tested, and which some studies suggest can adversely affect behavior and the ability to complete school tasks in some sensitive children.

PILLSBURY CINNAMON SWEET ROLLS WITH ICING
The Pillsbury Co.

Ingredients: enriched bleached flour (bleached flour, niacin, iron, thiamine mononitrate, riboflavin), water, sugar, beef fat and/or hydrogenated vegetable oil (cottonseed, palm, soybean), with BHA and citric acid, dextrose, wheat starch, baking powder (sodium acid pyrophosphate, baking soda), cornstarch, whey, salt, rice flour, mono- and diglycerides, cinnamon, corn syrup solids, cellulose gum, natural and artificial flavor, spice, polysorbate 60, artificial color, FD & C Yellow No. 5.

Amount: 1 roll			% USRDA
Calories	107	Protein	3
Protein, gm	1	Vitamin A	*
Carbohydrates, gm	16	Vitamin C	*
Fat, gm	4	Thiamine	5
Sodium, mg	241	Riboflavin	4
Cholesterol, mg	<5e	Niacin	3
Fiber, gm	<1e	Calcium	*
		Iron	3

THIS FOOD: Pillsbury Cinnamon Sweet Rolls with Icing are not a significant source of nutrients. They are high in sugar and fat, which contributes 34 percent of calories. This product is moderately high in sodium.

ADDITIVES: Contains artificial colors, which are inadequately tested, and which some studies suggest can adversely affect behavior and the ability to complete school tasks in some sensitive children; also contains Yellow No. 5, which can cause allergic reactions, especially in aspirin-sensitive individuals;

and artificial flavor, which can cause allergic reactions in sensitive individuals and which may also adversely affect behavior and the ability to complete school tasks in some sensitive children.

SOFT DRINKS

Following the attack on Pearl Harbor, Robert Woodruff, the president of Coca-Cola at the time, promised, "We will see that every man in uniform gets a bottle of Coca-Cola for five cents wherever he is and whatever it costs." By 1945 Coke had sixty-four plants overseas, established mostly at taxpayers' expense!

Today Coca-Cola is still the industry giant, with 24 percent of sales, followed closely by Pepsi, with 18 percent. Altogether Americans spend 25 billion dollars a year to quench their very big—40-gallon-a-person—thirst for soft drinks. Nobody pretends that soft drinks are nutritious. Their basic ingredients are carbonated water, some form of sugar (or artificial sweetener), and flavoring and coloring (natural or artificial). Consumed in moderation, soft drinks aren't actually bad for you, but they do have several drawbacks—empty sugar calories, caffeine (mostly in cola drinks), and artificial sweeteners—which may be cause for concern if you are a soda addict.

Soft drinks are the single largest source of sugar in the American diet (the typical 12-ounce can contains 5 to 10 teaspoons sugar). Sugar is nutritionally worthless, and also promotes tooth decay. Teeth are placed further at risk by the phosphoric acid in cola drinks (even sugar-free varieties), which erode teeth directly. Diet sodas, which are artificially sweetened with saccharin, aspartame, or a combination of the two, account for about twenty percent of the market. Many experts believe that both of these additives are inadequately tested for long-term safety.

All cola drinks (and many other popular soft drinks, such as Dr Pepper) also contain caffeine—typically 35 to 50 milligrams per 12-ounce can, which is about the same amount supplied by half a cup of brewed coffee. Most experts agree that caffeine intake should be limited by pregnant or nursing mothers and young children.

SODIUM GUIDELINES: In evaluating the sodium contents of soft drinks, we used the following standards:

less than 50 mg	low in sodium
50 mg to 100 mg	moderate in sodium
100 mg to 250 mg	high in sodium
more than 250 mg	very high in sodium

Remember, these guidelines are not for people following medically restricted low-sodium diets, but for healthy individuals who wish to monitor their sodium intake.

Canned Soft Drinks

CAFFEINE-FREE DIET COCA-COLA
The Coca-Cola Co.

Ingredients: carbonated water, caramel color, phosphoric acid, sodium saccharin, flavors, citric acid, sodium benzoate, aspartame.

Amount: 12 fl oz			% USRDA
Calories	0	Protein	*
Protein, gm	0	Vitamin A	*
Carbohydrates, gm	>1	Vitamin C	*
Fat, gm	0	Thiamine	*
Sodium, mg	36e	Riboflavin	*
Cholesterol, mg	0	Niacin	*
Fiber, gm	0	Calcium	*
		Iron	*

THIS FOOD: This artificially sweetened soft drink contains no nutrients.

ADDITIVES: Contains sodium saccharin, which causes cancer in laboratory animals. This additive is currently being investigated and should only be used in small amounts by healthy adults. Also contains aspartame (with phenylalanine), which should be avoided by people with PKU, a rare genetic disease, and which many experts believe has been inadequately tested for long-term safety.

NOTE: The letter "e" indicates that the data has been estimated; < means "less than" and is used for small amounts of sodium or cholesterol; * means food contains less than 2% of USRDA; "na" means that the information was not available and appears only when data is insufficient.

COCA-COLA
The Coca-Cola Co.

Ingredients: carbonated water, sugar, caramel color, phosphoric acid, natural flavorings, caffeine.

Amount: 12 fl oz			% USRDA
Calories	162	Protein	*
Protein, gm	0	Vitamin A	*
Carbohydrates, gm	40	Vitamin C	*
Fat, gm	0	Thiamine	*
Sodium, mg	14	Riboflavin	*
Cholesterol, mg	0	Niacin	*
Fiber, gm	0	Calcium	*
		Iron	*

THIS FOOD: All of the calories in this soft drink come from 10 teaspoons added sugar. Besides sugar calories, it contains no useful nutrients.

ADDITIVES: Contains caffeine, which may adversely affect behavior, motor activity, or sleep, especially in young children. Most experts agree that caffeine should be avoided by pregnant or nursing mothers and young children.

DR PEPPER
Dr Pepper Co.

Ingredients: carbonated water, sugar and/or corn sweetener, caramel color, artificial and natural flavoring, phosphoric acid, sodium benzoate, caffeine, monosodium phosphate, lactic acid, polyethylene glycol.

Amount: 12 fl oz			% USRDA
Calories	159	Protein	*
Protein, gm	0	Vitamin A	*
Carbohydrates, gm	41	Vitamin C	*
Fat, gm	0	Thiamine	*
Sodium, mg	36	Riboflavin	*
Cholesterol, mg	0	Niacin	*
Fiber, gm	0	Calcium	*
		Iron	*

THIS FOOD: All of the calories in this soft drink come from a whopping 10 teaspoons added sugar.

ADDITIVES: Contains artificial flavor, which can cause allergic reactions in sensitive individuals, and which some studies suggest may adversely affect behavior and the ability to complete school tasks in some sensitive children; also contains caffeine, which may adversely affect behavior, motor activity, or sleep, especially in young children. Most experts agree that caffeine should be avoided by pregnant or nursing mothers and young children.

FAYGO DIET GRAPE
Faygo Beverages, Inc.

Ingredients: carbonated water, citric acid, natural and artificial flavor, benzoate of soda, saccharin, aspartame.

Amount: 12 fl oz			% USRDA
Calories	0	Protein	*
Protein, gm	0	Vitamin A	*
Carbohydrates, gm	0	Vitamin C	*
Fat, gm	0	Thiamine	*
Sodium, mg	110	Riboflavin	*
Cholesterol, mg	0	Niacin	*
Fiber, gm	0	Calcium	*
		Iron	*

THIS FOOD: This artificially sweetened soft drink contains no nutrients. It contains more sodium than most of the other soft drinks profiled.

ADDITIVES: Contains artificial flavor, which some studies suggest may adversely affect behavior and the ability to complete school tasks in some sensitive children; may cause allergic reactions in sensitive individuals. Also contains sodium saccharin, which causes cancer in laboratory animals. This additive is currently being investigated and should only be used in small amounts by healthy adults. And aspartame (with phenylalanine), which should be avoided by people with PKU, a rare genetic disease, and which many experts believe has been inadequately tested for long-term safety.

FAYGO DIET ORANGE
Faygo Beverages, Inc.

Ingredients: carbonated water, citric acid, concentrated orange juice, orange peel flavoring and color, benzoate of soda, saccharin, aspartame.

Amount: 12 fl oz			% USRDA
Calories	0	Protein	*
Protein, gm	0	Vitamin A	*
Carbohydrates, gm	0	Vitamin C	*
Fat, gm	0	Thiamine	*
Sodium, mg	150	Riboflavin	*
Cholesterol, mg	0	Niacin	*
Fiber, gm	0	Calcium	*
		Iron	*

THIS FOOD: This artificially sweetened soft drink contains no nutrients. It contains two to three times more sodium than the other soft drinks profiled.

ADDITIVES: Contains sodium saccharin, which causes cancer in laboratory animals. This additive is currently being investigated and should only be used in small amounts by healthy adults. Also contains aspartame (with phenylalanine), which should be avoided by people with PKU, a rare genetic disease, and which many experts believe has been inadequately tested for long-term safety.

FAYGO PUNCH
Faygo Beverages, Inc.

Ingredients: carbonated water, sugar (and/or corn sweetener), concentrated orange juice, benzoate of soda, citric acid, orange peel flavor, artificial color, artificial flavor.

Amount: 12 fl oz			% USRDA
Calories	120	Protein	*
Protein, gm	0	Vitamin A	*
Carbohydrates, gm	30	Vitamin C	*
Fat, gm	0	Thiamine	*
Sodium, mg	66	Riboflavin	*
Cholesterol, mg	0	Niacin	*
Fiber, gm	0	Calcium	*
		Iron	*

THIS FOOD: All of the calories in this product come from 7 teaspoons added sugar. Besides sugar calories, it contains no nutrients.

ADDITIVES: Contains artificial color and flavor, which some studies suggest may adversely affect behavior and the ability to complete school tasks in some sensitive children; artificial colors are inadequately tested, and artificial flavor may cause allergic reactions in sensitive individuals.

DID YOU KNOW: Most sports doctors don't believe it is necessary to replace salt and other minerals lost in sweat unless an athlete loses 5 to 10 pounds during a workout or event. Plain tap water is usually recommended as the ideal fluid replacement.

FAYGO ROCK & RYE CREME COLA
Faygo Beverages, Inc.

Ingredients: carbonated water, sugar (and/or corn sweetener), citric acid, benzoate of soda, artificial color and flavor.

Amount: 12 fl oz			% USRDA
Calories	144	Protein	*
Protein, gm	0e	Vitamin A	*
Carbohydrates, gm	36	Vitamin C	*
Fat, gm	0	Thiamine	*
Sodium, mg	94	Riboflavin	*
Cholesterol, mg	0	Niacin	*
Fiber, gm	0	Calcium	*
		Iron	*

THIS FOOD: All of the calories in this product come from 9 teaspoons added sugar. Besides sugar calories, it contains no nutrients.

ADDITIVES: Contains artificial color and flavor, which some studies suggest may adversely affect behavior and the ability to complete school tasks in some sensitive children; artificial colors are inadequately tested, and artificial flavor may cause allergic reactions in some sensitive individuals.

GATORADE
Quaker Oats Co.

Ingredients: water, glucose, sucrose, citric acid, salt, sodium citrate, potassium, phosphate, natural flavor, ester gum, and artificial color.

Amount: 12 fl oz			% USRDA
Calories	75	Protein	*
Protein, gm	0	Vitamin A	*
Carbohydrates, gm	21	Vitamin C	*
Fat, gm	0	Thiamine	*
Sodium, mg	175	Riboflavin	*
Cholesterol, mg	0	Niacin	*
Fiber, gm	0	Calcium	*
		Iron	*

THIS FOOD: Gatorade is intended as a drink for athletes before, during, and after prolonged exertion. It has only about half the sugar of most sweetened juice drinks, which makes it preferable as a fluid replacement. It also contains sodium and potassium, intended to replace the minerals lost along with perspiration.

ADDITIVES: Contains artificial colors, which are inadequately tested, and which some studies suggest may adversely affect behavior and the ability to complete school tasks in some sensitive children.

PEPSI-COLA
PepsiCo, Inc.

Ingredients: carbonated water, sugar, caramel color, phosphoric acid, caffeine, citric acid, natural flavorings.

Amount: 12 fl oz			% USRDA
Calories	156	Protein	*
Protein, gm	0	Vitamin A	*
Carbohydrates, gm	39	Vitamin C	*
Fat, gm	0	Thiamine	*
Sodium, mg	9	Riboflavin	*
Cholesterol, mg	0	Niacin	*
Fiber, gm	0	Calcium	*
		Iron	*

THIS FOOD: All of the calories in this soft drink come from 9½ teaspoons added sugar. Besides sugar calories, it contains no nutrients.

ADDITIVES: Contains caffeine, which may adversely affect behavior, motor activity, or sleep, especially in young children. Most experts agree that caffeine should be avoided by pregnant or nursing mothers and young children.

7-UP
Philip Morris, Inc.

Ingredients: carbonated water, sugar and/or corn sweetener, citric acid, sodium citrate, natural lemon and lime flavors.

Amount: 12 fl oz			% USRDA
Calories	144	Protein	*
Protein, gm	0	Vitamin A	*
Carbohydrates, gm	36	Vitamin C	*
Fat, gm	0	Thiamine	*
Sodium, mg	4	Riboflavin	*
Cholesterol, mg	0	Niacin	*
Fiber, gm	0	Calcium	*
		Iron	*

THIS FOOD: Although a recent advertising campaign describes 7-Up as "less sweet," it actually contains more sugar than all of the major cola drinks. All of the calories in this product come from 9 teaspoons added sugar. Besides sugar calories, it contains no nutrients.

ADDITIVES: No questionable additives.

SHASTA COLA
Consolidated Foods, Inc.

Ingredients: carbonated water, high-fructose corn sweetener, caramel color, phosphoric acid, natural flavor, caffeine, gum arabic.

Amount: 12 fl oz			% USRDA
Calories	95	Protein	*
Protein, gm	0	Vitamin A	*
Carbohydrates, gm	26	Vitamin C	*
Fat, gm	0	Thiamine	*
Sodium, mg	1	Riboflavin	*
Cholesterol, mg	0	Niacin	*
Fiber, gm	0	Calcium	*
		Iron	*

THIS FOOD: All of the calories in this soft drink come from 6½ teaspoons added sugar. It contains no vitamins or minerals.

ADDITIVES: Contains caffeine, which may adversely affect behavior, motor activity, or sleep, especially in young children. Most experts agree that caffeine should be avoided by pregnant or nursing mothers, and young children.

SHASTA GINGER ALE
Consolidated Foods, Inc.

Ingredients: carbonated water, high-fructose corn sweetener, citric acid, natural flavor, caramel color, sodium benzoate.

Amount: 12 fl oz			% USRDA
Calories	78	Protein	*
Protein, gm	0	Vitamin A	*
Carbohydrates, gm	21	Vitamin C	*
Fat, gm	0	Thiamine	*
Sodium, mg	14	Riboflavin	*
Cholesterol, mg	0	Niacin	*
Fiber, gm	0	Calcium	*
		Iron	*

THIS FOOD: All of the calories in this soft drink come from 5 teaspoons added sugar. It contains no vitamins or minerals.

ADDITIVES: No questionable additives.

SHASTA ROOT BEER
Consolidated Foods, Inc.

Ingredients: carbonated water, high-fructose corn sweetener, caramel color, artificial and natural flavorings, yucca, propylene glycol, citric acid, sodium citrate, gum arabic, sodium benzoate.

Amount: 12 fl oz			% USRDA
Calories	100	Protein	*
Protein, gm	0	Vitamin A	*
Carbohydrates, gm	27	Vitamin C	*
Fat, gm	0	Thiamine	*
Sodium, mg	30	Riboflavin	*
Cholesterol, mg	0	Niacin	*
Fiber, gm	0	Calcium	*
		Iron	*

THIS FOOD: All of the calories in this soft drink come from 6¾ teaspoons added sugar. It contains no vitamins or minerals.

ADDITIVES: Contains artificial flavor, which may cause allergic reactions in sensitive individuals, and which some studies suggest may adversely affect behavior and the ability to complete school tasks in some sensitive children.

SHASTA SUGAR FREE DIET CHERRY COLA
Consolidated Foods, Inc.

Ingredients: carbonated water, caramel color, phosphoric acid, sodium saccharin, citric acid, sodium citrate, natural and artificial flavor, caffeine, gum arabic, sodium benzoate.

Amount: 12 fl oz			% USRDA
Calories	30	Protein	*
Protein, gm	0	Vitamin A	*
Carbohydrates, gm	0	Vitamin C	*
Fat, gm	0	Thiamine	*
Sodium, mg	53	Riboflavin	*
Cholesterol, mg	0	Niacin	*
Fiber, gm	0	Calcium	*
		Iron	*

THIS FOOD: This artificially flavored soft drink contains no nutrients.

ADDITIVES: Contains artificial color and flavor, which some studies suggest may adversely affect behavior and the ability to complete school tasks in some sensitive children; artificial colors are inadequately tested, and artificial flavor may cause allergic reactions in sensitive individuals. Also contains sodium saccharin, which causes cancer in laboratory animals. This additive is currently being investigated and should only be used in small amounts by healthy adults. Also contains caffeine, which may adversely affect behavior, motor activity, or sleep, especially in young children. Most experts agree that caffeine should be avoided by pregnant or nursing mothers and young children.

SHASTA SUGAR FREE DIET LEMON LIME SODA
Consolidated Foods, Inc.

Ingredients: carbonated water, citric acid, sodium saccharin, sodium citrate, natural flavor, sodium benzoate.

Amount: 12 fl oz			% USRDA
Calories	0	Protein	*
Protein, gm	0	Vitamin A	*
Carbohydrates, gm	0	Vitamin C	*
Fat, gm	0	Thiamine	*
Sodium, mg	49	Riboflavin	*
Cholesterol, mg	0	Niacin	*
Fiber, gm	0	Calcium	*
		Iron	*

THIS FOOD: This artificially sweetened soft drink contains no useful nutrients.

ADDITIVES: Contains sodium saccharin, which causes cancer in laboratory animals. This additive is currently being investigated and should only be used in small amounts by healthy adults.

SHASTA SUGAR FREE DIET ORANGE SODA
Consolidated Foods, Inc.

Ingredients: carbonated water, citric acid, gum arabic, sodium saccharin, sodium citrate, natural flavor, glycerol abietate, artificial color, brominated vegetable oil, sodium benzoate.

Amount: 12 fl oz			% USRDA
Calories	0	Protein	*
Protein, gm	0	Vitamin A	*
Carbohydrates, gm	0	Vitamin C	*
Fat, gm	0	Thiamine	*
Sodium, mg	52	Riboflavin	*
Cholesterol, mg	0	Niacin	*
Fiber, gm	0	Calcium	*
		Iron	*

THIS FOOD: This artificially sweetened soft drink contains no useful nutrients.

ADDITIVES: Contains artificial colors, which are inadequately tested, and which some studies suggest may adversely affect behavior and the ability to complete school tasks in some sensitive children, and sodium saccharin, which causes cancer in laboratory animals. This additive is currently being investigated and should only be used in small amounts by healthy adults.

DID YOU KNOW: A 12-ounce cola drink contains 30 to 65 milligrams caffeine. For a young child, this can equal the stimulant effect that 2 to 3 cups of coffee would have on an adult.

HELPFUL HINT: Instead of drinking additive-laden, sugary sodas, try mixing club soda or seltzer with an equal amount of orange or other unsweetened fruit juice. Remember, a mere 4 ounces of orange juice contains more than 3 teaspoons of naturally occurring sugar, so your sweet tooth shouldn't go unsatisfied with these healthful thirst quenchers.

Soft Drink Mixes

COUNTRY TIME LEMONADE FLAVOR SUGAR FREE DRINK MIX

General Foods Corp.

Ingredients: citric acid, aspartame (contains phenylalanine), calcium phosphate, maltodextrin (from corn), potassium citrate, natural lemon flavor with other natural flavors, vitamin C, artificial color (including FD & C Yellow No. 5), BHA.

Amount: 8 fl oz			% USRDA
Calories	4	Protein	*
Protein, gm	0	Vitamin A	*
Carbohydrates, gm	0	Vitamin C	15
Fat, gm	0	Thiamine	*
Sodium, mg	0	Riboflavin	*
Cholesterol, mg	0	Niacin	*
Fiber, gm	0	Calcium	*
		Iron	*

THIS FOOD: The flavoring in Country Time Lemonade Flavor Sugar Free Drink Mix is natural, but it is artificially sweetened and colored. This drink contains a small amount of added vitamin C.

ADDITIVES: Contains aspartame (with phenylalanine), which should be avoided by people with PKU, a rare genetic disease, and which many experts believe has been inadequately tested for long-term safety; and artificial color, which can cause allergic reactions in sensitive individuals, and which some studies suggest may adversely affect behavior and the ability to complete school tasks in some sensitive children. Also contains Yellow No. 5, which can cause allergic reactions, especially in aspirin-sensitive individuals, and BHA, whose long-term safety is currently being reexamined by FDA investigators.

CRYSTAL LIGHT ORANGE FLAVOR SUGAR FREE DRINK MIX
General Foods Corp.

Ingredients: citric acid, natural orange flavor, maltodextrin (from corn), tricalcium phosphate, potassium citrate, aspartame (contains phenylalanine), artificial flavor, xanthan gum, artificial color (including FD & C Yellow No. 5), vitamin C, orange juice solids, BHA, and alpha-tocopherol.

Amount: 8 fl oz			% USRDA
Calories	4	Protein	*
Protein, gm	0	Vitamin A	*
Carbohydrates, gm	0	Vitamin C	10
Fat, gm	0	Thiamine	*
Sodium, mg	0	Riboflavin	*
Cholesterol, mg	0	Niacin	*
Fiber, gm	0	Calcium	6
		Iron	*

THIS FOOD: Crystal Light Orange Flavor Sugar Free Drink Mix contains natural flavors along with artificial flavor, color, and sweetening. Like many drink mixes, it contains a small amount of added vitamin C.

ADDITIVES: Contains aspartame (with phenylalanine), which should be avoided by people with PKU, a rare genetic disease, and which many experts believe has been inadequately tested for long-term safety. Contains artificial color and flavor, which some studies suggest may adversely affect behavior and the ability to complete school tasks in some sensitive children; artificial colors are inadequately tested and artificial flavor may cause allergic reactions in sensitive individuals. Also contains Yellow No. 5, which can cause allergic reactions, especially in aspirin-sensitive individuals, and BHA, whose long-term safety is currently being reexamined by FDA investigators.

KOOL-AID GRAPE FLAVOR SUGAR-FREE SOFT DRINK MIX
General Foods Corp.

Ingredients: citric acid, monocalcium phosphate, aspartame (contains phenylalanine), maltodextrin (from corn), natural and artificial flavor, artificial color, vitamin C.

Amount: 8 fl oz			% USRDA
Calories	2	Protein	*
Protein, gm	0	Vitamin A	*
Carbohydrates, gm	0	Vitamin C	10
Fat, gm	0	Thiamine	*
Sodium, mg	0	Riboflavin	*
Cholesterol, mg	0	Niacin	*
Fiber, gm	0	Calcium	4
		Iron	*

THIS FOOD: Kool-Aid Sugar-Free Drink Mixes are almost entirely fake—an artificially colored, flavored, and sweetened soft drink. Apart from a small amount of added vitamin C, this product contains no nutrients at all.

ADDITIVES: Contains aspartame (with phenylalanine), which should be avoided by people with PKU, a rare genetic disease, and which many experts believe has been inadequately tested for long-term safety. Contains artificial color and flavor, which some studies suggest may adversely affect behavior and the ability to complete school tasks in some sensitive children; artificial colors are inadequately tested and artificial flavor may cause allergic reactions in sensitive individuals.

KOOL-AID RAINBOW PUNCH FLAVOR SUGAR-SWEETENED SOFT DRINK MIX
General Foods Corp.

Ingredients: sugar, citric acid, natural and artificial flavors, xanthan gum, artificial color, vitamin C, BHA.

Amount: 8 fl oz			% USRDA
Calories	90	Protein	*
Protein, gm	0	Vitamin A	*
Carbohydrates, gm	22	Vitamin C	10
Fat, gm	0	Thiamine	*
Sodium, mg	0	Riboflavin	*
Cholesterol, mg	0	Niacin	*
Fiber, gm	0	Calcium	*
		Iron	*

THIS FOOD: Kool-Aid sugar-sweetened drink mixes are almost all sugar, and the rest of the ingredients are almost entirely fake—an artificially colored and flavored soft drink. Apart from a small amount of added vitamin C, they contain no nutrients at all. One hundred percent of the calories in this product derive from sugar.

ADDITIVES: Contains artificial color and flavor, which some studies suggest may adversely affect behavior and the ability to complete school tasks in some sensitive children; artificial colors are inadequately tested and artificial flavor may cause allergic reactions in sensitive individuals. Also contains BHA, whose long-term safety is currently being reexamined by FDA investigators.

KOOL-AID STRAWBERRY FLAVOR UNSWEETENED SOFT DRINK MIX
General Foods Corp.

Ingredients: citric acid, calcium phosphates, artificial flavor, salt, sodium citrate, artificial color, vitamin C.

Amount: 8 fl oz			% USRDA
Calories	100	Protein	*
Protein, gm	0	Vitamin A	*
Carbohydrates, gm	25	Vitamin C	15
Fat, gm	0	Thiamine	*
Sodium, mg	35	Riboflavin	*
Cholesterol, mg	0	Niacin	*
Fiber, gm	0	Calcium	4
		Iron	*

THIS FOOD: Kool-Aid unsweetened drink mixes are almost entirely fake—an artificially colored and flavored soft-drink. Apart from a small amount of added vitamin C, they contain no nutrients at all. One hundred percent of the calories in this product derive from sugar.

ADDITIVES: Contains artificial color and flavor, which some studies suggest may adversely affect behavior and the ability to complete school tasks in some sensitive children; artificial colors are inadequately tested and artificial flavor may cause allergic reactions in sensitive individuals.

KOOL-AID TROPICAL PUNCH FLAVOR SUGAR-FREE SOFT DRINK MIX
General Foods Corp.

Ingredients: citric acid, monocalcium phosphate, natural and artificial flavor, maltodextrin (from corn), aspartame (contains phenylalanine), xanthan gum and cellulose gum, artificial color, vitamin C, BHA.

Amount: 8 fl oz			% USRDA
Calories	4	Protein	*
Protein, gm	0	Vitamin A	*
Carbohydrates, gm	0	Vitamin C	10
Fat, gm	0	Thiamine	*
Sodium, mg	1	Riboflavin	*
Cholesterol, mg	0	Niacin	*
Fiber, gm	0	Calcium	4
		Iron	*

THIS FOOD: Kool-Aid Sugar-Free Drink Mixes are almost entirely artificial. Apart from a small amount of added vitamin C, they contain no nutrients at all.

ADDITIVES: Contains aspartame (with phenylalanine), which should be avoided by people with PKU, a rare genetic disease, and which many experts believe has been inadequately tested for long-term safety. Contains artificial color and flavor, which some studies suggest may adversely affect behavior and the ability to complete school tasks in some sensitive children; artificial colors are inadequately tested and artificial flavor may cause allergic reactions in sensitive individuals; and BHA, whose long-term safety is currently being reexamined by FDA investigators.

LIPTON ICED TEA MIX
Unilever United States, Inc.

Ingredients: sugar, citric acid, instant tea, natural lemon flavor, tricalcium phosphate.

Amount: 2 tbsp (+ 8 fl oz water)			% USRDA
Calories	60	Protein	*
Protein, gm	0	Vitamin A	*
Carbohydrates, gm	16	Vitamin C	*
Fat, gm	0	Thiamine	*
Sodium, mg	0e	Riboflavin	*
Cholesterol, mg	0	Niacin	*
Fiber, gm	0	Calcium	*
		Iron	*

THIS FOOD: Lipton Iced Tea Mix supplies sugar calories but no nutrients. It contains about 30 mg caffeine per serving.

ADDITIVES: Contains naturally occurring caffeine. Many experts believe that caffeine intake should be avoided by pregnant and nursing mothers, young children, and anyone with gastrointestinal or heart ailments.

LIPTON SUGAR-FREE LEMON ICED TEA MIX
Unilever United States, Inc.

Ingredients: citric acid, instant tea, maltodextrin, sodium saccharin, natural lemon flavor.

Amount: 2 tbsp (+ 8 fl oz water)			% USRDA
Calories	2	Protein	*
Protein, gm	0	Vitamin A	*
Carbohydrates, gm	0	Vitamin C	*
Fat, gm	0	Thiamine	*
Sodium, mg	na	Riboflavin	*
Cholesterol, mg	0	Niacin	*
Fiber, gm	0	Calcium	*
		Iron	*

THIS FOOD: Lipton's Sugar-Free Lemon Iced Tea Mix is artificially sweetened and supplies about 35 mg caffeine per serving. Like most teas, it is extremely low in nutrients.

ADDITIVES: Contains naturally occurring caffeine. Many experts believe that caffeine intake should be avoided by pregnant and nursing mothers, young children, and anyone with gastrointestinal or heart ailments.

NESTEA SUGAR AND LEMON FLAVORED ICED TEA MIX
Nestlé, S.A.

Ingredients: sugar, citric acid, instant tea, natural lemon flavor.

Amount: 8 fl oz			% USRDA
Calories	90	Protein	*
Protein, gm	0	Vitamin A	*
Carbohydrates, gm	22	Vitamin C	*
Fat, gm	0	Thiamine	*
Sodium, mg	<10	Riboflavin	*
Cholesterol, mg	0	Niacin	*
Fiber, gm	0	Calcium	*
		Iron	*

THIS FOOD: Nestlé Iced Tea Mix supplies sugar calories but no nutrients. It contains about 30 mg caffeine per serving.

ADDITIVES: Contains naturally occurring caffeine. Many experts believe that caffeine intake should be avoided by pregnant and nursing mothers, young children, and anyone with gastrointestinal or heart ailments.

TANG ORANGE FLAVOR BREAKFAST BEVERAGE CRYSTALS
General Foods Corp.

Ingredients: sugar, citric acid, maltodextrin (from corn), potassium citrate, vitamin C, orange juice solids, monocalcium phosphate, artificial color (including FD & C Yellow No. 5), natural orange flavor, xanthan and cellulose gums, artificial flavor, vitamin A palmitate, folic acid, BHA and alpha-tocopherol.

Amount: 8 fl oz			% USRDA
Calories	120	Protein	*
Protein, gm	0	Vitamin A	13
Carbohydrates, gm	29	Vitamin C	133
Fat, gm	0	Thiamine	*
Sodium, mg	0	Riboflavin	*
Cholesterol, mg	0	Niacin	*
Fiber, gm	0	Calcium	3
		Iron	*

THIS FOOD: Tang Orange Flavor Breakfast Beverage contains natural flavors, along with artificial flavor and color. All of its calories come from sugar—5½ teaspoons per 6-ounce glass. It is rich in added vitamin C and is also supplemented with vitamin A.

ADDITIVES: Contains artificial color and flavor, which some studies suggest may adversely affect behavior and the ability to complete school tasks in some sensitive children; artificial colors are inadequately tested, and artificial flavor may cause allergic reactions in sensitive individuals. Also contains Yellow No. 5, which can cause allergic reactions, especially in aspirin-sensitive individuals; and BHA, whose long-term safety is currently being reexamined by FDA investigators.

WYLER'S SUGAR FREE WILD GRAPE DRINK MIX
Borden, Inc.

Ingredients: malic acid, dextrin, aspartame (contains phenylalanine), artificial and natural flavors, salt, ascorbic acid, artificial colors.

Amount: 8 fl oz			% USRDA
Calories	4	Protein	*
Protein, gm	0	Vitamin A	*
Carbohydrates, gm	1	Vitamin C	15
Fat, gm	0	Thiamine	*
Sodium, mg	20	Riboflavin	*
Cholesterol, mg	0	Niacin	*
Fiber, gm	0	Calcium	*
		Iron	*

THIS FOOD: Wyler's Sugar Free Wild Grape Drink Mix also contains some natural flavors, along with artificial color and sweetening. Like many drink mixes, it contains a small amount of added vitamin C.

ADDITIVES: Contains aspartame (with phenylalanine), which should be avoided by people with PKU, a rare genetic disease, and which many experts believe has been inadequately tested for long-term safety. Contains artificial color and flavor, which some studies suggest may adversely affect behavior and the ability to complete school tasks in some sensitive children; artificial colors are inadequately tested, and artificial flavor may cause allergic reactions in sensitive individuals.

HELPFUL HINT: If you must use soft-drink mixes, you are better off using unsweetened varieties and consciously cutting down on the amount of sugar you add.

SOUP

It probably comes as no surprise that Campbell's dominates a full 80 percent of this nearly $2-billion-a-year industry. Anyone who has been in a supermarket and seen the entire soup aisle filled with row upon row of familiar red-and-white labels can't help noticing Campbell's obvious strength in this market.

It's hard to discuss the nutritional value of soup in general, because it changes from variety to variety. For example, in nutritional terms, Campbell's two best sellers, Tomato Soup and Chicken Noodle Soup, are low in nutrients compared to Progresso's version of the same soups—or to other varieties within the Campbell's line. At its best, soup can be a good source of protein, complex carbohydrates, dietary fiber, vitamin A, vitamin C, and iron—but none of the brands profiled provide all these nutrients at once. Generally, the legume-based soups, such as Campbell Chunky Old-Fashioned Bean Soup, Progresso Green Split Pea, and Progresso Minestrone, are richest in nutrients. Almost without exception, soups made from dry mixes are less nutritious than soup in cans. Amid all this variety, there is one reliable constant: commercially prepared soup is high in salt.

So what does all this mean? Is soup good for you? The New York attorney general's office has its doubts. In October 1984, in the wake of an investigation into Campbell's allegedly misleading advertising practices, Attorney General Robert Abrams stated: "Failing to mention the sodium content in an advertisement geared to promote soup as a component of a healthy diet is dangerously misleading. . . ." Typical canned soups contain 800 to more than 1,000 mg sodium per 1-cup serving, or up to a half teaspoon of salt. Since the recommended daily intake for sodium is only 1,100–3,300 mg, it's easy to see why the vast majority of prepared soups are a poor choice for anyone interested in reducing their sodium intake.

In response to consumer concern about sodium, Campbell's introduced a low-sodium line of soups—a welcome addition to their many regular varieties.

SODIUM GUIDELINES: In evaluating the sodium content of canned and packaged soups, we used the following standards:

500 mg to 750 mg	high in sodium
more than 750 mg	very high in sodium

Remember, these guidelines are not for people following medically restricted low sodium diets, but for healthy individuals who wish to monitor their sodium intake.

SUPER SOURCES OF VITAMIN A

These soups contain more than 75 percent of the USRDA for vitamin A:

Campbell's Chunky Beef Soup
Campbell's Chunky Minestrone Soup
Campbell's Chunky Old Fashioned Bean 'n Ham Soup
Campbell's Chunky Vegetable Soup

SODIUM LOSERS

These soups contain more than 900 mg sodium, or nearly ½ teaspoon salt per cup:

Campbell's Beefy Mushroom Soup
Campbell's Chicken Noodle Soup
Campbell's Chunky Chicken Noodle Soup

Campbell's Chunky Old Fashioned Bean 'n Ham Soup
Campbell's French Onion Soup
Campbell's Minestrone Soup
Campbell's New England Clam Chowder
Lipton Chicken Noodle Soup with Chicken Meat Mix
Lipton Chicken Rice Soup Mix
Lipton Country Vegetable Soup Mix
Progresso Tomato Soup

CAMPBELL'S BEEF SOUP
Campbell Soup Co.

Ingredients: beef stock, water, beef, tomatoes, barley, carrots, potatoes, celery, salt, yeast extract and hydrolyzed plant protein, cornstarch, peas, potato starch, wheat flour, caramel color, beef fat, natural flavoring.

Amount: 1 cup			% USRDA
Calories	80	Protein	8
Protein, gm	5	Vitamin A	20
Carbohydrates, gm	10	Vitamin C	2
Fat, gm	2	Thiamine	*
Sodium, mg	855	Riboflavin	2
Cholesterol, mg	7e	Niacin	4
Fiber, gm	1e	Calcium	*
		Iron	4

THIS FOOD: Campbell's Beef Soup is a low-calorie product that also supplies 20 percent of the USRDA for vitamin A. Compared to other soups it is relatively high in protein. Like most canned soups, it is very high in sodium.

ADDITIVES: No questionable additives.

CAMPBELL'S BEEFY MUSHROOM SOUP
Campbell Soup Co.

Ingredients: beef stock, water, beef, mushrooms, modified food starch, salt, yeast extract and hydrolyzed plant protein, vegetable oil, wheat flour, potato starch, monosodium glutamate, dehydrated onions, beef fat, caramel color, natural flavoring.

NOTE: The letter "e" indicates that the data has been estimated; < means "less than" and is used for small amounts of sodium or cholesterol; * means food contains less than 2% of USRDA; "na" means that the information was not available and appears only when data is insufficient.

Amount: 1 cup			% USRDA
Calories	60	Protein	8
Protein, gm	4	Vitamin A	*
Carbohydrates, gm	5	Vitamin C	*
Fat, gm	3	Thiamine	*
Sodium, mg	990	Riboflavin	2
Cholesterol, mg	7e	Niacin	4
Fiber, gm	<1	Calcium	*
		Iron	2

THIS FOOD: Campbell's Beefy Mushroom Soup is higher than average in protein, but does not provide other nutrients. Forty-five percent of its calories derive from fat. Like most soups, it is very high in sodium.

ADDITIVES: Contains monosodium glutamate (MSG), which many authorities believe should be avoided by infants and very young children; causes adverse reactions in some sensitive individuals.

CAMPBELL'S CHICKEN NOODLE SOUP
Campbell Soup Co.

Ingredients: chicken stock, enriched egg noodles, chicken, water, salt, margarine, cornstarch, monosodium glutamate, dehydrated onions, yeast extract, natural flavoring, dehydrated garlic.

Amount: 1 cup			% USRDA
Calories	70	Protein	4
Protein, gm	3	Vitamin A	6
Carbohydrates, gm	8	Vitamin C	*
Fat, gm	3	Thiamine	4
Sodium, mg	935	Riboflavin	2
Cholesterol, mg	7e	Niacin	6
Fiber, gm	<1e	Calcium	*
		Iron	2

THIS FOOD: Campbell's Chicken Noodle Soup has been a perennial favorite for more than half a century. Unfortunately, it is low in nutrients, and contains 38 percent fat calories—which is higher than average for this category.

ADDITIVES: Contains monosodium glutamate (MSG), which many authorities believe should be avoided by infants and very young children; causes adverse reactions in some sensitive individuals.

OTHER BRANDS: Campbell's Low Sodium Chicken with Noodles Soup has only 67 mg sodium, contains no MSG, and derives only 28 percent of its calories from fat.

CAMPBELL'S CHICKEN VEGETABLE SOUP
Campbell Soup Co.

Ingredients: chicken stock, potatoes, carrots, tomatoes, enriched egg noodles, chicken meat, green beans, peas, zucchini, celery, salt, potato starch, lima beans, margarine, yeast extract and hydrolyzed plant protein, monosodium glutamate, dehydrated onions, chicken fat, natural flavoring, dehydrated garlic, dehydrated parsley.

Amount: 1 cup			% USRDA
Calories	70	Protein	4
Protein, gm	3	Vitamin A	50
Carbohydrates, gm	8	Vitamin C	*
Fat, gm	3	Thiamine	2
Sodium, mg	880	Riboflavin	2
Cholesterol, mg	17e	Niacin	4
Fiber, gm	1e	Calcium	*
		Iron	2

THIS FOOD: Campbell's Chicken Vegetable Soup is rich in vitamin A and low in calories, but 38 percent of those calories derive from fat. Like most soups, it is very high in sodium.

ADDITIVES: Contains monosodium glutamate (MSG), which many authorities believe should be avoided by infants and very young children; causes adverse reactions in some sensitive individuals.

OTHER BRANDS: Progresso Home Style Chicken Soup derives 27 percent of its calories from fat, substantially less than Campbell's.

CAMPBELL'S CHUNKY BEEF SOUP
Campbell Soup Co.

Ingredients: beef stock, potatoes, carrots, tomatoes, cooked beef, peas, water, potato starch, cornstarch, wheat flour, beef fat, yeast extract and hydrolyzed plant protein, salt, caramel color, natural flavoring.

Amount: 1 cup			% USRDA
Calories	141	Protein	19
Protein, gm	10	Vitamin A	89
Carbohydrates, gm	17	Vitamin C	7
Fat, gm	4	Thiamine	3
Sodium, mg	886	Riboflavin	7
Cholesterol, mg	14e	Niacin	7
Fiber, gm	2e	Calcium	*
		Iron	7

THIS FOOD: This soup is a very good source of protein and complex carbohydrates, an excellent source of vitamin A, and also supplies some dietary fiber. Like most soups, it is very high in sodium.

ADDITIVES: No questionable additives.

FOR SODIUM WATCHERS: If you are concerned with your sodium intake, choose from Campbell's low-sodium line of soups, which have no more than 100 milligrams sodium per serving:

FOR SODIUM WATCHERS: If you are concerned with your sodium intake, choose from Campbell's low-sodium line of soups, which have no more than 100 milligrams sodium per serving:

CAMPBELL'S CHUNKY CHICKEN NOODLE SOUP
Campbell Soup Co.

Ingredients: chicken stock, chicken, enriched egg noodles, mushrooms, carrots, celery, Sauterne wine, cornstarch, water, salt, sweet peppers, potato starch, yeast extract and hydrolyzed plant protein, monosodium glutamate, natural flavoring, dehydrated parsley.

Amount: 1 cup			% USRDA
Calories	152	Protein	21
Protein, gm	10	Vitamin A	17
Carbohydrates, gm	15	Vitamin C	3
Fat, gm	6	Thiamine	*
Sodium, mg	901	Riboflavin	3
Cholesterol, mg	18e	Niacin	13
Fiber, gm	1e	Calcium	*
		Iron	3

Contains about 1 teaspoon fat and ½ teaspoon salt.

THIS FOOD: Campbell's Chunky Chicken Noodle Soup is a very good source of protein, vitamin A, and niacin. Like most soups, it is very high in sodium.

ADDITIVES: Contains monosodium glutamate (MSG), which many authorities believe should be avoided by infants and very young children; causes adverse reactions in some sensitive individuals.

CAMPBELL'S CHUNKY MINESTRONE SOUP
Campbell Soup Co.

Ingredients: water, tomatoes, potatoes, carrots, celery, green beans, butter beans, zucchini, enriched macaroni product (enriched with niacin, ferrous sulfate, thiamine mononitrate, riboflavin), potato starch, Parmesan cheese, pork, peas, rutabagas, spinach, salt, dehydrated onion, yeast extract, natural flavoring, dehydrated parsley, dehydrated garlic.

Amount: 1 cup			% USRDA
Calories	118	Protein	5
Protein, gm	3	Vitamin A	84
Carbohydrates, gm	18	Vitamin C	5
Fat, gm	4	Thiamine	*
Sodium, mg	829	Riboflavin	3
Cholesterol, mg	5e	Niacin	3
Fiber, gm	2e	Calcium	5
		Iron	5

Contains about 1 teaspoon naturally occurring sugar, nearly 1 teaspoon fat, and more than ⅓ teaspoon salt.

THIS FOOD: One serving of this soup supplies 84 percent of the USRDA for vitamin A, along with a small amount of dietary fiber and complex carbohydrates. It is very high in sodium.

ADDITIVES: No questionable additives.

OTHER BRANDS: Progresso Minestrone has 35 percent less sodium (531 milligrams per serving) and twice as much protein, iron, and fiber as Campbell's Chunky Minestrone. If you are concerned with your sodium intake, choose from Campbell's low-sodium soups, which have less than 100 milligrams sodium per serving.

CAMPBELL'S CHUNKY OLD FASHIONED BEAN 'N HAM SOUP
Campbell Soup Co.

Ingredients: water, cooked beans, ham (cured with water, salt, sugar, sodium phosphate, sodium ascorbate, sodium nitrite), carrots, celery, potato starch, vegetable oil, wheat flour, salt, cornstarch, dextrose, monosodium glutamate, yeast extract, natural flavoring, smoke flavoring.

Amount: 1 cup			% USRDA
Calories	237	Protein	20
Protein, gm	11	Vitamin A	82
Carbohydrates, gm	30	Vitamin C	6
Fat, gm	7	Thiamine	8
Sodium, mg	965	Riboflavin	5
Cholesterol, mg	22e	Niacin	8
Fiber, gm	6e	Calcium	8
		Iron	12

Contains about 1 teaspoon sugar, 1½ teaspoons fat, and ½ teaspoon salt.

THIS FOOD: An excellent source of vitamin A, and a good source of dietary fiber, complex carbohydrates, protein, and iron. It supplies 237 calories (25 percent of them from fat), which is higher than average. Overall, the calories are well worth it in terms of the excellent nutritional values supplied. This product is very high in sodium.

ADDITIVES: Contains sodium nitrite, which can be converted into cancer-causing substances called nitrosamines; also contains monosodium glutamate (MSG), which many authorities believe should be avoided by infants and very young children; causes adverse reactions in some sensitive individuals.

OTHER BRANDS: Progresso Green Split Pea is another legume soup rich in fiber, iron, protein, and complex carbohydrates but without questionable additives. For those concerned with their salt intake, choose from Campbell's eight low-sodium varieties.

CAMPBELL'S CHUNKY STEAK 'N POTATO SOUP
Campbell Soup Co.

Ingredients: beef stock, potatoes, cooked beef, mushrooms, tomatoes, water, modified food starch, wheat flour, Burgundy wine, vegetable oil, salt, potato starch, monosodium glutamate, yeast extract and hydrolyzed plant protein, caramel color, beef fat, natural flavoring.

Amount: 1 cup			% USRDA
Calories	216	Protein	19
Protein, gm	10	Vitamin A	74
Carbohydrates, gm	27	Vitamin C	6
Fat, gm	7	Thiamine	7
Sodium, mg	878	Riboflavin	4
Cholesterol, mg	16e	Niacin	7
Fiber, gm	2e	Calcium	7
		Iron	11

THIS FOOD: Rich in vitamin A, protein, complex carbohydrates, iron; has some dietary fiber. It is very high in sodium.

ADDITIVES: Contains monosodium glutamate (MSG), which many authorities believe should be avoided by infants and very young children; causes adverse reactions in some sensitive individuals.

CAMPBELL'S CHUNKY VEGETABLE SOUP
Campbell Soup Co.

Ingredients: water, carrots, potatoes, celery, green beans, tomatoes, peas, zucchini, corn, lima beans, cornstarch, partially hydrogenated vegetable oil, (soybean, cottonseed), cabbage, salt, yeast extract and hydrolyzed plant protein, sweet peppers, monosodium glutamate, natural flavoring, caramel color.

Amount: 1 cup			% USRDA
Calories	104	Protein	4
Protein, gm	3	Vitamin A	126
Carbohydrates, gm	17	Vitamin C	7
Fat, gm	3	Thiamine	*
Sodium, mg	837	Riboflavin	3
Cholesterol, mg	0	Niacin	4
Fiber, gm	3e	Calcium	4
		Iron	6

THIS FOOD: An excellent source of vitamin A and also supplies dietary fiber. Like most prepared soups, it is very high in sodium.

ADDITIVES: Contains monosodium glutamate (MSG), which many authorities believe should be avoided by infants and very young children; causes adverse reactions in some sensitive individuals.

CAMPBELL'S CREAM OF CELERY SOUP
Campbell Soup Co.

Ingredients: water, celery, wheat flour, partially hydrogenated vegetable oil (soybean, palm, or cottonseed oil), cream, salt, cornstarch, dried dairy blend (whey, calcium caseinate), margarine (partially hydrogenated soybean oil, water, beta carotene), whey, monosodium glutamate, soy protein isolate, natural flavoring, yeast extract.

Amount: 1 cup			% USRDA
Calories	100	Protein	2
Protein, gm	1	Vitamin A	4
Carbohydrates, gm	8	Vitamin C	*
Fat, gm	7	Thiamine	*
Sodium, mg	875	Riboflavin	*
Cholesterol, mg	15e	Niacin	*
Fiber, gm	<1e	Calcium	2
		Iron	*

THIS FOOD: Campbell's Cream of Celery Soup is relatively low in desirable nutrients, and, with 63 percent fat calories, it is extremely high in fat. Like most canned soups, it is very high in sodium.

ADDITIVES: Contains monosodium glutamate (MSG), which many authorities believe should be avoided by infants and very young children; causes adverse reactions in some sensitive individuals.

CAMPBELL'S CREAM OF CHICKEN SOUP
Campbell Soup Co.

Ingredients: chicken stock, chicken, wheat flour, cornstarch, cream, vegetable oil, salt, chicken fat, water, margarine, dried dairy blend (whey, calcium casein-ate), dried whey, monosodium glutamate, soy protein isolate, yeast extract, natural flavoring.

Amount: 1 cup			% USRDA
Calories	110	Protein	4
Protein, gm	3	Vitamin A	10
Carbohydrates, gm	9	Vitamin C	*
Fat, gm	7	Thiamine	*
Sodium, mg	860	Riboflavin	2
Cholesterol, mg	10e	Niacin	2
Fiber, gm	<1	Calcium	2
		Iron	*

THIS FOOD: Campbell's Cream of Chicken Soup is relatively low in desirable nutrients, and, with 57 percent fat calories, is extremely high in fat. Like most canned soups, it is very high in sodium.

ADDITIVES: Contains monosodium glutamate (MSG), which many authorities believe should be avoided by infants and very young children; causes adverse reactions in some sensitive individuals.

CAMPBELL'S CREAM OF MUSHROOM SOUP
Campbell Soup Co.

Ingredients: water, mushrooms, partially hydrogenated vegetable oil (soybean, palm or cottonseed oil), wheat flour, cream, salt, cornstarch, dried dairy blend (whey, calcium caseinate), modified food starch, whey, monosodium gluta-mate, soy protein isolate, natural flavoring, yeast extract and dehydrated garlic.

Amount: 1 cup			% USRDA
Calories	100	Protein	2
Protein, gm	1	Vitamin A	*
Carbohydrates, gm	9	Vitamin C	*
Fat, gm	7	Thiamine	*
Sodium. mg	825	Riboflavin	4
Cholesterol, mg	<5e	Niacin	2
Fiber, gm	<1e	Calcium	2
		Iron	*
Contains 2 teaspoons sugar.			

THIS FOOD: Higher in fat and lower in nutrients than most soups. When prepared with water, it gets 63 percent of total calories from fat, much of it saturated. It is not a good source of any nutrient and is very high in sodium.

ADDITIVES: Contains monosodium glutamate (MSG), which many authorities believe should be avoided by infants and very young children; causes adverse reactions in some sensitive individuals.

CAMPBELL'S FRENCH ONION SOUP
Campbell Soup Co.

Ingredients: onions, beef stock, salt, yeast extract and hydrolyzed plant protein, vegetable oil, potato starch, monosodium glutamate, water, enzyme-modified Cheddar cheese, caramel color, beef fat, citric acid, natural flavoring.

Amount: 1 cup			% USRDA
Calories	70	Protein	2
Protein, gm	2	Vitamin A	*
Carbohydrates, gm	9	Vitamin C	2
Fat, gm	2	Thiamine	2
Sodium, mg	960	Riboflavin	*
Cholesterol, mg	5e	Niacin	2
Fiber, gm	1e	Calcium	2
		Iron	2
Contains 1 teaspoon sugar and nearly ½ teaspoon salt.			

THIS FOOD: Has no useful amounts of any nutrient. It is very high in sodium.

ADDITIVES: Contains monosodium glutamate (MSG), which many authorities believe should be avoided by infants and very young children; causes adverse reactions in some sensitive individuals.

CAMPBELL'S LOW SODIUM CHICKEN WITH NOODLES SOUP
Campbell Soup Co.

Ingredients: chicken stock, chicken meat, enriched egg noodles, carrots, celery, water, potato starch, Sauterne wine, yeast extract, chicken fat, sweet peppers, sugar, dehydrated onions, dehydrated garlic, natural flavoring, dehydrated parsley.

Amount: 1 cup			% USRDA
Calories	127	Protein	19
Protein, gm	10	Vitamin A	30
Carbohydrates, gm	13	Vitamin C	6
Fat, gm	4	Thiamine	7
Sodium, mg	67	Riboflavin	15
Cholesterol, mg	18e	Niacin	19
Fiber, gm	na	Calcium	*
		Iron	7
Contains 1 teaspoon sugar.			

THIS FOOD: Compared to most other soups, Campbell's Low Sodium Chicken with Noodles Soup is richer in nutrients. It is high in protein and is an excellent source of vitamin A, and a very good provider of niacin and riboflavin. It contains no added salt.

ADDITIVES: No questionable additives.

CAMPBELL'S LOW SODIUM TOMATO WITH TOMATO PIECES SOUP

Campbell Soup Co.

Ingredients: tomatoes, corn syrup, water, wheat flour, unsalted butter, Sauterne wine, yeast extract, partially hydrogenated vegetable oils (soybean or cottonseed oil), citric acid, natural flavoring, vitamin C.

Amount: 1 cup			% USRDA
Calories	137	Protein	5
Protein, gm	11	Vitamin A	19
Carbohydrates, gm	30	Vitamin C	38
Fat, gm	4	Thiamine	6
Sodium, mg	30	Riboflavin	6
Cholesterol, mg	0	Niacin	11
Fiber, gm	<1	Calcium	3
		Iron	6
Contains 5 teaspoons sugar.			

THIS FOOD: This low-sodium soup contains significant amounts of vitamin C and vitamin A. But to compensate for the flavor loss due to lack of added salt, Campbell's has added more sugar! One serving of this product contains an extraordinary 5 teaspoons of sugar—more than twice the amount in Campbell's regular tomato soup.

ADDITIVES: No questionable additives.

CAMPBELL'S MINESTRONE SOUP

Campbell Soup Co.

Ingredients: beef stock, carrots, potatoes, tomatoes, water, celery, peas, enriched spaghettini, green beans, pea beans, zucchini, salt, vegetable oil, potato starch, cabbage, yeast extract and hydrolyzed plant protein, spinach, rutabagas, monosodium glutamate, enzyme modified Cheddar cheese, natural flavoring.

Amount: 1 cup			% USRDA
Calories	80	Protein	4
Protein, gm	3	Vitamin A	50
Carbohydrates, gm	11	Vitamin C	2
Fat, gm	.2	Thiamine	2
Sodium, mg	930	Riboflavin	2
Cholesterol, mg	2e	Niacin	4
Fiber, gm	1e	Calcium	2
		Iron	2

THIS FOOD: Campbell's Minestrone Soup provides 50 percent of the USRDA for vitamin A. Like most soups it is very high in sodium.

ADDITIVES: Contains monosodium glutamate (MSG), which many authorities believe should be avoided by infants and very young children; causes adverse reactions in some sensitive individuals.

OTHER BRANDS: Progresso Minestrone contains 43 percent less sodium than Campbell's and substantially more fiber and iron.

CAMPBELL'S NATURAL CREAMY BROCCOLI SOUP
Campbell Soup Co.

Ingredients: chicken broth, broccoli, cream, wheat flour, water, butter, eggs, salt, cornstarch, dehydrated onions, natural flavoring.

Amount: 1 cup (prepared with water)			% USRDA
Calories	70	Protein	2
Protein, gm	1	Vitamin A	4
Carbohydrates, gm	8	Vitamin C	20
Fat, gm	4	Thiamine	*
Sodium, mg	820	Riboflavin	2
Cholesterol, mg	26e	Niacin	4
Fiber, gm	2e	Calcium	2
		Iron	4

THIS FOOD: Campbell's Natural Creamy Broccoli Soup proves that "natural" does not necessarily mean "healthful." This soup is low in calories, but more than half of them derive from fat, too much of it saturated. The broccoli makes it a very good source of vitamin C. Like many canned soups, this product is very high in sodium.

ADDITIVES: No questionable additives.

CAMPBELL'S NATURAL CREAMY BROCCOLI SOUP
Campbell Soup Co.

Ingredients: chicken broth, broccoli, cream, wheat flour, water, butter, eggs, salt, cornstarch, dehydrated onions, natural flavoring.

Amount: 1 cup (prepared with ½ cup milk)			% USRDA
Calories	140	Protein	10
Protein, gm	5	Vitamin A	6
Carbohydrates, gm	13	Vitamin C	20
Fat, gm	8	Thiamine	2
Sodium, mg	875	Riboflavin	10
Cholesterol, mg	40e	Niacin	4
Fiber, gm	2e	Calcium	10
		Iron	4

THIS FOOD: Campbell's Natural Creamy Broccoli Soup proves that "natural" ingredients do not necessarily make a product especially healthful. When prepared with whole milk, this soup is moderate in calories, but more than half of them derive from fat, too much of it saturated. The broccoli makes this soup a very good source of vitamin C, and the added milk, a fair source of protein, riboflavin, and calcium. Like many canned soups, this product is very high in sodium.

ADDITIVES: No questionable additives.

CAMPBELL'S NATURAL CREAMY POTATO SOUP
Campbell Soup Co.

Ingredients: potatoes, cream, chicken stock, butter, wheat flour, water, salt, onions, whey, cornstarch, white pepper, nutmeg.

Amount: 1 cup (prepared with water)			% USRDA
Calories	150	Protein	2
Protein, gm	1	Vitamin A	*
Carbohydrates, gm	11	Vitamin C	2
Fat, gm	11	Thiamine	2
Sodium, mg	810	Riboflavin	*
Cholesterol, mg	40e	Niacin	6
Fiber, gm	2e	Calcium	*
		Iron	2

THIS FOOD: The ingredients list for Campbell's Natural Creamy Potato Soup reads like a home recipe. But unfortunately, with 66 percent fat calories, and too much cholesterol and saturated fat from butter and cream, it is not a very healthful one. Like most canned soups, this product is very high in sodium. It is not a good source of protein, vitamins, or minerals.

ADDITIVES: No questionable additives.

CAMPBELL'S NATURAL CREAMY POTATO SOUP
Campbell's Soup Co.

Ingredients: potatoes, cream, chicken stock, butter, wheat flour, water, salt, onions, whey, cornstarch, white pepper, nutmeg.

Amount: 1 cup (prepared with ½ cup milk)			% USRDA
Calories	220	Protein	10
Protein, gm	5	Vitamin A	2
Carbohydrates, gm	16	Vitamin C	4
Fat, gm	15	Thiamine	4
Sodium, mg	865	Riboflavin	10
Cholesterol, mg	56e	Niacin	6
Fiber, gm	2e	Calcium	10
		Iron	2

THIS FOOD: The ingredients list for Campbell's Natural Creamy Potato Soup reads like a home recipe. But unfortunately, with 61 percent fat calories, and too much cholesterol and saturated fat from butter cream and the whole milk with which it is prepared, it is not a very healthful one. Like most canned soups, this product is very high in sodium. It is a fair source of protein, riboflavin, and calcium, all from the added milk.

ADDITIVES: No questionable additives.

CAMPBELL'S NEW ENGLAND CLAM CHOWDER
Campbell Soup Co.

Ingredients: clam broth, potatoes, clams, wheat flour, partially hydrogenated vegetable oil (soybean or cottonseed oil), water, salt, monosodium glutamate, yeast extract, natural flavoring.

Amount: 1 cup (prepared with ½ cup milk)			% USRDA
Calories	150	Protein	10
Protein, gm	7	Vitamin A	2
Carbohydrates, gm	17	Vitamin C	4
Fat, gm	7	Thiamine	2
Sodium, mg	940	Riboflavin	10
Cholesterol, mg	22e	Niacin	2
Fiber, gm	<1e	Calcium	15
		Iron	4

THIS FOOD: The clam chowder itself is very low in nutrients, but most people prepare this product using milk, which is a good source of calcium, protein, and also of unwanted fat. In fact, 42 percent of the calories in this product derive from fat when whole milk is added. Like most canned soups, this product is very high in sodium.

ADDITIVES: Contains monosodium glutamate (MSG), which many authorities believe should be avoided by infants and very young children; causes adverse reactions in some sensitive individuals.

CAMPBELL'S OLD FASHIONED TOMATO RICE SOUP
Campbell Soup Co.

Ingredients: tomatoes, water, high-fructose corn syrup, rice, wheat flour, salt, partially hydrogenated vegetable oil (soybean, palm, cottonseed), citric acid, enzyme-modified Cheddar cheese, natural flavoring, ascorbic acid.

Amount: 1 cup			% USRDA
Calories	110	Protein	2
Protein, gm	1	Vitamin A	6
Carbohydrates, gm	22	Vitamin C	20
Fat, gm	2	Thiamine	*
Sodium, mg	780	Riboflavin	*
Cholesterol, mg	2	Niacin	2
Fiber, gm	1e	Calcium	*
		Iron	2

Contains 2¾ teaspoons sugar.

THIS FOOD: Campbell's Old Fashioned Tomato Rice Soup provides 20 percent of the USRDA for vitamin C and little else. A full 40 percent of the calories in this soup derive from sugar (some of it naturally occurring). Like most soups, this variety is very high in sodium.

ADDITIVES: No questionable additives.

CAMPBELL'S TOMATO SOUP
Campbell Soup Co.

Ingredients: tomatoes, high-fructose corn syrup, wheat flour, salt, partially hydrogenated vegetable oil (soybean, palm, cottonseed), natural flavoring, ascorbic acid, citric acid.

Amount: 1 cup (with water)			% USRDA
Calories	90	Protein	2
Protein, gm	1	Vitamin A	8
Carbohydrates, gm	17	Vitamin C	40
Fat, gm	2	Thiamine	*
Sodium, mg	750	Riboflavin	*
Cholesterol, mg	e	Niacin	4
Fiber, gm	1e	Calcium	*
		Iron	2

Contains 2¼ teaspoons sugar.

THIS FOOD: A serving of Campbell's number-one best seller, Tomato Soup, provides 40 percent of the USRDA for vitamin C. Like most canned soups, it is high in sodium, but it is also unusually high in sugar.

ADDITIVES: No questionable additives.

CAMPBELL'S TOMATO SOUP
Campbell Soup Co.

Ingredients: tomatoes, high-fructose corn syrup, wheat flour, salt, partially hydrogenated vegetable oil (soybean, palm, or cottonseed oil), natural flavoring, ascorbic acid, citric acid.

Amount: 1 cup (prepared with ½ cup milk)			% USRDA
Calories	160	Protein	10
Protein, gm	5	Vitamin A	10
Carbohydrates, gm	22	Vitamin C	40
Fat, gm	6	Thiamine	2
Sodium, mg	800	Riboflavin	10
Cholesterol, mg	17e	Niacin	4
Fiber, gm	1e	Calcium	10
		Iron	2
Contains 3½ teaspoons sugar.			

THIS FOOD: Campbell's Tomato Soup is an excellent source of vitamin C and, when prepared with milk, becomes a fair source of protein, vitamin A, riboflavin, and calcium as well. Even when whole milk is used, it remains moderate in fat. Those concerned with their sugar intake should be aware that this product contains 3½ teaspoons sugar per serving. Like many canned soups, this product is very high in sodium.

ADDITIVES: No questionable additives.

NOTE: The letter "e" indicates that the data has been estimated; < means "less than" and is used for small amounts of sodium or cholesterol; * means food contains less than 2% of USRDA; "na" means that the information was not available and appears only when data is insufficient.

CAMPBELL'S TURKEY VEGETABLE SOUP
Campbell Soup Co.

Ingredients: turkey stock, potatoes, carrots, tomatoes, turkey meat, enriched macaroni product, celery, water, potato starch, peas, green beans, salt, turkey fat, margarine, yeast extract and hydrolyzed plant protein, monosodium glutamate, dehydrated onions, natural flavoring, dehydrated garlic, dehydrated parsley.

Amount: 1 cup			% USRDA
Calories	70	Protein	4
Protein, gm	2	Vitamin A	60
Carbohydrates, gm	8	Vitamin C	*
Fat, gm	3	Thiamine	2
Sodium, mg	825	Riboflavin	2
Cholesterol, mg	<5e	Niacin	4
Fiber, gm	1e	Calcium	*
		Iron	2

THIS FOOD: This low-calorie soup is an excellent source of vitamin A. Like most canned soups, it is very high in sodium.

ADDITIVES: Contains monosodium glutamate (MSG), which many authorities believe should be avoided by infants and very young children; causes adverse reactions in some sensitive individuals.

CAMPBELL'S VEGETABLE SOUP
Campbell Soup Co.

Ingredients: beef stock, tomatoes, carrots, potatoes, water, peas, enriched alphabet macaroni, high-fructose corn syrup, sweet peppers, corn, green beans, salt, barley, potato starch, vegetable oil, lima beans, celery, okra, sweet potatoes, yeast extract and hydrolyzed plant protein, monosodium glutamate, rutabagas, parsnips, cabbage, natural flavoring, caramel color, oleoresin, paprika, dry parsley.

Amount: 1 cup			% USRDA
Calories	80	Protein	2
Protein, gm	2	Vitamin A	60
Carbohydrates, gm	12	Vitamin C	4
Fat, gm	2	Thiamine	2
Sodium, mg	770	Riboflavin	2
Cholesterol, mg	5e	Niacin	4
Fiber, gm	1e	Calcium	*
		Iron	4

THIS FOOD: Campbell's Vegetable Soup provides 60 percent of the USRDA for vitamin A along with only 80 calories per serving. Like most soups, this product is very high in sodium.

ADDITIVES: Contains monosodium glutamate (MSG), which many authorities believe should be avoided by infants and very young children; causes adverse reactions in some sensitive individuals.

LIPTON CHICKEN NOODLE SOUP WITH CHICKEN MEAT MIX
Unilever United States, Inc.

Ingredients: enriched egg noodles, salt, dehydrated chicken (BHA, propyl gallate), dried corn syrup, hydrogenated vegetable oil, monosodium glutamate, hydrolyzed vegetable protein, chicken fat, dehydrated onions, wheat starch, sugar, dehydrated parsley, flavoring, coloring, natural flavors.

Amount: 1 cup			% USRDA
Calories	50	Protein	4
Protein, gm	3	Vitamin A	*
Carbohydrates, gm	1	Vitamin C	*
Fat, gm	2	Thiamine	6
Sodium, mg	940	Riboflavin	2
Cholesterol, mg	<5e	Niacin	4
Fiber, gm	<1e	Calcium	*
		Iron	2

THIS FOOD: Low in calories and nutrition. It contains more salt than chicken. One-cup serving does not provide useful amounts of any nutrient. It is very high in sodium.

ADDITIVES: Contains monosodium glutamate (MSG), which many authorities believe should be avoided by infants and very young children; causes adverse reactions in some sensitive individuals. Also contains BHA, whose long-term safety is currently being reexamined by FDA investigators.

LIPTON CHICKEN RICE SOUP MIX
Unilever United States, Inc.

Ingredients: quick-cooking rice, salt, dehydrated chicken (BHA, propyl gallate, citric acid), dried corn syrup, hydrogenated vegetable oil, monosodium glutamate, isolated soy protein, hydrolyzed vegetable protein, chicken fat, powdered onions, wheat starch, sugar, egg white solids, dehydrated parsley, flavoring, coloring, natural flavors.

Amount: 1 cup			% USRDA
Calories	60	Protein	4
Protein, gm	3	Vitamin A	*
Carbohydrates, gm	8	Vitamin C	*
Fat, gm	2	Thiamine	2
Sodium, mg	950	Riboflavin	*
Cholesterol, mg	<5e	Niacin	4
Fiber, gm	<1e	Calcium	*
		Iron	2

THIS FOOD: Lipton's Chicken Rice Soup Mix is low in calories—and nutrition. It actually contains more salt than chicken, so it is hardly surprising that a 1-cup serving does not provide useful amounts of any nutrient. This product, like most soups, is very high in sodium.

ADDITIVES: Contains monosodium glutamate (MSG), which many authorities believe should be avoided by infants and very young children; causes adverse reactions in some sensitive individuals. Also contains BHA, whose long-term safety is currently being reexamined by FDA investigators.

LIPTON COUNTRY VEGETABLE SOUP MIX
Unilever United States, Inc.

Ingredients: enriched macaroni product, dehydrated vegetables (potatoes, carrots, onions, peas, green beans, celery, tomatoes, green bell peppers), natural flavors, potato starch, salt, wheat flour, sugar, palm oil, monosodium glutamate, dehydrated tomatoes, cornstarch, onion powder, dehydrated garlic, oleoresin paprika, dehydrated parsley, caramel color.

Amount: 1 cup			% USRDA
Calories	80	Protein	4
Protein, gm	3	Vitamin A	25
Carbohydrates, gm	14	Vitamin C	2
Fat, gm	1	Thiamine	6
Sodium, mg	990	Riboflavin	4
Cholesterol, mg	na	Niacin	4
Fiber, gm	1e	Calcium	*
		Iron	2

THIS FOOD: Lipton's Country Vegetable Soup Mix is low in calories and provides 25 percent of the USRDA for vitamin A. It is very high in sodium.

ADDITIVES: Contains monosodium glutamate (MSG), which many authorities believe should be avoided by infants and very young children; causes adverse reactions in some sensitive individuals.

LIPTON CREAM OF MUSHROOM CUP-A-SOUP
Unilever United States, Inc.

Ingredients: nondairy creamer (hydrogenated coconut, soybean oils, dried corn syrup, sodium caseinate, mono- and diglycerides, dipotassium phosphate), modified tapioca starch, hydrogenated vegetable oil (cottonseed, soybean, palm), dried corn syrup, natural flavors, salt, whey solids, monosodium glutamate, guar gum, nonfat dry milk, dehydrated mushrooms, buttermilk solids, mono- and diglycerides, artificial mushroom flavor, dehydrated onion, dehydrated garlic, caramel color, disodium inosinate, disodium guanylate, oleoresin turmeric.

Amount: ¾ cup			% USRDA
Calories	80	Protein	2
Protein, gm	2	Vitamin A	*
Carbohydrates, gm	10	Vitamin C	*
Fat, gm	4	Thiamine	*
Sodium, mg	820	Riboflavin	2
Cholesterol, mg	na	Niacin	2
Fiber, gm	<1e	Calcium	*
		Iron	*

THIS FOOD: This is almost entirely a fake product. Dried mushrooms and dairy products (nonfat dry milk and buttermilk solids) are indeed present, but in such tiny amounts that they actually follow salt and MSG in the ingredients list. The largest single ingredient is nondairy creamer, which is mostly saturated fat, followed by hydrogenated vegetable oil, which is also highly saturated. Thus this soup supplies a high percentage of fat calories (45 percent of the total) without useful amounts of any other nutrients. Like most prepared soups, it is very high in sodium.

ADDITIVES: Contains monosodium glutamate (MSG), which many authorities believe should be avoided by infants and very young children; causes adverse reactions in some sensitive individuals. Also contains artificial flavor, which may cause allergic reactions in sensitive individuals, and which some studies suggest may adversely affect behavior and the ability to complete school tasks in some sensitive children.

LIPTON GREEN PEA CUP-A-SOUP
Unilever United States, Inc.
Ingredients: green split peas, hydrogenated vegetable oil (cottonseed, soybean, palm), dried corn syrup, modified food starch, salt, natural flavors, artificial ham flavor, monosodium glutamate, sugar, lactose, guar gum, artificial bacon flavor, whey solids, nonfat milk solids, dehydrated onion, locust bean gum, dehydrated garlic.

Amount: ¾ cup			% USRDA
Calories	120	Protein	6
Protein, gm	4	Vitamin A	*
Carbohydrates, gm	16	Vitamin C	*
Fat, gm	4	Thiamine	30
Sodium, mg	680	Riboflavin	2
Cholesterol, mg	<5e	Niacin	2
Fiber, gm	2e	Calcium	2
		Iron	*

THIS FOOD: Lipton's Green Pea Cup-a-Soup supplies 2 grams valuable dietary fiber and 30 percent of the USRDA for thiamine. It is high in sodium.

ADDITIVES: Contains monosodium glutamate (MSG), which can cause allergic reactions in sensitive individuals; and artificial ham and bacon flavor, which may cause allergic reactions in sensitive individuals, and which some studies suggest may adversely affect behavior and the ability to complete school tasks in some sensitive children.

OTHER BRANDS: Progresso Green Split Pea Soup contains substantially more protein, fiber, complex carbohydrates, and iron.

LIPTON ONION SOUP MIX
Unilever United States, Inc.

Ingredients: dehydrated onions, salt, natural flavors, hydrogenated vegetable oil (contains one or more of the following oils: cottonseed, soybean, palm), modified food starch, dried corn syrup, potato flour, wheat flour, cornstarch, caramel color, sugar, disodium inosinate, disodium guanylate.

Amount: 1 cup			% USRDA
Calories	35	Protein	2
Protein, gm	1	Vitamin A	*
Carbohydrates, gm	6	Vitamin C	*
Fat, gm	1	Thiamine	*
Sodium, mg	640	Riboflavin	*
Cholesterol, mg	0	Niacin	*
Fiber, gm	<1e	Calcium	*
		Iron	*

THIS FOOD: Lipton's Onion Soup Mix is low in calories and nutrition. A 1-cup serving does not provide useful amounts of any of the nutrients you need. It is high in sodium.

ADDITIVES: No questionable additives.

LIPTON TOMATO CUP-A-SOUP
Unilever United States, Inc.

Ingredients: dehydrated tomatoes, dried corn syrup, sugar, modified food starch, salt, nonfat dry milk, monosodium glutamate, natural flavor, hydrogenated vegetable oil (cottonseed, soybean, palm), butterfat, lactose, dehydrated onions, mono- and diglycerides, paprika and carrot oleoresins, citric acid, dehydrated garlic.

Amount: ¾ cup			% USRDA
Calories	80	Protein	*
Protein, gm	1	Vitamin A	*
Carbohydrates, gm	17	Vitamin C	4
Fat, gm	1	Thiamine	*
Sodium, mg	680	Riboflavin	*
Cholesterol, mg	<5e	Niacin	2
Fiber, gm	<1e	Calcium	2
		Iron	2

THIS FOOD: Lipton's Tomato Cup-a-Soup is high in sugar and salt without providing useful amounts of any of the nutrients you need.

ADDITIVES: Contains monosodium glutamate (MSG), which many authorities believe should be avoided by infants and very young children; causes adverse reactions in some sensitive individuals.

OTHER BRANDS: Campbell's Tomato Soup is high in added sugar and even higher in sodium, but it provides 40 percent of the USRDA for vitamin C.

PROGRESSO GREEN SPLIT PEA SOUP
Ogden Food Products Corp.
Ingredients: water, green split peas, celery, bacon, salt, sugar, dehydrated onions, hydrolyzed plant protein, natural flavorings, natural smoke flavor.

Amount: 1 cup			% USRDA
Calories	180	Protein	15
Protein, gm	11	Vitamin A	6
Carbohydrates, gm	29	Vitamin C	*
Fat, gm	2	Thiamine	15
Sodium, mg	839	Riboflavin	8
Cholesterol, mg	2	Niacin	8
Fiber, gm	5e	Calcium	2
		Iron	15

THIS FOOD: Rich in complex carbohydrates, fiber, vegetable protein, thiamine, and iron—a fairly nutritious soup. It is very high in sodium. Served with a slice of whole grain bread, an ounce of cheese, and a salad, this soup could be the basis of a complete, well-balanced meal.

ADDITIVES: No questionable additives.

PROGRESSO HOME STYLE CHICKEN SOUP
Ogden Food Products Corp.
Ingredients: chicken broth, macaroni product, chicken, carrots, celery, salt, chicken fat, hydrolyzed plant protein, monosodium glutamate, sugar, dehydrated chicken meat, soy flour, torula yeast, natural flavoring, turmeric.

Amount: 1 cup			% USRDA
Calories	70	Protein	10
Protein, gm	8	Vitamin A	30
Carbohydrates, gm	7	Vitamin C	*
Fat, gm	2	Thiamine	6
Sodium, mg	875	Riboflavin	2
Cholesterol, mg	10	Niacin	15
Fiber, gm	1e	Calcium	2
		Iron	6

THIS FOOD: Progresso Home Style Chicken Soup is low in calories, higher than average in protein and supplies 30 percent of the USRDA for vitamin A. Like most canned soups, it is very high in sodium.

ADDITIVES: Contains monosodium glutamate (MSG), which many authorities believe should be avoided by infants and very young children; causes adverse reactions in some sensitive individuals.

PROGRESSO MINESTRONE SOUP
Ogden Food Products Corp.

Ingredients: water, red kidney beans, great northern beans, green lima beans, green peas, carrots, potatoes, celery, cabbage, green beans, tomato paste, chick peas, macaroni product, salt, soybean oil, dehydrated onions, olive oil, dehydrated garlic, spices, natural flavorings.

Amount: 8 oz			% USRDA
Calories	130	Protein	8
Protein, gm	6	Vitamin A	50
Carbohydrates, gm	23	Vitamin C	4
Fat, gm	2	Thiamine	4
Sodium, mg	531	Riboflavin	2
Cholesterol, mg	0e	Niacin	15
Fiber, gm	5e	Calcium	6
		Iron	10

THIS FOOD: Progresso Minestrone Soup is one of the most nutritious vegetable soups available. High in vegetable protein, fiber, and complex carbohydrates, one serving of this product also supplies 50 percent of the USRDA for vitamin A and 10 percent of the USRDA for iron. Compared to most soups, it is only moderately high in sodium. Served with a slice of whole grain bread, an ounce of cheese, and a salad, this soup could be the cornerstone of a complete, well-balanced meal.

ADDITIVES: No questionable additives.

PROGRESSO TOMATO SOUP
Ogden Food Products Corp.

Ingredients: water, tomato paste, green beans, zucchini, macaroni product, carrots, sugar, salt, green peppers, soybean oil, wheat flour, dehydrated onions, dehydrated garlic, natural flavorings.

Amount: 8 oz			% USRDA
Calories	110	Protein	4
Protein, gm	3	Vitamin A	30
Carbohydrates, gm	21	Vitamin C	2
Fat, gm	2	Thiamine	10
Sodium, mg	929	Riboflavin	15
Cholesterol, mg	0	Niacin	6
Fiber, gm	1e	Calcium	2
		Iron	10

THIS FOOD: Progresso Tomato Soup provides 30 percent of the USRDA for vitamin A and small amounts of the B vitamins, including 15 percent of the USRDA for riboflavin. Like most canned soups, it is very high in sodium.

ADDITIVES: No questionable additives.

WYLER'S CHICKEN FLAVOR BOUILLON CUBES
Borden, Inc.

Ingredients: salt, chicken, corn syrup solids, sugar, chicken fat, monosodium glutamate, hydrolyzed vegetable protein, onion powder, garlic powder, turmeric, natural flavorings, corn oil, glyceryl mono-oleate and propylene glycol, BHA, BHT, propyl gallate, citric acid, l-cysteine hydrochloride, thiamine hydrochloride.

Amount: 1 cube (with 8 oz water)			% USRDA
Calories	8	Protein	*
Protein, gm	<1	Vitamin A	*
Carbohydrates, gm	1	Vitamin C	*
Fat, gm	1	Thiamine	*
Sodium, mg	850	Riboflavin	*
Cholesterol, mg	1	Niacin	*
Fiber, gm	0e	Calcium	*
		Iron	*

THIS FOOD: Wyler's Chicken Flavor Bouillon Cubes, like other popular brands, is little more than flavored salty water. One serving supplies 8 calories and no other useful nutrients. This product is very high in sodium.

ADDITIVES: Contains BHA and BHT, whose long-term safety is currently being reexamined by FDA investigators.

SPAGHETTI SAUCE

Ragú, Prego, and Aunt Millie's are the leading names in spaghetti sauce, an extremely popular convenience food. Eaten with low-fat, high-carbohydrate enriched pasta, most of these sauces will make a nutritionally well-balanced entrée. All of the national brands list tomatoes or tomato paste as their first ingredient, so it's somewhat surprising to find fairly significant differences in their nutrient content. Prego and Aunt Millie sauces contain about twice as much vitamin A and vitamin C as Ragú sauces, and Aunt Millie's has substantially less sodium than the other brands.

SODIUM GUIDELINES: In evaluating the sodium content of spaghetti sauce, we used the following standards:

less than 400 mg	moderate in sodium
400 mg to 600 mg	high in sodium
more than 600 mg	very high in sodium

Remember, these guidelines are not for people following medically restricted low-sodium diets, but for healthy individuals who wish to monitor their sodium intake.

SODIUM LOSERS

These spaghetti sauces contain over 800 mg sodium (more than ⅓ teaspoon salt) per serving:

Ragú Extra Thick and Zesty Plain Spaghetti Sauce
Ragú Extra Thick and Zesty Spaghetti Sauce, Flavored with Meat
Ragú Plain Spaghetti Sauce
Ragú Spaghetti Sauce Flavored with Meat

AUNT MILLIE'S MEATLESS TRADITIONAL SPAGHETTI SAUCE
Prince Macaroni Manufacturing Co.

Ingredients: tomato sauce, tomatoes in tomato juice, tomato paste, vegetable oil (peanut oil, imported olive oil), salt, imported Romano cheese made from sheep's milk, basil, dehydrated garlic, oregano, black pepper, bay.

Amount: ½ cup			% USRDA
Calories	70	Protein	0
Protein, gm	2	Vitamin A	22
Carbohydrates, gm	9	Vitamin C	20
Fat, gm	2	Thiamine	5e
Sodium, mg	302	Riboflavin	2e
Cholesterol, mg	<5e	Niacin	5e
Fiber, gm	<1e	Calcium	*e
		Iron	5e

THIS FOOD: Aunt Millie's Meatless Traditional Spaghetti Sauce is a very good source of vitamins A and C. It has no added sugar and is low in calories, 26 percent of which derive from fat. Compared to other prepared spaghetti sauces, it contains a moderate amount of sodium.

ADDITIVES: No questionable additives.

AUNT MILLIE'S SPAGHETTI SAUCE WITH SWEET PEPPERS AND ITALIAN SAUSAGE
Prince Macaroni Manufacturing Co.

Ingredients: tomato sauce, tomatoes in tomato puree, tomato paste, sweet green and red bell peppers, Italian sausage (pork, fennel seed, salt, black pepper), vegetable oil (peanut oil, imported olive oil), salt, imported Romano cheese made from sheep's milk, dehydrated onion, dehydrated garlic, black pepper, basil.

Amount: ½ cup			% USRDA
Calories	64	Protein	0
Protein, gm	3	Vitamin A	22
Carbohydrates, gm	6	Vitamin C	20
Fat, gm	3	Thiamine	5e
Sodium, mg	352	Riboflavin	2e
Cholesterol, mg	0	Niacin	5e
Fiber, gm	<1e	Calcium	*e
		Iron	5e

THIS FOOD: Aunt Millie's Spaghetti Sauce with Sweet Peppers and Italian Sausage is a very good source of vitamins A and C. It has no added sugar and is low in calories, 42 percent of which derive from fat. Compared to other prepared spaghetti sauces, it contains a moderate amount of sodium.

ADDITIVES: No questionable additives.

NOTE: The letter "e" indicates that the data has been estimated; < means "less than" and is used for small amounts of sodium or cholesterol; * means food contains less than 2% of USRDA; "na" means that the information was not available and appears only when data is insufficient.

PREGO NO-SALT ADDED SPAGHETTI SAUCE
Campbell Soup Co.

Ingredients: tomato paste, water, tomatoes, corn and/or cottonseed oil, dehydrated onions, concentrated lemon juice, dehydrated garlic, spices (basil, oregano, and other spices), and dehydrated parsley.

Amount: ½ cup			% USRDA
Calories	100	Protein	2
Protein, gm	2	Vitamin A	30
Carbohydrates, gm	10	Vitamin C	25
Fat, gm	6	Thiamine	4
Sodium, mg	25	Riboflavin	4
Cholesterol, mg	0e	Niacin	8
Fiber, gm	<1e	Calcium	4
		Iron	6

THIS FOOD: Prego No-Salt Added Spaghetti Sauce is an excellent source of vitamins A and C. About 54 percent of its calories derive from fat, which is much higher than in the other brands profiled. This product is low in sodium.

ADDITIVES: No questionable additives.

PREGO SPAGHETTI SAUCE
Campbell Soup Co.

Ingredients: tomato paste, water, tomatoes, corn syrup, cottonseed oil, salt, dehydrated onions, dehydrated garlic, concentrated lemon juice, dehydrated parsley, oregano, basil, and other spices.

Amount: ½ cup			% USRDA
Calories	140	Protein	2
Protein, gm	2	Vitamin A	15
Carbohydrates, gm	20	Vitamin C	20
Fat, gm	6	Thiamine	2
Sodium, mg	670	Riboflavin	2
Cholesterol, mg	0	Niacin	6
Fiber, gm	<1e	Calcium	2
		Iron	4

THIS FOOD: Prego Spaghetti Sauce is a very good source of vitamins A and C. It is relatively high in added sugar and calories, 38 percent of which derive from fat. Like most spaghetti sauces, this product is high in sodium.

ADDITIVES: No questionable additives.

PREGO SPAGHETTI SAUCE WITH MUSHROOMS
Campbell Soup Co.

Ingredients: tomato paste, tomatoes, water, corn syrup, cottonseed oil, mushrooms, salt, concentrated lemon juice, dehydrated onions, dehydrated garlic, oregano, basil, dehydrated parsley, and other spices.

Amount: ½ cup			% USRDA
Calories	140	Protein	2
Protein, gm	2	Vitamin A	20
Carbohydrates, gm	21	Vitamin C	25
Fat, gm	5	Thiamine	2
Sodium, mg	640	Riboflavin	4
Cholesterol, mg	0	Niacin	6
Fiber, gm	<1e	Calcium	2
		Iron	6

THIS FOOD: Prego Spaghetti Sauce with Mushrooms is a very good source of vitamins A and C. It is relatively high in added sugar and calories, 32 percent of which are derived from fat. Like most spaghetti sauces, this product is high in sodium.

ADDITIVES: No questionable additives.

RAGÚ EXTRA THICK AND ZESTY PLAIN SPAGHETTI SAUCE
Chesebrough-Pond's, Inc.

Ingredients: water, tomato paste, soybean oil, sugar, tomatoes with tomato puree, salt, corn syrup, Romano cheese made from cow's milk, dried onions, spices, olive oil, garlic powder.

Amount: ½ cup			% USRDA
Calories	100	Protein	2
Protein, gm	2	Vitamin A	10
Carbohydrates, gm	15	Vitamin C	10
Fat, gm	4	Thiamine	*
Sodium, mg	829	Riboflavin	6
Cholesterol, mg	0	Niacin	6
Fiber, gm	<1e	Calcium	2
		Iron	8
Contains ⅓ teaspoon salt.			

THIS FOOD: Ragú Extra Thick and Zesty Plain Spaghetti Sauce is relatively low in added sugar and provides some quantity of the vitamins A and C. About 36 percent of its calories derive from fat. Compared to other spaghetti sauces, it is extremely high in sodium.

ADDITIVES: No questionable additives.

BEST BET: Aunt Millie's Meatless Traditional Spaghetti Sauce is low in calories and contains moderate amounts of sodium: 64 percent less than Ragú Extra Thick and Zesty Sauces and about 50 percent less than Prego Spaghetti Sauces (not counting the No-Salt Added variety, of course). It contains only 26 percent fat calories, less than the other sauces profiled.

RAGÚ EXTRA THICK AND ZESTY SPAGHETTI SAUCE, FLAVORED WITH MEAT
Chesebrough-Pond's, Inc.

Ingredients: water, tomato paste, soybean oil, beef, sugar, tomatoes with tomato puree, salt, corn syrup, dried onions, Romano cheese (made from cow's milk), spices, olive oil, garlic powder.

Amount: ½ cup			% USRDA
Calories	100	Protein	2
Protein, gm	2	Vitamin A	10
Carbohydrates, gm	14	Vitamin C	10
Fat, gm	4	Thiamine	*
Sodium, mg	835	Riboflavin	6
Cholesterol, mg	2	Niacin	6
Fiber, gm	na	Calcium	2
		Iron	4
Contains ⅓ teaspoon salt.			

THIS FOOD: Ragú Extra Thick and Zesty Spaghetti Sauce, Flavored with Meat, is relatively low in added sugar and provides some quantity of the vitamins A and C. About 36 percent of its calories derive from fat. Compared to other spaghetti sauces, it is extremely high in sodium.

ADDITIVES: No questionable additives.

RAGÚ HOMESTYLE SPAGHETTI SAUCE WITH MUSHROOMS
Chesebrough-Pond's, Inc.

Ingredients: water, tomato paste, tomatoes in tomato juice, mushrooms, soybean oil, salt, dried onions, parsley, garlic powder, olive oil, basil, oregano, black pepper, thyme, bay.

Amount: ½ cup			% USRDA
Calories	70	Protein	2
Protein, gm	2	Vitamin A	10
Carbohydrates, gm	12	Vitamin C	10
Fat, gm	2	Thiamine	*
Sodium, mg	685	Riboflavin	10
Cholesterol, mg	0	Niacin	8
Fiber, gm	<1e	Calcium	2
		Iron	10

THIS FOOD: Ragú Homestyle Spaghetti Sauce with Mushrooms provides a fair amount of vitamins A, C, riboflavin, and iron. It contains no added sugar and derives 26 percent of its calories from fat. This product is very high in sodium.

ADDITIVES: No questionable additives.

RAGÚ PLAIN SPAGHETTI SAUCE
Chesebrough-Pond's, Inc.

Ingredients: water, tomato paste, soybean oil, salt, sugar, corn syrup, dried onions, Romano cheese made from cow's milk, olive oil, spice, garlic powder.

Amount: ½ cup			% USRDA
Calories	80	Protein	2
Protein, gm	2	Vitamin A	10
Carbohydrates, gm	11	Vitamin C	10
Fat, gm	3	Thiamine	*
Sodium, mg	820	Riboflavin	6
Cholesterol, mg	0	Niacin	6
Fiber, gm	<1e	Calcium	2
		Iron	6

THIS FOOD: Ragú Plain Spaghetti Sauce provides some vitamins A and C. It contains added sugar and derives 34 percent of its calories from fat. Like many Ragú sauces, this product is extremely high in sodium.

ADDITIVES: No questionable additives.

RAGÚ SPAGHETTI SAUCE FLAVORED WITH MEAT
Chesebrough-Pond's, Inc.

Ingredients: water, tomato paste, soybean oil, beef, salt, sugar, corn syrup, dried onion, Romano cheese (made from cow's milk), olive oil, spices, garlic powder.

Amount: ½ cup			% USRDA
Calories	80	Protein	2
Protein, gm	2	Vitamin A	10
Carbohydrates, gm	11	Vitamin C	10
Fat, gm	2	Thiamine	*
Sodium, mg	852	Riboflavin	6
Cholesterol, mg	2	Niacin	6
Fiber, gm	<1e	Calcium	2
		Iron	6
Contains ⅓ teaspoon salt.			

THIS FOOD: Ragú Spaghetti Sauce Flavored with Meat provides some vitamins A and C. It contains no added sugar and derives only 22 percent of its calories from fat. This product is extremely high in sodium.

ADDITIVES: No questionable additives.

RAGÚ TRADITIONAL PIZZA QUICK SAUCE
Chesebrough-Pond's, Inc.
Ingredients: water, tomato paste, soybean oil, salt, modified food starch, dried onions, sugar, spices, corn syrup, garlic powder.

Amount: 3 tbsp			% USRDA
Calories	35	Protein	*
Protein, gm	1	Vitamin A	6
Carbohydrates, gm	6	Vitamin C	4
Fat, gm	1	Thiamine	*
Sodium, mg	300e	Riboflavin	2
Cholesterol, mg	0	Niacin	4
Fiber, gm	<1e	Calcium	*
		Iron	2

THIS FOOD: Ragú Traditional Pizza Quick Sauce contains added sugar and derives about 26 percent of its calories from fat. A 3-tablespoon serving is not a significant source of vitamins or minerals. This product is extremely high in sodium.

ADDITIVES: No questionable additives.

NOTE: We've used a smaller portion size for Ragú Traditional Pizza Quick Sauce, since people use less sauce on a slice of pizza than they would on spaghetti. An equivalent amount of sauce would be nutritionally comparable to the other Ragú products profiled.

SUGAR AND SUGAR SUBSTITUTES

Babies have an inborn preference for sweet-tasting foods, and our liking for sugar may originally have been a survival mechanism: sweet berries and fruits are generally ripe and good to eat, while bitter-tasting plants are unripe or even poisonous. Clearly the occasional ice-cream sundae or sugar-laden slice of cake or pie won't destroy a habitually sound diet. But America's consumption of sweets is not moderate. On average each of us consumes 600 calories of sugar each day—only 6 percent of which occur naturally in the foods we eat. Most of this daily dose of sugar—about 400 calories' worth—is present in processed foods. Soft drinks are probably the single largest source of sugar in the American diet. But often the sugar in brand name foods is "hidden" in products we don't think of as being sweet. For instance, ketchup is fully one-third sugar by weight and Campbell's Tomato Rice Soup contains nearly three teaspoons of sugar per serving. The balance of sugar—about 6 teaspoons per day—is added at home.

Eating too much sugar can cause tooth decay and obesity. Yet many people are sugar addicts and still maintain normal weight. The real problem stems from the fact that sugar provides nutritionally worthless calories. So if you are eating lots of sugar and still do not have a weight problem, your diet, though not excessive in calories, may also not contain enough essential nutrients for optimum health. In other words, sugary foods may be replacing more desirable nutrient-rich foods in your diet.

C AND H GRANULATED SUGAR
California and Hawaiian Sugar Co.

Ingredients: granulated sugar.

Amount: 1 tsp			% USRDA
Calories	16	Protein	*
Protein, gm	0	Vitamin A	*
Carbohydrates, gm	4	Vitamin C	*
Fat, gm	0	Thiamine	*
Sodium, mg	0	Riboflavin	*
Cholesterol, mg	0	Niacin	*
Fiber, gm	0	Calcium	*
		Iron	*

THIS FOOD: Sugar is a clear example of worthless food in that it provides calories without significant amounts of any nutrient. Eating too much sugar can cause a number of health problems, including obesity and tooth decay.

ADDITIVES: None.

DOMINO BROWNULATED SUGAR
Amstar Corp.

Ingredients: brown sugar, cane caramel color.

Amount: 1 tsp			% USRDA
Calories	12	Protein	*
Protein, gm	0	Vitamin A	*
Carbohydrates, gm	3	Vitamin C	*
Fat, gm	0	Thiamine	*
Sodium, mg	0	Riboflavin	*
Cholesterol, mg	0	Niacin	*
Fiber, gm	0	Calcium	*
		Iron	*

THIS FOOD: Brown sugar is simply refined table sugar, colored with a little molasses. Like other forms of sucrose, brown sugar is a clear example of worthless food in that it provides calories without significant amounts of any nutrient. Eating too much sugar can cause a number of health problems, including obesity and tooth decay. Among susceptible individuals, heavy sugar consumption is associated with diabetes and an increased risk of developing heart disease.

ADDITIVES: None.

DOMINO GRANULATED SUGAR
Amstar Corp.

Ingredients: granulated sugar.

Amount: 1 tsp			% USRDA
Calories	16	Protein	*
Protein, gm	0	Vitamin A	*
Carbohydrates, gm	4	Vitamin C	*
Fat, gm	0	Thiamine	*
Sodium, mg	0	Riboflavin	*
Cholesterol, mg	0	Niacin	*
Fiber, gm	0	Calcium	*
		Iron	*

THIS FOOD: Sugar is a clear example of worthless food in that it provides calories without significant amounts of any nutrient. Eating too much sugar can cause a number of health problems, including obesity and tooth decay. Among susceptible individuals, heavy sugar consumption is associated with diabetes and an increased risk of developing heart disease.

ADDITIVES: None.

DOMINO LIQUID BROWN SUGAR
Amstar Corp.

Ingredients: brown sugar, water.

Amount: 1 tsp			% USRDA
Calories	16	Protein	*
Protein, gm	0	Vitamin A	*
Carbohydrates, gm	4	Vitamin C	*
Fat, gm	0	Thiamine	*
Sodium, mg	0	Riboflavin	*
Cholesterol, mg	0	Niacin	*
Fiber, gm	0	Calcium	*
		Iron	*

THIS FOOD: Brown sugar is simply refined table sugar, colored with a little molasses. Like other forms of sucrose, brown sugar is a pure example of worthless food in that it provides calories without significant amounts of any nutrient. Eating too much sugar can cause a number of health problems, including obesity and tooth decay. Among susceptible individuals, heavy sugar consumption is associated with diabetes and an increased risk of developing heart disease.

ADDITIVES: None.

DID YOU KNOW: There is no evidence that artificial sweeteners help people to lose weight and keep it off. In fact, nutritionists believe that they merely perpetuate one's cravings for sweets, and animal studies indicate that the use of sugar substitutes may raise a person's "set point." This is the weight you tend to stay at if you're not making any special effort to lose or gain.

NOTE: The letter "e" indicates that the data has been estimated; < means "less than" and is used for small amounts of sodium or cholesterol; * means food contains less than 2% of USRDA; "na" means that the information was not available and appears only when data is insufficient.

AUNT JEMIMA LITE SYRUP
Quaker Oats Co.

Ingredients: sugar syrup, water, cellulose gum, salt, natural and artificial flavors, sorbic acid, sodium benzoate, caramel color, sodium hexametaphosphate.

Amount: 3 tbsp			% USRDA
Calories	75	Protein	*
Protein, gm	0	Vitamin A	*
Carbohydrates, gm	14	Vitamin C	*
Fat, gm	0	Thiamine	*
Sodium, mg	97	Riboflavin	*
Cholesterol, mg	0	Niacin	*
Fiber, gm	0e	Calcium	*
		Iron	*
Contains 3½ teaspoons sugar.			

THIS FOOD: Aunt Jemima Lite Syrup contains one third the sugar and calories of regular Aunt Jemima Syrup, and is clearly the more healthful product, especially since the manufacturer has not replaced sugar with artificial sweeteners.

ADDITIVES: Contains artificial flavors, which may cause allergic reactions in sensitive individuals, and which some studies suggest may adversely affect behavior and the ability to complete school tasks in some sensitive children.

EQUAL
G.D. Searle & Co.

Ingredients: dextrose with dried corn syrup, aspartame, silicon dioxide, cellulose, tribasic calcium phosphate, cellulose derivatives.

Amount: 1 packet/1 gm			% USRDA
Calories	4	Protein	*
Protein, gm	0	Vitamin A	*
Carbohydrates, gm	<1	Vitamin C	*
Fat, gm	0	Thiamine	*
Sodium, mg	0	Riboflavin	*
Cholesterol, mg	0	Niacin	*
Fiber, gm	0	Calcium	*
		Iron	*

THIS FOOD: One packet of this sugar substitute has the sweetening power of two teaspoons of sugar. It contains 4 calories and a trace amount of carbohydrate.

ADDITIVES: Contains aspartame (with phenylalanine), which should be avoided by people with PKU, a rare genetic disease, and which many experts believe has been inadequately tested for long-term safety.

SWEET 'N LOW
Cumberland Packing, Inc.

Ingredients: nutritive dextrose, 4 percent soluble saccharin, cream of tartar, calcium silicate.

Amount: 1 packet/1 gm			% USRDA
Calories	4	Protein	*
Protein, gm	0	Vitamin A	*
Carbohydrates, gm	<1	Vitamin C	*
Fat, gm	0	Thiamine	*
Sodium, mg	4	Riboflavin	*
Cholesterol, mg	0	Niacin	*
Fiber, gm	0	Calcium	*
		Iron	*

THIS FOOD: One packet of this sugar substitute has the sweetening power of two teaspoons of sugar. It contains 4 calories and a trace amount of carbohydrate.

ADDITIVES: Contains saccharin, which causes cancer in laboratory animals. This additive is currently being investigated and should only be used in small amounts by healthy adults.

SYRUPS AND HONEY

In nutritional terms, both syrups and honey are identical to sugar. Both provide nutritionally empty calories. Some honeys, however, are as much as 40 percent sweeter than table sugar, so that teaspoon for teaspoon, you'll be able to use less honey than sugar and still satisfy your sweet tooth. It's true that honey contains tiny amounts of potassium, calcium, phosphorus, and vitamin B_{12}, but they are too small to be of value. Because honey sticks to your teeth, it is a potent cause of tooth decay.

NOTE: Throughout this section you'll notice that some syrups contain a larger amount of sugar than the serving size. This is possible because the syrups are sweeter than sugar and contain sugar in concentrated form.

AUNT JEMIMA SYRUP
Quaker Oats Co.

Ingredients: corn syrup, water, corn syrup solids, cellulose gum, natural and artificial flavors, sodium benzoate, and sorbic acid, caramel color.

Amount: 3 tbsp

			% USRDA
Calories	150	Protein	*
Protein, gm	0	Vitamin A	*
Carbohydrates, gm	39	Vitamin C	*
Fat, gm	0	Thiamine	*
Sodium, mg	38	Riboflavin	*
Cholesterol, mg	0	Niacin	*
Fiber, gm	0	Calcium	*
		Iron	*

Contains about 10 teaspoons sugar.

THIS FOOD: Aunt Jemima Syrup is basically a processed sugar, which provides no nutritional benefits besides calories.

ADDITIVES: Contains artificial flavor, which can cause allergic reactions in some sensitive individuals and which may also contribute to hyperactivity in sensitive children.

KARO LIGHT CORN SYRUP
CPC International, Inc.

Ingredients: light corn syrup with high-fructose corn syrup, salt, vanilla.

Amount: 3 tbsp

			% USRDA
Calories	180	Protein	*
Protein, gm	0	Vitamin A	*
Carbohydrates, gm	45	Vitamin C	*
Fat, gm	0	Thiamine	*
Sodium, mg	90	Riboflavin	*
Cholesterol, mg	0	Niacin	*
Fiber, gm	0	Calcium	*
		Iron	*

Contains 11 teaspoons sugar.

THIS FOOD: Corn syrup is processed sugar. Like most sugars, it supplies calories without anything else of nutritional value.

ADDITIVES: No questionable additives.

NOTE: The letter "e" indicates that the data has been estimated; < means "less than" and is used for small amounts of sodium or cholesterol; * means food contains less than 2% of USRDA; "na" means that the information was not available and appears only when data is insufficient.

LOG CABIN SYRUP
General Foods Corp.

Ingredients: corn syrup, sugar syrup, maple sugar syrup, artificial flavor, sodium benzoate and sorbic acid, caramel color.

Amount: 3 tbsp			% USRDA
Calories	150	Protein	*
Protein, gm	0	Vitamin A	*
Carbohydrates, gm	39	Vitamin C	*
Fat, gm	0	Thiamine	*
Sodium, mg	15	Riboflavin	*
Cholesterol, mg	0	Niacin	*
Fiber, gm	0	Calcium	*
		Iron	*

Contains about 10 teaspoons sugar.

THIS FOOD: Log Cabin Syrup is basically a processed sugar, which provides no nutritional benefits other than calories.

ADDITIVES: Contains artificial flavor, which may cause allergic reactions in sensitive individuals, and which some studies suggest may adversely affect behavior and the ability to complete school tasks in some sensitive children.

MRS. BUTTERWORTH'S PANCAKE SYRUP
Lever Brothers Co., Inc.

Ingredients: corn syrups, sugar syrup, grade A butter, artificial maple flavor, algin derivative, salt, sodium benzoate and sorbic acid, sodium citrate, citric acid, caramel color.

Amount: 3 tbsp			% USRDA
Calories	165	Protein	*
Protein, gm	0	Vitamin A	*
Carbohydrates, gm	40	Vitamin C	*
Fat, gm	.5	Thiamine	*
Sodium, mg	77	Riboflavin	*
Cholesterol, mg	2e	Niacin	*
Fiber, gm	0	Calcium	*
		Iron	*

Contains 10 teaspoons sugar.

THIS FOOD: Mrs. Butterworth's Pancake Syrup is basically a processed sugar flavored with butter, which provides no nutritional benefits other than calories.

ADDITIVES: Contains artificial flavor, which may cause allergic reactions in sensitive individuals, and which some studies suggest may adversely affect behavior and the ability to complete school tasks in some sensitive chldren.

SUE BEE HONEY
Sioux Honey Assn.

Ingredients: honey.

Amount: 3 tbsp			% USRDA
Calories	192	Protein	*
Protein, gm	<1	Vitamin A	*
Carbohydrates, gm	52	Vitamin C	*
Fat, gm	0	Thiamine	*
Sodium, mg	<5	Riboflavin	*
Cholesterol, mg	0	Niacin	*
Fiber, gm	0	Calcium	*
		Iron	*

THIS FOOD: Honey is a form of sugar which contains tiny, nutritionally insignificant amounts of potassium, calcium, phosphorus, and vitamin B_{12}. Some honeys are 40 percent sweeter than table sugar, so ounce for ounce, you can use less honey and still satisfy your sweet tooth.

ADDITIVES: None.

HELPFUL HINT: Because honey sticks to your teeth, it is a potent cause of tooth decay. Be sure to brush after eating honey, or at the very least rinse your mouth thoroughly with water.

TOMATO PRODUCTS

Tomatoes are naturally high in vitamin A and vitamin C. Not surprisingly, the most popular brand name products, including Del Monte, Hunt's, and Contadina tomato sauce, tomato paste, and stewed tomatoes, are also high in these nutrients. Most tomato pastes do not contain added salt, and Del Monte Peeled Tomatoes contain a moderate amount of added sodium, but all of the other items in this category are high, or very high, in sodium. Among the vitamin-rich juices, only V-8 No Salt Added Vegetable Juice is low in sodium.

SODIUM GUIDELINES: In evaluating the sodium content of tomato products, we have used the following standards:

sauce and paste:

less than 100 mg	low in sodium
100 mg to 250 mg	moderate in sodium
250 mg to 500 mg	high in sodium
more than 500 mg	very high in sodium

juice:

less than 100 mg	moderate in sodium
100 mg to 250 mg	high in sodium

Remember, these guidelines are not for people following medically restricted low-sodium diets, but for healthy individuals who wish to monitor their sodium intake.

CAMPBELL'S TOMATO JUICE
Campbell Soup Co.

Ingredients: water, tomato concentrate, salt, ascorbic acid.

Amount: 6 oz			% USRDA
Calories	35	Protein	2
Protein, gm	1	Vitamin A	15
Carbohydrates, gm	8	Vitamin C	35
Fat, gm	0	Thiamine	2
Sodium, mg	625	Riboflavin	2
Cholesterol, mg	0	Niacin	6
Fiber, gm	0	Calcium	*
		Iron	2

Contains nearly ⅓ teaspoon salt.

THIS FOOD: Campbell's Tomato Juice is low in calories, an excellent source of vitamin C, and a very good source of vitamin A. Like most tomato juices, this product is very high in sodium.

ADDITIVES: No questionable additives.

BEST BETS: V-8 Juice contains a whopping 45 percent of the USRDA for vitamins A and C—and all for just 35 calories a serving! The No Salt Added variety contains only 50 milligrams sodium per serving.

NOTE: The letter "e" indicates that the data has been estimated; < means "less than" and is used for small amounts of sodium or cholesterol; * means food contains less than 2% of USRDA; "na" means that the information was not available and appears only when data is insufficient.

CONTADINA TOMATO PASTE
Carnation Co.

Ingredients: tomatoes.

Amount: ¼ cup			% USRDA
Calories	50	Protein	2
Protein, gm	2	Vitamin A	30
Carbohydrates, gm	12	Vitamin C	28
Fat, gm	0	Thiamine	5
Sodium, mg	45	Riboflavin	3
Cholesterol, mg	0	Niacin	9
Fiber, gm	<1	Calcium	*
		Iron	5

THIS FOOD: Contadina Tomato Paste is rich in vitamins A and C, and low in unwanted fat, calories, and sodium.

ADDITIVES: None.

CONTADINA TOMATO SAUCE
Carnation Co.

Ingredients: tomatoes, salt, spices, garlic powder.

Amount: ½ cup			% USRDA
Calories	45	Protein	2
Protein, gm	2	Vitamin A	25
Carbohydrates, gm	9	Vitamin C	15
Fat, gm	0	Thiamine	4
Sodium, mg	510	Riboflavin	2
Cholesterol, mg	0	Niacin	6
Fiber, gm	1	Calcium	*
		Iron	4

Contains ¼ teaspoon salt.

THIS FOOD: Contadina Tomato Sauce provides vitamins A and C in a low-calorie, low-fat product. This sauce is high in sodium.

ADDITIVES: None.

DEL MONTE PEELED TOMATOES
R. J. Reynolds Industries, Inc.

Ingredients: tomatoes, tomato juice, salt, calcium chloride.

Amount: ½ cup			% USRDA
Calories	25	Protein	*
Protein, gm	1	Vitamin A	10
Carbohydrates, gm	5	Vitamin C	30
Fat, gm	0	Thiamine	2
Sodium, mg	220	Riboflavin	*
Cholesterol, mg	0	Niacin	2
Fiber, gm	1.5	Calcium	2
		Iron	2

THIS FOOD: Del Monte Peeled Tomatoes is an excellent source of vitamin C and a good source of vitamin A. Compared to most canned tomato products, it contains a moderate amount of sodium.

ADDITIVES: No questionable additives.

DEL MONTE TOMATO SAUCE
R. J. Reynolds Industries, Inc.

Ingredients: tomatoes, salt, peppers, corn sweetener, spice.

Amount: ½ cup			% USRDA
Calories	35	Protein	2
Protein, gm	2	Vitamin A	25
Carbohydrates, gm	8	Vitamin C	40
Fat, gm	.5	Thiamine	5
Sodium, mg	665	Riboflavin	3
Cholesterol, mg	0	Niacin	5
Fiber, gm	1	Calcium	*
		Iron	5
Contains ⅓ teaspoon salt.			

THIS FOOD: Compared to other popular brands, Del Monte Tomato Sauce is especially rich in vitamin C. It is also an excellent source of vitamin A. Like most canned tomato products, it is low in fat and calories and very high in sodium.

ADDITIVES: None.

HUNT'S STEWED TOMATOES
Hunt-Wesson Foods, Inc.

Ingredients: vine-ripened tomatoes, tomato juice, sugar, salt, dried onions, celery, and peppers, citric acid, calcium chloride, natural flavorings.

Amount: ½ cup			% USRDA
Calories	35	Protein	2
Protein, gm	1	Vitamin A	15
Carbohydrates, gm	8	Vitamin C	30
Fat, gm	0	Thiamine	4
Sodium, mg	460	Riboflavin	2
Cholesterol, mg	0	Niacin	4
Fiber, gm	1	Calcium	4
		Iron	6

THIS FOOD: Hunt's Stewed Tomatoes is rich in vitamin C and a very good source of vitamin A. Like most canned tomato products, it is high in sodium.

ADDITIVES: No questionable additives.

HUNT'S TOMATO SAUCE
Hunt-Wesson Foods, Inc.

Ingredients: vine-ripened tomatoes, salt, dextrose, citric acid, spice, natural flavors.

Amount: ½ cup			% USRDA
Calories	30	Protein	2
Protein, gm	1	Vitamin A	20
Carbohydrates, gm	7	Vitamin C	25
Fat, gm	0	Thiamine	4
Sodium, mg	665	Riboflavin	2
Cholesterol, mg	0	Niacin	6
Fiber, gm	1	Calcium	*
		Iron	15
Contains ⅓ teaspoon salt.			

THIS FOOD: Hunt's Tomato Sauce is a very good source of vitamins A and C. Like most canned tomato products, it is low in fat and calories and high in sodium.

ADDITIVES: No questionable additives.

V-8 NO SALT ADDED VEGETABLE JUICE
Campbell Soup Co.

Ingredients: tomato juice from concentrate (water, tomato concentrate), reconstituted juice of carrots,celery, beets, parsley, lettuce, watercress, spinach, with ascorbic acid, natural flavoring, and citric acid.

Amount: 6 oz			% USRDA
Calories	40	Protein	2
Protein, gm	1	Vitamin A	45
Carbohydrates, gm	8	Vitamin C	45
Fat, gm	0	Thiamine	*
Sodium, mg	50	Riboflavin	2
Cholesterol, mg	0	Niacin	6
Fiber, gm	0	Calcium	2
		Iron	4

THIS FOOD: V-8 No Salt Added Vegetable Juice is a nutritional bonanza: low in salt, fat, and calories and very rich in valuable vitamins A and C.

ADDITIVES: No questionable additives.

V-8 VEGETABLE JUICE
Campbell Soup Co.

Ingredients: tomato juice from concentrate (water, tomato concentrate), reconstituted juices of carrots, celery, beets, parsley, lettuce, watercress, spinach, with salt, ascorbic acid, natural flavoring, and citric acid.

Amount: 6 oz			% USRDA
Calories	35	Protein	2
Protein, gm	1	Vitamin A	45
Carbohydrates, gm	8	Vitamin C	45
Fat, gm	0	Thiamine	*
Sodium, mg	625	Riboflavin	2
Cholesterol, mg	0	Niacin	6
Fiber, gm	0	Calcium	2
		Iron	4

Contains nearly ⅓ teaspoon salt.

THIS FOOD: V-8 Vegetable Juice is very low in calories and very rich in vitamin C and vitamin A. Like most tomato juices, this product is very high in sodium.

ADDITIVES: No questionable additives.

See "Basic Foods" on page 566 for fresh tomato listings.

VEGETABLES & LEGUMES

If you eat like most Americans, tripling or quadrupling your consumption of vegetables, while cutting back on sweets and fatty protein foods, would go a long way toward correcting two major faults of your diet: too much fat, and not enough complex carbohydrates and fiber. At the same time, you'd be lowering your risk of heart disease, high blood pressure, diabetes, and certain types of cancer.

There's more good news as well. Naturally low in calories and sodium, vegetables are an excellent source of many valuable vitamins and minerals. Nutritionists say they have high "nutrient density" because they are low in calories yet still contain a variety of essential vitamins and minerals—especially vitamin A, vitamin C, potassium, and iron.

While vegetables ripened on the vine and cooked within hours of picking have the best nutrient content of all, few of us today enjoy the luxury of truly fresh produce. For most of us, frozen vegetables are a perfectly acceptable choice. All of the most popular brands, such as Birds Eye, Green Giant, and Seabrook, offer vitamin-rich, no-salt-added vegetables. Canned vegetables, whether from Del Monte, Green Giant, or Libby's, should always be your last choice. Typically

---

FIBER WINNERS

These vegetables contain at least 5 grams fiber per serving:

B & M Brick Oven Baked Beans
Birds Eye Green Peas
Birds Eye Little Ears of Corn
Bush's Best Light Red Kidney Beans
Bush's Showboat Pork and Beans
Campbell's Home Style Beans
Campbell's Pork and Beans in Tomato Sauce
Del Monte Early Garden Spinach
Del Monte Early Garden Sweet Peas
Green Giant Sweet Peas
Le Sueur Early June Peas
Van Camp's Pork and Beans

---

these products are high in added sodium and retain only about half of many vitamins and minerals.

The increasingly popular frozen sauced vegetables—some of them quite exotic—are a different story. Generally loaded with fatty sauces, additives, artificial coloring and flavoring, these convenience products are almost always a poor nutritional choice, when compared to plain frozen vegetables.

See "Basic Foods" on pages 552–55, 557–68 for fresh vegetable listings.

Beans/Pork and Beans

Plain beans, or legumes, are one of the most healthful foods. Kidney, pinto, navy, and lima are the most popular varieties and all are low in fat, extremely high in dietary fiber, and an excellent source of protein and iron. Currently the average American consumes only about one half of the 30 grams dietary fiber that health authorities believe we should eat each day. An easy way to increase the fiber in your diet is to eat more beans, a much neglected, extremely nutritious food. Every time you eat a cup of beans, you are getting 15 grams or more of dietary fiber, or 50 percent of the recommended daily intake. Research indicates that a diet high in fiber is associated with a lower incidence of intestinal disorders, and of colon cancer, a major killer. Beans are especially high in soluble fiber, which new studies indicate may help to lower cholesterol levels.

Campbell's, Van Camp's, and B & M Baked Beans are also nutritious inexpensive convenience foods, but these popular brands are higher in added salt and sugar than plain beans. For instance, Campbell's Pork and Beans in Tomato Sauce contains 3 teaspoons added sugar and 945 milligrams sodium per 8-ounce serving. Also each serving is usually made up of about 60 percent nutrient-rich beans and 40 percent sugary, salty sauce, which is the ratio suggested by the U.S. Department of Agriculture. It is interesting to note that despite their name, pork-and-bean products typically contain only about 1 percent pork by weight while beans-and-franks products must contain 20 percent wiener before processing. The iron and sodium content of canned beans in sauce varies widely, so be sure to check the label before you buy. Plain canned beans contain far less sodium than beans in sauce. For still less sodium, you can rinse the beans before using.

SODIUM GUIDELINES: In evaluating the sodium content of canned beans, we have used the following standards:

250 mg to 500 mg	moderate in sodium
500 mg to 750 mg	high in sodium
more than 750 mg	very high in sodium

Remember, these guidelines are not for people following medically restricted low-sodium diets, but for healthy individuals who wish to monitor their sodium intake.

B & M BRICK OVEN BAKED BEANS
Pet, Inc., Grocery Group

Ingredients: small pea beans with pork in sauce containing: water, brown sugar, salt, white sugar, mustard.

Amount: 1 cup			% USRDA
Calories	330	Protein	25
Protein, gm	16	Vitamin A	*
Carbohydrates, gm	49	Vitamin C	*
Fat, gm	8	Thiamine	2
Sodium, mg	1,051e	Riboflavin	6
Cholesterol, mg	na	Niacin	6
Fiber, gm	12e	Calcium	10
		Iron	40
Contains ½ teaspoon salt.			

THIS FOOD: All baked beans are a rich source of dietary fiber, complex carbohydrates, vegetable protein, and iron, but B & M Brick Oven Baked Beans are especially rich in iron and protein. This product is also higher in calories than most other brands—probably as it contains more beans relative to the amount of sauce.

ADDITIVES: None.

NUTRITION TIP: To enhance iron absorption, eat baked beans and other vegetable sources of iron with a vitamin-C rich food such as tomatoes, broccoli, cole slaw, or orange juice.

BUSH'S BEST LIGHT RED KIDNEY BEANS
Bush Brothers and Co.

Ingredients: kidney beans, water, sugar and salt, calcium chloride, disodium EDTA.

NOTE: The letter "e" indicates that the data has been estimated; < means "less than" and is used for small amounts of sodium or cholesterol; * means food contains less than 2% of USRDA; "na" means that the information was not available and appears only when data is insufficient.

Amount: 1 cup (with liquid)		% USRDA	
Calories	204	Protein	20
Protein, gm	13	Vitamin A	*
Carbohydrates, gm	37	Vitamin C	*
Fat, gm	1	Thiamine	8
Sodium, mg	264	Riboflavin	5
Cholesterol, mg	0	Niacin	7
Fiber, gm	20	Calcium	7
		Iron	23

THIS FOOD: Kidney beans, like many dried legumes, are close to being an ideal food. They are one of the richest and least expensive sources of dietary fiber, complex carbohydrates, and iron as well as being a low-fat source of vegetable protein. Because of added salt, Bush's Best Light Red Kidney Beans contain a moderate amount of sodium.

ADDITIVES: No questionable additives.

SERVING SUGGESTION: A cup of beans mixed with a half a can of water-packed tuna and tossed with a tablespoon of vinegar-and-oil dressing makes a tasty, fiber-rich and inexpensive luncheon dish.

BUSH'S SHOWBOAT PORK AND BEANS
Bush Brothers and Co.

Ingredients: prepared small white beans, water, sugar, tomato paste, salt, dextrose, pork, flavorings, and spices.

Amount: 1 cup		% USRDA	
Calories	277	Protein	22
Protein, gm	14	Vitamin A	16
Carbohydrates, gm	43	Vitamin C	8
Fat, gm	6	Thiamine	12
Sodium, mg	1,051	Riboflavin	4
Cholesterol, mg	<5	Niacin	7
Fiber, gm	10e	Calcium	12
		Iron	23

Contains ½ teaspoon salt.

THIS FOOD: Bush's Showboat Pork and Beans supply valuable dietary fiber, complex carbohydrates, calcium, and iron. They are also an inexpensive source of vegetable protein. Like most canned pork and beans they are very high in added salt and sugar.

ADDITIVES: No questionable additives.

CAMPBELL'S HOME STYLE BEANS
Campbell Soup Co.

Ingredients: cooked pea beans, water, tomatoes, brown sugar, molasses, sugar, bacon (cured with water, salt, sugar, sodium phosphate, sodium erythorbate, sodium nitrite), salt, high-fructose corn syrup, modified food starch, distilled vinegar, dehydrated onions, citric acid, natural flavors, smoke flavor.

Amount: 1 cup			% USRDA
Calories	270	Protein	15
Protein, gm	11	Vitamin A	4
Carbohydrates, gm	48	Vitamin C	6
Fat, gm	4	Thiamine	4
Sodium, mg	1,150	Riboflavin	2
Cholesterol, mg	<5	Niacin	4
Fiber, gm	10e	Calcium	10
Contains ½ teaspoon salt.		Iron	20

THIS FOOD: Campbell's Home Style Beans are a very good source of iron, one of the best possible sources of dietary fiber, and also provide complex carbohydrates and calcium. They are also an inexpensive source of vegetable protein. Like most canned beans they are very high in added salt and sugar.

ADDITIVES: Contains sodium nitrite, which can be converted into cancer-causing nitrosamines.

BEST BET: One serving of B & M Brick Oven Baked Beans contains a whopping 40 percent of the USRDA for iron, and 25 percent of the USRDA for protein, substantially more than the other popular brands.

CAMPBELL'S PORK AND BEANS IN TOMATO SAUCE
Campbell Soup Co.

Ingredients: prepared pea beans, water, tomatoes, corn syrup, sugar, pork, salt, modified food starch, distilled vinegar, natural flavors, citric acid, oleoresin, paprika.

Amount: 1 cup			% USRDA
Calories	250	Protein	15
Protein, gm	11	Vitamin A	4
Carbohydrates, gm	44	Vitamin C	4
Fat, gm	4	Thiamine	6
Sodium, mg	945	Riboflavin	2
Cholesterol, mg	<5	Niacin	4
Fiber, gm	10e	Calcium	10
		Iron	15
Contains 3 teaspoons sugar and ½ teaspoon salt.			

THIS FOOD: Campbell's Pork and Beans in Tomato Sauce are a good source of iron, one of the best possible sources of valuable dietary fiber and also provide complex carbohydrates and calcium. Like most canned beans, they are very high in added salt and sugar.

ADDITIVES: No questionable additives.

VAN CAMP'S PORK AND BEANS
Quaker Oats Co.

Ingredients: prepared small white beans, water, sugar, concentrated tomatoes, corn sweetener, salt, pork, vinegar, bicarbonate of soda, onion powder, spice, and natural and artificial flavorings.

Amount: 1 cup			% USRDA
Calories	220	Protein	15
Protein, gm	11	Vitamin A	2
Carbohydrates, gm	41	Vitamin C	4
Fat, gm	2	Thiamine	8
Sodium, mg	995	Riboflavin	6
Cholesterol, mg	<5	Niacin	4
Fiber, gm	10e	Calcium	10
		Iron	20

Contains ½ teaspoon salt.

THIS FOOD: This product is an excellent source of fiber, and a very good source of vegetable protein, complex carbohydrates, and iron. It is also a fair source of calcium. Like most canned pork and beans, this food is very high in added sodium and sugar. Van Camp's is the only popular brand to use artificial flavorings in its recipe.

ADDITIVES: Contains artificial flavor, which may cause allergic reactions in sensitive individuals, and which some studies suggest may adversely affect behavior and the ability to complete school tasks in some sensitive children.

DID YOU KNOW: The average American consumes only half of the dietary fiber that health authorities believe we should eat each day. Beans are one of the very best sources of fiber. One cup of this much neglected, extremely nutritious food will supply at least half the recommended intake of 30 grams fiber per day.

Canned Vegetables

Frozen or fresh vegetables are almost always superior in nutrition to canned produce. Although sales of canned vegetables have declined in recent years, there will always be a market for this convenience food since it requires no refrigeration. If you must use canned vegetables, always store them at 65 degrees Fahrenheit or less and heat them just through to minimize nutrient loss. Also remember to keep cans away from the stove.

SODIUM GUIDELINES: In evaluating the sodium content of canned vegetables, we used the following standards:

less than 100 mg	low in sodium
100 mg to 250 mg	moderate in sodium
250 mg to 600 mg	high in sodium
more than 600 mg	very high in sodium

Remember, these guidelines are not for people following medically restricted low-sodium diets, but for healthy individuals who wish to monitor their sodium intake.

DEL MONTE CREAM STYLE GOLDEN SWEET CORN
R. J. Reynolds Industries, Inc.

Ingredients: corn, water, sugar, modified food starch, salt.

Amount: ½ cup			% USRDA
Calories	80	Protein	2
Protein, gm	2	Vitamin A	2
Carbohydrates, gm	18	Vitamin C	8
Fat, gm	1	Thiamine	2
Sodium, mg	355	Riboflavin	2
Cholesterol, mg	0	Niacin	4
Fiber, gm	2.5	Calcium	*
		Iron	2

THIS FOOD: Many people may be surprised to find that "Cream Style" corn contains no cream or dairy product of any kind—only food starch, sugar, and salt. While canned corn in this form is still a source of fiber and complex carbohydrates, the added ingredients contribute calories without any additional nutrients. This product is high in sodium.

ADDITIVES: No questionable additives.

DEL MONTE EARLY GARDEN SPINACH

R. J. Reynolds Industries, Inc

Ingredients: whole leaf spinach, water, salt

Amount: ½ cup			% USRDA
Calories	25	Protein	2
Protein, gm	2	Vitamin A	110
Carbohydrates, gm	4	Vitamin C	20
Fat, gm	0	Thiamine	*
Sodium, mg	355	Riboflavin	6
Cholesterol, mg	0	Niacin	*
Fiber, gm	6.5e	Calcium	10
		Iron	8

THIS FOOD: Del Monte Early Garden Spinach is a rich storehouse of nutrients—even after the substantial losses which occur during processing. A half-cup serving supplies more than 600 mg of potassium, which is about 30 percent of the minimum recommended daily intake of this valuable mineral, and fair amounts of calcium and iron. Canned spinach is also very high in vitamin A and dietary fiber. Like most canned vegetables, this product is high in sodium.

ADDITIVES: None.

DEL MONTE EARLY GARDEN SWEET PEAS

R. J. Reynolds Industries, Inc.

Ingredients: peas, water, sugar, salt.

Amount: ½ cup			% USRDA
Calories	60	Protein	4
Protein, gm	3	Vitamin A	8
Carbohydrates, gm	10	Vitamin C	20
Fat, gm	0	Thiamine	6
Sodium, mg	355	Riboflavin	4
Cholesterol, mg	0	Niacin	4
Fiber, gm	5e	Calcium	2
		Iron	6

NOTE: The letter "e" indicates that the data has been estimated; < means "less than" and is used for small amounts of sodium or cholesterol; * means food contains less than 2% of USRDA; "na" means that the information was not available and appears only when data is insufficient.

THIS FOOD: Del Monte Early Garden Sweet Peas are a very good source of dietary fiber and vitamin C. Unfortunately, the canning process results in significant losses of vitamins and minerals. Like most canned vegetables, this product is high in added sodium.

ADDITIVES: None.

DEL MONTE WHOLE GREEN BEANS
R. J. Reynolds Industries, Inc.

Ingredients: green beans, water, salt.

Amount: ½ cup			% USRDA
Calories	20	Protein	*
Protein, gm	1	Vitamin A	10
Carbohydrates, gm	4	Vitamin C	10
Fat, gm	0	Thiamine	8
Sodium, mg	355	Riboflavin	2
Cholesterol, mg	0	Niacin	4
Fiber, gm	2	Calcium	*
		Iron	2

THIS FOOD: Del Monte Whole Green Beans are a fair source of vitamin A, vitamin C, and fiber. Like most canned foods, this product is high in sodium.

ADDITIVES: None.

OTHER BRANDS: Green Giant Kitchen Cut and French Style Green Beans contain substantially less sodium per serving than Del Monte Green Beans.

DEL MONTE WHOLE KERNEL FAMILY STYLE CORN
R. J. Reynolds Industries, Inc.

Ingredients: corn, water, sugar, salt.

Amount: ½ cup			% USRDA
Calories	70	Protein	2
Protein, gm	2	Vitamin A	2
Carbohydrates, gm	17	Vitamin C	10
Fat, gm	1	Thiamine	2
Sodium, mg	355	Riboflavin	4
Cholesterol, mg	0	Niacin	4
Fiber, gm	4e	Calcium	*
		Iron	2

THIS FOOD: Corn is a source of complex carbohydrates and fiber. Those concerned with their sodium intake should choose fresh or frozen corn. This product contains added sugar.

ADDITIVES: None.

OTHER BRANDS: Green Giant Whole Kernel Corn contains 72 percent less sodium per serving.

GREEN GIANT ASPARAGUS CUTS
The Pillsbury Co.

Ingredients: asparagus cuts, water, salt.

Amount: ½ cup			% USRDA
Calories	20	Protein	4
Protein, gm	3	Vitamin A	6
Carbohydrates, gm	2	Vitamin C	25
Fat, gm	0	Thiamine	2
Sodium, mg	450	Riboflavin	6
Cholesterol, mg	0	Niacin	2
Fiber, gm	2	Calcium	*
		Iron	4

THIS FOOD: Canned asparagus are naturally low in calories, and are a source of dietary fiber and an excellent source of vitamin C. As with most canned vegetables, the sodium content is extremely high, and most of the B vitamins have been destroyed during processing.

ADDITIVES: None.

GREEN GIANT CREAM STYLE CORN
The Pillsbury Co.

Ingredients: golden corn, water, sugar, modified cornstarch, salt.

Amount: ½ cup			% USRDA
Calories	100	Protein	2
Protein, gm	2	Vitamin A	*
Carbohydrates, gm	21	Vitamin C	8
Fat, gm	1	Thiamine	2
Sodium, mg	320	Riboflavin	2
Cholesterol, mg	0	Niacin	6
Fiber, gm	2.5e	Calcium	*
		Iron	*

THIS FOOD: Many people may be surprised to find that "Cream Style" corn contains no cream or dairy product of any kind—only cornstarch, salt, and sugar. While corn in this form is still a source of fiber and complex carbohydrates, the added ingredients contribute calories without any additional nutrients. Those concerned with their sodium intake should note that this product contains 72 percent more sodium than Green Giant Whole Kernel Corn.

ADDITIVES: No questionable additives.

GREEN GIANT FRENCH STYLE CUT GREEN BEANS
The Pillsbury Co.

Ingredients: French-cut green beans, water, sugar, salt.

Amount: ½ cup			% USRDA
Calories	18	Protein	*
Protein, gm	1	Vitamin A	4
Carbohydrates, gm	3	Vitamin C	4
Fat, gm	0	Thiamine	*
Sodium, mg	270	Riboflavin	2
Cholesterol, mg	0	Niacin	*
Fiber, gm	2	Calcium	2
		Iron	4

THIS FOOD: Compared to other canned vegetables, this product is low in nutrients. Like most canned foods, this product is high in sodium.

ADDITIVES: None.

GREEN GIANT KITCHEN CUT GREEN BEANS
The Pillsbury Co.

Ingredients: ½-diagonal-cut green beans, water, salt.

Amount: ½ cup			% USRDA
Calories	20	Protein	2
Protein, gm	2	Vitamin A	6
Carbohydrates, gm	3	Vitamin C	6
Fat, gm	0	Thiamine	2
Sodium, mg	260	Riboflavin	2
Cholesterol, mg	0	Niacin	*
Fiber, gm	2	Calcium	2
		Iron	4

THIS FOOD: Compared to other canned vegetables, this product is low in nutrients. Like most canned foods, this product is high in sodium.

ADDITIVES: None.

GREEN GIANT MUSHROOMS
The Pillsbury Co.

Ingredients: mushrooms, water, salt, ascorbic acid.

Amount: 2 oz			% USRDA
Calories	14	Protein	2
Protein, gm	1	Vitamin A	*
Carbohydrates, gm	2	Vitamin C	4
Fat, gm	0	Thiamine	*
Sodium, mg	260	Riboflavin	6
Cholesterol, mg	0	Niacin	2
Fiber, gm	1	Calcium	*
		Iron	2

THIS FOOD: Canned mushrooms do not provide significant amounts of the nutrients you need. Like most canned vegetables, this product is high in added sodium.

ADDITIVES: No questionable additives.

GREEN GIANT SWEET PEAS
The Pillsbury Co.

Ingredients: sweet peas, water, sugar, salt.

Amount: ½ cup			% USRDA
Calories	60	Protein	6
Protein, gm	4	Vitamin A	6
Carbohydrates, gm	11	Vitamin C	8
Fat, gm	0	Thiamine	8
Sodium, mg	375	Riboflavin	4
Cholesterol, mg	0	Niacin	4
Fiber, gm	5	Calcium	2
		Iron	6

THIS FOOD: Green Giant Sweet Peas are a good source of dietary fiber and vegetable protein. Unfortunately, the canning process results in significant losses of vitamins and minerals. Like most canned vegetables, this product is high in added sodium.

ADDITIVES: None.

GREEN GIANT WHOLE KERNEL CORN
The Pillsbury Co.

Ingredients: whole kernel corn, water, sugar, salt.

Amount: ½ cup			% USRDA
Calories	90	Protein	2
Protein, gm	2	Vitamin A	2
Carbohydrates, gm	20	Vitamin C	10
Fat, gm	0	Thiamine	2
Sodium, mg	230	Riboflavin	4
Cholesterol, mg	0	Niacin	4
Fiber, gm	4	Calcium	*
		Iron	2

THIS FOOD: Corn is a good source of complex carbohydrates and fiber. Those concerned with their sodium intake should choose fresh or frozen corn. This product contains added sugar.

ADDITIVES: None.

LE SUEUR EARLY JUNE PEAS
The Pillsbury Co.

Ingredients: early June peas, water, sugar, salt.

Amount: ½ cup			% USRDA
Calories	60	Protein	4
Protein, gm	3	Vitamin A	10
Carbohydrates, gm	11	Vitamin C	10
Fat, gm	<1	Thiamine	8
Sodium, mg	375	Riboflavin	4
Cholesterol, mg	0	Niacin	2
Fiber, gm	5	Calcium	2
		Iron	6

THIS FOOD: Le Sueur Early June Peas are a good source of dietary fiber and contain more protein than most vegetables (but somewhat less than other peas, because they are picked when slightly immature). The canning process, however, has resulted in significant losses of vitamin and mineral content. This product, like most canned items, has too much added salt.

ADDITIVES: None.

LIBBY'S NATURAL PACK MIXED VEGETABLES
Seneca Foods Corp.

Ingredients: water, carrots, potatoes, peas, corn, green beans, celery, baby lima beans.

Amount: ½ cup			% USRDA
Calories	40	Protein	2
Protein, gm	1	Vitamin A	90
Carbohydrates, gm	9	Vitamin C	8
Fat, gm	0	Thiamine	2
Sodium, mg	20	Riboflavin	2
Cholesterol, mg	0	Niacin	2
Fiber, gm	3	Calcium	2
		Iron	2

THIS FOOD: Libby's Natural Pack Mixed Vegetables are an excellent source of vitamin A and a fair source of dietary fiber and complex carbohydrates. This product contains only 20 mg naturally occurring sodium per serving.

ADDITIVES: None.

OTHER BRANDS: Libby's Natural Pack Mixed Vegetables contain no added sodium.

VEG-ALL
The Larsen Co.

Ingredients: water, carrots, potatoes, celery, sweet peas, green beans, corn, lima beans, salt and onion flavoring. Trace of calcium chloride added.

Amount: ½ cup			% USRDA
Calories	35	Protein	2
Protein, gm	2	Vitamin A	120
Carbohydrates, gm	7	Vitamin C	8
Fat, gm	0	Thiamine	2
Sodium, mg	330	Riboflavin	2
Cholesterol, mg	0	Niacin	4
Fiber, gm	2.5	Calcium	2
		Iron	2

THIS FOOD: Veg-All is an excellent source of vitamin A and also supplies some dietary fiber per serving. Like most canned foods, it is high in sodium.

ADDITIVES: No questionable additives.

Frozen Vegetables

How you store and cook frozen vegetables can radically affect their nutrient content. To minimize losses, frozen vegetables should be kept at 0 degrees Fahrenheit or less in your freezer. Even at that temperature, vitamin loss occurs so it's best to consume frozen produce within a month or two. Steam or cook vegetables in as little water and as briefly as possible to help preserve nutrients, and do not overcook.

SODIUM GUIDELINES: In evaluating the sodium content of frozen vegetables in sauce, we used the following standards:

100 mg to 250 mg	moderate in sodium
more than 250 mg	high in sodium

Remember, these guidelines are not for people following medically restricted low-sodium diets, but for healthy individuals who wish to monitor their sodium intake.

BIRDS EYE BROCCOLI SPEARS
General Foods Corp.
Ingredients: broccoli spears.

Amount: ½ cup			% USRDA
Calories	25	Protein	4
Protein, gm	3	Vitamin A	25
Carbohydrates, gm	5	Vitamin C	100
Fat, gm	0	Thiamine	4
Sodium, mg	20	Riboflavin	6
Cholesterol, mg	0	Niacin	2
Fiber, gm	3.5	Calcium	4
		Iron	4

THIS FOOD: Broccoli in this form is one of the most nutritious vegetables. Frozen spears are a rich source of vitamin A, vitamin C, and contain a fair amount of dietary fiber. Like most vegetables, they are naturally low in sodium.

ADDITIVES: None.

BIRDS EYE COOKED WINTER SQUASH
General Foods Corp.
Ingredients: cooked winter squash.

Amount: ½ cup			% USRDA
Calories	45	Protein	*
Protein, gm	1	Vitamin A	90
Carbohydrates, gm	11	Vitamin C	20
Fat, gm	0	Thiamine	2
Sodium, mg	0	Riboflavin	4
Cholesterol, mg	0	Niacin	2
Fiber, gm	3	Calcium	2
		Iron	4

THIS FOOD: Winter squash supplies fiber and is an excellent source of vitamin A—a mere half-cup serving provides 90 percent of the USRDA—as well as a good source of vitamin C. Winter squash is also an unusually rich source of potassium.

ADDITIVES: None.

BIRDS EYE CUT GREEN BEANS
General Foods Corp.

Ingredients: cut green beans.

Amount: ½ cup			% USRDA
Calories	25	Protein	2
Protein, gm	1	Vitamin A	10
Carbohydrates, gm	6	Vitamin C	15
Fat, gm	0	Thiamine	2
Sodium, mg	5	Riboflavin	4
Cholesterol, mg	0	Niacin	*
Fiber, gm	2	Calcium	4
		Iron	4

THIS FOOD: Green beans are low in calories, fat, and sodium, and contain fair amounts of vitamins, minerals, and fiber.

ADDITIVES: None.

NUTRITION TIP: Winter squash is one of the richest sources of carotene, a precursor of vitamin A, which gives carrots, sweet potatoes, squash, and other vegetables their rich orange coloring. Recent research suggests that consuming large quantities of carotenoids from natural sources may help to protect against cancer. If your family doesn't like winter squash, try pureeing and mixing half and half with mashed potatoes.

BIRDS EYE GREEN PEAS
General Foods Corp.

Ingredients: green peas, trace of salt.

Amount: ½ cup			% USRDA
Calories	80	Protein	8
Protein, gm	5	Vitamin A	15
Carbohydrates, gm	13	Vitamin C	30
Fat, gm	0	Thiamine	20
Sodium, mg	130	Riboflavin	6
Cholesterol, mg	0	Niacin	10
Fiber, gm	6	Calcium	2
		Iron	8

THIS FOOD: Peas are a very good source of fiber, complex carbohydrates, vitamin C, and thiamine. They are also relatively high in vegetable protein and contain small but useful amounts of iron. Even with a trace of added salt, Birds Eye frozen peas remain low in sodium.

ADDITIVES: None.

BIRDS EYE ITALIAN STYLE VEGETABLES
General Foods Corp.

Ingredients: Italian green beans, chick peas, red peppers, onions, ripe olives, partially hydrogenated soybean and cottonseed oils, dextrin, water, modified cornstarch, salt, hydrolyzed vegetable protein, onion powder, oregano flakes, sodium carbonate, natural flavor, sodium benzoate, artificial color, artificial flavor, vitamin A.

Amount: 3.3 oz/½ cup			% USRDA
Calories	110	Protein	4
Protein, gm	2	Vitamin A	15
Carbohydrates, gm	11	Vitamin C	40
Fat, gm	7	Thiamine	2
Sodium, mg	575	Riboflavin	4
Cholesterol, mg	0	Niacin	2
Fiber, gm	2.5e	Calcium	4
		Iron	4

THIS FOOD: The vegetables in this combination contain valuable nutrients, including a fair amount of fiber and a great deal of vitamin C. But artificial flavor and color as well as too much added fat and salt make this product a poor choice. About 57 percent of the calories in this product come from fat.

ADDITIVES: Contains artificial color and flavor, which some studies suggest may adversely affect behavior and the ability to complete school tasks in some sensitive children; artificial colors are inadequately tested and artificial flavor may cause allergic reactions in sensitive individuals.

BIRDS EYE JAPANESE STYLE VEGETABLES
General Foods Corp.

Ingredients: French-style green beans, broccoli, pearl onions, mushrooms, red peppers. *Sauce made from:* partially hydrogenated soybean and cottonseed oils, dextrin, water, modified cornstarch, sugar, salt, monosodium glutamate, natural flavor, hydrolyzed vegetable protein, wheat starch, sodium carbonate, chicken fat, dextrose, onion powder, sodium benzoate and benzoic acid, artificial color, turmeric and extractives of turmeric, artificial flavor, vitamin A palmitate.

Amount: 3.3 oz			% USRDA
Calories	100	Protein	4
Protein, gm	2	Vitamin A	15
Carbohydrates, gm	10	Vitamin C	60
Fat, gm	6	Thiamine	2
Sodium, mg	505	Riboflavin	4
Cholesterol, mg	<5e	Niacin	*
Fiber, gm	2e	Calcium	2
		Iron	2

THIS FOOD: Birds Eye Japanese Style Vegetables contain some valuable dietary fiber and vitamin C along with a long list of additives. Fifty-four percent of this product's calories derive from fat, and it contains a whopping 505 mg sodium per serving.

ADDITIVES: Contains artificial color and flavor, which some studies suggest may adversely affect behavior and the ability to complete school tasks in some sensitive children; artificial colors are inadequately tested, and artificial flavor may cause allergic reactions in sensitive individuals. Also contains monosodium glutamate (MSG), which many authorities believe should be avoided by infants and very young children; causes adverse reactions in sensitive individuals.

HELPFUL HINT: If you want Oriental-style vegetables, without too much fat or additives, try adding a few drops of fragrant dark sesame oil and a dash of low-sodium soy sauce, now available in most supermarkets.

BIRDS EYE LITTLE EARS OF CORN
General Foods Corp.
Ingredients: cob corn.

Amount: 2 ears			% USRDA
Calories	130	Protein	6
Protein, gm	4	Vitamin A	6
Carbohydrates, gm	30	Vitamin C	15
Fat, gm	1	Thiamine	10
Sodium, mg	5	Riboflavin	6
Cholesterol, mg	0	Niacin	10
Fiber, gm	5	Calcium	*
		Iron	4

THIS FOOD: Corn is a very good source of complex carbohydrates and dietary fiber. It is also relatively high in vegetable protein. Like most vegetables, it is low in fat and sodium.

ADDITIVES: None.

BIRDS EYE SAN FRANCISCO STYLE VEGETABLES
General Foods Corp
Ingredients: French-style green beans, bean sprouts, celery, partially hydrogenated soybean and cottonseed oils, mushrooms, red peppers, dextrin, wheat flour, water, salt, monosodium glutamate, natural flavor, hydrolyzed vegetable protein, wheat starch, sodium carbonate, chicken fat, dextrose, onion powder, sodium benzoate, benzoic acid, TBHQ, citric acid, artificial color, turmeric, artificial color and flavor.

Amount: ½ cup			% USRDA
Calories	100	Protein	4
Protein, gm	2	Vitamin A	10
Carbohydrates, gm	11	Vitamin C	15
Fat, gm	5	Thiamine	4
Sodium, mg	395	Riboflavin	4
Cholesterol, mg	<5e	Niacin	2
Fiber, gm	2e	Calcium	2
		Iron	2

THIS FOOD: Contains a mixture of nutritious and appetizing vegetables, but too much fat, as well as artificial color and flavor, are real drawbacks. A full 45 percent of this product's calories come from added oils and fats.

ADDITIVES: Contains artificial color and flavor, which some studies suggest may adversely affect behavior and the ability to complete school tasks in some sensitive children; artificial colors are inadequately tested, and artificial flavor may cause allergic reactions in sensitive individuals. Also contains monosodium glutamate (MSG), which many authorities believe should be avoided by infants and very young children; causes adverse reactions in sensitive individuals.

BIRDS EYE SWEET CORN
General Foods Corp.

Ingredients: sweet corn.

Amount: ½ cup			% USRDA
Calories	80	Protein	4
Protein, gm	3	Vitamin A	4
Carbohydrates, gm	20	Vitamin C	8
Fat, gm	1	Thiamine	4
Sodium, mg	5	Riboflavin	4
Cholesterol, mg	0	Niacin	8
Fiber, gm	5	Calcium	*
		Iron	2

THIS FOOD: Corn is a very good source of complex carbohydrates and dietary fiber. It is also relatively high in vegetable protein. Like most vegetables, it is low in fat and sodium.

ADDITIVES: None.

GREEN GIANT BROCCOLI, CAULIFLOWER, AND CARROTS IN CHEESE SAUCE
The Pillsbury Co.

Ingredients: cut broccoli, cut cauliflower, cut carrots, water, whey, hydrogenated vegetable oil (soy and/or cottonseed), modified cornstarch, buttermilk, salt, dried Cheddar cheese, natural flavors, nonfat milk, sodium phosphate, sodium alginate, sodiuim hexametaphosphate, dried Parmesan cheese, hydrolyzed plant protein, dried blue cheese, onion powder, monoglycerides, garlic powder, cream, artificial color, including FD & C Yellow No. 5, lactic acid, citric acid, disodium inosinate, disodium guanylate.

Amount: ½ cup			% USRDA
Calories	60	Protein	4
Protein, gm	3	Vitamin A	80
Carbohydrates, gm	8	Vitamin C	50
Fat, gm	2	Thiamine	4
Sodium, mg	465	Riboflavin	8
Cholesterol, mg	5e	Niacin	2
Fiber, gm	2e	Calcium	6
		Iron	*

THIS FOOD: Green Giant Broccoli, Cauliflower, and Carrots in Cheese Sauce is relatively low in fat and calories, probably because the cheese itself is scarcely present. A glance at the ingredients list tells the real story: dried Cheddar appears tenth on the list, after such ingredients as water, hydrogenated vegetable oil, modified cornstarch, and salt. In other words, there is more salt (465 mg per serving!) than Cheddar cheese, more sodium alginate (a thickener/emulsifier) and sodium phosphate than Parmesan and blue cheese. On the positive side, this product is very rich in vitamin A and vitamin C.

ADDITIVES: Contains Yellow No. 5, which can cause allergic reactions, primarily among aspirin-sensitive individuals. Also contains artificial color, which is inadequately tested and which some studies suggest may adversely affect behavior and the ability to complete school tasks in some sensitive children.

GREEN GIANT BROCCOLI SPEARS IN BUTTER SAUCE
The Pillsbury Co.

Ingredients: broccoli spears, water, butter, sugar, salt, modified cornstarch.

Amount: ½ cup			% USRDA
Calories	40	Protein	4
Protein, gm	2	Vitamin A	8
Carbohydrates, gm	5	Vitamin C	30
Fat, gm	1	Thiamine	2
Sodium, mg	325	Riboflavin	4
Cholesterol, mg	<5e	Niacin	2
Fiber, gm	3e	Calcium	2
		Iron	*

THIS FOOD: This low-fat, low-calorie convenience product is perhaps the best choice among the presauced frozen vegetables. It is an excellent source of vitamin C and a fair source of dietary fiber. In addition, some scientists believe that broccoli, like other members of the cabbage family, may help protect against colon cancer.

ADDITIVES: No questionable additives.

OTHER BRANDS: Birds Eye Broccoli Spears in Butter Sauce have three times more of vitamins A and C and twice as much iron, without any added sodium.

HELPFUL HINT: If you enjoy the taste of cheese, try adding a teaspoon of Parmesan to each cup of cooked vegetables. You probably won't need more salt, and you'll end up with an additive-free dish of low-fat, low-calorie, and low-cost vegetables.

GREEN GIANT CAULIFLOWER IN CHEESE SAUCE
The Pillsbury Co.

Ingredients: cut cauliflower, water, whey, hydrogenated vegetable oil (soy and/or cottonseed), modified cornstarch, buttermilk, salt, dried Cheddar cheese, natural flavors, nonfat milk, sodium phosphate, sodium alginate, sodium hexametaphosphate, dried Parmesan cheese, dried blue cheese, hydrolyzed plant protein, onion powder, monoglycerides, garlic powder, cream, artificial color (including FD & C Yellow No. 5), lactic acid, citric acid, disodium inosinate, disodium guanylate.

Amount: ½ cup			% USRDA
Calories	60	Protein	2
Protein, gm	2	Vitamin A	15
Carbohydrates, gm	10	Vitamin C	50
Fat, gm	2	Thiamine	2
Sodium, mg	450	Riboflavin	8
Cholesterol, mg	5e	Niacin	*
Fiber, gm	1e	Calcium	6
		Iron	2

THIS FOOD: Green Giant Cauliflower in Cheese Sauce is relatively low in fat and calories, probably because the cheese itself is scarcely present. A glance at the ingredients list tells the real story: dried Cheddar appears eighth on the list, after such ingredients as water, hydrogenated vegetable oil, modified cornstarch, and salt. In other words, there is more salt (450 mg per serving!) than Cheddar cheese, more sodium alginate (a thickener/emulsifier) and sodium phosphate than Parmesan and blue cheese. On the positive side, this product supplies 50 percent of the USRDA for vitamin C.

ADDITIVES: This product is colored with Yellow No. 5, which can cause allergic reactions, primarily among aspirin-sensitive individuals. Also contains artificial color, which is inadequately tested and which some studies suggest may adversely affect behavior and the ability to complete school tasks in some sensitive children.

BEST BETS: Plain frozen vegetables, with no added salt, are always the best nutritional choice. Among the already sauced frozen vegetables, Green Giant Green Beans in Butter Sauce, Green Giant Broccoli Spears in Butter Sauce, and Green Giant Cut Leaf Spinach in Butter Sauce are the best bets. These products are high in sodium, but contain a scant ⅓ teaspoon butter per serving—without other questionable additives.

GREEN GIANT CUT LEAF SPINACH IN BUTTER SAUCE
The Pillsbury Co.

Ingredients: spinach, water, butter, salt, modified cornstarch.

Amount: ½ cup			% USRDA
Calories	50	Protein	4
Protein, gm	3	Vitamin A	190
Carbohydrates, gm	6	Vitamin C	40
Fat, gm	2	Thiamine	8
Sodium, mg	465	Riboflavin	15
Cholesterol, mg	<5e	Niacin	2
Fiber, gm	4e	Calcium	10
		Iron	8

THIS FOOD: Green Giant Cut Leaf Spinach in Butter Sauce is a very good supplier of dietary fiber as well as many of the nutrients you need. One serving supplies a whopping 190 percent of the USRDA for vitamin A and is a very good source of vitamin C, riboflavin, calcium, and iron. Sodium content is rather high at 465 mg per serving. This product is one of the best choices among sauced frozen vegetables.

ADDITIVES: No questionable additives.

GREEN GIANT FRENCH STYLE AND CUT GREEN BEANS IN BUTTER SAUCE
The Pillsbury Co.

Ingredients: French-cut green beans, water, butter, salt, xanthan gum.

Amount: ½ cup			% USRDA
Calories	40	Protein	2
Protein, gm	1	Vitamin A	8
Carbohydrates, gm	6	Vitamin C	10
Fat, gm	1	Thiamine	2
Sodium, mg	355	Riboflavin	4
Cholesterol, mg	<5e	Niacin	*
Fiber, gm	2e	Calcium	2
		Iron	2

THIS FOOD: Low in fat and calories, this convenience product is one of the better choices among the already sauced vegetables. It contains a fair amount of vitamins A and C and some dietary fiber. Like most processed foods, it is relatively high in sodium.

ADDITIVES: No questionable additives.

GREEN GIANT MIXED VEGETABLES IN BUTTER SAUCE
The Pillsbury Co.

Ingredients: corn, peas, green beans, carrots, lima beans, water, butter, modified cornstarch, salt, xanthan gum, sodium stearoyl lactylate, artificial color.

Amount: ½ cup			% USRDA
Calories	80	Protein	4
Protein, gm	3	Vitamin A	80
Carbohydrates, gm	12	Vitamin C	15
Fat, gm	2	Thiamine	6
Sodium, mg	345	Riboflavin	2
Cholesterol, mg	<5e	Niacin	4
Fiber, gm	2.5e	Calcium	2
		Iron	4

THIS FOOD: Green Giant Mixed Vegetables in Butter Sauce provide dietary fiber, and are an excellent source of vitamin A and provide useful amounts of vitamin C. This product is artificially colored and contains 345 mg sodium per serving.

ADDITIVES: Contains artificial colors, which are inadequately tested, and which some studies suggest may adversely affect behavior and the ability to complete school tasks in some sensitive children.

GREEN GIANT NIBLETS CORN IN BUTTER SAUCE
The Pillsbury Co.

Ingredients: niblets of corn, water, butter, sugar, salt, modified cornstarch, xanthan gum, sodium stearoyl lactylate, artificial flavor.

Amount: ½ cup			% USRDA
Calories	100	Protein	4
Protein, gm	2	Vitamin A	*
Carbohydrates, gm	18	Vitamin C	10
Fat, gm	2	Thiamine	4
Sodium, mg	280	Riboflavin	2
Cholesterol, mg	<5e	Niacin	6
Fiber, gm	3e	Calcium	*
		Iron	2

THIS FOOD: Corn in this form is a very good source of dietary fiber and complex carbohydrates. Less than 20 percent of its calories derive from fat—well within the recommended guidelines. Although high in sodium, with 280 mg per serving, many other sauced vegetables are much saltier.

ADDITIVES: Contains artificial flavor, which may cause allergic reactions in sensitive individuals, and which some studies suggest may adversely affect behavior and the ability to complete school tasks in some sensitive children.

SEABROOK FARMS BABY BRUSSELS SPROUTS
Seabrook Foods, Inc.

Ingredients: baby Brussels sprouts.

Amount: ½ cup			% USRDA
Calories	35	Protein	5
Protein, gm	3	Vitamin A	15
Carbohydrates, gm	6	Vitamin C	100
Fat, gm	0	Thiamine	6
Sodium, mg	<5e	Riboflavin	4
Cholesterol, mg	0e	Niacin	2
Fiber, gm	3e	Calcium	2
		Iron	4

THIS FOOD: In addition to being low in calories and sodium, Brussels sprouts are a good source of vitamin A and dietary fiber and a super source of vitamin C. As members of the cabbage family, they are a cruciferous vegetable, and considered to have anticancer properties.

ADDITIVES: None.

HELPFUL HINT: If you want to cut down on salt and avoid possibly harmful additives, try seasoning your own vegetables with a little butter or oil, and herbs and spices. If you still miss the salt, try seasoning with a dash of low-sodium soy sauce. You'll save money this way too.

NUTRITION TIP: Eating lots of broccoli, along with other members of the cabbage family, such as Brussels sprouts and cauliflower (and of course cabbage), may lower your risk of colon cancer, according to some studies.

YOGURT

Yogurt is a cultured milk product in which some of the lactose, or milk sugar, has been partially digested by harmless bacteria. Does yogurt deserve its healthy image? Plain yogurt—especially the low-fat kind—is clearly a nutritious food. Like milk, it is a good source of protein and potassium and an excellent source of riboflavin and calcium. Low-fat yogurts such as Dannon contain added nonfat milk solids and provide as much as 40 percent of the USRDA for calcium per 8-ounce carton. Unfortunately, the vast majority of yogurt eaters choose the fruit-flavored varieties, which typically contain about 6 teaspoons added sugar per carton—and proportionally less calcium. As much as 50 percent of the calories in these products derive from added sugar. If you are eating fruit-flavored yogurt for dessert, instead of a rich piece of pie or cake, you've made a wise choice. But you'd be still better off eating plain yogurt with naturally sweet fruit and perhaps a little honey. Yogurt can also be a valuable food for the many individuals who have "lactose intolerance" or other digestive difficulties when consuming fresh milk.

BREYER'S ALL NATURAL PINEAPPLE YOGURT
Kraft, Inc.

Ingredients: milk, pineapple, sugar, skim milk, yogurt culture, pectin, lemon juice concentrate.

Amount: 1 cup			% USRDA
Calories	270	Protein	20
Protein, gm	9	Vitamin A	2
Carbohydrates, gm	45	Vitamin C	4
Fat, gm	5	Thiamine	2
Sodium, mg	125	Riboflavin	20
Cholesterol, mg	10e	Niacin	*
Fiber, gm	e	Calcium	30
		Iron	*

THIS FOOD: Breyer's All Natural Pineapple Yogurt derives nearly half its calories from added sugar. While this product is still a very good source of protein, vitamin C, and riboflavin and an excellent source of calcium, it cannot be recommended, since other yogurts provide similar nutrient content without excessive sweetening.

ADDITIVES: No questionable additives.

BREYER'S ALL NATURAL STRAWBERRY YOGURT
Kraft, Inc.

Ingredients: milk, strawberries, sugar, skim milk, yogurt culture, pectin, lemon juice concentrate.

Amount: 1 cup			% USRDA
Calories	270	Protein	20
Protein, gm	9	Vitamin A	2
Carbohydrates, gm	46	Vitamin C	15
Fat, gm	5	Thiamine	2
Sodium, mg	120	Riboflavin	20
Cholesterol, mg	10e	Niacin	*
Fiber, gm	< 1	Calcium	30
		Iron	*
Contains 8 teaspoons added sugar.			

THIS FOOD: Breyer's All Natural Strawberry Yogurt derives nearly half its calories from added sugar. While this product is still a very good source of protein, vitamin C, and riboflavin and an excellent source of calcium, it cannot be recommended, since other yogurts provide similar nutrient content without excessive sweetening.

ADDITIVES: No questionable additives.

DANNON BLUEBERRY LOWFAT YOGURT
The Dannon Co.

Ingredients: cultured pasteurized grade A milk, skim milk, blueberries, sugar, corn sweeteners, nonfat milk solids, pectin, natural flavors, lemon juice.

Amount: 1 cup (8 oz)			% USRDA
Calories	240	Protein	20
Protein, gm	9	Vitamin A	2
Carbohydrates, gm	43	Vitamin C	*
Fat, gm	3	Thiamine	8
Sodium, mg	120	Riboflavin	30
Cholesterol, mg	10e	Niacin	*
Fiber, gm	<1	Calcium	35
		Iron	*
Contains 7 teaspoons added sugar.			

NOTE: The letter "e" indicates that the data has been estimated; < means "less than" and is used for small amounts of sodium or cholesterol; * means food contains less than 2% of USRDA; "na" means that the information was not available and appears only when data is insufficient.

THIS FOOD: This yogurt is an excellent source of protein, riboflavin, and calcium. Unfortunately, the popular fruit-flavored varieties are highly sweetened. Nearly 50 percent of the calories in Dannon Blueberry Lowfat Yogurt derive from added sugar.

ADDITIVES: No questionable additives.

DANNON COFFEE LOWFAT YOGURT
The Dannon Co.
Ingredients: cultured pasteurized grade A milk, skim milk, sugar, nonfat milk solids, coffee, natural flavors.

Amount: 1 cup			% USRDA
Calories	200	Protein	25
Protein, gm	11	Vitamin A	2
Carbohydrates, gm	32	Vitamin C	*
Fat, gm	4	Thiamine	4
Sodium, mg	80	Riboflavin	20
Cholesterol, mg	11e	Niacin	*
Fiber, gm	< 1	Calcium	35
		Iron	*
Contains 4 teaspoons added sugar.			

THIS FOOD: Dannon Coffee Lowfat Yogurt is an excellent source of protein, riboflavin, and calcium. Like most flavored yogurts, it is highly sweetened; about 32 percent of calories come from sugar. Still, compared to other snack foods which tend to be high in sodium and fat, this product is a nutritional bargain.

ADDITIVES: May contain trace amounts of caffeine.

HELPFUL HINT: To cut down on empty sugar calories, try adding fresh fruit or a little honey to plain yogurt. Chances are you'll need much less sweetening than the whopping 6 to 8 teaspoons sugar that is generally added to fruit-flavored varieties.

DANNON PLAIN LOWFAT YOGURT
The Dannon Co.

Ingredients: cultured pasteurized grade A milk, skim milk, nonfat milk solids.

Amount: 1 cup			% USRDA
Calories	150	Protein	30
Protein, gm	12	Vitamin A	2
Carbohydrates, gm	17	Vitamin C	*
Fat, gm	4	Thiamine	4
Sodium, mg	115	Riboflavin	30
Cholesterol, mg	14	Niacin	*
Fiber, gm	< 1	Calcium	40
		Iron	*
Contains no added sugar.			

THIS FOOD: Dannon Plain Lowfat Yogurt is an extremely nutritious food. Like most yogurts, it is low in fat, but because it contains nonfat milk solids, this product is especially high in protein, riboflavin, and calcium. If you add a teaspoon or two of honey or fruit preserves, you'll still be consuming a fraction of the sugar contained in flavored yogurts, which typically contain 4 to more than 7 teaspoons of sugar per cup.

ADDITIVES: None.

LIGHT N' LIVELY STRAWBERRY FRUIT CUP LOWFAT YOGURT
Kraft, Inc.

Ingredients: low-fat milk, sugar, skim milk, strawberries, water, food starch–modified, pineapple, black cherries, yogurt culture, peaches, natural flavors, concentrated pineapple juice, gelatin, corn syrup, sorbic acid, citric acid, artificial color.

Amount: 1 cup			% USRDA
Calories	160	Protein	15
Protein, gm	7	Vitamin A	*
Carbohydrates, gm	29	Vitamin C	4
Fat, gm	2	Thiamine	*
Sodium, mg	95	Riboflavin	15
Cholesterol, mg	10	Niacin	*
Fiber, gm	<1	Calcium	25
		Iron	*
Contains 4 teaspoons added sugar.			

THIS FOOD: Light n' Lively Strawberry Fruit Cup Lowfat Yogurt is low in fat, an excellent source of calcium, and a very good source of protein and riboflavin. Compared to many other snack foods, yogurt is quite nutritious.

Like most fruit-flavored yogurts, this product is highly sweetened; it derives 37 percent of its calories from added sugar.

ADDITIVES: Contains artificial color, which is inadequately tested, and which some studies suggest may adversely affect behavior and the ability to complete school tasks in some sensitive children.

YOPLAIT BANANA CUSTARD STYLE YOGURT
General Mills, Inc.

Ingredients: cultured pasteurized grade A milk, sugar, nonfat milk solids, banana puree, natural flavors, cornstarch, gelatin, colored with turmeric.

Amount: 6 oz			% USRDA
Calories	190	Protein	15
Protein, gm	7	Vitamin A	2
Carbohydrates, gm	32	Vitamin C	*
Fat, gm	4	Thiamine	4
Sodium, mg	95	Riboflavin	15
Cholesterol, mg	10	Niacin	*
Fiber, gm	<1	Calcium	20
		Iron	*

Contains 5 teaspoons added sugar.

THIS FOOD: Yogurt is a very good source of protein, riboflavin, and calcium. Unfortunately, the popular fruit-flavored varieties are highly sweetened. About 50 percent of the calories in Yoplait Banana Custard Style Yogurt derive from added sugar.

ADDITIVES: No questionable additives.

YOPLAIT BOYSENBERRY YOGURT
General Mills, Inc.

Ingredients: cultured pasteurized grade A milk, sugar, boysenberries, nonfat milk solids, natural flavors.

Amount: 6 oz			% USRDA
Calories	190	Protein	15
Protein, gm	7	Vitamin A	*
Carbohydrates, gm	32	Vitamin C	*
Fat, gm	4	Thiamine	6
Sodium, mg	105	Riboflavin	20
Cholesterol, mg	10	Niacin	*
Fiber, gm	<1	Calcium	25
		Iron	*

Contains 5 teaspoons added sugar.

THIS FOOD: Yogurt is a very good source of protein, riboflavin, and calcium. Unfortunately, the popular fruit-flavored varieties are highly sweetened. About 50 percent of the calories in Yoplait Boysenberry Yogurt derive from added sugar.

ADDITIVES: No questionable additives.

YOPLAIT STRAWBERRY YOGURT
General Mills, Inc.

Ingredients: cultured pasteurized grade A milk, sugar, strawberries, nonfat milk solids, natural flavors.

Amount: 6 oz			% USRDA
Calories	190	Protein	15
Protein, gm	7	Vitamin A	*
Carbohydrates, gm	32	Vitamin C	*
Fat, gm	4	Thiamine	6
Sodium, mg	105	Riboflavin	20
Cholesterol, mg	10	Niacin	*
Fiber, gm	<1	Calcium	25
		Iron	*
Contains 5 teaspoons added sugar.			

THIS FOOD: Yogurt is a very good source of protein, riboflavin, and calcium. Unfortunately, the popular fruit-flavored varieties are highly sweetened. About 50 percent of the calories in Yoplait Strawberry Yogurt derive from added sugar.

ADDITIVES: No questionable additives.

BASIC FOODS:
A NUTRITION COUNTER

While the main purpose of this book is to provide nutrition information for brand name convenience foods, no reference is complete without information on basic foods. These are foods, such as baked potatoes, apples, or peaches, that we eat in more or less the same form as they occur in nature, or minimally processed foods, such as milk. Sometimes basic foods, such as rice or frozen vegetables, are packaged and sold as brand name products. Since most people think of Uncle Ben's Rice and Birds Eye Vegetables, these products are listed in the brand name profile section, even though they could also be considered basic foods. Whenever this occurs, we have referred the reader to the appropriate page.

The basic foods in this section are arranged in simple alphabetical order—not by category. Each entry provides the same nutrition data as the brand name food profiles, but does not include a text evaluation.

APPLES

Amount: 1 medium			% USRDA
Calories	81	Protein	*
Protein, gm	<1	Vitamin A	*
Carbohydrates, gm	21	Vitamin C	13
Fat, gm	<1	Thiamine	*
Sodium, mg	1	Riboflavin	*
Cholesterol, mg	0	Niacin	*
Fiber, gm	3	Calcium	*
		Iron	*

ASPARAGUS

Amount: ½ cup

			% USRDA
Calories	15	Protein	3
Protein, gm	2	Vitamin A	14
Carbohydrates, gm	3	Vitamin C	33
Fat, gm	<1	Thiamine	8
Sodium, mg	1	Riboflavin	8
Cholesterol, mg	0	Niacin	5
Fiber, gm	1	Calcium	2
		Iron	3

AVOCADOS

Amount: 1 medium

			% USRDA
Calories	306	Protein	6
Protein, gm	3.6	Vitamin A	21
Carbohydrates, gm	4	Vitamin C	23
Fat, gm	30	Thiamine	12
Sodium, mg	7	Riboflavin	12
Cholesterol, mg	0	Niacin	17
Fiber, gm	3	Calcium	*
		Iron	11

BANANAS

Amount: 1 medium

			% USRDA
Calories	105	Protein	*
Protein, gm	1	Vitamin A	*
Carbohydrates, gm	27	Vitamin C	17
Fat, gm	< 1	Thiamine	3
Sodium, mg	1	Riboflavin	6
Cholesterol, mg	0	Niacin	3
Fiber, gm	3	Calcium	*
		Iron	*

BEANS, KIDNEY

Amount: 1 cup

			% USRDA
Calories	295	Protein	31
Protein, gm	20	Vitamin A	*
Carbohydrates, gm	54	Vitamin C	*
Fat, gm	1	Thiamine	18
Sodium, mg	3	Riboflavin	9
Cholesterol, mg	0	Niacin	9
Fiber, gm	20	Calcium	10
		Iron	33

BEANS, LIMA

Amount: ½ cup			% USRDA
Calories	90	Protein	9
Protein, gm	6	Vitamin A	4
Carbohydrates, gm	16	Vitamin C	22
Fat, gm	< 1	Thiamine	9
Sodium, mg	< 1	Riboflavin	4
Cholesterol, mg	0	Niacin	5
Fiber, gm	7.5	Calcium	4
		Iron	11

BEANS, STRING

Amount: ½ cup			% USRDA
Calories	16	Protein	*
Protein, gm	1	Vitamin A	7
Carbohydrates, gm	3	Vitamin C	12
Fat, gm	< 1	Thiamine	3
Sodium, mg	5	Riboflavin	3
Cholesterol, mg	0	Niacin	*
Fiber, gm	2	Calcium	3
		Iron	2

BEEF, GROUND CHUCK

Amount: 6 oz			% USRDA
Calories	561	Protein	99
Protein, gm	45	Vitamin A	*
Carbohydrates, gm	0	Vitamin C	*
Fat, gm	40	Thiamine	6
Sodium, mg	102	Riboflavin	20
Cholesterol, mg	106	Niacin	34
Fiber, gm	0	Calcium	*
		Iron	31

BEEF, T-BONE, BROILED

Amount: 6 oz			% USRDA
Calories	421	Protein	96
Protein, gm	43	Vitamin A	*
Carbohydrates, gm	0	Vitamin C	*
Fat, gm	26	Thiamine	12
Sodium, mg	88	Riboflavin	12
Cholesterol, mg	160	Niacin	52
Fiber, gm	0	Calcium	*
		Iron	36

BEEF TENDERLOIN, BROILED

Amount: 6 oz			% USRDA
Calories	381	Protein	98
Protein, gm	44	Vitamin A	*
Carbohydrates, gm	0	Vitamin C	*
Fat, gm	21	Thiamine	12
Sodium, mg	77	Riboflavin	45
Cholesterol, mg	160	Niacin	28
Fiber, gm	0	Calcium	*
		Iron	37

BEETS

Amount: ½ cup			% USRDA
Calories	27	Protein	*
Protein, gm	1	Vitamin A	*
Carbohydrates, gm	6	Vitamin C	8
Fat, gm	< 1	Thiamine	2
Sodium, mg	36	Riboflavin	*
Cholesterol, mg	0	Niacin	*
Fiber, gm	2	Calcium	*
		Iron	2

BROCCOLI: See "Brand Name Profiles" on pages 534, 540.

BUTTER: See "Brand Name Profiles" on page 66.

CABBAGE, GREEN

Amount: ½ cup			% USRDA
Calories	17	Protein	*
Protein, gm	1	Vitamin A	2
Carbohydrates, gm	4	Vitamin C	46
Fat, gm	< 1	Thiamine	2
Sodium, mg	12	Riboflavin	*
Cholesterol, mg	0	Niacin	*
Fiber, gm	3	Calcium	4
		Iron	*

CANTALOUPE

Amount: 1 cup			% USRDA
Calories	57	Protein	*
Protein, gm	1	Vitamin A	103
Carbohydrates, gm	13	Vitamin C	113
Fat, gm	<1	Thiamine	4
Sodium, mg	14	Riboflavin	*
Cholesterol, mg	0	Niacin	5
Fiber, gm	1	Calcium	*
		Iron	*

CARROTS, COOKED

Amount: ½ cup			% USRDA
Calories	32	Protein	*
Protein, gm	<1	Vitamin A	158
Carbohydrates, gm	5	Vitamin C	8
Fat, gm	<1	Thiamine	3
Sodium, mg	25	Riboflavin	2
Cholesterol, mg	0	Niacin	*
Fiber, gm	2	Calcium	2
		Iron	3

CAULIFLOWER, COOKED

Amount: ½ cup			% USRDA
Calories	13	Protein	*
Protein, gm	1	Vitamin A	*
Carbohydrates, gm	2	Vitamin C	52
Fat, gm	<1	Thiamine	3
Sodium, mg	5	Riboflavin	3
Cholesterol, mg	0	Niacin	*
Fiber, gm	1	Calcium	*
		Iron	2

CELERY, RAW

Amount: 1 stalk			% USRDA
Calories	8	Protein	*
Protein, gm	<1	Vitamin A	2
Carbohydrates, gm	2	Vitamin C	8
Fat, gm	<1	Thiamine	*
Sodium, mg	63	Riboflavin	*
Cholesterol, mg	0	Niacin	*
Fiber, gm	1	Calcium	2
		Iron	*

CHEESE: See "Brand Name Profiles" on page 137.

CHERRIES, RAW

Amount: 10 cherries			% USRDA
Calories	49	Protein	*
Protein, gm	<1	Vitamin A	2
Carbohydrates, gm	11	Vitamin C	8
Fat, gm	<1	Thiamine	2
Sodium, mg	0	Riboflavin	2
Cholesterol, mg	0	Niacin	*
Fiber, gm	1	Calcium	*
		Iron	*

CHICKEN, DARK MEAT, ROASTED WITHOUT SKIN

Amount: 6 oz			% USRDA
Calories	351	Protein	104
Protein, gm	47	Vitamin A	2
Carbohydrates, gm	0	Vitamin C	*
Fat, gm	17	Thiamine	8
Sodium, mg	159	Riboflavin	7
Cholesterol, mg	159	Niacin	57
Fiber, gm	0	Calcium	3
		Iron	13

CHICKEN, LIGHT MEAT, FRIED WITH SKIN

Amount: 6 oz			% USRDA
Calories	421	Protein	116
Protein, gm	52	Vitamin A	2
Carbohydrates, gm	3	Vitamin C	*
Fat, gm	21	Thiamine	9
Sodium, mg	132	Riboflavin	13
Cholesterol, mg	149	Niacin	103
Fiber, gm	0	Calcium	3
		Iron	1

CHICKEN, LIGHT MEAT, ROASTED WITHOUT SKIN

Amount: 6 oz			% USRDA
Calories	296	Protein	118
Protein, gm	53	Vitamin A	*
Carbohydrates, gm	0	Vitamin C	*
Fat, gm	8	Thiamine	8
Sodium, mg	132	Riboflavin	12
Cholesterol, mg	146	Niacin	106
Fiber, gm	0	Calcium	3
		Iron	10

CHICK PEAS

Amount: 4 oz			% USRDA
Calories	205	Protein	18
Protein, gm	12	Vitamin A	*
Carbohydrates, gm	35	Vitamin C	*
Fat, gm	3	Thiamine	11
Sodium, mg	na	Riboflavin	5
Cholesterol, mg	0	Niacin	6
Fiber, gm	7	Calcium	9
		Iron	19

COD, BROILED

Amount: 6 oz			% USRDA
Calories	278	Protein	99
Protein, gm	44.7	Vitamin A	6
Carbohydrates, gm	0	Vitamin C	*
Fat, gm	9	Thiamine	9
Sodium, mg	180	Riboflavin	10
Cholesterol, mg	86e	Niacin	24
Fiber, gm	0	Calcium	5
		Iron	9

CORN: See "Brand Name Profiles" on pages 526, 528, 529, 532, 538, 539, 543.

COTTAGE CHEESE

Amount: ½ cup			% USRDA
Calories	117	Protein	31
Protein, gm	14	Vitamin A	4
Carbohydrates, gm	3	Vitamin C	*
Fat, gm	5	Thiamine	*
Sodium, mg	457	Riboflavin	11
Cholesterol, mg	17	Niacin	*
Fiber, gm	0	Calcium	7
		Iron	*

CREAM, HEAVY

Amount: 1 tbsp			% USRDA
Calories	52	Protein	*
Protein, gm	<1	Vitamin A	4
Carbohydrates, gm	<1	Vitamin C	*
Fat, gm	6	Thiamine	*
Sodium, mg	6	Riboflavin	*
Cholesterol, mg	21	Niacin	*
Fiber, gm	0	Calcium	*
		Iron	*

CREAM, LIGHT

Amount: 1 tbsp			% USRDA
Calories	29	Protein	*
Protein, gm	<1	Vitamin A	2
Carbohydrates, gm	<1	Vitamin C	*
Fat, gm	3	Thiamine	*
Sodium, mg	6	Riboflavin	*
Cholesterol, mg	10	Niacin	*
Fiber, gm	0	Calcium	*
		Iron	*

CUCUMBER

Amount: ½ medium			% USRDA
Calories	8	Protein	*
Protein, gm	<1	Vitamin A	2
Carbohydrates, gm	2	Vitamin C	9
Fat, gm	<1	Thiamine	*
Sodium, mg	3	Riboflavin	*
Cholesterol, mg	0	Niacin	*
Fiber, gm	<1	Calcium	*
		Iron	3

EGGS

Amount: 1 egg			% USRDA
Calories	79	Protein	13
Protein, gm	6	Vitamin A	5
Carbohydrates, gm	<1	Vitamin C	*
Fat, gm	6	Thiamine	3
Sodium, mg	69	Riboflavin	9
Cholesterol, mg	274	Niacin	*
Fiber, gm	0	Calcium	3
		Iron	6

FLOUR: See "Brand Name Profiles" on page 189.

GRAPEFRUIT

Amount: ½ medium			% USRDA
Calories	39	Protein	*
Protein, gm	<1	Vitamin A	6
Carbohydrates, gm	10	Vitamin C	72
Fat, gm	<1	Thiamine	3
Sodium, mg	0	Riboflavin	*
Cholesterol, mg	0	Niacin	*
Fiber, gm	1	Calcium	*
		Iron	*

GRAPES, WHITE

Amount: 1 cup			% USRDA
Calories	58	Protein	*
Protein, gm	<1	Vitamin A	*
Carbohydrates, gm	16	Vitamin C	*
Fat, gm	<1	Thiamine	6
Sodium, mg	2	Riboflavin	3
Cholesterol, mg	0	Niacin	*
Fiber, gm	<1	Calcium	*
		Iron	*

HAM: See "Brand Name Profiles" on page 308.

LAMB, LEG, ROASTED

Amount: 6 oz			% USRDA
Calories	414	Protein	78
Protein, gm	35	Vitamin A	*
Carbohydrates, gm	0	Vitamin C	*
Fat, gm	25	Thiamine	18
Sodium, mg	105	Riboflavin	22
Cholesterol, mg	170	Niacin	45
Fiber, gm	0	Calcium	*
		Iron	30

LENTILS

Amount: 1 cup			% USRDA
Calories	159	Protein	18
Protein, gm	12	Vitamin A	*
Carbohydrates, gm	28	Vitamin C	*
Fat, gm	<1	Thiamine	8
Sodium, mg	6	Riboflavin	6
Cholesterol, mg	0	Niacin	4
Fiber, gm	6	Calcium	*
		Iron	18

LETTUCE, ICEBERG

Amount: 1 cup			% USRDA
Calories	7	Protein	*
Protein, gm	<1	Vitamin A	4
Carbohydrates, gm	2	Vitamin C	6
Fat, gm	<1	Thiamine	2
Sodium, mg	5	Riboflavin	*
Cholesterol, mg	0	Niacin	*
Fiber, gm	1	Calcium	*
		Iron	*

LETTUCE, ROMAINE

Amount: 1 cup			% USRDA
Calories	10	Protein	*
Protein, gm	<1	Vitamin A	21
Carbohydrates, gm	2	Vitamin C	17
Fat, gm	<1	Thiamine	*
Sodium, mg	5	Riboflavin	3
Cholesterol, mg	0	Niacin	*
Fiber, gm	1	Calcium	4
		Iron	4

LIVER, CALF, FRIED

Amount: 6 oz			% USRDA
Calories	447	Protein	113
Protein, gm	51	Vitamin A	1,121
Carbohydrates, gm	7	Vitamin C	106
Fat, gm	23	Thiamine	27
Sodium, mg	202	Riboflavin	421
Cholesterol, mg	751	Niacin	141
Fiber, gm	0	Calcium	2
		Iron	135

MARGARINE: See "Brand Name Profiles" on page 67.

MILK, LOWFAT, 2-PERCENT FAT

Amount: 1 cup			% USRDA
Calories	121	Protein	18
Protein, gm	8	Vitamin A	10
Carbohydrates, gm	12	Vitamin C	4
Fat, gm	5	Thiamine	6
Sodium, mg	122	Riboflavin	24
Cholesterol, mg	18	Niacin	*
Fiber, gm	0	Calcium	30
		Iron	*

MILK, SKIM

Amount: 1 cup			% USRDA
Calories	86	Protein	18
Protein, gm	8	Vitamin A	10
Carbohydrates, gm	12	Vitamin C	4
Fat, gm	<1	Thiamine	6
Sodium, mg	126	Riboflavin	20
Cholesterol, mg	4	Niacin	*
Fiber, gm	0	Calcium	30
		Iron	*

MILK, WHOLE, 3.3-PERCENT FAT

Amount: 1 cup			% USRDA
Calories	150	Protein	18
Protein, gm	8	Vitamin A	6
Carbohydrates, gm	11	Vitamin C	4
Fat, gm	8	Thiamine	6
Sodium, mg	120	Riboflavin	23
Cholesterol, mg	33	Niacin	*
Fiber, gm	0	Calcium	29
		Iron	*

MUSHROOMS, FRESH

Amount: 10 small			% USRDA
Calories	28	Protein	5
Protein, gm	3	Vitamin A	*
Carbohydrates, gm	4	Vitamin C	5
Fat, gm	<1	Thiamine	7
Sodium, mg	15	Riboflavin	27
Cholesterol, mg	0	Niacin	21
Fiber, gm	2.5	Calcium	*
		Iron	4

NECTARINES

Amount: 1 medium			% USRDA
Calories	67	Protein	*
Protein, gm	1	Vitamin A	20
Carbohydrates, gm	16	Vitamin C	12
Fat, gm	<1	Thiamine	*
Sodium, mg	0	Riboflavin	4
Cholesterol, mg	0	Niacin	7
Fiber, gm	3	Calcium	*
		Iron	*

NUTS: See "Brand Name Profiles" on page 359.

OLIVES: See "Brand Name Profiles" on page 369.

ONIONS, RAW

Amount: 1 medium			% USRDA
Calories	38	Protein	2
Protein, gm	2	Vitamin A	*
Carbohydrates, gm	9	Vitamin C	17
Fat, gm	<1	Thiamine	2
Sodium, mg	10	Riboflavin	2
Cholesterol, mg	0	Niacin	*
Fiber, gm	2	Calcium	3
		Iron	3

ORANGES, NAVEL

Amount: 1 medium			% USRDA
Calories	65	Protein	*
Protein, gm	1	Vitamin A	5
Carbohydrates, gm	16	Vitamin C	133
Fat, gm	<1	Thiamine	8
Sodium, mg	1	Riboflavin	4
Cholesterol, mg	0	Niacin	2
Fiber, gm	2	Calcium	6
		Iron	*

PEACHES

Amount: 1 medium			% USRDA
Calories	37	Protein	*
Protein, gm	<1	Vitamin A	9
Carbohydrates, gm	10	Vitamin C	10
Fat, gm	<1	Thiamine	*
Sodium, mg	0	Riboflavin	2
Cholesterol, mg	0	Niacin	5
Fiber, gm	2	Calcium	*
		Iron	*

PEARS

Amount: 1 medium			% USRDA
Calories	98	Protein	*
Protein, gm	<1	Vitamin A	*
Carbohydrates, gm	25	Vitamin C	12
Fat, gm	<1	Thiamine	2
Sodium, mg	1	Riboflavin	4
Cholesterol, mg	0	Niacin	*
Fiber, gm	4	Calcium	*
		Iron	2

PEAS: See "Brand Name Profiles" on pages 527, 531, 532, 536.

PEPPER, GREEN BELL, RAW

Amount: 1 large			% USRDA
Calories	22	Protein	*
Protein, gm	1	Vitamin A	8
Carbohydrates, gm	5	Vitamin C	213
Fat, gm	<1	Thiamine	5
Sodium, mg	13	Riboflavin	5
Cholesterol, mg	0	Niacin	3
Fiber, gm	1.5	Calcium	*
		Iron	4

PERCH: See "Brand Name Profiles" on page 183.

PLUMS

Amount: 1 medium			% USRDA
Calories	36	Protein	*
Protein, gm	< 1	Vitamin A	4
Carbohydrates, gm	9	Vitamin C	10
Fat, gm	< 1	Thiamine	2
Sodium, mg	0	Riboflavin	4
Cholesterol, mg	0	Niacin	*
Fiber, gm	1.5	Calcium	*
		Iron	*

PORK LOIN

Amount: 6 oz			% USRDA
Calories	612	Protein	111
Protein, gm	50	Vitamin A	*
Carbohydrates, gm	0	Vitamin C	*
Fat, gm	44	Thiamine	135
Sodium, mg	103	Riboflavin	19
Cholesterol, mg	150	Niacin	47
Fiber, gm	0	Calcium	2
		Iron	42

PORK RIBS, ROASTED

Amount: 6 medium ribs			% USRDA
Calories	396	Protein	42
Protein, gm	19	Vitamin A	*
Carbohydrates, gm	0	Vitamin C	*
Fat, gm	35	Thiamine	25
Sodium, mg	na	Riboflavin	11
Cholesterol, mg	80e	Niacin	15
Fiber, gm	0	Calcium	*
		Iron	13

POTATOES, BAKED

Amount: 1 medium			% USRDA
Calories	95	Protein	4
Protein, gm	3	Vitamin A	*
Carbohydrates, gm	21	Vitamin C	33
Fat, gm	< 1	Thiamine	7
Sodium, mg	4	Riboflavin	2
Cholesterol, mg	0	Niacin	9
Fiber, gm	2.5	Calcium	*
		Iron	4

RASPBERRIES

Amount: 1 cup			% USRDA
Calories	61	Protein	*
Protein, gm	1	Vitamin A	3
Carbohydrates, gm	14	Vitamin C	52
Fat, gm	< 1	Thiamine	3
Sodium, mg	0	Riboflavin	6
Cholesterol, mg	0	Niacin	6
Fiber, gm	9	Calcium	3
		Iron	4

RICE: See "Brand Name Profiles" on page 425.

SOLE: See "Brand Name Profiles" on pages 183, 187.

SPINACH, COOKED

Amount: ½ cup			% USRDA
Calories	21	Protein	4
Protein, gm	3	Vitamin A	146
Carbohydrates, gm	3	Vitamin C	42
Fat, gm	< 1	Thiamine	4
Sodium, mg	45	Riboflavin	8
Cholesterol, mg	0	Niacin	3
Fiber, gm	5.5	Calcium	3
		Iron	11

SPINACH, RAW

Amount: 1 cup			% USRDA
Calories	14	Protein	3
Protein, gm	2	Vitamin A	89
Carbohydrates, gm	2	Vitamin C	47
Fat, gm	< 1	Thiamine	4
Sodium, mg	39	Riboflavin	6
Cholesterol, mg	0	Niacin	*
Fiber, gm	2	Calcium	5
		Iron	9

SQUASH, SUMMER, BOILED

Amount: ½ cup			% USRDA
Calories	14	Protein	*
Protein, gm	< 1	Vitamin A	8
Carbohydrates, gm	3	Vitamin C	17
Fat, gm	< 1	Thiamine	3
Sodium, mg	1	Riboflavin	5
Cholesterol, mg	0	Niacin	4
Fiber, gm	2	Calcium	3
		Iron	2

SQUASH, WINTER, BAKED

Amount: ½ cup			% USRDA
Calories	63	Protein	3
Protein, gm	2	Vitamin A	84
Carbohydrates, gm	15	Vitamin C	22
Fat, gm	< 1	Thiamine	3
Sodium, mg	1	Riboflavin	8
Cholesterol, mg	0	Niacin	4
Fiber, gm	3	Calcium	3
		Iron	4

STRAWBERRIES

Amount: 1 cup			% USRDA
Calories	45	Protein	*
Protein, gm	< 1	Vitamin A	*
Carbohydrates, gm	11	Vitamin C	142
Fat, gm	< 1	Thiamine	2
Sodium, mg	2	Riboflavin	6
Cholesterol, mg	0	Niacin	*
Fiber, gm	3	Calcium	2
		Iron	3

SUGAR: See "Brand Name Profiles" on page 507.

SWEET POTATO, BAKED

Amount: 1 large			% USRDA
Calories	254	Protein	6
Protein, gm	4	Vitamin A	292
Carbohydrates, gm	59	Vitamin C	67
Fat, gm	< 1	Thiamine	11
Sodium, mg	22	Riboflavin	8
Cholesterol, mg	0	Niacin	7
Fiber, gm	5	Calcium	7
		Iron	9

TOMATOES, RAW

Amount: 1 medium			% USRDA
Calories	33	Protein	2
Protein, gm	2	Vitamin A	27
Carbohydrates, gm	7	Vitamin C	57
Fat, gm	< 1	Thiamine	6
Sodium, mg	4	Riboflavin	4
Cholesterol, mg	0	Niacin	5
Fiber, gm	2	Calcium	2
		Iron	4

TURKEY, DARK MEAT, ROASTED, WITHOUT SKIN

Amount: 6 oz			% USRDA
Calories	321	Protein	109
Protein, gm	49	Vitamin A	*
Carbohydrates, gm	0	Vitamin C	*
Fat, gm	12	Thiamine	7
Sodium, mg	135	Riboflavin	25
Cholesterol, mg	146	Niacin	31
Fiber, gm	0	Calcium	5
		Iron	22

TURKEY, LIGHT MEAT, ROASTED, WITHOUT SKIN

Amount: 6 oz			% USRDA
Calories	269	Protein	113
Protein, gm	51	Vitamin A	*
Carbohydrates, gm	0	Vitamin C	*
Fat, gm	5	Thiamine	7
Sodium, mg	109	Riboflavin	13
Cholesterol, mg	118	Niacin	58
Fiber, gm	0	Calcium	3
		Iron	13

TURNIPS

Amount: ½ cup			% USRDA
Calories	17	Protein	*
Protein, gm	< 1	Vitamin A	*
Carbohydrates, gm	4	Vitamin C	28
Fat, gm	< 1	Thiamine	2
Sodium, mg	26	Riboflavin	2
Cholesterol, mg	0	Niacin	*
Fiber, gm	2	Calcium	3
		Iron	*

VEAL CUTLET

Amount: 6 oz			% USRDA
Calories	475	Protein	127
Protein, gm	57	Vitamin A	*
Carbohydrates, gm	0	Vitamin C	*
Fat, gm	26	Thiamine	14
Sodium, mg	92	Riboflavin	32
Cholesterol, mg	154	Niacin	55
Fiber, gm	0	Calcium	*
		Iron	40

WATERMELON

Amount: 1 cup			% USRDA
Calories	50	Protein	*
Protein, gm	1	Vitamin A	12
Carbohydrates, gm	12	Vitamin C	25
Fat, gm	< 1	Thiamine	9
Sodium, mg	3	Riboflavin	*
Cholesterol, mg	0	Niacin	*
Fiber, gm	1	Calcium	*
		Iron	*

WHEAT GERM, TOASTED

Amount: ¼ cup			% USRDA
Calories	107	Protein	12
Protein, gm	8	Vitamin A	*
Carbohydrates, gm	14	Vitamin C	*
Fat, gm	3	Thiamine	31
Sodium, mg	1	Riboflavin	14
Cholesterol, mg	0	Niacin	8
Fiber, gm	2.5	Calcium	*
		Iron	14

YOGURT: See "Brand Name Profiles" on page 545.

ZUCCHINI, RAW

Amount: ½ cup			% USRDA
Calories	11	Protein	*
Protein, gm	< 1	Vitamin A	4
Carbohydrates, gm	2	Vitamin C	21
Fat, gm	< 1	Thiamine	2
Sodium, mg	1	Riboflavin	3
Cholesterol, mg	0	Niacin	3
Fiber, gm	2	Calcium	*
		Iron	*

GLOSSARY
OF BASIC TERMS

Additives are chemicals added to food to enhance appearance, texture, taste, and nutritive value; preservatives, the most important class of additives, are used by manufacturers to prevent spoilage in processed foods and keep them free of disease-causing microorganisms. The safety of some commonly used additives has been questioned by consumer groups and independent scientists, but the vast majority are not believed to be harmful. Apart from the possible dangers from the chemicals themselves, additive-rich foods are often low in nutritional value.

Calories are used to measure the energy value of food. One calorie is the amount of heat needed to raise the temperature of one gram of water one degree centigrade. If a person consumes more calories than he or she expends each day, the excess will be stored as fat.

Carbohydrates are an essential nutrient found most abundantly in grains, starchy vegetables, fruit, and milk. In their natural form, simple carbohydrates (sugars) and complex carbohydrates (starches) are found in foods rich in vitamins, minerals, and fiber, and fairly low in calories. Americans do not eat enough naturally occurring carbohydrates for optimum health. One gram of carbohydrate supplies 4 calories.

Cholesterol is a fatty substance contained in animal foods and is also produced by humans, primarily in the liver. Cholesterol is essential for many important body functions, but people do not have to consume dietary cholesterol since the body can produce more than enough for its needs. The average American consumes about 600 milligrams of cholesterol from animal foods such as meat, chicken, dairy products, and eggs, or twice as much as the recommended amount. High levels of cholesterol in the blood are associated with an increased risk of developing atherosclerosis, a condition characterized by clogged arteries, and a major cause of heart attacks.

Cruciferous vegetables are members of the cabbage family. They are generally high in dietary fiber and may also help to protect against certain forms of cancer. Brussels sprouts, broccoli, cauliflower, kale, and cabbage are all cruciferous vegetables. Many nutritionists recommend increased consumption of these vegetables.

Fat is an essential nutrient, but only one tablespoon of polyunsaturated fat each day is needed for good nutrition. Too much dietary fat is associated with an increased risk of heart disease and certain kinds of cancer. Fat supplies 9 calories per gram, which makes it more than twice as "fattening" as protein or carbohydrate.

   Saturated fat, found in animal and dairy foods, is hard at room temperature and raises cholesterol levels in the blood. Hydrogenated fats, which are added to many processed foods, also raise cholesterol levels.
   Polyunsaturated and *monounsaturated* fats are liquid at room temperature. Both help to lower cholesterol levels.

Fiber is a type of complex carbohydrate that passes through the intestinal tract without being digested. There are many kinds of fiber, but they all come from plant foods—fruits, vegetables, and whole grains. Most Americans consume about 15 grams of dietary fiber each day— about half the recommended amount. Eating more fiber may reduce the risk of certain types of cancer. Soluble fiber, which is found in legumes, oat bran, and certain fruits and vegetables, may help to lower cholesterol levels in the blood.

Minerals are inorganic substances that exist in nature and in plant and animal foods. Like vitamins, they help the body to perform a wide range of essential body functions. Sixteen minerals are considered essential in the diet. Calcium, phosphorus, magnesium, potassium, sulfur, sodium, and chloride are called macrominerals because they are needed in fairly large amounts. The trace minerals—iron, zinc, selenium, manganese, molybdenum, copper, iodine, chromium and fluorine—are needed only in very small amounts. Most minerals can be stored by the body.

Nutrients are substances the body needs to function but cannot manufacture on its own. Protein, fat, carbohydrates, vitamins, and minerals are all nutrients contained in foods. These substances are needed for tissue growth and repair and to help regulate body processes. Protein, fat, and carbohydrates also provide energy in the form of calories. Strictly speaking, fiber and water are not nutrients, even though they also help the body to function properly.

Protein is an essential nutrient made up of amino acids and used for tissue growth and repair as well as for scores of other body functions. Protein from animal foods contains all the amino acids the body needs for growth and repair. Protein from vegetable sources generally lacks one or more essential amino acid. To obtain high quality protein from vegetable sources, it is important to combine grains, nuts, and seeds with legumes, or any vegetable protein with a small amount of animal protein. Most Americans consume at least twice as much protein as they need each day. Protein supplies 4 calories per gram.

P/S ratio expresses the relative amount of polyunsaturated fat as compared to saturated fat in margarines and oils. The higher the number, the more polyunsaturated fat a product contains.

Salt is the common name given to sodium chloride. Numerous studies have shown that a high intake of sodium is associated with an increased risk of developing high blood pressure, among people at risk for this disease. High blood pressure affects some 60 million Americans and has potentially fatal consequences. The average American consumes too much salt, mostly from processed foods.

Sodium. See entry for *salt*.

USRDA are initials which stand for United States Recommended Daily Allowance and were devised by the Food and Drug Administration for use on product labels. They specify the level of intake for nineteen nutrients considered adequate for healthy individuals, but they are only a rough guide that does not take into account different requirements based on age and sex. Still, these standards provide a reasonable margin of safety for most people.

Vitamins are organic substances obtained from plant or animal foods and help to regulate body metabolism. There are thirteen vitamins required in the diet, either fat soluble or water soluble. Each has a different chemical structure and each has several functions. The fat-soluble vitamins A, D, E, and K can be stored in body fat, so they do not necessarily have to be eaten every day. On the other hand, vitamin C and the eight B vitamins are water soluble, which means they pass through the body in the form of urine or sweat. Because the body does not usually store these vitamins, they must be supplied daily in the diet.

SOURCES

General Reference

Brody, Jane. *Jane Brody's Good Food Book*. New York: W. W. Norton, 1985.

Brody, Jane. *Jane Brody's Nutrition Book*. New York: Bantam, 1981.

Code of Federal Regulations, 21 CFR 100.120. Food and Drug Administration, Department of Health and Human Services. Washington, D.C.: U.S. Government Printing Office.

Consumer Reports, food articles, 1979–84. Mt. Vernon, N.Y.: Consumers Union of the United States, Inc.

Food Marketing Institute. *Trends: Consumer Attitudes and the Supermarket*. Washington, D.C.: Food Marketing Institute, 1984.

Freydberg, Nicholas, and Willis A. Gortner. *The Food Additives Book*. New York: Bantam, 1982.

Hightower, Jim. *Eat Your Heart Out*. New York: Crown, 1975.

Laws Enforced By the U.S. Food and Drug Administration. Washington, D.C.: U.S. Government Printing Office.

Moskowitz, Milton, Michael Katz, and Robert Levering, eds. *Everybody's Business*. Philadelphia: Harper and Row, 1980.

Natow, Annette, and Jo-Ann Heslin. *Nutrition for the Prime of Your Life*. New York: McGraw-Hill, 1983.

Pyke, Magnus. *Technological Eating*. London: John Murray, 1972.

Senate Select Committee on Nutrition and Human Needs. *Dietary Goals for the United States*. Washington, D.C.: U.S. Government Printing Office, 1977.

Trager, James. *The Enriched, Fortified, Concentrated, Country-Fresh, Lip-Smacking, Finger-Licking, International Unexpurgated Foodbook*. New York: Grossman, 1970.

Nutrition Data

In addition to using data available on product labels or supplied by the food manufacturer, we referred to the following sources:

Anderson, James W., et al., "Composition of Foods Used in Diets," *Diabetes Care*, 1:5 (1978).

Anderson, James W., Wen-Ju Lin Chen, and Beverly Sieling. *Plant Fiber in Foods*. Lexington: HCF Diabetes Foundation, 1980.

Bowes, Anna dePlanter, and Charles Frederick Church. *Bowes and Church's Food Values of Portions Commonly Used*, revised by Jean A. T. Pennington and Helen Nichols Church. Philadelphia: J.B. Lippincott, 1985.

Composition of Foods—Raw, Processed, Prepared. USDA Handbook No. 8. Washington, D.C.: U.S. Government Printing Office. Handbook No. 8, 1963

        8-1, Dairy and Egg Products, 1976
        8-3, Baby Foods, 1978
        8-4, Fats and Oils, 1979
        8-5, Poultry Products, 1979
        8-6, Soups, Sauces, and Gravies, 1980
        8-7, Sausages and Luncheon Meats, 1980
        8-8, Breakfast Cereals, 1982
        8-10, Pork Products, 1983

Feeley, R. M., P. E. Criner, and B. K. Watt. "Cholesterol Content of Foods," *Research*, Vol. 61 (August 1972).

Southgate, D. A. T., B. Bailey, E. Collinson, and A. F. Walker. "A Guide to Calculating Intakes of Dietary Fiber," *Journal of Human Nutrition*, 30:303 (1976).

USDA Nutrient Research Group for Dietary Fiber, unpublished data, 1986.

Diet and Health

Anderson, J. W., and W. L. Chen, "Legumes and Their Soluble Fiber: Effects on Cholesterol-Rich Lipoproteins." A Chemical Society Symposium series, No. 214: Unconventional Sources of Dietary Fiber. American Chemical Society, 1983.

Blackburn, H., "Diet and Atherosclerosis: Epidemiologic Evidence and Public Health Implications," *Preventive Medicine*, 12:1 (1983).

Kirby, R. W., J. W. Anderson, B. Sieling, et al., "Oat-Bran Intake Selectively Lowers Serum Low-Density Lipoprotein Cholesterol Concentrations of Hypercholesteromic Men," *American Journal of Clinical Nutrition*, 34:824–829 (1981).

Palmer and Bakshi, "Diet, Nutrition, and Cancer: Interim Dietary Guidelines," *Journal of the National Cancer Institute*, 70:6 (1984).

Reddy, B., "Dietary Fat and Its Relationship to Large Bowel Cancer," *Cancer Research*, 41:9 (1981).

Suzuki, K. and T. Mitsuoka, "Increase in Fecal Nitrosamines in Japanese Individuals Given a Western Diet," *Nature*, Vol. 294 (December 1981).

Trevison, M., et. al., "Dietary Salt and Blood Pressure," *Preventive Medicine*, 12:1 (1983).

INDEX

A

Added ingredients included in nutrient
   data, 9
Additives, 1, 7
   allergies, 17–18
   information in profiles, 8
   on labels of food products, 14
All-Bran, 104
Almond Joy, 146
Alpha-Bits, 104–105
American Heart Association, 2, 16
Apple Jacks, 105
Argo Corn Starch, 190
Arm & Hammer Baking Soda,
   191
Armour Beef Hot Dogs, 312–13
Armour Chicken Burgundy Classic
   Lite Dinner, 255
Armour Chicken Fricassee Dinner
   Classic, 255–56
Armour Cooked Salami, 318–19
Armour Golden Star Canned Ham,
   309
Armour Seafood Natural Herbs
   Classic Lite Dinner, 256–57
Armour Seafood Newburg Dinner
   Classic, 257

Armour Sliced Beef with Broccoli
   Classic Lite Dinner, 258
Arnold Brick Oven White Bread, 42
Arnold Brick Oven Whole Wheat
   Bread, 42–43
Arnold Extra Crisp Muffins, 349–50
Arnold Honey Wheat Berry Bread, 43
Arnold Hot Dog Buns, 44
Arnold Original Bran'nola Bread, 44
Arnold Pumpernickel, 45
Aunt Jemima Blueberry Waffles, 379–
   80
Aunt Jemima Complete Buttermilk
   Pancake Mix, 380–81
Aunt Jemima Lite Syrup, 510
Aunt Jemima Original Pancake Mix,
   381
Aunt Jemima Original Waffles, 381–82
Aunt Jemima's Enriched Yellow Corn
   Meal, 191
Aunt Jemima Syrup, 512
Aunt Millie's Meatless Traditional
   Spaghetti Sauce, 500–501
Aunt Millie's Spaghetti Sauce with
   Sweet Peppers and Italian
   Sausage, 501

B

Baby food, 25–35
  cereals, 25–27
  fruits and fruit juices, 27–30
  meat and vegetables, 31–35
Bacon, 297–300
Baker's Premium Shred Coconut, 358–59
Baker's Semi-Sweet Chocolate, 146
Baker's Unsweetened Chocolate, 147
Baking needs. *See* Flour and baking needs
Ball Park Beef Franks, 313
Ball Park Franks, 314
B & M Brick Oven Baked Beans, 522
Banquet American Favorites Beans and Franks Dinner, 258–59
Banquet American Favorites Fish Dinner, 259–60
Banquet Buffet Supper Gravy and Sliced Beef, 271
Banquet Buffet Supper Gravy & Sliced Turkey Main Dish, 272
Banquet Chicken Pie, 272–73
Banquet Cookin' Bag Chicken à la King Entrée, 273–74
Banquet Cookin' Bag Salisbury Steak Entrée, 274
Banquet International Favorites Veal Parmigiana Buffet Supper, 275
Banquet Macaroni and Cheese Casserole, 276
Barnum's Animal Crackers, 157
Basic foods nutrition counter, 551–68
Beans, grains, and nuts group, 3
  See also Legumes
Beech-Nut Stage 1 Chicken and Chicken Broth, 31
Beech-nut Stage 1 Golden Delicious Applesauce, 27
Beech-Nut Stage 1 Mohawk Valley Green Beans, 31
Beech-Nut Stage 2 Oatmeal with Applesauce and Bananas, 25–26
Beech-Nut Stage 2 Turkey Dinner Supreme, 32
Beech-Nut Stage 2 Vegetable Beef Dinner, 32
Bertolli Olive Oil, 364–65
Best Foods Real Mayonnaise, 293
Betty Crocker Au Gratin Potatoes, 414
Betty Crocker Classic Boston Cream Pie Mix, 78
Betty Crocker Coconut Pecan Frosting Mix, 91
Betty Crocker Corn Muffin Mix, 350–51
Betty Crocker Creamy Deluxe Cherry Frosting, 91–92
Betty Crocker Creamy Deluxe Chocolate Chip Frosting, 92
Betty Crocker Creamy Vanilla Frosting Mix, 93
Betty Crocker Hamburger Helper for Cheeseburger Macaroni, 248
Betty Crocker Hamburger Helper for Chili Tomato, 248–49
Betty Crocker Piecrust Mix, 399
Betty Crocker Potato Buds, 415
Betty Crocker Supermoist German Chocolate Cake Mix, 79
Betty Crocker Walnut Brownie Mix, 80
Betty Crocker Wild Blueberry Muffin Mix, 351
Birds Eye Broccoli Spears, 534
Birds Eye Cooked Winter Squash, 534–35
Birds Eye Cool Whip Extra Creamy Dairy Whipped Topping, 174
Birds Eye Cool Whip Non-Dairy Whipped Topping, 174–75
Birds Eye Cut Green Beans, 535
Birds Eye Frozen Strawberries in Syrup, 196–97
Birds Eye Green Peas, 536
Birds Eye Italian Style Vegetables, 536–37
Birds Eye Japanese Style Vegetables, 537
Birds Eye Little Ears of Corn, 538
Birds Eye San Francisco Style Vegetables, 538–39
Birds Eye Sweet Corn, 539

Biscuits and biscuit mixes, 36–40
  butter, 39
  buttermilk, 36–37, 38–39
  country style, 40
  flaky, 38
Bisquick Buttermilk Baking Mix, 36–37
Blue Bonnet Soft Margarine, 67
Blue Bonnet Stick Margarine, 67–68
Blue Diamond Blanched Almonds, 359
Blue Plate Mayonnaise, 294
Bologna, 301–304
Brach Royals, 96
Brach Toffees, 96–97
Bread and rolls, 40–60
  bagels, 49–50
  with bran, 44
  butter and egg, 51
  croissants, 54–55
  dinner rolls, 58
  French, 53
  honey wheat berry, 43, 54
  hot dog buns, 44, 55, 59–60
  protein, 59
  pumpernickel, 45
  rye, 45–46, 50–51, 53
  7 grain, 48–49
  wheat, 42–43, 46–47, 48, 51–52, 55–56, 56–57, 58–59
  wheatberry, 49
  white, 42, 47, 52, 56, 58, 60
Bread crumbs and stuffing mixes, 61–64
  cheddar and Romano cheese croutons, 61–62
  cornbread, 64
  herb seasoned, 62
  New England style, 63–64
  plain, 63
Breakfasts, instant, 233–35
Breast cancer, 17
Breyer's All Natural Pineapple Yogurt, 545
Breyer's All Natural Strawberry Yogurt, 546
Buddig Smoked Sliced Beef, 323
Buddig Smoked Sliced Chicken, 323

Buddig Smoked Sliced Corned Beef, 324
Buitoni High-Protein Spinach Linguine, 385–86
Bumble Bee Chunk Lite Tuna in Water, 178
Bumble Bee Pink Salmon, 179
Bumble Bee Red Sockeye Salmon, 179
Bumble Bee Solid White Tuna in Water, 180
Bundt Pound Cake Supreme, 80–81
Bush's Best Light Red Kidney Beans, 522–23
Bush's Showboat Pork and Beans, 523
Butter, 65–66
  salted, 66
  sweet, 66
  unsalted, 66
Butterfinger, 147

C

Caffeine-Free Diet Coca-Cola, 459
Cake icings, 91–95
  cherry, 91–92
  chocolate, 94
  chocolate chip, 92
  chocolate fudge, 95
  coconut pecan, 91
  vanilla, 93, 94–95
Cakes and cake mixes, 77–90
  angel food, 81
  banana, 89
  Boston cream, 78, 86
  cake mixes, 78–86
  carrot, 82
  carrot nut, 83–84
  cheesecake, 89–90
  chocolate, 79, 85–86, 87–88
  chocolate mint, 85–86
  chocolate mousse Bavarian, 88
  date bread, 84
  devil's food, 82–83
  Dutch apple streusel swirl, 84–85
  German chocolate, 79
  layer, 86–87

Cakes and cake mixes *(cont.)*
  pound, 80–81, 90
  ready-to-eat cakes, 86–90
  walnut brownie, 80
  See also Snack cakes and pies
Calcium, 17, 18
Calorie content:
  information in profiles, 8
  weight watchers and, 15–16
Calumet Baking Powder, 192
Campbell's Beefy Mushroom Soup, 477–78
Campbell's Chicken Noodle Soup, 478
Campbell's Chicken Vegetable Soup, 479
Campbell's Chunky Beef Soup, 479–80
Campbell's Chunky Chicken Noodle Soup, 480
Campbell's Chunky Minestrone Soup, 480–81
Campbell's Chunky Old Fashioned Bean 'N Ham Soup, 481–82
Campbell's Chunky Steak 'N Potato Soup, 482
Campbell's Chunky Vegetable Soup, 482–83
Campbell's Cream of Celery Soup, 483
Campbell's Cream of Chicken Soup, 484
Campbell's Cream of Mushroom Soup, 484–85
Campbell's French Onion Soup, 485
Campbell's Home Style Beans, 524
Campbell's Low Sodium Chicken with Noodles Soup, 485–86
Campbell's Low Sodium Tomato with Tomato Pieces Soup, 486
Campbell's Minestrone Soup, 486–87
Campbell's Natural Creamy Broccoli Soup, 487, 488
Campbell's Natural Creamy Potato Soup, 488, 489
Campbell's New England Clam Chowder, 489–90
Campbell's Old Fashioned Tomato Rice Soup, 490
Campbell's Pork and Beans in Tomato Sauce, 524–25

Campbell's Tomato Juice, 515
Campbell's Tomato Soup, 490–91
Campbell's Turkey Vegetable Soup, 492
Campbell's Vegetable Soup, 492–93
Cancer, 1, 8, 17
C and H Granulated Sugar, 507–508
Candy (nonchocolate), 95–100
  bubble gum, 97–98
  chewing gum, 97–98, 100
  Cracker Jack, 97
  marshmallows, 98–99
  Spear O Mint, 99
  toffees, 96–97
  wild cherry, 99
  See also Chocolate
Cap'n Crunch, 106
Cap'n Crunch's Crunchberries, 106–107
Capri Sun Fruit Punch Natural Fruit Drink, 205
Capri Sun Orange Natural Fruit Drink, 206
Carbohydrates, complex, 1, 2
Carnation Chocolate Breakfast Bar, 233–34
Carnation Coffee-Mate, 155
Carnation Evaporated Milk, 346
Carnation Evaporated Skimmed Milk, 346–47
Carnation Honey Nut Breakfast Bar, 234
Carnation Instant Natural Malted Milk, 342
Carnation Instant Nonfat Dry Milk, 347
Carnation 70 Calorie Hot Cocoa Mix, 342–43
Carnation Sugar Free Hot Cocoa Mix, 343
Carnation Sweetened Condensed Milk, 348
Carnation Vanilla Instant Breakfast, 234–35
Carolina Extra Long Grain Enriched Rice, 425
Casino Brand Monterey Jack Cheese, 137–38

Celentano Eggplant Parmigiana, 276–77
Celentano Lasagna, 277
Celentano 9 Slice Pizza, 406–407
Celentano Stuffed Shells, 277–78
Celentano Thick Crust Pizza, 407
Celeste Cheese Pizza, 408
Center for Science in the Public Interest, 3–6
Cereals, 100–36
  apple-flavored, 105
  baby food, 25–27
  bran, 104, 110, 120–21, 126–27
  with cocoa, 108–109
  cold, 102–34
  with corn, 110–12, 113–14, 116, 120, 125, 127–28
  Cream of Wheat, 135
  with dates, 115
  hot, 134–36
  with marshmallows, 123–24
  oatmeal, 134–35
  with raisins, 112–13, 115, 117, 119, 121
  with rice, 108, 115–16, 123–24, 129–30, 131
  with rolled oats, 128–29, 134–35, 136
  with walnuts, 115
  whole wheat, 114–15, 119, 124, 125, 133–34
Cheerios, 107
Cheese, 137–45
  Cheddar, 139, 140, 143–44
  Colby, 140
  cream, 142–43
  low-cholesterol, 141
  Monterey Jack, 137–38
  reduced-sodium, 142, 144
  spread, 138, 144–45
  Swiss, 143
Cheez-Whiz Pasteurized Process Cheese Spread, 138
Chef Boy-Ar-Dee Beef Ravioli in Tomato and Meat Sauce, 243–44
Chef Boy-Ar-Dee Lasagna, 244
Chicken of the Sea Chunk Light Tuna in Water, 180

Chicken of the Sea Low Sodium Chunk White Tuna in Water, 181
Chicken of the Sea Solid White Tuna in Oil, 181
Chicken Rice-A-Roni, 426
Chiffon Soft.Margarine, 68
Chinese food. See Oriental food
Chocolate, 145–54
  milk chocolate, 148–51, 152–54
  with nuts, 146, 147, 148–49, 150, 152
  with rice, 151
  semi-sweet, 146, 152
  unsweetened, 147
  See also Candy (nonchocolate)
Cholesterol, 1, 2, 7
  information in profiles, 8, 12
  reducing intake of, 16
Chun King Beef Pepper Oriental Divider Pak, 372
Chun King Chicken Chow Mein Divider Pak, 373
Chun King Chicken Chow Mein Pouch, 373–74
Chun King Egg Foo Yung Stir Fry Dinner, 374
Chun King Sweet and Sour Pork Pouch, 374–75
Claussen Kosher Pickles, 394
Claussen Sweet 'n Sour Pickles, 395
Coca-Cola, 460
Cocoa Crispies, 108
Cocoa Pebbles, 108–109
Cocoa Puffs, 109
Coconut, 358–59
Coffee creamers, 154–56
Colon cancer, 17
Complex carbohydrates, 1, 2
Contadina Tomato Paste, 516
Contadina Tomato Sauce, 516
Cookie Crisps, 109–10
Cookies and granola bars, 156–68
  with almonds, 162
  animal crackers, 157
  chocolate, 164, 165
  chocolate chip, 157–58, 160, 166
  with figs, 158–59
  fudge, 158

Cookies and granola bars *(cont.)*
  graham crackers, 159
  honey and oats, 163, 168
  mint, 161–62
  oatmeal, 160–61
  peanut butter, 158
  shortbread, 161
Corn Bran, 110
Corn Chex, 111
Corn chips, 418
Corn Pops, 111–12
Country Time Lemonade Flavor Sugar
    Free Drink Mix, 468–69
Cracker Barrel Sharp Cheddar
    Cheese, 139
Cracker Jack, 97
Crackers, 169–73
  rye, 173
  wheat, 169–73
Cremora Non-Dairy Creamer, 155–56
Crisco Oil, 365
Crisco Shortening, 365–66
Crispy Wheats 'n Raisins, 112–13
Crystal Light Orange Flavor Sugar
    Free Drink Mix, 469

D

Dannon Blueberry Lowfat Yogurt, 546
Dannon Coffee Lowfat Yogurt, 547
Dannon Plain Lowfat Yogurt, 548
Del Monte Bartlett Pear Halves, 197
Del Monte Cream Style Golden Sweet
    Corn, 526
Del Monte Early Garden Spinach, 527
Del Monte Early Garden Sweet Peas,
    527–28
Del Monte Fruit Cocktail, 197–98
Del Monte Peeled Tomatoes, 517
Del Monte Pineapple Chunks in
    Pineapple Juice, 198
Del Monte Sliced Pineapple in
    Pineapple Juice, 199
Del Monte Tomato Catsup, 241
Del Monte Tomato Sauce, 517
Del Monte Whole Green Beans, 528

Del Monte Whole Kernel Family Style
    Corn, 528–29
Del Monte Yellow Cling Peach Halves,
    199
Dessert toppings, 173–77
  butterscotch-flavored, 176
  non-dairy, 174–75
  strawberry, 176–77
Diamond Baking Walnuts, 360
Dinners. *See* Main dishes and dinners
Dinty Moore Beef Stew, 244–45
Dr Pepper, 460–61
Dole Pineapple Juice, 212
Dole Sliced Pineapple, 200
Dole Sliced Pineapple in Pineapple
    Juice, 200
Domino Brownulated Sugar, 508
Domino Granulated Sugar, 508–509
Domino Liquid Brown Sugar, 509
Downyflake Buttermilk Waffles, 382–
    83
Drake's Devil Dogs, 449
Drake's Ring Ding Jr., 450
Duncan Hines Angel Food Cake Mix,
    81
Duncan Hines Chocolate Chip
    Cookies, 157–58
Duncan Hines Creamy Chocolate
    Frosting, 94
Duncan Hines Creamy Vanilla
    Frosting, 94–95
Duncan Hines Deluxe Carrot Cake
    Mix, 82
Duncan Hines Deluxe Devil's Food
    Cake Mix, 82–83
Duncan Hines Peanut Butter 'n Fudge
    Cookies, 158
Duncan Hines Wild Blueberry Muffin
    Mix, 352

E

Eagle Brand Sweetened Condensed
    Milk, 348–49
Earth Grains Devil's Food Doughnuts,
    450–51

Earth Grains Light Rye Bread, 45–46
Earth Grains Old Fashioned Glazed
    Doughnuts, 451–52
Earth Grains Stone Ground Wheat
    Bread, 46
Eckrich Beef Franks, 314
Eckrich Bologna, 302
Eckrich Franks, 315
Eckrich Garlic Bologna, 302–303
Eckrich Hard Salami, 319
Eckrich Olive Loaf, 325
Eggo Homestyle Waffles, 383
Eggs, poultry, fish, and meat food
    group, 5
Elio's Pepperoni Pizza, 408–409
Elio's Round Family Style Cheese
    Pizza, 409
Equal, 510–11
Estimated values in *The Food Book*
    profiles, 9–10

F

Farmer John Wieners, 315–16
Farmland Sliced Bacon, 297–98
Fats, 1, 16
    reducing intake of, 2, 16, 17
Faygo Diet Grape, 461
Faygo Diet Orange, 461–62
Faygo Punch, 462
Faygo Rock & Rye Creme Cola, 463
Fiber, 1, 2, 7, 15–16, 17
    information in profiles, 8, 11, 12–13
Fig Newtons, 158–59
Fish, 2, 16, 177–89
    canned, 178–83
    clams, 186
    cod, 185
    flounder, 186–87, 189
    frozen, 183–89
    perch, 183
    pollock, 185–86
    poultry, meat, and eggs food group,
        5
    salmon, 179
    scallops, 188

scrod, 184
    sole, 183–84, 187–88
    tuna, 178, 180–83
Fleischmann's Active Dry Yeast, 192
Fleischmann's Diet Margarine, 69
Fleischmann's Stick Margarine, 69–70
Fleischmann's Unsalted Stick
    Margarine, 70
Flour and baking needs, 189–95
    all-purpose, 193, 196
    baking powder, 192
    baking soda, 191
    corn meal, 191
    corn starch, 190
    rye, 195
    whole wheat, 193, 195
    yeast, 192
Food and Drug Administration, 13, 14
*Food Values of Portions Commonly
    Used* (Bowes and Church), 12
Franco-American Beef RavioliOs in
    Meat Sauce, 245
Franco-American Chicken Gravy, 222–
    23
Franco-American Mushroom Gravy, 223
Franco-American Spaghetti with
    Meatballs in Tomato Sauce, 246
Franco-American SpaghettiOs with
    Sliced Beef Franks in Tomato
    Sauce, 246–47
French's Bold 'N Spicy Mustard, 356
French's Brown Gravy Mix, 223–24
French's Mushroom Gravy Mix, 224
French's Mustard with Horseradish,
    357
French's Prepared Yellow Mustard,
    357
Fresh Horizons Wheat Bread, 46–47
Fritos Corn Chips, 418
Froot Loops, 113
Frosted Flakes, 114
Frosted Mini-Wheats, 114–15
Frosting. *See* Cake icings
Frozen desserts. *See* Ice cream and
    frozen desserts
Frozfruit, Pineapple, 226
Fruit and Fiber with Dates, Raisins,
    and Walnuts, 115

Fruit baby food, 27–30
Fruit drinks, 205–11
    citrus, 210
    cranberry, 208–209, 211
    grape, 207, 211
    grapefruit, 209
    lemonade, 207
    mixed, 205, 206, 210
    orange, 206
Fruit juice, 212–19
    apple, 213, 214, 215, 216–17
    grape, 218–19
    grapefruit, 214
    lemon, 215
    orange, 213, 217
    pineapple, 212
    prune, 216
Fruits, 2, 17, 196–204
    applesauce, 202–203
    cocktail, 197–98, 201
    cranberry sauce, 203
    food group, vegetables and, 4
    peaches, 199, 201
    pears, 197
    pineapple, 198–99, 200
    prunes, 204
    raisins, 204
    strawberries, 196–97
    See also Basic foods nutrition
        counter
Fruity Pebbles, 115–16

G

Gallo Pepperoni, 320
Gatorade, 463
Gelatin desserts, 219–21
    cherry flavor, 219–21
    strawberry-banana flavor, 221
Gerber Dry Barley Cereal, 26
Gerber High Protein Dry Cereal, 27
Gerber Strained Apple Juice, 28
Gerber Strained Applesauce, 28
Gerber Strained Beef, 33
Gerber Strained Mixed Fruit Juice, 29
Gerber Strained Mixed Vegetables, 33

Gerber Strained Orange Juice, 29
Gerber Strained Peach Cobbler, 30
Gerber Strained Turkey with
    Vegetable, 34
Gerber Strained Vegetables with
    Chicken, 34
Glossary of basic terms, 569–71
Golden Grahams, 116
Golden Grain Macaroni and Cheddar,
    249
Gold Medal All-Purpose Flour, 193
Gold Medal Whole Wheat Flour, 193
Good Humor Chocolate Eclair, 226–27
Good Humor Ice Cream Sandwich,
    227
Gorton's Fishmarket Fresh Ocean
    Perch Fillets, 183
Gorton's Fishmarket Fresh Sole
    Fillets, 183–84
Gorton's Light Recipe Baked Stuffed
    Scrod, 184
Gorton's Light Recipe Entrée-Size
    Fish Fillets, 185
Grains, beans, and nuts food group, 3
    See also Legumes
Granola bars. See Cookies and granola
    bars
Grape-Nuts, 117
Gravy and gravy mixes, 222–25
    brown, 223–24
    chicken, 222–23, 224–25
    mushroom, 223, 224
Green Giant Asparagus Cuts, 529
Green Giant Broccoli, Cauliflower, and
    Carrots in Cheese Sauce, 539–
    40
Green Giant Broccoli Spears in Butter
    Sauce, 540
Green Giant Cauliflower in Cheese
    Sauce, 541
Green Giant Cream Style Corn, 529–30
Green Giant Cut Leaf Spinach in
    Butter Sauce, 542
Green Giant French Style and Cut
    Green Beans in Butter Sauce,
    542
Green Giant French Style Cut Green
    Beans, 530

Green Giant Kitchen Cut Green Beans, 530
Green Giant Mixed Vegetables in Butter Sauce, 543
Green Giant Mushrooms, 531
Green Giant Niblets Corn in Butter Sauce, 543
Green Giant Sweet Peas, 531
Green Giant Whole Kernel Corn, 532
Guidelines for healthy eating, 2–6

H

Häagen-Dazs Coffee Ice Cream, 228
Hain Safflower Margarine, 70–71
Ham, 308–11
Hawaiian Punch, Fruit Juicy Red, 206
Health Valley Sprouts 7 with Raisins, 117
Heart disease, 1, 3, 8
  eating to prevent, 16
Heinz Bananas and Pineapple with Tapioca, 30
Heinz Beef and Beef Broth, 35
Heinz Bread 'n Butter Cucumber Slices, 395
Heinz Cider Vinegar, 369
Heinz 57 Sauce, 440–41
Heinz Ketchup, 241
Heinz Low Sodium Lite Ketchup, 242
Heinz Sweet Gherkins, 396
Heinz Sweet Relish, 396
Heinz Vegetables, Egg Noodles, and Chicken, 35
Hellmann's Real Mayonnaise, 294–95
Hershey's Kisses, 148
Hershey's Milk Chocolate with Almonds, 148
HI-C Grape Drink, 207
Hidden Valley Ranch Garden Herb Salad Dressing, 430
Hidden Valley Ranch Original Ranch Salad Dressing, 430–31
High blood pressure, diet and, 17
Hollywood Safflower Oil, 366
Home Pride Butter Top White Bread, 47

Home Pride 100% Whole Wheat Bread, 48
Home Pride 7 Grain Bread, 48–49
Home Pride Wheatberry Bread, 49
Honey, 511, 514
Honeycomb, 118
Honey Maid Graham Crackers, 159
Honey Nut Cheerios, 118–19
Honey Nut Crunch Raisin Bran, 119
Honey Smacks, 119–20
Hostess Blueberry Pie, 452
Hostess Cherry Pie, 452–53
Hostess Chocolate Cupcakes, 453–54
Hostess Crumb Cakes, 454
Hostess Ding Dongs, 454–55
Hostess Twinkies, 455–56
Hot dogs, 312–18
How to use *The Food Book,* 18–19
Hubba Bubba Original Flavor Bubble Gum, 97–98
Hungry Jack Buttermilk Pancake and Waffle Mix, 384
Hungry Jack Extra Lights Pancake and Waffle Mix, 384–85
Hungry Jack Extra Rich Buttermilk Biscuits, 37
Hungry Jack Flaky Biscuits, 38
Hungry Jack Instant Mashed Potatoes, 415–16
Hunt's All-Natural Hot and Zesty Barbecue Sauce, 441
Hunt's All-Natural Original Flavor Barbecue Sauce, 441–42
Hunt's Chocolate Flavor Snack Pack, 421–22
Hunt's Original Manwich, 442
Hunt's Stewed Tomatoes, 518
Hunt's Tomato Sauce, 518
Hunt's Vanilla Flavor Snack Pack, 422
Hygrade's West Virginia Brand Bacon, 298

I

Ice cream and frozen desserts, 225–32
  chocolate, 226–27, 232
  coffee, 228

Ice cream and frozen desserts *(cont.)*
  pecan, 231
  pineapple, 226
  pudding pops, 228–29
  sandwich, 227
  vanilla, 230, 231–32
  yogurt, frozen, 232
Icing. *See* Cake icings
Imperial Stick Margarine, 71
Imperial Whipped Margarine, 72
Instant breakfasts and diet bars, 233–35
Instant Quaker Oatmeal with Apples and Cinnamon, 134
Instant Quaker Oatmeal with Maple and Brown Sugar, 134–35
Iron, 18

J

Jams, jellies, and preserves, 235–40
  blackberry, 236
  grape, 237, 239–40
  orange, 238
  raspberry, 238
  strawberry, 236, 239
Japanese food. *See* Oriental food
Jell-O Americana Tapioca Pudding Mix, 422–23
Jell-O Banana Flavor Pudding Pops, 228–29
Jell-O Brand Cherry Flavor Gelatin, 219–20
Jell-O Chocolate Flavor Pudding Pops, 229
Jell-O Sugar-Free Cherry Flavor Gelatin, 220–21
Jell-O Vanilla Pudding Mix, 423
Jell-O Vanilla Sugar-Free Instant Pudding Mix, 424
Jelly. *See* Jams, jellies, and preserves
Jif Creamy Peanut Butter, 390
Jiffy Bran Date Muffin Mix, 352
Jiffy Corn Muffin Mix, 353
Jimmy Dean Pork Sausages, 332–33
Jones Little Sausages, 333
Jones Original Liverwurst, 325

K

Karo Light Corn Syrup, 512
Keebler Chips Deluxe Cookies, 160
Keebler Harvest Wheat Crackers, 169
Keebler Oatmeal Cremes Sandwich Cookies, 160–61
Kellogg's Blueberry Pop-Tarts, 456
Kellogg's Corn Flakes, 120
Kellogg's 40% Bran Flakes, 120–21
Kellogg's Frosted Strawberry Pop-Tarts, 456–57
Kellogg's Raisin Bran, 121
Ketchup, 240–42
Kikkoman Soy Sauce, 442
Kit Kat, 148–49
Kix, 122
Knudsen Party Time Vanilla Ice Cream, 230
Kool-Aid Grape Flavor Sugar-Free Soft Drink Mix, 470
Kool-Aid Rainbow Punch Flavor Sugar-Sweetened Soft Drink Mix, 470–71
Kool-Aid Strawberry Flavor Unsweetened Soft Drink Mix, 471
Kool-Aid Tropical Punch Flavor Sugar-Free Soft Drink Mix, 471–72
Kraft American Singles Pasteurized Process Cheese Food, 139
Kraft Bacon and Tomato Dressing, 431
Kraft Barbecue Sauce, 443
Krafty Creamy Cucumber Reduced Calorie Dressing, 431–32
Kraft Egg Noodle with Chicken Dinner, 250
Kraft French Dressing, 432
Kraft French Reduced Calorie Dressing, 433
Kraft Italian Reduced Calorie Dressing, 433–34
Kraft Jet-Puffed Marshmallows, 98–99
Kraft Macaroni and Cheese Dinner, 250–51
Kraft Natural Colby Cheese, 140
Kraft Natural Mild Cheddar Cheese, 140

Kraft Oil-Free Italian Dressing, 434
Kraft Onion Bits Barbecue Sauce,
    443–44
Kraft Real Mayonnaise, 295
Kraft Strawberry Preserves, 236
Kraft Tangy Italian Style Spaghetti
    Dinner, 251
Kraft Tartar Sauce, 444

L

Labels on food products, 6–7, 13–15
La Choy Chinese Style Fried Rice, 375
La Choy Fancy Chinese Mixed
    Vegetables, 376
La Choy Shrimp Chow Mein, 376
La Choy Sukiyaki, 377
La Creme Whipped Topping, 175
Land O' Frost Beef, 326
Land O' Frost Chicken, 326–27
Land O' Frost Ham, 309–10
Land O' Frost Pastrami, 327
Land O' Lakes Country Blend Lightly
    Salted Margarine, 72–73
Land O' Lakes Lightly Salted Sweet
    Butter, 66
Land O' Lakes Margarine Stick, 73
Land O' Lakes Unsalted Sweet Cream
    Butter, 66
Legumes, 521–25
    beans/pork and beans, 521–25
    See also Vegetables
Le Menu Beef Sirloin Tips Dinner, 260
Le Menu Breast of Chicken
    Parmigiana Dinner, 260–61
Le Menu Yankee Pot Roast Dinner,
    261–62
Lender's Plain Bagels, 49–50
Lender's Raisin 'N Honey Bagels, 50
Le Sueur Early June Peas, 532
Levy's Real Unseeded Jewish Rye, 50–
    51
Libby's Corned Beef, 305
Libby's Fruit Cocktail, 201
Libby's Lite Yellow Cling Peached
    Packed in Fruit Juice, 201

Libby's Natural Pack Mixed
    Vegetables, 533
Life, 122–23
Life Savers, Spear O Mint, 99
Life Savers, Wild Cherry, 99
Light n' Lively Reduced Calorie
    Mayonnaise, 295–96
Light n' Lively Strawberry Fruit Cup
    Lowfat Yogurt, 548–49
Lindsay Ripe Olives, 370
Lipton Chicken Noodle Soup with
    Chicken Meat Mix, 493
Lipton Chicken Rice Soup Mix, 493–
    94
Lipton Country Vegetable Soup Mix,
    494
Lipton Cream of Mushroom Cup-a-
    Soup, 494
Lipton Egg Noodles and Sauce, Beef
    Flavor, 251–52
Lipton Egg Noodles and Sauce,
    Chicken Flavor, 252
Lipton Green Pea Cup-a-Soup, 495–96
Lipton Iced Tea Mix, 472
Lipton Onion Soup Mix, 496
Lipton Sugar-Free Lemon Iced Tea
    Mix, 473
Lipton Tomato Cup-a-Soup, 496–97
Lite-Line Cholesterol Cheese Food
    Substitute, 141
Lite-Line Pasteurized Process Cheese
    Product, 141–42
Lite-Line Reduced Sodium
    Pasteurized Process Cheese
    Product, 142
Log Cabin Syrup, 513
Lorna Doone Shortbread, 161
Louis Rich Turkey Bologna, 303
Louis Rich Turkey Breast Slices, 327–
    28
Louis Rich Turkey Cotto Salami, 320–
    21
Louis Rich Turkey Ham, 310
Louis Rich Turkey Luncheon
    Loaf, 328
Louis Sherry Vanilla Ice Cream, 230
Lucky Charms, 123
Lucky Leaf Apple Juice, 213

M

Mahatma Long Grain Enriched Rice, 426
Mahatma Natural Long Grain Brown Rice, 427
Main dishes and dinners, 242–92
  beans and franks, 258–59
  beef, 244–45, 258, 260, 261–62, 265, 267, 269, 271, 274, 276–78, 283, 286–87
  beef stew, 244–45
  canned prepared, 243–47
  chicken, 255–56, 260–61, 262, 264–65, 272–74, 281–82, 284–85, 286, 289–92
  corned beef hash, 247
  dry prepared, 247–53
  egg noodles, 250, 251–52
  eggplant Parmigiana, 276–77
  fish, 256–57, 259–60, 285, 288
  frozen prepared dinners, 253–70
  frozen prepared entrées, 271–92
  Hamburger Helper, 248–49
  lasagna, 244, 270, 277, 283–84
  low-calorie, 256–57, 258, 269–70
  macaroni and beef, 267
  macaroni and cheese, 249, 250–51, 267–68, 276
  pork, 266–67
  ravioli, 243–44, 245
  spaghetti, 251, 282, 287–88
  spaghetti with meatballs, 246
  SpaghettiOs with beef franks, 246–47
  stuffed shells, 277–78
  turkey, 263, 265–66, 268, 272, 280
  veal, 263–64, 275, 287–88, 292
  vegetable lasagna, 283–84
M & M's Peanut Chocolate Candies, 150
M & M's Plain Chocolate Candies, 150–51
Margarine, 65–77
  corn oil, 76
  diet, 69, 74
  safflower, 70–71
  salted, 72–73
  soft, 67, 68, 75–76
  stick, 67–68, 69–70, 71, 73
  unsalted, 70, 75
  whipped, 72
Marie's Blue Cheese Refrigerated Dressing, 434
Marie's Italian Refrigerated Dressing, 435
Marie's Thousand Island Refrigerated Dressing, 435–36
Marshmallow Krispies, 123–24
Martha White All-Purpose Plain Flour, 194
Mary Kitchen Corned Beef Hash, 247
Mayonnaise, 293–96
  reduced-calorie, 295–96
  salad dressing, 296
Mazola Corn Oil, 366
Mazola Diet Imitation Margarine, 74
Mazola Margarine, 74
Mazola Unsalted Margarine, 75
McCormick's Chicken Gravy Mix, 224–25
McCormick's Chili Seasoning Mix, 444
McGovern Committee, Dietary Goals of the, 2, 3, 17
Meadow Gold Butter Pecan Ice Cream, 231
Meadow Gold French Vanilla Ice Cream, 231–32
Meat and poultry products, 2, 297–335
  baby food, 31–35
  bacon, 297–301
  bologna, 301–304
  canned, 305–308
  food group, fish, eggs, and, 5
  ham, 308–11
  hot dogs, 312–18
  salami, 318–322
  sandwich meats, 322–32
  sausages, 332–35
  See also Basic foods nutrition counter
Mexican food, 335–41
  burritos, 337
  combination dinners, 337–39
  enchiladas, 339–41
  refried beans, 335–36
  tamales, 336–37

blueberry, 379–80
buttermilk, 380–81, 382–83, 384
extra light, 384
Parkay Margarine, 76–77
Pasta, 385–89
egg noodles, 386, 388
macaroni, 386–87
spaghetti, 387, 388–89
spinach linguine, 385–86
Pastries. *See* Pies and pastries
Patio Beef and Bean Burrito, 337
Patio Mexican Style Combination
Dinner, 337–38
Peanut butter, 389–93
chunky, 392
creamy, 390, 391
crunchy, 391
natural, 392–93
no salt, 392
Pepperidge Farm Boston Cream Cake
Supreme, 86
Pepperidge Farm Brown 'N Serve
French Enriched Rolls, 53
Pepperidge Farm Cheddar and
Romano Cheese Croutons, 61–
62
Pepperidge Farm Chocolate-Laced
Pirouettes, 164
Pepperidge Farm English Muffins, 353
Pepperidge Farm Family Rye Bread,
53
Pepperidge Farm Frozen Blueberry
Turnovers, 401
Pepperidge Farm Frozen Cheese
Danish, 402
Pepperidge Farm Golden Layer Cake,
86–87
Pepperidge Farm Herb Seasoned
Stuffing Mix, 62
Pepperidge Farm Honey Wheat Berry
Bread, 54
Pepperidge Farm Hot Frozen Old
Fashioned Corn Muffin Mix,
354
Pepperidge Farm Large Old Fashioned
Granola Cookies, 165
Pepperidge Farm Milano Distinctive
Cookies, 165

Pepperidge Farm Petite All Butter
Croissants, 54
Pepperidge Farm Salted Tiny Goldfish,
170
Pepperidge Farm Side-Sliced Enriched
Frankfurter Rolls, 55
Pepperidge Farm Sprouted Wheat
Sliced Bread, 55–56
Pepperidge Farm White Thin Sliced
Enriched Bread, 56
Pepperidge Farm Whole Wheat Thin
Sliced Bread, 56–57
Pepsi-Cola, 464
Peter Pan Crunchy Peanut Butter, 391
Pet Ritz Pie Crust, 402–403
Philadelphia Brand Cream Cheese,
142–43
Pickled meats, 2
Pickles, 393–98
bread and butter, 395
dill, 397, 398
gherkins, 396
kosher, 394, 397, 398
reduced-salt, 397
sweet and sour, 395
Pies and pastries, 398–405
apple Danish, 403–404
apple pie filling, 404, 405
blueberry turnover, 401
cheese Danish, 402
cherry pie filling, 404
peach pie, 399–400
pie crust, 402–403
piecrust mix, 399
pumpkin custard pie, 400–401
See also Snack cakes and pies
Pillsbury Big Country Buttermilk
Biscuits, 38–39
Pillsbury Butter Biscuits, 39
Pillsbury Carrot Nut Bread Mix, 83–84
Pillsbury Chocolate Chip Cookie
Dough, 166
Pillsbury Chocolate Chip Oatmeal
Fudge Jumbles, 166–67
Pillsbury Chocolate Fudge Flavor
Frosting Supreme, 95
Pillsbury Cinnamon Sweet Rolls with
Icing, 457–58

Pillsbury Country Style Biscuits, 40
Pillsbury Date Bread Mix, 84
Pillsbury Dutch Apple Streusel Swirl
    Cake Mix, 84–85
Pillsbury Plus Chocolate Mint Cake,
    85–86
Pillsbury Best All-Purpose Enriched
    Flour, 194
Pillsbury Best Apple Danish, 403–404
Pillsbury Best Medium Rye Flour, 195
Pillsbury Best Whole Wheat Flour, 195
Pipin' Hot Wheat Loaf Dinner Rolls,
    57
Pipin' Hot White Loaf Dinner Rolls, 58
Pizza, 405–13
    cheese, 408, 409–10, 411–13
    diet, 413
    French bread, 409–11
    pepperoni, 408–409, 410–11
    thick crust, 407
Pizza Flavor Combos, 419
Planter's Cocktail Peanuts, 360
Planter's Dry Roasted Peanuts, 361
Planter's SnackNuts, Mixed Nuts with
    Peanuts, 361–62
Planter's Spanish Peanuts, 362
Planter's Unsalted Cashews, 362
Planter's Unsalted Peanuts, 363
Polyunsaturated fats, 16
Popcorn, 417–19
Portions, 9
Post 40% Bran Flakes, 126–27
Post Raisin Bran, 127
Post Toasties Corn Flakes, 127–28
Potassium, 17
Potato chips, 417–18, 420–21
Potatoes, 413–17
    with cheese, 414
    cubed, 416–17
    dried, 415–16
    French fries, 416
Poultry. See Meat and poultry
    products
Prego No-Salt Added Spaghetti Sauce,
    502
Prego Spaghetti Sauce, 502
Prego Spaghetti Sauce with
    Mushrooms, 503

Premium Saltine Crackers, 170–71
Preserves. See Jams, jellies, and
    preserves
Pretzels, 419–20
Prince Enriched Macaroni and
    Spaghetti, 387
Prince Superoni, 387–88
Processed meats, 2
Product 19, 128
Profiles, The Food Book, 6–12
    added ingredients included in
        nutrient data, 9
    estimated values, 9–10
    portions, 9
    rating system, 11–12
    sample, 7–8
    symbols, 11
    tips for using, 15–18
    vitamins and minerals, 10
Progresso Green Split Pea Soup, 497
Progresso Home Style Chicken Soup,
    497–98
Progresso Minestrone Soup, 498
Progresso Plain Bread Crumbs, 63
Progresso Tomato Soup, 499
Protein, 2
Pudding, 421–24
    chocolate, 421–22
sugar-free instant, 424
    tapioca, 422–23
    vanilla, 422, 423, 424
Puritan Oil, 367

Q

Quaker Chewy Chocolate Chip
    Granola Bars, 167
Quaker Chewy Honey and Oats
    Granola Bars, 168
Quaker 100% Natural Cereal, 128–29
Quick Quaker Oats, 136

R

Ragú Extra Thick and Zesty Plain
    Spaghetti Sauce, 503–504

Ragú Extra Thick and Zesty Spaghetti Sauce, Flavored with Meat, 504
Ragú Homestyle Spaghetti Sauce with Mushrooms, 504–505
Ragú Plain Spaghetti Sauce, 505
Ragú Spaghetti Sauce Flavored with Meat, 505–506
Ragú Traditional Pizza Quick Sauce, 506
Rating system, *The Food Book,* 11–12
Realemon Brand Natural Strength Lemon Juice from Concentrate, 215
Reese's Peanut Butter Cups, 152
Regular Swiss Miss, 345–46
Relish, 393–94, 396, 397
  hot dog, 397
  sweet, 396
Rice, 425–29
  brown, 427
  chicken-flavored, 426
  long grain enriched, 425, 426
  Minute, 427
  Spanish-style, 428
Rice Chex, 129
Rice Krispies, 130
Ritz Crackers, 171
Roka Brand Blue Cheese Dressing, 436
Rold Gold Pretzel Twists, 420
Rolls. *See* Bread and rolls
Roman Meal, 58–59
Ronzoni Egg Noodles, 388
Ronzoni Spaghetti, 388
Royal Strawberry-Banana Flavor Gelatin, 221

S

Salad dressing, 429–39
  bacon and tomato, 431
  blue cheese, 434, 436, 437
  creamy cucumber, 431–32
  French, 432–33, 438
  herb, 430
  Italian, 433–34, 435, 436–37
  ranch, 430–31
  reduced-calorie, 431–32, 433–34, 437–38
  Russian, 439
  Thousand Island, 435–36, 438, 439
Salami, 318–22
Salt, 445–46. *See also* Sodium
Salt-cured meat, 2
Sandwich meats, 322–32
  beef, 323, 326, 331–32
  chicken, 323, 326–27
  corned beef, 324
  liverwurst, 325
  olive loaf, 325, 330–31
  pastrami, 327
  picnic loaf, 331
  turkey, 327–29
S & W Mammoth Queen Olives, Medium, 317
San Giorgio Spaghetti, 389
Sara Lee Chocolate Cake, 87-88
Sara Lee Chocolate Mousse Bavarian, 88
Sara Lee Fresh Banana Cake, 89
Sara Lee Original Cheesecake, 89–90
Sara Lee Original Pound Cake, 90
Sargento Sliced Swiss Cheese, 143
Saturated fats, 2, 14, 16
  profile information on, 8
Sauces and seasonings
  barbecue sauce, 440–42, 443–44, 446–47
  chicken seasoning mix, 447–48
  chili seasoning, 444
  pork seasoning mix, 448
  salt, 445–46
  soy sauce, 442
  tartar sauce, 444
Sausages, 332–35
Schrafft's Chocolate Ice Cream, 232
Seabrook Farms Baby Brussels Sprouts, 544
Seasonings. *See* Sauces and seasoning
Seneca Frozen Apple Juice, 215
7-Up, 464
Shake 'n Bake for Pork, 448
Shake 'n Bake Original Chicken, 447–48
Shasta Cola, 465

Shasta Ginger Ale, 465
Shasta Root Beer, 466
Shasta Sugar Free Diet Cherry Cola,
    466–67
Shasta Sugar Free Diet Lemon Lime
    Soda, 467
Shasta Sugar Free Diet Orange Soda,
    467–68
Shellfish. *See* Fish
Skippy Creamy Peanut Butter, 391
Skippy Super Chunk Peanut Butter,
    392
Smucker's Blackberry Spread, 236
Smucker's Butterscotch Flavored
    Topping, 176
Smucker's Concord Grape Jelly, 237
Smucker's Imitation Grape Jelly, 237
Smucker's Natural No Salt Added
    Peanut Butter, 392
Smucker's Natural Peanut Butter, 393
Smucker's Orange Marmalade, 238
Smucker's Raspberry Preserves, 238
Smucker's Strawberry Jam, 239
Smucker's Strawberry Topping,
    176–77
Smurf-Berry Crunch, 130–31
Snack cakes and pies, 448–58
    blueberry, 452, 456
    cherry, 452–53
    chocolate, 449–51, 453–55
    crumb cakes, 454
    glazed, 451–52
    strawberry, 456–57
    sweet rolls, 457–58
    Twinkies, 455–56
    See also Cakes and cake mixes;
        Pies and pastries
Snickers Bar, 153
Sodium, 1
    high blood pressure and, 17
    information in profiles, 8, 12
    reducing intake of, 2
Soft drinks, 458–75
    for athletes, 463
    caffeine-free, 459
    canned, 459–68
    cherry, 466–67
    colas, 459–61, 463, 464, 465

diet, 459, 461–62, 466–68, 468–70,
    471–72, 474–75
ginger ale, 465
grape, 461, 470, 474–75
iced tea, 472–73
lemonade, 468–69
lemon lime, 467
mixes, 468–75
orange, 461–62, 467–68, 469, 474
punch, 462, 470–72
root beer, 466
7-Up, 464
strawberry, 471
Soup, 475–99
    bean and ham, 481–82
    beef, 477, 479–80, 482
    broccoli, 487–88
    celery, 483
    chicken, 478–79, 480, 484, 485–86,
        493–94, 497–98
    chicken flavor bouillon cubes, 499
    clam chowder, 489–90
    creamed, 483–85, 487–89
    green pea, 495–96, 497
    low-sodium, 485–86
    minestrone, 480–81, 486–87, 498
mushroom, 477–78, 484–85, 494–95
    onion, 485, 496
    potato, 488–89
    tomato, 486, 490–91, 496–97, 499
    turkey, 492
    vegetable, 482–83, 492, 494
Spaghetti sauce, 500–506
    extra thick, 503–504
    flavored with meat, 504, 505–506
    meatless, 500–501
    with mushrooms, 503, 504–505
    with no salt added, 502
    pizza sauce, 506
    with sweet peppers and sausage, 501
Spam, 306
Spanish Rice-A-Roni, 428
Special K, 131
Star-Kist Chunk Light Tuna in Oil, 182
Star-Kist Solid White Tuna in Water,
    182–83
Steam-Um Frozen Steak Sandwich
    Meat, 331–32

Stouffer's Chicken Chow Mein Without Noodles, 377–78
Stouffer's Chicken Divan, 281
Stouffer's Chinese Green Pepper Steak, 378
Stouffer's French Bread Cheese Pizza, 409–10
Stouffer's French Bread Pepperoni Pizza, 410–11
Stouffer's Glazed Chicken with Vegetable Rice Lean Cuisine, 281–82
Stouffer's Spaghetti with Beef and Mushroom Sauce Lean Cuisine, 282
Stouffer's Swedish Meatballs with Parsley Noodles, 283
Stouffer's Vegetable Lasagna, 283–84
Stove Top Americana New England Style Stuffing Mix, 63–64
Stove Top Cornbread Stuffing Mix, 64
Stuffing mixes. *See* Bread crumbs and stuffing mixes
Sue Bee Honey, 514
Sugar and sugar substitutes, 2, 507–11
  brown sugar, 508, 509
  diet syrup, 510
  Equal, 510
  granulated sugar, 507, 508–509
  Sweet 'N Low, 511
Sunlite Oil, 368
Sun-Maid Natural Thompson Seedless Raisins, 204
Sunny Delight Florida Citrus Punch, 210
Sunsweet Prune Juice, 216
Sunsweet Whole Prunes, 204
Surgeon General's Report on Preventive Medicine, 2
Swanson Chicken Pie, 284–85
Swanson Fish 'n' Chips Entrée, 285
Swanson Fried Chicken Breast Dinner, 264–65
Swanson Fried Chicken Entrée, 286
Swanson Hungry-Man Chopped Beef Steak Dinner, 265
Swanson Hungry-Man Sliced Beef, 286–87

Swanson Hungry-Man Turkey Dinner, 265–66
Swanson Loin of Pork Dinner, 266–67
Swanson Macaroni and Beef Dinner, 267
Swanson Macaroni and Cheese Dinner, 267–68
Swanson Meatballs with Brown Gravy Entrée, 287
Swanson Mexican Style Combination Dinner, 338–39
Swanson Premium Chunk White Chicken, 306–307
Swanson Spaghetti in Tomato Sauce with Breaded Veal Entrée, 287–88
Swanson Turkey Dinner, 268–69
Sweet 'N Low, 511
Swift Original Brown 'n Serve Beef Links, 333–34
Swift Original Brown 'n Serve Pork Links, 334–35
Swift Premium Sizzlean, 300
Symbols used in *The Food Book*, 11
Syrups, 511–13

T

Tang Orange Flavor Breakfast Beverage Crystals, 474
Taste O'Sea Batter Dipt Scallops, 188
Taste O'Sea Flounder Fillets, 189
Taste O'Sea Perch Dinner, 288
Thank You Apple Pie Filling, 404
Thank You Cherry Pie Filling, 404
Thank You Lite Apple Pie Filling, 405
Thomas' Honey Wheat English Muffins, 354
Thomas' Protogen Protein Bread, 59
Thomas' Regular English Muffins, 355
Three Musketeers Bar, 153
Tillamook Cheddar Cheese, 143
Tillamook Low Sodium Cheddar Cheese, 144
Tomato products, 514–19
  juice, 515, 519

Tomato products *(cont.)*
  paste, 516
  peeled tomatoes, 517
  sauce, 516, 517, 518
  stewed, 518
  vegetable juice, 519
Total, 131–32
Totino's My Classic Deluxe Cheese
    Pizza, 411
Totino's Party Cheese Pizza, 412
Treet, 307
Tree Tavern Frozen Cheese Pizza,
    412–13
Tree Top Apple Juice from
    Concentrate, 216
Tree Top Frozen Apple Juice
    Concentrate, 217
Triscuit Wafers, 171–72
Trix, 132–33
Tropicana Orange Juice, 217
Tuscan Pops Lowfat Chocolate Frozen
    Yogurt, 232
Twix Caramel Cookies Bars, 154
Tyson Chicken Franks, 317–18
Tyson Chick'n Quick Thick & Crispy
    Dinner Patties, 289
Tyson Heat 'N Serve Oven Ready
    Fully Cooked Chicken, 289–90

U

Uncle Ben's Converted Rice, 428–29
Underwood Deviled Ham, 307–308
Uneeda Biscuits, 172–73
U.S. Department of Agriculture
    (USDA), 14
  food tables, 12
  Nutrient Data Research Group, 12
USRDA information in profiles, 6, 13

V

Van Camp's Pork and Beans, 525
Van de Kamp's Cheese Enchiladas
    Ranchero, 339

Van de Kamp's Chicken Enchiladas
    Suiza, 340
Van de Kamp's Shredded Beef
    Enchiladas, 340–41
Veg-All, 533
Vegetable oils, 14, 16
Vegetables, 2, 17, 520–21, 526–44
  asparagus, 529
  baby food, 31–35
  broccoli, 534, 539–40, 540
  Brussels sprouts, 544
  in butter sauce, 540, 542–43
  canned, 526–33
  carrots, 539–40
  cauliflower, 539–40, 541
  in cheese sauce, 539–40, 541
  corn, 526, 528–29, 529–30, 532, 538,
    539, 543
  creamed, 526, 529–30
  food group, fruits and, 4
  frozen, 534–44
  green beans, 528, 530, 535, 542
  Italian style, 536–37
  Japanese style, 537
  mixed, 533, 536–37, 537, 538–39,
    539–40, 543
  mushrooms, 531
  peas, 527–28, 531, 532, 536
  San Francisco style, 538–39
  spinach, 527, 542
  winter squash, 534–35
  See also Basic foods nutrition
    counter
V-8 No Salt Added Vegetable Juice,
    519
V-8 Vegetable Juice, 519
Velveeta Pasteurized Process Cheese
    Spread, 144
Velveeta Pasteurized Process Cheese
    Spread Slices, 145
Vinegar, 368–69
Vitamin A, 2, 13, 17
Vitamin C, 2, 17, 18
Vitamin information in *The Food Book*
    profiles, 10, 11, 13
Vlasic Half the Salt Kosher Crunchy
    Dills, 397
Vlasic Hot Dog Relish, 397

Vlasic Kosher Dill Spears, 398

W

Waffles. *See* Pancakes and waffles
Wasa Lite Rye Crispbread, 173
Weaver Good 'N Wholesome Whole
    Wheat Recipe Fried Chicken,
    290
Weaver Italian Style Chicken
    Rondolets, 291
Weight watchers, advice for, 15–16
Weight Watchers Cheese Pizza, 413
Weight Watchers Chopped Beef Steak
    and Green Pepper in Mushroom
    Sauce, 269
Weight Watchers Lasagna with Meat,
    Tomato Sauce and Cheese, 270
Weight Watchers Southern Fried
    Chicken Patty, Vegetable
    Medley, 291–92
Weight Watchers Veal Patty
    Parmigiana Zucchini in Tomato
    Sauce, 292
Welchade Frozen Grape Drink
    Concentrate, 211
Welch's Frozen Cranberry Juice
    Cocktail, 211
Welch's Frozen Sweetened Grape
    Juice, 218
Welch's Grape Jam, 239
Welch's Grape Jelly, 240
Welch's Purple Grape Juice, 218
Welch's Red Grape Juice, 219
Wesson Oil, 368
Wheat Chex, 133
Wheaties, 133–34
Wheat Thins, 172

Wise Regular Potato Chips, 420–21
Wish-Bone Italian Salad Dressing,
    436–37
Wish-Bone Lite-Line Chunky Blue
    Cheese Salad Dressing,
    437
Wish-Bone Lite-Line French Style
    Salad Dressing, 438
Wish-Bone Lite-Line Thousand Island
    Salad Dressing, 438
Wish-Bone Russian Salad Dressing,
    439
Wish-Bone Thousand Island Salad
    Dressing, 439
Women, dietary needs of, 18
Wonder Hot Dog Rolls, 59–60
Wonder White Bread, 60
Wrigley's Doublemint Gum, 100
Wyler's Chicken Flavor Bouillon
    Cubes, 499
Wyler's Sugar Free Wild Grape Drink
    Mix, 474–75

Y

Yogurt, 545–50
    banana, 549
    blueberry, 546–47
    boysenberry, 549–50
    coffee, 547
    low-fat, 546–49
    pineapple, 545
    strawberry, 546, 548–49, 550
Yoplait Banana Custard Style Yogurt,
    549
Yoplait Boysenberry Yogurt, 549–50
Yoplait Strawberry Yogurt, 550

ABOUT THE CONTRIBUTORS

BERT STERN and LAWRENCE D. CHILNICK are publisher and editor in chief of Bookmark Books, Inc., a company that produces medical and health reference books, tapes, and videos. Their previously published books include the best seller *The Pill Book, Beat the Odds, The Good News About Depression,* and *Wonder Drugs.*

LYNN SONBERG is a writer and book packager specializing in medical, health, and nutrition topics. She graduated with honors from the University of Chicago, and worked for several years as a senior editor at a New York publishing house. Her next book on nutrition is *The Fiber and Calorie Counter.*

SHARRON DALTON, Asst. Professor of Nutrition at New York University, is a registered dietitian with degrees in food and nutrition: a B.S. from Iowa State University, an M.S. from Rutgers University, and a Ph.D. from New York University.
  Her original research has been published in academic journals, and she has taught in medical, classroom, and consumer settings abroad and in the United States. She currently teaches undergraduate and graduate courses at New York University in the Department of Home Economics and Nutrition.